Weird Words

Weird Words

A Lovecraftian Lexicon

Dan Clore

Hippocampus Press

New York

Published by Hippocampus Press
P.O. Box 641, New York, NY 10156.
http://www.hippocampuspress.com

Cover art by Howard Wandrei © 2009 by Harold Hughesdon.
Cover design by Barbara Briggs Silbert. Hippocampus Press logo
designed by Anastasia Damianakos.

First Edition
1 3 5 7 9 8 6 4 2
ISBN 978-0-9824296-4-8

Word collecting is a chronic illness, a pleasurable malady but nonetheless impossible to cure.

Susan Kelz Sperling, *Poplollies & Bellibones: A Celebration of Lost Words* (1977)

Surely one of the primary rules for writing an effective tale of horror is never to use any of these words [. . .]

Edmund Wilson, "Tales of the Marvellous and the Ridiculous" (1945)

Mr. Wilson affirms that "the only characteristic Nabokov trait" in my translation (aside from an innate "sado-masochistic" urge "to torture both the reader and himself," as Mr. Wilson puts it in a clumsy attempt to stick a particularly thick and rusty pin into my effigy) is my "addiction to rare and unfamiliar words." It does not occur to him that I may have rare and unfamiliar things to convey; that is his loss.

Vladimir Nabokov, "Reply to My Critics" (1966)

How will all my undignified language look a century hence?

H. P. Lovecraft, letter to Samuel Loveman (29 April 1923)

It were impossible to list all the works consulted in the compilation of this volume; however, the following proved of especial value:

Isaac Asimov's little study of *Words from the Myths*; Samuel Henley's notes to William Beckford's *History of the Caliph Vathek: An Arabian Tale*; Jorge Luís Borges' *The Book of Imaginary Beings*, in the revised, enlarged, and translated edition prepared by Margarita Guerrero in collaboration with the author; Peter Bowler's authoritative guide to proper usage, *The Superior Person's Book of Words*; Ambrose Bierce's satirical classic *Write It Right*, as well as his definitive guide to proper usage, *The Devil's Dictionary*; the first and second editions of Daniel Harms' *Encyclopedia Cthulhuiana*; the revised and expanded edition of Daniel Harms' and John Wisdom Gonce's *The Necronomicon Files: The Truth Behind Lovecraft's Legend*; the annotated editions of the works of H. P. Lovecraft prepared by S. T. Joshi, Peter Cannon, and David E. Schultz; Scott J. Osterhage's on-line Collation of Theosophical Glossaries, incorporating works by H. P. Blavatsky, William Quan Judge, Gottfried de Purucker, and others; version 3.0 of the CD-ROM second edition of the *Oxford English Dictionary*; Stephen Peithman's annotated edition of the tales of Edgar Allan Poe; Stuart Levine and Susan Levine's annotated edition of the tales of Edgar Allan Poe; Thomas Ollive Mabbott's edition of Poe's *Complete Poems*; Robert M. Price's essay on "Lovecraft's Concept of Blasphemy"; *The Encyclopedia of the Occult: A Compendium of Information on the Occult Sciences, Occult Personalities, Psychic Science, Magic, Spiritism and Mysticism*, compiled by Lewis Spence; and J. E. Zimmerman's *Dictionary of Classical Mythology*.

While every effort has been made to ensure that quotations follow the intentions of the authors, it must be recognized that printed texts differ from edition to edition, due to various factors including auctorial revision, editorial tampering, typesetters' errors, and the use of faulty copy-texts. When variants of a text are known, it is not always possible to determine which variant should be preferred. Because of these factors, the quotations presented here may not always match other copies of the texts in the reader's possession; the reader may rest assured, however, that these quotations accurately represent *some* published variant of the text in question—except in those very few cases in which it has been felt advisable to combine features of different editions. *Caveat lector.*

Quotation dates refer to the year of composition, if known; otherwise, to the year of first publication, if known. Readers should bear in mind that many quotations therefore give a year later than composition; in addition, many authors incorporate earlier texts into their works, so that even where the time of composition is known, portions of the work had been written earlier. Also, some texts have undergone later revisions; here, the author's preferred version has been used, but in general only the earlier date has been given. For translations, the year given refers to the year of the English translation used, rather than to the original foreign language text.

Quotations are generally organized chronologically by the authors' birthdates. One should beware of the fallacy of presuming that one quotation served as the source for another, simply because it is given or dated before it.

Abbreviations Used in This Work

adj.	adjective		*n.*	noun
adv.	adverb		OE	Old English
Ar	Arabic		*OED*	*Oxford English Dictionary*
F	French		OF	Old French
Gr	Greek		ppl. adj.	participial adjective
Hb	Hebrew		*pr.n.*	proper noun
It	Italian		Skr	Sanskrit
L	Latin		*v.intr.*	verb, intransitive
LL	Late Latin		*v.tr.*	verb, transitive

Weird Words

A

Abaddon, *pr.n.* [< Hb ABDVN, destruction; abyss < ABD, lost, ruined] A personification of the idea of destruction, or of Hell or the bottomless pit; Hell or the bottomless pit itself; Satan, the devil, or a lesser devil or demon; also referred to by the equivalent Greek term *Apollyón*, "destroyer." Cf. **Apollyon.**

Lucifer signified his assent; and *Copernicus*, without muttering a word, was as quiet, as he thinks the sunne, when he which stood next him, entred into his place. To whom *Lucifer* said: "And who are you?" Hee answered, "*Philippus Aureolus Theophrastus Paracelsus Bombast of Hohenheim*." At this *Lucifer* trembled, as if it were a new *Exorcisme*, and he thought it might well be the first verse of Saint *John*, which is alwaies imployed in *Exorcismes*, and might now bee taken out of the *Welsh*, or *Irish Bibles*. But when hee understood that it was but the webbe of his name, hee recollected himselfe, and raising himselfe upright, asked what he had to say to the great *Emperour Sathan, Lucifer, Belzebub, Leviathan, Abaddon.*

John Donne, *Ignatius His Conclave; or, His Introduction in a Late Election in Hell: Wherein Many Things Are Mingled by Way of Satyr* (1611)

> But thou, infernal serpent, shalt not long
> Rule in the clouds; like an autumnal star
> Or lightning thou shalt fall from heaven trod down
> Under his feet: for proof, ere this thou feel'st
> Thy wound, yet not thy last and deadliest wound
> By this repulse received, and hold'st in hell
> No triumph; in all her gates Abaddon rues
> Thy bold attempt; hereafter learn with awe
> To dread the Son of God: he all unarmed
> Shall chase thee with the terror of his voice
> From thy demoniac holds, possession foul,
> Thee and thy legions, yelling they shall fly,
> And beg to hide them in a herd of swine,
> Lest he command them down into the deep
> Bound, and to torment sent before their time.

John Milton, *Paradise Regained* (1671)

On the threshold stood the fulminant figure of Evil, the Horror of emptiness, with his ghastly eyes like poisonous wells. He stood, and the chamber was corrupt; the air stank. He was an old and gnarled fish more hideous than the shells of Abaddon. He enveloped me with his demon tentacles; yea, the eight fears took hold upon me.

> Aleister Crowley, *Liber Cordis Cincti Serpenti vel LXV* (1907)

Shells or Qliphoth are lifeless excrement; and Abaddon is the destroyer or disperser—the destroyer by dispersion.

> Aleister Crowley, commentary to *Liber Cordis Cincti Serpenti vel LXV* (1907)

"And then—a nightmare of crawling up infinite stretches of steps—memories of dull horror while hidden within caves with the lights pulsing without and whisperings that called and called me—memory of a time when I awoke to find that my body was obeying the call and had carried me half way out between the guardians of the portals while thousands of gleaming globes rested in the blue haze and watched me. Glimpses of bitter fights against sleep and always, always—a climb up along infinite distances of steps that led from Abaddon to a Paradise of blue sky and open world!"

> A. Merritt, "The People of the Pit" (1918)

Their eyes met, clashed, burned into each other—black flame from Abaddon and golden flame from Paradise.

> A. Merritt, *The Moon Pool* (1919)

From the black deck the thunder of the serpent drum redoubled; the brazen conches shrieked. Drum-thunder and shrieking horn mingled; they became the pulse of Abaddon, lair of the damned.

> A. Merritt, *The Ship of Ishtar* (1924)

Faint at first and far away began a keen edged shrieking; louder it grew as though from racing hordes fresh loosed from Abaddon.

> A. Merritt, *The Ship of Ishtar* (1924)

Only the grim brooding desert gods know what really took place—what indescribable struggles and scrambles in the dark I endured or what Abaddon guided me back to life, where I must always remember and shiver in the night-wind till oblivion—or worse—claims me.

> H. P. Lovecraft, "The Nameless City" (1921)

And yet, as I have said, vague new fears hovered menacingly over us; as if giant bat-winged gryphons squatted invisibly on the mountain-tops and leered with Abaddon-eyes that had looked on trans-cosmic gulfs.

> H. P. Lovecraft, "The Lurking Fear" (1922)

I think I shrieked, and my hands flew up to shut out that intolerable vision of lost Abaddon—the dimension of the Invaders.

> Henry Kuttner, "The Invaders" (1939)

ab-human, abhuman, *adj.* & *n.* [< L *ab-*, from, away, off of + *human*] Non-human, departing from the human. Coined by William Hope Hodgson. Used by critic Kelly Hurley in *The Gothic Body: Sexuality, Materialism, and Degeneration at the Fin de Siècle* to refer to "a not-quite-human subject, characterized by its morphic variability, continually in danger of becoming not-itself, becoming other." [Not in *OED*.]

But, of course, this had been taken with just about the same amount of seriousness that people take most ghost-tales, and that is not usually of a worryingly *real* nature. I mean, that most people never quite know how much or how little they believe of matters ab-human or abnormal, and generally they never have an opportunity to learn.

William Hope Hodgson, "The Thing Invisible" (1910) in
Carnacki the Ghost-Finder

"One other thing," said Arkright, "have you any idea what governs the use of the Unknown Last Line of the Saaamaaa Ritual? I know, of course, that it was used by the Ab-human Priests in the Incantation of Raaaee; but what used it on your behalf, and what made it?"

William Hope Hodgson, "The Whistling Room" (1910) in
Carnacki the Ghost-Finder

And round by the House of Silence, wound the Road Where The Silent Ones Walk. And concerning this Road, which passed out of the Unknown Lands, nigh by the Place of the Ab-humans, where was always the green, luminous mist, nothing was known; save that it was held that, of all the works about the Mighty Pyramid, it was, alone, the one that was bred, long ages past, of healthy human toil and labour. And on this point alone, had a thousand books, and more, been writ; and all contrary, and so to no end, as is ever the way in such matters.

William Hope Hodgson, *The Night Land: A Love Tale* (1912)

A dim record there was of olden sciences (that are yet far off in *our* future) which, disturbing the unmeasurable Outward Powers, had allowed to pass the Barrier of Life some of those Monsters and Ab-human creatures, which are so wondrously cushioned from us at this normal present.

William Hope Hodgson, *The Night Land: A Love Tale* (1912)

Preserving the cold and evilly cryptic nature of reptiles, they had made themselves the masters of an abhuman science.

Clark Ashton Smith, "The Flower-Women" (1933)

"A thought came to me—one of those guesses in the dark. The answer is, I said to myself, that the blue Vampire is Fthaggua, Lord of Ktynga. And there is only *one* Fire Vampire in all! Somehow, this monstrous ab-human entity grew up as a

unit composed of individuals, a disconnected organism that nevertheless might
die if its main member were killed."

Donald Wandrei, "The Fire Vampires" (1933)

Even as the Yorkshireman yelled the voice of the thing that had been Gordon
Finch screamed from Peaslee's handset:

"I am STRICKEN!—Na-ngh . . . ngh . . . ngh-ya—Great Ubbo-sathla, your
child dies—but give me now strength for a final drinking—let me stretch myself
this one last time—DEFY the sigils of the Elder Gods—na-argh . . . ngh . . .
ngh!—Arghhh-k-k-k!—Hyuh, yuh, h-yuh-yuh!"

As these monstrous, utterly abhuman exhortations and syllables crackled in
hideously distorted cacophony from the walkie-talkie, so I witnessed the final
abomination.

Brian Lumley, *The Burrowers Beneath* (1974; ellipses in original)

"My strategy," Smythe continued presently, "was to lure the manifestation into the
open so it might be exorcized by the Ritual of the Astral League. You need damnably supple limbs for that ritual, but it has great power over elementals, manifestations and parking meters. But how to lure this ab-human entity into sight?"

David Langford, "The Thing in the Bedroom" (1984)

"The horror of it! These solid manifestations are the most terrible and inarguable
of spiritual perils—it's infinitely easier to deal with an astral entity which *can't* re-
spond with a sudden blow to your solar plexus. And worst of all, something which
might have sent my hair white if I hadn't already dyed it this rather fetching color,
the Thing had now fallen *inside* the pentacle, with me! Again, imagine the horror of
it, the feeling of spiritual violation: already my outer defenses had been penetrated.
The ab-human embodiment reared up, questing this way and that like a cobra
readying its strike—and then it began to move my way."

David Langford, "The Thing in the Bedroom" (1984)

You're a morbid abhuman bastard, Holmes . . . where were you when they built
Treblinka and Dachau?

Keri Hulme, *The Bone People* (1983; ellipsis in original)

Acheron, *pr.n.* [< L < Gr *Akhérôn*] In Græco-Roman mythology, the river of
woe in Hades.

> Contorted lock of furies I could tear,
> Kick Hercules from damned Acheron,
> And make the triple-headed bandog roar;
> Pluto confront within his jetty throne,
> And sink cursed Charon in his ferry boat.

Alexander Hart, *The Tragi-Comical History of
Alexto and Angelica; or, Love's Metaphor* (1640)

Against th' opposing will and arm of Heav'n
May never this just sword be lifted up,
But for that damn'd magician, let him be girt
With all the greisly legions that troop
Under the sooty flag of Acheron,
Harpyies and Hydras, or all the monstrous forms
'Twixt Africa and Inde, Ile find him out,
And force him to restore his purchase back,
Or drag him by the curls, to a foul death,
Curs'd as his life.

John Milton, *Comus (A Masque Presented at Ludlow Castle, 1634)*

[For "forms", the original MS. reads "buggs"—cf. entry under **bug**.]
Likewise, devils are distinguished according to the elements: for some are called earthy devils, other fiery, some airy, and others watery. Hence, also, those four infernal rivers: fiery Phlegethon, airy Cocytus, watery Styx, earthy Acheron.

Francis Barrett, *The Magus; or, Celestial Intelligencer:*
Being a Complete System of Occult Philosophy (1801)

"You know I am yours, were you bound for the slimy strand of Acheron."

E. R. Eddison, *Mistress of Mistresses* (1930–35)

That at least two of the fear's embodiments were destroyed, formed but a slight guarantee of mental and physical safety in this Acheron of multiform diabolism; yet I continued my quest with even greater zeal as events and revelations became more monstrous.

H. P. Lovecraft, "The Lurking Fear" (1922)

Somewhere, on rose and rosemary,
On lotus red and lotus wan,
Distill the dews of Acheron:
Not yet, not yet, for you and me
To find the placid fields of death
And spend our sighs upon the breath
Of poppies of Persephone.

Christophe des Laurières (Clark Ashton Smith), "Tristan to Iseult" (1927)

Acherontian, *adj.* Of, pertaining to, or resembling Acheron (q.v.); Acherontic; hellish, infernal; dark, dismal, gloomy. [Not in *OED*.]

All the pains induced by the total abandonment of hasheesh were spiritual. From the ethereal heights of Olympus I had been dropped into the midst of an Acherontian fog.

Fitz Hugh Ludlow, *The Hasheesh Eater:*
Being Passages from the Life of a Pythagorean (1857)

Acherontic, acherontic, *adj.* [< *Acheron* (root: *Acheront-*)] Of, pertaining to, or resembling Acheron (q.v.); Acherontian; hellish, infernal; dark, dismal, gloomy; moribund, on the brink of death, with one foot in the grave.

[. . .] an old Acherontic disard, that hath one foot in his grave [. . .]
> Robert Burton, *The Anatomy of Melancholy: What It Is, With All the Kinds,*
> *Causes, Symptomes, Prognostickes & Severall Cures of It* (1621)

From what black wells of Acherontic fear or feeling, from what unplumbed gulfs of extra-cosmic consciousness or obscure, long-latent heredity, were those half-articulate thunder-croakings drawn?
> H. P. Lovecraft, "The Dunwich Horror" (1928)

Or, wandering through ashen fields of perennial autumn, we sought the rare and mystic immortelles, with sombre leaves and pallid petals, that bloomed beneath willows of wan and veil-like foliage: or wept with a sweet and nepenthe-laden dew by the flowing silence of Acherontic waters.
> Clark Ashton Smith, "From the Crypts of Memory" (1917)

> At an inn called the Sign
> Of the Acherontic Pump,
> Two poets drank their ebon wine
> In memory of the rose and amber
> Essence of the vine.
>> Clark Ashton Smith, "Poets in Hades" in "Quintrains"

> I offer thee such dreams
>   As thou hast never known;
> I offer thee the moan
> Of Acherontic streams;
>   I offer thee the vague, vast Hadean domain
>   For thee to reign.
>> Donald Wandrei, "Death and the Poet: A Fragment"

aconite, aconitum, *n.* [< L *aconītum* < Gr *akóniton*] A plant of the species *Aconitum lycoctonum* (and also, by extension, other species of the genus *Aconitum*, such as *Aconitum napellus*); also, a poisonous and psychotropic alkaloid derived from the dried leaves and roots of such a plant. Also known as monk's-hood and wolf's-bane. In Græco-Roman mythology, aconite was supposed to have sprung from the slobber of Cerberus when Hercules brought him from Hades.

> I thrust in *eleoselinum* lately
> Aconitum, frondes populeas, and soot—
> You may see that, he looks so black i' th' mouth—
> Then sium, acorum vulgare too,

Pentaphyllon, the blood of a flitter-mouse,
Solanum somnificum et oleum.

Thomas Middleton, *The Witch* (1604)

"From pharmacy to pharmacy she has gone, like a hypochondriac seeking for a cure. Consider what she bought"—he checked the items off upon his fanned-out fingers—"aconitum, belladonna, solanin, mandragora officinalis. Not in any one, or even any two places did she buy these things. No, she was shrewd, she was clever, by blue, but she was subtle! Here she bought a *flacon* of perfume, there a box of powder, again, a cake of scented soap, but mingled with her usual purchases would be occasionally one of these strange things which no young lady can possibly be supposed to want or need."

Seabury Quinn, "The Hand of Glory" (1933)

The lolling weeds of Lethe, green or wan,
Exhale their fatal languors on the light;
From out infernal grails of aconite
Poisons and dews are proffered to the dawn.

Clark Ashton Smith, "Duality" (1923)

My impatience to attempt the Ritual of the Bell would brook no delay, so I began the experiment that very evening. According to the notes of my ancestor, a certain potion must be imbibed in preparation, the recipe for which was given in those portions of his papers which were not encoded. The formula involved certain drugs and poisonous alkaloids such as belladonna and aconite, but as I had sampled these and other potent narcotics earlier while striving to systematically derange my senses, I fortunately had liberal supplies of such chemicals on hand.

Lin Carter, "The Bell in the Tower"

"For your information, Potter, asphodel and wormwood make a sleeping potion so powerful it is known as the Draught of Living Death. A bezoar is a stone taken from the stomach of a goat and it will save you from most poisons. As for monkshood and wolfsbane, they are the same plant, which also goes by the name of aconite."

J. K. Rowling, *Harry Potter and the Philosopher's Stone*
(1995; aka *Harry Potter and the Sorcerer's Stone*)

adjectivies, *n.* An inflammation of the adjectives. [Not in *OED*.]

A good many years back, you started selling yarns that had a lot of "mood," and they went pretty well. They were in a way, rather like the Gothic horror story the "Fall of the House of Usher" sort of thing, built up with *Roget's Thesaurus*, and various sources of adjectives. Lovecraft did the same kind. I did some of 'em myself. As of the time and the slant of the field, they were right.

That was a dozen years ago, and the field's changed far and fast since then. We're older, too, you and I and we've got to change with the change.

In this story, you have, 95% of the way through. But some of the older style still lingers—and to the extent the adjectivies, or *Roget's* Disease, lingers, the whole is weakened.

John W. Campbell, letter to Robert Moore Williams (14 August 1952)

adjectivitis, *n*. An inflammation of the adjectives. [Not in *OED*.]

Titles: Donald R. Burleson, "Lovecraft and Adjectivitis: A Deconstructionist View" (criticism)

Then they went on to praise Pompeo Stromboli with the very words they usually applied to her. His voice was full, rich, tender, vibrating, flexible, soft, powerful, stirring, natural, cultivated, superb, phenomenal, and perfectly fresh. The critics had a severe attack of "adjectivitis."

F. Marion Crawford, The Primadonna: A Sequel to Fair Margaret (1907)

Adjectivitis is a common fault of tyronic writers, who might write: "a brutal-looking, short-necked, thick-bodied, bestially hairy man with long dangling arms, short bowed legs, a broad flattened nose, and sinister little eyes scowling under beetling eyebrows . . ." when they could simply say "an apelike man" and let it go at that.

L. Sprague de Camp & Catherine Crook de Camp, Science Fiction Handbook, Revised:
A Guide to Writing Imaginative Literature (1953/1975; ellipsis in original)

Ægipan (*pl*. **Ægipanes, Ægipans**); (**Ægypan, Œgipan**); *n*. [< Gr *aigipan*, goat + Pan.] In Græco-Roman mythology, a satyr or faun, represented as a human male with the horns, ears, tail, legs, and hooves of a goat. (According to some sources, one of a race of centaur-like beings with the torso of a man joined to the body of a goat.) [Not in *OED*.]

As for the Demigods, *Fauns, Satyrs, Sylvans, Hobgoblins, Ægipanes, Nymphs, Heroes*, and *Dæmons*, several Men have, from the total Sum, which is the result of the divers Ages Calculated by *Hesiod*, reckon'd their Life to be 9720 Years, that sum, consisting of four special numbers orderly arising from one, the same added together and multiplied by four every way, amounts to forty; these forties being reduced into Triangles by five times, make up the total of the foresaid Number. See *Plutarch*, in his Book about the Cessation of Oracles.

François Rabelais (trans. Pierre Le Motteux & Sir Thomas Urquhart),
The Lives, Heroick Deeds, and Sayings of Gargantua and His Son Pantagruel (1653/1694)

Among the rest, they descanted with great Prolixity on the Pyramids and Hieroglyphics of *Egypt*, of the *Nile*, of *Babylon*, of the *Troglodytes*, the *Hymantapodes* or *Crumpfooted Nation*; the *Blæmiæ* People that wear their Heads in the middle of their Breasts, the *Pygmies*, the *Cannibals*, the *Hyperborei* and their Mountains, the

Ægypanes with their Goat's-feet, and the Devil and all of others: every individual word of it by *Hear-say*.

François Rabelais (trans. Pierre Le Motteux & Sir Thomas Urquhart),
The Lives, Heroick Deeds, and Sayings of Gargantua and His Son Pantagruel (1653/1694)

In his Left hand he held a Pipe, and a crooked Stick in his Right. His Forces consisted also wholly of Satyrs, Ægipanes, Agripanes, Sylvans, Fauns, Lemures, Lares, Elves, and Hobgoblins, and their Number was Seventy eight thousand one hundred and fourteen. The Signal or Word common to all the Army was Euohe.

François Rabelais (trans. Pierre Le Motteux & Sir Thomas Urquhart),
The Lives, Heroick Deeds, and Sayings of Gargantua and His Son Pantagruel (1653/1694)

We pored together over such works as the Ververt et Chartreuse of Gresset; the Belphegor of Machiavelli; the Heaven and Hell of Swedenborg; the Subterranean Voyage of Nicholas Klimm by Holberg; the Chiromancy of Robert Flud, of Jean D'Indaginé, and of De la Chambre; the Journey into the Blue Distance of Tieck; and the City of the Sun of Campanella. One favourite volume was a small octavo edition of the *Directorium Inquisitorum*, by the Dominican Eymeric de Gironne; and there were passages in Pomponius Mela, about the old African Satyrs and Œgipans [some texts correct to "Ægipans"], over which Usher would sit dreaming for hours. His chief delight, however, was found in the perusal of an exceedingly rare and curious book in quarto Gothic—the manual of a forgotten church—the *Vigiliæ Mortuorum secundum Chorum Ecclesiæ Maguntinæ*.

Edgar Allan Poe, "The Fall of the House of Usher" (1839)

Villiers turned page after page, absorbed, in spite of himself, in the frightful Walpurgis Night of evil, strange monstrous evil, that the dead artist had set forth in hard black and white. The figures of Fauns and Satyrs and Ægipans danced before his eyes, the darkness of the thicket, the dance on the mountain-top, the scenes by lonely shores, in green vineyards, by rocks and desert places, passed before him: a world before which the human soul seemed to shrink back and shudder.

Arthur Machen, "The Great God Pan" (1890)

Goats leaped to the sound of thin accursed flutes, and ægipans chased endlessly after misshapen fauns over rocks twisted like swollen toads.

H. P. Lovecraft, "The Horror at Red Hook" (1925)

Once in his ascent Randolph crossed a rushing stream whose falls a little was off sang runic incantations to the lurking fauns and ægipans and dryads.

H. P. Lovecraft, "The Silver Key" (1926)

"And God! The shapes of nightmare that float around in that perpetual dæmon twilight! The blasphemies that lurk and leer and hold a Witches' Sabbat with that

woman as a high-priestess! The black shaggy entities that are not quite goats—
the crocodile-headed beast with three legs and a dorsal row of tentacles—and
the flat-nosed ægipans dancing in a pattern that Egypt's priests knew and called
accursed!"

> H. P. Lovecraft & Zealia Bishop, "Medusa's Coil" (1930)

Quaint quills whereon the ægipan has played.

> Clark Ashton Smith, *The Black Book of Clark Ashton Smith*

From out its winding tube
The serpent sobs a music old and quaint
As antic quills blown by the ægipan.

> Clark Ashton Smith, *The Black Book of Clark Ashton Smith*

PAN: Physically the largest of all the gods. In his troupe were lemures, ægipanes,
bassarides, bacchides, evantes, mænades, fauns, and sylvans. They all adored
him.

> Charles G. Finney, *The Circus of Dr. Lao* (1934)

ægipanic, *adj.* Of, pertaining to, or resembling an ægipan (q.v.). [Not in *OED*.]

In their rhythmic piping, droning, rattling, and beating I felt an element of terror
beyond all the known terrors of earth—a terror peculiarly dissociated from personal fear, and taking the form of a sort of objective pity for our planet, that it
should hold within its depths such horrors as must lie beyond these ægipanic cacophonies.

> H. P. Lovecraft & Harry Houdini, "Under the Pyramids" (1924)

ægritude, egritude, *n.* [< L *ægritūdŏ*] Illness, sickness.

Good work—that recovery stuff! May ægritude long shun your honour'd door,
& health triumphant reign for evermore!

> H. P. Lovecraft, letter to Samuel Loveman (24 March 1923)

Æolian, æolian, Eolian, eolian, *adj.* [< L *Æolus* < Gr *Aíolos,* the god of the
winds] Of or pertaining to the wind. Often found in the phrase **Æolian harp**
(also **harp of Æolus, Æolian lyre,** etc.): A musical instrument consisting of a
stringed box, whose strings are sounded by the action of the wind.

a. General:

'Tis the deep music of the rolling world,
Kindling within the strings of the waved air
Æolian modulations.

> Percy Bysshe Shelley, *Prometheus Unbound: A Lyrical Drama* (1819)

At last the day arriv'd, the sky o'erspread
With dark'ning messengers and clouds of lead;

Each neighb'ring grove Æolian warnings sigh'd,
And thick'ning terrors broadcast seem'd to bide.

H. P. Lovecraft, "Psychopompos: A Tale in Rhyme" (1917–18)

b. In Æolian harp, Æolian lyre, etc.:

A silver trumpet Spenser blows,
And as its martial notes to silence flee,
From a virgin Chorus flows
A hymn in praise of spotless Chastity.
'Tis still!—Wild warblings from the Æolian lyre
Enchantment softly breathe, and tremblingly expire.

John Keats, "Ode to Apollo" (1815)

The golden and silver fish haunted the river, out of the bosom of which issued, little by little, a murmur that swelled, at length, into a lulling melody more divine than that of the harp of Æolus—sweeter than all save the voice of Eleonora.

Edgar Allan Poe, "Eleonora" (1841)

The song rose louder; impossible to describe its effect, in the midst of the tranquil night, chiming over the serried rooftops, and under the solitary moon. It was not like the artful song of man, for it was defective in the methodical harmony of tune; it was not like the song of the wild-bird, for it had no monotony in its sweetness: it was wandering and various as the sounds from an Æolian harp.

Sir Edward Bulwer-Lytton, *A Strange Story* (1861)

Who can so relate a dream that it shall seem one? No poet has so light a touch. As well try to write the music of an Æolian harp.

Ambrose Bierce, "Visions of the Night" (1887)

æon, eon, *n.* [< L *æōn* < Gr *aiōn*] An indefinitely or immeasurably long period of time. In Gnostic mythology, the Æons are members of the celestial hierarchy emanating from the absolute. In current scientific use, a period of a billion years.

Titles: H. P. Lovecraft & Hazel Heald, "Out of the Æons"; Robert Bloch, *Strange Eons*

Names: Æ. or A. E. (George William Russell); Homer Eon Flint (Homer Flindt)

For then forthwith some thing beside our God
We did conceive our parted selves to be,
And loosened, first from that simple Good,
Then from great *Æon*, then from *Psyche* free,
We after fell into low phantasie,
And after that into corporeall sense,

And after sense embarkd as in a tree,
  (First sown in earthly slime, then sprung from thence)
A fading life we lead in deadly influence.

Henry More, The Præexistency of the Soul (1647)

So Los lamented over Satan, who triumphant divided the Nations
He set his face against Jerusalem to destroy the Eon of Albion

William Blake, Milton (1804)

That is not dead which can eternal lie,
  And with strange æons even death may die.

Abdul Alhazred, Necronomicon, as quoted in
H. P. Lovecraft, "The Nameless City" (1921) & "The Call of Cthulhu" (1926)

"Some call it folklore," Colin agreed. "But others know that many forgotten truths live on as folklore. 'That is not dead which can eternal lie ... and with strange eons, even Death may die.' *Af baraldim Azathoth! Ad baraldim asdo galoth Azathoth! Iä Cthulhu fthagn!*"

Marion Zimmer Bradley, Heartlight (1998; ellipsis in original)

æonian, eonian, *adj.* Of or pertaining to an æon or eon; lasting for an indefinitely or immeasurably long period of time; indefinitely or immeasurably old.

But I should turn my ear and hear

The moanings of the homeless sea,
  The sound of streams that swift or slow
  Draw down Æonian hills, and sow
The dust of continents to be;

And Love would answer with a sigh,
  "The sound of that forgetful shore
  Will change my sweetness more and more,
Half-dead to know that I shall die."

Alfred, Lord Tennyson, In Memoriam (1850)

A smattering of theosophical lore, and a fondness for the speculations of such writers as Colonel Churchward and Lewis Spence concerning lost continents and primal forgotten civilisations, made Reynolds especially alert to any æonian relic like the unknown mummy.

H. P. Lovecraft & Hazel Heald, "Out of the Æons" (1933)

The thing was so perfect and complete and all-sufficing, so independent of lesser life in its world-enmeshing growth. It poured forth the sense of eonian longevity, perhaps of immortality.

Clark Ashton Smith, "Seedling of Mars" (1931)

Of course, the strangeness of our situation, and the weird proximity of those æonian walls and towers may in some measure have contributed to my unrest.

Clark Ashton Smith, "The Vaults of Yoh-Vombis" (1931)

From out the light of many a mightier day,
From Pharaonic splendour, Memphian gloom,
And from the night æonian of the tomb
They brought him forth, to meet the modern ray—
Upon his brow the unbroken seal of clay,
While gods have to a forgotten doom,
And desolation and the dust assume
Temple and cot immingling in decay.

Clark Ashton Smith, "The Mummy" (1919)

æra, *n.* An era.

Then, whispered Castro, those first men formed the cult around small idols which the Great Ones shewed them; idols brought in dim æras from dark stars. That cult would never die till the stars came right again, and the secret priests would take great Cthulhu from His tomb to revive His subjects and resume His rule of earth. The time would be easy to know, for then mankind would have become as the Great Old Ones; free and wild and beyond good and evil, with laws and morals thrown aside and all men shouting and killing and revelling in joy. Then the liberated Old Ones would teach them new ways to shout and kill and revel and enjoy themselves, and all the earth would flame with a holocaust of ecstasy and freedom.

H. P. Lovecraft, "The Call of Cthulhu" (1926)

æsthete, esthete, *n.* An individual with an especially refined sense of the beautiful.

"The place for an artist to live is the North End. If any æsthete were sincere, he'd put up with the slums for the sake of the massed traditions. God, man! Don't you realise that places like that weren't merely *made*, but actually *grew*?"

H. P. Lovecraft, "Pickman's Model" (1926)

Afrit, Afrite, Afreet, *n.* [<Ar *'ifrīt*] In Islamic mythology, a powerful Djinn, spirit, or demon. Cf. **Efreet, Ifrit.** [Beckford antedates *OED* by 15 years.]

Immediately a cloud descended, which, gradually dissipating, discovered Carathis on the back of an afrit, who grievously complained of his burden.

William Beckford, *The History of the Caliph Vathek: An Arabian Tale* (1786)

These were a kind of Medusæ, or Lamiæ, supposed to be the most terrible and cruel of all the orders of the dives.—D'HERBELOT, p. 66.

Samuel Henley, note to William Beckford,
The History of the Caliph Vathek: An Arabian Tale (1786)

Wet with thine own best blood shall drip,
Thy gnashing tooth and haggard lip;
Then stalking to thy sullen grave—
Go—and with Gouls and Afrits rave;
Till these in horror shrink away
From spectre more accursed than they!

Lord Byron, *The Giaour: A Fragment of a Turkish Tale* (1813)

The Shadow had fallen—but too late, a bare instant too late. And shrinking as we fled from it, still it seemed to strain like some fettered Afrit from Eblis, throbbing with wrath, seeking with every malign power it possessed to break its bonds and pursue.

A. Merritt, *The Moon Pool* (1919)

I shall never forget that hideous summer sixteen years ago, when like a noxious afrite from the halls of Eblis typhoid stalked leeringly through Arkham.

H. P. Lovecraft, "Herbert West—Reanimator" (1922)

Of my birth, my youth, and the appellation by which I was known and perhaps renowned among men, it would now be bootless to speak: for those days are one in remoteness with the reign of Al Raschid, they have gone by like the Afrit-builded halls of Suleiman.

Clark Ashton Smith, "Told in the Desert" (1930)

Everywhere there was a loud beating as of metal pulses, a mutter as of prisoned Afrits and servile iron titans.

Clark Ashton Smith, "Vulthoom" (1933)

aglaophotis, aglauphotis, *n.* [< Gr, literally "bright light" < *aglaós*, bright + *phôs* (root: *phôt-*), light] According to most authorities, peony (*Pæonia officinalis*), known in herbal lore for protection from evil spirits. According to Lewis Spence in *The Encyclopedia of the Occult: A Compendium of Information on the Occult Sciences, Occult Personalities, Psychic Science, Magic, Spiritism and Mysticism,* an herb that grows in the Arabian deserts, and which is made use of by sorcerers in the evocation of dæmons. According to Pliny, it grows in the marble quarries of Arabia and is also known as *marmaritis* and is used by the Magi to summon the gods. [Not in *OED.*]

The like doth the herb aglauphotis do, which is called marmorites, growing upon the marbles of Arabia, as saith *Pliny,* and the which magicians use.

Henry Cornelius Agrippa (trans. James Freake),
Three Books of Occult Philosophy (1651)

And to summon these and other Demons, the herb AGLAOPHOTIS must be burnt in a new bowl that has a crack, and the Incantations recited clearly. And it must be the Evil Times, and at Night.

> Abdul Alhazred (trans. "Simon"), *Necronomicon* (1977)

agrestic, *adj.* Of or pertaining to the country; rural, rustic.

I have begun to emerge from hibernation, and took a long scenic ramble (both urban and agrestic) night before last, during the course of which I discovered one of the most hellish slums ever imagined by mankind.

> H. P. Lovecraft, letter to Wilfred Blanch Talman (23 April 1926)

ague, *n.* [< OF *(fievre) ague,* sharp (fever)] A malarial illness characterized by intermittent fever, chills, and fits of shaking and shivering. This disease rarely occurs in fantasy and weird fiction, but characters not infrequently suffer symptoms similar to its effects.

a. Literal:

b. Figurative (simile, metaphor, etc.):

> Fear is an ague, that forsakes
> And haunts, by fits, those whom it takes;
> And they'll opine they feel the pain
> And blows they felt to-day, again.
>
> Samuel Butler, *Hudibras* (1663–78)

One evening, about the season of corn harvest, the maids that went out for water returned pale and affrighted, with their pitchers empty; their teeth chattered, and every limb quivered as if they were shaken by the shivering fit of an ague.

> William Beckford, "The Nymph of the Fountain" (1791)

"I have no curiosity to see him at all," said the Baronet, whose courage seemed, from a certain quaver in his accent, to have taken a fit of the ague.

> Sir Walter Scott, *The Antiquary* (1816)

Oh, grief! thou art classed amongst the depressing passions. And true it is, that thou humblest to the dust, but also thou exaltest to the clouds. Thou shakest as with ague, but also thou steadiest like frost. Thou sickenest the heart, but also thou healest its infirmities.

> Thomas De Quincey, *Suspiria de Profundis:*
> *Being a Sequel to the Confessions of an English Opium-Eater* (1845)

I was feeble in the extreme—so much so that I shook all over, as with an ague, at the slightest movement or exertion.

> Edgar Allan Poe, *The Narrative of Arthur Gordon Pym of Nantucket* (1838)

Towards night my companions awoke, one by one, each in an indescribable state of weakness and horror, brought on by the wine, whose fumes had now evaporated. They shook as if with a violent ague, and uttered the most lamentable cries for water.

> Edgar Allan Poe, *The Narrative of Arthur Gordon Pym of Nantucket* (1838)

"No one will ever know what my feelings were at that moment. I shook from head to foot as if I had had the most violent fit of the ague."

> Edgar Allan Poe, "A Descent into the Maelström" (1841)

The heat rapidly increased, and once again I looked up, shuddering as with a fit of the ague.

> Edgar Allan Poe, "The Pit and the Pendulum" (1842)

When he first heard that the horse had come home without his master, and without his master's saddle-bags, and all bloody from a pistol-shot, that had gone clean through and through the poor animal's chest without quite killing him,—when he heard all this, he turned as pale as if the missing man had been his own dear brother or father, and shivered and shook all over as if he had had a fit of the ague.

> Edgar Allan Poe, "Thou Art the Man" (1844)

Some key to that inscrutable appeal,
Which made the very frame of Nature quiver,
And every thrilling nerve and fibre feel
So ague-like a shiver.

> Thomas Hood, "The Haunted House: A Romance"

"Yes, but I do know quite enough to warrant my confidence," interrupted the soldier, "don't I know that all your annoyance proceeds from the occasional appearance of a certain little man in a cap and greatcoat, with a red vest and a bad face, who follows you about, and pops upon you at corners of lanes, and throws you into ague fits."

> J. S. LeFanu, "The Familiar" (1847)

Her face underwent a change that alarmed and even terrified me for a moment. It darkened, and became horribly livid; her teeth and hands were clenched, and she frowned and compressed her lips, while she stared down upon the ground at her feet, and trembled all over with a continued shudder as irrepressible as ague.

> J. S. LeFanu, "Carmilla" (1871)

He was shivering with a kind of ague.

> Oscar Wilde, *The Picture of Dorian Gray* (1890)

It frightened and amazed me somewhat; and as for Arthur, he fell a-trembling, and finally was shaken with doubt as with an ague.

Bram Stoker, *Dracula* (1897)

I stood shuddering and quaking as with the grip of ague, sick with unspeakable agonies of fear and loathing, and for five minutes I could not summon force or motion to my limbs.

Arthur Machen, "Novel of the White Powder" in
The Three Impostors; or, The Transmutations (1894)

The next circumstance that I now observed was a trembling of the ground on which I lay, the which trembled greatly, as with a very grave ague.

M. P. Shiel, "Dark Lot of One Saul" (1912)

Maitland roared for my help; and at that moment, I, poor wretch, in greater misery than he, stood shivering in an ague: for all at once one of those wrangles of the voices of my destiny was filling my bosom with commotion, one bidding me dash to Maitland's aid, one passionately commanding me be still.

M. P. Shiel, *The Purple Cloud* (1901)

The pallor of his face grew ghastly as he neared the end. He began to shake all over as with ague.

Algernon Blackwood, "The Man Who Found Out (A Nightmare)" (1912)

"And then," said Tip to himself, with a laugh, "she'll squeal louder than the brown pig does when I pull her tail, and shiver with fright worse than I did last year when I had the ague!"

L. Frank Baum, *The Marvelous Land of Oz* (1904)

"A glance at Nils dispelled this thought in a flash. In the pale light of the high stars he was the embodiment of all possible human fear, quaking with an ague, his jaw fallen, his tongue out, his eyes protruding like those of a hanged man."

Ralph Adams Cram, "The Dead Valley" (1895)

Burke, shaking like a man with an ague, sat on the lower step, pathetically drumming his palms upon his uplifted knees.

Sax Rohmer (Arthur Sarsfield Ward),
The Return of Dr. Fu-Manchu (1916; aka *The Devil Doctor*)

The King's hand shook as with an ague as he turned the pages of the mighty book.

E. R. Eddison, *The Worm Ouroboros* (1922)

Of their purport I did not need to be told, and I shivered as with ague.

H. P. Lovecraft, "The Whisperer in Darkness" (1930)

Carnby went back to his chair, tottering a little with weakness. His lineaments were agonized by the gnawing of some inward horror, and he shook visibly like an ague patient.

Clark Ashton Smith, "The Return of the Sorcerer" (1931)

Dropping the whip he reeled back and fell up against the table, clutching blindly at its edge. He shook as with an ague. His hair was plastered across his brow in dank strands, and sweat dripped from his livid countenance which was like a carven mask of Fear.

Robert E. Howard, "The Black Stranger" (c. 1934;
aka "The Treasure of Tranicos")

At the thought he shook as with an ague and his dark skin grew ashy.

Robert E. Howard, "Red Nails" (1935)

And Bran stood aghast, for Gonar's face was white as driven snow and he shook as with ague.

Robert E. Howard, "Worms of the Earth" (1930)

I found myself shaking as with ague and cold sweat stood upon my body as in a nightmare.

Robert E. Howard, "The Hoofed Thing" (1932)

I freed her in an instant and she threw her arms convulsively about me, shaking as with an ague.

Robert E. Howard, "The Hoofed Thing" (1932)

And even as I spoke, icy sweat stood out on my body and I shook as with an ague.

Robert E. Howard, "Dig Me No Grave"

"In God's name, who comes by so late?" cried Jabez Stone in an ague of fear.

Stephen Vincent Benét, "The Devil and Daniel Webster" (1937)

With grim foreboding I lifted the heavy oaken lid. It was mossy and dank and my hands trembled as if I had an ague.

W. J. Stamper, "Ti Michel" (1926)

The cold was the taste of lemons and the vacuum was a rake of talons on his skin. The sun and the stars were a shaking ague that racked his bones.

Alfred Bester, *Tiger! Tiger!* (1956; aka *The Stars My Destination*)

He could almost picture his own slight body shaking as though under an ague, the sweat rolling off him, the fear a live thing around his body, his eyes large and white-ringed as they looked for a way out.

Harlan Ellison, "Run for the Stars" (1955)

One kiss of that tongue and the Darter boy reeled back, eyes bulging. He shook with a fatal ague while the serpent wrapped its coils round and round his neck.

John Jakes, "The Unspeakable Shrine" (1967) in *Brak the Barbarian*

The fat little man was crouched in his kingly robes, quivering with fright. His eyes bulged, his mottled jowls shook in the ague of terror that held him in his grasp.

Gardner F. Fox, *Kyrik: Warlock Warrior* (1975)

"And it isn't just that; a kind of dread haunts my bones like an ague."

Janet Fox, "Demon and Demoiselle" (1978)

Moments later the earth shook as with ague, and the serpent-folk were flung from their mounts to the slime of the jungle floor, many crushed in a moment by toppling conifers.

John R. Fultz, "The Devouring of S'lithik Hhai:
The History of X'hyl the Apothecary" (1997)

Aidenn, Aidenne, Aiden, aden, *pr.n.* & *n.* [< Ar *Adn*, the Muslim paradise or heaven, cognate with Hb ODN, Eden] The heavenly or paradisiacal world of the afterlife. [Not in *OED*. Coined by Edgar Allan Poe(?).]

Titles: Thomas Holley Chivers, "The Vigil of Aiden"

"Prophet!" said I, "thing of evil!—prophet still, if bird or devil!
By that Heaven that bends above us—by that God we both adore—
Tell this soul with sorrow laden if, within the distant Aidenn,
It shall clasp a sainted maiden whom the angels name Lenore—
Clasp a rare and radiant maiden whom the angels name Lenore."
Quoth the Raven "Nevermore."

Edgar Allan Poe, "The Raven" (1844)

"But the nucleus of the destroyer was now upon us;—even here in Aidenn, I shudder while I speak."

Edgar Allan Poe, "The Conversation of Eiros and Charmion" (1839)

There are *no* dreams in Aidenn—but it is here whispered that, of this infinity of matter, the *sole* purpose is to afford infinite springs, at which the soul may allay the thirst *to know* which is for ever unquenchable within it—since to quench it would be to extinguish the soul's self.

Edgar Allan Poe, "The Power of Words" (1845)

In the Rosy Bowers of Aiden
With her ruby lips love-laden
Dwelt the mild, the modest maiden
    Whom Politian calls Lenore.
As the churches, with their whiteness

Clothe the earth with their uprightness,
Clothes she now his soul with brightness,
    Breathing out her heart's love-lore;
For her lily limbs so tender,
Like the moon in her own splendor
Seemed all earthly things to render
    Bright as Eden was of yore.

                    Thomas Holley Chivers, "The Vigil of Aiden" (1851)

Not with ware of worth unladen,
    Sailed my bark in days of yore,
When, seafarer bound for Aidenn,
By the singing siren-maiden,
    Tempted, I forsook the shore.

                    Richard Garnett, "Prelude" in *Poems* (1893)

And we that joy in this month joy-laden,
    The gladdest thing that our eyes have seen,
Oh thou, proud mother and much proud maiden—
Maid yet mother as May hath been—
To thee we tender the beauties all
Of the month by men called virginal
And, where thou dwellest in deep-groved Aidenn,
    Salute thee, mother, the maid-month's Queen!

                    Gerard Manly Hopkins, "*Ad Mariam*" (1884)

Come, my demon-spouse, to fashion
    The fantastic marriage-bed!
Let the starry billows splash on
    Both our bodies, let them shed
Dewfall, as the streams Thalassian
    On Selene's fallen head!
Let us mingle magic passion,
    Interpenetrating, dead,
Deathless, O my dead sweet maiden!
Lifeless, in the secret Aidenn!
Let our bodies meet and mix
On the spirit's crucifix!

                    Aleister Crowley, *The Temple of the Holy Ghost* (1901)

This word is taken direct from Poe's "Raven" in the sense in which it is used by
him.

                    Aleister Crowley, note to *The Temple of the Holy Ghost* (1901)

The caravans that in the desert, heavy-laden,
By unknown oases pitch their sun-blacken'd tents,
Shall bring thee all sweet scents
Wherein delight in heaven the houris ever-maiden—
Patchouli, nard, and myrrh, from many a distant aden
Of heavenly indolence.

> David Park Barnitz, "Song of India" in *The Book of Jade* (1901)

"O Pow'rs of Light and Space and Aidenn,
Is *Life* with such foul horrors laden?
Pray hide no more the wondrous plan,
But shew the living glory—Man!"

> H. P. Lovecraft, "Astrophobos" (1917)

In a vale of light and laughter,
    Smiling 'neath the friendly sun,
Where fulfillment follow'd after
    Ev'ry hope or dream begun;
Where an Aidenn, gay and glorious,
    Beckon'd down the winsome way;
There my soul, o'er pain victorious,
    Laugh'd and linger'd—yesterday.

> H. P. Lovecraft, "Revelation" (1919)

No, Zara, no! Such beauty reigns
Immortal in immortal fanes;
Radiant for ever, ever laden
With beams of uncorrupted Aidenn,
And naught that slumbers here tonight
Can perish from a lover's sight.

> H. P. Lovecraft, "To Zara" (1922)

How oft would we float in the twilight
O'er flow'r-cover'd pastures and hillsides
All white with the lowly astalthon;
The lowly yet lovely astalthon,
And dream in a world made of dreaming
The dreams that are fairer than Aidenn;
Bright dreams that are truer than reason!

> H. P. Lovecraft, "Nathicana"

They have captured and chained you, my brother, from Aidenne beyond
    the blue,
The Fates and the vast All-Mother, to laugh at an hour or two.

> H. P. Lovecraft, "To an Infant" (1925)

Your distant vales are blue as Aidenn, yet no ease
I find therein, but pain against my coming stored:
Autumn, whose heart is one with all lost things adored,
By you I am betrayed to all my memories.

Clark Ashton Smith, "October" (1935)

Aidennic, *adj.* Of, pertaining to, or resembling Aidenn (q.v.). [Not in *OED*.]

Long as a leaping flame, exalted over all,
Across the sun
Her banners bear Aidennic blooms armorial
And beasts infernal on a field of ciclaton;
Amid her agate courts,
Like to a demon ichor, towering proud and tall,
A scarlet fountain spurts,
To fall upon parterres of dwale and deathly hebenon.

Clark Ashton Smith, "The Saturnienne" (1925)

For such—the peacock, and the poppy, and the rose—
Still wax within some dim Aidennic garden-close.

Donald Sidney-Fryer, "Spenserian Stanza-Sonnet Empoupré"

ailurophile, *n.* [< Gr *aílouros,* cat + *phílos,* loving] A lover of cats.

The word was ailurophile, and signifies one who, like myself, possesses an extreme fondness for the feline species. It is, of course, derived from the Greek
[*aílouros*], a cat—this term meaning literally "wag-tail", from [*aiólos*], quick-
moving or changeable (cf. [*Aíolos*]—Lat. Æolus—the God of the Winds), and
[*ourá*], tail.

H. P. Lovecraft, letter to M. F. Bonner (1 April 1936)

HPL's article is delighting the Sullys who, like myself, are fervent ailurophiles.

Clark Ashton Smith, letter to R. H. Barlow (9 September 1937)

But now, at this very instant, by Death's crooked, dark-alleyed plotting hidden
almost but not quite from himself, the thin wrists of the benign monarch of
Lankhmar were being pricked in innocent play be his favoritest cat's needle-
sharp claws, which had by a jealous, thin-nosed nephew of the royal ailurophile
been late last night envenomed with the wind-swift poison of the rare emperor
snake of tropical Klesh.

Fritz Leiber, "The Sadness of the Executioner" (1973)

Aklo, ?. See quotations. [Not in *OED*.]

I must not write down the real names of the days and months which I found
out a year ago, nor the way to make the Aklo letters, or the Chian language, or
the great beautiful Circles, nor the Mao Games, nor the chief songs. I may write

something about all these things but not the way to do them, for peculiar reasons. And I must not say who the Nymphs are, or the Dôls, or Jeelo, or what voolas mean. All these are most secret secrets, and I am glad when I remember what they are, and how many wonderful languages I know, but there are some things that I call the secrets of the secrets of the secrets that I dare not think of unless I am quite alone, and then I shut my eyes, and put my hands over them and whisper the word, and the Alala comes.

> Arthur Machen, "The White People" (1899)

Today learned the Aklo for the Sabaoth, which did not like, it being answerable from the hill and not from the air.

> Wilbur Whateley, diary, as quoted in
> H. P. Lovecraft, "The Dunwich Horror" (1928)

I wonder how I shall look when the earth is cleared and there are no earth beings on it. He that came with the Aklo Sabaoth said I may be transfigured, there being much of outside to work on.

> Wilbur Whateley, diary, as quoted in
> H. P. Lovecraft, "The Dunwich Horror" (1928)

It was in June that Blake's diary told of his victory over the cryptogram. The text was, he found, in the dark Aklo language used by certain cults of evil antiquity, and known to him in a halting way through previous researches.

> H. P. Lovecraft, "The Haunter of the Dark" (1935)

That tentacle suggests very ominously one which groped fumblingly about my own study eighty years ago, upon the one occasion when I attempted to read the *entire* Aklo ritual. I paused in time—but I shudder to think of what may have happened to a younger man too bold, too curious, or too enthusiastic to cease at the right moment.

> H. P. Lovecraft, letter to Henry Kuttner (30 November 1936)

The ants came marching hundred by hundred. The door to Chapel Perilous swung open again and the buzzing increased. All power to the Soviets: a *vagina dentata* myth. It was the Aklo chants being howled and gibbered and shrieked and grunted by thousands of dholes and shoggoths. There are sacraments of evil as well as of good: only the madman is absolutely sure. Azathoth, the Demon-Sultan who is the primal Chaos at the center of Infinity, howled: I know all about those garters, you two perverts! The ants came marching thousand by thousand.

> Robert Anton Wilson, *Masks of the Illuminati* (1981)

akman, *n.* [< Forrest J *Ackerman*, active in various controversies amongst science fiction fandom.] A slimy, wriggling creature native to the planet Venus. [Not in *OED*.]

Not another living thing higher than the wriggling akmans and skorahs, or the flying tukahs of the other continent—unless of course those holes in the Dionæan Plateau hide something.

> H. P. Lovecraft & Kenneth Sterling, "In the Walls of Eryx" (1936)

That body is simply a writhing mass of vermin now—the odour has begun to draw some of the slimy akmans from the far-off jungle.

> H. P. Lovecraft & Kenneth Sterling, "In the Walls of Eryx" (1936)

alabandine, alabraundine, alabraundyne, *n.* [< L *alabandīna* < *Alabanda,* a city of Caria] The precious stone almandine.

                    If I will
    I am at once the vision and the seer,
    And mingle with my ever-streaming pomps,
    And still abide their suzerain; I am
    The neophyte who serves a nameless god,
    Within whose fane the fanes of Hecatompylos
    Were arks the Titan worshippers might bear,
    Or flags to pave the threshold; or I am
    The god himself, who calls the fleeing clouds
    Into the nave where suns might congregate
    And veils the darkling mountain of his face
    With fold on solemn fold; for whom the priests
    Amass their monthly hecatomb of gems—
    Opals that are a camel-cumbering load,
    And monstrous alabraundines, won from war
    With realms of hostile serpents; which arise,
    Combustible, in vapors many-hued
    And myrrh-excelling perfumes.

> Clark Ashton Smith, *The Hashish-Eater; or, The Apocalypse of Evil* (1920)

alabastrine, alabastine, *adj.* Of, pertaining to, or resembling alabaster.

            Ah! more than voice hath said
            They speak of revels fled—
    The alabastine and exultant thighs,
            The vine-encircled head,
    The rose-face lifted, lyric, to the skies,
    The loins by leaping roses garlanded.

> George Sterling, "To a Girl Dancing" (1920)

Her hair was knotted in a long golden-brown braid, heavy as the glistening coils of some eastern serpent. Her eyes were a strange amber, her lips a vermilion touched with the coolness of woodland shadow, and her skin was of alabastrine fairness. Ambrose saw that she was beautiful; but she inspired him with the same awe that he would have felt before a queen, together with something of the fear and consternation which a virtuous young monk would conceive in the perilous presence of an alluring succubus.

Clark Ashton Smith, "The Holiness of Azédarac" (1931)

Alastor, alastor, *pr.n.* & *n.* [< Gr *alástōr* < *alastos*, unforgettable] A spirit or personification of vengeance; the masculine equivalent of the feminine Nemesis (q.v.).

Titles: Percy Bysshe Shelley, *Alastor; or, The Spirit of Solitude* (verse); Jack Vance, three novels set in the Alastor Cluster—*Marune: Alastor 933, Wyst: Alastor 1716,* and *Trullion: Alastor 2262*

At this time Shelley wrote his *Alastor.* He was at a loss for a title, and I proposed that which he adopted: *Alastor; or, The Spirit of Solitude.* The Greek word, [*Alastōr*], is an evil genius, [*kakodaimōn*], though the sense of the two words is somewhat different [. . .] The poem treated the spirit of solitude as a spirit of evil. I mention the true meaning of the word because many have supposed Alastor to be the name of the hero of the poem.

Thomas Love Peacock, *Memoirs of Shelley* (1858–60)

We may picture him in the traditional state of the sorcerer—poor, proscribed, envious, ambitious, and having no capacity for legitimate enterprises. Unable to earn money, he hankers after hidden treasures, and haunts those spots up and down the country-side which are reputed to conceal them. He has done this presumably for a long time before determining to betake himself to Magic, but the earth will not yield up her hoards, for the gnomes and the Earth-Spirits, the Alastors and the Demons of the Solitudes, stand guard over the secrets of dead misers when the human ghost has ceased to walk in the neighbourhood.

A. E. Waite, *The Book of Ceremonial Magic* (1898/1911; aka *The Book of Black Magic, The Book of Black Magic and of Pacts,* & *The Book of Black Magic and Ceremonial Magic*)

Apart from this general signification there is a personal allusion to 666 who is Alastor, the Spirit of Solitude. Foolish Rabbins have included this symbol in their list of demons. To the well-fed Pharisee as to the modern bourgeois nothing seems more frightful than solitude in which the mind is compelled to face reality.

Aleister Crowley, commentary to *Liber Cordis Cincti Serpenti vel LXV* (1907)

Much was made of the obscure nativity of Nathaire and his dubitable wanderings before he had settled, six years previous, in Vyones. People said that he was fiend-begotten, like the fabled Merlin: his father being no less a personage than Alastor, demon of revenge; and his mother a deformed and dwarfish sorceress. From the former, he had taken his spitefulness and malignity; from the latter, his squat, puny physique.

Clark Ashton Smith, "The Colossus of Ylourgne" (1932)

Love, can you see, as I,
The corpses, ghosts and demons mingled with the crowd?
The djinns that men have freed, grown turbulent and proud?
Alastor, Asmodai?
And all-unheeded envoys from the stars on high?

Clark Ashton Smith, "Interrogation" (1925)

Waste not thy knightliness in wars unworthy,
For time and his alastors shall destroy
Full soon, and bring to stuffless, cloudy ruin
All things that fret thy spirit, riding down
This pass with pandemonian walls, this Hinnom
Where Moloch and where Mammon herd the doomed.

Clark Ashton Smith, "Don Quixote on Market Street" (1950)

Algol, *pr.n* [< Ar *al-ghûl,* the ghoul or demon] The beta star of the constellation Perseus, known as the Demon Star.

"You on earth have unwittingly felt its distant presence—you who without knowing idly gave to its blinking beacon the name of Algol, the Dæmon-Star."

H. P. Lovecraft, "Beyond the Wall of Sleep" (1919)

Unlike the heroes in my own tales, who were wont to visit the Fifth Dimension or the worlds of Algol with perfect *sangfroid,* I did not feel in the least adventurous, and I shrank back with man's instinctive recoil before the unknown.

Clark Ashton Smith, "The City of the Singing Flame" (1931)

alienist, *n.* A psychiatrist; in particular, one legally empowered to certify patients insane and have them committed to an asylum.

Of course I couldn't pass any alienist's examination—but could any alienist?

Charles Fort, *Lo!* (1931)

Ward, it is true, was always a scholar and an antiquarian; but even his most brilliant early work did not shew the prodigious grasp and insight displayed during his last examinations by the alienists.

H. P. Lovecraft, *The Case of Charles Dexter Ward* (1927)

The beginning of Ward's madness is a matter of dispute among alienists.

H. P. Lovecraft, *The Case of Charles Dexter Ward* (1927)

People in general would have laughed if they had known what I was trying to do. Also there were cousins and other relations, all enviously watchful of my inherited wealth . . . and a country full of lawyers, alienists, and lunatic asylums. I have always had a reputation for eccentricity; and I did not choose to give my

dear relatives an opportunity which might have been considered legally sufficient for the well-known process of "railroading."

> Clark Ashton Smith, "The Letter from Mohaun Los" (1931;
> aka "Flight into Super-Time"; ellipsis in original)

In my capacity of alienist and physician I have often committed patients to the
selfsame institution in which I myself am now confined, and today—irony of
ironies!—I find myself their brother in misfortune.

> Robert Bloch, "The Grinning Ghoul" (1936)

What follows is an exact account of the circumstances which have led me to a
noisome dungeon, under constant observation by alienists, brutally misused by
simian thugs in white coats should I so much as refer to the hateful knowledge
in my brain.

> John Brunner, "Concerning the Forthcoming Inexpensive
> Paperback Translation of the *Necronomicon* of Abdul Alhazred" (1992)

an, an if, *conj.* If, and if.

Strive ever more! and if thou art truly mine—and doubt it not, an if thou art
ever joyous!—death is the crown of all.

> Aleister Crowley, *Liber AL vel Legis* (1904)

Thither would I go were I old enough to find the way, and thither shouldst thou
go an thou wouldst sing and have men listen to thee.

> H. P. Lovecraft, "The Quest of Iranon" (1921; misprinted as *and* in many editions)

> "Well, old man, what are you doing here?"
> "Looking at the fish, an it please Your Lordship."

> John Bellairs, *The Face in the Frost* (1969)

anarch, *n.* [< *anarchy*, through backformation by analogy with *monarch*] (1) A
lawless and anarchic ruler; a tyrant, despot. (2) A partisan of anarchy or anarchism; an anarchist. Coined by John Milton, who applied the term to Chaos in
Paradise Lost.

Titles: David Humphreys, Joel Barlow, John Trumbull, and Dr. Lemuel Hop-
kins, *The Anarchiad: A Poem on the Restoration of Chaos and Substantial Night*; Malcolm Jameson, "The Anarch"; A. Bertram Chandler, *The Anarch Lords*

> Thus *Satan*; and him thus the Anarch old
> With falt'ring speech and visage incompos'd
> Answer'd.

> John Milton, *Paradise Lost* (1667)

> Lo! thy dread Empire, CHAOS! is restor'd;
> Light dies before thy uncreating word:
> Thy hand, great Anarch! lets the curtain fall;

And Universal Darkness buries All.

> Alexander Pope, *The Dunciad in Four Books* (1728)

In visions fair the scenes of fate unroll,
And Massachusetts opens on my soul;
There Chaos, Anarch old, asserts his sway,
And mobs in myriads blacken all the way:
See Day's stern port—behold the martial frame
of Shays' and Shattuck's mob-compelling name:
See the bold Hampshirites on Springfield pour,
The fierce Tauntonians crowd the alewife shore.

> David Humphreys, Joel Barlow, John Trumbull, and Dr. Lemuel Hopkins,
> *The Anarchiad: A Poem on the Restoration of Chaos and Substantial Night* (1786–87)

Look where the second Cæsar's trophies rose!
Now, like the hands that rear'd them, withering:
Imperial Anarchs, doubling human woes!
GOD! was thy globe ordain'd for such to win and lose?

> Lord Byron, *Childe Harold's Pilgrimage: A Romaunt* (1809–18)

Is it that now my inexperienced fingers
But strike the prelude of a loftier strain?
Or must the lyre on which my spirit lingers
Soon pause in silence, ne'er to sound again,
Though it might shake the Anarch Custom's reign,
And charm the minds of men to Truth's own sway,
Reply in hope—but I am worn away,
And Death and Love are yet contending for their prey.

> Percy Bysshe Shelley, *The Revolt of Islam: A Poem* (1817)

[. . .]
But if Freedom should awake
In her omnipotence, and shake
From the Celtic Anarch's hold
All the keys of dungeons cold,
Where a hundred cities lie
Chained like thee, ingloriously,
Thou and all thy sister band
Might adorn this sunny land,
Twining memories of old time
With new virtues more sublime;
If not, perish thou and they!—

> Percy Bysshe Shelley, "Lines Written Among the Eugenean Hills" (1818)

This human living multitude
Was savage, cunning, blind, and rude,

For thou wert not; but o'er the populous solitude,
    Like one fierce cloud over a waste of waves
        Hung tyranny; beneath, sate deified
    The sister-pest, congregator of slaves;
        Into the shadow of her pinions wide
Anarchs and priests, who feed on gold and blood
    Till with the stain their inmost souls are dyed,
    Dyed the astonished herds of men from every side.
            Percy Bysshe Shelley, "Ode to Liberty" (1820)

[Referring to Napoleon:]

When one, like them, but mightier far than they,
    The Anarch of thine own bewildered powers,
        Rose: armies mingled in obscure array,
    Like clouds with clouds, darkening the sacred bowers
Of serene heaven. He, by the past pursued,
    Rests with those dead, but unforgotten hours,
    Whose ghosts scare victor kings in their ancestral towers.
            Percy Bysshe Shelley, "Ode to Liberty" (1820)

What though Cimmerian anarchs dare blaspheme
    Freedom and thee? thy shield is as a mirror
To make their blind slaves see, and with fierce gleam
    To turn his hungry sword upon the wearer;
        A new Actæon's error
Shall theirs have been—devoured by their own hounds!
    Be thou like the imperial Basilisk,
Killing thy foe with unapparent wounds!
            Percy Bysshe Shelley, "Ode to Naples" (1820)

Dissonant threats kill Silence far away,
    The serene Heaven which wraps our Eden wide
        With iron light is dyed,
The Anarchs of the North lead forth their legions
    Like Chaos o'er creation, uncreating;
An hundred tribes nourished on strange religions
And lawless slaveries,—down the aërial regions
        Of the white Alps, desolating;
        Famished wolves that bide no waiting,
Blotting the glowing footsteps of old glory,
Trampling our columned cities into dust,
        Their dull and savage lust
        On Beauty's corse to sickness satiating—
They come! The fields they tread look black and hoary

With fire—from their red feet the streams run gory!
Percy Bysshe Shelley, "Ode to Naples" (1820)

In the great Morning of the world
The spirit of God with might unfurled
The flag of Freedom over chaos,
    And all the banded anarchs fled
Like Vultures frighted from Imaus
    Before an Earthquake's tread.—
Percy Bysshe Shelley, Hellas: A Lyrical Drama (1821)

    What anarch wears a crown or mitre,
Or bears the sword, or grasps the key of gold,
Whose friends are not thy friends, whose foes thy foes?
Percy Bysshe Shelley, Hellas: A Lyrical Drama (1821)

Shout in the jubilee of death! the Greeks
Are as a brood of lions in the net
Round which the kingly hunters of the earth
Stand smiling. Anarchs, ye whose daily food
Are curses, groans and gold, the fruit of death
From Thule to the Girdle of the World,
Come, feast! the board groans with the flesh of men;
The cup is foaming with a nation's blood,
Famine and Thirst await! eat, drink and die!
Percy Bysshe Shelley, Hellas: A Lyrical Drama (1821)

    "Dost thou behold,"
Said then my guide, "those spoilers spoiled, Voltaire,

    "Frederic, and Kant, Catherine, and Leopold,
Chained hoary anarchs, demagogue and sage
    Whose name the fresh world thinks already old—

"For in the battle Life and they did wage
    She remained conqueror—I was overcome
By my own heart alone, which neither age

    "Nor tears nor infamy nor now the tomb
Could temper to its object."—
Percy Bysshe Shelley, "The Triumph of Life" (1822)

    Could I remake me! or set free
This sexless bound in sex, then plunge
Deeper than Sappho, in a lunge
Piercing Pan's paramount mystery!

For, Nature, in no shallow surge
Against thee either sex may urge,
Why hast thou made us but in halves—
Co-relatives? This makes us slaves.
If these co-relatives never meet
Self-hood itself seems incomplete.
And such the dicing of blind fate
Few matching halves here meet and mate.
What Cosmic jest or Anarch blunder
The human integral clove asunder
And shied the fractions through life's gate?

Herman Melville, "After the Pleasure Party" (185-)

"A torpedo," cried Zero, brightening, "a torpedo in the Thames! Superb, dear fellow! I recognize in you the marks of an accomplished anarch."

Robert Louis Stevenson & Fanny Van de Grift Stevenson, *The Dynamiter* (1885)

People begin to find Shelley—for all his melody—noisy and ill-conditioned now because his Anarchs have vanished, yet there was a time when novel thought *had* to go to that tune of breaking glass.

H. G. Wells, *In the Days of the Comet* (1912)

Hail! passionate rebel, great anarch of Nazareth, slitter of masks,
Announcer of Self procreate from a self—
Halloo! Halloo! from me to thee!

Benjamin De Casseres, "The Cynic of Nazareth"
in *The Shadow-Eater* (1916)

O Thou wild anarch of the Hills, pale glooming above the mists of the Earth! I adore Thee, Evoe! I adore Thee, IAO!

J. F. C. Fuller, *The Treasure House of Images* (1913)

You were bred, fed, fostered and fattened from holy childhood up in this two easter island on the piejaw of hilarious heaven and roaring the other place (plunders to night of you, blunders what's left of you, flash as flash can!) and now, forsooth, a nogger among the blankards of this dastard century, you have become of twosome twiminds forenenst gods, hidden and discovered, nay, condemned fool, anarch, egoarch, hiresiarch, you have reared your disunited kingdom on the vacuum of your own most intensely doubtful soul.

James Joyce, *Finnegans Wake* (1922–39)

And from their riven pomp and sundered dust
    Arose imperial in their print of flame
Œdipus, Agamemnon ever just,
    And hoar Tiresias wearily the same;

One rises with a face of suffering,
    Beautiful as a god with golden hair,
Austerely saying: "I am Louis Lingg,
    I am the priest whose gospel was despair,
We, on that terrible eve forever gone,
    Draped with the anarch red your fleeting altar,
      We dared—O holy Mother—even we;
    Lied on and spied on, never once to cease or falter,
And I, who perished without word or moan,
      I cry aloud your name, O Liberty!"
                  Samuel Loveman, "Debs in Prison" (c. 1919)

Beautiful souls, unquenched dooms of men,
Crying, "Who calls us from our anarch ken?
Is it the night hath ta'en your hope immortal,
    O miserablest of earth's unwary ones?
None gaze upon this adamantine portal,
    Unblinded by the sapphire-lighted suns!"
             Samuel Loveman, "A Triumph in Eternity" (1921)

                Then I would urge
The strong contention and conflicting might
Of Chaos and Creation—matching them,
Those immemorial powers inimical,
And all their stars and gulfs subservient,
Dynasts of time, and anarchs of the dark—
In closer war reverseless, and would set
New discord at the universal core—
A Samson-principle to bring it down
In one magnificence of ruin. Yea,
The monster, Chaos, were mine unleashed hound,
And all my power Destruction's own right arm!
             Clark Ashton Smith, "Nero" (1912)

Upon their heavenly precipice,
The gathered suns shrink back aghast
From that interminate abyss,
And threat of sightless anarchs vast.

             Clark Ashton Smith, "Ode on Imagination"

androsphinx (*pl.* **androsphinges, androsphinxes**), *n.* A male sphinx.

    Stone colossi marched in endless night and drove herds of grinning androsphinxes down to the shores of illimitable stagnant rivers of pitch.
             H. P. Lovecraft & Harry Houdini, "Under the Pyramids" (1924)

The opaque, jet-like orbs of their huge eyes were impassive as the carven eyes of androsphinxes, and they uttered no sound from their heavy, straight, expressionless lips.

Clark Ashton Smith, "The City of the Singing Flame" (1931)

antediluvian, *adj.* [< L *ante,* before + *dīluvium,* flood, deluge] Dating from before the Noachian deluge of Biblical mythology; extremely old or ancient.

There was silence supreme! Not a shriek, not a scream,
Scarcely even a howl or a groan,
As the man they called "Ho!" told his story of woe
In an antediluvian tone.

Lewis Carroll, *The Hunting of the Snark* (1876)

For a short mile it was visible, pouring in and out among the islands, and then disappearing with a huge sweep into the willows, which closed about it like a herd of monstrous antediluvian creatures crowding down to drink.

Algernon Blackwood, "The Willows"

We went into the moonless and tortuous network of that incredibly ancient town; went out as the lights in the curtained windows disappeared one by one, and the Dog Star leered at the throng of cowled, cloaked figures that poured silently from every doorway and formed monstrous processions up this street and that, past the creaking signs and antediluvian gables, the thatched roofs and diamond-paned windows; threading precipitous lanes where decaying houses overlapped and crumbled together, gliding across open courts and churchyards where the bobbing lanthorns made eldritch drunken constellations.

H. P. Lovecraft, "The Festival" (1923)

"That was his original theory. In later years he apparently cloaked it with a pattern of demonology and what amounted to a modern adaptation of prehistoric superstition and folklore. He believed that these super undersea species are the incarnation of those Elder Gods who ruled the antediluvian deep and whose existence has been brought down to us in the dark myths and legends of primitive man; that commanded by the great Cthulhu, they have lain dormant these eons in the sunken city of Flann, awaiting the time they would rise again to feed and rule. He believed further that this metempsychosis of the Elder Gods carried with it a latent incredible power and that if he could aid them to their destiny some of that power would be transmitted to him. Oh, Horatio really went all out in this mystic fol-de-rol. I even overheard him promise his brother, Edmund, all kinds of maledictions if he continued to ridicule his beliefs."

Carl Jacobi, "The Aquarium" (1962)

antemundane, ante-mundane, *adj.* Of, belonging to, or pertaining to a period before the creation of the world.

The power of Zhothaqquah was still feared; and it was said that those who were willing to forgo their humanity by serving him would become the heritors of antemundane secrets, and the masters of a knowledge so awful that it could only have been brought from outlying planets coeval with night and chaos.

Clark Ashton Smith, "The Door to Saturn" (1930)

Again he became the sorcerer Zon Mezzamalech in Mhu Thulan; again he dreamt to retrieve the wisdom of the antemundane gods; again he drew back from the deepening crystal with the terror of one who fears to fall; and once more—but doubtfully and dimly, like a failing wraith—he was Paul Tregardis.

Clark Ashton Smith, "Ubbo-Sathla" (1932)

Antenora, *pr.n.* In Dante's *Inferno,* the second division of the ninth circle of Hell, named for Antenor, who betrayed Troy in the Trojan War, and in which the souls of traitors are frozen neck-deep in a lake of ice. [Not in *OED.*]

> Through doors
> Enlaid with lilies twined luxuriously,
> I enter, dazed and blinded with the sun,
> And hear, in gloom that changing colors cloud,
> A chuckle sharp as crepitating ice
> Upheaved and cloven by shoulders of the damned
> Who strive in Antenora.

Clark Ashton Smith, *The Hashish-Eater; or, The Apocalypse of Evil* (1920)

antholite, *n.* A fossil flower.

"Before you is one of the flowers of which I have spoken. It is not, as you have perhaps surmised, a work of sculpture, but it is an antholite, or fossil blossom, brought, with others of the same kind, from the world to which I am native."

Clark Ashton Smith, "Vulthoom" (1933)

Aonian, *adj.* Of or pertaining to Aonia, the region of ancient Bœotia which contains Mts. Helicon and Cithæron, sacred to the "Aonian maids," the Muses.

> Each eve he sought his bashful Muse to wake
> With overdoses of ice-cream and cake;
> But tho' th' ambitious youth a dreamer grew,
> Th' Aonian Nymph declin'd to come to view.

H. P. Lovecraft, "The Poe-et's Nightmare: A Fable" (1916)

Apollyon, *pr.n.* [< Gr *apollýōn,* destroyer] See under **Abaddon.**

So he went on, and *Apollyon* met him; now the Monster was hidious to behold, he was clothed with scales like a Fish (and they are his pride) he had Wings like a Dragon, feet like a Bear, and out of his belly came Fire and Smoak, and his mouth was as the mouth of a Lion.

John Bunyan, *The Pilgrim's Progress from This World to That Which Is to Come, Delivered under the Similitude of a Dream* (1678–84)

And just as far as ever from the end!
   Naught in the distance but the evening, naught
   To point my footstep further! At the thought,
A great black bird, Apollyon's bosom-friend,
Sailed past, nor beat his wide wing dragon-penned
   That brushed my cap—perchance the guide I sought.

Robert Browning, "'Childe Roland to the Dark Tower Came'" (1852)

Then, when he had apparently convinced himself of Gaspard's identity, the look of maniacal wrath returned, flooding his eyes with Tartarean fire and twisting his lineaments into a mask of Apollyon-like malignity.

Clark Ashton Smith, "The Colossus of Ylourgne" (1932)

O, foulness born as of the ninefold curse
Of dragon-mouthed Apollyon, plumed with darts
And armed with horns of incandescent bronze!

Clark Ashton Smith, "The Ghoul and the Seraph" (1919)

arabesque, Arabesque, *adj.* & *n.* (1) Arabian or Moorish; of, pertaining to, or resembling the style of art known as arabesque (see following). (2) A complex, interlaced pattern in which geometric, floral, and foliate figures are fantastically interwoven. The style takes its name from its employment in Moorish and Arabian decorative art.

Titles: Edgar Allan Poe, *Tales of the Grotesque and the Arabesque*; Clark Ashton Smith, "Arabesque" (verse)

a. As *adj.*:

Let me not be supposed to prefer the rhythm in which it is written, abstractedly considered, to the regular blank verse; the noblest measure, in my judgement, of which our admirable language is capable. For the following Poem I have preferred it, because it suits the varied subject: it is the *Arabesque* ornament of an Arabian tale.

Robert Southey, Preface to *Thalaba the Destroyer* (1800)

"Like these arabesque censers, my spirit is writhing in fire, and the delirium of this scene is fashioning me for the wilder visions of that land of real dreams whither I am now rapidly departing."

Edgar Allan Poe, "The Assignation" (1834)

The silken hair, too, had been suffered to grow all unheeded, and as, in its wild gossamer texture, it floated rather than fell about the face, I could not, even with effort, connect its Arabesque expression with any idea of simple humanity.

Edgar Allan Poe, "The Fall of the House of Usher" (1839)

He had directed, in great part, the moveable embellishments of the seven chambers, upon occasion of this great *fête*; and it was his own guiding taste which had given character to the masqueraders. Be sure they were grotesque. There were much glare and glitter and piquancy and phantasm—what has been since seen in "Hernani." There were arabesque figures with unsuited limbs and appointments. There were delirious fancies such as the madman fashions. There was much of the beautiful, much of the wanton, much of the bizarre, something of the terrible, and not a little of that which might have excited disgust.

> Edgar Allan Poe, "The Masque of the Red Death" (1842)

Then, employing a flint and steel which I found on one of the small tables, I lit the many candles reposing about the walls in Arabesque sconces.

> H. P. Lovecraft & Winifred Virginia Jackson, "The Crawling Chaos" (1920–21)

De Quincey more than once revels in grotesque and arabesque terrors, though with a desultoriness and learned pomp which deny him the rank of specialist.

> H. P. Lovecraft, "Supernatural Horror in Literature" (1925–27)

Pardon my flight of fancy—but mysteries always arouse my imagination. It seems too bad to let them pass without providing material for a tale of the grotesque or arabesque. I fear if I were to become a lady's man like you, I should offend all my charmers at the very outset by weaving them into weird and horrible tales! But fortunately horror-writers are not often ladies' men—notwithstanding Mr. Poe's fondness for the fair.

> H. P. Lovecraft, letter to Reinhardt Kleiner (27 December 1719) [*sic*]

Of the drawings & water-colours I lack a vocabulary adequate to express my enthusiastic admiration. What a world of opiate phantasy & horror is here unveiled, & what an unique power & perspective must lie behind it! I speak with especial sincerity & enthusiasm, because my own especial tastes centre almost wholly around the grotesque & the arabesque. I have tried to write short stories & sketches affording glimpses into the unknown abysses of terror which leer beyond the boundaries of the known, but have never succeeded in evoking even a fraction of the stark hideousness conveyed by any one of your ghoulishly potent designs.

> H. P. Lovecraft, letter to Clark Ashton Smith (12 August 1922)

I thanked my courteous host and followed the silent black automaton up the great stone staircase. The flickering torch of the giant servitor cast arabesque shadows upon bare stone walls of great age and advanced decrepitude; clearly the structure was very old.

> Robert Bloch, "The Feast in the Abbey" (1934)

The room blazed with the coruscating brilliance of the glowing gems, which were set in walls and ceiling in bizarre arabesque patterns.

> Henry Kuttner, "Spawn of Dagon" (1938)

[Hakim] Bey has a potpourri of penchants—anarchy, speculative physics, fanzines, dope, heretical Islam and comely boys—which are somehow all of a piece in his hands. Bey put the sin back into syncretism. He has written numerous essays as well as *Crowstone*, the world's finest—and only—pornographic sword 'n' sorcery man-boy love novel; and *Chaos: The Broadsheets of Ontological Anarchism*, an ecstatic anarcho-arabesque vision. *Crowstone* as fantasy (in the rococo decadent mode of, say, Jack Vance), like *Crowstone* as hard-core porn, astonishes by the way it at once realizes and synthesizes these genres; his parody, like Fielding's, actually displaces the object of parody.

Bob Black, "The Marginals Marco Polo"

Maria had been reading a chrystelephantinely over-written book called *Moll Flanders* in the coach, and very definitely she thought the somber, passionate, tragicomic, and picaresque story was most absorbing, and certainly presented the dark, sinister, underground side of English life in a vivacious and veridical manner that carried conviction, but she wished Mr. Defoe were not so in love with ornamentally excessive adjectives and long, stentorian, and somewhat inchoate sentences that, even by the standards of the time, seemed to twist and turn through curlicues and arabesques and wind on and on through ever-increasing clauses and sub-clauses, including abrupt changes of subject and total *non sequiturs*, even if he did seem to be making a unique effort to understand a woman's perspective on the world, which was all to the good, of course, and it was less monochromatically monotonous (she had to admit) than the other one he wrote with virtually nobody in it but that one ingenious mechanic on the island, living in total isolation until he found that mute but ineluctuctable footprint; and yet it could all be told as well and be more pleasant to read if those sentences did get so totally out of control and sprawl all over the page so often in positive apotheosis of the lugubrious style, and then she wondered if reading so much of such labyrinthine and arabesque prose for so long in the hot carriage had affected her own mind and she were starting to think like that herself, instead of just enjoying the shade of the oak trees and resting from thought in the dense cool quiet of the mid-afternoon English summer.

Robert Anton Wilson, *Nature's God* (1991)

b. As noun:

Its walls were hung with tapestry and bedecked with manifold and multiform armorial trophies, together with an unusually great number of very spirited modern paintings in frames of rich golden arabesque.

Edgar Allan Poe, "The Oval Portrait" (1842)

The material was the richest cloth of gold. It was spotted all over, at irregular intervals, with arabesque figures, about a foot in diameter, and wrought upon the cloth in patterns of the most jetty black. But these figures partook of the true character of the arabesque only when regarded from a single point of view. By a contrivance now common, and indeed traceable to a very remote period of antiquity, they were made changeable in aspect. To one entering the room, they bore the appearance of simple monstrosities; but upon a farther advance, this appearance gradually departed; and step by step, as the visitor moved his station in the chamber, he saw himself surrounded by an endless succession of the ghastly forms which belong to the superstition of the Norman, or arise in the guilty slumbers of the monk. The phantasmagoric effect was vastly heightened by the artificial introduction of a strong continual current of wind behind the draperies—giving a hideous and uneasy animation to the whole.

Edgar Allan Poe, "Ligeia" (1838)

> Like strange mechanical grotesques,
> Making fantastic arabesques,
> The shadows raced across the blind.

Oscar Wilde, "The Harlot's House" (1883)

From the mouths of the dragon and the Loves, from the swans' eyes, from the breasts of the doves, from the satyrs' horns and lips, from the masks at many points, and from the children's curls, the water played profusely, cutting strange arabesques and subtle figures.

Aubrey Beardsley, The Story of Venus and Tannhäuser: A Romantic Novel (1894–98)

The outside pattern is a florid arabesque, reminding one of a fungus. If you can imagine a toadstool in joints, an interminable string of toadstools, budding and sprouting in endless convolutions—why, that is something like it.

Charlotte Perkins Gilman, "The Yellow Wall-Paper" (1892)

The Sub-Cantor looked over his shoulder at the pinned-down sheet where the first words of the magnificat were built up in gold washed with red-lac for a background to the Virgin's hardly yet fired halo. She was shown, hands joined in wonder, at a lattice of infinitely intricate arabesque, round the edges of which sprays of orange-bloom seemed to load the blue air that carried back over the minute parched landscape in the middle distance.

Rudyard Kipling, "The Eye of Allah" (1926)

He rattled on about his wedding and the graces of Constance, and their future prospects, calling my attention to his captain's shoulder-straps, and the triple gold arabesque on his sleeve and fatigue cap.

Robert W. Chambers, "The Repairer of Reputations" (1895)

At the far side was a low, wide divan of ivory inlaid with the milky crystals and patterned with golden arabesques.

A. Merritt, The Ship of Ishtar (1924)

Inside, wrapped in a discoloured parchment, was a huge key of tarnished silver covered with cryptical arabesques; but of any legible explanation there was none.

H. P. Lovecraft, "The Silver Key" (1926)

Certainly, I look forward impatiently to the sight of that great silver key, for in its cryptical arabesques there may stand symbolised all the aims and mysteries of a blindly impersonal cosmos.

H. P. Lovecraft, "The Silver Key" (1926)

Gilman sometimes compared the inorganic masses to prisms, labyrinths, clusters of cubes and planes, and Cyclopean buildings; and the organic things struck him variously as groups of bubbles, octopi, centipedes, living Hindoo idols, and intricate Arabesques roused into a kind of ophidian animation.

H. P. Lovecraft, "The Dreams in the Witch House" (1932)

Nathaire, propped among Saracenic cushions with arabesques of sullen gold and fulgurant scarlet, was peering upon him from a kind of improvised couch, made with bales of Orient rugs and arrases, to whose luxury the rude walls of the castle, stained with mold and mottled with dead fungi, offered a grotesque foil.

Clark Ashton Smith, "The Colossus of Ylourgne" (1932)

We returned to the study, and Carnby brought out from a locked drawer the volume of which he had spoken. It was enormously old, and was bound in ebony covers arabesqued with silver and set with darkly glowing garnets.

Clark Ashton Smith, "The Return of the Sorcerer" (1931)

The fire was green and dazzling, pure as the central flame of a star; it blinded me, and when I turned my eyes away, the air was filled with webs of intricate colour, with swiftly changing arabesques whose numberless, unwonted hues and patterns were such as no mundane eye had ever beheld.

Clark Ashton Smith, "The City of the Singing Flame" (1931)

The globe had grown enormous. From it, there issued palpable ropes and filaments, pearly, shuddering into strange colors, that appeared to fasten themselves to the ruined floor and walls and roof, like the weaving of a spider. Thickly and more thickly they multiplied, forming a curtain between Grotara and the chasm, and falling upon Thirlain Ludoch and himself, till he saw the sanguine burning of the globe as through arabesques of baleful opal.

Clark Ashton Smith, "The Weaver in the Vault" (1933)

> Like arabesques of ebony,
> The cypresses in silhouette,
> Fantastically cleave and fret
> A moon of yellow ivory.

Clark Ashton Smith, "Arabesque"

On Earth

He comes no more: the very worms have died
In the scarce-nibbled carrion; the thin wind
Will write man's epitaph in shifting sand,
And the pale unfading arabesques of frost
Adorn and fret his ghoul-forgotten tomb.

Clark Ashton Smith, "The Flight of Azrael"

For the tetrahedra were restless, were weaving aimlessly in and out among the boulders in weird arabesques as of some unearthly dance of the crystal folk, were condensing in little groups of half a dozen or less that formed and broke again even as do restless humans, waiting impatiently for some anticipated event.

P. Schuyler Miller, "Tetrahedra of Space" (1931)

And the mosaic seemed to follow some definite pattern, unfamiliar to Carson; there were curves of purple and violet mingled with angled lines of green and blue, intertwining in fantastic arabesques.

Henry Kuttner, "The Salem Horror" (1937)

The scream shot out of his flesh through empty locker rooms and barracks, musty resort hotels, and spectral, coughing corridors of T.B. sanitariums, the muttering, hawking, grey dishwater smell of flophouses and Old Men's Homes, great, dusty custom sheds and warehouses, through broken porticoes and smeared arabesques, from urinals worn paper thin by the urine of a million fairies, deserted weed-grown privies with a musty smell of shit turning back to the soil, erect wooden phallus on the grave of dying peoples plaintive as leaves in the wind, across the great brown river where whole trees float with green snakes in the branches and sad-eyed lemurs watch the shore out over a vast plain (vulture wings husk in the dry air).

William S. Burroughs, *Naked Lunch* (1955–59)

Catatonic youths dressed as women in gowns of burlap and rotten rags, faces heavily and crudely painted in bright colors over a strata of beatings, arabesques of broken, suppurating scars to the pearly bone, push against the passer-by in silent clinging insistence.

William S. Burroughs, *Naked Lunch* (1955–59)

"Shahryar bid her fetch me in to sit at the foot of the bed; almost in a faint I watched him help her off with the pretty nightie I'd crocheted for her myself, place a white silk cushion under her bottom, and gently open her legs; as I'd never seen a man erect before, I groaned despite myself when he opened his robe and I saw what he meant to stick her with: the hair done up in pearls, the shaft like a minaret decorated with arabesques, the head like a cobra's spread to strike."

John Barth, "Dunyazadiad" in *Chimera* (1972)

Each of those who enter the realm of the *Imam-of-one's-own-being* becomes a sultan of inverted revelation, a monarch of abrogation & apostasy. In a central chamber scalloped with light and hung with tapestried arabesques they lean on bolsters & smoke long chibouks of haschisch scented with opium & amber.

> Hakim Bey (Peter Lamborn Wilson), "The Assassins" in
> *T.A.Z.: The Temporary Autonomous Zone, Ontological Anarchy, Poetic Terrorism*

arborescence, *n.* A tree-like growth or formation.

"I can't tell you now whether it's an exterior or an interior—whether those hellish Cyclopean vaultings are seen from the outside or the inside, or whether they are indeed carven stone and not merely a morbid fungous arborescence. The geometry of the whole thing is crazy—one gets the acute and obtuse angles all mixed up."

> H. P. Lovecraft & Zealia Bishop, "Medusa's Coil" (1930)

arcade, *n.* [< Fr < It *arcata* < *arco,* arch] A long, arched passageway or gallery.

But at the time it was all horribly real, and nothing can ever efface the memory of those nighted crypts, those titan arcades, and those half-formed shapes of hell that strode gigantically in silence holding half-eaten things whose still surviving portions screamed for mercy or laughed with madness.

> H. P. Lovecraft, "The Horror at Red Hook" (1925)

Reluctant even to be left alone again, each one of the cowed squatters refused point-blank to advance another inch toward the scene of unholy worship, so Inspector Legrasse and his nineteen colleagues plunged on unguided into black arcades of horror that none of them had ever trod before.

> H. P. Lovecraft, "The Call of Cthulhu" (1926)

arcanic, *adj.* Of or pertaining to arcana (q.v.); arcane.

Gaillard, especially, felt himself in the presence of ultramundane mystery and marveled as he neared the coppery-golden bulk: his feeling amounted almost to an actual vertigo, such as would be experienced by one who gazes athwart unfathomable gulfs upon the arcanic secrets and the wit-transforming wonders of a foreign sphere.

> Clark Ashton Smith, "Seedling of Mars" (1931)

arcanum (*pl.* **arcana**), *n.* A profound secret or mystery; in particular, and especially when in the plural, the specialized knowledge or information known only to a defined group and inaccessible to the general public. Frequently used in the plural.

If this slight and casual hint of a secret is felt by both Marguerite and myself with so much uneasiness and embarrassment, what will be our situation, if I go on to accept the stranger's confidence, and become the depository of an arcanum so important as he represents his to be?

William Godwin, *St. Leon: A Tale of the Sixteenth Century* (1799)

As I publish the case, in this volume, simply to interest the "laity," I shall forestal the intelligent lady, who relates it, in nothing; and after due consideration, I have determined, therefore, to abstain from presenting any *précis* of the learned Doctor's reasoning, or extract from his statement on a subject which he describes as "involving, not improbably, some of the profoundest arcana of our dual existence, and its intermediaries."

J. S. Le Fanu, "Carmilla" (1871–72)

After that it was that his researches, which at the beginning had been directed mainly to Poor Law institutions for defective and malformed children, asylums, wonder children, and the more grotesque arcana of gynæcology, turned rather to schools and universities and the ascertainable characteristics of exceptional and gifted people.

H. G. Wells, *Star-Begotten: A Biological Fantasia* (1937)

So Carter bought stranger books and sought out deeper and more terrible men of fantastic erudition; delving into arcana of consciousness that few have trod, and learning things which disturbed him ever afterward.

H. P. Lovecraft, "The Silver Key" (1926)

Old Providence! It was this place and the mysterious forces of its long, continuous history which had brought him into being, and which had drawn him back toward marvels and secrets whose boundaries no prophet might fix. Here lay the arcana, wondrous or dreadful as the case might be, for which all his years of travel and application had been preparing him.

H. P. Lovecraft, *The Case of Charles Dexter Ward* (1927)

All through late August he fortified himself with the massed lore of cryptography; drawing upon the fullest resources of his own library, and wading night after night amidst the arcana of Trithemius' *Poligraphia*, Giambattista Porta's *De Furtivis Literarum Notis*, De Vigénère's *Traité des Chiffres*, Falconer's *Cryptomenysis Patefacta*, Davys' and Thicknesse's eighteenth-century treatises, and such fairly modern authorities as Blair, von Marten, and Klüber's *Kryptographik*.

H. P. Lovecraft, "The Dunwich Horror" (1928)

Never was a sane man more dangerously close to the arcana of basic entity—never was an organic brain nearer to utter annihilation in the chaos that transcends form and force and symmetry.

H. P. Lovecraft, "The Whisperer in Darkness" (1930)

It was as if the bus were about to keep on its ascent, leaving the sane earth altogether and merging with the unknown arcana of upper air and cryptical sky.

H. P. Lovecraft, "The Shadow over Innsmouth" (1931)

Far over the city towered the great Roman dome of the new museum; and beyond it—across the cryptic yellow Nile that is the mother of æons and dynasties—lurked the menacing sands of the Libyan Desert, undulant and iridescent and evil with older arcana.

H. P. Lovecraft & Harry Houdini, "Under the Pyramids" (1924)

Here I was arrested mainly by the great temple of the Scottish Rite Masons, whose striking architecture lifts it out of the commonplace and mundane into the realm of the cosmick and mystical. Gazing upon it, I could well believe all the vague legends connected with the Masonick order; for here surely dwelt arcana whose sources are not of this earth. I saw it first at night, when only the twin cryptick braziers beside the great bronze door lit up the grim guardian sphinxes and the huge windowless façade.

H. P. Lovecraft, "Observation on Several Parts of America" (1928)

Surely I, as an enlightened and educated man, must admit the veiled and subtle truths so furtively revealed in such tomes as Ludvig Prinn's *Mysteries of the Worm*, or the grotesque *Black Rites* of mystic Luveh-Keraphf, the priest of cryptic Bast. He had made some studies recently of the mad and legendary *Necronomicon* of Abdul Alhazred. I could not refute the arcana behind such things as the banned and infamous Fable of Nyarlathotep, or the Legend of the Elder Saboth.

Robert Bloch, "The Grinning Ghoul" (1936)

Occultism is all right for a study, but the nightmare arcana of *Cultes des Goules* and the *Dæmonolorum* are not conducive to a healthy state of mind.

Robert Bloch, "The Dark Demon" (1936)

archon, *n.* [< Gr *árkhôn*, a ruler or chief magistrate < *arkhein*, to rule] A high ruler or official; in particular, a chief magistrate of a city-state; in Gnosticism, the Archons or Archontes were powers subordinate to God, who had created the world.

"Who so pleased as Theocles now? He takes the chair as archon with Leæna by his side, and off goes every soul in the place, except Pannychis, who cannot bear the sight of blood, and Porphyry, who is an outrageous humanitarian, and us poor devils left in charge of this old dreamer."

Richard Garnett, "The City of Philosophers" (1888)

—Dialectic, Stephen answered: and from his mother how to bring thoughts into the world. What he learnt from his other wife Myrto (*absit nomen!*), Socratididion's Epipsychidion, no man, not a woman, will ever know. But neither the midwife's lore nor the caudlelectures saved him from the archons of Sinn Fein and their naggin of hemlock.

James Joyce, *Ulysses* (1914–21)

That night the men of Teloth lodged the stranger in a stable, and in the morning an archon came to him and told him to go to the shop of Athok the cobbler, and be apprenticed to him.

> H. P. Lovecraft, "The Quest of Iranon" (1921)

"All in Teloth must toil," replied the archon, "for that is the law."

> H. P. Lovecraft, "The Quest of Iranon" (1921)

argosy, *n.* [< It < *Ragusa,* an ancient seaport (modern Dubrovnik)] A large merchant ship; a fleet of large merchant ships.

So, our adieus made and our affairs arranged, we begin our adventure, embark on our argosies.

> Leonard Cline, *The Dark Chamber* (1927)

From far shores came those white-sailed argosies of old; from far Eastern shores where warm suns shine and sweet odours linger about strange gardens and gay temples.

> H. P. Lovecraft, "The White Ship" (1919)

arras (*pl.* **arras, arrases**), **Arras**, *n.* [< *Arras,* France, a famous tapestry-center in the Middle Ages] A rich wall-hanging or tapestry, hand-woven with pictorial designs. An essential item of weird fiction and fantasy décor.

> Now night is come, now soone her disaray,
> And in her bed her lay;
> Lay her in lillies and in violets,
> And silken courteins over her display,
> And odourd sheetes, and Arras coverlets.
>
> Edmund Spenser, "Epithalamion" (1594)

But fie, what a smell is here! I'll not speak another word unless the ground be perfumed and covered with cloth of Arras.

> Christopher Marlowe, *The Tragical History of the
> Life and Death of Doctor Faustus* (1588–9)

> False glozing pleasures, casks of happinesse,
> Foolish night-fires, womens and childrens wishes,
> Chases in Arras, guilded emptinesse,
> Shadows well mounted, dreams in a career,
> Embroider'd lyes, nothing between two dishes;
>   These are the pleasures here.
>
> George Herbert, "Dotage" (1633)

> Yea truth, and Justice then
> Will down return to men,

Th'enameled *Arras* of the Rain-bow wearing,
And Mercy set between,
Thron'd in Celestiall sheen,
    With radiant feet the tissued clouds down staring,
And Heav'n as at som festivall,
With wide open Gates of her high Palace Hall.

John Milton, "On the Morning of Christ's Nativity" (1629)

These latter quillets are so minced with divisions and distinctions that their very patrons are dubious how to state them. I could compare their physiology to a chase in arras, where there is much of similitude but nothing of truth. 'Tis the child of fancy, a romance in syllogisms, a texture of their own brain, like that cobweb campagna which Lucian's spiders planted betwixt the Moon and Venus.

Thomas Vaughan, *Anima Magica Abscondita; or, A Discourse of the Universal Spirit of Nature, with His Strange, Abstruse, Miraculous Ascent and Descent* (1650)
[quillet: quirk, quibble; campagna: field, plain]

But this is a subject foreign to my present purposes: it is sufficient to say, that a chorus, &c., of elaborate harmony, displayed before me, as in a piece of arras work, the whole of my past life—not as if recalled by an act of memory, but as if present and incarnated in the music; no longer painful to dwell upon, but the detail of its incidents removed or blended in some hazy abstraction; and its passions exalted, spiritualized, and sublimed.

Thomas De Quincey, *Confessions of an English Opium-Eater: Being an Extract from the Life of a Scholar* (1821)

So was supper served well and abundantly: the meat and drink was of the best, and the vessel and all the plenishing was as good as might be; and the walls of that chamber were hung with noble arras-cloth picturing the Pilgrimage of the Soul of Man.

William Morris, *The Well at the World's End* (1893)

"To the Baron's lodging I went, which was not right great, but hung goodly with arras of Troy."

William Morris, *The Sundering Flood* (1896)

"There *is* a real world, but it is beyond this glamour and this vision, beyond these 'chases in Arras, dreams in a career,' beyond them all as beyond a veil."

Arthur Machen, "The Great God Pan" (1890)

Whether the arras actually moved I cannot say. I think it did, very slightly.

H. P. Lovecraft, "The Rats in the Walls" (1923)

In a vast room hung with strangely figured arras and carpeted with Bokhara rugs of impressive age and workmanship four men were sitting around a document-strown table.

> H. P. Lovecraft & E. Hoffmann Price,
> "Through the Gates of the Silver Key" (1932–33)

The clock's abnormal ticking was hideous, and the tripod fumes and swaying arras danced a dance of death.

> H. P. Lovecraft & E. Hoffmann Price,
> "Through the Gates of the Silver Key" (1932–33)

Silence hung everywhere, like a funereal, unstirred arras.

> Clark Ashton Smith, "The Treader of the Dust" (1935)

Behind the arras of cryptic silence, time and again, they seemed to hear a faint whisper, like the sigh of sunken seas far down at some hemispheric depth.

> Clark Ashton Smith, "The Dweller in the Gulf" (1932)

All men spoke of her, as if conspiring tacitly to keep her in his thoughts; and it seemed that even the heavy arrases whispered her name as they rustled in the lost winds that wandered through the gloomy and interminable halls.

> Clark Ashton Smith, "The Witchcraft of Ulua" (1933)

Silently the three came to the portals of the chamber, where entrance was barred only by a black arras wrought with the Signs of night in silver, and bordered with a repetition of the five names of the archfiend Thasaidon in scarlet thread. The brothers paused, as if fearing to lift the arras; but Yadar, unhesitating, held it aside and passed into the chamber; and the twain followed him quickly as if for shame of their poltroonery.

> Clark Ashton Smith, "Necromancy in Naat" (1935)

Even as he passed into the building, the arras-like silence before him was burst asunder by a frightful hubbub.

> Clark Ashton Smith, "The Black Abbot of Puthuum" (1935)

Here, in porticoes, halls and chambers the cressets where thick as stars in a cloudless vault. It seemed that Famurza wished to dissipate all shadows, except those in arrased alcoves set apart for the fitful amours of his guests.

> Clark Ashton Smith, "Morthylla" (1952)

arthame, athame, athalme, *n.* [< L *arthame, artamus, arthanus*; (found in some French recensions of the *Key of Solomon*; a British recension calls the black-handled knife the *arclavum* or *arthanus*, and the white-handled knife the *arthany*) ?< OF *attame*, to cut, or ?< Ar *al-dhammé*, bloodletter.] A long, black-handled knife used in sorcery and witchcraft. [Not in *OED*.]

She is moving with a regal gait, grasping the *arthame*, or magic knife, with the point of which she can instantly dissolve any of the evil spirits who should dare to attack her.

Grillot de Givry (trans. J. Courtenay Locke), *Witchcraft, Magic, and Alchemy* (1931)

There is also a description of the essential clothing and footgear, of the knife, or *arthame*, of the needle, or burin, the ring, the sceptre, the fire, the Holy Water, the lights, the perfumes, the virgin parchment and the pen, and of the ink and blood to write with; all these instruments are indispensable to the operation, for the evocation of a demon is not so easy a business as some idle and curious amateurs might suppose.

Grillot de Givry (trans. J. Courtenay Locke), *Witchcraft, Magic, and Alchemy* (1931)

With hands tightening on the hilts of our arthames, we went cautiously and circumspectly toward the cavern and paused a little short of its entrance.

Clark Ashton Smith, "The Master of the Crabs" (1947)

"Aye, and your neophyte is also armed with an arthame. However, it matters little. I shall feast on your liver, Mior Lumivix, and wax stronger by such power of sorcery as was yours."

Clark Ashton Smith, "The Master of the Crabs" (1947)

At the end of the long room he had cleared the cluttered floor of its equipment, leaving only an immense globe of crystal glass that suggested an aquarium. About the globe he had traced with a consecrated knife, the sorcerers' arthame, a circle inscribed with pentagrams and the various Hebrew names of the Deity. Also, at a distance of several feet, a smaller circle, similarly inscribed.

Clark Ashton Smith, "Schizoid Creator" (1952)

Wearing a seamless and sleeveless robe of black, he stood now within the smaller, protective circle. Upon his breast and forehead was bound the Double Triangle, wrought perfectly from several metals. A silver lamp, engraved with the same sign, afforded the sole light, shining on a stand beside him. Aloes, camphor and storax burned in censers set about him on the floor. In his right hand he held the arthame; in his left, a hazel staff with a core of magnetized iron.

Clark Ashton Smith, "Schizoid Creator" (1952)

Then she jammed the dagger—arthame, Jedson called it—with which she had scribed the figures into the ground at the top of the big circle so hard that it quivered. It continued to vibrate the whole time.

Robert A. Heinlein, "Magic, Inc." (1940)

She drew a T between our two circles. It followed closely behind the arthame, like a cat at an opening door.

Robert A. Heinlein, "Magic, Inc." (1940)

The only circle that matters is the one drawn before every ceremony with either a duly consecrated Magic Sword or a Knife, the latter being the Witches' Athame or Black-Hilted Knife, with magic signs on the hilt, and this is most generally used.

Gerald B. Gardner, *Witchcraft Today* (1954)

There are no witch's supply stores, so a poor witch usually has to make or improvise her own tools; a novice is often presented with an Athame, and of course in a witch family there are often old tools to be had. Old tools are always preferred, as they are supposed to have *Power*.

Gerald B. Gardner, *Witchcraft Today* (1954)

In one hand she held some sort of hilted knife. I did not realize until much later that it was an athame.

Margeret St. Clair, *The Sign of the Labrys* (1963)

She went to the cupboard and got out a strong cloth shopping bag. With it in one hand and the athame in the other, she walked to the door. "I'll be back soon," she said reassuringly, and went out.

Margeret St. Clair, *The Sign of the Labrys* (1963)

I went by cautious ways now, for these shadowy regions were haunted by obscene and monstrous Things which shambled squealing from my path, driven hence by the potent runes etched by acids distilled from the slobber of basilisks, wherewith my arthame (or wizard's sword) was rendered repellent to That which dwelleth in these vales.

Lin Carter, "In the Vale of Pnath" (1975)

The unaccustomed heat I kept at bay by use of a cantrip learned from the dwarves of Hyperborea who spend much time amid subterranean magmic fires forging rune-inscribed arthama-swords like the one that even now slapped my hip as I walked.

Robert M. Price, "The Burrower Beneath" (1997)

Asianic, Asiatic, *adj.* Of, pertaining to, or resembling the florid and imaginative literary style of the Greeks of Asia Minor in the first three centuries BCE.

"But in the presence of these famous fair ones now departed from me for ever, with what glowing words I ought to have spoken! upon a wondrous ladder of tropes, metaphors and recondite allusions, to what stylistic heights of Asiatic prose I ought to have ascended! and instead, I twaddled like a schoolmaster."

James Branch Cabell, *Jurgen: A Comedy of Justice* (1919)

astral, *adj.* [< LL *astrālis* < L *astrum*, star] In Theosophy, of or pertaining to a supersensible plane of being parallel to the physical. **astral body, astral spirit:** The ethereal double or counterpart of the physical body, which may separate from it and wander through the astral plane. **astral projection**: the projection of the astral body outside of the physical body.

Luridan, a familiar, did for many years inhabit the Island Pomonia, the largest of the Orcades in Scotland, supplying the place of Man-servant and maid-servant with wonderful diligence to these Families whom he did haunt, sweeping their rooms, and washing their dishes and making their fires before any were up in the morning. This Luridan affirmed, That he was the Genius Astral, of that Island, that his place or residence in the dayes of Solomon and David was at Jerusalem; That then he was called by the Jewes Belelah, and after that he remained Long in the Dominion of Wales, instructing their Bards in Brittish Poesy and Prophesies, being called Urthin, Wadd, Elgin: And now said he, I have removed hither, and alas my continuance is but short, for in 70 years I must resign my place to Balkin, Lord of the Northern Mountains.

"Discourse upon Divils and Spirits",
appended to the 1665 edition of Reginald Scot, *The Discoverie of Witchcraft*

Others, that what the Low-countrey Scot calls a Wreath, and the Irish eug or deaths Messenger, (appearing somtimes as a litle rough dog, and if crossed, and conjur'd in tim will be pacified by the death of any other creature instead of the sick Man) is only exuvious fumes of the Man approaching death, exhal'd and congeal'd into a various sickness, (as Ships and armies are somtimes shapt in the air) and called Astral Bodies, agitated as wild-fire with wind, and are neither Souls nor Counterfeiting Spirits.

Robert Kirk, *Secret Commonwealth; or, A Treatise Displayeing the Chiefe Curiosities as They Are in Useamong Diverse of the People of Scotland to This Day, Singularities for the Most Part Peculiar to That Nation* (1691)

The inquisitor demanded of me, Whether I had never seen or held conversation with any supernatural being, or the spirit of a man departed? Whether I had never practised diabolical arts to raise the dead? Whether I had never had a familiar in the form of some insect, domestic animal, or reptile? He was particularly subtle and copious in his questions respecting the history of my unfortunate dog, endeavouring to surprise me in some slip or contradiction in what I affirmed on the subject. He asked, Whether I had never assumed a form different from my real one, either a different age and appearance, or a different species of animal? Whether I had never, by the agency of my demon, inflicted sickness, convulsion-fits, or death? Whether I had never caused the mortality of cattle? Whether I had not the power of being in two places at once? Whether I had never been seen riding through the air? Whether I had never been wounded in my absence, by a blow aimed at my astral spirit or apparition? Whether I had never possessed books of conjuration or the art magic? Whether it had never happened to me that an indifferent person, indiscreetly perusing a spell or incantation in my possession, had been maimed or killed by the spirits he had undesignedly evoked?

William Godwin, *St. Leon: A Tale of the Sixteenth Century* (1799)

The Astral Body is not always of the same sex as the terrestrial, that is, the proportions of the two forces, varying from right to left, seem frequently to belie the visible organisation, producing seeming aberrations of human passion and explaining, while in no wise morally justifying, the amorous peculiarities of Anacreon and Sappho.

Éliphas Lévi (trans. A. E. Waite), *Transcendental Magic: Its Doctrine and Ritual* (1896)

When I tell my story most people call me a plain liar. Others lay it to abnormal psychology—and heaven knows I *was* overwrought—while still others talk of "astral projection" of some sort.

H. P. Lovecraft & Adolphe de Castro, "The Electric Executioner" (1929)

This creature pursued him amid the archetypal ferns and club-mosses; and overtaking him after five or six bounds, it proceeded to ingest him with the celerity of any latter-day saurian of the same species. Luckily, the ingestment was not permanent: for the tyrannosaurus' body-plasm, though fairly opaque, was more astral than material; and Ralibar Vooz, protesting stoutly against his confinement in its maw, felt the dark walls give way before him and tumbled out on the deeply resilient ground.

Clark Ashton Smith, "The Seven Geases" (1933)

"Cheers," said the Major. "Now where *have* you been these last three months? Living abroad with some woman, I suppose, as you did for half a year after laying the ghost in that 'Astral Buffalo' case? Ah, you randy devil—"

David Langford, "The Thing in the Bedroom" (1984)

astral, *n.* The astral body. See under **astral**.

Certainly Edmond described the pamphlet plainly enough, and it is strange, therefore, that no bibliophile could identify it. According to the diary, it was quite small, about four by five inches, bound in coarse brown paper, and yellowed and crumbling with age. The printing—in eighteenth century type with the long *s*—was crudely done, and there was neither a dateline nor a publisher's imprint. There were eight pages, seven of them filled with what Edmond called the usual banal sophisms of mysticism, and on the last page were the specific directions for what would nowadays be known as "projecting one's astral."

Henry Kuttner, "Hydra" (1939)

aureate, *adj.* Characterized by a golden color; gilded; elaborately ornamented.

Far away some little hills blazed like an aureate bulwark broken off by age and fallen from the earthward rampart of Paradise.

Lord Dunsany, "The Little City" (1915)

The sea of crimson lacquer, with its floating moons of luminous colour—this bow of prismed stone leaping to the weird isle crowned by the anomalous, aureate—excrescence—the half human batrachians—the elfland through which we had passed, with all its hidden wonders and terrors—I felt the foundations of my cherished knowledge shaking. Was this all a dream? Was this body of mine lying somewhere, fighting a fevered death, and all these but images floating through the breaking chambers of my brain?

A. Merritt, The Moon Pool (1919)

> In the midnight heavens burning
> Thro' ethereal deeps afar,
> Once I watch'd with restless yearning
> An alluring, aureate star;
> Ev'ry eye aloft returning,
> Gleaming nigh the Arctic car.

H. P. Lovecraft, "Astrophobos" (1917)

The golden sun sank languorously on it blue couch of the horizon, and perfumed breezes swooned through the aureate rays, caressing the lean hard yellow cheek of the Emperor Po Ko, stirring the peacock plumes of the fan which he carelessly waved in one set of lacquered claws.

Hannes Bok, "Jewel Quest" (1974)

austral, *adj.* Of or pertaining to the south; from the south; southern.

And going South they went by glittering fog-banks and saw old islands lifting their heads above them; they saw the slow quests of the wandering ships, and divers seeking pearls, and lands at war, till there came in view the mountains that they sought and the sight of the peaks they knew; and they descended into an austral valley, and saw Summer sometimes sleeping and sometimes singing song.

Lord Dunsany, "The Hen" (1915)

Further exploration was hardly feasible in view of our tragic decimation and the ruin of our drilling machinery; and the doubts and horrors around us—which we did not reveal—made us wish only to escape from this austral world of desolation and brooding madness as swiftly as we could.

H. P. Lovecraft, At the Mountains of Madness (1931)

He had beheld many marvels, and things incredible to relate: the uncouthly carven gods of the South, to whom blood was spilt on sun-approaching towers; the plumes of the huusim, which were many ells in length and were colored like pure flame; the mailed monsters of the austral swamps; the proud argosies of Mu and Antillia, which moved by enchantment, without oar or sail; the fuming peaks that were shaken perpetually by the struggles of imprisoned demons.

Clark Ashton Smith, "The White Sybil" (1932)

> below the dead Sixties
> right whales with maws of krill
> veils of austral light ripped from the sky

flagged & folded across the mongoloid darkness
under an Arthur-Gordon-Pym-like curse
hexed & abandoned on the shelf ice

> Hakim Bey (Peter Lamborn Wilson),
> "The Antarctic Autonomous Zone: A Science-Fiction Story" (1989)

Avernian, *adj.* Of or pertaining to Avernus (q.v.); Avernal.

Not luminous
With lodestar, or with star calamitous,
The Past is closed as by the night-black spate
Of planet-gulfing seas—its keyless gate
Lost in Avernian shadows cavernous.

> Clark Ashton Smith, "The Unremembered" (1912)

Avernus, Averno, *pr.n.* [< L ?< Gr *áornis* (*límên*), birdless (lake)] In Roman mythology, a lake placed at the entrance to Hell or Hades. Virgil's *Æneid* famously tells us that *facilis descensus Averni,* "easy is the descent to Hell." [Not in *OED.*]

Titles: H. P. Lovecraft, "A Descent to Avernus" (nonfiction)

His looks do menace heaven and dare the gods.
His fiery eyes are fixed upon the earth
As if he now devised some strategem,
Or meant to pierce Avernus' darksome vaults
To pull the triple-headed dog from hell.

> Christopher Marlowe, *Tamburlaine the Great* (1590)

It is all very well to talk about the *facilis descensus Averni*; but in all kinds of climbing, as Catalani said of singing, it is far more easy to get up than to come down.

> Edgar Allan Poe, "The Purloined Letter" (1844)

The first change I experienced was rather agreeable. It was very near the turning point from which began the descent of Avernus.

> J. S. LeFanu, "Carmilla" (1871)

I have dreamed like this ever since I was old enough to remember dreams, & probably shall till I descend to Avernus.

> H. P. Lovecraft, letter to Rheinhart Kleiner (21 May 1920)

With blood rilling heavily upon their faces, with the somnolent, vigilant, implacable and eyeless Shape at their heels, herding them on, restraining them when they tottered at the brink, the three began their second descent of the road that went down forever to a night-bound Avernus.

> Clark Ashton Smith, "The Dweller in the Gulf" (1932)

The myth of the Pied Piper is a fable that hides a blasphemous horror, and the black pits of Avernus have brought forth hell-spawned monstrosities that never venture into the light of day.

> Henry Kuttner, "The Graveyard Rats" (1939)

Azrael, Asrael, *pr.n.* [< Hb, AZRAL help of God] In Jewish and Islamic mythology, the angel of death. [Not in *OED*.]

Titles: Clark Ashton Smith, "The Flight of Azrael" (verse); Robert E. Howard, "The Road of Azrael"

The name of this exterminating angel is *Azrael,* and his office is to conduct the dead to the abode assigned them; which is said by some to be near the place of their interment. Such was the office of Mercury in the Grecian mythology.

> Samuel Henley, note to William Beckford,
> *The History of the Caliph Vathek: An Arabian Tale* (1786)

I saw that she must die—and I struggled desperately in spirit with the grim Azrael.

> Edgar Allan Poe, "Ligeia" (1838)

Khaled stood in the third heaven, which is the heaven of precious stones, and of Asrael, the angel of Death. In the midst of the light shed by the fruit of the trees Asrael himself is sitting, and will sit until the day of the resurrection from the dead, writing in his book the names of those who are to be born, and blotting out the names of those who have lived their years and must die. Each of the trees has seventy thousand branches, each branch bears seventy thousand fruits, each fruit is composed of seventy thousand diamonds, rubies, emeralds, carbuncles, jacinths, and other precious stones. The stature and proportions of Asrael are so great that his eyes are seventy thousand days journey apart, the one from the other.

> F. Marion Crawford, *Khaled: A Tale of Arabia* (1891)

All but myself, indeed, had perished; and sorely wounded in the side, I lay among the dead as one on whom there descends the pall-like shadow of Azrael.

> Clark Ashton Smith, "Told in the Desert" (1930)

B

Baaras, *pr.n.*[?< Hb BOR, "the burning"] A marvellous, flame-colored plant mentioned by Josephus, which is held to be of great use to alchemists. By some considered an alternative name for the mandrake (q.v.). [Not in *OED*.]

> It is wonderfull, and scarce credible, but that that grave and worthy Author *Josephus* relates it in his history of *Jerusalem*, of a root of *Baaras*, so called from a place neer *Machernus*, a Town of *Judea*, being of a yellow colour, that in the night it did shine, and was hard to be taken, that it did oftentimes deceive the hands of them that went to take it, and go out of their sight, never stood still, till the urine of a menstrous woman was sprinkled on it. Neither yet being thus retained, is it pulled up without danger, but suddain death fals upon him that drawes it up, unless he were fortified with an amulet of the said root; which they that want, sacrificing about the earth do bind the root to a dog by a cord, and presently depart: at length the dog with a great deal of pains drawes up the root, and as it were supplying the place of his master presently dies, after which anyone may handle the root without danger; the power of which is much excellent in expiations, as is manifest for the delivery of those that are vexed with unclean spirits; now that these kind of matters should act upon spirituall substances by putting them to flight, or by alluring them, or mitigating them, or by inciting them, they are of no other opinion then that the fire of *Sicilia* acts upon souls: which (*William* of *Paris* being witness) not hurting the bodies, doth most intolerably torment the souls of them that are neer.
>
> Henry Cornelius Agrippa (trans. James Freake),
> *Three Books of Occult Philosophy* (1651)

> That there is any power in *Bitumen*, Pitch, or Brimstone, to purifie the air from his uncleanness; that any vertue there is in *Hipericon* to make good the name of *fuga Dæmonis*, any such Magick as is ascribed unto the Root *Baaras* by *Josephus*, or *Cynospastus* by *Ælianus*, it is not easie to believe; nor is it naturally made out what is delivered of *Tobias*, that by the fume of a Fishes liver, he put to flight *Asmodeus*.
>
> Sir Thomas Browne, *Pseudodoxia Epidemica; or, Enquiries into Very Many Received Tenents and Commonly Presumed Truths* (1646)

Josephus (*ob.* A.D. 100) relates that God taught Solomon how demons were to be expelled, a "science useful and sanitative to men." He also gives an account of Eleazar, a celebrated exorcist of the time, whom, in the presence of the Emperor Vespasian, the historian actually saw casting out evil spirits. The operator applied to the nose of the possessed a ring having attached to it a root which Solomon is said to have prescribed—"Baaras," a herb of magical properties, and one dangerous for the uninitiated to handle.

Montague Summers, The History of Witchcraft and Demology (1925)

> Amid thy garden blooms the Tree which bears
> Unnumbered heads of demons for its fruit;
> And, like a slithering serpent, runs the root
> That is called Baaras;
> And there the forky, pale mandragoras,
> Self-torn from out the soil, go to and fro,
> Calling upon they name:
> Till men new-damned will deem that devils pass,
> Crying in wrathful frenzy and strange woe.

"Ludar's Litany to Thasaidon", as quoted in
Clark Ashton Smith, "The Garden of Adompha" (1937)

babel, Babel, *n.* [< *Babel* < Hb BBL < Assyrian, *bab-ilu*, gate of god, cf. Gr *Babylon*] A confused mixture of voices or other noises, as of many speakers talking at once.

Dyson made his way slowly along, mingling with the crowd on the cobblestones, listening to the queer babel of French and German, and Italian and English, glancing now and again at the shop-windows with their levelled batteries of bottles, and had almost gained the end of the street, when his attention was arrested by a small shop at the corner, a vivid contrast to its neighbours.

Arthur Machen, "The Inmost Light" (1892)

A minute later, the gardens lay silent. From the Pit, came a deep, hoarse Babel of swine-talk.

William Hope Hodgson, The House on the Borderland (1908)

Her story was about fairies and gnomes; and the gently-flowing moonlight of the narrative seemed to illumine the white pages, and she could hear in fancy fairy voices, so silent was the great many-roomed house, and so mellifluent were the words of the story. Presently she put out her candle, and, with a confused babel of voices close to her ears, and faint swift pictures before her eyes, she fell asleep.

Walter de la Mare, "The Riddle"

I think I screamed frantically near the last—I was almost mad—but if I did so my cries were lost in the hell-born babel of the howling wind-wraiths.

H. P. Lovecraft, "The Nameless City" (1921)

The population is a hopeless tangle and enigma; Syrian, Spanish, Italian, and negro elements impinging upon one another, and fragments of Scandinavian and

American belts lying not far distant. It is a babel of sound and filth, and sends out strange cries to answer the lapping of oily waves at its grimy piers and the monstrous organ litanies of the harbour whistles.

H. P. Lovecraft, "The Horror at Red Hook" (1925)

Indeed, there was much to listen to, for beyond the closed door at the head of the stone steps was a veritable nightmare of feline yelling and clawing, whilst Nigger-Man, unmindful of his kindred outside, was running excitedly around the bare stone walls, in which I heard the same babel of scurrying rats that had troubled me the night before.

H. P. Lovecraft, "The Rats in the Walls" (1923)

The stench waxed overpowering, and the noises swelled to a bestial babel of croaking, baying, and barking without the least suggestion of human speech.

H. P. Lovecraft, "The Shadow over Innsmouth" (1931)

There was a hideous fall through incalculable leagues of viscous, sentient darkness, and a babel of noises utterly alien to all that we know of the earth and its organic life.

H. P. Lovecraft, "The Shadow out of Time" (1935)

The babel of a myriad tongues smote on the Cimmerian's ears as the restless pattern of the Zamboula streets weaved about him—cleft now and then by a squad of clattering horsemen, the tall, supple warriors of Turan, with dark hawk-faces, clinking metal and curved swords.

Robert E. Howard, "Shadows in Zamboula" (1935)

A hurried babel of grisly tongues rose and the shadows heaved in turmoil.

Robert E. Howard, "Worms of the Earth" (1930)

Colton's discomfiture had been noticed by his confreres; and all at once, as if their tongues had been loosed by this happening, a babel of discussion arose among them.

Clark Ashton Smith, "Seedling of Mars" (1931)

The others had kept to the main catacombs; and I heard far off a muffled babel of mad cries, as if several of them had been seized by their pursuers.

Clark Ashton Smith, "The Vaults of Yoh-Vombis" (1931)

Or to know it's life still, a form of life, ordained to end, as others ended and will end, till life ends, in all its forms. Words, mine was never more than that, than this pell-mell babel of silence and words, my viewless form described as ended, or to come, or still to progress, depending on the words, the moments, long may it last in that singular way. Apparitions, keepers, what childishness, and ghouls, to think I said ghouls, do I as much as know what they are, of course I don't, and how the intervals are filled, as if I didn't know, as if there were two things, some other thing besides this thing, what is it, this unnamable thing that I name and name and never wear out, and I call that words.

Samuel Beckett, "Texts for Nothing 6" (1950–52)

Babelian, *adj.* [< *Babel*] Of, pertaining to, or resembling Babel. [Not in *OED*.]

It walked undulously in ante-human streets, in strange crooked vaults; it peered at primeval stars from high, Babelian towers; it bowed with hissing litanies to great serpent-idols.

Clark Ashton Smith, "Ubbo-Sathla" (1932)

Indeed, the world that had once flourished beneath a living sun was little more than a legend now, a tradition preserved by art and literature and history. Its beetling Babelian cities, its fecund hills and plains, were swathed impenetrably in snow and ice and solidified air. No living man had gazed upon it, except from the night-bound towers maintained as observatories.

Clark Ashton Smith, "Phœnix" (1953)

Its mountain-passing ramparts climb exalted from the nadir flats
In black, Babelian ziggurats that tier the dusk of nether time.

Clark Ashton Smith, "The City of Destruction"

Bacchæ (*pl.*, *sing.* **Baccha**), *n.* [< L < Gr *bákkhē*] Bacchanals, Bacchantes, Bassarides, Edonides, Euhyades, Evantes, Mænades, Mimallonides, Ogygiæ, Thyiades, Trietherides. [Not in *OED*.]

Titles: Euripides, *The Bacchæ* (play)

We then saw the *Indian* Army, who had at last taken the Field, to prevent the Devastation of the rest of their Country. In the Front were the Elephants with Castles well garison'd on their backs. But the Army and themselves were put into Disorder; the dreadful Cries of the *Bacchæ* having fill'd them with Consternation, and those huge Animals turn'd Tail, and trampled on the Men of their Party.

François Rabelais (trans. Pierre Le Motteux & Sir Thomas Urquhart),
The Lives, Heroick Deeds, and Sayings of Gargantua and His Son Pantagruel (1653/1694)

Gentle breezes from the tower of Aiolos wafted them high above warm, scented seas, till suddenly they came upon Zeus holding court on the double-headed Parnassus; his golden throne flanked by Apollo and the Muses on the right hand, and by ivy-wreathed Dionysus and pleasure-flushed Bacchæ on the left hand.

H. P. Lovecraft & Anna Helen Crofts, "Poetry and the Gods" (1920)

The howling, insensate cries of the Bacchæ grew louder in their ears and, turning in the saddle, Simon saw behind him the dim shapes of their pursuers— shapes which grew stronger with the deepening darkness.

Michael Moorcock, "The Greater Conqueror" (1963)

Bacchanal, bacchanal, Bacchanale, *n.* A Bacchanalia (q.v.); a participant in the Bacchanalia; any drunken reveler.

Titles: Samuel Loveman, "Bacchanale" (verse); Leonard Cline, "Bacchanale Solo" (verse)

a. A Bacchanalia:

Once more I threaded the mazy sphere-harmony of the minuet, reeled in the waltz, long pomps of candelabra, the noon-day of the bacchanal, about me. Cosmo was the very tsar and maharajah of the Sybarites! the Priap of the *détraqués!*

M. P. Shiel, "Xélucha" (1896)

They hung high poised, nodding and swaying—like goblins hovering over *Titania's* court; cacophony of Cathay accenting the *Flower Maiden* music of "Parsifal"; *bizarrerie* of the angled, fantastic beings that people the Javan pantheon watching a bacchanal of houris in Mohammed's paradise!

A. Merritt, *The Moon Pool* (1919)

It was inside this circle that the ring of worshippers jumped and roared, the general direction of the mass motion being from left to right in endless Bacchanal between the ring of bodies and the ring of fire.

H. P. Lovecraft, "The Call of Cthulhu" (1926)

Madness rides the star-wind . . . claws and teeth sharpened on centuries of corpses . . . dripping death astride a Bacchanale of bats from night-black ruins of buried temples of Belial. . . .

H. P. Lovecraft, "The Hound" (1922; ellipses in original)

> Like torchy fires you footsteps leap
> Where covens of lost dreamers keep
> Their sabbat and their bacchanal;
> Your breasts are moons that mount and fall
> Through the dim, turbulent climes of sleep.

Clark Ashton Smith, "Madrigal of Memory" (1941)

b. A participant in the Bacchanalia:

> But now, o Pan, the whole world falls
> With its reeling rout of Bacchanals
> Into the gulf, and thy wild note
> Shrills up from the black Nothing's throat
> Like an enchanted harp that playeth
> Melodies, melodies magniloquent of death.

Aleister Crowley, *The World's Tragedy* (1908)

In the centre yawns a great open door, reached by an impressive flight of steps, and surrounded by exquisite carvings like the figure of Bacchanals in relief.

> H. P. Lovecraft, "The Temple" (1920)

Louder and louder, wilder and wilder, mounted the shrieking and whining of that desperate viol. The player was dripping with an uncanny perspiration and twisted like a monkey, always looking frantically at the curtained window. In his frenzied strains I could almost see shadowy satyrs and Bacchanals dancing and whirling insanely through seething abysses of clouds and smoke and lightning.

> H. P. Lovecraft, "The Music of Erich Zann" (1921)

> From west to east the things advanc'd—
> A mocking train that leap'd and danc'd
> Like Bacchanals with joined hands
> In endless file thro' airy lands.

> H. P. Lovecraft, "Clouds" in "A Cycle of Verse" (1918)

Bacchanalia, bacchanalia, *n.* An ancient Roman festival held in honor of the god Bacchus; a wild, drunken, orgiastic feast or revel.

Titles: Donald Wandrei, "Bacchanalia" (verse)

Bacchanalian, *adj.* Of, pertaining to, or resembling a Bacchanalia (q.v.) or bacchanal (q.v.).

> Less wild the Bacchanalian dames appear,
> When, from afar, their nightly god they hear,
> And howl about the hills, and shake the wreathy spear.

> Virgil (trans. John Dryden), *Æneid*

Bacchant, *n.* & *adj.* A Bacchante, Mænad.

> "This was their token:
> Beautiful bodies, white and broken,
> Fauns that still held the cup of drouth
> Pressed wearily pale mouth to mouth,
> Bacchant and Satyr, chill in death,
> The Mænads moaning a last breath,
> Their spears with arbute-blossoms pied,
> Plunged in each stark and bleeding side;
> But those that fled wailed as the leaves
> Some vast autumnal spirit grieves,
> When in the nadir, sick with light,
> A ponderous wind proclaims the night."

> Samuel Loveman, *The Hermaphrodite* (1922)

Bacchante, *n.* & *adj.* A Mænad.

Titles: Clark Ashton Smith, "Bacchante" (verse)

Bacchic, *adj.* Of, pertaining to, or resembling Bacchus or his worship.

Titles: Donald Wandrei, "At the Bacchic Revel" (verse)

> It is his theory that the fearful and shocking rites of the Bacchic cultus survive in this disillusioned age; that Panic lechery and wickedness did not cease with the Agony, as Mrs. Browning and others would have us believe.
>
> Vincent Starrett, "Arthur Machen: A Novelist of Ecstasy and Sin" (1917) in
> *Buried Cæsars: Essays in Literary Appreciation* (1923)

bale, *n.* [< OE *bealu,* evil, malice, suffering] An evil or pernicious influence; something causing grievous harm; misery, misfortune, calamity.

> Mother of God! be with me in success,
> Abide with me if peradventure fail
> These faint songs, murmurs of a summer gale
> That my heart clothes within a mortal dress;
> And with thy sympathy, their bliss or bale
> Shall be too light to shake my happiness.
>
> Aleister Crowley, "Sonnet to the Virgin Mary" in *White Stains: The Literary Remains of*
> *George Archibald Bishop, A Neuropath of the Second Empire* (1898)

> "The wonderful disorder and distresses of his army must, if thou amend it not, swing all our fortune at one chop from bliss to bale."
>
> E. R. Eddison, *The Worm Ouroboros* (1922)

> "Upon which matters," he said, and the voice of him was now as very frostbite in the air, "and upon whether they shall seem fit to you to be embraced and followed or (by contraries) to be eschewed and renounced, resteth (I suppose) your bliss or bale unto everlasting."
>
> E. R. Eddison, *The Mezentian Gate* (1941–45)

> Reading the horoscopic stars, we found no future ill in their aspect; nor was any shadow of bale foreshown to us through geomancy, or such other modes of divination as we employed.
>
> Clark Ashton Smith, "The Double Shadow" (1932)

> Deeming that this thing was no natural occurrence, but a sorcery that had been exerted by the great glacier, and that the glacier itself was a live, malignant entity with powers of unknown bale, they did not slacken their flight.
>
> Clark Ashton Smith, "The Ice-Demon" (1932)

> Peace and pallor of the flowers
> They have fevered, they have marred
> With the poison of their light,
> With distillèd bale and blight

Of a red, accurst regard:
All the toil of sunlight hours
They undo
With their wild eyes—
Eldritch and ecstatic eyes,
Stooping timeward from the skies,
Burning redly in the dew.

Clark Ashton Smith, "The Land of Evil Stars" (1913)

I am that messenger whose call
Convenes dark mage and banished lord
And branded witch and whip-flayed thrall,
To plot, amid the madness poured
On the black Sabbat's frothing horde,
The bale of realms, the planet's fall.

Clark Ashton Smith, "Cambion" (1943)

Deep is the night and slow
Whose gulf obscurely swarms
Mad, somber, faceless forms,
Blind masks of bale and woe.

Clark Ashton Smith, "Before Dawn" (1942)

On falcon banners never furled,
Beyond the marches of the world,
They blazon forth the heraldries
Of dream-established sovereignties
Whose princes wage immortal wars
For beauty with the bale-red stars.

Clark Ashton Smith, "Amithaine" (1950)

They ride the night-wind when the Demon Star
Over the dim horizon burns bale-red,
Come from the charnel-pits of the undead,
Nadir of nightmare, where the shoggoths are.

Lin Carter, "Spawn of the Black Goat" in *Dreams from R'lyeh*

baleful, *adj.* [< *bale* (q.v.)] Deadly, destructive, pernicious; portending evil, ominous, sinister; sad, sorrowful, mournful.

a. General:

His breastplate first, that was of substance pure,
Before his noble heart he firmly bound,
That mought his life from yron death assure,
And ward his gentle corpes from cruell wound:

For it by arte was framed, to endure
The bit of balefull steele and bitter stownd,
No lesse than that, which *Vulcane* made to sheild
Achilles life from fate of *Troyan* field.

> Edmund Spenser, *Muiopotmos; or, The Fate of the Butterflie* (1590)

[stownd: stroke]

When those accursed messengers of hell,
    That feigning dreame, and that faire-forged Spright
Came to their wicked maister, and gan tell
    Their bootelesse paines, and ill succeeding night:
    Who all in rage to see his skilfull might
Deluded so, gan threaten hellish paine
    And sad *Proserpines* wrath, them to affrighte.
    But when he saw his threatning was but vaine,
He cast about, and searcht his balefull books againe.

> Edmund Spenser, *The Faërie Queene* (159-)

Little suspected the good knight and his gentle lady what a baleful banquet was preparing for them, for the envious and angry queen, instead of tender paps to give the infant nourishment, she commanded it to be made food for that womb that gave it first life.

> *The Famous and Renowned History of Morindos a King of Spain* (1609)

"Fill high the sparkling bowl,
The rich repast prepare,
Reft of a crown, he yet may share the feast:
Close by the regal chair
Fell Thirst and Famine scowl
A baleful smile upon their baffled guest."

> Thomas Gray, "The Bard: A Pindaric Ode"

"I love to scale the thundercloud; to ride on the topmost billow of the storm; to roost by the cataract, or croon the anthem of hell at the gate of heaven. But *thou* delightest to see blood,—rank, reeking, and baleful Christian blood."

> James Hogg, "Fairies, Deils, and Witches" (1828)

She fails—she sinks—as dies the lamp
In charnel airs or cavern-damp,
So quickly do his baleful sighs
Quench all the sweet light of her eyes!

> Thomas Moore, "Paradise and the Peri" in *Lalla Rookh* (1817)

On the lone bleak moor,   At the midnight hour,
Beneath the Gallows Tree,

Hand in hand   The Murderers stand,
By one, by two, by three!
And the Moon that night   With a grey, cold light
Each baleful object tips;
One half of her form   Is seen through the storm,
The other half's hid in Eclipse!

Thomas Ingoldsby (Richard Harris Barham),
"The Nurse's Story—The Hand of Glory" in *The Ingoldsby Legends* (1840)

Somehow the hut appeared to expand, to change luminously about him. He hardly recognized its squalid furnishings, its litter of baleful oddments, on which a torrid splendor was shed by the black candles, tipped with ruddy fire, that towered and swelled gigantically into the soft gloom.

Clark Ashton Smith, "Mother of Toads" (1937)

A scorner of such things in my normal moments, I was now ready to believe in the most baleful creations of superstitious fancy.

Clark Ashton Smith, "The Return of the Sorcerer" (1931)

Heedless of each other or of anything but the urgency of flight, we plunged into the ramifying passages at random. Behind me, I heard someone stumble and go down, with a curse that mounted to an insane shrieking; but I knew that if I halted and went back, it would be only to invite the same baleful doom that had overtaken the hindmost of our party.

Clark Ashton Smith, "The Vaults of Yoh-Vombis" (1931)

Conscious of gulfs in which I dared not gaze,
I passed on faltering and imperilled ways,
Through lands where hoary mountains danced and roared
To baleful pygmies piping hellish lays.

Clark Ashton Smith, "Said the Dreamer" (1912; rev. 1944)

Crowley is surely a picturesque character, to have inspired anything like Clinton! I know little about Crowley myself, but wouldn't be surprised if many of the more baleful elements in his reputation were akin to those in the Baudelaire legend . . . that is to say, largely self-manufactured or foisted upon him by the credulous bourgeoisie.

Clark Ashton Smith, letter to H. P. Lovecraft (late January 1934) (ellipsis in original)

For a moment I despaired, since I was unwilling to approach any local classical or Latin scholar in connection with so hideous and blasphemous a text. Then came an inspiration. Why not take it east and seek the aid of my friend? He was a student of the classics, and would be less likely to be shocked by the horrors of Prinn's baleful revelations.

Robert Bloch, "The Shambler from the Stars" (1935)

He felt indescribably small and lonely there in the night,. and he was conscious of strange and baleful powers that were weaving the threads of his destiny into a final tragic pattern.

Robert Bloch, "The Faceless God" (1936)

Here were gathered a number of men in robes which bore a curious similarity to those of Carteret's present guide. They were conversing with a tall, white-bearded man whose crudely drawn figure seemed to exude an uncanny aura of black and baleful power.

Robert Bloch, "Fane of the Black Pharaoh" (1937)

"Centuries in the past, before the Scroll of History was even a little way unrolled, one of these two powerful gods ruled all the world. Yob-Haggoth." Jerome's lips curled, as though the word were filth upon his tongue. "This very monument, as you have heard, is one of his baleful images, a relic of those lost times when he was worshipped publicly in loathsome rites."

John Jakes, "The Unspeakable Shrine" (1967) in Brak the Barbarian

Kyrik knew the name and power of that dread being. Absothoth lived in the nether worlds of Absora and Absoron, he was baleful, malignant. Hate was in his heart, his head, and he obeyed only those who fed his life with human blood.

Gardner F. Fox, Kyrik: Warlock Warrior (1975)

I remember all these things because, as it turned out, this was a special day: the day I saw, for the second time, the black man and his baleful horn.

T. E. D. Klein, "Black Man with a Horn" (1980)

b. Of eyes (gaze, glare, etc.):

> Nine times the Space that measures Day and Night
> To mortal men, hee with his horrid crew
> Lay vanquisht, rolling in the fiery Gulf
> Confounded though immortal; But his doom
> Reserv'd him to more wrath; for now the thought
> Both of lost happiness and lasting pain
> Torments him; round he throws his baleful eyes
> That witness'd huge affliction and dismay
> Mixt with obdurate pride and steadfast hate
> At once as far as Angels' ken he views
> The dismal Situation waste and wild,
> A Dungeon horrible, on all sides round
> As one great Furnace flam'd, yet from those flames
> No light, but rather darkness visible
> Serv'd only to discover sights of woe,
> Regions of sorrow, doleful shades, where peace
> And rest can never dwell, hope never comes

That comes to all; but torture without end
Still urges, and a fiery Deluge, fed
With ever-burning Sulphur unconsum'd:
Such place Eternal Justice had prepar'd
For those rebellious, here thir Prison ordained
In utter darkness, and thir portion set
As far remov'd from God and light of Heav'n
As from the Center thrice to th' utmost Pole.

John Milton, Paradise Lost (1667)

But the thought of the serpent within a few feet of his head, yet unseen—perhaps in the very act of springing upon him and throwing its coils about his throat—was too horrible! He lifted his head, stared again into those baleful eyes and was again in bondage.

Ambrose Bierce, "The Man and the Snake" (1890)

No matter what unclean shape each hateful monstrosity might bear, all alike had fiery, malignant eyes; and in every case in these baleful orbs there dwelt an awful demoniac power of fascination—an expression of bitter unrelenting hostility to the human race. Each noisome abomination, as it writhed slowly past, fixed its fearful eyes on mine, and seemed to be exerting some formidable power against me.

C. W. Leadbeater, "A Test of Courage" (1911)

The great yellow eyes were fixed upon him with a wicked and baleful gleam, and the red tongue licked the longing lips as Sabor crouched, worming her stealthy way with belly flattened against the earth.

Edgar Rice Burroughs, Tarzan of the Apes (1912)

Out of the mists had flown a great bird. It hovered fifty feet over us, glaring down with baleful yellow eyes. A great bird—a white bird . . .

A. Merritt, Dwellers in the Mirage (1932; ellipsis in original)

The green moon, shining through broken windows, shewed me the hall door half open; and as I rose from the plaster-strown floor and twisted myself free from the sagged ceiling, I saw sweep past it an awful torrent of blackness, with scores of baleful eyes glowing in it.

H. P. Lovecraft, "He" (1925)

He and Geoffrey both saw a movement on the writing-table, and before their incredulous eyes the rattlesnake coiled on the pile of paper slowly raised its arrow-shaped head and darted forth its forky tongue! Its cold, unwinking eyes, with a fixation of baleful intensity well-nigh hypnotic, were upon the intruders, and as they stared in unbelieving horror, they heard the sharp rattling of its tail, like withered seeds in a wind-swung pod.

Clark Ashton Smith, "The Resurrection of the Rattlesnake" (1929)

They could hear the shuffling of the first lizard-monster on the incline and could see the baleful glaring of its single eye as it came forward.

Clark Ashton Smith, "Marooned in Andromeda" (1930)

> Her all-deleting hand
> Seems promise that her reign awhile shall stand,
> When Day, with baleful Cyclopean eye,
> Upleaps in flame, and of his sway the sand
> Grows ostent, swift.

Clark Ashton Smith, "Imagination"

Frodo and Sam, horror-stricken, began slowly to back away, their own gaze held by the dreadful stare of those baleful eyes; but as they backed so the eyes advanced.

J. R. R. Tolkien, *The Two Towers* in *The Lord of the Rings* (1936–49)

One shiny bit of carnelian fell and rolled under the bed, gleaming out of the dark like a baleful eye.

Mary Elizabeth Counselman, "The Lamashtu Amulet" (1980)

The tentacles one by one slid thrashing back into the pool. The baleful yellow eyes began to pulse and dim, pulse and dim. With its whistling rising higher and higher, until Brak's ears began to ache and throb, the Hellarms sank downward into water darkening with the tarry ichor.

John Jakes, "The Girl in the Gem" (1965)

Even as that whisper floated through the chamber, a leathery rustle was heard and a darkness came, shot with brownish gleamings, where something— crouched low to the floor and two baleful green eyes glittered.

Gardner F. Fox, *Kyrik: Warlock Warrior* (1975)

For what seemed an age they followed into the regions of Stygian dark, into the cellers and sub-cellers and still deeper. There were shallow stone steps leading down, and arches too low for the passage of men. Baleful-eyed rats watched them avidly.

Gary Myers, "The Feast in the House of the Worm" (1970)

Kane's baleful eyes held him in cold speculation for a moment, wondering how much of this was a chance taunt.

Karl Edward Wagner, "The Dark Muse" (1975)

> Upon these wastes there broods the baleful Eye
> Of Barad-dûr, dark citadel of Night,
> Where ancient evil stirs and grows in might
> And lifts again its death-black banners high.

Richard Tierney, "Mordor" (1976)

It was fearful to enter that dark place, with the quakes rumbling and shuddering at the floor, to approach that knot of shadow that huddled in the corner, wherein baleful and angry eyes watched: he had to remember that Death is a serpent-child, and it was a serpent-shape that seemed imprisoned there, earthwise and ancient, and unlike his twin, cold.

C. J. Cherryh, "The Dark King" (1977)

"Don't say it," said Mavis, giving him a warning look, and George remembered the tattoo he had seen between her breasts. He looked down again. They were above the pyramid now and George could see the side that had been hidden from him as they approached. He saw what he had half-feared, half-expected to see: a blood-red design in the shape of a baleful eye.

Robert Anton Wilson & Robert Shea,
The Eye in the Pyramid in The Illuminatus! Trilogy (1969–71)

c. Of a heavenly body, or other light-source or light:

> How sweet a scene will earth become!
> Of purest spirits, a pure dwelling-place,
> Symphonious with the planetary spheres;
> When man, with changeless Nature coalescing,
> Will undertake regeneration's work,
> When its ungenial poles no longer point
> > To the red and baleful sun
> > That faintly twinkles there.

Percy Bysshe Shelley, Queen Mab: A Philosophical Poem (1813)

Gauracy's baleful sun was gone, and the dislodged and incinerated worlds, with all their satellites, were revolving trimly in their proper places, undamaged.

James Branch Cabell, The Silver Stallion: A Comedy of Redemption (1925)

The crown of Witchland shed baleful sparkles above the darkness of the dark fortress-face of Gorice the King, the glitter of his dread eyeballs, the deadly line of his mouth, the square black beard jutting beneath.

E. R. Eddison, The Worm Ouroboros (1922)

And while he beheld these things, there was torn a ragged rift in the clouds, and there fled there a bearded star, baleful in the abyss of night.

E. R. Eddison, Mistress of Mistresses (1930–35)

> O lover, thy black prayer unsay,
> Who called baleful Anteros!
> Crown thee with nettles, kneel, and lay
> Thy brows upon love's altar close,
> To the departing Eros pray
> Against the wrath of Anteros.

Clark Ashton Smith, "Anteros"

The poppy yielded you demented dreams,
   Death-fevers mottled you with lurid shades,
Mars poured on you the bane of baleful beams,
   You stain vermilion vipers in dank glades.

                              Donald Wandrei, "Red" (1928)

Orion with his jewelled buckler was vaulting up out of the east, Mars bore the baleful flare of his torch down into the west, in a sky one glitter of stars when I looked out of the window.

                              Leonard Cline, *The Dark Chamber* (1927)

Across a flaming desert's sun-scorched ways
I journeyed far into a land unknown
And found a crumbling fane of night-black stone
Crouching beneath the white sun's baleful rays.

                              Richard Tierney, "The Pilgrimage" (1972)

Had I kept these ancient revelations to myself I might now rest easy in my mind and not mortally dread every dark shadow I see silhouetted against the baleful moon or evilly winking stars, whether it be merely a passing cloud or something more substantial and fearful.

                              John S. Glasby, "The Brooding City"

In the east, like a great cyclopean beast lifting its huge head, the moon rose majestically above the treetops, casting long gigantic shadows across the lawn. It was full tonight, the second full moon of the month, and very bright. To Freirs, without his glasses, there seemed something new in its face, something baleful and malign.

                              T. E. D. Klein, *The Ceremonies* (1984)

d. Of an influence:

"Before I can aid you in any experiment that may serve to prolong your life, I must know how far that life has been a baleful and destroying influence?"

                              Sir Edward Bulwer-Lytton, *A Strange Story* (1861)

Even this hypothesis was not a very pleasant one; yet it was plain that if Barton could ever be convinced that there was nothing preternatural in the phenomenon which he had hitherto regarded in that light, the affair would lose all its terrors in his eyes, and wholly cease to exercise upon his health and spirits the baleful influence which it had hitherto done.

                              J. S. LeFanu, "The Familiar" (1847)

"What a distinction it is to provide our own light, instead of being dependent on a thing hung up in the air—a most disagreeable contrivance—intended no doubt to blind us when we venture out under its baleful influence!"

                              George MacDonald, *The Princess and the Goblin* (1872)

A baleful malignant influence that seemed to emanate from the corpse itself held me with magnetic fascination.

> C. M. Eddy, Jr. & H. P. Lovecraft, "The Loved Dead" (1923)

"I was saying, my dear, that you were clearly born under the baleful influence of Saturn," said Professor Trelawney, a faint note of resentment in her voice at the fact that he had obviously not been hanging on her words.

> J. K. Rowling, *Harry Potter and the Goblet of Fire* (2000)

e. Poisonous:

> Behind St Luke's, as the dead men know,
> A pale apothecary dwells,
> Who deals in death both quick and slow,
> And baleful philtres, withering spells.
> He sells alike to rich and poor
> Who know what knocks to give his door,
> The yellow powder that rings the knells.

> Eugene Lee-Hamilton, "Ipsissimus"

f. Of trees or other vegetation (in the sense of melancholy, not poisonous):

> The water Nymphs, that wont with her to sing and daunce,
> And for her girlond Olive braunches beare,
> Now balefull boughes of Cypres doen advaunce
> The Muses, that were wont greene bayes to weare,
> Now bringen bitter Eldre braunches seare:
> The fatall sisters eke repent,
> Her vitall threde so soone was spent.
> O heavie herse,
> Morne now my Muse, now morne with heavie cheare.
> O carefull verse.

> Edmund Spenser, November in *The Shepheardes Calender* (1579)

> Without, where baleful cypresses make rich
> The bleeding sun's phantasmagoric gules,
> Are fungus-tapers of the twilight witch
> (Seen by the bat above unfathomed pools)
> And tiger-lilies known to silent ghouls,
> Whose king has digged a somber carcanet
> And necklaces with fevered opals set.

> George Sterling, "A Wine of Wizardry" (1907)

So frightful was the situation—the mysterious light burned with so silent and awful a menace; the noxious plants, the trees that by common consent are invested with a melancholy or baleful character, so openly in his sight conspired against his peace; from overhead and all about came so audible and startling whispers and the sighs of creatures so obviously not of earth—that he could endure it no longer, and with a great effort to break some malign spell that bound his faculties to silence and inaction, he shouted with the full strength of his lungs!

> Ambrose Bierce, "The Death of Halpin Frayser" (1891)

Baleful primal trees of unholy size, age, and grotesqueness leered above me like the pillars of some hellish Druidic temple; muffling the thunder, hushing the clawing wind, and admitting but little rain.

> H. P. Lovecraft, "The Lurking Fear" (1922)

The forest became suddenly malignant and malefic. The baleful creepers twined insidiously about his leg, and all along his path the wounded ones howled in swelling ululations that made the forest echo with waves of fiendish sound.

> Donald Wandrei, "A Fragment of a Dream" (1926)

Into the shadowland I made my way
Where writhing trees loomed tall to shroud the sky,
And baleful boles of strange misshapen growths
Uprose gigantic in the endless gloom,
Where silence ruled yet something waited me
And brooded in that vast and soundless grove.

> Donald Wandrei, "The Woodland Pool"

g. A bunch of baleful bowers:

Soone as thou gynst to sette thy notes in frame,
O how the rurall routes to thee doe cleave:
Seemeth thou dost their soule of sence bereave,
All as the shepherd, that did fetch his dame
From *Ph*utoes balefull bowre withouten leave:
His musicks might the hellish hound did tame.

> Edmund Spenser, October in *The Shepheardes Calender* (1579)

Where my high steeples whilom usde to stand,
On which the lordly Faulcon wont to towre,
There now is but an heap of lyme and sand,
For the Shriche-owle to build her balefull bowre:
And where the Nightingale wont forth to powre
Her restles plaints, to comfort wakefull Lovers,
There now haunt yelling Mewes and whining Plovers.

> Edmund Spenser, *The Ruines of Time* (1590)

In haste Duessa from her place arose,
    And to him running said, O prowest knight,

That euer Ladie to her loue did chose,
 Let now abate the terror of your might,
 And quench the flame of furious despight,
 And bloudie vengeance; lo th'infernall powres
 Couering your foe with cloud of deadly night,
 Haue borne him hence to Plutoes balefull bowres.
The conquest yours, I yours, the shield, and glory yours.

Edmund Spenser, The Faërie Queene (159-)

And if thou euer happen that same way
  To trauell, goe to see that dreadfull place:
  It is an hideous hollow caue (they say)
  Vnder a rocke that lyes a little space
  From the swift Barry, tombling downe apace,
  Emongst the woodie hilles of Dyneuowre:
  But dare thou not, I charge, in any cace,
  To enter into that same balefull Bowre,
For fear the cruell Feends should thee vnwares deuowre.

Edmund Spenser, The Faërie Queene (159-)

Ere long they came neere to a balefull bowre,
Much like the mouth of that infernall cave,
That gaping stood all Commers to devoure,
Darke, dolefull, dreary, like a greedy grave,
That still for carrion carkasses doth crave.
  The ground no hearbs, but venomous did beare,
  Nor ragged trees did leave, but every whear
Dead bones, and skulls wear cast, and bodies hanged wear.

Giles Fletcher, Christ's Victorie on Earth (1610)

The other was a fell, despiteful fiend:
Hell holds none worse in baleful bower below:
By pride, and wit, and rage, and rancour keen'd;
Of man alike, if good or bad, the foe:
With nose up-turn'd, he always made a show
As if he smelt some nauseous scent; his eye
Was cold and keen, like blast from boreal snow,
And taunts he casten forth most bitterly.
Such were the twain that off drove this ungodly fry.

James Thomson, The Castle of Indolence:
An Allegorical Poem in Imitation of Spenser (1748)

But here 'twixt rock and river grew
A dismal grove of sable yew,
With whose sad tints were mingled seen

> The blighted fir's sepulchral green.
> Seemed that the trees their shadows cast
> The earth that nourished them to blast;
> For never knew that swarthy grove
> The verdant hue that fairies love,
> Nor wilding green nor woodland flower
> Arose within its baleful bower;
> The dank and sable earth receives
> Its only carpet from the leaves
> That, from the withering branches cast,
> Bestrewed the ground with every blast.

> Sir Walter Scott, *Rokeby* (1812)

balefully, *adv.* In a baleful (q.v.) manner.

a. General:

> Yonder, where parching Sirius set in drought,
> Balefully glares red Arson—there—and there.

> Herman Melville, "The House-Top: A Night Piece"

The crouching image with its cuttlefish head, dragon body, scaly wings, and hieroglyphed pedestal, was preserved in the Museum at Hyde Park; and I studied it long and well, finding it a thing of balefully exquisite workmanship, and with the same utter mystery, terrible antiquity, and unearthly strangeness of material which I had noted in Legrasse's smaller specimen.

> H. P. Lovecraft, "The Call of Cthulhu" (1926)

Even in the bleak nights of winter, the globe yielded a genial warmth; and it fell never from its weird suspension, though without palpable support; and beneath it the garden flourished balefully, lush and exuberant as some parterre of the nether circles.

> Clark Ashton Smith, "The Garden of Adompha" (1937)

b. Of the eyes (gaze, etc.):

His serpent eyes glittered balefully.

> Robert E. Howard, *Skull-Face* (1929)

Out of the blackness beyond the fire two enormous crimson eyes glared balefully; Koto calmly arose, stepped across the glowing line of the Fire of Safety, and walked off in the darkness toward those glowing orbs.

> Nictzin Dyalhis, "The Sapphire Siren" (1934)

Paradine regarded his wife balefully and crossed his long legs. "You sound like one of my students."

> Lewis Padgett (Henry Kuttner & C. L. Moore),
> "Mimsy Were the Borogoves" (1943)

His eyes glared balefully under his shaggy brows as Kazazael glanced at Kothar.

> Gardner F. Fox, "The Sword of the Sorcerer" in
> *Kothar—Barbarian Swordsman* (1969)

Hate was in his balefully glinting eyes as he dragged himself forward across the stone to where the sword lay.

> John Jakes, "The Unspeakable Shrine" (1967) in *Brak the Barbarian*

"Eh?" said Mundungus, peering balefully at Harry through his matted ginger hair.

> J. K. Rowling, *Harry Potter and the Order of the Phœnix* (2003)

c. Of a heavenly body:

Between the sun's departure and return, the Silver Death had fallen upon Yoros. Its advent, however, had been foretold in many prophecies, both immemorial and recent. Astrologers had said that this mysterious malady, heretofore unknown on earth, would descend from the great star, Achernar, which presided balefully over all the lands of the southern continent of Zothique; and having sealed the flesh of a myriad men with its bright, metallic pallor, the plague would still go on in time and space, borne by the dim currents of ether to other worlds.

> Clark Ashton Smith, "The Isle of the Torturers" (1932)

bane, *n.* [< OE *bana*, murderer, slayer, killer] Death or destruction; the cause of death, destruction, ruin, injury, or misery; a source of persistent annoyance. In combined forms, a deadly poison, as henbane, wolf's-bane, rat's-bane, etc.

Titles: Robert E. Howard, "Dermod's Bane"; Michael Moorcock, *The Bane of the Black Sword*

Who hesitates to destroy a venomous serpent that has crept near his sleeping friend, except the man who selfishly dreads lest the malignant reptile should turn his fury on himself? And if the poisoner has assumed a human shape, if the bane be distinguished only from the viper's venom by the excess and extent of its devastation, will the saviour and avenger here retract and pause entrenched behind the superstition of the indefeasible divinity of man? Is the human form, then, the mere badge of a prerogative for unlicensed wickedness and mischief?

> Percy Bysshe Shelley, "The Assassins" (1814)

> Nature rejects the monarch, not the man;
> The subject, not the citizen: for kings
> And subjects, mutual foes, for ever play
> A losing game into each other's hands,
> Whose stakes are vice and misery. The man
> Of virtuous soul commands not, nor obeys.
> Power, like a desolating pestilence,
> Pollutes whate'er it touches; and obedience,
> Bane of all genius, virtue, freedom, truth,

Makes slaves of men, and, of the human frame,
A mechanized automaton.

> Percy Bysshe Shelley, *Queen Mab: A Philosophical Poem* (1813)

She was a careless, fearless girl,
  And made her answer plain,
Outspoken she to earl or churl,
  Kindhearted in the main,
But somewhat heedless with her tongue
  And apt at causing pain;
A mirthful maiden she and young,
  Most fair for bliss or bane.

> Christina Rossetti, "Jessie Cameron"

"But where did he come from, the little dark thing, harboured by a good man to his bane?" muttered superstition, as I dozed into unconsciousness.

> Emily Brontë, *Wuthering Heights: A Novel* (1847)

But she knew in her heart darkly that he was either boon or bane to her, for of his coming she had been warned without words, as it will happen to those that have the gift: and this also darkly, that his looking and his speaking were both to her mind, whereby she was the more cast down at his breaking from her.

> Sir Henry Newbolt, *Aladore* (1914)

Long ago had Gorice VII. practised forbidden arts therein, and folk said that in that chamber he raised up those spirits whereby he gat his bane. Sithence was the chamber sealed, nor had the late Kings need of it, since little faith they placed in art magical, relying rather on the might of their hands and the sword of Witchland.

> E. R. Eddison, *The Worm Ouroboros* (1922)

Lady Margaret Trevor from Cornwall, wife of Godfrey, the second son of the fifth baron, became a favourite bane of children all over the countryside, and the dæmon heroine of a particularly horrible old ballad not yet extinct near the Welsh border.

> H. P. Lovecraft, "The Rats in the Walls" (1923)

"You need not thank me," said the lady, with a dulcet smile. "I am Moriamis, the enchantress, and the Druids fear my magic, which is more sovereign and more excellent than theirs, though I use it only for the welfare of men and not for their bale or bane."

> Clark Ashton Smith, "The Holiness of Azédarac" (1931)

Sluggish drops of sullen balm;
Blood-red wine from fruits of bane,

> Subtly mixed with polar snows
> Melted in a harlot's palm;
> Attar from the firstling rose
> On the grave of lovers slain:—
>
> Clark Ashton Smith, "The Love-Potion" (1923)

According to popular wisdom, the company of magicians was usually more bane than benefit.

Jack Vance, *Lyonesse: Suldrun's Garden* (1983)

baneful, *adj.* Causing death, destruction, ruin, injury, or misery; poisonous or venomous.

a. General:

Architecturally and in point of "furnishing" the Snakery had a severe simplicity befitting the humble circumstances of its occupants, many of whom, indeed, could not safely have been intrusted with the liberty that is necessary to the full enjoyment of luxury, for they had the troublesome peculiarity of being alive. In their own apartments, however, they were under as little personal restraint as was compatible with their protection from the baneful habit of swallowing one another; and, as Brayton had thoughtfully been apprised, it was more than a tradition that some of them had at divers times been found in parts of the premises where it would have embarrassed them to explain their presence.

Ambrose Bierce, "The Man and the Snake" (1890)

As I rose, I fell flat: and what I did thereafter I did in a state of existence whose acts, to the waking intellect, seem unreal as dream. I must immediately, I think, have been conscious that here was the cause of the destruction of organisms, conscious that it still surrounded its own neighborhood with baneful emanations, conscious that I was approaching it: and I must have somehow crawled or won myself forward.

M. P. Shiel, *The Purple Cloud* (1901)

And as I raised my glance it was without preparation that I saw glistening in the distance two dæmoniac reflections of my expiring lamp; two reflections glowing with a baneful and unmistakable effulgence, and provoking maddeningly nebulous memories.

H. P. Lovecraft, "The Lurking Fear" (1922)

b. Of the eyes (gaze, glare, etc.):

I knew now that we were lost, indeed; these were confidences which our graves should hold inviolate! He suddenly opened fully those blazing green eyes and directed their baneful glare upon Nayland Smith.

Sax Rohmer (Arthur Sarsfield Ward),
The Return of Dr. Fu-Manchu (1916; aka *The Devil Doctor*)

There he lay, writhing, for a moment, his baneful eyes turned up, revealing the whites; and the great grey rats, released, began leaping about the room.

> Sax Rohmer (Arthur Sarsfield Ward),
> *The Return of Dr. Fu-Manchu* (1916; aka *The Devil Doctor*)

c. Of an influence:

> The page gave the flasket, which Walwayn had filled
> With the juice of wild roots that his heart had distilled—
> So baneful their influence on all that had breath,
> One drop had been frenzy and two had been death.

> Sir Walter Scott, *Harold the Dauntless: A Poem in Six Cantos* (1816)

There is nothing more baneful than the influence which privileged nurses and other attendants upon young children exercise over their untutored imaginations, through the medium of superstitious dread.

> Daniel Keyes Sanford, "A Night in the Catacombs" (1818)

The parent at all times exercises mighty influence over the mind of his offspring; but were I to attempt to describe that which my father possessed over me, it would seem as if I were penning some romantic tale to make old women bless their stars and crouch nearer to the blazing Christmas log, rather than simply narrating the prime source of all those curseful events that have made me the wretch I am. Nor need I here describe his power; for each page that I have to write will more and more develope the entireness of his baneful influence over my mind, and shew how he employed it to my irretrievable undoing.

> William Godwin the Younger, "The Executioner" (1832)

"I went on,—Derval's murder; the missing contents of the casket; the apparition seen by the maniac assassin guiding him to the horrid deed; the luminous haunting shadow; the positive charge in the murdered man's memoir connecting Margrave with Louis Grayle, and accusing him of the murder of Haroun; the night in the moonlit pavilion at Derval Court; the baneful influence on Lilian; the struggle between me and himself in the house by the sea-shore,—the strange All that is told in this Strange Story."

> Sir Edward Bulwer-Lytton, *A Strange Story* (1861)

"Your novels have interested me for this reason: you are aware of the baneful influences which surround us, which so often sway or actuate us. I have followed the working of these agencies even in chemical reactions, in the growth and decay of trees, flowers, minerals. I feel that the processes of physical decomposition, as well as the similar mental and moral processes, are due entirely to them."

> Clark Ashton Smith, "The Devotee of Evil" (1930)

Suddenly a thought came to me—a recollection of that night when a certain glass of water had glowed with iridescent fire; when, through the baneful influence of the fog, my own mind had skirted the borderland of lunacy. I began to understand.

Bertram Russell, "The Scourge of B'Moth" (1929)

bas-relief, *n.* [< Fr] A low-relief; a sculpture in which figures project less than one half of their true proportions from the background (contrasted with **alto-relievo** or **high-relief**). An essential style of art in weird fiction and fantasy décor.

I approached and saw, as if graven in *bas relief* upon the white surface, the figure of a gigantic *cat*.

Edgar Allan Poe, "The Black Cat" (1843)

The first thing I noticed was that the walls were covered with sculptures in bas-relief, for the most part of a sort similar to those upon the vases that I have described—love-scenes principally, then hunting pieces, pictures of executions, and of the torture of criminals by the placing of a pot upon the head, presumably red-hot, thus showing whence our hosts had derived this pleasant practice.

H. Rider Haggard, *She: A History of Adventure* (1886)

Lamps that were milky opals self-effulgent filled all the chamber with a soft radiance, in which the bas-reliefs of the high dado, delicately carved, portraying those immortal blooms of amaranth and nepenthe and moly and Elysian asphodel, were seen in all their delicate beauty, and the fair painted pictures of the Lord of Krothering and his lady sister, and of Lord Juss above the great open fireplace with Goldry and Spitfire on his left and right. A few other pictures there were, smaller than these: the Princess Armelline of Goblinland, Zigg and his lady wife, and others; wondrous beautiful.

E. R. Eddison, *The Worm Ouroboros* (1922)

So it was upon Walburga's Eve, when almost anything is rather more than likely to happen, that Jurgen went hastily out of Heaven, without having gained or wasted any love there. St. Peter unbarred for him, not the main entrance, but a small private door, carved with innumerable fishes in bas-relief, because this exit opened directly upon any place you choose to imagine.

James Branch Cabell, *Jurgen: A Comedy of Justice* (1919)

The face of the terrace was about ten feet high, and all over it ran a bas-relief of what looked like short-trailing vines, surmounted by five stalks, on the tip of each of which was a flower.

A. Merritt, *The Moon Pool* (1919)

"The Snake Mother!" her gaze returned to him; she touched a bracelet on her right wrist. Graydon, drawing close, saw that this bracelet held a disk on which was carved in bas-relief a serpent with a woman's head and woman's breast and arms.

A. Merritt, The Face in the Abyss (1923)

Plainly visible across the intervening water on account of their enormous size, were an array of bas-reliefs whose subjects would have excited the envy of a Doré.

H. P. Lovecraft, "Dagon" (1917)

"It's the billionaire, Claud Wishhaven, who wants me to do a bas-relief in pseudo-jade and neo-jasper for the hall of his country mansion. He wants something really advanced and futuristic. We're to talk it over tonight—decide on the motifs, etc."

Clark Ashton Smith, "The Plutonian Drug" (1932)

And more than once I was found huddled and still asleep in our cellar alongside the grotesquely floor-set "Gate of Dreams" bas-relief—to which, incidentally, my mother had taken a dislike which she tried to conceal from my father.

Fritz Leiber, "The Terror from the Depths" (1975)

The designer chuckled, and went to work sketching the bronze scene—a vividly-done bas-relief unearthed at the Ur dig, in the 1920s by Woolley, among the jewels of Queen Shub-ad and her lesbian ladies-in-waiting.

Mary Elizabeth Counselman, "The Lamashtu Amulet" (1980)

Brak's rapid impression convinced him that here was a different kind of chariot from those he had distantly observed rolling away to the north. Upon the front of this car, in rich bronzed bas-relief, was the device of a goddess.

John Jakes, "The Barge of Souls" (1967) in *Brak the Barbarian*

As they padded noiselessly up the steps to the yawning entrance to the mysterious edifice, the two observed it was windowless, and its granite face was covered with intricate bas-reliefs depicting scenes of unspeakable and obscene cruelty.

Charles R. Saunders, "The City of Madness" (1974)

batrachian, *adj.* [< Gr *bátrakhos,* frog] Of, pertaining to, or resembling the Batrachia, the order of amphibians including frogs and toads.

Titles: Kermit Marsh III, "Derleth's Use of the Terms 'Ichthyic' and 'Batrachian'"

I saw no other pet animals among this community except some very amusing and sportive creatures of the Batrachian species, resembling frogs, but with very intelligent countenances, which the children were fond of, and kept in their private gardens.

Sir Edward Bulwer-Lytton, *The Coming Race* (1871; aka *Vril: The Power of the Coming Race*)

The portrait of the grandfather had the features and aspect of the philosopher, only much more exaggerated: he was not dressed, and the colour of his body was singular; the breast and stomach yellow, the shoulders and legs of a dull bronze hue: the great-grandfather was a magnificent specimen of the Batrachian genus, a Giant Frog, *pur et simple*.

Sir Edward Bulwer-Lytton, *The Coming Race* (1871; aka *Vril: The Power of the Coming Race*)

Among these reliefs were fabulous monsters of abhorrent grotesqueness and malignity—half ichthyic and half batrachian in suggestion—which one could not dissociate from a certain haunting and uncomfortable sense of pseudo-memory, as if they called up some image from deep cells and tissues whose re-tentive functions are wholly primal and awesomely ancestral.

H. P. Lovecraft, "The Shadow over Innsmouth" (1931)

Her witchcraft had made her feared among the peasantry of that remote province, where belief in spells and philtres was still common. The people of Averoigne called her *La Mère des Crapauds*, Mother of Toads, a name given for more than one reason. Toads swarmed innumerably about her hut; they were said to be her familiars, and dark tales were told concerning their relationship to the sorceress, and the duties they performed at her bidding. Such tales were all the more readily believed because of those batrachian features that had always been remarked in her aspect.

Clark Ashton Smith, "Mother of Toads" (1937)

"Suppose—it is an awful thought, I know—suppose that some creature closely resembling what Ulman became was *once* our ancestor, that a hundred million years ago a gigantic batrachian shape with trunk-like appendages and great flapping ears paddled through the warm primeval seas or stretched its leathery length on banks of Permian slime!"

Frank Belknap Long, "The Horror from the Hills" (1930)

"But you are familiar with art. And I wonder whether you can explain why the primitives of the South Pacific should emphasize the batrachian and ichthyic in their artifacts and arts, while the primitives of the North Pacific, for example, emphasize characteristics which are clearly avian. There are exceptions, of course; you will recognize them. The lizard figures of Easter Island and the batrachian pieces from Melanesia and Micronesia are common to these areas; the avian masks and headdresses of the North Pacific Indian tribes are common to the Canadian coast. But we find on occasion among those coastal Indian tribes disturbingly familiar motifs; consider, for instance, the markedly batrachian aspects of the shaman's headdress of the Haida tribe common to Prince of Wales Island and the ceremonial shark headdress of the Tlingit of Ketchikan, Alaska."

August Derleth, "The Black Island" (1952) in *The Trail of Cthulhu*

For there were in his notes far more than strange references, which I found oddly disturbing; there were crude, yet effective drawings of shockingly outré settings and alien creatures, such beings as I could never, in my wildest dreams, have conceived. Indeed, for the most part, the creatures beggared description; they were winged, bat-like beings of the size of a man; they were vast, amorphous bodies, hung with tentacles, looking at first glance octopoid, but very definitely far more intelligent than an octopus; they were clawed half-man, half-bird creatures; they were horrible, batrachian-faced things walking erect, with scaled arms and a hue of pale green, like sea-water.

August Derleth (as H. P. Lovecraft & August Derleth),
"The Gable Window" (1957)

"Deadloin!" they croaked in terrified batrachian voices. "The deadloin is coming!"

James Blish & Judith Ann Lawrence, "Getting Along" (1972)

batrachian (*pl.* **batrachians, batrachia**), *n.* A member of the Batrachia, the order of amphibians including frogs and toads.

"I think," I said cautiously, "that we face an evolution of highly intelligent beings from ancestral sources radically removed from those through which mankind ascended. These half-human, highly developed batrachians they call the *Akka* prove that evolution in these caverned spaces has certainly pursued one different path than on earth. The Englishman, Wells, wrote an imaginative and very entertaining book concerning an invasion of earth by Martians, and he made his Martians enormously specialized cuttlefish. There was nothing inherently improbable in Wells's choice. Man is the ruling animal of earth today solely by reason of a series of accidents; under another series spiders or ants, or even elephants, could have become the dominant race."

A. Merritt, *The Moon Pool* (1919)

This drawing took up the majority of the page, and the jotting accompanying it I assumed to be a notation of an encounter—evidently in research, for it could hardly have been in the flesh—with a sub-human type—(could the "D.O." have been a reference to the "Deep Ones," mention of which I had previously encounted?), which, doubtless, Dr. Charriere looked upon as a verification of the trend of his research, a trend to support a belief he probably held that some kinship with batrachia, and hence very probably also saurians, could be traced.

August Derleth (as H. P. Lovecraft & August Derleth), "The Survivor" (1954)

There were large insects, huge spiders, and great, goggle-eyed frogs here aplenty. The batrachians evidently fed on the insects and arachnids, keeping them in relatively low numbers, and there were monstrous cranes and other gigantic wading birds that must have found the fish and frogs of the marsh most beneficial.

Gary Gygax, *Artifact of Evil* (1986)

batrachoid, *adj.* [< Gr *bátrakhos,* frog] Of, pertaining to, or resembling the Batrachia, the order of amphibians including frogs and toads.

> It was full of monstrous hints of the obscure traffic Persis Winthorp had had with the abnormal beings that dwelt in the North Swamp, and in particular her dealings with the batrachoid creature who had sired her—a demon whom the Indians had worshiped ages ago, Dobson said.
>
> Henry Kuttner, "The Frog" (1939)

> The artist had a glimpse of a shining hideous countenance protruding through the window; a dreadful mask that was neither batrachoid nor human, but partook monstrously of the attributes of both.
>
> Henry Kuttner, "The Frog" (1939)

Behemoth, Beemoth, *pr.n.* & *n.* [< Hb BHMVTh, beasts (intensive plural); or < Hb, assimilated from < Egyptian *p-ehe-mau,* water-ox] In Biblical mythology, an enormous beast of indefinite description, perhaps a gigantic hippopotamus, though sometimes identified as an elephant. Frequently paired with Leviathan (q.v.). [Form beemoth not in *OED.*]

Titles: Bertram Russell, "The Scourge of B'Moth"; Michael Shea, *The Mines of Behemoth*

> The Sixt, and of Creation last arose
> With Ev'ning Harps and Matin, when God said,
> Let th' Earth bring forth Soul living in her kind,
> Cattle and Creeping things, and Beast of the Earth,
> Each in their kind. The Earth obey'd, and straight
> Op'ning her fertile Womb teem'd at a Birth
> Innumerous living Creatures, perfect forms,
> Limb'd and full grown: out of the ground up rose
> As from his Lair the wild Beast where he wons
> In Forest wild, in Thicket, Brake, or Den;
> Among the Trees in Pairs they rose, they walk'd:
> The Cattle in the Fields and Meadows green:
> Those rare and solitary, these in flocks
> Pasturing at once, and in broad Herds upsprung.
> The grassy Clods now Calv'd, now half appear'd
> The Tawny Lion, pawing to get free
> His hinder parts, then springs as broke from Bonds,
> And Rampant shakes his Brinded mane; the Ounce,
> The Libbard, and the Tiger, as the Mole
> Rising, the crumbl'd Earth above them threw
> In Hillocks; the swift Stag from under ground
> Bore up his branching head: scarce from his mould
> *Behemoth* biggest born of Earth upheav'd

His vastness: Fleec't the Flocks and bleating rose,
As Plants: ambiguous between Sea and Land
The River Horse and scaly Crocodile.

John Milton, *Paradise Lost* (1667)

Let Aquila rejoice with Beemoth who is Enoch, no fish but a stupendous creeping Thing.

Christopher Smart, *Jubilate Agno* (1759–63)

Let Priscilla rejoice with Cythera. As earth increases by Beemoth so the sea likewise emerges.

Christopher Smart, *Jubilate Agno* (1759–63)

The wrecks beside of many a city vast,
Whose population which the Earth grew over
Was mortal but not human; see, they lie,
Their monstrous works and uncouth skeletons,
Their statues, homes, and fanes; prodigious shapes
Huddled in grey annihilation, split,
Jammed in the hard black deep; and over these
The anatomies of unknown winged things,
And fishes which were isles of living scale,
And serpents, bony chains, twisted around
The iron crags, or within heaps of dust
To which the tortuous strength of their last pangs
Had crushed the iron crags;—and over these
The jagged alligator and the might
Of earth-convulsing behemoth, which once
Were monarch beasts, and on the slimy shores
And weed-overgrown continents of Earth
Increased and multiplied like summer worms
On an abandoned corpse, till the blue globe
Wrapt Deluge round it like a cloak, and they
Yelled, gaspt and were abolished; or some God
Whose throne was in a Comet, past, and cried—
"Be not!"—and like my words they were no more.

Percy Bysshe Shelley, *Prometheus Unbound: A Lyrical Drama* (1819)

Far had he roam'd,
With nothing save the hollow vast, that foam'd
Above, around, and at his feet; save things
More dead than Morpheus' imaginings:
Old rusted anchors, helmets, breast-plates large
Of gone sea-warriors; brazen beaks and targe;
Rudders that for a hundred years had lost

The sway of human hand; gold vase emboss'd
With long-forgotten story, and wherein
No reveller had ever dipp'd a chin
But those of Saturn's vintage; mouldering scrolls,
Writ in the tongue of heaven, by those souls
Who first were on the earth; and sculptures rude
In ponderous stone, developing the mood
Of ancient Nox;—then skeletons of man,
Of beast, behemoth, and leviathan,
And elephant, and eagle, and huge jaw
Of nameless monster.

John Keats, *Endymion: A Poetic Romance* (1817–18)

"And the hippopotami heard my call, and came, with the behemoth, unto the foot of the rock, and roared loudly and fearfully beneath the moon."

Edgar Allan Poe, "Silence—A Fable" (1838)

Something of awe now stole over me, as I gazed upon this inflexible iron animal. Always, more or less machinery of this ponderous, elaborate sort strikes, in some moods, strange dread into the human heart, as some living, panting Behemoth might.

Herman Melville, "The Paradise of Bachelors and the Tartarus of Maids" (1855)

Nay, more, where there is no record, and history is either lost, or was never written, Criticism can re-create the past for us from the very smallest fragment of language or art, just as surely as the man of science can from some tiny bone, or the mere impress of a foot upon a rock, re-create for us the winged dragon or Titan lizard that once made the earth shake beneath its tread, can call Behemoth out of his cave, and make Leviathan swim once more across the startled sea.

Oscar Wilde, "The Critic as Artist"

"The world we live in today is a meager spectacle beside the abundance of the earlier Tertiary time, when Behemoth in a thousand forms, Deinotherium, Titanotherium, Helladotherium, saber-toothed tiger, a hundred sorts of elephant, and the like, pushed through the jungles that are now this mild world of today."

H. G. Wells, *The Undying Fire: A Novel Based on the Book of Job* (1919)

I rushed toward her. The word "Madman!" hissed as by the tongues of ten thousand serpents through the chamber, I heard; for a moment to my wild eyes there seemed to rear itself, swelling to the roof, a tower of ragged cloud, and, as my arms closed upon emptiness, I was tossed by the operation of some Behemoth potency backward to a wall of the chamber, where I fell, shocked into insensibility.

M. P. Shiel, "Xélucha" (1896)

The rose-red light shone warm on the walls and floor of that passage, but none might say whence it shone. Strange sculptures glimmered overhead, bull-headed men, stags with human faces, mammoths, and behemoths of the flood: vast forms and uncertain carved in the living rock.

E. R. Eddison, *The Worm Ouroboros* (1922)

In the centre of the palace Miramon had set like a tower one of the tusks of Behemoth: the tusk was hollowed out into five large rooms, and in the inmost room, under a canopy with green tassels, they found the magician.

James Branch Cabell, *Figures of Earth: A Comedy of Appearances* (1920)

BEHEMOTH—According to the legends of the Jews, Behemoth is the greatest of created animals. He requires the produce of a thousand mountains for his food, and all the water that flows through Jordan in a year he can drink at a single gulp. At the end he will fight Leviathan and, the animals killing each other, both will be served to the pious on the Judgment Day. Behemoth is described in the Bible in Job XL, 15–24.

John Philips Cranwell & James P. Cover, *Notes on* Figures of Earth (1929)

But, lo, as you would quaffoff his fraudstuff and sink teeth through that pyth of a flowerwhite bodey behold of him as behemoth for he is noewhemoe.

James Joyce, *Finnegans Wake* (1922–39)

It flew with the claw-tipped wings of a pterodactyl, it swam in tepid seas with the vast, winding bulk of an ichthyosaurus, it bellowed uncouthly with the armored throat of some forgotten behemoth to the huge moon through primordial mists.

Clark Ashton Smith, "Ubbo-Sathla" (1932)

Wings that were too broad for those of the bat flew vaguely overhead; and at whiles, in the shadowy caverns, he beheld great fearsome bulks having a likeness to those behemoths and giant reptiles which burdened the Earth in earlier times; but because of the dimness he could not tell if these were living shapes or forms that the stone had taken.

Clark Ashton Smith, "The Seven Geases" (1933)

The forest continued almost to the city walls. Peering from behind the final boscage, I saw their overwhelming battlements in the sky above me, and noted the flawless jointure of their prodigious blocks. I was near the great road, which entered an open gate large enough to admit the passage of behemoths.

Clark Ashton Smith, "The City of the Singing Flame" (1931)

It was the Year of the Behemoth, the Month of the Hedgehog, the Day of the Toad.

Fritz Leiber, "The Jewels in the Forest" (1939)

"Oh, by Glaggerk and by Kos!" he roared. "By the Behemoth! Oh, by the Cold Waste and the guts of the Red God! Oh! Oh! Oh!" Again the insane bellowing burst out. "Oh, by the Killer Whale and the Cold Woman and her spawn!"

Fritz Leiber, "The Jewels in the Forest" (1939)

He found himself disliking the texture and consistency of the tarry mixture gouged from the cracks, which somehow he could only liken to wholly imaginary substances, such as the dung of dragons or the solidified vomit of the Behemoth.

Fritz Leiber, "The Jewels in the Forest" (1939)

Being of a mind to discover the Ultimate, I sought diligently into the works of historians, and wise men of all ages. In my studies, I chanced upon a manuscript written by one, Joachim of Cannes. He had gathered a wealth of lore from men of every clime. He said the name of the Devourer was Behemoth, which, indeed, is translated into "he who devours the souls of men." This monster is of great antiquity, and was well perceived by the ancients.

Johannes of Madgeburg, untitled manuscript, as quoted in
Bertram Russell, "The Scourge of B'Moth" (1929)

In the white glare of moonlight, the dark city brooded like some vast behemoth of the night.

Charles R. Saunders, "The City of Madness" (1974)

behemothic, *adj.* Of, pertaining to, or resembling a behemoth. [Not in *OED*.]

After all, it was not a long thing to tell. Oozing and surging up out of that yawning trap-door in the Cyclopean crypt I had glimpsed such an unbelievable behemothic monstrosity that I could not doubt the power of its original to kill with its mere sight.

H. P. Lovecraft & Hazel Heald, "Out of the Æons" (1933)

beleaguer, *v.tr.* [< Dutch *belegeren,* to besiege < *be-,* around + *legeren,* to camp; spelling influenced by *league*] To lay siege to; to surround with troops so as to prevent escape.

The Celt assailed him, beckoning from the weird wood he called the world, and his far-off ancestors, the "little people," crept out of their caves, muttering charms and incantations in hissing inhuman speech; he was beleaguered by desires that had slept in his race for ages.

Arthur Machen, *The Hill of Dreams* (1897)

The lodge was a fortress beleaguered by the woods, a fortress whose garrison sallied forth with axe and torch to take their toll of the besiegers.

A. Merritt, "The Women of the Wood" (1926)

I tingled at the thought of what he might now have to tell me—there was an almost paralyzing fascination in the thought of sitting in that lonely and lately beleaguered farmhouse with a man who had talked with actual emissaries from outer space; sitting there with the terrible record and the pile of letters in which Akeley had summarised his earlier conclusions.

H. P. Lovecraft, "The Whisperer in Darkness" (1930)

be-nightmared, benightmared, *ppl. adj.* Afflicted with nightmare.

> That night the Baron dreamt of many a woe,
> And all his warrior-guests, with shade and form
> Of witch, and demon, and large coffin-worm,
> Were long be-nightmar'd. Angela the old
> Died palsy-twitch'd, with meagre face deform;
> The Beadsman, after thousand aves told,
> For aye unsought for slept among his ashes cold.

John Keats, "The Eve of St. Agnes" (1818)

He saw the wretched agony of his being as the drug wore off its potency and left his body racked with spasms of exquisite pain. His head seemed to swell as if about to burst; his rotting, benightmared brain seemed to grow inside his skull and split his head asunder.

Robert Bloch, "Black Lotus" (1935)

betimes, *adv.* Early, soon, in good time; from time to time.

When he did, the answer was plain and decisive, "No, never, never. When his honor sat in the kitchen in winter, to save a fire in his own room, he could never bear the talk of the old women that came in to light their pipes *betimes*, (from time to time)."

Charles Maturin, *Melmoth the Wanderer: A Tale* (1820)

Many and multiform are the dim horrors of Earth, infesting her ways from the prime. They sleep beneath the unturned stone; they rise with the tree from its root; they move beneath the sea and in subterranean places; they dwell in the inmost adyta; they emerge betimes from the shutten sepulchre of haughty bronze and the low grave that is sealed with clay.

Abdul Alhazred, *Necronomicon*, as quoted in
Clark Ashton Smith, "The Nameless Offspring" (1931)

Bhole, (Dhole), *n.* A fabulous creature in the Dreamlands of H. P. Lovecraft. (Long mistranscribed *dhole*.) [Not in *OED*.]

At last far below him he saw faint lines of grey and ominous pinnacles which he knew must be the fabled Peaks of Thok. Awful and sinister they stand in the haunted dusk of sunless and eternal depths; higher than man may reckon, and guarding terrible valleys where the bholes crawl and burrow nastily.

H. P. Lovecraft, *The Dream-Quest of Unknown Kadath* (1927)

Now Carter knew from a certain source that he was in the vale of Pnath, where crawl and burrow the enormous bholes; but he did not know what to expect, because no one has ever seen a bhole or even guessed what such a thing may be like. Bholes are known only by dim rumour, from the rustling they make amongst mountains of bones and the slimy touch they have when they wriggle past one. They cannot be seen because they creep only in the dark.

H. P. Lovecraft, *The Dream-Quest of Unknown Kadath* (1927)

The note said: "Machen's *dols* = Lovecraft's *dholes?*"

Robert Anton Wilson & Robert Shea,
The Eye in the Pyramid in *The Illuminatus! Trilogy* (1969–71)

"The money is gone," Carl Jung said, wearing Freud's beard. "What totem will you use now to ward off insecurity and the things that go bump in the night?" He sneered. "What childish codes! M.A.F.I.A.—*Morte Alla Francia Italia Anela.* French Canadian bean soup—the Five Consecrated Bavarian Seers. *Annuit Coeptis Novus Ordo Seclorum*—Anti-Christ Now Our Saviour. A boy has never wept nor dashed a thousand kim—Asmodeus Belial Hastur Nyarlathotep Wotan Niggurath Dholes Azathoth Tindalos Kadith. Child's play! *Glasspielen!*"

Robert Anton Wilson & Robert Shea, *The Golden Apple* in
The Illuminatus! Trilogy (1969–71)

blaspheme, *v.intr.* & *v.tr.* To commit blasphemy (q.v.); to utter profane, impious speech; to transcend and transgress against the normal bounds and categories of reality.

There were, in such voyages, incalculable local dangers; as well as that shocking final peril which gibbers unmentionably outside the ordered universe, where no dreams reach; that last amorphous blight of nethermost confusion which blasphemes and bubbles at the centre of all infinity—the boundless dæmon-sultan Azathoth, whose name no lips dare speak aloud, and who gnaws hungrily in inconceivable, unlighted chambers beyond time amidst the muffled, maddening beating of vile drums and the thin, monotonous whine of accursed flutes; to which detestable pounding and piping dance slowly, awkwardly, and absurdly the gigantic ultimate gods, the blind, voiceless, tenebrous, mindless Other Gods whose soul and messenger is the crawling chaos Nyarlathotep.

H. P. Lovecraft, *The Dream-Quest of Unknown Kadath* (1927)

"Who exactly are the Great Old Ones?" Chandler asked.

"There are lots of them," Deborah said. "One is Azathoth, the blind idiot god. He is depicted as an amorphous blight of confusion which bubbles and blasphemes at the centre of infinity."

Michael Slade, *Ghoul* (1987)

blasphemous, *adj.* Characterized by blasphemy (q.v.); transcending and transgressing against the normal bounds and categories of reality.

Titles: Thomas Ligotti, "The Blasphemous Enlightenment of Prof. Francis Wayland Thurston of Boston, Providence, and the Human Race"

"Who dares?" he demanded hoarsely of the courtiers who stood near him— "who dares insult us with this blasphemous mockery? Seize him and unmask him—that we may know whom we have to hang at sunrise, from the battlements!"

Edgar Allan Poe, "The Masque of the Red Death" (1842)

Our museum was a blasphemous, unthinkable place, where with the satanic taste of neurotic virtuosi we had assembled an universe of terror and decay to excite our jaded sensibilities. It was a secret room, far, far underground; where huge winged dæmons carven of basalt and onyx vomited from wide grinning mouths weird green and orange light, and hidden pneumatic pipes ruffled into kaleidoscopic dances of death the lines of red charnel things hand in hand woven in voluminous black hangings. Through these pipes came at will the odours our moods most craved; sometimes the scent of pale funeral lilies, sometimes the narcotic incense of imagined Eastern shrines of the kingly dead, and sometimes—how I shudder to recall it!—the frightful, soul-upheaving stenches of the uncovered grave.

H. P. Lovecraft, "The Hound" (1922)

Amorphous shadows seemed to lurk in the darker recesses of the weed-choked hollow and to flit as in some blasphemous ceremonial procession past the portals of the mouldering tombs in the hillside; shadows which could not have been cast by that pallid, peering crescent moon.

H. P. Lovecraft, "The Statement of Randolph Carter" (1919)

It was certainly nervous waiting, and the blasphemous book in my hands made it doubly so.

H. P. Lovecraft, "The Festival" (1923)

There's no use in my trying to tell you what they were like, because the awful, the blasphemous horror, and the unbelievable loathsomeness and moral fœtor came from simple touches quite beyond the power of words to classify.

H. P. Lovecraft, "Pickman's Model" (1926)

Armitage, half-ready to tell him he might make a copy of what parts he needed, thought suddenly of the possible consequences and checked himself. There was too much responsibility in giving such a being the key to such blasphemous outer spheres.

H. P. Lovecraft, "The Dunwich Horror" (1928)

Of course they might be fraudulent, for others besides myself had read the monstrous and abhorred *Necronomicon* of the mad Arab Abdul Alhazred; but it nevertheless made me shiver to recognise certain ideographs which study had taught me to link with the most blood-curdling and blasphemous whispers of things that had had a kind of mad half-existence before the earth and the other inner worlds of the solar system were made.

H. P. Lovecraft, "The Whisperer in Darkness" (1930)

Blasphemous influences seemed to surround me and press chokingly upon my senses.

H. P. Lovecraft, "The Whisperer in Darkness" (1930)

Hideous though the idea was, I knew that I was under the same roof with nameless things from abysmal space; for those two voices were unmistakably the blasphemous buzzings which the Outside Beings used in their communication with men.

H. P. Lovecraft, "The Whisperer in Darkness" (1930)

"Tell me, Daniel Upton—*what devilish exchange was perpetrated in the house of horror where that blasphemous monster had his trusting, weak-willed, half-human child at his mercy?*"

H. P. Lovecraft, "The Thing on the Doorstep" (1933)

I was willing enough to stay mute while the affair was fresh and uncertain; but now that it is an old story, with public interest and curiosity gone, I have an odd craving to whisper about those few frightful hours in that ill-rumoured and evilly shadowed seaport of death and blasphemous abnormality.

H. P. Lovecraft, "The Shadow over Innsmouth" (1931)

At times I fancied that every contour of these blasphemous fish-frogs was overflowing with the ultimate quintessence of unknown and inhuman evil.

H. P. Lovecraft, "The Shadow over Innsmouth" (1931)

Nothing that I could have imagined—nothing, even, that I could have gathered had I credited old Zadok's crazy tale in the most literal way—would be in any way comparable to the dæmoniac, blasphemous reality that I saw—or believe I saw.

H. P. Lovecraft, "The Shadow over Innsmouth" (1931)

I knew too well what they must be—for was not the memory of that evil tiara at Newburyport still fresh? They were the blasphemous fish-frogs of the nameless design—living and horrible—and as I saw them I knew also of what that humped, tiaraed priest in the black church basement had so fearsomely reminded me.

H. P. Lovecraft, "The Shadow over Innsmouth" (1931)

One or two of the cases had an added ring of faint, blasphemous familiarity, as if I had heard of them before through some cosmic channel too morbid and frightful to contemplate.

> H. P. Lovecraft, "The Shadow out of Time" (1935)

I recall glimpsing the archway to the room of machines and almost crying out as I saw the incline leading down to where one of those blasphemous trap-doors must be yawning two levels below.

> H. P. Lovecraft, "The Shadow out of Time" (1935)

Nearly paralysed with fright, I glanced at the huge rusty lock, and at the alien, cryptic hieroglyphs graven upon it. They were signs I could not recognise, and something in their vaguely Mongoloid technique hinted at a blasphemous and indescribable antiquity. At times I fancied I could see them glowing with a greenish light.

> H. P. Lovecraft & William Lumley, "The Diary of Alonzo Typer" (1935)

It was as if I had quaffed deep draughts of some exotic elixir—some abominable concoction brewed from blasphemous formulæ in the archives of Belial.

> C. M. Eddy, Jr. & H. P. Lovecraft, "The Loved Dead" (1923)

One of Lovecraft's worst faults is his incessant effort to work up the expectations of the reader by sprinkling his stories with such adjectives as "horrible," "terrible," "frightful," "awesome," "eerie," "weird," "forbidden," "unhallowed," "unholy," "blasphemous," "hellish" and "infernal." Surely one of the primary rules for writing an effective tale of horror is never to use any of these words—especially if you are going, at the end, to produce an invisible whistling octopus.

> Edmund Wilson, "Tales of the Marvellous and the Ridiculous" (1945)

On each of the five walls there hung one of the parchment paintings, all of which seemed to be the work of some aboriginal race. Their themes were blasphemous and repellent; and Zhothaqquah figured in all of them, amid forms and landscapes whose abnormality and sheer uncouthness may have been due to the half-developed technique of the primitive artists.

> Clark Ashton Smith, "The Door to Saturn" (1930)

The thing was like some blasphemous dream of a mad devil.

> Clark Ashton Smith, "The Tomb-Spawn" (1933)

"Choose now! Rise up against that ancient devil and his blasphemous gods, receive your rightful queen and deity again and you shall regain some of your former greatness. Refuse, and the ancient prophecy shall be fulfilled and the sun will set on the silent and crumbled ruins of Bal-Sagoth!"

> Robert E. Howard, "The Gods of Bal-Sagoth" (1931)

The slavering jaws closed on the arm Conan flung up to guard his throat, but the monster made no effort to secure a death-grip. Over his mangled arm it glared fiendishly into the king's eyes, in which there began to be mirrored a likeness of the horror which stared from the eyes of Ascalante. Conan felt his soul shrivel and begin to be drawn out of his body, to drown in the yellow wells of cosmic horror which glimmered spectrally in the formless chaos that was growing about him and engulfing all life and sanity. Those eyes grew and became gigantic, and in them the Cimmerian glimpsed the reality of all the abysmal and blasphemous horrors that lurk in the outer darkness of formless voids and nighted gulfs.

Robert E. Howard, "The Phœnix on the Sword" (1932)

And we fell to, tearing like hungry beasts at the succulent white meat in the jeweled trenchers. Strange monsters served us, and at a chill touch on my arm I turned to find a dreadful crimson thing, like a skinned child, refilling my goblet. Strange, strange and utterly blasphemous was our feast.

Henry Kuttner, "The Secret of Kralitz" (1936)

Still the iron disk lifted; still the withered horror stood with its skeleton arms raised in blasphemous benediction; still the blackness oozed out in slow amœboid movement.

Henry Kuttner, "The Salem Horror" (1937)

Good God! What was this thing—this nightmare spawn of ancient horror that came leaping at Hartley out of the night? What blasphemous creature had been buried beneath the Witch Stone—and what dark forces had Hartley unknowingly unleashed?

Henry Kuttner, "The Frog" (1939)

Their faces were hideous staring masks, fish-like in contour, with parrot-like beaks and great staring eyes covered with a filmy glaze. Their bodies were amorphous things, half solid and half gelatinous ooze, like the iridescent slime of jellyfish; writhing tentacles sprouted irregularly from the ghastly bodies of the things. They were the offspring of no sane universe, and they came in a blasphemous hissing rush across the room.

Henry Kuttner, "Spawn of Dagon" (1938)

In his great library were such names as Sinistrari, Zancherius, and the ill-famed Gougenot des Mousseau; in his library safe he had, it was rumored, an immense scrapbook filled with excerpts copied from such fantastic sources as the *Book of Karnak*, the monstrous *Sixtystone*, and the blasphemous *Elder Key*, of which only two copies are reputed to exist on Earth.

Henry Kuttner, "Hydra" (1939)

The Franciscans were praying. But what availed their prayers while in the tower the bells were sending out their blasphemous summons?

Henry Kuttner, "Bells of Horror" (1939)

Black loathsome foulness seemed to wash his brain, indescribable but fearfully real, making him shudder with nausea. It was as though unutterable evil were pouring into his body, his mind, his very soul, through the blasphemous kiss on his lips. He felt loathsome, contaminated.

Robert Bloch & Henry Kuttner, "The Black Kiss" (1937)

At that moment Dean would gladly have welcomed death, for the stark, blasphemous horror of his discovery was too much to bear.

Robert Bloch & Henry Kuttner, "The Black Kiss" (1937)

One of his influential friends in the Home Office, hearing of his interest, managed to obtain for him a portion of Ludvig Prinn's evil and blasphemous *De Vermis Mysteriis*, known more familiarly to students of recondite arcana as *Mysteries of the Worm*.

Robert Bloch, "Fane of the Black Pharaoh" (1937)

Captain Carteret did not greatly wish to believe in such utterly blasphemous abominations as Nyarlathotep.

Robert Bloch, "Fane of the Black Pharaoh" (1937)

I could scarcely wait for the ensuing week to pass, realizing that Baldwyn was alone in that upstairs room, browsing in a blasphemous book from the past and composing weird music on his devil's machine.

Duane W. Rimel, "Music of the Stars" (1943)

blasphemously, *adv.* In a blasphemous (q.v.) manner; in a manner that transcends and transgresses against the normal bounds and categories of reality.

As before, the sides of the road shewed a bruising indicative of the blasphemously stupendous bulk of the horror; whilst the conformation of the tracks seemed to argue a passage in two directions, as if the moving mountain had come from Cold Spring Glen and returned to it along the same path.

H. P. Lovecraft, "The Dunwich Horror" (1928)

No chance had been left me for merciful mistake. Here, indeed, in objective form before my own eyes, and surely made not many hours ago, were at least three marks which stood out blasphemously among the surprising plethora of blurred footprints leading to and from the Akeley farmhouse. *They were the hellish tracks of the living fungi from Yuggoth.*

H. P. Lovecraft, "The Whisperer in Darkness" (1930)

It is absolutely necessary, for the peace and safety of mankind, that some of earth's dark, dead corners and unplumbed depths be let alone; lest sleeping abnormalities wake to resurgent life, and blasphemously surviving nightmares squirm and splash out of their black lairs to newer and wider conquests.

H. P. Lovecraft, *At the Mountains of Madness* (1931)

"Fright became pure awe, and what had seemed blasphemously abnormal seemed now only ineffably majestic."

H. P. Lovecraft & E. Hoffmann Price,
"Through the Gates of the Silver Key" (1932–33)

Truly, there are terrible arcana of earth which had better be left unknown and unevoked; dread secrets which have nothing to do with man, and which man may learn only in exchange for peace and sanity; cryptic truths which make the knower evermore an alien among his kind, and cause him to walk alone on earth. Likewise are there dread survivals of things older and more potent than man; things that have blasphemously straggled down through the æons to ages never meant for them; monstrous entities that have lain sleeping endlessly in incredible crypts and remote caverns, outside the laws of reason and causation, and ready to be waked by such blasphemers as shall know their dark forbidden signs and furtive passwords.

H. P. Lovecraft & William Lumley, "The Diary of Alonzo Typer" (1935)

He glared fearsomely at the out gloom, and thought of all the grisly tales he had heard of Tsotha's necromantic cruelty, and it was with an icy sensation down his spine that he realized that these must be the very Halls of Horror named in shuddering legendry, the tunnels and dungeons wherein Tsotha performed horrible experiments with beings human, bestial, and, it was whispered, demoniac, tampering blasphemously with the naked basic elements of life itself. Rumor said that the mad poet Rinaldo had visited these pits, and been shown horrors by the wizard, and that the nameless monstrosities of which he hinted in his awful poem, *The Song of the Pit*, were no mere fantasies of a disordered brain.

Robert E. Howard, "The Scarlet Citadel" (1933)

blasphemousness, *n.* The state or property of being blasphemous (q.v.).

There was a vast room—a chamber of Cyclopean masonry—and I seemed to be viewing it from one of its corners. On the walls were carvings so hideous that even in this imperfect image their stark blasphemousness and bestiality sickened me.

H. P. Lovecraft & Hazel Heald, "Out of the Æons" (1933)

blasphemy, *n.* Profane and impious language or speech; the action or event of transcending and transgressing against the normal bounds and categories of reality; an object or entity which, by its mere existence, transcends and transgresses against the normal bounds and categories of reality.

Titles: Robert M. Price, "Lovecraft's Concept of Blasphemy"

"It is not true," Jurgen protested. "What you have shown me is a pack of nonsense. It is the degraded lunacy of a so-called Realist. It is sorcery and pure childishness and abominable blasphemy. It is, in a word, something I do not choose to believe. You ought to be ashamed of yourself!"

James Branch Cabell, *Jurgen: A Comedy of Justice* (1919)

He seemed like a walking blasphemy, a blend of the angel and the ape.

G. K. Chesterton, *The Man Who Was Thursday: A Nightmare* (1907)

Moreover, so far as æsthetic theory was involved, if the psychic emanations of human creatures be grotesque distortions, what coherent representation could express or portray so gibbous and infamous a nebulosity as the spectre of a malign, chaotic perversion, itself a morbid blasphemy against Nature?

H. P. Lovecraft, "The Unnamable" (1923)

Age-old horror is a hydra with a thousand heads, and the cults of darkness are rooted in blasphemies deeper than the well of Democritus.

H. P. Lovecraft, "The Horror at Red Hook" (1925)

It was a colossal and nameless blasphemy with glaring red eyes, and it held in bony claws a thing that had been a man, gnawing at the head as a child nibbles at a stick of candy.

H. P. Lovecraft, "Pickman's Model" (1926)

And the day wore on, and still Olney listened to rumours of old times and far places, and heard how the Kings of Atlantis fought with the slippery blasphemies that wriggled out of rifts in ocean's floor, and how the pillared and weedy temple of Poseidonis is still glimpsed at midnight by lost ships, who know by its sight that they are lost.

H. P. Lovecraft, "The Strange High House in the Mist" (1926)

No one will ever know what was abroad that night; and though the blasphemy from beyond had not so far hurt any human of unweakened mind, there is no telling what it might not have done at that last moment, and with its seemingly increased strength and the special signs of purpose it was soon to display beneath the half-clouded moonlit sky.

H. P. Lovecraft, "The Colour Out of Space" (1927)

At the foot of the hill, and along the narrow mounting lanes of its side, the old town dreamed; Old Providence, for whose safety and sanity so monstrous and colossal a blasphemy was about to be wiped out.

H. P. Lovecraft, *The Case of Charles Dexter Ward* (1927)

Johansen, thank God, did not know quite all, even though he saw the city and the Thing, but I shall never sleep calmly again when I think of the horrors that lurk ceaselessly behind life in time and in space, and of those unhallowed blasphemies from elder stars which dream beneath the sea, known and favoured by a nightmare cult ready and eager to loose them on the world whenever another earthquake shall heave their monstrous stone city again to the sun and air.

H. P. Lovecraft, "The Call of Cthulhu" (1926)

Night would soon fall, and it was then that the mountainous blasphemy lumbered upon its eldritch course. *Negotium perambulans in tenebris.* . . .

> H. P. Lovecraft, "The Dunwich Horror" (1928; ellipsis in original)

There seemed to be an awful, immemorial linkage in several definite stages betwixt man and nameless infinity. The blasphemies which appeared on earth, it was hinted, came from the dark planet Yuggoth, at the rim of the solar system; but this was itself merely the populous outpost of a frightful interstellar race whose ultimate source must lie far outside even the Einsteinian space-time continuum or greatest known cosmos.

> H. P. Lovecraft, "The Whisperer in Darkness" (1930)

"A minute before I was locked in the library, and then I was there where she had gone with my body—in the place of utter blasphemy, the unholy pit where the black realm begins and the watcher guards the gate. . . . I saw a shoggoths—it changed shape. . . . I can't stand it. . . . I won't stand it. . . . I'll kill her if she ever sends me there again. . . . I'll kill that entity . . . her, him, it . . . I'll kill it! I'll kill it with my own hands!"

> H. P. Lovecraft, "The Thing on the Doorstep" (1933; ellipses in original)

The actual sights and vague impressions were bad enough, but what was hinted or asserted by some of the other dreamers savoured of madness and blasphemy.

> H. P. Lovecraft, "The Shadow out of Time" (1935)

They had borne enough, God knows, without the countryside guessing what a dæmon of the pit—what a gorgon of the elder blasphemies—had come to flaunt their ancient and stainless name.

> H. P. Lovecraft & Zealia Bishop, "Medusa's Coil" (1930)

Wild tales and suggestions of rites and sacrifices to nameless elder gods continued, and now and then Rogers would lead his guest to one of the hideous blasphemies in the screened-off alcove and point out features difficult to reconcile with even the finest human craftsmanship.

> H. P. Lovecraft & Hazel Heald, "The Horror in the Museum" (1932)

Only a stout sanity could resist the insidious suggestion that the blasphemy was—or had once been—some morbid and exotic form of actual life.

> H. P. Lovecraft & Hazel Heald, "The Horror in the Museum" (1932)

To be brief—the hapless invader, who less than an hour before had been a sturdy living Melanesian bent on unknown evils, was now a rigid, ash-grey figure of stony, leathery petrification, in every respect identical with the crouching, æon-old blasphemy in the violated glass case.

> H. P. Lovecraft & Hazel Heald, "Out of the Æons" (1933)

By what hellish arts had Tsotha brought this unnatural being into life? Conan felt vaguely that he had looked on blasphemy against the eternal laws of nature.

Robert E. Howard, "The Scarlet Citadel"

The shriveled and corroded patches that he had seen sloughed off from that being of insane blasphemy had unaccountably disappeared, although they had left black stains upon the stones.

Henry Kuttner, "The Salem Horror" (1937)

From the gaping mouth of the thing came a ghastly outpouring of croaking shrieks, a monstrous bellowing that suddenly grew horribly familiar, articulate, thick and guttural: a frenzied outcry of blasphemy such as might come from the rotting tongue of a long-dead corpse.

Henry Kuttner, "The Frog" (1939)

It was he who initiated me into the mysteries and arcana to be found amid the shuddery speculations of such blasphemies as the *Necronomicon*, the *Book of Eibon*, the *Cabala of Saboth*, and that pinnacle of literary madness, Ludvig Prinn's *Mysteries of the Worm*. There were grim treatises on anthropomancy, necrology, lycanthropical and vampiristic spells and charms, witchcraft, and long, rambling screeds in Arabic, Sanskrit and prehistoric ideography, on which lay the dust of centuries.

Robert Bloch, "The Secret in the Tomb" (1934)

He quoted guardedly from the legendary *Necronomicon*, and spoke timidly of a certain *Book of Eibon* that was reputed to surpass it in the utter wildness of its blasphemy.

Robert Bloch, "The Shambler from the Stars" (1935)

In a few moments there was a loud cry from the gang of laborers, as a black and sinister head came into view. It was a triple-crowned blasphemy. Great spiky cones adorned the top of the ebony diadem, and beneath them were hidden intricately executed designs.

Robert Bloch, "The Faceless God" (1936)

What does matter is the necessity for immediate investigation of the horror below those moors; that blasphemy that broods beneath.

Robert Bloch, "The Brood of Bubastis" (1937)

The terrible things of their former days together were forgotten by Vanny, and Edmond guarded carefully against the vision of the inexpressible, marshaling his thoughts selected channels lest she sense implications dangerous to her tense little mind. He was not always successful. One afternoon he returned to the library to find her trembling and tearful over a very ancient French translation of the *Necronomicon* of the Arab. She had gathered enough of the meaning of that blasphemy colossal to revive the almost vanished terrors of her old thoughts. Edmond soothed her by ancient and not at all superhuman means, but later she noticed that half a dozen volumes had been removed from the library, probably to his laboratory. One of these, she recalled, was the *Krypticon* of the Greek Silander in which Edmond had once during the old days pointed out to her certain horrors, and another was a nameless little volume in scholastic Latin by one who signed himself Ferus Magnus.

> Stanley Weinbaum, *The New Adam* (193-)

I pored for hours over Young's synopsis of the monstrous and alien myth-cycle—the legends of how Cthulhu came from an indescribable milieu beyond the furthest bounds of this universe—of the polar civilizations and abominably unhuman races from black Yuggoth on the rim—of hideous Leng and its monastery-prisoned high priest who had to cover what should be its face—and of a multitude of blasphemies only rumored to exist, save in certain forgotten places of the world.

> Ramsey Campbell, "The Church in High Street" (1962)

The vicar began to shout about Creatures of the Night and Unholy Practices and Living Blasphemies and Things Like That.

> Roger Zelazny, *A Night in the Lonesome October* (1993)

blasted heath, *n.* A balefully blown upon or stricken tract of open, uncultivated ground.

Titles: Brian Lumley, "The Thing from the Blasted Heath"

> Say from whence
> You owe this strange Intelligence, or why
> Vpon this blasted Heath you stop our way
> With such Prophetique greeting?
>
> William Shakespeare, *The Tragedie of Macbeth* (1606)

> As when Heaven's Fire
> Hath scath'd the Forest Oaks, or Mountain Pines,
> With singed top their stately growth though bare
> Stands on the blasted Heath.
>
> John Milton, *Paradise Lost* (1667)

Half-formed, the words of my song burst forth upon the wind. So hears a tree, on the vale, the voice of spring around. It pours its green leaves to the sun. It shakes its lonely head. The hum of the mountain-bee is near it; the hunter sees it, with joy, from the blasted heath.

> Ossian (trans. James Macpherson), *Temora: An Epic Poem* (1765)

"We rushed on either side of a stream, which roared through a blasted heath. High broken rocks were round, with all their bending trees. Near were two circles of Loda, with the stone of power; where spirits descended, by night, in dark-red streams of fire. There, mixed with the murmur of waters, rose the voice of aged men; they called the forms of night to aid them in their war."

Ossian (trans. James Macpherson), "Sul-malla of Lumon: A Poem" (1765)

Fierce in dread silence on the blasted heath
Fell UPAS sits, the HYDRA-TREE of Death.
Lo! from one root, the envenom'd soil below,
A thousand vegetative serpents grow;
In shining rays the scaly monster spreads
O'er ten square leagues his far-diverging heads;
Or in one trunk entwists his tangled form;
Looks o'er the clouds, and hisses in the storm.
Steep'd in fell poison, as his sharp teeth part,
A thousand tongues in quick vibration dart,
Snatch the proud Eagle towering o'er the heath,
Or pounce the Lion, as he stalks beneath;
Or strew, as marshall'd hosts contend in vain,
With human skeletons the whiten'd plain.

Erasmus Darwin, *The Botanic Garden, Part II: The Loves of the Plants* (1798)

Oh! it breathes awe and rapture o'er the soul
To mark the surge in wild confusion roll,
And when the forest groans, and tempest lours,
To wake Imagination's darkest powers!
How throbs the breast with terror and delight,
Filled with rude scenes of Europe's barbarous night!
When restless war with papal craft combined,
To shut each softening ray from lost mankind;
When nought but Error's fatal light was shown,
And taste and science were alike unknown;
To mark the soul, benumbed its active powers,
Chained at the foot of Superstition's towers;
To view the pale-eyed maid in penance pine,
To watch the votary at the sainted shrine;
And, while o'er blasted heaths the night-storm raves,
To hear the wizard wake the slumb'ring graves;
To view war's glitt'ring front, the trophied field,
The hallowed banner, and the rec-cross shield;
The tourney's knights, the tyrant baron's crimes,
"Pomp, pride, and circumstance," of feudal times!

"Introductory Dialogue" in *Tales of Terror* (1801)

When the rich soil teemed with youth's generous flowers—
I felt thee sunshine—now thy rayless light
Falls like the cold moon on a blasted heath

Mocking its desolation—speak thy vow—
I will not chide thee if the words should kill me—
Charles Maturin, *Bertram; or, The Castle of St. Aldobrand: A Tragedy* (1816)

During the most stormy weather, when the spirits of the air were supposed to be wreaking their fury on the elements—in the depth of night, at what hour the departed were supposed to revisit the earth, and forms obscure and terrific to appear to the unfortunate traveller who should be bewildered on his way,—even at such seasons would Albert venture into the recesses of the woods, enjoy the conflict of nature on the blasted heath, and explore the wildest solitudes around his domain.

"The Water Lady—A Legend" (1822)

At length, deserted as this wild region had always been, it became still more gloomy. Strange rumours arose, that the path of unwary travellers had been beset on this "blasted heath," and that treachery and murder had intercepted the solitary stranger as he traversed its dreary extent.

Catherine Sinclair, "The Murder Hole" (1829)

Roused by its voice the ghastly Wars arise,
Mars reddens earth, the Valkyrs pale the skies;
Dim Superstition from her hell escapes,
With all her shadowy brood of monster shapes;
Here life itself the scowl of Typhon takes;
There Conscience shudders at Alecto's snakes;
From Gothic graves at midnight yawning wide,
In gory cerements gibbering spectres glide;
And where o'er blasted heaths the lightnings flame,
Black secret hags "do deeds without a name!"
Sir Edward Bulwer-Lytton, "The Ideal World" (1849)

But what most puzzled and confounded you was a long, limber, portentous, black mass of something hovering in the centre of the picture over three blue, dim, perpendicular lines floating in a nameless yeast. A boggy, soggy, squitchy picture truly, enough to drive a nervous man distracted. Yet was there a sort of indefinite, half-attained, unimaginable sublimity about it that fairly froze you to it, till you involuntarily took an oath with yourself to find out what that marvellous painting meant. Ever and anon a bright but, alas, deceptive idea would dart you through.—It's the Black Sea in a midnight gale.—It's the unnatural combat of the four primal elements.—It's a blasted heath.—It's a Hyperborean winter scene.—It's the breaking-up of the ice-bound stream of Time. But at last all these fancies yielded to that one portentous something in the picture's midst. *That* once found out, and all the rest were plain. But stop; does it not bear a faint resemblance to a gigantic fish? even the great leviathan himself?

Herman Melville, *Moby-Dick; or, The Whale* (1851)

Two Blighted Beings, haggard, lacrymose and detested, met on a blasted heath in the light of a struggling moon.

Ambrose Bierce, "Two of the Damned" (1890) in *Fantastic Fables*

Man, in Carlyle, is a poor wretch in thin and ragged clothes, out on a blasted heath, with all the heavens and all the clouds crashing and pouring upon him; blackness over him, hailstorms and fire showers his portion in the world.

Arthur Machen, *Far Off Things* (1922)

On and on I raced through the wood, each step a nightmare. I felt hands stretching out to clutch me . . . heard shrill whisperings. . . . Sweating, trembling, I broke out of the wood and raced over a vast plain that stretched, treeless, to the distant horizon. The plain was trackless, pathless, and covered with brown and withered grass. It was like, it came to me, the blasted heath of Macbeth's three witches. No matter . . . it was better than the haunted wood.

A. Merritt, *Burn, Witch, Burn!* (1932; ellipses in original)

The name "blasted heath" seemed to me very odd and theatrical, and I wondered how it had come into the folklore of a Puritan people.

H. P. Lovecraft, "The Colour Out of Space" (1927)

But even all this was not so bad as the blasted heath. I knew it the moment I came upon it at the bottom of a spacious valley; for no other name could fit such a thing, or any other thing fit such a name. It was as if the poet had coined the phrase from having seen this one particular region.

H. P. Lovecraft, "The Colour Out of Space" (1927)

Boreal, boreal, *adj.* [< L *Boreālis* < *Boreas,* the north wind < Gr *Boréas,* coming from the north] Of or pertaining to the north wind; of or pertaining to the far north, northern. **Boreal Pole:** the pole of a magnetic compass pointing toward the south; hence, the South Pole.

> Ev'n yet preserv'd, how often may'st thou hear,
> Where to the pole the Boreal mountains run,
> Taught by the father to his list'ning son
> Strange lays, whose power had charm'd a SPENCER'S ear.

William Collins, "An Ode on the Popular Superstitions of the Highlands of Scotland, Considered as the Subject of Poetry" (1749)

> These were days when my heart was volcanic
> As the scoriac rivers that roll—
> As the lavas that restlessly roll
> Their sulphurous currents down Yaanek,
> In the ultimate climes of the Pole—

That groan as they roll down Mount Yaanek,
In the realms of the Boreal Pole.

Edgar Allan Poe, "Ulalume—A Ballad" (1847)

He paused. He scratched his head. The boreal word of power was Cabinet or Cabochon or Capricorn or something of the kind, he knew: but what it was exactly was exactly what Ninzian had forgotten. He would have to try something else.

James Branch Cabell, *The Silver Stallion: A Comedy of Redemption* (1925)

Still tingled the fingers of the passers-by and still their breath was visible, and still they huddled their chins into their coats when turning a corner they met with a new wind, still windows lighted early sent out into the street the thought of romantic comfort by evening fires; these things still were, yet the throne of Winter tottered, and every breeze brought tidings of further fortresses lost on lakes or boreal hill-slopes.

Lord Dunsany, "Spring in Town" (1915)

In the Orient, the weird tale tended to assume a gorgeous colouring and sprightliness which almost transmuted it into sheer phantasy. In the West, where the mystical Teuton had come down from his black Boreal forests and the Celt remembered strange sacrifices in Druidic groves, it assumed a terrible intensity and convincing seriousness of atmosphere which doubled the force of its half-told, half-hinted horrors.

H. P. Lovecraft, "Supernatural Horror in Literature" (1925–27)

And legends there were, of awful crevasses that yawned abruptly and closed like monstrous mouths upon them that dared the frozen waste; of winds like the breath of boreal demons, that blasted men's flesh with instant, utter cold and turned them into statues hard as granite.

Clark Ashton Smith, "The Ice-Demon" (1932)

brachiate, *adj.* Equipped with arms or arm-like appendages, such as branches.

She lived in a phosphorescent palace of many terraces, with gardens of strange leprous corals and grotesque brachiate efflorescences, and welcomed me with a warmth that may have been sardonic.

H. P. Lovecraft, "The Shadow over Innsmouth" (1931)

brachycephalic, *adj.* Short-headed. Cf. **dolichocephalic.**

Modern Indians are brachycephalic—round-headed—and you can't find any dolichocephalic or long-headed skulls except in ancient Pueblo deposits dating back 2500 years or more; yet this man's long-headedness was so pronounced that I recognised it at once, even at his vast distance and in the uncertain field of the binoculars.

H. P. Lovecraft & Zealia Bishop, "The Mound" (1930)

bucolic, *adj.* [< L *bucolicus* < Gr *boukolikós* < *boukólos,* herdsman] Of or pertaining to shepherds or herdsmen, pastoral; of or pertaining to country life, rural, rustic.

There is nothing more absurd, as I view it, than that conventional association of the homely and the wholesome which seems to pervade the psychology of the multitude. Mention a bucolic Yankee setting, a bungling and thick-fibred village undertaker, and a careless mishap in a tomb, and no average reader can be brought to expect more than a hearty albeit grotesque phase of comedy.

H. P. Lovecraft, "In the Vault" (1925)

bug, *n.* [< OE < Welsh *bwg* or *bwgan,* a hobgoblin, bogey, bugbear] A hobgoblin, bugbear, bugaboo, bogey; an object of terror.

Eccentric translations, rather than printing errors, make armfuls of other Bibles worthy of note. There are, for example, two "Bug Bibles." Miles Coverdale's Bible of 1535 has earned that creepy sobriquet; and so has the Bible printed in Antwerp two years later as the translation of a certain Thomas Matthews, which was probably a pen name for one John Rogers. In both editions, a passage in Psalm 91 is presented as "Thou shalt not nede to be afrayed for eny bugges by night." In most other English-language Bibles, it's *terror by night.*

Ray Russell, "The 'Wicked' Bibles; or,
Let Him Who Is without Sin among You Cast the First Line of Type"

This is but a little, yet it makes thee seem a great bug.

Richard Edwards, *The Excellent Comedie of Two the Most
Faithfullest Freendes, Damon and Pythias* (1571)

It is observable that, in the fifth verse of the Ninety-first Psalm, "the terror by night," is rendered, in the old English version, "the bugge by night." In the first settled parts of North America, every nocturnal fly of a noxious quality is still generically named a bug; whence the term bugbear signifies one that carries terror wherever he goes. Beelzebub, or the Lord of Flies, was an Eastern appellative given to the Devil; and the nocturnal sound called by the Arabians *azif* was believed to be the howling of demons. Analogous to this is a passage in [John Milton's] *Comus* as it stood in the original copy:—

> But for that damn'd magician, let him be girt
> With all the grisly legions that troop
> Under the sooty flag of Acheron,
> Harpies and Hydras, or all the monstrous buggs
> 'Twixt Africa and Inde, I'll find him out.

Samuel Henley, note to William Beckford, *The History of the Caliph Vathek:
An Arabian Tale* (1786)

> Till that they come vnto a forrest greene,
>   In which they shroud themselues from causelesse feare;
>   Yet feare them followes still, where so they beene,

Each trembling leafe, and whistling wind they heare,
As ghastly bug their haire on end does reare:
Yet both doe striue their fearfulnesse to faine.

Edmund Spenser, *The Faërie Queene* (159-)

All these, and thousand thousands many more,
 And more deformed Monsters thousand fold,
 With dreadfull noise, and hollow rombling rore,
 Came rushing in the fomy waues enrold,
 Which seem'd to fly for feare, them to behold:
 Ne wonder, if these did the knight appall;
 For all that here on earth we dreadfull hold,
 Be but as bugs to fearen babes withall,
Compared to the creatures in the seas entrall.

Edmund Spenser, *The Faërie Queene* (159-)

How now, ye petty kings? Lo, here are bugs
Will make the hair stand upright on your heads,
And cast your crowns in slavery at their feet.

Christopher Marlowe, *Tamburlaine the Great* (1590)

Vp from my Cabin
My sea-gowne scarft about me in the darke,
Grop'd I to finde out them; had my desire,
Finger'd their Packet, and in fine, withdrew
To mine owne roome againe, making so bold,
(My feares forgetting manners) to vnseale
Their grand Commission, where I found *Horatio,*
Oh royall knauery: An exact command,
Larded with many seuerall sorts of reason;
Importing Denmarks health, and Englands too,
With hoo, such Bugges and Goblins in my life,
That on the superuize no leasure bated,
No not to stay the grinding of the Axe,
My head shoud be struck off.

William Shakespeare, *The Tragedy of Hamlet, Prince of Denmark* (1602)

"Yea," quoth Ralph laughing, "even as the tales of the ghosts and bugs that abide the wayfarer on the other side of yonder white moveless cloud."

William Morris, *The Well at the World's End* (1893)

Most children have a touch of poetry and believe in what I hate to call psychic phenomena, at least to the extent of fancying they see fairies or being scared of "bugges by night".

Aleister Crowley, *The Confessions of Aleister Crowley: An Autohagiography* (1923)

buopoth, *n.* A fantastic creature that inhabitants the Dreamlands of H. P. Lovecraft. [Not in *OED.*]

> In former dreams he had seen quaint lumbering buopoths come shyly out of that wood to drink, but now he could not see any.
>
> > H. P. Lovecraft, *The Dream-Quest of Unknown Kadath* (1927)

burden, burthen, *n.* An oft-recurring idea or theme; the central meaning or message of a song or literary composition.

> It is quite a common thing to be thus annoyed with the ringing in our ears, or rather in our memories, of the burthen of some ordinary song, or some unimpressive snatches from an opera.
>
> > Edgar Allan Poe, "The Imp of the Perverse" (1845)

> This bore regular fruit, for after the first interview the manuscript records daily calls of the young man, during which he related startling fragments of nocturnal imagery whose burden was always some terrible Cyclopean vista of dark and dripping stone, with a subterrene voice or intelligence shouting monotonously in enigmatical sense-impacts uninscribable save as gibberish.
>
> > H. P. Lovecraft, "The Call of Cthulhu" (1926)

burgess, *n.* An inhabitant of a borough, a townsman.

> In Ulthar, before ever the burgesses forbade the killing of cats, there dwelt an old cotter and his wife who delighted to trap and slay the cats of their neighbours.
>
> > H. P. Lovecraft, "The Cats of Ulthar" (1920)

burgomaster, *n.* The chief magistrate of a Flemish or Dutch town, roughly corresponding to an English mayor.

> Old Kranon, the burgomaster, swore that the dark folk had taken the cats away in revenge for the killing of Menes' kitten; and cursed the caravan and the little boy.
>
> > H. P. Lovecraft, "The Cats of Ulthar" (1920)

C

Cabalism, cabalism, cabbalism, *n.* The study and practice of the Qabalah.

Titles: William Child Green, "Secrets of Cabalism; or, Ravenstone and Alice of Huntingdon"

> Masters, for that learned Burden's skill is deep,
> And sore he doubts of Bacon's cabalism,
> I'll show you why he haunts to Henley oft:
> Not, doctors, for to taste the fragrant air,
> But there to spend the night in alchemy,
> To multiply with secret spells of art;
> Thus private steals he learning from us all.
>
> Robert Greene, *The Honorable History of Friar Bacon and Friar Bungay* (1594)

Cabbalism itself, so prominent during the Middle Ages, is a system of philosophy explaining the universe as emanations of the Deity, and involving the existence of strange spiritual realms and beings apart from the visible world, of which dark glimpses may be obtained through certain secret incantations. Its ritual is bound up with mystical interpretations of the Old Testament, and attributes an esoteric significance to each letter of the Hebrew alphabet—a circumstance which has imparted to Hebrew letters a sort of spectral glamour and potency in the popular literature of magic.

> H. P. Lovecraft, "Supernatural Horror in Literature" (1925–27)

cabalist, *n.* A student of the Qabalah.

For, first of all, as eminent a cabalist as his disciples would represent him [*sc.,* Homer], his account of the *opus magnum* is extremely poor and deficient; he seems to have read but very superficially either Sendivogius, Behmen, or *Anthroposophia Theomagica.* He is also quite mistaken about the *sphæra pyroplastica,* a neglect not to be atoned for; and (if the reader will admit so severe a censure), *vix crederem autorem hunc, unquam audivisse ignis vocem.*

> Jonathan Swift, *A Tale of a Tub, Written for the Universal Improvement of Mankind* (1697)

cabalistic, cabbalistic, kabbalistic, qabalistic, *adj.* Of or pertaining to the Qabalah (q.v.); conveying or containing an occult or secret meaning; of use in magick, sorcery, or wizardry.

115

These charms consisted of oblong slips of vellum, with cabalistic ciphers and diagrams upon them.

J. S. Le Fanu, "Carmilla" (1871–72)

"As I was destined to find, there lay a deeper more cabalistic meaning in the motto than any I had been able to dream of."

M. P. Shiel, "The S.S." (1895)

Having heard old Mombi pronounce the magic words, and having also suc-ceeded in bringing the Saw-Horse to life, Tip did not hesitate an instant in speaking the three cabalistic words, each accompanied by the peculiar gesture of the hands.

L. Frank Baum, *The Marvelous Land of Oz* (1904)

So that was it. The ring and the maiden. What was the bond? There was weird-ness in its colour, almost cabalistic—a call out of the occult.

Austin Hall & Homer Eon Flint, *The Blind Spot* (1921)

Hopelessly at bay, weaponless, and knowing that any show of physical violence would bring a score of attendants to the doctor's rescue, Joseph Curwen had re-course to his one ancient ally, and began a series of cabbalistic motions with his forefingers as his deep, hollow voice, now unconcealed by feigned hoarseness, bellowed out the opening words of a terrible formula.

H. P. Lovecraft, *The Case of Charles Dexter Ward* (1927)

He appealed to the curio-dealer, a dwarfish Hebrew with an air of dusty antiq-uity, who gave the impression of being lost to commercial considerations in some web of cabalistic revery.

"Can you tell me anything about this?"

Clark Ashton Smith, "Ubbo-Sathla" (1932)

For at the base of the wall, behind the baseboard, there lay, among long yel-lowed papers half gnawed away by mice, yet still bearing on their surfaces the unmistakably cabalistic designs of some bygone day, among wicked implements of death and destruction—short, dagger-like knives rusted by what must surely have been blood—*the small skulls and bones of at least three children!*

August Derleth (as H. P. Lovecraft & August Derleth),
"The Peabody Heritage" (1957)

I searched amid the satanic spells and cabalistic incantations of a thousand for-gotten necromancers, delved into pages of impassioned prophecy, burrowed into secret legendary lore whose written thoughts writhed through me like ser-pents from the pit. It was in vain.

Robert Bloch, "The Secret in the Tomb" (1934)

Wizards nowadays are not garbed in cabalistic robes of silver and black; instead they wear purple dressing-gowns.

Robert Bloch, "The Suicide in the Study" (1935)

Death writhed his thin, smiling lips and moved his bony fingertips in tiny, cabalistic curves, as he worked a small but difficult magic.

Fritz Leiber, "Trapped in the Shadowland" (1973)

Fair could not restrain himself, and by degrees returned to a study of green magic. Rather than again invoke the sprite whose air of indulgent contempt he found exasperating, he decided to seek knowledge by an indirect method, employing the most advanced concepts of technical and cabalistic science.

Jack Vance, "Green Magic" (1963)

And of the eldritch sign which was clumsily engraved in each wall of the concrete riverside building, Brichester folk do not like to think. If one asks the professors at the University, they will answer vaguely that it is an extremely ancient cabalistic symbol, but one is never told exactly what the symbol is supposed to invoke, or against what it may be intended as a protection.

Ramsey Campbell, "The Horror from the Bridge" (1964)

One day, the Meridian having been closely enough establish'd, and with an hour or two of free time available to them, one heads north, one south, and 'tis Dixon's luck to discover The Rabbi of Prague, headquarters of a Kabbalistick Faith, in Correspondence with the Elect Cohens of Paris, whose private Salute they now greet Dixon with, the Fingers spread two and two, and the Thumb held away from them likewise, said to represent the Hebrew letter *Shin* and to signify, "Live long and prosper."

Thomas Pynchon, *Mason & Dixon* (1997)

cabalistical, *adj.* Cabalistic (q.v.).

"I've called them to Earth," he muttered dully, his shoulders drooping. "The *Mysteries of the Worm* gave a list of precautions to be taken before using the drug—the Pnakotic pentagon, the cabalistical signs of protection—things you wouldn't understand. The book gave terrible warnings of what might happen if those precautions weren't taken—specifically mentioned those things—'the dwellers in the Hidden World', it called them."

Henry Kuttner, "The Invaders" (1939)

cabalistically, *adv.* In a cabalistic manner; in a manner according with the Qabalah.

The sword hung above an ancient cloak in which it had been wrapped when the furtive Arab had slipped into his tent. Unknown centuries had softened the azure of that cloak, through whose web and woof great silver serpents writhed, cabalistically entwined.

A. Merritt, *The Ship of Ishtar* (1924)

cabalistics, *n.* The study of the Qabalah. [Not in *OED*.]

There were Lully's *Ars Magna et Ultima,* Fludd's *Clavis Alchimiæ,* the *Liber Ivonis,* Albertus Magnus, Artephous' [*sic*] *Key of Wisdom,* the Comte d'Erlette's *Culte des Goules,* Ludvig Prinn's *De Vermis Mysteriis,* and many other tomes hoary with age, having to do with philosophy, thaumaturgy, demonology, cabalistics, mathematics, and the like, among them several sets of Paracelsus and Hermes Trismogistus [*sic*], which bore the marks of much usage.

August Derleth (as H. P. Lovecraft & August Derleth),
The Lurker at the Threshold (1945)

cachinnate, *v.intr.* To laugh harshly and immoderately.

Then the brown man stamped his foot, and the striking of his foot upon the moss made a new noise such as Jurgen had never heard: for the noise seemed to come multitudinously from every side, at first as though each leaf in the forest were tinily cachinnating; and then this noise was swelled by the mirth of larger creatures, and echoes played with this noise, until there was a reverberation everywhere like that of thunder.

James Branch Cabell, *Jurgen: A Comedy of Justice* (1919)

Two claws, cold as flames of icy hell, fastened around my throat, two eyes bored like maggots through my frenzied being, a laughter born of madness alone cachinnated in my ears like the thunder of doom.

Robert Bloch, "The Secret in the Tomb" (1934)

cachinnation, *n.* Harsh and immoderate laughter.

I began to laugh, Larry joined me, and then Kra and Gulk joined in our merriment with deep batrachian cachinnations and gruntings.

A. Merritt, *The Moon Pool* (1919)

Miriam beckoned me on, with an eerie ripple of cachinnation.

Leonard Cline, *The Dark Chamber* (1927)

He laughed abruptly, with a mirthless, jarring note that was like the cachinnation of a sorcerer.

Clark Ashton Smith, "The Hunters from Beyond" (1931)

Cacodæmon, Cacodemon, Cacodaimon, Kakodæmon, Kakodaimon, *n.* [< Gr *kakodaímôn* < *kakós,* evil, bad + *daimôn*] An evil spirit; a devil or demon. In neo-Platonism and Gnosticism, the Cacodæmon is the evil genius (or evil angel, etc.). In both senses, opposed to the *Agathodæmon* or *Eudæmon,* a good spirit or good genius (or guardian angel, etc). In astrology, the twelfth house, considered to have a baleful significance. The word is also an archaic medical term for nightmare, perhaps following Nashe; a fair number of uses retain this association.

Questionless, this is an unrefutable consequence, that the man who is mocked of his fortune, he that hath consumed his brains to compass prosperity and meets with no countervailment in her likeness, but hedge wine and lean mutton and peradventure some half-eyed good looks that can hardly be discerned from winking; this poor piteous perplexed miscreant either finally despairs, or like a lank frostbitten plant loseth his vigour or spirit by little and little; any terror, the least illusion in the earth, is a Cacodæmon unto him. His soul hath left his body; for why, it is flying after these airy incorporate courtly promises, and glittering painted allurements, which when they vanish to nothing, it likewise vanisheth with them.

Thomas Nashe, "The Terrors of the Night; or, A Discourse of Apparitions" (1593)

Hie thee to hell for shame and leaue the world
Thou Cacodemon, there thy kingdome is.

William Shakespeare, *The Tragedy of King Richard III*

To this, quoth Sidrophello, Sir,
Agrippa was no conjurer,
Nor Paracelsus, no, nor Behmen;
Nor was the dog a caco-dæmon,
But a true dog, that would shew tricks
For th' emp'ror, and leap o'er sticks;
Would fetch and carry, was more civil
Than other dogs, but yet no devil;
And whatsoe'er he's said to do,
He went the self-same way we go.

Samuel Butler, *Hudibras* (1663–78)

Ai! but now the monster splits me
Struggling in his bloody cage.
Is it in his sport or rage?
Answer that, thou doting sage!
For his cacodæmon shape
Twisting round no longer fits me.
This is like some hellish rape
Of one's soul the grisly ape!

Aleister Crowley, *The World's Tragedy* (1908)

Crimson burn'd the star of sadness
    As behind the beams I peer'd;
All was woe that seem'd but gladness
    Ere my gaze with truth was sear'd;
Cacodæmons, mir'd with madness,
    Thro' the fever'd flick'ring leer'd.

H. P. Lovecraft, "Astrophobos" (1917)

I went on blindly in the direction the car was headed for; nothing was in my mind but to get away from that frightful region of nightmares and cacodæmons—to get away as quickly and as far as gasoline could take me.

H. P. Lovecraft & Zealia Bishop, "Medusa's Coil" (1930)

The potent nightmarishness of these creations was not calculated to reassure my trembling nerves; and all at once I felt an imperative desire to escape from the studio, to flee from the baleful throng of frozen cacodemons and chiseled chimeras.

Clark Ashton Smith, "The Hunters from Beyond" (1931)

He pushed against it with herculean effort, raging like a trapped lion, but the mass was immovable. For hours, it seemed, he strove as with some monstrous cacodemon.

Clark Ashton Smith, "The Weaver in the Vault" (1933)

Here the queen faltered, for it seemed that black, unseen cacodemons rose all about her from the graveyard ground, towering higher than the shafts and boles, and standing in readiness to assail her if she went farther. Nevertheless, she came anon to the dark adit that she sought.

Clark Ashton Smith, "The Death of Ilalotha" (1937)

I had hoped to write ere this and render my thanks for the foursquare sybilline image (prequickened) that I received around New Year's. It has long since gone the way of such eidola, with additional libations of port or burgundy, and was always partaken of a little before the hour of retiring. I don't remember any kakodæmones as a result of such evocation: but I did have some exceedingly pleasant dreams on those nights.

Clark Ashton Smith, letter to Ray & Margaret St. Clair (20 January 1937)

Once again we viewed the monsters I was trying to forget; the snake-men, the satyr-creatures, the deformed cacodemons we found in the upper tombs. But now we saw them pictured in life, and it was worse than any imagining.

Robert Bloch, "The Brood of Bubastis" (1937)

Sleep if maintained with cacodemons making waking in light and dark if this maintained faint sweet relief and the longing for it again and to be gone again a folly to be resisted again in vain.

Samuel Beckett, "All Strange Away" (1963–64)

There were dancers in the center of the womb, dozens of them, nude and painted luminously into vampires, ghouls, cacodemons, succubi, harpies, ogresses, satyrs, furies. They wore confusing contrasting masks, front and back. They glowed, writhed, entwined, and contorted to the music.

Alfred Bester, Golem[100] (1980)

A great magician was Luthanimor, one versed in the spells and cantraips of his world. But he was fearful, for odd tales had come to his ears of late concerning the deaths of other necromancers, men as great or even greater than he when it came to dooming a man or a maid to the seven hells of Eldrak or summoning up the cacodemons to destroy a warrior or a castle.

Gardner F. Fox, *Kothar and the Wizard Slayer* (1970)

Sooner or later he would meet some snuffling cacodemon in this blackness and be forced to fight for his life.

Gardner F. Fox, "Shadow of a Demon" (1976)

Lok the Depressor lived by himself in a stone cot on the edge of the Great Fokmah Waste. Because demands for his services remained ever constant, no day passed without an accompaniment of visitors. But deep night drew cacodemons, wasted spirits, and ghouls out of the fens, and travelers seldom ventured near.

Philip Coakley, "Lok the Depressor" (1978)

cacodæmoniacal, cacodemoniacal, kakodemoniacal, kakodaimoniacal,
adj. [after *cacodæmon* + *dæmoniacal*] Of, pertaining to, or resembling a Cacodæmon (q.v.). [Not in *OED*.]

Men, also, who at first hand have studied modern recrudescences of devil-worship, modern flirtations with kakodaimoniacal agencies, the Luciferianism of modern France, will not mutter with patronizing superiority of superstitions and old wives' fables; but perfectly well will know that hideous abnormality with which the Pope's Holiness had to deal.

Frederick Baron Corvo, Chonicles of the House of Borgia (1901)

And as the gigantic edifice of the Christian Church was the child of the neuropathic mystagogues of the dark ages of religion, so now the colossal fabric of Scientific Utilitarianism, offspring of a distorted and epileptic steam-mania, has bemerded us with its panting slime, and wound us tight in the arachnoid meshes of its kakodemoniacal web, until we stand before ourselves, no long *homo sapiens*, but alone, naked and unadorned, a cinder-sprinkled, soot-besmeared, spider-legged, *homo ridiculissimus*!

J. F. C. Fuller, *The Star in the West:*
A Critical Essay Upon the Works of Aleister Crowley (1906)

I have said that the fury of the rushing blast was infernal—cacodæmoniacal—and that its voices were hideous with the pent-up viciousness of desolate eternities.

H. P. Lovecraft, "The Nameless City" (1921)

There were nauseous musical instruments, stringed, brass, and wood-wind, on which St. John and I sometimes produced dissonances of exquisite morbidity and cacodæmoniacal ghastliness; whilst in a multitude of inlaid ebony cabinets reposed the most incredible and unimaginable variety of tomb-loot ever assembled by human madness and perversity.

H. P. Lovecraft, "The Hound" (1922)

It is cold. Unseasonably cold! As if inspired by the cacodemoniacal presences that harass me, the breeze that was so friendly a few minutes ago growls angrily about my ears—an icy gale that rushes in from the swamp and chills me to the bone.

C. M. Eddy, Jr. & H. P. Lovecraft, "Deaf, Dumb, and Blind" (1924)

I read some of the pieces aloud to my aunt; & despite her general leaning toward the realists she could not escape the breathless spell of your cacodæmoniacal incantations, but ended up by becoming an admirer!

H. P. Lovecraft, letter to Clark Ashton Smith (25 March 1923)

Up the long slope to the north of that accursed lake, stumbling over boulders of basanite, and ledges that were sharp with verdigris-covered metals; floundering in pits of salt or innominable ashes, on terraces wrought by the receding tide in ancient æons, I fled as a man flees from dream to baleful dream of some cacodemoniacal night.

Clark Ashton Smith, "The Abominations of Yondo" (1925)

Their slumber was disturbed by a series of cacodemoniacal dreams in which they both thought they had been recaptured by the Bhlemphroims and were forced to espouse the Djhenquomh.

Clark Ashton Smith, "The Door to Saturn" (1930)

From a moral standpoint, I had every reason to sleep the sleep of the virtuous; but, even as on the preceding night, I was made the victim of one cacodemoniacal dream after another.

Clark Ashton Smith, "The Testament of Athammaus" (1931)

cacodæmonic, cacodemonic, *adj.* Of, pertaining to, or resembling a Cacodæmon (q.v.).

> Poe! Frankenstein! Shelley thy Prophecy,
> What Demiurge assembles Matter-Factories
>   to blast the Cacodemonic Planet-Mirror apart
> Split atoms & Polarize Consciousness &
>   let the eternal Void leak thru Pentagon
>   & cover White House with Eternal Vacuum-Dust!

Allen Ginsberg, "To Poe: Over the Planet, Air Albany-Baltimore" (1969)

cacography, *n.* Ugly handwriting.

Having abandoned all hope of getting a fountain pen to suit my aging claw and crabbed cacography, I have returned to the pencils of my infancy.

H. P. Lovecraft, letter to Wilfrid Blanch Talman (5 March 1932)

cacophony, *n.* Discordant and jarring noise.

On a balcony, a jazz band was emitting ear-splitting cacophonies, and dancing was in full swing.

> Arthur Machen, *The Green Round* (1932)

Not more unutterable could have been the chaos of hellish sound if the pit itself had opened to release the agony of the damned, for in one inconceivable cacophony was centred all the supernal terror and unnatural despair of animate nature.

> H. P. Lovecraft, "Herbert West—Reanimator" (1922)

Strange mists of unconsciousness began to shred and part. And Brak heard a cacophony of weird, marrow-chilling sounds.

> John Jakes, "The Barge of Souls" (1967) in *Brak the Barbarian*

Cambion (*pl.* **Cambion, Cambiones**), **cambion,** *n.* [< LL] The offspring of an incubus (q.v.) and a human woman. Also, a changeling (q.v.). [Not in *OED*.]

Titles: Clark Ashton Smith, "Cambion" (verse)

This beggar was the proprietor of one those Imps called the Cambion (or Devil's-brat)—the natural child of those two very agreeable demons, the Incubus and the Succubus—a creature of extraordinary weight that always drains its nurses dry and never, by any chance, gets fat.

> "Superstitions and Traditions" in *Household Words:*
> *A Weekly Journal* (ed. Charles Dickens), Vol. XVI (1857)

A short time afterwards, the beggar, who had run away on witnessing this catastrophe was captured, and he acknowledged that the child was a Cambion, and had been very useful to him in his calling, and turned people's minds towards alms-givings. What became of the Cambion is not stated, but I believe the beggar was burnt. These heavy little devils are the same as the German Wechselkinder, the changelings of the old English ballad.

> "Superstitions and Traditions" in *Household Words:*
> *A Weekly Journal* (ed. Charles Dickens), Vol. XVI (1857)

In general he was regarded as a *Marcou:* some went so far as to believe him to be *Cambion.* A cambion is the child of a woman begotten by a devil.

> Victor Hugo (trans. ?), *The Toilers of the Sea: A Novel* (1866)

Those who obstinately regarded him as a cambion, or son of the devil, were evidently in error. They ought to have known that cambions scarce exist outside of Germany.

> Victor Hugo (trans. ?), *The Toilers of the Sea: A Novel* (1866)

> Some believe he is
> A cambion, devil-sired though woman-whelped.
>> Clark Ashton Smith, *The Dead Will Cuckold You* (1951)

Iuz had many concubines—human, semi-human, and demon-spawn as well. Who could say which he enjoyed most—beautiful, or horrifyingly malformed and ugly? Mammalian or reptilian? Iuz was a cambion, after all, the bastard son of a demon mated with a woman.
>> Gary Gygax, *Artifact of Evil* (1986)

As the trembling chamberlain rushed to do Iuz's bidding, the form seated on the massive heap of bones and skulls that formed his throne seemed to flow and change. One minute he was a wrinkled, toothless old man: the next, he was a massive, demoniac monster—a cambion, as those of his ilk were called—with pale reddish skin and pointed fangs lining his jaws.
>> Gary Gygax, *Sea of Death* (1987)

Candlemas, *pr.n.* February 2; one of the four nights of the year on which witches are reputed to celebrate their Sabbat.

Titles: Robert Graves, "An Appointment for Candlemas"

> The final nightmare came before Candlemas—heralded, in cruel irony, by a false gleam of hope.
>> H. P. Lovecraft, "The Thing on the Doorstep" (1933)

> 'Twas Candlemas, the dreariest time of year,
> With fall long gone, and spring too far to cheer,
> When little Jean, the bailiff's son and heir,
> Fell sick and threw the doctors in despair.
>> H. P. Lovecraft, "Psychopompos: A Tale in Rhyme" (1917–18)

cannabis, *n.* [< Gr *kánnabis*, hemp < Scythian or Thracian] The hemp or marijuana plant, known in the varieties *Cannabis sativa* and *Cannabis indica.* Cf. *bhang*, **cannabine, dacha, ganja, hashish, hemp, majoon, marihuana**.

> From Time's remotest dawn where China brings
> In proud succession all her Patriot-Kings;
> O'er desert-sands, deep gulfs, and hills sublime,
> Extends her massy walls from clime to clime;
> With bells and dragons crests her Pagod-bowers,
> Her silken palaces, and porcelain towers;
> With long canals a thousand nations laves;
> Plants all her wilds, and people's her waves;
> Slow treads fair CANNABIS the breezy strand,
> The distaff streams dishevell'd in her hand;
> Now to the left her ivory neck inclines,

And leads in Paphian curves its azure lines;
Dark waves the fringed lid, the warm cheek glows,
And the fair ear the parting locks disclose;
Now to the right with airy sweep she bends,
Quick join the threads, the dancing spole depends.

Erasmus Darwin, *The Botanic Garden, Part II: The Loves of the Plants* (1798)

"Cannabis sativa produces an intoxicant that in Turkey is known as hadschy, in Arabia and India as hashish, and to the Hottentots as dacha, and serves as a drunkard's food in other lands."

John Uri Lloyd, *Etidorhpa; or, The End of Earth: The Strange History of a Mysterious Being and the Account of a Remarkable Journey* (1894)

"This *Cannabis indica*," the author went on, "came into my possession last autumn while my wife was away. I need not explain how I got it, for that has no importance; but it was the genuine fluid extract, and I could not resist the temptation to make an experiment. One of its effects, as you know, is to induce torrential laughter—"

Algernon Blackwood, "A Psychical Invasion" (1908)

As one entranced by dint of cannabis,
  Whose sense of time is changed past recognition,
  Whether he suffer woe or taste of bliss,
  He loses both his reason and volition.

Aleister Crowley, *Clouds Without Water* (1909)

Cannabis.—Indian hemp, a drug producing maniacal intoxication.

Rev. C. Verey (Aleister Crowley), note to *Clouds Without Water* (1909)

"*Cannabis indica*," I said—"Indian hemp. That is what you were drugged with. I have no doubt that now you experience a feeling of nausea and intense thirst, with aching muscles, particularly the deltoid? I think you must have taken at least fifteen grains."

Sax Rohmer (Arthur Sarsfield Ward),
The Mystery of Dr. Fu-Manchu (1913; aka *The Insidious Dr. Fu-Manchu*)

All this dreaming comes without the stimulus of *cannabis indica*. Should I take that drug, who can say what worlds of unreality I might explore?

H. P. Lovecraft, letter to Reinhardt Kleiner (17 September 1919)

Thus it was that he served as a cupbearer at bacchanalian revels, but remained abstemious throughout, pouring night after night in the ruby-crusted cup of Famorgh the maddening wines that were drugged with cannabis and the stupefying arrack with its infusion of poppy.

Clark Ashton Smith, "The Witchcraft of Ulua" (1933)

Bring hashish, cannabis, or sleepy opium,
And of the empty dreams that were not worth desiring,
When of this pastime tiring,
O Cyrenaya, take away the sweet, dark gum,
Unclothe you, scent you with nard, myrrh, olibanum,
Make you fair for admiring.

Donald Wandrei, "Somewhere Past Ispahan"

Where they secured the *cannabis indica* later discovered on the scene of the tragedy is a mystery, but not, of course, one impossible of a solution.

Henry Kuttner, "Hydra" (1939)

He extracted and refined the stimulating factors in alcohol, cocoa, heroin, and Mother Nature's prize dope runner, *cannabis indica*. Like the scientist who, in analyzing the various clotting agents for blood treatments, found that oxalic acid and oxalic acid alone was the active factor, Kidder isolated the accelerators and decelerators, the stimulants and soporifics, in every substance that ever undermined a man's morality and/or caused a "noble experiment."

Theodore Sturgeon, "Microcosmic God" (1941)

Now you are mine! The joys of cannabis
Are vapid dreams beside the fiery storm
That roars within my veins at the first kiss
I press upon your warm, compliant form.

Richard Tierney, "Fulfillment" (1972)

Winter dawdled by the window, looking. It was truly amazing what people had been able to buy without a prescription at the turn of the century: opium and morphine and cocaine, all packaged in pretty blue and amber glass bottles, or wrapped in boxes with labels written in serious Spencerian script. Extract of cannabis. Tincture of arsenic. Cyanide.

Marion Zimmer Bradley, *Witchlight* (1996)

As a scientist, Washy Bridge, of course, regarded Von Junzt as a mental case and the *Necronomicon* as the ravings of a deranged cannabis abuser.

Robert Anton Wilson, *The Trick Top Hat* in the *Schrödinger's Cat Trilogy* (1979)

cantrip, cantrap, cantraip, *n.* [?] A spell, incantation, charm, or enchantment.

Coffins stood round like open presses,
That shaw'd the Dead in their last dresses,
And (by some devilish cantraip slight)
Each in its cauld hand held a light.—

Robert Burns, "Tam O'Shanter: A Tale" (1790)

So extraordinary were her powers, that the country people began to put them in competition with those of the Master, and say, that in some *cantraps* she surpassed him.

James Hogg, note to *The Queen's Wake: A Legendary Poem* (1813)

Consequently, Colin was nurtured in sin, and inured to iniquity, until all the kindly and humane principles of his nature were erased, or so much distorted, as to appear like their very opposites; and when this was accomplished, his wicked aunt and her associate hags, judging him fairly gained, without the pale of redemption, began to exercise cantrips, the most comical, and, at the same time, the most refined in cruelty, at his expense; and at length, on being assured of every earthly enjoyment, he engaged to join their hellish community, only craving three days to study their mysteries, bleed himself, and, with the blood extracted from his veins, extinguish the sign of the cross, thereby renouncing his hope in mercy, and likewise make some hieroglyphics of strange shapes and mysterious efficacy, and finally subscribe his name to the whole.

James Hogg, "Fairies, Deils, and Witches" (1828)

Then, with cantrip kisses seven,
   Three times round with kisses seven,
Warped and woven there spun we
Arms and legs and flaming hair,
Like a whirlwind in the sea.

William Bell Scott, "The Witch's Ballad"

Methought I had recover'd of the Becket,
That all was plan'd and bevell'd smooth again,
Save from some hateful cantrip of thine own.

Alfred, Lord Tennyson, *Becket* (1884)

He cam' a step nearer to the corp; an' then his heart fair whammled in his inside. For by what cantrip it was illbeseem a man to judge, she was hingin' frae a single nail an' by a single wursted thread for darnin' hose.

Robert Louis Stevenson, "Thrawn Janet" (1881)

This is he on the gallows tree
   Whom shadows long befriended,
Stiff and stark at the edge of dark
   With all his cantrips ended.

Leslie Barringer, "The Lay of Fastingal" in *Joris of the Rock* (1928)

"Now, if you ask my opinion, Jurgen, your cantrap is nonsense, and can never be of any earthly use to anybody. Without boasting, dear, I have handled a great deal of black magic in my day, but I never encountered a spell at all like this."

James Branch Cabell, *Jurgen: A Comedy of Justice* (1919)

"Yet three of Toupan's servitors endure upon earth, where they who were once lords of the Vendish have now no privilege remaining save to creep humbly as insects: the use of their wings is denied them here among the things which were made by Koshchei, and the charmed stone holds them immutably. Oho, but wife, there is a cantrap which would free them, and to their releaser will be granted whatever his will may desire—"

James Branch Cabell, *The Silver Stallion: A Comedy of Redemption* (1925)

Gerald had begun this tale in the days when he had intended to endow America with a literature superior to that of other countries; but for months now he had neglected it: and, in fact, ever since he set up as a student of magic he had lacked time somehow, with every available moment given over to runes and cantraps and suffumigations, to get back to any really serious work upon this romance.

James Branch Cabell, *Something About Eve: A Comedy of Fig-Leaves* (1927)

A particularly loathly annoyance whereby witches tormented their victims was through an uncouth spell to render them verminous. This filthy cantrip persists to-day.

Montague Summers, *A Popular History of Witchcraft* (1936)

[. . .] his cantraps of fermented words, abracadabra calubra culorum, [. . .]

James Joyce, *Finnegans Wake* (1922–39)

[colubra culorum: "serpent (adder) of the buttocks" (L)]

Scarcely less credible were von Junzt's conjectures on the whereabouts of the stolen scroll of cantrips against Ghatanothoa, and on the ultimate uses to which this scroll might be put.

H. P. Lovecraft & Hazel Heald, "Out of the Æons" (1933)

Presently, as he laboured with his useless cantrips, he felt on his face the breathing of a wind that was not air but a subtler and rarer element cold as the moon's ether.

Clark Ashton Smith, "The Coming of the White Worm" (1933)

Almost, in the marvel of new tests and cantraips, I forgot the ineffectual conjuration; and I deemed that Avyctes had forgotten it.

Clark Ashton Smith, "The Double Shadow" (1932)

He fumbled in his pouch to make sure he had not lost his good-luck talismans and amulets. His lips moved rapidly as he murmured two or three prayers and cantrips. But all the while he held his sling ready, and his eyes never once ceased their quick shifting.

Fritz Leiber, "The Jewels in the Forest" (1939)

"In ages gone," the Sage had said, his eyes fixed on a low star, "a thousand spells were known to sorcery and the wizards effected their wills. Today, as

Earth dies, a hundred spells remain to man's knowledge, and these have come to us through the ancient books . . . But there is one called Pandelume, who knows all the spells, all the incantations, cantraps, runes, and thaumaturgies that have ever wrenched and molded space . . ."

Jack Vance, "Turjan of Miir" in *The Dying Earth* (1950; ellipses in original)

Faucelme picked up the loose rope. "Should I wish to seize upon something, I toss it high and use the cantrap '*Tzip!*', in this fashion—"

"Halt!" cried Cugel, raising his sword. "I want no demonstrations!"

Jack Vance, *Cugel's Saga* (1984)

"He has set spells and cantraips on all the doors and windows so nothing can catch him unawares."

Gardner F. Fox, "Shadow of a Demon" (1976)

The enormous throbbing in his groin suggested that he would henceforth need a bag to contain the pulp of his manly parts. He had heard gossip lately about the cantrips of a foul necromancer, and he suspected that his corpse had been imperfectly revived by that villain.

Brian McNaughton, "Reunion in Cephalune" (1997)

Carcassonne, *pr.n.* [< L Colonia Julia *Carcaso*] A city of 45,000 in southeastern France, featuring the finest surviving mediæval fortifications extant. [Not in *OED*.]

> One sees it dimly from the height
>   Beyond the mountain blue:
> Fain would I walk five weary leagues—
> I do not mind the road's fatigues—
>   Through morn and evening dew;
> But bitter frosts would fall at night,
> And on the grapes that yellow blight;
> I could not go to Carcassonne,
> I never went to Carcassonne.

Gustave Nadaud (trans. M. E. W. Sherwood), "Carcassone"

In a letter from a friend whom I have never seen, one of those that read my books, this line was quoted—"But he never came to Carcassonne." I do not know the origin of the line, but I made this tale about it.

Lord Dunsany, "Carcassonne" (1910)

Then it had lighted up window by window above the shimmering tides where lanterns nodded and glided and deep horns bayed weird harmonies, and itself become a starry firmament of dream, redolent of faery music, and one with the marvels of Carcassonne and Samarcand and El Dorado and all glorious and half-fabulous cities.

H. P. Lovecraft, "He" (1925)

Carcassonne or the Acropolis itself would be deadwood to me if I knew weeks ahead just *when* I was going to see it, just *how* I was going to see it, and just *how long* I was going to see it.

H. P. Lovecraft, letter to James Ferdinand Morton (12 March 1930)

Suddenly, in the midst of this interstellar engagement, it was as if a curtain had been drawn across the scene; it faded away abruptly, and slowly another took its place, or, rather, a succession of scenes—a strange, black-watered lake, lost among crags in an utterly alien landscape, certainly not terrestrial, with a boiling, churning disturbance in the water and the rising of a thing too hideous to be named; a bleak, dark, windswept landscape with snow-covered crags ringing in a great plateau, in the center of which rose a black structure suggesting a many-turreted castle, within which sat enthroned a quartet of sombre beings in the guise of men, attended by huge bat-winged birds; a sea-kingdom, a far cry from Carcassone, similar to that of which I had previously dreamed; a snowy land-scape, suggestive of Canadian regions, with a great shape striding across it, as on the wind, blotting out the stars, showing in their place great shining eyes, a gro-tesque caricature on mankind in the Arctic wastes.

August Derleth, "The Black Island" (1952) in *The Trail of Cthulhu*

Ever the quiet whisper comes, stealing across the graves;
Night is within the whisper, and the silence of sunless caves,
Purple and onyx of Carcassonne, satyr and nymph of Pan,
Orcus, god of the underworld—the shadowed soul of man . . .

Henry Kuttner, "Where He Walked" (1936; ellipsis in original)

casement, *n.* [< *encasement*] A window hinged with a sash that opens outward; the sash of such a window. An essential feature of architectural style in Gothic romance, weird fiction, and fantasy.

a. General:

Manfred rose to pursue her; when the moon, which was now up, and gleamed in at the opposite casement, presented to his sight the plumes of the fatal helmet, which rose to the height of the windows, waving backwards and forwards in a tempestuous manner, and accompanied with a hollow and rustling sound.

Horace Walpole, *The Castle of Otranto: A Gothic Story* (1764)

"It was a beautiful and fearful sight to see her as she stood;—her marble face—her moveless features—her eyes in which burned the fixed and livid light of de-spair, like a lamp in a sepulchral vault—the lips that half opened, and remaining unclosed, appeared as if the speaker was unconscious of the words that had es-caped them, or rather, as if they had burst forth by involuntary and incontrou-lable impulse;—so she stood, like a statue, at her casement, the moonlight giving her white drapery the appearance of stone, and her wrought-up and determined mind lending the same rigidity to her expression."

Charles Maturin, *Melmoth the Wanderer: A Tale* (1820)

It was an early dawn of the third day; I was leaning from the casement, watching the misty jewel-fires of the luminous lilies fade, the mist wraiths that were the slaves of the waterfall rise slowly and more slowly.

A. Merritt, Dwellers in the Mirage (1932)

Into the north window of my chamber glows the Pole Star with uncanny light. All through the long hellish hours of blackness it shines there. And in the autumn of the year, when the winds from the north curse and whine, and the red-leaved trees of the swamp mutter things to one another in the small hours of the morning under the horned waning moon, I sit by the casement and watch that star.

H. P. Lovecraft, "Polaris" (1918)

b. With reference to Keats's "Ode to a Nightingale":

> Thou wast not born for death, immortal Bird!
> No hungry generations tread thee down;
> The voice I hear this passing night was heard
> In ancient days by emperor and clown:
> Perhaps the self-same song that found a path
> Through the sad heart of Ruth, when, sick for home,
> She stood in tears amid the alien corn;
> The same that oft-times hath
> Charm'd magic casements, opening on the foam
> Of perilous seas, in faëry lands forlorn.

John Keats, "Ode to a Nightingale" (1819)

Since then music has frankly beome a "mixed" art, a "criticism of life" in the medium of sound, we who try to understand literature may well insist that our fine prose and our fine poetry have a part in them, and that part the most precious, which is wholly super-intellectual, non-intelligible, occult. The lines of Keats, the "magic casements, opening on the foam Of perilous seas, in faëry lands forlorn," will occur to every one as an instance of this mysterious element.

Arthur Machen, "The Literature of Occultism" (1899)

I think, on the contrary, that children, especially young children before they have been defiled by the horrors of "education," possess the artistic emotion in remarkable purity, that they reproduce, in a measure, the primitive man before he was defiled, artistically, by the horrors of civilisation. The ecstasy of the artist is but a recollection, a remnant from the childish vision, and the child undoubtedly looks at the world through "magic casements."

Arthur Machen, Hieroglyphics: A Note upon Ecstasy in Literature (1902)

There is a certain confusion in the narrative of "Kubla Khan"; and the magic casements charmed by the song of the nightingale are misty.

Arthur Machen, "The Line of Terror" (1930)

Writing while Cowper was composing evangelical hymns under the influence of the Rev. Dr. Newton, and while Burns was celebrating his Highland Mary, Blake anticipates many of the profoundest thoughts of Nietzsche, and opens the "charmed magic casements" upon these perilous fairy seas, voyaged over by Verlaine and Hauptmann and Maeterlinck and Mallarmé.

John Cowper Powys, "William Blake" in
Suspended Judgments: Essays on Books and Sensations (1916)

For Mr. Tarkington has not mere talent but an uncontrollable wizardry that defies concealment, even by the livery of a popular novelist. The winding-up of the William Sylvanus Baxter stories, for example, is just the species of necromancy attainable by no other living author; so that a theatre wherein but now the humor of sitting upon wet paint and the mirthful aspect of a person vomiting have made their bids for popular applause, is shaken to its low foundation by the departing rumble of a "pompous train," and unsuspected casements open upon Fairy Land.

James Branch Cabell, *Beyond Life: Dizain des Démiurges* (1919)

For it seemed to me—as it still seems,—that the opening of this particular magic casement, upon an outlook rather more perilous than the bright foam of fairy seas, was alike the climax and the main "point" of my book.

James Branch Cabell, "Author's Note" (1927) to
Figures of Earth: A Comedy of Appearances

"It was, instead, for the great generality, who combine a taste for travel with a dislike for leaving home, that books were by the luckiest hit invented, to confound the restrictions of geography and the almanac. In consequence, from the Ptolemies to the Capets, from the twilight of a spring dawn in Sicily to the uglier shadow of Montfaucon's gibbet, there intervenes but the turning of a page, a choice between Theocritus and Villon. From the Athens of Herodotus to the Versailles of Saint-Simon, from Naishapur to Cranford, it is equally quick traveling. All times and lands that ever took the sun, indeed, lie open, equally, to the explorer by the grace of Gutenberg; and transportation into Greece or Rome or Persia or Chicago, equally, is the affair of a moment. Then, too, the islands of Avalon and Ogygia and Theleme stay always accessible, and magic casements open readily upon the surf of Sea-coast Bohemia. For the armchair traveler alone enjoys enfranchisement of a chronology, and of a geography, that has escaped the wear-and-tear of ever actually existing."

James Branch Cabell, *The Cream of the Jest: A Comedy of Evasion* (1911–15)

> At ease behind thy lofty casement,
>   Charm'd magick, op'ning on the foam
> Of perilous seas wherein have placement
>   The faery spire and island dome,
> Accept these maund'rings, dull and charmless,
>   Such as old men in dotage whine;

Assur'd that they at least are harmless,
 Pat to the season, and benign!

> H. P. Lovecraft, (Christmas greetings to Samuel Loveman)

Beneath the Polar Mountain
Rose cross and crosser there
Symbols of the swan
Aerial races
In rotation over
The magical casement
Visions of a parallel world

> Blue Öyster Cult, "*Les Invisibles*" (1988)

catafalque, catafalk, *n.* [< Fr < It *catafalco,* scaffold] A temporary structure
erected for use in a funeral ceremony.

Calmly he said that her lot was cast,
That the door she had passed was shut on her
Till the final catafalk repassed.

> Robert Browning, "The Statue and the Bust" (1855)

Round the earth still and stark
Heaven's death-lights kindle, yellow spark by spark,
Beneath the dreadful catafalque of the dark.

> Francis Thompson, A Corymbus for Autumn

And did you mark the Cyprian kiss white Adon on his catafalque?
And did you follow Amenalk, the God of Heliopolis?

> Oscar Wilde, "The Sphinx" (1894)

Worse than this, if possible, there were newly ceremented corpses that leaped
from their biers or catafalques, and disregarding the horrified watchers, ran with
great bounds of automatic frenzy into the night, never to be seen again by those
who lamented them.

> Clark Ashton Smith, "The Colossus of Ylourgne" (1932)

Above all was a dead, unchanging sky, with its catafalque of oppressive and su-
perincumbent grayness.

> Clark Ashton Smith, "The Gorgon" (1930)

cephalic, *adj.* Of or pertaining to the head.

"Duck!" roared the Doctor, spinning away upon his cephalic pivot:—the Black
Cat cocked his tail, and seemed to mew the word "Duck!"

> Thomas Ingoldsby (Richard Harris Barham),
> "The Leech of Folkestone" in *The Ingoldsby Legends* (1840)

But unlike most people, they did not regard their current stage of development with unqualified complacency. Indeed, their headlessness was a source of national regret; they deplored the retrenchment of nature in this regard; and the arrival of Eibon and Morghi, who were looked upon as ideal exemplars of cephalic evolution, had served to quicken their eugenic sorrow.

> Clark Ashton Smith, "The Door to Saturn" (1930)

But of such things I was still oblivious when I sallied forth that morning to the place of execution, where three criminals of a quite average sort, whose very cephalic contours I have forgotten along with their offenses, were to meet their well-deserved doom beneath my capable arm.

> Clark Ashton Smith, "The Testament of Athammaus" (1931)

Smith's method of self-education was to read an unabridged dictionary through, word for word, studying not only the definitions of the words but also their derivations from ancient languages. [. . .] When he became a commercial writer, he constantly disconcerted his readers by dropping in rare words like "fulvous," "cerement," and "mignard." [. . .] No other writer, I am sure, ever called a man's head his "cephalic appendage."

> L. Sprague de Camp, *Literary Swordsmen and Sorcerers:*
> *The Makers of Heroic Fantasy* (1976)

[But cf. quotation under **cephaloid**.]

cephaloid, *adj.* Resembling a head in shape.

Because of the virtual non-existence of a nape, the third beheading called for a precision of eye and a nicety of touch which, in all likelihood, no other headsman than myself could have shown. I rejoice to say that my skill was adequate to the demand thus made upon it; and once again the culprit was shorn of his vile cephaloid appendage. But if the blade had gone even a little to either side, the dismemberment entailed would have been technically of another sort than decapitation.

> Clark Ashton Smith, "The Testament of Athammaus" (1931)

changeling, *n.* (1) A turncoat, traitor. (2) One thing exchanged for another. (3) A child secretly exchanged for another child in infancy by the fairies. (4) A fool, oaf.

Titles: John Greenleaf Whittier, "The Changeling" (verse); James Russell Lowell, "The Changeling" (verse); Walter de la Mare, "The Changeling"; the Doors, "Changeling" (song)

> For well I wote, thou springst from ancient race
> Of Saxon kings, that haue with mightie hand
> And many bloudie battailes fought in place
> High reard their royall throne in Britane land,

And vanquisht them, vnable to withstand:
From thence a Faerie thee unweeting reft,
There as thou slepst in tender swadling band,
And her base Elfin brood there for thee left.
Such men do Chaungelings call, so chaungd by Faeries theft.

Edmund Spenser, *The Faërie Queene* (159-)

Doe you amend it then: it lyes in you.
Why should *Titania* crosse her *Oberon*?
I doe but begge a little Changeling boy,
To be my Henchman.

William Shakespeare, *A Midsummer Night's Dream*

It is in the same way that in ignorant ages the notion of changelings has been produced. The weak and fascinated mother sees every feature with a turn of expression unknown before, all the habits of the child appear different and strange, till the parent herself denies her offspring, and sees in the object so lately cherished and doated on, a monster uncouth and horrible of aspect.

William Godwin, *Lives of the Necromancers; or, An Account of the Most Eminent Persons in Successive Ages Who Have Claimed for Themselves, or to Whom Has Been Imputed by Others, the Exercise of Magical Power* (1834)

"Ah, na, na, madam! ye canna be auld. It is impossible! But goodness kens! there are sad changelings now-a-days. I hae seen an auld wrinkled wife blooming o'er night like a cherub."

James Hogg, "Fairies, Deils, and Witches" (1828)

The old man took the oars, and soon the bark
Smote on the beach beside a tower of stone.
It was a crumbling heap whose portal dark
With blooming ivy-trails was overgrown;
Upon whose floor the spangling sands were strown,
And rarest sea-shells, which the eternal flood,
Slave to the mother of the months, had thrown
Within the walls of that gray tower, which stood
A changeling of man's art nursed amid Nature's brood.

Percy Bysshe Shelley, *The Revolt of Islam: A Poem* (1817)

Mrs Owen brought with her into the family her little child by her first husband, a boy nearly three years old. He was one of those elfish, observant, mocking children, over whose feelings you seem to have no control; agile and mischievous, his little practical jokes, at first performed in ignorance of the pain he gave, but afterward proceeding to a malicious pleasure in suffering, really seemed to afford some ground to the superstitious notion of some of the common people that he was a fairy changeling.

Elizabeth Gaskell, "The Doom of the Griffiths" (1858)

"You mocking changeling—fairy-born and human-bred!"

Charlotte Brontë, *Jane Eyre: An Autobiography* (1847)

"Joe! *You* aren't by any chance a sort of fairy changeling?"

H. G. Wells, *Star-Begotten: A Biological Fantasia* (1937)

It was one or another old hero from out of Poictesme, Nero had heard, who had first modeled these earthen images; and Freydis, as occasion served, gave life to these images and set them to live upon earth, as changelings.

James Branch Cabell, *Something About Eve: A Comedy of Fig-Leaves* (1927)

Creative writers of every kind, in brief, appear to me to be rather fantastically gifted children—like changelings who as yet remember a little magic picked up in their faëry nurseries,—and they do not ever, except in exteriors, become mature.

Branch Cabell, *Special Delivery: A Packet of Replies* (1932)

To all but my soft-voiced, deep-bosomed, Norse mother I had been a stranger in that severely conventional, old house where I had been born. The youngest son, and an unwelcome intruder; a changeling. It had been no fault of mine that I had come into the world a throwback to my mother's yellow-haired, blue-eyed, strong-thewed Viking forefathers.

A. Merritt, *Dwellers in the Mirage* (1932)

She was more changeling than I. A changeling of the mirage! Nurtured on food from Goblin Market!

A. Merritt, *Dwellers in the Mirage* (1932)

Listen—can you fancy a squatting circle of nameless dog-like things in a church-yard teaching a small child how to feed like themselves? The price of a change-ling, I suppose—you know the old myth about how the weird people leave their spawn in cradles in exchange for the human babes they steal.

H. P. Lovecraft, "Pickman's Model" (1926)

Great God! That whisperer in darkness with its morbid odour and vibrations! Sorcerer, emissary, changeling, outsider ... that hideous repressed buzzing ... and all the time in that fresh, shiny cylinder on the shelf ... poor devil ... "pro-digious surgical, biological, chemical, and mechanical skills". ...

H. P. Lovecraft, "The Whisperer in Darkness" (1930; ellipses in original)

I am that swart, unseen pursuer
Whose lust begets a changeling breed:
All women know me for their wooer:
Mine is the whisper maidens heed
At twilight; mine the spells that lead
The matron to the nighted moor.

Clark Ashton Smith, "Cambion" (1943)

But this changeling, this waif of darkness, this horror who bears the noble name of Ketrick, the brand of the serpent is upon him, and until he is destroyed there is no rest for me.

Robert E. Howard, "The Children of the Night" (1930)

charnel, *n.* [< OF *charnel* < L *carnāle*] A building or room in which the remains of the dead are placed. (Not always differentiable from its use as an adjective. See next entry.)

a. General:

How many holy liars and parasites, in solemn guise, would his saviour arm drag from their luxurious couches, and plunge in the cold charnel, that the green and many-legged monsters of the slimy grave might eat off at their leisure the lineaments of rooted malignity and detested cunning.

Percy Bysshe Shelley, "The Assassins" (1814)

> I have made my bed
> In charnels and on coffins, where black death
> Keeps record of the trophies won from thee.

Percy Bysshe Shelley, "Alastor; or, The Spirit of Solitude" (1815)

> One day the dreary old King of Death
>   Inclined for some sport with the carnal,
> So he tied a pack of darts on his back,
>   And quietly stole from his charnel.

Thomas Hood, "Death's Ramble"

The ancient city of Lara was a charnel. Of all the rulers not twoscore had escaped, and these into regions of peril which to describe as sanctuary would be mockery.

A. Merritt, *The Moon Pool* (1919)

Perhaps the city differed little from others, except in being older and darker; but to Phariom, in his extremity of anguish, the ways that he followed were like subterrene corridors that led only to some profound and monstrous charnel.

Clark Ashton Smith, "The Charnel God" (1932)

b. In **charnel-house, charnel house:**

> And I ha'been choosing out this Scull,
> From Charnel Houses, that were full;
> From private Grots, and publick Pits,
> And frighted a Sexton out of his Wits.

Ben Jonson, *The Masque of Queens* (1609)

At the upper end of the vault, at a rude table formed of a decaying coffin, or something which once served the same purpose, sat three monks. They were among the oldest corpses in the charnel house, for the inquisitive brother knew their faces well; and the cadaverous hue of their cheeks seemed still more cadaverous in the dim light shed upon them, while their hollow eyes gave forth what looked to him like flashes of flame.

"The Monk of Horror; or, The Conclave of Corpses" (1798)

'Twas from a scene, a witching trance like this,
He hurried her away, yet breathing bliss,
To the dim charnel-house;—through all its steams
Of damp and death, led only by those gleams
Which foul Corruption lights, as with design
To show the gay and proud *she* too can shine!—

Thomas Moore, "The Veiled Prophet of Khorassan" in *Lalla Rookh* (1817)

To examine the causes of life, we must first have recourse to death. I became acquainted with the science of anatomy: but this was not sufficient; I must also observe the natural decay and corruption of the human body. In my education my father had taken the greatest precautions that my mind should be impressed with no supernatural horrors. I do not ever remember to have trembled at a tale of superstition, or to have feared the apparition of a spirit. Darkness had no effect upon my fancy; and a churchyard was to me merely the receptacle of bodies deprived of life, which, from being the seat of beauty and strength, had become food for the worm. Now I was led to examine the cause and progress of this decay, and forced to spend days and nights in vaults and charnel-houses.

Mary Shelley, *Frankenstein; or, The Modern Prometheus* (1816–17)

"In the very charnel-house is the nursery of production and animation. Is that true?"

Edward Bulwer-Lytton, *Zanoni: A Rosicrucian Tale* (1842)

My eyesight waxed gradually dull to all but the fleshless skulls that were glaring in the yellow light of the tapers—the hum of human voices was stifled in my ears, and I thought myself alone, already with the dead. The guide thrust the light he carried into a huge skull that was lying separate in a niche; but I marked not the action or the man, but only the fearful glimmering of the transparent bone, which I thought a smile of triumphant malice from the presiding spectre of the place, while imagined accents whispered, in my hearing, "Welcome to our charnel-house, for THIS shall be your chamber!"

Daniel Keyes Sanford, "A Night in the Catacombs" (1818)

"Would they have me make of a charnel-house my bed-chamber?" I cried aloud. "I will not. I will lie abroad on the heath. It cannot be colder there!"

George MacDonald, *Lilith: A Romance* (1895)

I sighed with sadness. I, too, was a dead soul—and I had given up the Lord of Resurrection that morning out of loyalty to another dead soul. And—the same afternoon! Faugh! what a charnel-house Life is! How chill and damp and poisonous is the air! How the walls sweat the agony of the damned!

Aleister Crowley, *The Diary of a Drug Fiend* (1922)

I daresay the soil would be quite fat with corpsemanure, bones, flesh, nails. Charnelhouses. Dreadful. Turning green and pink decomposing. Rot quick in damp earth. The lean old ones tougher. Then a kind of tallowy kind of a cheesy. Then begin to get black, black treacle oozing out of them. Then dried up. Deathmoths. Of course the cells or whatever they are go on living. Changing about. Live for ever practically. Nothing to feed on feed on themselves.

James Joyce, *Ulysses* (1914–21)

We were in quest of new lands of silks and spices. In truth, we found fevers, violent deaths, pestilential paradises where death and beauty kept charnel-house together. That old Johannes Maartens, with no hint of romance in that stolid face and grizzly square head of his, sought the islands of Solomon, the mines of Golconda—ay, he sought old lost Atlantis which he hoped to find still afloat unscuppered. And he found head-hunting, tree-dwelling anthropophagi instead.

Jack London, *The Star Rover* (1915)

It was as if the old, good-easy, meek-eyed man of science, dying, had left his effectual curse on all the world, and had thereby converted civilization into one omnivorous grave, one universal charnel-house.

M. P. Shiel, "The S.S." (1895)

As I closed the door behind me and descended the dripping steps by the light of my lone candle, I seemed to know the way; and though the candle sputtered with the stifling reek of the place, I felt singularly at home in the musty, charnel-house air.

H. P. Lovecraft, "The Tomb" (1917)

This stench was nothing which any of the Fenners had ever encountered before, and produced a kind of clutching, amorphous fear beyond that of the tomb or the charnel-house.

H. P. Lovecraft, *The Case of Charles Dexter Ward* (1927)

A foul charnel-house scent flowed out of the aperture and the dim sunlight seemed less to illuminate the cavern-like opening than to be fouled by the rank darkness which clung there.

Robert E. Howard, "Worms of the Earth" (1930)

And there was something else: in spite of the wind that was blowing away from me, I caught a scent, a charnel-house reek of death and decay and corruption that rose from the blossoms.

Robert E. Howard, "The Garden of Fear"

A tiger skull grinned up at him with jaws that seemed to widen hungrily. The vertebræ of a huge python lay in disjointed coils on the planks, twisted as if in agony. He discerned the skeletonic remains of tigers, tapirs, and jungle beasts of unknown identity. And human heads, many of them, scattered about like an assembly of mocking, dead-alive faces, leering at him, watching him with hellish anticipation. The place was a morgue—a charnel house!

Hugh B. Cave, "Stragella" (1932)

Yes, an old fœtus, that's what I am now, hoar and impotent, mother is done for, I've rotted her, she'll drop me with the help of gangrene, perhaps papa is at the party too, I'll land headforemost mewling in the charnel-house, not that I'll mewl, not worth it. All the stories I've told myself, clinging to the putrid mucus, and swelling, swelling, saying, Got it at last, my legend.

Samuel Beckett, Malone Dies (1948)

Yes, if I could, but I can't, whatever it is, I can't any more, there was perhaps a time I could, in the days when I was bursting my guts, as per instructions, to bring back to the fold the dear lost lamb, I'd been told he was dear, that he was dear to me, that I was dear to him, that we were dear to each other, all my life I've pelted him with twaddle, the dear departed, wondering what he could possibly be like, well, almost, damn the almost, all my life, until I joined him, and now it's I am dear to them, now its they are dear to me, glad to hear it, they'll join us, one by one, what a pity they are numberless, so are we, dear charnel-house of renegades, this evening decidedly everything is dear, no matter, the ancients hear nothing, and my old quarry, there beside me, for him it's all over, beside me how are you, underneath me, we're piled up in heaps, no, that won't work either, no matter, it's a detail, for him it's all over, him the second-last, and for me too, me the last, it will soon be all over, I'll hear nothing more, I've nothing more to do, simply wait, it's a slow business, he'll come and lie on top of me, lie beside me, my dear tormentor, his turn to suffer what he made me suffer, mine to be at peace.

Samuel Beckett, The Unnamable (1949)

The tomb-herd confer no benefits upon their worshippers. Their powers are few, for they can but disarrange space in small regions and make tangible that which cometh forth from the dead in other dimensions. They have power wherever the chants of Yog-Sothoth have been cried out at their seasons, and can draw to them those who open their gates in the charnel-houses. They have no substance in this dimension, but enter earthly tenants to feed through them while they await the time when the stars become fixed and the gate of infinite sides opens to free That Which Claws at the Barrier.

Abdul Alhazred, *Necronomicon*, as quoted in
Ramsey Campbell, "The Church in High Street" (1962)

Graff pointed downward, and his crooked finger wandered in an arc through the sepulchral dimness of the room. Arthur Emerson now saw that the place had been turned into a charnel house for the remains of small animals: mice, rats, birds, squirrels, even a few young possums and raccoons. He already knew the cat to be an obsessive hunter, but it seemed strange that these carcasses had all been brought to this room, as if it were a kind of sanctum of mutilation and death.

Thomas Ligotti, "The Prodigy of Dreams"

"No, Howard. Think of it: our own collection of death. A catalogue of pain, of human frailty—all for us. Set against a backdrop of tranquil loveliness. Think what it would be to walk through such a place, meditating, reflecting upon your own ephemeral essence. Think of making love in a charnel house! We have only to assemble the parts—they will create a whole into which we may fall."

Poppy Z. Brite, "His Mouth Will Taste of Wormwood" (1990)

c. In other combined forms or as modifier:

> Such are those thick and gloomy shadows damp
> Oft seen in Charnell vaults, and Sepulchers
> Lingering, and sitting by a new made grave,
> As loath to leave the body that it lov'd,
> And link't it self by carnal sensualty
> To a degenerate and degraded state.

John Milton, *Comus (A Masque Presented at Ludlow Castle, 1634)*

> When the long-sounding curfew from afar
> Loaded with loud lament the lonely gale,
> Young Edwin, lighted by the evening star,
> Lingering and listening, wandered down the vale.
> There would he dream of graves, and corses pale;
> And ghosts that to the charnel-dungeon throng,
> And drag a length of clanking chain, and wail,
> Till silenced by the owl's terrific song,
> Or blast that shrieks by fits the shuddering aisles along.

James Beattie, "The Minstrel" (1771–74)

> All stood together on the deck,
> For a charnel-dungeon fitter:
> All fixed on me their stony eyes,
> That in the Moon did glitter.

S. T. Coleridge, "The Rime of the Ancient Mariner" (1798)

And when he bent, the earthy lips
  A kiss of horror gave;
'Twas like the smell from charnel vaults,
  Or from the mouldering grave!

Thomas Moore, "The Ring: A Tale" (1801)

Reeks not the charnel-stream of murder from me?

Charles Maturin, *Bertram; or, The Castle of St. Aldobrand: A Tragedy* (1816)

My God!
The beautiful blue heaven is flecked with blood!
The sunshine on the floor is black! The air
Is changed to vapours such as the dead breathe
In charnel pits! Pah! I am choked!

Percy Bysshe Shelley, *The Cenci: A Tragedy* (1819)

His books have become a monument. His laurel so largely mixed with cypress, a charnel-breath so mingles with the temple incense, that boys and maids will shun the spot.

Ralph Waldo Emerson, "Swedenborg; or, The Mystic" in *Representative Men*

It lies uncover'd in the pesty gloom,
Eyeless and earless, on the charnel-floor,
While in its nameless corpse the wormlets hoar
Make in its suppurated brain their room.

David Park Barnitz, "The Grotesques" in *The Book of Jade* (1901)

This is th' abyss. Behold wherein I lurk
The lazar-house my mind, wherein do work
The horrid charnel-priests, whose loathly song
Sickens my soul, and quells the spirit strong.

Aleister Crowley, "Abysmos" in *White Stains: The Literary Remains of George Archibald Bishop, A Neuropath of the Second Empire* (1898)

"Methinks that the royal house of Tasuun rots and totters to its fall. Harlots and sorcerers swarm in the palace of Famorgh like charnel-worms; and now, in this princess Lunalia of Xylac whom he has taken to wife, he has found a harlot and a witch in one."

Clark Ashton Smith, "The Weaver in the Vault" (1933)

Then began another lengthy journey through endless labyrinthine caverns and charnel vaults.

Robert Bloch, "The Grinning Ghoul" (1936)

charnel, charnal, *adj.* [< OF *charnel* < L *carnāle*] Gruesomely reminiscent of death or the dead. (Not always differentiable from its use as a noun. See preceding entry.)

Titles: Clark Ashton Smith, "The Charnel God"

> The hues of life flushed up with unwonted energy into the countenance—the limbs relaxed—and, save that the eyelids were yet pressed heavily together, and that the bandages and draperies of the grave still imparted their charnel character to the figure, I might have dreamed that Rowena had indeed shaken off, utterly, the fetters of Death.
>
> Edgar Allan Poe, "Ligeia" (1838)

> The entire surface of this metallic enclosure was rudely daubed in all the hideous and repulsive devices to which the charnel superstition of the monks has given rise. The figures of fiends in aspects of menace, with skeleton forms, and other more really fearful images, overspread and disfigured the walls.
>
> Edgar Allan Poe, "The Pit and the Pendulum" (1842)

> My fancy grew charnel. I talked "of worms, of tombs, and epitaphs." I was lost in reveries of death, and the idea of premature burial held continual possession of my brain.
>
> Edgar Allan Poe, "The Premature Burial" (1844)

> The world may not like to see these ideas dissevered, for it has been accustomed to blend them; finding it convenient to make external show pass for sterling worth—to let whitewashed wall vouch for clean shrines. It may hate him who dares to scrutinize and expose, to raise the gilding and show base metal under it, to penetrate the sepulchre and reveal charnal relics; but hate as it will, it is indebted to him.
>
> Charlotte Brontë, *Jane Eyre: An Autobiography* (1847)

> Far and wide is my charnel range,
>   And rich carousal I keep;
> Till back I come to my gibbet home,
>   To be merrily rocked to sleep.
>
> Eliza Cook, "Song of the Carrion Crow" (1856)

> "Then the flame went out, in a brief sizzle, yet at the last moment, I had seen an extraordinary raw look, become visible upon the end of that monstrous, protruding lappet. It had become dewed with a hideous, purplish sweat. And with the darkness, there came a sudden charnel-like stench."
>
> William Hope Hodgson, "The Derelict" (1912)

For a week I tasted to the full the joys of that charnel conviviality which I must not describe, when the *thing* happened, and I was borne away to this accursed abode of sorrow and monotony.

H. P. Lovecraft, "The Tomb" (1917)

The wind grew stronger, and the air was filled with the lethal, charnel odour of plague-stricken towns and uncovered cemeteries.

H. P. Lovecraft, "The White Ship" (1919)

The scene I cannot describe—I should faint if I tried it, for there is madness in a room full of classified charnel things, with blood and lesser human debris almost ankle-deep on the slimy floor, and with hideous reptilian abnormalities sprouting, bubbling, and baking over a winking bluish-green spectre of dim flame in a far corner of black shadows.

H. P. Lovecraft, "Herbert West—Reanimator" (1922)

Then I saw a small black aperture, felt a ghoulish wind of ice, and smelled the charnel bowels of a putrescent earth.

H. P. Lovecraft, "Herbert West—Reanimator" (1922)

And then, because that nightmare's position barred me from the stone staircase down which we had come, I flung myself into the oily underground river that bubbled somewhere to the caves of the sea; flung myself into that putrescent juice of earth's inner horrors before the madness of my screams could bring down upon me all the charnel legions these pest-gulfs might conceal.

H. P. Lovecraft, "The Festival" (1923)

They were sometimes shewn in groups in cemeteries or underground passages, and often appeared to be in battle over their prey—or rather, their treasure-trove. And what damnable expressiveness Pickman sometimes gave the sightless faces of this charnel booty!

H. P. Lovecraft, "Pickman's Model" (1926)

A fiendish and ululant corpse-gurgle or death-rattle now split the very atmosphere—the charnel atmosphere poisonous with naphtha and bitumen blasts—in one concerted chorus from the ghoulish legion of hybrid blasphemies.

H. P. Lovecraft & Harry Houdini, "Under the Pyramids" (1924)

> I was afraid when thro' the vaulted space
> Of the old tow'r, the clock-ticks died away
> Into a silence so profound and chill
> That my teeth chatter'd—giving yet no sound,
> Then flicker'd low the light, and all dissolv'd,
> Leaving me floating in the hellish grasp

Of body'd blackness, from whose beating wings
Came ghoulish blasts of charnel-scented mist.

> H. P. Lovecraft, "Aletheia Phrikodes" in
> "The Poe-et's Nightmare: A Fable" (1916)

But at midnight, when we sat together by the silver lamps, pondering the blood-writ runes of Hyperborea, I saw that the shadow had drawn closer to the shadow of Avyctes, towering behind his chair on the wall. And the thing was a streaming ooze of charnel pollution, a foulness beyond the black leprosies of hell; and I could bear it no more; and I cried out in my fear and loathing, and informed the master of its presence.

> Clark Ashton Smith, "The Double Shadow" (1932)

Phariom, sick at heart with the charnel terror and cruelty of the doom that impended for his girlish wife in this unknown city of nightmare, heard an evil, stealthy creaking on the stairs that led to the attic of the inn.

> Clark Ashton Smith, "The Charnel God" (1932)

There was, it seemed, a diabolic fatality about the whole train of circumstances through which Elaith, still living, though with that outward aspect of the tomb which her illness involved, had fallen into the grasp of the devotees of the charnel god.

> Clark Ashton Smith, "The Charnel God" (1932)

Unchilled and undismayed, he entered those always-open portals of death, where ghoul-headed monsters of black marble, glaring with hideously pitted eyes, maintained their charnel postures before the crumbling pylons.

> Clark Ashton Smith, "The Death of Ilalotha" (1937)

Beware! the voices float and fall
Half-heard, and haply sweet to thee
As are the runes of memory
And murmurs of a voice foreknown
In days when love dwelt not alone:
Beware! for where the voices call,
Slow waters weave thy charnel pall.

> Clark Ashton Smith, "Warning" (1928)

What nightmare bore you, hateful blight of red?
What evil source your awful scarlet flood?
Of desolation and the livid dead,
Whence came your charnel hue of pain and blood?

> Donald Wandrei, "Red" (1928)

There was about this dream one aspect which had a more disturbing bond to reality. In the course of the way through the woods to the meeting place of the coven, the path led beside a marsh to fœtid sloughs in a place where there was a charnel odor of decay; I sank into the mud repeatedly in that place, though neither the cat nor great-grandfather seemed to more than float upon its surface.

> August Derleth (as H. P. Lovecraft & August Derleth),
> "The Peabody Heritage" (1957)

It was a skeleton-thin, parchment-brown corpse, and it looked a skeleton with the hide of some great lizard stretched over its bones. It stirred, it crept forward, and its long nails scratched audibly against the stone. It crawled out into the Witch Room, its passionless face pitilessly revealed in the white light, and its eyes were gleaming with charnel life. He could see the serrated ridge of its brown, shrunken back—

> Henry Kuttner, "The Salem Horror" (1937)

A monstrous thought assailed Allington. Was *this* his other self—this ghoul-spawned, charnel horror of corpse-accursed dread?

> Robert Bloch, "The Suicide in the Study" (1935)

And yet another sense informed him that he was surrounded by a stench of decay, an aura of charnel rot so strong, so intimate, that he could not long resist the conclusion that it rose from his own vile body.

> Anthony Boucher, "The Scrawny One" (1949)

It is inevitable that we read these sad histories as we do, as a catalogue of missed opportunities and broken communications. A present generation righteously declares the errors of its forefathers. But it is unlikely that any human effort would have changed the course of events. There would still have come about the re-awakening of Dzhaimbú and the other worse gods, under whose charnel dominion we now suffer and despair.

> Fred Chappell, "Weird Tales" (1984)

Piles of yellowed hymnals squatted against a pillar like grotesque huddled shapes of crouching beings, long forsaken—here and there the pews were broken with age—and the air in that enclosed place was thick with a kind of charnel musk.

> Ramsey Campbell, "The Church in High Street" (1962)

Often vaults would be opened, and newly buried corpses might be dug forth and reanimated by certain horrendous formulæ. There were even hints that these living cadavers were taken as wives or husbands by favored members of the cult, for the children resulting from such charnel betrothals would have primal powers which properly belonged only to alien deities.

> Ramsey Campbell, "The Horror from the Bridge" (1964)

We spent a happy time refurbishing the museum, polishing the inlaid precious metals of the wall fixtures, brushing away the dust that frosted the velvet designs of the wallpaper, alternately burning incense and charring bits of cloth we had saturated with our blood, in order to give the rooms the odor we desired—a charnel perfume strong enough to drive us to frenzy.

> Poppy Z. Brite, "His Mouth Will Taste of Wormwood" (1990)

charneled, *ppl. adj.* Placed as in a charnel or tomb. [Not in *OED*.]

> They strode upon the swooning pave,
> They towered by the trembling spires,
> Tall as apocalyptic fires
> Above the peoples of the grave:
> But, sightless and inveterate,
> To Mammon vowed, the throng went by,
> Charneled beneath an iron sky.

> Clark Ashton Smith, "The Envoys" (1925)

Ecstatically, I fingered the lovely shape whose secret I must know or die, whose maze I must thread as best I can or go mad for if I am to prevail I must soon come face to face with the Minotaur of dreams and confound him in his charneled lair, and in our heroic coupling know the last mystery; total power achieved not over man, not over woman but over the heraldic beast, the devouring monster, the maw of creation itself that spews us forth and sucks us back into the black oblivion where stars are made and energy waits to be born in order to begin once more the cycle of destruction and creation at whose apex now I stand, once man, now woman, and soon to be privy to what lies beyond the uterine door, the mystery of creation that I mean to shatter with the fierce thrust of a will that alone separates me from the nothing of eternity; and as I have conquered the male, absorbed and been absorbed by the female, I am at last outside the human scale, and so may render impotent even familiar banal ubiquitous death whose mouth I see smiling at me with moist coral lips between the legs of my beloved girl who is the unwitting instrument of victory, and the beautiful fact of my life's vision made all too perfect flesh.

> Gore Vidal, *Myra Breckinridge* (1968)

Charonian, *adj.* [< *Charon,* in Græco-Roman mythology, the ferryman who conveys the dead across the river Styx into Hades] Of or pertaining to Charon or the river Styx; hellish, infernal; dark, dismal, gloomy. [Not in *OED*.]

The Elysian plain, near the Catacombs in Egypt, stood upon the foul Charonian canal; which was so noisome, that every fetid ditch and cavern was from it called Charonian.

> Jacob Bryant, *A New System; or, An Analysis of Antient Mythology* (1774)

And the shadow answered, "I am SHADOW, and my dwelling is near to the Catacombs of Ptolemais, and hard by those dim plains of Helusion which border upon the foul Charonian canal."

> Edgar Allan Poe, "Shadow—A Parable" (1835)

[Helusion: Elysium]

I do not remember exactly how I managed to reach the motorcar, start it, and slip unobserved back to the village; for I retain no distinct impression save of wild-armed titan trees, dæmoniac mutterings of thunder, and Charonian shadows athwart the low mounds that dotted and streaked the region.

> H. P. Lovecraft, "The Lurking Fear" (1922)

For the thing within that cage was hideous to look upon, and was covered with foul yellow mud and dank Charonian vegetation, and it uttered little feeble cries which reminded me of the cries which Heth had uttered when he had been attacked by the lampreys in his master's garden, and had suffered his blood to be drawn off in eighteen different directions at the same time.

> Frank Belknap Long, "The Eye Above the Mantel" (1921)

Oh God, the loathsome thing within covered with dank Charonian vegetation was flesh of my flesh, and bone of my bone!

> Frank Belknap Long, "The Eye Above the Mantel" (1921)

chhaya, *n.* [< Skr *chāyā*, shadow] In Theosophy, the astral body. [Not in *OED*.]

Says the Commentary explaining the verse:—

> *"The holy youths (the gods) refused to multiply and create species after their likeness, after their kind. They are not fit forms (rupas) for us. They have to grow. They refuse to enter the chhayas (shadows or images) of their inferiors. Thus had selfish feeling prevailed from the beginning, even among the gods, and they fell under the eye of the Karmic Lipikas."*

> H. P. Blavatsky, *The Secret Doctrine:*
> *The Synthesis of Science, Religion, and Philosophy* (1888)

Chhaya-birth, or that primeval mode of *sexless* procreation, the first Race having *oozed out*, so to say, from the bodies of the Pitris, is hinted at in a Cosmic allegory in the Purânas. It is the beautiful allegory and story of Sanjnâ, the daughter of Viswakarman—married to the Sun, who, "unable to endure the fervours of her lord," gave him her *chhaya* (shadow, image, or *astral* body), while she herself repaired to the jungle to perform religious devotions, or *Tapas*. The Sun, supposing the "chhaya" to be his wife begat by her children, like Adam with Lilith—an *ethereal shadow* also, as in the legend, though an actual living female monster millions of years ago.

> H. P. Blavatsky, *The Secret Doctrine:*
> *The Synthesis of Science, Religion, and Philosophy* (1888)

In the *"Great Book of the Mysteries"* we are told that: "Seven Lords created Seven men; three Lords (Dhyan Chohans or Pitris) were holy and good, four less heavenly and full of passion. . . . The *chhayas* (phantoms) of the Fathers were as they."

H. P. Blavatsky, *The Secret Doctrine:*
The Synthesis of Science, Religion, and Philosophy (1888; ellipsis in original)

Scott was a strange man. Slender, sharp-eyed, and taciturn, he spent most of his time in an old brownstone house in Baltimore. His knowledge of esoteric matters was little short of phenomenal; he had read the *Chhaya Ritual,* and in his letters to Ludwig and Edmond had hinted at the real meanings behind the veiled hints and warnings in that half-legendary manuscript. In his great library were such names as Sinistrari, Zancherius, and the ill-famed Gougenot des Mouseau; in his library safe he had, it was rumoured, an immense scrapbook filled with excerpts copied from such fantastic sources as the *Book of Karnak,* the monstrous *Sixtystone,* and the blasphemous *Elder Key,* of which only two copies are reputed to exist on Earth.

Henry Kuttner, "Hydra" (1939)

"It's here, in the *Book of Karnak*—and in the other books, *La Trés Sainte Trinoso-phie,* the *Chhaya Ritual,* the *Dictionnaire Infernal* of de Plancy. But man won't believe, because he doesn't want to believe. He has forced belief from his mind. From ancient times the only memory that has come down is fear—fear of those ultra-human entities which once walked the Earth."

Henry Kuttner, "Hydra" (1939)

chiaroscuro, *n.* [< It, clear + dark] The arrangement and interplay of the elements of light and dark in the pictorial arts.

Upon everything was a haze of restlessness and oppression; a touch of the unreal and the grotesque, as if some vital element of perspective or chiaroscuro were awry. I did not wonder that the foreigners would not stay, for this was no region to sleep in. It was too much like a landscape of Salvator Rosa; too much like some forbidden woodcut in a tale of terror.

H. P. Lovecraft, "The Colour out of Space" (1927)

chimæra (*pl.* **chimæræ, chimæras**), **chimera** (*pl.* **chimeræ, chimeras**), **chi-mere, chymera,** *n.* [< L < Gr *khímaira,* a nanny goat] In Græco-Roman mythology, a monster with a goat's body, a serpent's tail, and a fire-breathing lion's head; hence, any monster compounded from the parts of various disparate animals; in common figurative use, an idle or vain fancy.

Titles: Charles Baudelaire, "To Each His Chimera" (prose-poem); Clark Ashton Smith, "The Chimera" (verse), "To the Chimera" (verse); John Barth, *Chimera*

Only the poet, disdaining to be tied to any such subjection, lifted up with the vigor of his own invention, doth grow in effect another nature, in making things either better than nature bringeth forth, or, quite anew, forms such as never were in nature, as the Heroes, Demigods, Cyclopes, Chimeras, Furies, and such like: so as he goeth hand in hand with nature, not enclosed within the narrow warrant of her gifts, but freely ranging only within the zodiac of his own wit.

Sir Philip Sidney, *An Apology for Poetry* (1583)

He shall inspire my verse with gentle mood
Of Poets Prince, whether he woon beside
Faire *Xanthus* sprincled with *Chimæras* blood;
Or in the woods of *Astery* abide;
Or whereas mount *Parnasse*, the Muses brood,
Doth his broad forhead like two hornes divide,
And the sweete waves of sounding *Castaly*
With liquid foote doth slide downe easily.

Edmund Spenser, *Virgils Gnat* (1590)

His cloaths wear ragged clouts, with thornes pind fast,
And as he musing lay, to stonie fright
A thousand wild Chimera's would him cast:
As when a fearefull dreame, in mid'st of night,
Skips to the braine, and phansies to the sight
Some winged furie, strait the hasty foot,
Eger to flie, cannot plucke up his root,
The voyce dies in the tongue, and mouth gapes without boot.

Giles Fletcher, *Christ's Victorie on Earth* (1610)

In the middle of these Cogitations, Apprehensions and Reflections, it came into my Thought one Day, that all this might be a meer Chimera of my own; and that the Foot might be the Print of my own Foot, when I came on Shore from my Boat: This chear'd me up a little too, and I began to perswade my self it was all a Delusion; that it was nothing else but my own Foot, and why might not I come that way from the Boat, as well as I was going that way to the Boat; again, I consider'd also that I could by no Means tell for certain where I had trod, and where I had not; and that if at last this was only the Print of my own Foot, I had play'd the Part of those Fools, who strive to make stories of Spectres, and Apparitions; and then are frighted at them more than any body.

Daniel Defoe, *The Life and Surprising Adventures of*
Robinson Crusoe, of York, Mariner (1719)

In the Fairyland of Fancy, Genius may wander wild; there it has a creative power, and may reign arbitrarily over its own empire of Chimeras.

Edward Young, *Conjectures on Original Composition*

Drear is the state of the benighted wretch
Who then bewildered wanders through the dark

Full of pale fancies and chimeras huge;
Nor visited by one directive ray
From cottage streaming or from airy hall.

James Thomson, "Autumn" in *The Seasons*

Hell is but the chimera of priests, to bubble idiots and cowards.

William Godwin, *St. Leon: A Tale of the Sixteenth Century* (1799)

"If men of powerful and vigorous minds, a Rousseau and others, have surrendered themselves to the chimeras of a disturbed imagination, and have believed that they were every where at the disposal of some formidable and secret confederacy, what wonder that I, a boy of eight years old, should be subject to similar alarm?"

William Godwin, *Fleetwood; or, The New Man of Feeling* (1804)

In this congenial solitude of Nightmare Abbey, the distempered ideas of metaphysical romance and romantic metaphysics had ample time and space to germinate into a fertile crop of chimeras, which rapidly shot up into vigorous and abundant vegetation.

Thomas Love Peacock, *Nightmare Abbey* (1817)

Persons of feeble, nervous, melancholy temperament, exhausted by fever, by labour, or by spare diet, will readily conjure up, in the magic ring of their own phantasy, spectres, gorgons, chimæras, and all the objects of their hatred and their love. We are most of us like Don Quixote, to whom a windmill was a giant, and Dulcinea a magnificent princess: all more or less the dupes of our own imagination, though we do not all go so far as to see ghosts, or to fancy ourselves pipkins and teapots.

Thomas Love Peacock, *Nightmare Abbey* (1817)

"'Be damned to all eternity!' said the priest, tossing on his feverish bed, and dreaming, in the intervals of his troubled sleep, of Don Fernan coming to confession with a drawn sword, and Donna Clara with a bottle of Xeres' in her hand, which she swallowed at a draught, while his parched lips were gaping for a drop in vain,—and of the Inquisition being established in an island off the coast of Bengal, and a huge partridge seated with a cap on at the end of a table covered with black, as chief Inquisitor,—and various and monstrous chimeras, the abortive births of repletion and indigestion."

Charles Maturin, *Melmoth the Wanderer: A Tale* (1820)

Gorgons, and Hydras, and Chimæras dire—stories of Celæno and the Harpies—may reproduce themselves in the brain of superstition—but they were there before. They are transcripts, types—the archetypes are in us, and eternal. How else should the recital of that, which we know in a waking sense to be false, come to affect us at all? [. . .] Is it that we naturally conceive terror from such objects, considered in their capacity of being able to inflict upon us bodily injury?—O, least of all! These terrors are of older standing. They date beyond body—or, without the body, they would have been the same. All the cruel, tormenting, defined devils in Dante—tearing, mangling, choking, stifling, scorching demons—are they one half so fearful to the spirit of a man, as the simple idea of a spirit unembodied following him? [. . .] That the kind of fear here treated of is purely spiritual—that it is strong in proportion as it is objectless upon earth—that it predominates in the period of sinless infancy—are difficulties, the solution of which might afford some probable insight into our ante-mundane condition, and a peep at least into the shadow-land of pre-existence.

Charles Lamb, "Witches, and Other Night-Fears" (1821)

"Thus we, instead of Friends, are Dinner-guests; and here as elsewhere have cast away chimeras."

Thomas Carlyle, *Sartor Resartus: The Life and Opinions of Herr Teufelsdröckh* (1831)

"The ancient teachers of this science," said he, "promised impossibilities, and performed nothing. The modern masters promise very little; they know that metals cannot be transmuted, and that the elixir of life is a chimera."

Mary Shelley, *Frankenstein; or, The Modern Prometheus* (1816–17)

Haroun led his wild guest to boast of his own proficiency in magic, and, despite my incredulity, I could not overcome the shudder with which fictions, however extravagant, that deal with that dark Unknown abandoned to the chimeras of poets, will, at night and in solitude, send through the veins of men the least accessible to imaginary terrors.

Sir Edward Bulwer-Lytton, *A Strange Story* (1861)

I am almost ashamed to own—yes, even in this felon's cell, I am almost ashamed to own—that the terror and horror with which the animal inspired me, had been heightened by one of the merest chimæras it would be possible to conceive.

Edgar Allan Poe, "The Black Cat" (1843)

Never can I forget what I saw. Many terrible memories are mine, memories stranger and more terrible than those of the average man; but this *thing* which now moved slowly down upon us through the impenetrable gloom of that haunted place was (if the term be understood) almost absurdly horrible. It was a mediæval legend come to life in modern London; it was as though some horrible chimera of black and ignorant past was become created and potent in the present.

Sax Rohmer (Arthur Sarsfield Ward),
The Return of Dr. Fu-Manchu (1916; aka *The Devil Doctor*)

"Yes—the image of Mallare stands saluting his charming chimera with an interesting Ethiopian erection."

Ben Hecht, *Fantazius Mallare: A Mysterious Oath* (1918)

"Come inside," Julian cried suddenly. "You, Sebastien! Come inside. And bring them all in—the entire army of chimeras that flow from your waxen eyes. I will destroy them one by one to the last of your abominations. I will tear down each tower you breathe into the air. Come, my glowering monster, bring in your lecherous bride and your androgynous slaves to defend you. I am going to tear your little Kingdom down."

Ben Hecht, The Kingdom of Evil: A Continuation of the
Journal of Fantazius Mallare (1924)

They soared high, swerved and swooped upon the lance-throwers! Beneath their onslaught those chimeræ tottered. I saw living projectiles and living target fuse where they met—melt and weld in jets of lightnings.

A. Merritt, The Metal Monster (1920)

Vornikoff, the Russian, and Schwartz, the German, had experimented with still higher forms of life, producing *chimeræ*, nightmare things they had been forced to slay—and quickly.

A. Merritt, The Face in the Abyss (1923)

You recall that Pickman's forte was faces. I don't believe anybody since Goya could put so much of sheer hell into a set of features or a twist of expression. And before Goya you have to go back to the mediæval chaps who did the gargoyles and chimæras on Notre Dame and Mont Saint-Michel. They believed all sorts of things—and maybe they saw all sorts of things, too, for the Middle Ages had some curious phases.

H. P. Lovecraft, "Pickman's Model" (1926)

O, who will slay the last chimera, Time?

Clark Ashton Smith, "The Chimera" (1918)

Brave spectre, what chimera shares thy saddle,
Pointing thee to this place?

Clark Ashton Smith, "Don Quixote on Market Street" (1950)

Ashton Smith hovers over the corpse of matter like a beautiful, ironic Chimera over a Sphinx that is silent because it has nothing but imbecility in its eyes and an eternal vacuity in its brain—the Sphinx of "modernity".

Benjamin DeCasseres, "Clark Ashton Smith: Emperor of Shadows" in
Clark Ashton Smith, Selected Poems

chimærical, chimerical, *adj.* Having the nature of a chimæra or chimera; in particular, illusory, imaginary, or wildly fanciful.

Persons after a debauch of liquor, or under the influence of terror, or in the deleria of a fever, or in a fit of lunacy, or even walking in their sleep, have had their brains as deeply impressed with chimerical representations, as they could possibly have been, had these representations struck their senses.

William Shenstone, "An Opinion of Ghosts" in
Essays on Men, Manners, and Things

Books like Ignatius Donnelly's chimerical account of Atlantis he absorbed with zest, and a dozen obscure precursors of Charles Fort enthralled him with their vagaries.

H. P. Lovecraft, "The Descendant" (1927?)

There had, it seems, been some truth in chimerical old Borellus when he wrote of preparing from even the most antique remains certain "Essential Saltes" from which the shade of a long-dead living thing might be raised up.

H. P. Lovecraft, *The Case of Charles Dexter Ward* (1927)

My conception of time—my ability to distinguish between consecutiveness and simultaneousness—seemed subtly disordered; so that I formed chimerical notions about living in one age and casting one's mind all over eternity for knowledge of past and future ages.

H. P. Lovecraft, "The Shadow out of Time" (1935)

chirography, *n.* Handwriting.

Upon attempting to read the manuscript I at first found myself puzzled by a style of chirography very peculiar and characteristic, but execrably bad. Vainly did I attempt to read it; even the opening sentence was not deciphered without long inspection and great difficulty.

John Uri Lloyd, *Etidorhpa; or, The End of Earth: The Strange History of a Mysterious Being and the Account of a Remarkable Journey* (1894)

When first we had seen it we had gazed upon a sea of radiance pierced with lanced forests, swept with gigantic gonfalons of mists of flame; we had seen it emptied of its fiery mists—a vast slate covered with the chirography of the Metal Hordes and dominated by the colossal integrate hieroglyph of the City—the Metal Monster; we had seen it as a radiant lake over which brooded weird suns; a lake of yellow flame froth upon which a sparkling hail fell, within which reared islanded towers and a drowning mount running with cataracts of sun fires; here we had watched a Goddess woman, a being half of earth, half of the unknown immured within a living tomb—a dying tomb—of flaming mysteries; had seen a cross-shaped metal Satan, a sullen flaming crystal Judas betray—itself!

A. Merritt, *The Metal Monster* (1920)

There were cryptic formulæ and diagrams in his and other hands which Ward now either copied with care or had photographed, and one extremely mysterious letter in a chirography that the searcher recognised from items in the Registry of Deeds as positively Joseph Curwen's.

H. P. Lovecraft, *The Case of Charles Dexter Ward* (1927)

chlorotic, *adj.* Of, pertaining to, or afflicted with chlorosis or green sickness.

And in the Stygian grotto I saw them do the rite, and adore the sick pillar of flame, and throw into the water handfuls gouged out of the viscous vegetation which glittered green in the chlorotic glare. I saw this, and I saw something amorphously squatted far away from the light, piping noisomely on a flute; and as the thing piped I thought I heard noxious muffled flutterings in the fœtid darkness where I could not see.

H. P. Lovecraft, "The Festival" (1923)

chymist, *n.* An alchemist.

"He had not been at Oxford for nothing, nor talked to no account with an ancient chymist and astrologer in Paris."

H. P. Lovecraft, "He" (1925)

Curious porters and teamers who delivered bottles, bags, or boxes at the small rear door would exchange accounts of the fantastic flasks, crucibles, alembics, and furnaces they saw in the low shelved room; and prophesied in whispers that the close-mouthed "chymist"—by which they meant *alchemist*—would not be long in finding the Philosopher's Stone.

H. P. Lovecraft, *The Case of Charles Dexter Ward* (1927)

cicerone (*pl.* **ciceroni, cicerones**), *n.* [< Marcus Tullus *Cicero,* the famous Roman orator] A guide who conducts sightseers.

"I was led to expect that one of these visits would be paid on the look-out in company with my cicerone at a quarter to ten, and the hour and the lady came with equal punctuality."

Arthur Machen, "The Great God Pan" (1890)

"They are looking for the bleeding corpse," whispered the invisible cicerone, and the words filled Master Nathaniel with an unspeakable horror.

Hope Mirrlees, *Lud-in-the-Mist* (1926)

Guided by our Bædeker, we had struck east past the Ezbekiyah Gardens along the Mouski in quest of the native quarter, and were soon in the hands of a clamorous cicerone who—notwithstanding later developments—was assuredly a master at his trade.

H. P. Lovecraft & Harry Houdini, "Under the Pyramids" (1924)

"Dear God—what is it, Tillinghast?" I gasped. My subterranean cicerone seemed to sneer as he replied. "Nothing at all, Brainard. A mere bagatelle."

Harry S. Robbins, "The Smoker from the Shadows" (1990)

Cimmerian, *adj.* Of or pertaining to Cimmeria, a land of perpetual darkness in which Odysseus consulted the spirits of the dead on his voyage home from Troy; hellish or infernal; dark, dismal, gloomy.

> First let Cimmerian darkness be my onl' habitation:
> First be mine eyes pull'd out, first be my brain perished,
> Ere that I should consent to do so excessive a damage
> Unto the earth, by the hurt of this her heavenly jewel.
>
> Sir Philip Sidney, *The Countess of Pembroke's Arcadia* (1580)

Philosophers, dynasts, monarchs, all were involved and overshadowed in this mist, in more than Cimmerian darkness.

> Robert Burton, *The Anatomy of Melancholy: What It Is, With All the Kinds,*
> *Causes, Symptomes, Prognostickes & Severall Cures of It* (1621)

> But now well-wearied with our too long stay
> In these Cimmerian fogs and hatefull mists
> Of Ghosts, of Goblins, and drad sorcery,
> From nicer allegations we'll desist.
>
> Henry More, *The Præexistency of the Soul* (1647)

In the Cimmerian gloom of the stairway the voice of a pursuer hailed me.

> Joseph Conrad & Ford Madox Ford (Ford Madox Hueffer),
> *The Inheritors: An Extravagant Story* (1901)

> The Spirit's profanation who would know:—
> Behold, eclipsed are heaven's last rays, that light
> Its sculptured fane, and in Cimmerian night
> It shall lie desolate, a Mystery of Woe;
> Archdeacons of abandonment shall haunt
> Its holiest shrine; nor death nor dread shall daunt
> Their blood-wrought ritual, evoking so
> A strange creation, shaped in Heaven's despite.
>
> John Allan, "L'Évocation de Scorphael"

Then she extinguished the lamp and all within the cabin was wrapped in Cimmerian darkness.

> Edgar Rice Burroughs, *Tarzan of the Apes* (1912)

Stylistically, Burroughs is—how shall I put it?—uneven. He has moments of ornate pomp, when the darkness is "Cimmerian"; of redundancy, "she was hideous and ugly"; of extraordinary dialogue: "Name of a name," shrieked Rokoff. "Pig, but you shall die for this!"

> Gore Vidal, "Tarzan Revisited" (1963)

—In Summerian sunshine?
—And in Cimmerian shudders.

James Joyce, *Finnegans Wake* (1922–39)

For a brief while, he still seemed to see the star he had been watching, far down in the terrible Cimmerian void; and then he forgot, and could find it no more.

Clark Ashton Smith, "The Planet of the Dead"
(1930; aka "The Doom of Antarion")

But silence brimmed the Cimmerian channel, troubled only by the clatter and crunch of their own footsteps.

Clark Ashton Smith, "Vulthoom" (1933)

Regressive, through what realms of elder doom
Where even the swart vans of Time are stunned,
Seek thou some tall Cimmerian citadel,
And proud demonian capitals unsunned
Whose ramparts, ominous with horrent gloom,
Heave worldward on the unwaning light of hell.

Clark Ashton Smith, "The Medusa of Despair" (1913)

I wandered down Sleep's vast and sunless vale,
Where silence and Cimmerian darkness lay
That never moon nor stars disturb, nor Day
With sword of golden light.

Clark Ashton Smith, "The Dream-God's Realm"

Iced in for the winter
the floes grind against the hull
HMS Terror & the son of Chaos
Erebus, brother & husband of Night
lord of the Cimmerian darkness
the leprosy of the ice

Hakim Bey (Peter Lamborn Wilson), "The Antarctic Autonomous Zone:
A Science-Fiction Story" (1989)

Cimmerian (*pl.* **Cimmerii, Cimmerians**), *n.* An inhabitant of Cimmeria.

None other saw them when they came
Across the many-clangored mart,
But in mine eyes and in my heart
They passed as might the pillared flame
Of lightning loosened on the tombs,-
Or errant suns that wander by
To dawn on the Cimmerii.

Clark Ashton Smith, "The Envoys" (1925)

cincture, *v.tr.* To gird, encompass, or encircle, as with a belt or girdle.

And the cities of Cathuria are cinctured with golden walls, and their pavements also are of gold.

H. P. Lovecraft, "The White Ship" (1919)

cincture, *n.* A belt, girdle.

> Return, with all the ancient loves,
> Like Venus and her circling doves,
> With Cyprian cinctures to unweave,
> And snatches of some Lesbian air
> To lighten this my long despair
> Upon a saffron-bordered eve.

Clark Ashton Smith, "To One Absent" (1941/43)

cinerarium (*pl.* **cineraria**), *n.* A place reserved for the deposition of the ashes of the dead.

He flashed the beam of his torch forward to reveal a chamber carved from plutonic basalt. A vessel of unidentifiable design reposed in a niche in the seamless black wall as do cineraria in a mausoleum.

Harry S. Robbins, "The Smoker from the Shadows" (1990)

clavicle, *n.* [< L *clāvicula,* dim. *clavis,* key; with reference to the grimoires known as the Greater and Lesser Keys of Solomon, the *Clavicula Salomonis* and the *Lemegeton vel Clavicula Salomonis Regis.*] A key. [Not in *OED.*]

But I am not unreadie for for harde ffortunes, as I haue tolde you, and haue long work'd upon yᵉ Way of gett'g Backe after yᵉ Laste. I laste Night strucke on yᵉ Wordes that bringe up YOGGE-SOTHOTHE, and sawe for yᵉ firste Time that fface spoke of by Ibn Schacabao in yᵉ ———. And IT said, that yᵉ III Psalme in yᵉ Liber-Damnatus holdes yᵉ Clauicle. With Sunne in V House, Saturne in Trine, drawe yᵉ Pentagram of Fire, and saye yᵉ ninth Uerse thrice. This Uerse repeate eache Roodemas and Hallow's Eue; and yᵉ Thing will breede in yᵉ Outside Spheres.

Joseph Curwen, letter to Simon Orne (c. 1750), as quoted in H. P. Lovecraft,
The Case of Charles Dexter Ward (1927)

I thought I knew what books I was studying, but the voices now are telling me, "The runes of Nug-Soth, the clavicle of Nyarlathotep, the litanies of Lomar, the secular meditations of Pierre-Louis Montagny, the *Necronomicon*, the chants of Crom-Ya, the overviews of Yiang-Li . . .")

Fritz Leiber, "The Terror from the Depths" (1975; ellipsis in original)

clepsammia (*pl.* **clepsammiæ**), *n.* A device which measures time by the graduated flow of sand; a sand-clock, sand-glass, hour-glass. [Not in *OED.*]

It is not to be denied that before the daies of *Jerom* there were Horologies, and several accounts of time; for they measured the hours not only by drops of water in glasses called Clepsydræ, but also by sand in glasses called Clepsammia.

Sir Thomas Browne, *Pseudodoxia Epidemica; or, Enquiries into
Very Many Received Tenents and Commonly Presumed Truths* (1646)

And there I mark the tall clepsammiæ
That time has overthrown,
And empty clepsydræ,
And dials drowned in umbrage never-lifting;
And there, on rusty parapegms,
I read the ephemerides
Of antique stars and elder planets drifting
Oblivionward in night
And there, with purples of the tomb bedight
And crowned with funereal gems,
I hold awhile the throne
Whereon mine immemorial selves have sate,
Canopied by the triple-tinted glory
Of the three suns forever paled and flown.

Clark Ashton Smith, "Revenant" (1933)

clepsydra (*pl.* **clepsydræ, clepsydras**), *n.* A device which measures time by the graduated flow of a liquid; a water clock or water glass.

Before him in the undetermined shadows he discerned the dim and puzzling contours of an object that he could liken only to some enormous clepsydra or fountain surrounded with grotesque carvings.

Clark Ashton Smith, "The Tomb-Spawn" (1933)

cloaca (*pl.* **cloacæ**), *n.* A sewer.

Suddenly Graydon seemed to behold a whole new world of appalling *grotesquerie*—spider-men and spider-women spread upon huge webs and weaving with needled fingers wondrous fabrics, mole-men and mole-women burrowing, opening mazes of subterranean passages, *cloaca,* for those who had wrought phantasmagoria of humanity, monstrously twinned with Nature's perfect machine, while still plastic in the womb!

A. Merritt, *The Face in the Abyss* (1923)

cloacal, *adj.* Of, pertaining to, or resembling a sewer or sewers.

The Roman, like the Englishman who follows in his footsteps, brought to every new shore on which he set his foot (on our shore he never set it) only his cloacal obsession.

James Joyce, *Ulysses* (1914–21)

Burlap and all, the burden went down to the oblivion of a cloacal labyrinth.

> H. P. Lovecraft & Hazel Heald, "The Horror in the Museum" (1932)

"Consider him!" spoke Kerlin. "His lineaments, his apparatus. He is nothing else but anthropoid, and such is his origin, together with all the demons, frits and winged glowing-eyed creatures that infest latter-day Earth. Blikdak, like the others, is from the mind of man. The sweaty condensation, the stench and vileness, the cloacal humors, the brutal delights, the rapes and sodomies, the scatophilac whims, the manifold tittering lubricities that have drained through humanity form a vast tumor; so Blikdak assumed his being, so now this is he. You have seen how he molds his being, so he performs his enjoyments. But of Blikdak, enough. I die, I die!"

> Jack Vance, "Guyal of Sfere" in *The Dying Earth* (1950)

codex (*pl.* **codices**), *n.* [< L *cōdex* < *caudex,* tree-trunk, wooden tablet, book] A manuscript volume.

I must not delay in expressing my well-nigh delirious delight at *The Tale of Satampra Zeiros*—which has veritably given me the one arch-kick of 1929! Yug! n'gha k'yun bth'gth R'lyeh gllur ph'ngui Cthulhu yzkaa . . . . what an atmosphere! I can see & feel & smell the jungle around immemorial Commoriom, which I am sure must lie buried today in glacial ice near Olathoë, in the land of Lomar! It is of this crux of elder horror, I am certain, that the mad Arab Abdul Alhazred was thinking when he—even he—left something unmention'd & signify'd by a row of stars in the surviving codex of his accursed & forbidden *Necronomicon!*

> H. P. Lovecraft, letter to Clark Ashton Smith (3 December 1929)

Great winds whipping across a black plain scattered the codices and hieroglyphs to rubbish heaps of the earth—(A Mexican boy whistling Mambo, drops his pants by a mud wall and wipes his ass with a page from the Madrid codex)—

> William S. Burroughs, *Nova Express* (1961–63)

Joe was a chess puzzle and logical paradox addict; like William S. Burroughs, he was perpetually poring over the Mayan codices, trying to unscrew those inscrutable glyphs for which no Rosetta Stone has yet been found.

> Robert Anton Wilson, *The Trick Top Hat* in the
> *Schrödinger's Cat Trilogy* (1979)

colloquy, *n.* A conversation or dialogue; in particular, a formal one.

To complete the eldritch colloquy there were two actually human voices—one the crude speech of an unknown and evidently rustic man, and the other the suave Bostonian tones of my erstwhile guide Noyes.

> H. P. Lovecraft, "The Whisperer in Darkness" (1930)

conceit, *n.* [< Fr < L *conceptus,* concept, idea] An odd, fanciful, and extravagant notion or idea.

"Poets and philosophers, that take a pride in inventing new opinions, have sought to renown their wits by hunting after strange conceits of heaven and hell; all generally agreeing that such places there are, but how inhabited, by whom governed, or what betides them that are transported to the one or other, not two of them jump in one tale."

Thomas Nashe, *Pierce Penniless his Supplication to the Devil* (1592)

> But Isabel had nothing seen,
>   She look'd around in vain;
> And much she mourned the mad conceit
>   That rack'd her Rupert's brain.

Thomas Moore, "The Ring: A Tale" (1801)

He knew how foolish it had been in the first place to trouble his mind with such conceits of a dreary cottage on the outskirts of London. and it was more foolish now to meditate these things, fantasies, feigned forms, the issue of a sad mood and a bleak day of spring.

Arthur Machen, *The Hill of Dreams* (1897)

That flyaway lady, supporting one corner of the pulpit canopy, which looked like a fringed damask table-cloth in a high wind, at the first attempt of a basilisk to pose up there in the organ loft, she would point her gold trumpet at him, and puff him out of existence! I laughed to myself over this conceit, which, at the time, I thought very amusing, and sat and chaffed myself and everything else, from the old harpy outside the railing, who had made me pay ten centimes for my chair, before she would let me in (she was more like a basilisk, I told myself, than was my organist with the anæmic complexion): from that grim old dame, to, yes, alas! to Monseigneur C——, himself.

Robert W. Chambers, "In the Court of the Dragon" (1895)

It was after a night like this that I shocked the community with a queer conceit about the burial of the rich and celebrated Squire Brewster, a maker of local history who was interred in 1711, and whose slate headstone, bearing a graven skull and crossbones, was slowly crumbling to powder. In a moment of childish imagination I vowed not only that the undertaker, Goodman Simpson, had stolen the silver-buckled shoes, silken hose, and satin small-clothes of the deceased before burial; but that the Squire himself, not fully inanimate, had turned twice in his mound-covered coffin on the day after interment.

H. P. Lovecraft, "The Tomb" (1917)

I refer to a sort of cloudy whitish pattern on the dirt floor—a vague, shifting deposit of mould or nitre which we sometimes thought we could trace amidst the sparse fungous growths near the huge fireplace of the basement kitchen. Once in a while it struck us that this patch bore an uncanny resemblance to a doubled-up human figure, though generally no such kinship existed, and often there was no whitish deposit whatever. On a certain rainy afternoon when this illusion seemed phenomenally strong, and when, in addition, I had fancied I glimpsed a kind of thin, yellowish, shimmering exhalation rising from the nitrous pattern toward the yawning fireplace, I spoke to my uncle about the matter. He smiled at this odd conceit, but it seemed that his smile was tinged with reminiscence. Later I heard that a similar notion entered into some of the wild ancient tales of the common folk—a notion likewise alluding to ghoulish, wolfish shapes taken by smoke from the great chimney, and queer contours assumed by certain of the sinuous tree-roots that thrust their way into the cellar through the loose foundation-stones.

H. P. Lovecraft, "The Shunned House" (1924)

"No, we are not interested so much in their relation to other figures in the pantheon, as to the conceit which gave them being in the first place. And to its relation to so many batrachian or ichthyic figures and motifs which occur in the art work, ancient and modern, to be found in the South Pacific islands."

August Derleth, "The Black Island" (1952) in *The Trail of Cthulhu*

"I'm still here," the writer says, adjusting to the tone. (I've even stuck the requisite pipe in my mouth, stuffed with a plug of latakia.) "It's over now," he says. "I've lived through it."

A comforting premise, perhaps. Only, in this case, it doesn't happen to be true. Whether the experience is really "over now" no one can say; and if, as I suspect, the final chapter has yet to be enacted, then the notion of my "living through it" will seem a pathetic conceit.

T. E. D. Klein, "Black Man with a Horn" (1980)

conclave, *n.* A private or secret meeting, as of cardinals in the Roman Catholic Church.

Titles: "The Monk of Horror; or, The Conclave of Corpses"

A terrible and abnormal conclave, I felt certain, was assembled below me; but for what shocking deliberations I could not tell. It was curious how this unquestioned sense of the malign and the blasphemous pervaded me despite Akeley's assurances of the Outsiders' friendliness.

H. P. Lovecraft, "The Whisperer in Darkness" (1930)

condor, Condor, *n.* A large, flying bird of the vulture family, species of which are found in California and the Andes.

Like some huge and sable-feathered condor, we were slowly drifting towards the Bridge of Sighs, when a thousand flambeaux flashing from the windows, and down the staircases of the Ducal Palace, turned all at once that deep gloom into a livid and preternatural day.

Edgar Allan Poe, "The Assignation" (1834)

Of late, eternal Condor years
So shake the very Heaven on high
With tumult as they thunder by,
I have no time for idle cares
Through gazing on the unquiet sky.

Edgar Allan Poe, "Romance" (1829)

Mimes, in the form of God on high,
    Mutter and mumble low,
And hither and thither fly—
    Mere puppets they, who come and go
At bidding of vast formless things
    That shift the scenery to and fro,
Flapping from out their Condor wings
    Invisible Wo!

Edgar Allan Poe, "The Conqueror Worm" (1843)

I look'd and sigh'd, I knew not why,
As when a condor flutters by,
And thought the moonbeams on thy face
Timid to seek thy resting-place.

H. P. Lovecraft, "To Zara" (1922)

O condor, keep thy mountain-ways
Above the long Andean lands;
Gier-eagle, guard the eastern sands
Where the forsaken camel strays:
Beetle and worm and I will ward
The lardered graves of lout and lord.

Clark Ashton Smith, "The Ghoul and the Seraph" (1919)

In those mountains we were assailed by freezing winds and hunger, and by giant condors which swept down upon us with a thunder of gigantic wings.

Robert E. Howard, "The Garden of Fear" (1934)

congeries, *n.* [< L *congeriēs,* heap, pile, mass] An aggregation of miscellaneous bodies heaped together into a single mass.

"Life, believe me, is no simple thing, no mass of grey matter and congeries of veins and muscles to be laid naked by the surgeon's knife; man is the secret which I am about to explore, and before I can discover him I must cross over weltering seas indeed, and oceans and the mists of many thousand years."

Arthur Machen, "Novel of the Black Seal" in
The Three Impostors; or, The Transmutations (1895)

On my left, across a well-kept lawn which stretched to the road and flaunted a border of whitewashed stones, rose a white, two-and-a-half-story house of unusual size and elegance for the region, with a congeries of contiguous or arcade-linked barns, sheds, and windmill behind and to the right.

> H. P. Lovecraft, "The Whisperer in Darkness" (1930)

Two of the less irrelevantly moving things—a rather large congeries of iridescent, prolately spheroidal bubbles and a very much smaller polyhedron of unknown colours and rapidly shifting surface angles—seemed to take notice of him and follow him about or float ahead as he changed position among the titan prisms, labyrinths, cube-and-plane clusters, and quasi-buildings; and all the while the vague shrieking and roaring waxed louder and louder, as if approaching some monstrous climax of utterly unendurable intensity.

> H. P. Lovecraft, "The Dreams in the Witch House" (1932)

Imagination called up the shocking form of fabulous Yog-Sothoth—only a congeries of iridescent globes, yet stupendous in its malign suggestiveness.

> H. P. Lovecraft & Hazel Heald, "The Horror in the Museum" (1932)

> Small lozenge panes, obscured by smoke and frost,
> Just showed the books, in piles like twisted trees,
> Rotting from floor to floor—congeries
> Of crumbling elder lore at little cost.

> H. P. Lovecraft, "The Book" in *Fungi from Yuggoth* (1929–30)

"Let me put it as a hypothetical case," Ningauble replied imperturbably. "Let us suppose, My Gentle Son, that there is a man in a universe and that a most evil force comes to this universe from another universe, or perhaps from a congeries of universes, and that this man is a brave man who wants to defend his universe and who counts his life as a trifle and that moreover he has to counsel him a very wise and prudent and public-spirited uncle who knows all about these matters which I have been hypothecating—"

> Fritz Leiber, "Bazaar of the Bizarre" (1963)

The sea fog still wraps the sprawling suburbs below, its last vestiges are sliding out of high, dry Laurel Canyon, but far off to the south I can begin to discern the black congeries of scaffold oil wells near Culver City, like stiff-legged robots massing for the attack.

> Fritz Leiber, "The Terror from the Depths" (1975)

conium, *n.* [< L *conīum* < Gr *kóneion*] The common hemlock; an extract thereof, used as a drug or poison.

> I have drunk out of heavy goblets golden,
> As from some hellish tabernaculum
> Cannabis, conium;

> I know quite all the poisons, all the olden
> Sins, all the ténébreux dark secrets hid,
> And things forbid.
>
> David Park Barnitz, Prelude to *The Book of Jade* (1901)

[ténebreux: Fr, tenebrous]

> Hast heard the voices of the fen,
> That softly sing a lethal rune
> Where reeds have caught the fallen moon—
> A song more sweet than conium is,
> Or honey-blended cannabis,
> To draw the dreaming feet of men
> On ways where none goes forth again?
>
> Clark Ashton Smith, "Warning" (1928)

> From out her amber windows, gazing languidly
> On a weird land
> Where conium and cannabis and upas-tree
> Seem wrought in verdigris against the copper sand,
> She sees and sees again
> A trailing salt like leprous dragons from the sea
> Far-crawled upon the fen;
> And foam of monster-cloven gulfs beyond a fallow strand.
>
> Clark Ashton Smith, "The Saturnienne" (1925)

coronate, *adj.* Supplied with a crown or corona.

> I saw a mountain, coronate
> With cities populous and great,
> Whose habitants, a mighty number,
> Lay hid in deep nocturnal slumber,
> So that the moon for long dim hours
> Leer'd on lone streets and silent tow'rs.
>
> H. P. Lovecraft, "Astrophobos" (1917)

corpse-light, *n.* A corpse-candle (q.v.).

> "Where corpse-light
> Dances bright,
> Be it day or night,
> Be it by light or dark,
> There shall corpse lie stiff and stark."
>
> Sir Walter Scott, *The Pirate* (1821)

"They?" said Claud Halcro; "what mean you by they?—is it the corpse-lights?—No, they did not pass me by, but I think they have passed by you, and blighted you with their influence, for you are as pale as a spectre."

Sir Walter Scott, The Pirate (1821)

> Some said he had not plunged into the wave,
> But vanish'd like a corpse-light from a grave;
> Others, that something supernatural
> Glared in his figure, more than mortal tall;
> While all agreed that in his cheek and eye
> There was a dead hue of eternity.

Lord Byron, The Island; or, Christian and His Comrades (1823)

> But once a year, on the eve of All-Souls,
> Through these arches dishallowed the organ rolls,
> Fingers long fleshless the bell-ropes work,
> The chimes peal muffled with sea-mists mirk,
> The skeleton windows are traced anew
> On the baleful flicker of corpse-lights blue,
> And the ghosts must come, so the legend saith,
> To a preaching of Reverend Doctor Death.

James Russell Lowell, "The Black Preacher: A Breton Legend"

She stood still once, the fear upon her, for she saw three or four blurred yellow gleams moving beyond her eastward along the dyke. She knew what they were,—the corpse-lights that on the night of death go between the bier and the place of burial. More than once she had seen them before the last hour, and by that token had known the end to be near.

Fiona Macleod (William Sharp), "The Sin-Eater" (1895)

As though the memory fanned dead embers within him, a kind of corpse-light stirred in his pale eyes.

E. R. Eddison, The Mezentian Gate (1941–45)

Out of the fungus-ridden earth steamed up a vaporous corpse-light, yellow and diseased, which bubbled and lapped to a gigantic height in vague outlines half-human and half-monstrous, through which I could see the chimney and fire-place beyond. It was all eyes—wolfish and mocking—and the rugose insect-like head dissolved at the top to a thin stream of mist which curled putridly about and finally vanished up the chimney.

H. P. Lovecraft, "The Shunned House" (1924)

> I see
> The mound-stretched gossamers, cradles to the dew;
> Moon-wefted briers, and the cypress-trees

With shadow swathed, or cerements of the moon;
And corpse-lights borne from aisle to secret aisle
Within the footless forest. . . .

> Clark Ashton Smith, "The Witch in the Graveyard"
> (1913; ellipsis in original)

Here evil exhalations of decay
Give forth a corpse-light that illumines naught
Save a faint-gleaming road that slopes away
To a white bridge with hideous figures wrought.

> Richard Tierney, "Minas Morgul" (1979)

coruscate, *v.intr.* To give forth reflective flashes of light; to sparkle or glitter.

A hundred paces away was a dais, its rim raised a yard above the floor. From the edge of this rim streamed upward a steady, coruscating mist of the opalescence, veined even as was that of the Dweller's shining core and shot with milky shadows like curdled moonlight; up it stretched like a wall.

> A. Merritt, *The Moon Pool* (1919)

We were high above an ocean of living light—a sea of incandescent splendors that stretched mile upon uncounted mile away and whose incredible waves streamed thousands of feet in air, flew in gigantic banners, in tremendous streamers, in coruscating clouds of varicolored flame—as though torn by the talons of a mighty wind! And the place was one vast caldron of tempests; a titanic womb of the lightnings!

> A. Merritt, *The Metal Monster* (1920)

coruscation, *n.* A sudden flash or sparkle of reflective light.

I saw a blinding blue auroral coruscation, heard an ululating shriek more hideous than any of the previous cries of that mad, horrible journey, and smelled the nauseous odour of burning flesh. That was all my overwrought consciousness could bear, and I sank instantly into oblivion.

> H. P. Lovecraft & Adolphe de Castro, "The Electric Executioner" (1929)

crabbed, *adj.* Of handwriting: difficult to decipher due to the poor formation of the characters. A common style of handwriting in fantasy and weird fiction.

Then, just as I was giving up hope, I found it—a little green-backed book, filled with closely written and crabbed writing.

> William Hope Hodgson, "The Goddess of Death" (1904)

He also opened the diary at a page carefully selected for its innocuousness and gave Willett a glimpse of Curwen's connected handwriting in English. The doctor noted very closely the crabbed and complicated letters, and the general aura of the seventeenth century which clung round both penmanship and style despite the writer's survival into the eighteenth century, and became quite certain that the document was genuine.

H. P. Lovecraft, *The Case of Charles Dexter Ward* (1927)

Certainly, the change was radical and profound, and yet there was something damnably familiar about the new writing. It had crabbed and archaic tendencies of a very curious sort, and seemed to result from a type of stroke utterly different from that which the youth had always used.

H. P. Lovecraft, *The Case of Charles Dexter Ward* (1927)

The sheets were obviously from a long letter, written in a crabbed hand, and with some of the most awkward sentences imaginable.

August Derleth, "Beyond the Threshold" (1941)

"Among my Uncle Amos's papers there are many fearsome names written in his crabbed script: *Great Cthulhu, the Lake of Hali, Tsathoggua, Yog-Sothoth, Nyarlathotep, Azathoth, Hastur the Unspeakable, Yuggoth, Aldones, Thale, Aldebaran, the Hyades, Carcosa*, and others: and it is possible to divide some of those names into vaguely suggestive classes from those notes which are explicable to me—though many present insoluble mysteries I cannot hope as yet to penetrate; and many, too, are written in a language I do not know, together with cryptic and oddly frightening symbols and signs."

August Derleth, "The Return of Hastur" (1939) in *The Mask of Cthulhu*

He had reached almost his nadir of disappointment when he chanced upon a document penned in a crabbed hand, and only in part legible, which bore the arresting heading, *Of Evill Sorceries done in New-England of Dæmons in no Humane Shape.*

August Derleth (as H. P. Lovecraft & August Derleth),
The Lurker at the Threshold (1945)

"Those crabbed letters are devilish hard to read," said the red-haired wench, frowning.

Fritz Leiber, "Thieves' House" (1943)

On the wall above a leaden tablet displayed a set of crabbed black characters which altered as she watched: a remarkable object indeed!

Jack Vance, *Lyonesse: Suldrun's Garden* (1983)

The ink was much fresher and of a far poorer quality than the thick, rusted ink in the bulk of the book; on close inspection he would have said that it was of a modern manufacture and written quite recently, were it not for the fact it was in the same crabbed, late seventeenth-century handwriting.

Margaret Irwin, "The Book" (1935)

But now the desk was piled with books: fat tomes of geology, astrology and demonology, and one thin notebook lying open to pages closely written in Han's crabbed hand with the cryptic hieroglyphs he reserved for recording his most private thoughts.

> Gary Myers, "The Last Night of Earth" (1995)

crustaceous, *adj.* Of, pertaining to, or resembling a crustacean or crustaceans.

They were pinkish things about five feet long; with crustaceous bodies bearing vast pairs of dorsal fins or membraneous wings and several sets of articulated limbs, and with a sort of convoluted ellipsoid, covered with multitudes of very short antennæ, where a head would ordinarily be.

> H. P. Lovecraft, "The Whisperer in Darkness" (1930)

cutting, *n.* An article or picture cut from a newspaper or magazine. [Chiefly British.]

Usage: Many fantasy and weird fiction writers have preferred this term over the American usage *clipping.*

I have said my attention was attracted by an account of the death of a well-known airman. I have not the habit of preserving cuttings, I am sorry to say, so that I cannot be precise as to the date of this event.

> Arthur Machen, *The Terror* (1916)

Is it any matter for wonder that such a people had produced a Fu-Manchu? I pasted the cutting into a scrap-book, determined that, if I lived to publish my account of those days, I would quote it therein as casting a sidelight upon Chinese character.

> Sax Rohmer (Arthur Sarsfield Ward),
> *The Mystery of Dr. Fu-Manchu* (1913; aka *The Insidious Dr. Fu-Manchu*)

The press cuttings, as I have intimated, touched on cases of panic, mania, and eccentricity during the given period. Professor Angell must have employed a cutting bureau, for the number of extracts was tremendous and the sources scattered throughout the globe.

> H. P. Lovecraft, "The Call of Cthulhu" (1926)

Moved by some vague presentiment amidst the horrors of that period, Willett arranged with an international press-cutting bureau for accounts of notable current crimes and accidents in Prague and in eastern Transylvania; and after six months believed that he had found two very significant things amongst the multifarious items he received and had translated.

> H. P. Lovecraft, *The Case of Charles Dexter Ward* (1927)

The tales thus brought to my notice came mostly through newspaper cuttings; though one yarn had an oral source and was repeated to a friend of mine in a letter from his mother in Hardwick, Vermont.

> H. P. Lovecraft, "The Whisperer in Darkness" (1930)

"Why," replied my colleague, "that wretched press-cutting agency to which we made a subscription about a year ago has at last sent us something really useful—which saves us the trouble of wading through the columns of politics and other ignorant rubbish written by reporters."

M. P. Dare, "The Demoniac Goat" (1947)

"Ah . . . reading magazines under the table as well?" Snape added, snatching up the copy of *Witch Weekly*. "A further ten points from Gryffindor . . . oh but of course . . ." Snape's black eyes glittered as they fell on Rita Skeeter's article. "Potter has to keep up with his press cuttings. . . ."

J. K. Rowling, *Harry Potter and the Goblet of Fire* (2000; ellipses in original)

Cyclopean, cyclopean, Cyclopian, Cyclopæan, cyclopæan, *adj.* [< L *Cyclopēus, Cyclōpius* < Cyclōps (root: *Cyclōp-*) < Gr *Kýklōps*, circle + eye] Of, pertaining to, or resembling a Cyclops (or one-eyed giant) in any manner, as, for example, having a single eye. In particular, from the 19th century on, constructed in the manner of certain prehistoric ruins which the Classical Greeks believed had been built by the Cyclopes. The Cyclopean style uses stones of immense size, which are shaped to fit together without mortar. Apart from Greece, examples exist in various parts of the world including China, Japan, Peru, Ireland, and Micronesia. In a generalized sense, huge, enormous, gigantic, Gargantuan, Titanic. [The form Cyclopæan not in *OED;* Marlowe antedates the *OED's* first citation by about fifty years.]

Titles: Richard Shaver, "The Cyclopeans"

Usage: Most properly, the word should be capitalized, spelt Cyclopean, and the primary accent should fall on the third syllable.

> The flagging winds forsook us, with the sun;
> And, wearied, on Cyclopian shores we run.
>
> Virgil (trans. John Dryden), *Æneid*

> Our quivering lances shaking in the air
> And bullets like Jove's dreadful thunderbolts,
> Enrolled in flames and fiery smoldering mists,
> Shall threat the gods more than Cyclopian wars;
> And with our sun-bright armor, as we march
> We'll chase the stars from heaven and dim their eyes
> That stand and muse at our admirèd arms.
>
> Christopher Marlowe, *Tamburlaine the Great* (1590)

> And there are times when burning memory flows
> In on the mind, that saving it would slay,
> As did the lava-floods which choked yore

The Cyclopean cities—brimming up
Brasslike their mighty moulds.

Philip James Bailey, *Festus: A Poem* (1838)

Then it fluttered up, and perched on a bough of the old oak, from the deep labyrinth of whose branches the other birds had emerged; and from thence it flew down and lighted on the broad druidic stone, that stood like a cyclopean table on its sunken stone props, before the snakelike roots of the oak.

J. S. LeFanu, "The Haunted Baronet" (1870)

There was a striking resemblance between the architecture of the Peruvians and that of some of the nations of the Old World. It is enough for me to quote Mr. Ferguson's words, that the coincidence between the buildings of the Incas and the Cyclopean remains attributed to the Pelasgians in Italy and Greece, "is the most remarkable in the history of architecture."

Ignatius Donnelly, *Atlantis: The Antediluvian World* (1882)

The oldest remains of Cyclopean buildings were all the handiwork of the Lemurians of the last sub-races; and an occultist shows, therefore, no wonder on learning that the stone relics found on the small piece of land called Easter Island by Captain Cook, are "very much like the walls of the Temple of Pachacamac or the Ruins of Tia-Huanuco in Peru," ("*The Countries of the World*," *by Robert Brown, Vol. 4, p. 43*); and that they are in the CYCLOPEAN STYLE.

H. P. Blavatsky, *The Secret Doctrine:
The Synthesis of Science, Religion, and Philosophy* (1888)

Many harbours were successfully carried out: one, the harbour of Wick, the chief disaster of my father's life, was a failure; the sea proved too strong for man's arts; and after expedients hitherto unthought of, and on a scale hyper-cyclopean, the work must be deserted, and now stands a ruin in that bleak, God-forsaken bay, ten miles from John-o'-Groat's.

Robert Louis Stevenson, "Thomas Stevenson"

Heartless and hopeless I struggled on over the blasted and forbidding plain, and still the mighty structure grew until I could no longer compass it with a look, and its towers shut out the stars directly overhead; then I passed in at an open portal, between columns of cyclopean masonry whose single stones were larger than my father's house.

Ambrose Bierce, "Visions of the Night" (1887)

There were Cyclopean turbines athwart the mountain torrents and long, low, many windowed buildings that might serve some industrial purpose.

H. G. Wells, *Men Like Gods* (1923)

But she would dream of warmer gems, and so
Ere long her eyes in fastnesses look forth
O'er blue profounds mysterious whence glow
The coals of Tartarus on the moonless air,
As Titans plan to storm Olympus' throne,
'Mid pulse of dungeoned forges down the stunned,
Undominated firmament, and glare
Of Cyclopean furnaces unsunned.

George Sterling, "A Wine of Wizardry" (1907)

So that something preserves me: Something, Someone: *and for what?* . . . If I had slept in the cabin, I must most certainly have perished: for, stretched there on the chair, I dreamed a dream which once I had dreamed in snows yonder in the beyond of that hyperborean North: that I was in an Arab paradise; and I had a protracted vision of it, for I reached up amid the trees, and picked the peaches, and pressed the blossoms to my nostrils with breathless inhalations of fondness: until a sickness woke me, and when I opened my eyes the night was gloomy, the moon down, everything drenched with dew, the sky a jungle lush with stars, bazaar of maharajahs tiaraed, begums arrayed in garish trains, and all the air informed with that mortal afflatus; and high and wide uplifted before my sight—stretching from the northern to the southern limit—a row of eight or nine smokes, inflamed as from the chimneys of some Cyclopean forge which goes all night, most solemn, most great and dreadful in the solemn night: eight or nine, I should say, or it may be seven, or it may be ten, for I did not reckon them; and from those craters puffed up gusts of encrimsoned stuff, there a gust and there a gust, with tinselled fumes that convolved upon themselves, glittering with troops of sparks and flashes, all in a garish haze of glare: for the foundry was going, though languidly; and upon a land of rock four knots ahead, which no chart had ever marked, the *Speranza* drove straight with the sweep of the phosphorus sea.

M. P. Shiel, *The Purple Cloud* (1901; ellipsis in original)

Even as, to a climber, the mere vastness of the mountain becomes, as he goes higher, a presence, unite and palpable, built up of successive vastness of slabbed rock-face, vertiginous ice-cliff, eye-dazzling expanse of snow-field, up-soaring ultimate cornice chiselled by the wind to a sculptured perfection of line, sun-bright and remote against an infinite remoteness of blue heaven above it, so here was all gathered to an immobility of time-worn and storied magnificence: cyclopæan walls and gateways; flights of stairs six riders abreast might ride down on horseback and not touch knees; galleries, alcoves and clerestories cut from the rock; perspectives flattening the eye down distances of corbel and frieze and deep-mullioned windows six times the height of a man; colonnades with doric capitals curiously carved, supporting huge-timbered vaulted roofs; and domed roofs that seemed wide as the arch of day.

E. R. Eddison, *The Mezentian Gate* (1941–45)

And surmounting a higher ledge beyond this upthrust a huge dome of dull gold, Cyclopean, striking eyes and mind with something inhumanly alien, baffling; sending the mind groping, as though across the deserts of space, from some far-flung star, should fall upon us linked sounds, coherent certainly, meaningful surely, vaguely familiar—yet never to be translated into any symbol or thought of our own particular planet.

A. Merritt, *The Moon Pool* (1919)

The misty-edged circle had become an oval, a flattened ellipse another five hundred feet high and three times that in length. And in its exact center, shining forth as though it opened into a place of pale azure incandescene was a Cyclopean portal, rectangular, to which the huge megalithic gateway of that mysterious race whose fanes were time-worn before the Incas learned to build upon them were but doorways for pygmies!

A. Merritt, *The Metal Monster* (1920)

He looked out over a grass-covered plain strewn with huge, isolated rocks rising from the green like menhirs of the Druids. There were no trees. The plain was dish-shaped; an enormous oval as symmetrical as though it had been molded by the thumb of some Cyclopean potter.

A. Merritt, *The Face in the Abyss* (1923)

Across the chasm, the wavelets washed the base of the Cyclopean monolith; on whose surface I could now trace both inscriptions and crude sculptures.

H. P. Lovecraft, "Dagon" (1917)

With Cyclopean rage it tore through the soil above that damnable pit, blinding and deafening me, yet not wholly reducing me to a coma.

H. P. Lovecraft, "The Lurking Fear" (1922)

My coming to New York had been a mistake; for whereas I had looked for poignant wonder and inspiration in the teeming labyrinths of ancient streets that twist endlessly from forgotten courts and squares and waterfronts to courts and squares and waterfronts equally forgotten, and in the Cyclopean modern towers and pinnacles that rise blackly Babylonian under waning moons, I had found instead only a sense of horror and oppression which threatened to master, paralyse, and annihilate me.

H. P. Lovecraft, "He" (1925)

Upon retiring, he had had an unprecedented dream of great Cyclopean cities of titan blocks and sky-flung monoliths, all dripping with green ooze and sinister with latent horror.

H. P. Lovecraft, "The Call of Cthulhu" (1926)

Old Castro remembered bits of hideous legend that paled the speculations of theosophists and made man and the world seem recent and transient indeed. There had been æons when other Things ruled on the earth, and They had had great cities. Remains of Them, he said the deathless Chinamen had told him, were still to be found as Cyclopean stones on islands in the Pacific.

H. P. Lovecraft, "The Call of Cthulhu" (1926)

Randolph Carter's advance through that Cyclopean bulk of abnormal masonry was like a dizzy precipitation through the measureless gulfs between the stars.

H. P. Lovecraft & E. Hoffmann Price,
"Through the Gates of the Silver Key" (1932–33)

From below no sound came, but only a distant, undefinable fœtor; and it is not to be wondered at that the men preferred to stay on the edge and argue, rather than descend and beard the unknown Cyclopean horror in its lair.

H. P. Lovecraft, "The Dunwich Horror" (1928)

"To visit Yuggoth would drive any weak man mad—yet I am going there. The black rivers of pitch that flow under those mysterious Cyclopean bridges— things built by some elder race extinct and forgotten before the beings came to Yuggoth from the ultimate voids—ought to be enough to make any man a Dante or Poe if he can keep sane long enough to tell what he has seen."

H. P. Lovecraft, "The Whisperer in Darkness" (1930)

He talked about terrible meetings in lonely places, of Cyclopean ruins in the heart of the Maine woods beneath which vast staircases lead down to abysses of nighted secrets, of complex angles that lead through invisible walls to other re- gions of space and time, and of hideous exchanges of personality that permitted explorations in remote and forbidden places, on other worlds, and in different space-time continua.

H. P. Lovecraft, "The Thing on the Doorstep" (1933)

Great watery spaces opened out before me, and I seemed to wander through ti- tanic sunken porticos and labyrinths of weedy Cyclopean walls with grotesque fishes as my companions.

H. P. Lovecraft, "The Shadow over Innsmouth" (1931)

We shall swim out to that brooding reef in the sea and dive down through black abysses to Cyclopean and many-columned Y'ha-nthlei, and in that lair of the Deep Ones we shall dwell amidst wonder and glory for ever.

H. P. Lovecraft, "The Shadow over Innsmouth" (1931)

Later I had visions of sweeping through Cyclopean corridors of stone, and up and down gigantic inclined planes of the same monstrous masonry.

H. P. Lovecraft, "The Shadow out of Time" (1935)

Here and there I saw, half-shrouded by the sand, those primal Cyclopean blocks left from nameless and forgotten æons.

H. P. Lovecraft, "The Shadow out of Time" (1935)

A rain of curious javelins struck the galley as the prow hit the wharf, felling two ghouls and slightly wounding another; but at this point all the hatches were thrown open to emit a black cloud of whirring night-gaunts which swarmed over the town like a flock of horned and Cyclopean bats.

H. P. Lovecraft, *The Dream-Quest of Unknown Kadath* (1927)

Suddenly through the open window came the sound of a deep, hideous chuckle, and the flames of the burning clinic took fresh contours till they half resembled some nameless, Cyclopean creatures of nightmare.

H. P. Lovecraft & Adolphe de Castro, "The Last Test" (1927)

Among the scattered rubble were massive stones of manifestly artificial shaping, and a little examination disclosed the presence of some of that prehistoric Cyclopean masonry found on certain Pacific islands and forming a perpetual archæological puzzle.

H. P. Lovecraft & Hazel Heald, "Out of the Æons" (1933)

This preternatural landscape was appallingly distinct in every detail, under a greenish-black sky that was over-arched from end to end with a triple cyclopean ring of dazzling luminosity.

Clark Ashton Smith, "The Door to Saturn" (1930)

Fearfully, as one who confronts an apparition reared up from nether hell, Gaspard beheld the colossus that lay inert as if in Cyclopean sleep on the castle flags. The thing was no longer a skeleton: the limbs were rounded into bossed, enormous thews, like the limbs of Biblical giants; the flanks were like an insuperable wall; the deltoids of the mighty chest were broad as platforms; the hands could have crushed the bodies of men like millstones. . . . *But the face of the stupendous monster, seen in profile athwart the pouring moon, was the face of the Satanic dwarf, Nathaire—remagnified a hundred times, but the same in its implacable madness and malevolence!*

Clark Ashton Smith, "The Colossus of Ylourgne" (1932; ellipsis in original)

Geologists deny it a volcanic origin; yet its outcroppings of rough, nodular stone and enormous rubble heaps have all the air of scoriac remains—at least, to my non-scientific eye. They look like the slag and refuse of Cyclopean furnaces, poured out in prehuman years, to cool and harden into shapes of limitless grotesquerie.

Clark Ashton Smith, "The City of the Singing Flame" (1931)

He was standing on a road paven with cyclopean blocks of gray stone—a road that ran interminably before him into the vague, tremendous vistas of an inconceivable world.

Clark Ashton Smith, "The Planet of the Dead" (1930;
aka "The Doom of Antarion")

Mounting the marble steps, the jewelers entered a vast, roofless hall where cyclopean columns towered as if to bear up the desert sky.

Clark Ashton Smith, "The Tomb-Spawn" (1933)

Well, it seemed there was no place to land in that interminable bristling wilderness of cyclopean growths.

Clark Ashton Smith, "The Immeasurable Horror" (1930)

It was smaller but nearer than the igneous orb of history and legend. In its center, like a Cyclopean eye, there burned a single spot of dusky red fire, believed the mark the eruption of some immense volcano amid the measureless and cinder-blackened landscape.

Clark Ashton Smith, "Phœnix" (1953)

From out the everlasting womb sublime
Of cyclopean death, within a land
Of tombs and cities rotting the sun,
He is reborn to mock the might of time,
While kings have built against Oblivion
With walls and columns of the windy sand.

Clark Ashton Smith, "The Mummy" (1919)

The brazen empire of the bournless waste,
The unstayed dominions of the brazen sky—
These I desire, and all things wide and deep;
And, lifted past the level years, would taste
The cup of an Olympian ecstasy,
Titanic dream, and Cyclopean sleep.

Clark Ashton Smith, "Desire of Vastness"

I came to the cliffs and was somewhat disquieted to note that the illusive moonlight lent them a subtle appearance I had not noticed before—in the weird light they appeared less like natural cliffs and more like the ruins of cyclopean and Titan-reared battlements jutting from the mountain-slope.

Robert E. Howard, "The Black Stone" (1931)

As in twilight shadow I saw the ruined temple, cyclopean walls staggering up from masses of decaying masonry and fallen blocks of stone.

Robert E. Howard, "The Valley of the Worm"

"I could tell you things that would shatter your paltry brain! I could breathe into your ear names that would wither you like a burnt weed! What do you know of Yog-Sothoth, of Kathulos and the sunken cities? None of these names is even included in your mythologies. Not even in your dreams have you glimpsed the black cyclopean walls of Koth, or shriveled before the noxious winds that blow from Yuggoth!"

Robert E. Howard, "Dig Me No Grave"

To the resounding background of sea and wind that beat upon barren Easter Island, Graham started out in early morning and walked along the giants' memorial graveyard. The cyclopean monuments and statues seemed inordinately oppressive; their very presence was a burden that overcast his thoughts.

Donald Wandrei, *The Web of Easter Island* (1929–31)

The window goes blond slowly. Frostily clears.
From Cyclopean towers across Manhattan waters
—Two—three bright window-eyes aglitter, disk
The sun, released—aloft with cold gulls hither.

Hart Crane, *The Bridge* (1930)

In the gloom they could see nothing save faintly visible terraces of stone, like cyclopean steps on the mountainside, sheer expanses of white granite walls, and beyond, the black bulk of the mountain.

Lloyd Arthur Eshbach, "The City of Dread"

To one side a higher heap of stone, which was all that was left of the western wall, obstructed his view of what lay beyond. Over the fallen blocks before him he could see a vast paved square dotted with other buildings fallen into ruin. And beyond these, under a heavily clouded sky through which the obscured sun poured in a queer, grayly radiant light, buildings of barbaric colors and utterly alien architecture lifted their Cyclopean heights, massive as the walls of Karnak, but too strangely constructed to awake any memories.

C. L. Moore, "Tryst in Time" (1936)

Blazing white light blinded him. He had a flashing, indistinct vision of tremendous forces, leashed, cyclopean, straining mightily to burst the bonds that held them.

Henry Kuttner, "Spawn of Dagon" (1938)

I seemed to be standing in a vast amphitheater of jet, and around me, towering to a sky sprinkled with an infinite multitude of cold stars, I could see a colossal and shocking city of scalene black towers and fortresses, of great masses of stone and metal, arching bridges and cyclopean ruins. And with racking horror I saw teeming loathsomely in that nightmare city the spawn of that alien dimension.

Henry Kuttner, "The Invaders" (1939)

So in blind and trembling haste I chanted the obscure litany and performed the necessary obeisances demanded in the ritual I had learned, and at their conclusion the cyclopean portal swung open.

Robert Bloch, "The Secret in the Tomb" (1934)

Damn the heat! Sand all around him. Hills of it, mountains. All alike they were, like the crumbled, cyclopean ruins of titan cities. All were burning, smoldering in the fierce heat.

Robert Bloch, "The Faceless God" (1936)

Those forms—they were spawned only in delirium; only in nightmares and dreams of the Pit. There were grinning demons that skulked on padding claws across that endless moving plain; there were shapeless toadstools with tentacles ending in Cyclopean eyes; there were fanged heads that rolled towards me, laughing; great hands that curled and crawled like mad spiders. Ghouls, monsters, fiends—the words sprang to my consciousness. And a moment ago they had been mathematical figures!

Robert Bloch, "The Sorcerer's Jewel" (1939)

And I went into the sunset with Her sign, and into the night past accursed and desolate places and cyclopean ruins, and so came at last to the City of Chorazin. And there a great tower of Black Basalt was raised, that was part of a castle whose further battlements reeled over the gulf of stars.

Jack Parsons, *The Book of Antichrist* (1949)

Beyond this meadow to my certain knowledge a path, then a field and finally the ramparts, closing the prospect. Cyclopean and crenellated, standing out faintly against a sky scarcely less sombre, they did not seem in ruins, viewed from mine, but were, to my certain knowledge.

Samuel Beckett, "The Calmative" (1946)

He undressed and, after carefully laying his pants between the mattress and springs for pressing, fell asleep and began to dream his familiar dreams of vertiginous geometries and cyclopean half-gods, vivid dreams which would have been anyone else's sweat-drenched nightmares.

Fred Chappell, "Weird Tales" (1984)

What was most striking was that these "cyclopean cities" of the great old ones (not the polypus race, which they replaced) fitted what we now knew of our own underground city. According to Lovecraft, these cities had no stairs, only inclined planes, for their inhabitants were huge, cone-like creatures with tentacles; the base of the cone was "fringed with a rubbery grey substance, which moved the whole entity through expansion and contraction". The probe had revealed that this city below Karatepe had many inclined planes, but apparently no stairs. And its size certainly merited the adjective "cyclopean".

Colin Wilson, *The Mind Parasites* (1966)

I thought of those great underground cities, described by Lovecraft, cities with "cyclopean blocks" of masonry and huge inclined planes.

Colin Wilson, *The Philosopher's Stone* (1967–68)

K'tholo was one of the few men who ever their underground cities—the Old Ones built underground, because they knew that man would eventually penetrate to every corner of the earth. And what impressed me most when I "saw" these cities was the accuracy of Lovecraft's time-vision. For he had described them very much as they were—and as they still exist, miles below the surface of the earth. These cities were built of immense stone blocks—Lovecraft speaks of them as "cyclopean". It was easier for the Old Ones to handle huge blocks than small ones, so their buildings were somtimes a mile high.

Colin Wilson, *The Philosopher's Stone* (1967–68)

They all said it was genuine. But they could not say where the thing had come from. It was, however, native to the planet: thirty feet in height, Cyclopean, as hard as rhinoceros horn . . . but human.

Harlan Ellison, "On the Slab" (1981)

I was stiff and sore and tired from a night of driving. The only rest I'd gotten was fitful dozing in which cyclopean ruby eyes looked at me till I awoke in terror.

Robert Shea & Robert Anton Wilson, *The Illuminatus! Trilogy* (1969–71)

00005, in fact, was in an enormous marbled room deliberately designed to impress the bejesus out of any and all visitors. Pillars reached up to cyclopean heights, supporting a ceiling too high and murky to be visible, and every wall, of which there seemed to be five, was the same impenetrable ivory-grained marble.

Robert Shea & Robert Anton Wilson, *The Illuminatus! Trilogy* (1969–71)

The Novelist was working on a huge, Cyclopean sword-and-sorcery epic set in 18th-century Europe, full of duels and seductions and revolutions and a cast that included such egregious gentry as Napoleon and the Marquis de Sade.

Robert Anton Wilson, "The Persecution and Assassination of the Parapsychologists as Performed by the Inmates of the American Association for the Advancement of Science under the Direction of the Amazing Randi" (1980)

This is how the broadcast ended: "Mists are clearing—something big towering up dead ahead—is it a mountain range? No, the shapes are too regular. My God! It can't be! It's a city! Great tiers of terraced towers built of black stone—rivers of pitch that flow under cyclopean bridges, a dark world of fungoid gardens and windowless cities—an unknown world of fungous life—forbidden Yuggoth!"

James Wade, "Planetfall on Yuggoth" (1972)

Phipps then disappeared under the bridge, and through his continued chanting rang the sound of metal scraping on stone. Upon this sound came a subterranean commotion, with a rising chorus of voiceless croaking and a sound as if of Cyclopean bodies slithering against one another in some charnel pit, with a nauseating rise of that alien reptilian odor.

Ramsey Campbell, "The Horror from the Bridge" (1964)

"And what of the poisoned waste, Elwood? From beneath the cyclopean walls of our scores of power plants . . ."

Bruce Sterling, "The Unthinkable" (1991; ellipsis in original)

He told of Cyclopean ruins in the heart of the Maine woods, beneath which stone staircases lead down to abysses of antehuman secrets.

Harry S. Robbins, "The Smoker from the Shadows" (1990)

Subterranean regions of the continent excavated in cyclopæan caverns, cathedralspace fractal networks, labyrinthine gargantuan tunnels, slow black underground rivers, unmoving stygian lakes, pure & slightly luminiferous, slim waterfalls plunging down watersmooth rock, cataracting round petrified forests of stalactites & stalagmites in spelunker-bewildering blind-fish complexity & unfathomable vastness . . .

Hakim Bey (Peter Lamborn Wilson), "Hollow Earth" in *T.A.Z.:*
The Temporary Autonomous Zone, Ontological Anarchy, Poetic Terrorism (ellipsis in original)

Saxon closed his eyes as if that would somehow shut out the sound, and for a moment had a vision of great cyclopean cities and sky-flung monoliths all dripping green ooze and covered with hieroglyphics. From some undetermined source came a voice that was not really a voice but more a chaotic sensation uttering the gibberish *"Cthulhu fhtagn."*

Michael Slade, *Ghoul* (1987)

He gazed at the cyclopean thing in a trance of horror, until its mountainous mass began to move, slowly stretching out some part of itself, flexing what might have been a misshapen arm.

Thomas Ligotti, "The Prodigy of Dreams"

D

dæmon, demon, *n.* [< L *dæmōn* (Mediæval Latin *dēmōn*) & *dæmonium* < Gr *daímôn* & *daimónion*] Any spirit, whether good or evil, of a nature between that of men and the gods; in particular, the tutelary attendant spirit of an individual, corresponding to the Holy Guardian Angel, Genius, or Higher Self.

Titles: "The Dæmon Lover" (traditional ballad); Clark Ashton Smith, "To the Dæmon of Sublimity" (verse), "To the Dæmon"; Elizabeth Bowen, "The Demon Lover"; C. L. Moore, "Dæmon"; Shirley Jackson, "The Dæmon Lover"; Lin Carter, "The Dream-Dæmon" in *Dreams from R'lyeh* (verse)

"Socrates affirmeth that his *dæmon* did oftentimes talk with him, and that he saw him and felt him many times."

> Thomas Nashe, *Pierce Penniless his Supplication to the Devil* (1592)

> Therefore (oh *Antony*) stay not by his side
> Thy Dæmon that's thy spirit which keepes thee, is
> Noble, Couragious, high vnmatchable,
> Where *Caesars* is not. But neere him, thy Angell
> Becomes a feare: as being o're-powr'd, therefore
> Make space enough betweene you.

> William Shakespeare, *Antony and Cleopatra* (160-)

How much nobler, if he had resisted the temptation of that *Gothic Dæmon*, which modern Poesy tasting, became mortal?

> Edward Young, *Conjectures on Original Composition* (1759)

The soul which was to be emancipated was the divine emanation, the vital spark of heavenly flame, the principle of reason and perception, which was personified into the familiar dæmon, or genius, supposed to have the direction of each individual, and to dispose him to good or evil, wisdom or folly, and all their consequences of prosperity and adversity.

> Richard Payne Knight, *A Discourse on the Worship of Priapus and Its Connection with the Mystic Theology of the Ancients* (1786)

But the question which introduces his name into this volume is that of what is called the demon of Socrates. He said that he repeatedly received a divine premonition of dangers impending over himself and others; and considerable pains have been taken to ascertain the cause and author of these premonitions. Several persons, among whom we may include Plato, have conceived that Socrates re-

181

garded himself as attended by a supernatural guardian, who at all times watched over his welfare and concerns.

> William Godwin, *Lives of the Necromancers; or, An Account of the Most Eminent Persons in Successive Ages Who Have Claimed for Themselves, or to Whom Has Been Imputed by Others, the Exercise of Magical Power* (1834)

> But oh! that deep romantic chasm which slanted
> Down the green hill athwart a cedarn cover!
> A savage place! as holy and enchanted
> As e'er beneath a waning moon was haunted
> By woman wailing for her demon-lover!

> S. T. Coleridge, "Kubla Khan; or, A Vision in a Dream: A Fragment" (1797)

These incidents, for a time, occupied all our thoughts. In me they produced a sentiment not unallied to pleasure, and more speedily than in the case of my friends were intermixed with other topics. My brother was particularly affected by them. It was easy to perceive that most of his meditations were tinctured from this source. To this was to be ascribed a design in which his pen was, at this period, engaged, of collecting and investigating the facts which relate to that mysterious personage, the Dæmon of Socrates.

> Charles Brockden Brown, *Wieland; or, The Transformation: An American Tale* (1798)

"And thou knowest he thought much of heathen and Egyptian conjuration; but that is not my secret. Plato and Socrates had their attendant demons. I have seen, it may be, such a one in a dream last night. Methought there stood by me in an oratory a woman of queen-like beauty and strange beauty. She shewed me, as it were beyond a mist, a green tree growing near a fountain, and the star that shone on that fountain was the brightest in the sky; but presently the tree grew wide and broad, and the light of the star set behind it."

> William Child Green, "Secrets of Cabalism; or, Ravenstone and Alice of Huntingdon" (1809)

Over everything stands its dæmon, or soul, and, as the form of the thing is reflected by the eye, so the soul of the thing is reflected by a melody.

> Ralph Waldo Emerson, "The Poet"

The misery of man is to be baulked of the sight of essence, and to be stuffed with conjectures: but the supreme good is reality; the supreme beauty is reality; and all virtue and all felicity depend on this science of the real: for courage is nothing else than knowledge: the fairest fortune that can befall man, is to be guided by his dæmon to that which is truly his own.

> Ralph Waldo Emerson, *Representative Men*

The dæmons, according to this theory, are intermediate beings between the divine perfection and human sinfulness, and he divides them into classes, each subdivided into many others. But he states expressly that the individual or personal soul is the leading guardian dæmon of every man, and that no dæmon has more power over us than our own. Thus the *Daimonion* of Socrates is the god or Divine Entity which inspired him all his life. It depends on man either to open or close his perceptions to the Divine voice.

H. P. Blavatsky, *Isis Unveiled: A Master-Key to the Mysteries of Ancient and Modern Science and Theology* (1877)

DÆMONS.—A name given by the ancient people, and especially the philosophers of the Alexandrian school, to all kinds of spirits, whether good or bad, human or otherwise. The appellation is often synonymous with that of gods or angels. But some philosophers tried, with good reason, to make a just distinction between the many classes.

H. P. Blavatsky, *Isis Unveiled: A Master-Key to the Mysteries of Ancient and Modern Science and Theology* (1877)

"My guardian, my tutelary dæmon," he exclaimed, "visible manifestation of Æsculapius! Then I am not forsaken by the immortal gods."

Richard Garnett, "The City of Philosophers" (1888)

"Yes, that is the Demon of Socrates," the Friar from Oxford rumbled above his cup.

Rudyard Kipling, "The Eye of Allah"

"That's true, Mr.—Mr.—Demon," said the boy. "Excuse me if I don't get your name right, but I understood you to say you are a demon."

"Certainly. The Demon of Electricity."

"But electricity is a good thing, you know, and—and—"

"Well?"

"I've always understood that demons were bad things," added Rob, boldly.

"Not necessarily," returned his visitor. "If you will take the trouble to consult your dictionary, you will find that demons may be either good or bad, like any other class of beings. Originally all demons were good, yet of late years people have come to consider all demons evil. I do not know why. Should you read Hesiod you will find he says:

> *Soon was a world of holy demons made,*
> *Aerial spirits, by great Jove designed*
> *To be on earth the guardians of mankind."*

"But Jove was himself a myth," objected Rob, who had been studying mythology.

The Demon shrugged his shoulders.

"Then take the words of Mr. Shakespeare, to whom you all defer," he replied. "Do you not remember that he says:

> *Thy demon (that's thy spirit which keeps thee) is*
> *Noble, courageous, high, unmatchable.*"

"Oh, if Shakespeare says it, that's all right," answered the boy. "But it seems you're more like a genie, for you answer the summons of the Master Key of Electricity in the same way Aladdin's genie answered the rubbing of the lamp."

"To be sure. A demon is also a genie; and a genie is a demon," said the Being. "What matters a name? I am here to do your bidding."

L. Frank Baum, The Master Key: An Electrical Fairy Tale (1901)

Because he has lent himself the more innocently to the whispers of his subconscious dæmon, and because he has set those murmurs to purer and harder crystal than we others, by so much the longer will the poems of Clark Ashton Smith endure. Here indeed is loot against the forays of moth and rust.

George Sterling, Preface to Clark Ashton Smith, Ebony and Crystal (1922)

The knowledge suffices me (as I patiently explain over and yet over again to that ever-impatient flag) that I have never written about contemporary life because—for a reason, or for a concatenation of reasons, as to which I remain contentedly ignorant—that dæmon who in some sort both serves and controls my endless typing does not wish me to write about contemporary life.

Branch Cabell, These Restless Heads: A Trilogy of Romantics (1931)

Instead of the hillside tomb, it was the charred cellar on the crest of the slope whose presiding dæmon beckoned to me with unseen fingers.

H. P. Lovecraft, "The Tomb" (1917)

"I have seen beyond the bounds of infinity and drawn down dæmons from the stars. . . . I have harnessed the shadows that stride from world to world to sow death and madness. . . . Space belongs to me, do you hear?"

H. P. Lovecraft, "From Beyond" (1920; ellipses in original)

The Genie that haunts the moonbeams spake to the Dæmon of the Valley, saying, "I am old, and forget much. Tell me the deeds and aspect and name of them who built these things of stone."

H. P. Lovecraft, "Memory" (1919)

"I am His Messenger," the dæmon said,
As in contempt he struck his Master's head.

H. P. Lovecraft, "Azathoth" in Fungi from Yuggoth (1929–30)

I too intend to write some memorial verses which will evoke something of his daily life and surroundings together with the imagery and atmosphere of his literary work. It seems better, however, to wait a little for the required energy and inspiration which the Dæmon will supply presently.

Clark Ashton Smith, letter to August Derleth (30 March 1937)

The volume, selected at random, was not one calculated to rid my mind of haunting shadows. It was the extremely rare Düsseldorf edition of Von Junzt's *Nameless Cults*, called the Black Book, not because of its iron-clasped leather bindings, but because of its dark contents. Opening the volume at random, I began idly to read the chapter on the summoning of dæmons out of the Void. More than ever I sensed a deep and sinister wisdom behind the author's incredible assertions as I read of the unseen worlds of unholy dimensions which Von Junzt maintains press, horrific and dimly guessed, on our universe, and of the blasphemous inhabitants of those Outer Worlds, which he maintains at times burst terribly through the Veil at the bidding of evil sorcerers to blast the brains and feast on the blood of men.

Robert E. Howard, "The Hoofed Thing" (1932)

The captain's name was Jonah Stryker. He was a cruel man, dangerous to be near. The men hated him. They were at his mercy while we were at sea, and the captain was at the mercy of his dæmon. That was why I could not hate him as the others did.

C. L. Moore, "Dæmon" (1946)

dæmoniac, demoniac, *adj.* Of, pertaining to, or resembling a dæmon or demon; in particular, suggesting or resembling possession by a dæmon or demon; and in especial, characterized by a berserk, murderous frenzy, as if possessed by a dæmon or demon.

Titles: M. P. Dare, "The Demoniac Goat"

Often at midnight was she waked by the dismal shrieks of demoniac rage, or of excruciating despair, uttered in such wild tones of indescribable anguish as proved the total absence of reason, and roused phantoms of horror in her mind, far more terrific than all that dreaming superstition ever drew.

Mary Wollstonecraft, *The Wrongs of Woman; or, Maria: A Fragment* (1798)

All round seem'd tranquil—even the foe had ceased,
As if aware of that demoniac feast,
His fiery bolts; and though the heavens look'd red,
'Twas but some distant conflagration's spread.

Thomas Moore, "The Veiled Prophet of Khorassan" in *Lalla Rookh* (1817)

"Great G—d!" exclaimed Stanton, as he recollected the stranger whose demoniac laugh had so appalled him, while gazing on the lifeless bodies of the lovers, whom the lightning had struck and blasted.

Charles Maturin, *Melmoth the Wanderer: A Tale* (1820)

"He, whom he has for twelve hours been vociferating 'is the loveliest among ten thousand,' becomes the object of demoniac hostility and execration. He grapples with the iron posts of his bed, and says he is rooting out the cross from the very foundations of Calvary; and it is remarkable, that in proportion as his morning exercises are intense, vivid, and eloquent, his nightly blasphemies are outrageous and horrible.—Hark! Now he believes himself a demon; listen to his diabolical eloquence of horror!"

Charles Maturin, Melmoth the Wanderer: A Tale (1820)

Custom had banished my fears. In spite of the most painful vigilance, I had never detected the trace of a cloven foot; nor was the studious silence of our abode ever disturbed by demoniac howls.

Mary Shelley, "The Mortal Immortal" (1833)

But for what conceivable purpose had I been subjected as a victim to influences as much beyond my control as the Fate or Demoniac Necessity of a Greek Myth?

Sir Edward Bulwer-Lytton, A Strange Story (1861)

Deathlike the silence seemed, and unbroken, save by the herons
Home to their roosts in the cedar-trees returning at sunset,
Or by the owl, as he greeted the moon with demoniac laughter.

Henry Wadsworth Longfellow, Evangeline (1847)

"Ah, yes, what does the old poet say? Milton, is it?

"'Stab your demoniac smile to my brain,
Soak me in cognac, love, and cocaine.'"

"How silly you are," cried Lou. "Cocaine wasn't invented in the time of Milton."

"Was that Milton's fault?" retorted King Lamus.

Aleister Crowley, The Diary of a Drug Fiend (1922)

Iliel shuddered with the horror of the vision; it was to her a dread unspeakable, yet she was hypnotized and helpless. She felt in herself that one day she too must become the prey of that most dire and demoniac power of darkness.

Aleister Crowley, Moonchild (1917; aka The Butterfly-Net or The Net)

He had thought at first they were all of common stature and costume, with the evident exception of the hairy Gogol. But as he looked at the others, he began to see in each of them exactly what he had seen in the man by the river, a demoniac detail somewhere. That lop-sided laugh, which would suddenly disfigure the fine face of his original guide, was typical of all these types. Each man had something about him, perceived perhaps at the tenth or twentieth glance, which was not normal, and which seemed hardly human.

G. K. Chesterton, The Man Who Was Thursday: A Nightmare (1907)

Then, following chapters of incoherence, words end and drawings fill the pages; sketches of curious-shaped windows, apocryphal beasts, telescopic towers, serpentine designs that formalize into strange temples; a bizarre and tortured ornamentalization growing continually wilder until the unraveling lines become a demoniac pattern, sinister and illegible.

Ben Hecht, The Kingdom of Evil: A Continuation of the
Journal of Fantazius Mallare (1924)

The madness and monstrosity lay in the figures in the foreground—for Pickman's morbid art was preëminently one of dæmoniac portraiture.

H. P. Lovecraft, "Pickman's Model" (1926)

For yards about the steps extended an insane tangle of human bones, or bones at least as human as those on the steps. Like a foamy sea they stretched, some fallen apart, but others wholly or partly articulated as skeletons; these latter invariably in postures of dæmoniac frenzy, either fighting off some menace or clutching other forms with cannibal intent.

H. P. Lovecraft, "The Rats in the Walls" (1923)

By 1760 Joseph Curwen was virtually an outcast, suspected of vague horrors and dæmoniac alliances which seemed all the more menacing because they could not be named, understood, or even proved to exist.

H. P. Lovecraft, The Case of Charles Dexter Ward (1927)

As time went by I turned to architecture and gave up my design of illustrating a book of Edward's dæmoniac poems, yet our comradeship suffered no lessening.

H. P. Lovecraft, "The Thing on the Doorstep" (1933)

From that point forward my impressions are scarcely to be relied on—indeed, I still possess a final, desperate hope that they all form parts of some dæmoniac dream—or illusion born of delirium.

H. P. Lovecraft, "The Shadow out of Time" (1935)

It was the ecstasy of nightmare and the summation of the fiendish. The suddenness of it was apocalyptic and dæmoniac—one moment I was plunging agonizingly down that narrow well of million-toothed torture, yet the next moment I was soaring on bat-wings in the gulfs of hell; swinging free and swoopingly through illimitable miles of boundless, musty space; rising dizzily to measureless pinnacles of chilling ether, then diving gaspingly to sucking nadirs of ravenous, nauseous lower vacua. . . .

H. P. Lovecraft & Harry Houdini, "Under the Pyramids"
(1924; ellipsis in original)

As the old man had proceeded with his story, I had become more and more convinced that he must be telling me the truth, and not merely gibbering in drunkenness. Every detail fitted what Haines had told me. Fear was growing upon me by degrees. With the old wizard now shouting with demoniac laughter, I was tempted to bolt down the narrow stairway and leave that accursed neighborhood.

Wilfred Blanch Talman & H. P. Lovecraft, "Two Black Bottles" (1926)

Dæmoniac clouds, up-pil'd in chasmy reach
Of soundless heav'n, smother'd the brooding night;
Nor voice of autumn wind along the moor,
Nor mutter'd noises of th' insomnious grove
Whose black recesses never saw the sun.

H. P. Lovecraft, "Aletheia Phrikodes" in
"The Poe-et's Nightmare: A Fable" (1916)

The other guard, farther removed from the source of the sound, yet sensed the horror of what was taking place, the grisly threat that lay in that demoniac fifing.

Robert E. Howard, "Red Nails" (1935)

Surely on such nights in past centuries, my whimsical imagination told me, naked witches astride magic broomsticks had flown across this valley, pursued by jeering demoniac familiars.

Robert E. Howard, "The Black Stone" (1931)

Before I could take a half dozen steps a score of barbed spikes would be thrust into my flesh, their avid mouths sucking the flood from my veins to feed their demoniac lust.

Robert E. Howard, "The Garden of Fear"

The idol embodied in its utter, abysmal and sullen bestiality the whole soul of this demoniac city.

Robert E. Howard, "The Fire of Asshurbanipal" (1936)

"I don't know," I answered, "but this I do know—that demoniac lust is no stronger than human hate, and that I will match this blade, which in old days slew witches and warlocks and vampires and werewolves, against the foul legions of Hell itself. Go! Take the dog and run home as fast as you can!"

Robert E. Howard, "The Hoofed Thing" (1932)

"*Evohé!*" the demoniac rout thundered. "*Evohé!* All hail, O Pan!"

Henry Kuttner, "Cursed Be the City" (1939)

dæmoniac, demoniac, *n.* One possessed by a dæmon or demon; an energumen.

"Whether I was mad or not, they cared very little; to enroll a son of the first house of Spain among their converts, or to imprison him as a madman, or to exorcise him as a demoniac, was all the same to them."

Charles Maturin, Melmoth the Wanderer: A Tale (1820)

"'You,—you!' he exclaimed, after a burst of sound that seemed rather like the convulsion of a demoniac, than the mirth, however frantic, of a human being— 'you!—oh, there's metal more attractive!'"

Charles Maturin, Melmoth the Wanderer: A Tale (1820)

Within this hazy, quivering veil, the violinist was then seen, driving his bow furiously across the human chords, with the contortions of a demoniac, as we see them represented on mediæval cathedral paintings!

H. P. Blavatsky, "The Ensouled Violin" (1880)

I wondered how many of those who had known the legends realised that additional link with the terrible which my wider reading had given me; that ominous item in the annals of morbid horror which tells of the creature *Jacques Roulet, of Caude*, who in 1598 was condemned to death as a dæmoniac but afterward saved from the stake by the Paris parliament and shut in a madhouse.

H. P. Lovecraft, "The Shunned House" (1924)

dæmoniacal, demoniacal, *adj.* Dæmoniac (q.v.).

And he closed these and similar boasts of demoniacal arts, which I remember too obscurely to repeat, with a tumultuous imprecation on their nothingness to avail against the gripe of death.

Sir Edward Bulwer-Lytton, A Strange Story (1861)

Goaded, by the interference, into a rage more than demoniacal, I withdrew my arm from her grasp and buried the axe in her brain.

Edgar Allan Poe, "The Black Cat" (1843)

Under a narrow, arched doorway, surmounted by one of those demoniacal grotesques in which the cynical and ghastly fancy of old Gothic carving delights, I saw very gladly the beautiful face and figure of Carmilla enter the shadowy chapel.

J. S. LeFanu, "Carmilla" (1871)

I said that the old man had laid some curse on Andrew, and that that might explain his state of mind. After all demoniacal possession must be equivalent in law to insanity.

John Buchan, "The Green Wildebeest" (1927)

Life is a hideous thing, and from the background behind what we know of it peer dæmoniacal hints of truth which make it sometimes a thousandfold more hideous.

> H. P. Lovecraft, "Facts Concerning the Late Arthur Jermyn
> and His Family" (1920)

My heart gave a sudden leap of unholy glee, and pounded against my ribs with demoniacal force as if to free itself from the confining walls of my frail frame.

> C. M. Eddy, Jr. & H. P. Lovecraft, "The Loved Dead" (1923)

Returning to his chamber he busied himself with various conjurations. But his familiars had gone away in the night, forsaking the angles at which he had posted them; and no spirit either human or demoniacal made reply to his questions.

> Clark Ashton Smith, "The Coming of the White Worm" (1933)

Then Balthus forgot his exasperation as his ears were outraged by the most frightful cry he had ever heard. It was not human, this one; it was a demoniacal caterwauling of hideous triumph that seemed to exult over fallen humanity and find echo in black gulfs beyond human ken.

> Robert E. Howard, "Beyond the Black River" (1935)

The last few tiger cloaks gave up and went for the rail, leaping wide, disappearing into the foaming water with demoniacal howls of fright.

> John Jakes, "The Barge of Souls" (1967) in *Brak the Barbarian*

And as the three guests moved closer, he croaked in a whisper barely audible above the dæmoniacal flutes that *this* is the tomb where seethes and bubbles the unutterable *thing*, the evil he must forever watch over, and keep the seal of the Elder Gods inviolate for all of time.

> Gary Myers, "The Feast in the House of the Worm" (1970)

dæmoniacally, demoniacally, *adv.* In a dæmoniacal (q.v.) manner.

There is no passion in nature so demoniacally impatient, as that of him who, shuddering upon the edge of a precipice, thus meditates a plunge.

> Edgar Allan Poe, "The Imp of the Perverse" (1845)

Dismounting and warily picking my way down the dangerous declivity—horse and man both sliding now and then upon the icy ledges—at length I drove, or the blast drove me, into the largest square, before one side of the main edifice. Piercingly and shrilly the shotted blast blew by the corner; and redly and demoniacally boiled Blood River at one side.

> Herman Melville, "The Paradise of Bachelors and the Tartarus of Maids" (1855)

Bluebeard was no more a creation of Perrault or of Offenbach than Don Juan was a creation of Mozart or of Molière. Both really lived, but Bluebeard the more demoniacally.

Edgar Saltus, *Historia Amoris: A History of Love Ancient and Modern* (1906)

The thing was grotesquely like a crooked gnarled man in shape, but its face was bestial. It bared yellow fangs as it lurched silently toward him, and from under penthouse brows small reddened eyes gleamed demoniacally. Yet there was something of the human in its countenance; it was neither ape nor man, but an unnatural creature horribly compounded of both.

Robert E. Howard, "The Gods of Bal-Sagoth" (1931)

Dantean, *adj.* Of, pertaining to, or resembling the poet Dante Alighieri (1265–1321) or his works, such as the *Inferno*; in particular, hellish, infernal.

Winding along at the bottom of the gorge is a dangerously narrow wheel-road, occupying the bed of a former torrent. Following this road to its highest point, you stand as within a Dantean gateway. From the steepness of the walls here, their strangely ebon hue, and the sudden contraction of the gorge, this particular point is called the Black Notch.

Herman Melville, "The Paradise of Bachelors and the Tartarus of Maids" (1855)

On his part, the stranger looked at the thin Dantean features and slight frame of the poet with a cool unreadable air which seemed to indicate that he knew all that was essential to know about Alvor.

Clark Ashton Smith, "The Monster of the Prophecy" (1929)

There were long, tediously winding tunnels that went down into Cimmerian depth, or climbed at acclivitous angles. There were strait cubby-holes, dripping with unknown liquid ores, through which he crawled like a lizard on his belly; and Dantean gulfs that he skirted on slippery, perilous, broken ledges, hearing far below him the sullen sigh or the weirdly booming roar of sub-Mercutian waters.

Clark Ashton Smith, "The Immortals of Mercury" (1932)

daroh, *n.* [< Jack *Darrow*, science fiction fan] An obnoxious creature that inhabits the jungles of Venus. [Not in *OED*.]

I was always slashing ugrats and stepping on skorahs, and my leather suit was all speckled from the bursting darohs which struck it from all sides.

H. P. Lovecraft & Kenneth Sterling, "In the Walls of Eryx" (1936)

death-fire, *n.* A death-light; a phosphorescent glow seen over putrefying bodies in graveyards. A will-o'-the-wisp, corpse-candle, corpse-light.

> About, about, in reel and rout,
> The death-fires danced at night;

> The water, like a witch's oils,
> Burnt green, and blue and white.
>> S. T. Coleridge, *The Rime of the Ancient Mariner* (1798)

> See! hark!
> They come, they come! give way! Alas, ye deem
> Falsely—'t is but a troop of spectres, through the dark
> From the choked well, whence a bright death-fire sprung,
> A lurid earth-star, which dropped many a spark
> From its blue train, and, spreading widely, clung
> To their wild hair, like mist the topmost pines among.
>> Percy Bysshe Shelley, *The Revolt of Islam: A Poem* (1817)

At sill lower levels the death-fires in the air gave out, and one met only the primal blackness of the void save aloft where the thin peaks stood out goblin-like.
>> H. P. Lovecraft, *The Dream-Quest of Unknown Kadath* (1927)

> But the stream of Time, swift flowing,
> Brings the torment of half-knowing—
> Dimly rushing, blindly going
>> Past the never-trodden lea;
> And the voyager, repining,
> Sees the grisly death-fires shining,
> Hears the wicked petrel's whining
>> As he helpless drifts to sea.
>> H. P. Lovecraft, "Despair" (1919)

dedaim, *n.* [< Fr < Hb DVD (*pl.* DVDIM), the mandrake (literally "love apple")] Originally, the mandrake; in later use, various fabulous conceptions derived therefrom. [Not in *OED*.]

The Dedaims of Babylon, which are trees, bear human heads for fruit; Mandragoras sing,—the root Baaras runs through the grass.
>> Gustave Flaubert (trans. Lafcadio Hearn), *The Temptation of Saint Anthony* (1882)

A plant known as the *dedaim*, with a bulbous, pulpy, whitish-green bole from whose center rose and radiated several leafless reptilian boughs, dripped upon Thuloneah's bosom an occasional drop of yellowish-red ichor from incisions made in its smooth bark.
>> Clark Ashton Smith, "The Garden of Adompha" (1937)

"Nay," said Dwerulas, in a voice harsh as a rusty coffin-hinge, "but I have administered to her the drowsy and over-powering juice of the *dedaim*. Her heart beats impalpably, her blood flows with the sluggishness of that mingled ichor."
>> Clark Ashton Smith, "The Garden of Adompha" (1937)

"I woke too tardily from the swoon induced by the *dedaim*. A lesser adept would never have awakened at all."

Clark Ashton Smith, "The Master of the Crabs" (1947)

Just above the mouth of his cave they had planted a curious Dedaim tree, whose undying boughs bore ever a grisly fruit of human heads.

Lin Carter, *Kesrick* (1982)

demesne, *n.* An extensive landed property retained by the owner for his personal use; an estate, a manorial land, or the grounds of a mansion; an extent of territory over which rule or dominion is exercised; a realm or domain. Frequently used in the plural.

Filled with a feeling that our tangible world is only an atom in a fabric vast and ominous, and that unknown demesnes press on and permeate the sphere of the known at every point, Northam in youth and young manhood drained in turn the founts of formal religion and occult mystery.

H. P. Lovecraft, "The Descendant" (1926?)

I had the book that told the hidden way
Across the void and through the space-hung screens
That hold the undimensioned worlds at bay,
And keep lost æons to their own demesnes.

H. P. Lovecraft, "The Key" in *Fungi from Yuggoth* (1929–30)

deodamnate, *adj.* "Goddamned." [Not in *OED*.]

Revisory servitude has bowed me to the dust of illiteracy, so that I have not had time to peruse a deodamnate thing since Buchan's "Witch Wood", of which I think I told you.

H. P. Lovecraft, letter to Donald Wandrei (29 February 1928)

desiderate, *adj.* Desirable; desired, longed-for.

"That temple is in your desiderate sunset city, so steer for it before you heed the singing and are lost."

H. P. Lovecraft, *The Dream-Quest of Unknown Kadath* (1927)

Devachan, *n.* [< Skr, "dwelling of the gods"] In Theosophy ("Esoteric Buddhism"), a subjective, heavenly realm (or rather, state) experienced by an individual between two incarnations. [Not in *OED*.]

Therein you shall behold unshapen dooms,
And ghoul-astounding shadows of the tombs;
Oblivion, with blossoms plucked in Devachan,
In stillness of the santal-pillared woods;
But nevermore the moiling world of man.

Clark Ashton Smith, "Enchanted Mirrors" (1925)

"Devachan", as I understand it, is merely a temporary Paradise of beatific illusions—in which the discarnate soul is permitted to abide for a time before its return to mortal existence. The Buddhists have no conception of a *permanent* heaven, or "Eden." Their hells, too, are only temporary . . . The religions of the west are puerile compared to the esoteric doctrines of Buddhism.

> Clark Ashton Smith, letter to George Sterling (11 July 1922) (ellipsis in original)

Dis, *pr.n.* [< L, variant of *dives*, wealthy] The god of the underworld or the underworld itself; Pluto, Hades, Orcus. In Dante's *Divine Comedy*, Dis is the name of the capital city of Hell.

> In every ecstasy exalt my heart;
>   Let every trance make loose and light the wings
>   My soul must shake, ere her pure fabric springs
> Clothed in the secret dream-delights of Art
>   Transcendant into air, the tomb of Things;
>   Let every kiss
> Melt on my lips to flame, fling back the gates of Dis!

> Aleister Crowley, *Aceldama, A Place to Bury Strangers in:*
> *A Philosophical Poem* (1898)

A name contracted from Dives, sometimes given to Pluto and hence also to the lower world. But *vide* Dante, *Inferno*, Canto xxxiv.

> Aleister Crowley, note to *Aceldama, A Place to Bury Strangers in:*
> *A Philosophical Poem* (1898)

Then the boat from the slow, grey river loomed up to the coast of Dis and the little, silent shade still shivering stepped ashore, and Charon turned the boat to go wearily back to the world.

> Lord Dunsany, "Charon" (1915)

There was something about that immense ebon citadel that struck me with the same sense of fore-knowledge that I had felt when I had ridden into the ruins of the Gobi oasis. Also I thought it looked like that city of Dis which Dante glimpsed in Hades. And its antiquity hung over it like a sable garment.

> A. Merritt, *Dwellers in the Mirage* (1932)

Blue black, shining, sharply cut as though from polished steel, it reared full five thousand feet on high! How great it was I could not tell, for the height of its precipitous walls barred the vision. The frowning façade turned toward us was, I estimated, five miles in length. Its colossal scarp struck the eyes like a blow; its shadow, falling upon us, checked the heart. It was overpowering, gigantic— dreadful as that midnight city of Dis that Dante saw rising up from another pit!

> A. Merritt, *The Metal Monster* (1920)

Once, I think I half remember,
Ere the grey skies of November
Quench'd my youth's aspiring ember,
    Liv'd there such a thing as bliss;
Skies that now are dark were beaming,
Gold and azure, splendid seeming
Till I learn'd it all was dreaming—
    Deadly drowsiness of Dis.

H. P. Lovecraft, "Despair" (1919)

Perchance the fountains of the dolorous rivers four
In Dis, will quench the thirst thy wine assuages never;
And in my veins will mount a twice-infuriate fever
When the black, burning noons upon Cimmeria pour.

Clark Ashton Smith, "Farewell to Eros" (1937)

It is Dis; it is the damned city, and sad voices in the silent metropolis mourn for lost glory.

Henry Kuttner, "The Jest of Droom-avista" (1937)

And so Ludwig moved through awful abysses of pulsing, fearful darkness; he went through a place of curious violet light that sent tinkling, evil trills of goblin laughter after him; he went through a Cyclopean deserted city of ebon stone which he shudderingly recognized as fabled Dis.

Henry Kuttner, "Hydra" (1939)

docent, *adj.* Teaching.

The docent presence swell'd my strength of soul;
All things I knew, but knew with mind alone.

H. P. Lovecraft, "Aletheia Phrikodes" in
"The Poe-et's Nightmare: A Fable" (1916)

Doel, *n.* See quotations. [Not in *OED*.]

"I am waiting and watching," Chalmers wrote. "I sit by the window and watch walls and ceiling. I do not believe they can reach me, but I must beware of the Doels. Perhaps they can help them break through. The satyrs will help, and they can advance through the scarlet circles. The Greeks knew a way of preventing that. It is a great pity that we have forgotten so much."

Frank Belknap Long, "The Hounds of Tindalos" (1929)

He lay naked, his chest and arms covered with bluish pus gave off a smell like rotten solder. "Must beware of the Doels. They can help them break through, you know who they are, of course. The satyrs will help. They can gain entrance through the scarlet circle, the Greeks knew a way of preventing that. Good God, the plaster is falling. . . . It is getting dark in the room . . . their tongues."

William S. Burroughs, *The Place of Dead Roads* (1977–83; ellipses in original)

Were any child to be reared in isolation, and surrounded from infancy with the religious precepts of Tsathoggua, YOG-SOTHOTH, or the Doles, his inner emotions would all through life inform him positively of the truth of Tsathogguanism, Yog-Sothothery, or Dolatry, as the case might be. Iä! Shub-Niggurath! The Goat With a Thousand Young! God! I wonder if there *isn't* some truth in some of this? What is this my emotions are telling me about Great Cthulhu? Ya-R'lyeh! Ya-R'lyeh!—Cthulhu fhgthagn . . . . .n'ggah . . . ggll . . . . . Iä! Iä! And so it goes.

H. P. Lovecraft, letter to Frank Belknap Long
(22 November 1730) [*sic*] (ellipses as in original)

My contributions to the Mythos were of assorted shapes and sizes, ranging from the tiny, flesh-devouring Doels, who inhabited an alien dimension in night and chaos, to the monstrous Chaugnar Faugn, whom only the suicidally inclined would have mistaken for a pachyderm. I also contributed one scenic vista, the mysterious, perpetually mist-shrouded Plateau of Leng, and one forbidden book, John Dee's English translation of *The Necronomicon*, which I placed at the head of *The Space Eaters* when that story first appeared in *Weird Tales*, but later omitted when the story was reprinted in *The Magazine of Horror*, fearing that my invention might take on an appalling life of its own and appear on the shelves of some unsuspecting and defenseless book dealer!

Frank Belknap Long, *Howard Phillips Lovecraft: Dreamer on the Nightside* (1975)

dolichocephalic, *adj.* Long-headed. Cf. brachycephalic.

Their conformation of skull has marked differences from that of any known races in the upper world, though I cannot help thinking it a development, in the course of countless ages, of the Brachycephalic type of the Age of Stone in Lyell's *Elements of Geology*, c.x., p.113, as compared with the Dolichocephalic type of the beginning of the Age of Iron, correspondent with that now so prevalent amongst us, and called the Celtic type.

Sir Edward Bulwer-Lytton, *The Coming Race* (1871; aka
Vril: The Power of the Coming Race)

"And how," asked Clemants, "do you account for their brachycephalicism? The Mediterraneans were as long-headed as the Aryans: would admixture between these dolichocephalic peoples produce a broad-headed intermediate type?"

Robert E. Howard, "The Children of the Night" (1930)

Domdaniel, domdaniel, Dom-Daniel, *pr.n.* & *n.* [< Fr ?< Gr, *dôma Daniél*, hall of Daniel; or L, *domus Danielis*, house of Daniel; coined by Jacques Cazotte and Dom Dennis Chavis in their *Continuation des mille et une nuits* (1788–93;

trans. as *Arabian Tales*)] A fabled undersea cavern wherein a school of sorcerers held its meetings, which Cazotte places "under the sea near Tunis," and Southey places "under the roots of the ocean"; hence, any gathering-place or gathering of witches and wizards, a Witches' Sabbath; metaphorically, a hellish or infernal place, or a den of iniquity.

Titles: Peter Allen, "Domdaniel"

> In the continuation of the Arabian Tales, the Domdaniel is mentioned; a seminary for evil magicians, under the roots of the sea. From this seed the present romance has grown.
>
> Robert Southey, Preface to Thalaba the Destroyer (1800)

> In the Domdaniel caverns,
> Under the Roots of the Ocean,
> Met the Masters of the Spell.
> Before them from its floor of rock,
> Ten magic flames arose.
>
> Robert Southey, Thalaba the Destroyer (1800)

> Never, in short, did parallel
> Betwixt two heroes *gee* so well:
> And, among the points in which they fit,
> There's one, dear Bob, I can't omit.
> That hacking, hectoring blade of thine
> Dealt much in the *Domdaniel* line;
> And 'tis but rendering justice due,
> To say that ours and his Tory crew
> *Damn Daniel* most devoutly too.
>
> Thomas Moore, "Announcement of a New Thalaba"

> Next see tremendous Thalaba come on,
> Arabia's monstrous, wild, and wond'rous son;
> Domdaniel's dread destroyer, who o'erthrew
> More mad magicians than the world e'er knew.
>
> Lord Byron, English Bards and Scotch Reviewers: A Satire (1808)

His scheme of philosophy is a mere day-dream, a poetical creation, like the Domdaniel caverns, the Swerga, or Padalon; and indeed, it bears no inconsiderable resemblance to those gorgeous visions. Like them, it has something of invention, grandeur, and brilliancy. But like them, it is grotesque and extravagant, and perpetually violates even that conventional probability which is essential to the effect of works of art.

Lord Macauley, "Southey's Colloquies on Society"

He was just now enchanted with his first reading of "Thalaba," where he found all manner of deep meanings, to which the sisters listened with wonder and delight. He repeated, in a low, awful, thrilling tone, that made Amy shudder, the lines in the seventh book, ending with—

> "'Who comes from the bridal chamber!
> It is Azrael, angel of death.'"

"You have not been so taken up with any book since Sintram." said Laura.

"It is like Sintram," he replied.

"Like it?"

"So it seems to me. A strife with the powers of darkness; the victory, forgiveness, resignation, death.

> 'Thou know'st the secret wishes of my heart,
> Do with me as thou wilt, thy will is best.'"

"I wish you would not speak as if you were Thalaba yourself," said Amy, "you bring the whole Domdaniel round us."

"I am afraid he is going to believe himself Thalaba as well as Sintram," said Laura. "But you know Southey did not see all this himself, and did not understand it when it was pointed out."

"Don't tell us that," said Amy.

Charlotte M. Younge, The Heir of Redclyffe (1853)

Among other gross transgressions of the most ordinary rules, it may be remarked, that the accused, in what their judges called confessions, contradicted each other at every turn respecting the description of the Domdaniel in which they pretended to have assembled, and the fiend who presided there.

Sir Walter Scott, Letters on Demonology and Witchcraft,
Addressed to J. G. Lockheart, Esq. (1830)

Recognizing little Ned Higgins among them, Hepzibah put her hand into her pocket, and presented the urchin, her earliest and staunchest customer, with silver enough to people the Domdaniel cavern of his interior with as various a procession of quadrupeds, as passed into the ark.

Nathaniel Hawthorne, The House of the Seven Gables (1850–51)

Presently I saw myself a gnome imprisoned by a most weird enchanter, whose part I assigned to the doctor before me, in the Domdaniel caverns, "under the roots of the ocean." Here, until the dissolution of all things, was I doomed to hold the lamp that lit that abysmal darkness, while my heart, like a giant clock, ticked solemnly the remaining years of time.

Fitz-Hugh Ludlow, The Hasheesh Eater:
Being Passages from the Life of a Pythagorean (1857)

But then I remembered Hough's broad summary of Richard Pride's life, the most replete of all human careers, beyond even the dreams of romance; and I reflected what brave stories must be filed away in that mysterious domdaniel, what spectres must linger in its corridors, what pathos of beauty so desperately cherished.

Leonard Cline, *The Dark Chamber* (1927)

I saw this vista, I say, and heard as with the mind's ear the blasphemous domdaniel of cacophony which companioned it.

H. P. Lovecraft, "He" (1925)

dree, *v.tr.* [< OE *dréogan,* to endure, suffer, or work] To endure, to suffer. **To dree (a) weird:** to endure a fate. Revived by Sir Walter Scott.

a. General:

> When they go at length, with such a shaking
>   Of heads o'er the old delusion, sadly
> Each master his way through the black streets taking,
>   Where many a lost work breathes though badly—
> Why don't they bethink them of who has merited?
>   Why not reveal, while their pictures dree
> Such doom, how a captive might be out-ferreted?
>   Why is it they never remember me?

Robert Browning, "Old Pictures in Florence" (1855)

> Shulde this Ston stalen bee,
> Or shuld it chaunges dre,
> The Houss of Sawl and hys Hed anoon shal de.

Inscription on a sixteenth-century chalice, as quoted in
M. P. Shiel, "The Stone of the Edmundsbury Monks" (1895)

"The inscription assures us that if 'this stone be stolen,' or if it 'chaunges dre,' the House of Saul and its head 'anoon' (i.e., anon, at once) shall die. 'Dre,' I may remind you, is an old English word, used, I think, by Burns, identical with the Saxon '*dreogan,*' meaning to 'suffer.'"

M. P. Shiel, "The Stone of the Edmundsbury Monks" (1895)

b. In phrase **to dree (a) weird:**

"Ohon! we're dreeing a sair weird; we hae had a heavy dispensation!"

Sir Walter Scott, *The Antiquary* (1816)

The ceremony took place, and the apparition of Mr Kirke was visibly seen while they were seated at table; but Grahame of Duchray, in his astonishment, failed to perform the ceremony enjoined, and it is to be feared that Mr Kirke still "drees his weird in Fairy Land," the Elfin state declaring to him, as the Ocean to poor Falconer, who perished at sea, after having written his popular poem of the Shipwreck,—

"Thou hast proclaim'd our power—be thou our prey!"

Sir Walter Scott, *Letters on Demonology and Witchcraft,*
Addressed to J. G. Lockheart, Esq. (1830)

"Now, gallant and rightful Laird of Dalcastle," said Mrs. Logan, "what hast thou to say for thyself? Lay thy account to dree the weird thou hast so well earned. Now shalt thou suffer due penance for murdering thy brave and only brother."

James Hogg, *The Private Memoirs and Confessions of a Justified Sinner* (1824)

Had he foreseen whither that envy would have led him; had he foreseen the hideous and fratricidal day of February 22, 1071, and that fair boy's golden locks rolling in dust and blood, the wild Viking would have crushed the growing snake within his bosom, for he was a knight and a gentleman. But it was hidden from his eyes. He had to "dree his weird;" to commit great sins, do great deeds, and die in his bed, mighty and honoured, having children to his heart's desire, and leaving the rest of his substance to his babes. Heaven help and the like of him!

Charles Kingsley, *Hereward the Wake: "Last of the English"* (1865)

"O mither, I may not sleep nor stray,
    My weird is ill to dree;
For a fause faint lord of the south seaboard
    Wad win my bride of me."
        In, in, out and in,
        Blaws the wind and whirls the whin.

Algernon Charles Swinburne, "The Bride's Tragedy" (1889)

Scathe, and shame, and a waefu' name,
    And a weary time and strange,
Have they that seeing a weird for dreeing
    Can die, and cannot change.

Algernon Charles Swinburne, "A Jacobite's Exile" (1889)

Though he possess sweet babes and loving wife,
    A home of peace by loyal friendship cheered,
And love them more than death or happy life,
    They shall avail not; he must dree his weird;
Renounce all blessings for that imprecation,
Steal forth and haunt that builded desolation,
    Of woe and terrors and thick darkness reared.

James Thomson, "The City of Dreadful Night" (1870–74)

"Therefore I say, show to us a token; and if thou be the God, this shall be easy to thee; & if thou show it not, then is thy falsehood manifest, & thou shalt dree the weird."

William Morris, The Wood Beyond the World (1894)

> Below be miners fashioned fair,
>   And all that labour in the sea
> Sepulchred from the ambient air,
>   A fatal weird of dole to dree.
> No time to be, no light to live.
> Earth's need to these hath hope to give.

Aleister Crowley, Rodin in Rime (1907)

And oh dear! the conversations. Children don't talk bad metaphysics, nor do repatriated lumbermen. But Mr. Blackwood must dree his weird, I suppose.

Aleister Crowley, review of
Algernon Blackwood, The Education of Uncle Paul (1911)

My nature is peace-loving, it is even pigeon-livered, and must dree its weird.

Branch Cabell, Special Delivery: A Packet of Replies (1932)

"Y'see, Captain, I canna answer exactly, because my mind's sae bollixed up by the screen itsel', an' by all the weirds I've had tae dree since I began walkin' across this fearsome planet, that I hardly ken a quark from a claymore any mair."

James Blish, Spock Must Die! (1970)

Dryad (*pl.* **Dryades, Dryads**), *n.* [< Gr < *drŷs*, oak tree] In Greek mythology, a wood nymph.

Titles: William Diaper, *Dryades; or, The Nymphs Prophecy: A Poem*

Have you watched a willow bough swaying in spring above some clear sylvan pool, or a slender birch dancing with the wind in a secret woodland and covert, or the flitting green shadows in a deep forest glade which are dryads half-tempted to reveal themselves? I thought of them as she came toward us.

A. Merritt, Dwellers in the Mirage (1932)

Well did I come to know the presiding dryads of those trees, and often have I watched their wild dances in the struggling beams of a waning moon—but of these things I must not now speak. I will tell only of the lone tomb in the darkest of the hillside thickets; the deserted tomb of the Hydes, an old and exalted family whose last direct descendant had been laid within its black recesses many decades before my birth.

H. P. Lovecraft, "The Tomb" (1917)

It seems the selfsame wind is in the pine
That sighed or sand above
Our ecstasy and love. . . .
But now no dryad face, no dryad voice
Shall make my heart rejoice,
No dear Bacchante wear the wilding vine.

Clark Ashton Smith, "Wine of Summer" (1942; ellipsis in original)

So he was in no wise amazed when a great high-branched pine opened its snow-plastered bark and showed him its dryad—a merry, blue-eyed, blonde-haired girl's face, a dryad no more than seventeen years old.

Fritz Leiber, "The Snow Women" (1970)

"I came from the south, after great Pan was dead and the new god whose name I cannot speak was in Hellas. No place remained for the old gods and the old beings of our land. The priests cut down the sacred groves and built churches—Oh, I remember how the dryads screamed, unheard by them, screams that quivered on the hot still air as if to hang there forever. They ring yet in my ears, they always will."

Poul Anderson, *The Broken Sword* (1954)

"You've probably heard about it in a different way, though—the young of the Black Goat? *gof'nn hupadgh Shub-Niggurath?* But the dryads and fauns and satyrs are a lot different from the classical descriptions, so don't think you're prepared—"

Ramsey Campbell, "The Moon-Lens" (1964)

He himself felt less than totally miserable only when walking alone through the most heavily wooded sections of his 20,000 acres, thinking "green thoughts in a green shade," as the Poet said; there it sometimes seemed to him, especially when twilight was casting cinnamon and gold highlights into the emerald-green branches, that a door to another world would almost swing open and he could faintly discern the quick timid movements of dryads and the sulphurous sandalwood scent, beneath the earth, of vast caverns of trolls.

Robert Anton Wilson, *Masks of the Illuminati* (1981)

Dunsanian, Dunsanean, *adj.* Of, pertaining to, or resembling Lord Dunsany or his classic works of literary fantasy. [Not in *OED*.]

Distant mountains floated in the sky as enchanted cities, and often the whole white world would dissolve into a gold, silver, and scarlet land of Dunsanian dreams and adventurous expectancy under the magic of the low midnight sun. On cloudy days we had considerable trouble in flying, owing to the tendency of snowy earth and sky to merge into one mystical opalescent void with no visible horizon to mark the junction of the two.

H. P. Lovecraft, *At the Mountains of Madness* (1931)

How quickly you [*viz.*, H. P. Lovecraft] changed your mind! You arrived to find a gold Dunsanian city of arches and domes and fantastic spires … or so you told us. Yet when you fled two years later you could see only "alien hordes."

T. E. D. Klein, "Black Man with a Horn" (1980; ellipsis in original)

dwale, *n.* The deadly nightshade, belladonna (*Atropa belladonna*); frequently as a stupefying, soporific potion or as a deadly poison.

Façade!—that reeks of nightmare-dread and gloom!
Dwale, henbane, hemlock in its courtyard bloom;
Dumb walls; the speechless silence of the tomb.

Walter de la Mare, "Laid Low"

Before our feet depart,
With hemlock fill the cup
Our hands unto thy laden urn hold up;
With deadliest dwale bedew thy kiss
To leave a Stygian stillness in the heart
That begs no later bliss.

Clark Ashton Smith, "Supplication" (1942)

Dweurgarian, *adj.* [< *Duergar* (q.v.)] Of, pertaining to, or resembling the Duergar or dwarfs of Scandinavian mythology; dwarfish. [Not in *OED*.]

The house shook like a Dweurgarian cinder in the sieves of Niflheim.

C. M. Eddy, Jr. & H. P. Lovecraft, "Deaf, Dumb, and Blind" (1924)

dybbuk (*pl.* **dybbukim, dybbuks**), **dibbuk** (*pl.* **dibbukim, dibbuks**), *n.* [< Hb DBVQ] In Jewish mythology, the spirit of a deceased individual that possesses a living individual.

Titles: Ansky (Solomon Rappoport), *The Dybbuk*

Both golems and dybbuks are fixed types, and serve as frequent ingredients of later Jewish tradition.

H. P. Lovecraft, "Supernatural Horror in Literature" (1925–27)

Dzyan, *n.* [Arbitrary formation by H. P. Blavatsky from Skr *dhyān, dhyāna,* yogic meditation, from whence also Chinese *ch'an,* Japanese *zen*] Mystic meditation; a state of enlightenment resulting from meditation. [Not in *OED*.]

It is more than probable that the book will be regarded by a large section of the public as a romance of the wildest kind; for who has ever even heard of the book of Dzyan?

H. P. Blavatsky, Preface to *The Secret Doctrine:
The Synthesis of Science, Religion, and Philosophy* (1888)

Dan, now become in modern Chinese and Tibetan phonetics *ch'an*, is the general term for the esoteric schools, and for their literature. In the old books, the *Janna* is defined as "to reform one's self by meditation and knowledge," a second *inner* birth. Hence Dzan, *Djan* phonetically, the "Book of *Dzyan*."

H. P. Blavatsky, note to *The Secret Doctrine: The Synthesis of Science, Religion, and Philosophy* (1888)

Says the Book of Dzyan (Knowledge through meditation)—
  "The great mother lay with Δ, *and the , and the , the second and the* φ *in her bosom, ready to bring them forth, the valiant sons of the* □Δ| | *(or 4,320,000, the Cycle) whose two elders are the* ± *and the* ≅ *(Point)."*

H. P. Blavatsky, *The Secret Doctrine: The Synthesis of Science, Religion, and Philosophy* (1888)

The Book of Dzyan—from the Sanskrit word "Dhyân" (mystic meditation)—is the first volume of the Commentaries upon the seven secret folios of *Kiu-te*, and a Glossary of the public works of the same name. Thirty-five volumes of *Kiu-te* for exoteric purposes and the use of the laymen may be found in the possession of the Tibetan Gelugpa Lâmas, in the library of any monastery; and also four-teen books of Commentaries and Annotations on the same by the initiated Teachers.

H. P. Blavatsky, "The Secret Books of 'Lam-Rin' and Dzyan"

The work which I here translate forms part of the same series as that from which the "Stanzas" of the *Book of Dzyan* were taken, on the which the *Secret Doctrine* is based.

H. P. Blavatsky, Preface to *The Voice of the Silence: Being Chosen Fragments from the "Book of the Golden Precepts"* (1889)

Dzyan. (Tib) Also written *Dzyn* or *Dzen*. A corruption of Sk. *Dhyâna* and *Gnyâna*. In Chinese *Ch'an*, the name of one of the schools of *Yoga* or medita-tion which follow the same rules as these *Precepts*. Also a generic name of the Esoteric schools and their literature. See S.D. for Stanzas of the *Book of Dzyan* and *Commentaries*.

Alice Leighton Cleather & Basil Crump, note to *H. P. Blavatsky, The Voice of the Silence: Being Chosen Fragments from the "Book of the Golden Precepts"* (1927)

By the way, I might add here that this term *Dzyan* is but the Senzar term of what in Sanskrit meant spiritual meditation; the same word is used in the phrase Dhyâni-Buddhas, the Buddhas immersed in Dhyâna. *Dhyâna* therefore is the Sanskrit form of the Senzar *Dzyan*.

G. de Purucker, *Studies in Occult Philosophy* (1949)

The Book of Dzyan, as a physical roll or book or manuscript, or Tibetan type-print, call it what you like, as a physical thing, is, as H.P.B. says, not very old, probably about a thousand years, and is part of a well-known, more or less common Tibetan series of works, well-known even exoterically, called Kiu-te as a general title for all these volumes; just as *The Secret Doctrine* is in two volumes, etc.

The substance, however, of the Book of Dzyan, which is simply the Tibetan or Mongolian way of pronouncing the Sanskrit Dhyâna, is very ancient, even highly archaic, goes right back into Atlantean times, and even beyond as regards the doctrine taught.

G. de Purucker, Studies in Occult Philosophy (1949)

In the case of *The Book of Dzyan* the comprehension of the symbol is enormously assisted by the fact that the book itself is highly magnetized in a peculiar way, so that when the student who is privileged to see it takes one of the pages in his hand a remarkable effect is produced upon him. Before the mind's eye arises the picture of that which the page is intended to symbolize, and simultaneously he hears a sort of recitation of the stanza which describes it. It is very difficult to put this clearly into words, but the experience is a wonderful one.

I have myself seen and handled the copy which Madame Blavatsky describes—from the study of which she wrote *The Secret Doctrine*. That is of course not the original book, but the copy of it which is kept in the occult museum which is under the care of the Master K.H. The original document is at Shamballa, in the care of the Head of the Hierarchy, and is certainly the oldest book in the world. Indeed it has been said that part of it (the first six stanzas, I think) is even older than the world, for it is said to have been brought over from some previous chain. That most ancient part is regarded by some as not merely an account of the processes of the coming existence of a system, but rather a kind of manual of directions for such an act of creation. Even the copy must be millions of years old.

Charles W. Leadbeater, The Inner Life (1910)

The original of *The Book of Dzyan* is in the hands of the august Head of the Occult Hierarchy, and has been seen by none. None knows how old it is, but it is rumoured that the earlier part of it (consisting of the first six stanzas), has an origin altogether anterior to this world, and even that it is not a history, but a series of directions—rather a formula for creation than an account of it. A copy of it is kept in the museum of the Brotherhood, and it is that copy (itself probably the oldest book produced on this planet) which Madame Blavatsky and several of her pupils have seen—which she describes so graphically in *The Secret Doctrine*. The book has, however, several peculiarities which she does not there mention. It appears to be very highly magnetized, for as soon as a man takes a page into his hand he sees passing before his eyes a vision of the events which it is intended to portray, while at the same time he seems to hear a sort of rhythmic description of them in his own language, so far as that language will convey the ideas involved. Its pages contain no words whatever—nothing but symbols.

Annie Besant & C. W. Leadbeater, Commentary on The Voice of the Silence

The Dzyan is a Hindu book written in Sanskrit about 1500 B.C. The book is accredited to the Brahmins and it certainly looks like their work. In this book the Naacal copies of the Sacred Inspired Writings of the Motherland have been taken as a base to work on. The Dzyan is the most incomplete and the most ambiguous ancient work I have ever come across. It takes the Sacred Writings and with evident deliberateness misinterprets and adds to them. Misstatements permeate the whole text. The book reads as if it had been designed to breed distrust, fear and superstition in the people. There is very little symbolism in it. It is, rather, filled up with comparisons, unphilosophical and absolutely one-sided. No point is proven. Most sentences read like the headline of a chapter, leaving the chapter unwritten. There is no continuity of subjects, which leaves the whole thing indefinite. If the writer was only committing stray thoughts to writing, he admirably succeeded, but to follow the workings of his mind by his writings is absolutely impossible. It it was a work written with a view to breeding schisms and sects, without doubt it is admirable.

James Churchward, *The Children of Mu* (1931)

E

efjeh-weed, *n.* [< *Forrest J* Ackerman, active in various controversies amongst science fiction fandom. Cf. the "Effjay of Akkamin" in H. P. Lovecraft & Robert Barlow, "The Battle That Ended the Century (MS. Found in a Time Machine)"] An obnoxious weed that infests the jungles of Venus. [Not in *OED.*]

> It was a horrible sight, yet the man-lizards seemed quite unconcerned. Now and then one of them would brush away the farnoth-flies with its limbs or tentacles, or crush a wriggling sificligh or akman, or an out-reaching efjeh-weed, with the suction disks on its stumps.
>
> H. P. Lovecraft & Kenneth Sterling, "In the Walls of Eryx" (1936)

> I can understand how poor Dwight must have felt. His corpse is now just a skeleton, and the sificlighs and akmans and farnoth-flies are gone. The efjeh-weeds are nipping the leather clothing to pieces, for they were longer and faster-growing than I had expected.
>
> H. P. Lovecraft & Kenneth Sterling, "In the Walls of Eryx" (1936)

> I shall not last long, though I am resolved not to hasten matters as Dwight did. His grinning skull has just turned toward me, shifted by the groping of one of the efjeh-weeds that are devouring his leather suit.
>
> H. P. Lovecraft & Kenneth Sterling, "In the Walls of Eryx" (1936)

effluvium (*pl.* **effluvia**; also erroneously used as *sing.*), *n.* [< LL] An emanation or exhalation, as of gas or vapor, particularly when characterized by noisomeness and malodorousness. Frequently found in the plural.

> Though night unnumber'd worlds unfold to view;
> Boundless creation! what art thou? a beam,
> A mere effluvium of his majesty:
> And shall an atom of this atom world
> Mutter in dust and sin the theme of heaven?
>
> Edward Young, *The Complaint, and the Consolation; or, Night Thoughts* (1742)

> "Immalee withheld her breath, as if she inhaled the abominable effluvia of this mass of putrefaction, which is said to desolate the shores near the temple of Juggernaut, like a pestilence."
>
> Charles Maturin, *Melmoth the Wanderer: A Tale* (1820)

"Fool! Spawn of Noth-Yidik and effluvium of K'thun! Son of the dogs that howl in the maelstrom of Azathoth!"

> H. P. Lovecraft & Hazel Heald, "The Horror in the Museum" (1932)

Beneath the instruction of the Martian, before landing, they slew these reptiles, incinerating them completely with infrared beams, so that not even their carcasses would remain to taint the air with putrefactive effluvia.

> Clark Ashton Smith, "Seedling of Mars" (1931)

The air was singularly heavy, as if the lees of an ancient atmosphere, less tenuous than that of Mars to-day, had settled down and remained in that stagnant darkness. It was harder to breathe than the outer air; it was filled with unknown effluvia; and the light dust arose before us at every step, diffusing a faintness of bygone corruption, like the dust of powdered mummies.

> Clark Ashton Smith, "The Vaults of Yoh-Vombis" (1931)

Faintly at first, but more strongly as they went on, there came to them an insidious feeling of somnolence, such as might have been caused by mephitical effluvia.

> Clark Ashton Smith, "The Dweller in the Gulf" (1932)

Strange, terrible faces stared at me, half-heard voices moaned and gibbered in my ears, clammy hands grasped at my arms and clothing, yet could not hold. Once a pair of icy cold lips kissed me full on my mouth; and oh! the foul effluvium of that breath! . . .

> Nictzin Dyalhis, "The Sapphire Siren" (1934; ellipsis in original)

Like a vampire bat he gives off a narcotic effluvium, a dank green mist that anesthetizes his victims and renders them helpless in his enveloping presence.

> William S. Burroughs, Naked Lunch (1955–59)

But in the time it took him to slay the beasts, the demoniac effluvium would be upon him, wrapping him, choking him, killing him—

> John Jakes, "Devils in the Walls" (1963)

Beating its ribbed wings like a monstrous bat and belching a vile effluvia [sic] of sulphur and brimstone, it hurtled down upon him like a runaway locomotive.

> David Mallory, "St. George" (1978)

efreet, *n.* See under **afrit**.

I knew the *Saracenic Rituals* only too well. The account dealt with Prinn's mysterious sojourn in Egypt and the Orient in what he claimed were Crusader days. There is revealed the lore of the *efreet* and the *djinn*, the secrets of the Assassin sects, the myths of Arabian ghoul-tales, and the hidden practices of dervish cults.

> Robert Bloch, "The Secret of Sebek" (1937)

eidolon (*pl.* **eidola, eidolons**), **eidólon,** *n.* [< Gr *eídôlon* < *eîdos*, form, shape, idea] (1) An (immaterial) image, form, representation; a phantom, spectre, apparition, simulacrum. (2) In occultism and Theosophy, the astral body or phantom, a pale copy of the physical form that perseveres after death; according to many sources, this may be made visible by subjecting the essential salts preserved in the ashes of a burnt flower (or other body) to various chemical or alchemical processes. (3) A (material) statue, effigy; in particular, one of a deity, i.e., an idol; the concrete embodiment of an abstract ideal.

Usage: In English, the accent normally falls on the second syllable. Poe apparently wished to have the word pronounced with accentuation as in the Greek, putting a primary accent on the first syllable and a secondary accent on the third; some writers have followed him in this, as clearly exemplified by the prosody in verse by H. P. Lovecraft and Robert A. W. Lowndes.

Titles: Walt Whitman, "Eidólons" (verse); George Sterling, "Eidolon" (verse); H. P. Lovecraft, "The Eidolon" (verse); Clark Ashton Smith, "Eidolon" (verse), "Some Blind Eidolon" (verse), "The Dark Eidolon"; Harlan Ellison, "Eidolons"

> When it is recollected that Maupertuis died at a distance from Berlin, once the scene of his triumphs—overwhelmed by the petulant ridicule of Voltaire, and out of favour with Frederick, with whom to be ridiculous was to be worthless—we can hardly wonder at the imagination even a man of physical science calling up his Eidolon in the hall of his former greatness.
>
> Sir Walter Scott, *Letters on Demonology and Witchcraft,*
> *Addressed to J. G. Lockheart, Esq.* (1830)

> By a route obscure and lonely,
> Haunted by ill angels only,
> Where an Eidolon, named NIGHT,
> On a black throne reigns upright,
> I have reached these lands but newly
> From an ultimate dim Thule—
> From a wild weird clime that lieth, sublime,
> Out of Space—out of Time.
>
> Edgar Allan Poe, "Dream-Land" (1844)

"Let me illustrate what I mean from an experiment which Paracelsus describes as not difficult, and which the author of the *Curiosities of Literature* cites as credible: A flower perishes; you burn it. Whatever were the elements of that flower while it lived are gone, dispersed, you know not whither; you can never discover nor re-collect them. But you can, by chemistry, out of the burnt dust of that flower, raise a spectrum of the flower, just as it seemed in life. It may be the same with the human being. The soul has so much escaped you as the essence or elements of the flower. Still you may make a spectrum of it. And this phantom, though in the popular superstition it is held to be the soul of the departed, must not be confounded with the true soul; it is but the eidolon of the dead form."

Sir Edward Bulwer-Lytton,
"The Haunted and the Haunters; or, The House and the Brain" (1857)

> Thy body permanent,
> The body lurking within thy body,
> The only purport of the form thou art, the real I myself,
> An image, an eidólon.

Walt Whitman, "Eidólons" in *Leaves of Grass* (1881)

A wild shriek rang through the echoing place, and with the fall of her eidolon, the princess herself, till then standing like a statue in front of me, fell heavily, and lay still.

George MacDonald, *Lilith: A Romance* (1895)

"I would not be content to live again as I had lived before, to use the life principle which lies in love, only for pleasure or the bringing of eidolons on earth."

Mabel Collins, *The Blossom and the Fruit: A True Story of a Black Magician* (1888)

It was as if slab, gully, scree-slope, buttress, and mile-long train of precipice wall, cut off from all supports of earth and washed of all earthy superfluities which belong to appearances subject to secular change, stood revealed in their vast substantiality; the termless imperishable eidolon, laid up in Heaven, of all these things.

E. R. Eddison, *A Fish Dinner in Memison* (1936–40)

"Into Thalarion, The City of a Thousand Wonders, many have passed but none returned. Therein walk only dæmons and mad things that are no longer men, and the streets are white with the unburied bones of those who have looked upon the eidolon Lathi, that reigns over the city."

H. P. Lovecraft, "The White Ship" (1919)

He saw slip past him the glorious lands and cities of which a fellow-dreamer of earth—a lighthouse-keeper in ancient Kingsport—had often discoursed in the old days, and recognised the templed terraces of Zar, abode of forgotten dreams; the spires of infamous Thalarion, that dæmon-city of a thousand wonders where the eidolon Lathi reigns; the charnel gardens of Xura, land of pleasures unattained, and the twin headlands of crystal, meeting above in a resplendent arch, which guard the harbour of Sona-Nyl, blessed land of fancy.

H. P. Lovecraft, *The Dream-Quest of Unknown Kadath* (1927)

I cannot even hint at what it was like, for it was a compound of all that is un-clean, uncanny, unwelcome, abnormal, and detestable. It was the ghoulish shade of decay, antiquity, and desolation; the putrid, dripping eidolon of unwholesome revelation; the awful baring of that which the merciful earth should always hide.

H. P. Lovecraft, "The Outsider" (1921)

Well, I saw the same thing that poor Heaton saw—and I saw it after reading the manuscript, so I know more of its history than he did. That makes it worse—for I know all that it *implies*; all that must be still brooding and festering and waiting down there. I told you it had padded mechanically toward me out of the narrow passage and had stood sentry-like at the entrance between the frightful eidola of Yig and Tulu.

H. P. Lovecraft & Zealia Bishop, "The Mound" (1930)

> In this dark throng my sight could trace
> Beings from all ethereal space;
> A sentient chaos gather'd here
> From ev'ry immemorial sphere,
> Yet of one mind, with ardour rife
> To find the Eidolon call'd *Life*.

H. P. Lovecraft, "Astrophobos" (1917)

> And now the moon in heav'n stood still
> As if no more foreboding ill,
> Whereat the throngs aerial knew
> That *Life* at last was in their view;
> That the fair mount each gaz'd upon
> Was *Life*, the long-sought Eidolon!

H. P. Lovecraft, "Astrophobos" (1917)

The more superstitious and timid began leaving the city forthwith; and there was much revival of forgotten prophecies; and much talk among the various priesthoods anent the necessity of placating with liberal sacrifice their mystically angered gods and eidolons.

Clark Ashton Smith, "The Testament of Athammaus" (1931)

Unclean and bestial as a figment of some atavistic madness, the eidolon seemed to drowse on the altar. It troubled the mind with a slow, insidious horror; it assailed the senses with an emanating stupor, an effluence as of primal worlds before the creation of light, where life might teem and raven slothfully in the blind ooze.

Clark Ashton Smith, "The Dweller in the Gulf" (1932)

"The monks were but emanations of Ujuk," said Zobal. "They were mere phantasms, multiple eidola, that he sent forth and withdrew into himself at will; they had no real existence apart from him. With Ujuk's death they have become less than shadows."

Clark Ashton Smith, "The Black Abbot of Puthuum" (1935)

Chryselephantine, clear as carven flame,
Before my gaze thy soul's eidolon stands,
As on the threshold of the frozen lands
A frozen sun forevermore the same.

Clark Ashton Smith, "Eidolon" (1918)

Though proud as Babylon our bliss,
Mortal corruption is
The seed self-sown
Amid the rampant flowers and the founts. . . .
The laughter of some blind eidolon mounts
Where the self-deluded mourner sobs alone
Amid the ruined flowers and the founts.

Clark Ashton Smith, "Some Blind Eidolon" (1942; ellipsis in original)

In his enthusiasm he failed to notice the furtive whispers of the natives and the guides, and disregarded their fearsome glances at the unclean eidolon.

Robert Bloch, "The Faceless God" (1936)

Perhaps five feet in height, it was little more than a thick stone column with arms and legs cut into its roundness, and a head which was a stone ball set atop the indentations that represented shoulders. It had been that eidolon against which his sword had clanged, filling his body with its eerie power.

Gardner F. Fox, *Kothar and the Wizard Slayer* (1970)

The barbarian saw a stone statue—the eidolon of Afgorkon—grown to an immense height.

Gardner F. Fox, *Kothar and the Wizard Slayer* (1970)

From out of the caverns, mewling vashti came
To mock me in my terror, till the same
Fell whisper scattered them and grisly dawn
Destroyed me; yet, before I fell, I heard
The fearful courier's long-awaited word:
"Remember when you were the Eidolon!"

Robert A. W. Lowndes, "The Courier" in *Annals of Arkya*

I caught the name Vodalus in the air; but at that moment it seemed I was the only one who heard it, and suddenly I felt Vodalus had been only an eidolon created by my imagination from the fog, and only the man I had slain with his own ax real.

Gene Wolfe, *The Shadow of the Torturer* (1980)

Blake Williams became a regular at these *soirées*, and often retired sneakily to the kitchen to make notes, which later resulted in a scholarly article, "Priapism Recrudescent: Hellenic Religion in a Secular Contest." The "ithyphallic eidolon," as he insisted on calling Ms. Wildeblood's obscene joke, seemed to produce markedly different effects on various personality types. One football player, for instance, had to be removed in a straitjacket.

Robert Anton Wilson, The Universe Next Door in the
Schrödinger's Cat Trilogy (1979)

eikon, *n.* [< NL < Gr *eikôn*] An icon; a statue, idol, eidolon.

Not like the eikons of other gods were those of Zo-Kalar and Tamash and Lobon, for so close to life were they that one might swear the graceful bearded gods themselves sate on the ivory thrones.

H. P. Lovecraft, "The Doom That Came to Sarnath" (1919)

And when I saw that this reef was but the black basalt crown of a shocking eikon whose monstrous forehead now shone in the dim moonlight and whose vile hooves must paw the hellish ooze miles below, I shrieked lest the hidden face rise above the waters, and lest the hidden eyes look at me after the slinking away of that leering and treacherous yellow moon.

H. P. Lovecraft, "What the Moon Brings" (1922)

About both writing and image there hung an air of sinister evil so profound and pervasive that I could not think it the product of any one world or age. Rather must that monstrous shape be a focus for all the evil in unbounded space, throughout the æons past and to come—and those eldritch symbols be vile sentient eikons endowed with a morbid life or their own and ready to wrest themselves from the parchment for the reader's destruction.

H. P. Lovecraft & William Lumley, "The Diary of Alonzo Typer" (1935)

Those who had issued from the temple re-entered it, and came out once more carrying a huge image of Hziulquoigmnzhah, some smaller eikons of lesser though allied deities, and a very ancient-looking idol which both Eibon and Morghi recognized as having a resemblance to Zhothaqquah.

Clark Ashton Smith, "The Door to Saturn" (1930)

The many carven figures cast twisted and fantastic shadows on the wall as he shifted it about. Crude eikons from Africa that were but roughly shipped logs, and elaborately ornamented monstrosities from India. Squat, grotesque pottery images of ancient Mexico sat cheek by jowl with delicate translucent figurines of amber and jade from China.

R. H. Barlow, "The Eyes of the God" (1933)

eldritch, eldrich, (elritch, elrich), *adj.* [? < *elf* + *riche*, kingdom] Weird, eerie, spooky, spectral, strange, uncanny, unearthly, *unheimlich*.

Titles: Clark Ashton Smith, "The Eldritch Dark" (verse); Philip K. Dick, *The Three Stigmata of Palmer Eldritch*; Esther M. Friesner, "Love's Eldritch Ichor"

[. . .]
Thare was Pluto, the elrich incubus,
   In cloke of grene, his court usit no sable.

William Dunbar, The Goldyn Targe (1508)

His lengthen'd chin, his turned-up snout,
   His eldritch squeel an' gestures,
O how they fire the heart devout,
   Like cantharidian plasters,
     On sic a day!

Robert Burns, "The Holy Fair"

The creature grain'd an eldritch laugh,
And says, "Ye needna yoke the pleugh,
Kirk-yards will soon be till'd enough,
   Tak ye nae fear:
They'll a' be trench'd wi' mony a sheugh
   In twa-three year.

Robert Burns, "Death and Doctor Hornbook: A True Story"

I've heard my reverend Grannie say,
In lanely glens ye like to stray;
Or where auld, ruin'd castles, gray,
   Nod to the moon,
Ye fright the nightly wand'rer's way,
   Wi' eldritch croon.

Robert Burns, "Address to the Deil"

The cudgel in my nieve did shake,
Each bristl'd hair stood like a stake,
When wi' an eldritch stoor quaick, quaick,
   Amang the springs,
Awa ye squatter'd like a drake,
   On whistling wings.

Robert Burns, "Address to the Deil"

As eager rins the market-croud,
When "Catch the thief!" resounds aloud;
So Maggie rins, the witches follow,
Wi' monie an eldrich skreech and hollow.—

Robert Burns, "Tam O'Shanter: A Tale"

I look'd upon the rotting Sea,
 And drew my eyes away;
I look'd upon the eldritch deck,
 And there the dead men lay.

     S. T. Coleridge, "The Rime of the Ancyent Marinere"
[1798 version; later replaced by "ghastly", and finally by "rotting".]

On taking leave of Barbara, and promising to attend her on the following Sabbath, a burst of eldrich laughter arose close by, and a voice, with a hoarse and giggling sound, exclaimed, "No sae fast, canny lad—no sae fast. There will maybe be a whipping o' cripples afore that play be played."

     James Hogg, "Fairies, Deils, and Witches" (1828)

'Mid the sleet and the rain did St. Clair remain
 Till the evening star did rise;
And the rout so gay did dwindle away
 To the elritch dwarfy size.

     J. Leyden, "The Elfin-King" (1801)

In fact, adown the vista of the garden avenue a number of persons were seen approaching, towards the house. Pearl, in utter scorn of her mother's attempt to quiet her, gave an eldritch scream, and then became silent; not from any notion of obedience, but because the quick and mobile curiosity of her disposition was excited by the appearance of these new personages.

     Nathaniel Hawthorne, *The Scarlet Letter* (1850)

The huntsman has ridden too far on the chase,
And eldrich, and eerie, and strange is the place!

     Owen Meredith (Robert Bulwer-Lytton), *Lucile* (1860)

And the woman, whose voice had risen to a kind of eldritch singsong, turned with a skip, and was gone. I stood where she left me, with my hair on end. In those days folk still believed in witches and trembled at a curse; and this one, falling so pat, like a wayside omen, to arrest me ere I carried out my purpose, took the pith out of my legs.

     Robert Louis Stevenson, *Kidnapped* (1886)

As for Janet she cam' an' she gaed; if she didnae speak muckle afore, it was reason she should speak less then; she meddled naebody; but she was an eldritch thing to see, an' name wad hae mistrysted wi' her for Ba'weary glebe.

     Robert Louis Stevenson, "Thrawn Janet" (1881)

But Malachias' tale began to freeze them with horror. He conjured up the scene before them. The secret panel beside the chimney slid back and in the recess appeared—Haines! Which of us did not feel his flesh creep! He had a portfolio full of Celtic literature in one hand, in the other a phial marked *Poison*. Surprise, horror, loathing were depicted on all faces while he eyed them with a ghostly grin. I anticipated some such reception, he began with an eldritch laugh, for which, it seems, history is to blame. Yes, it is true. I am the murderer of Samuel Childs. And how I am punished! The inferno has no terrors for me. This is the appearance is on me. Tare and ages, what way would I be resting at all, he muttered thickly, and I tramping Dublin this while back with my share of songs and himself after me the like of a soulth or a bullawurrus? My hell, and Ireland's, is in this life. It is what I tried to obliterate my crime. Distractions, rookshooting, the Erse language (he recited some), laudanum (he raised the phial to his lips), camping out. In vain! His spectre stalks me. Dope is my only hope. . . . Ah! Destruction! The black panther!

James Joyce, Ulysses (1914–21; ellipsis in original)

[soulth: ghost, apparition; bullawurrus: smell of murder]

A flute woke a thread of melody amid the tapping and shouts and laughter. A horn warbled throatily, and an eldritch din of bagpipes broke out; Yaan was striding about the inner ring, wielding now a little whip, but Red Anne sat alone on the altar, her cow's mask pulled again over her face.

Leslie Barringer, Joris of the Rock (1928)

Therewith up rose an eldritch cry, "Rejoice, for this earth-born is mad!"

E. R. Eddison, The Worm Ouroboros (1922)

The Senators were certainly not loved by the rabble. However, not having heard Moonlove's eldritch shrieks nor her wild remarks, they supposed that her father had been bullying her for some mild offence, and that, in consequence, she had taken to her heels.

Hope Mirrlees, Lud-in-the-Mist (1926)

And lying now alone in my bed, with the candle guttering on the low table at the bedside and the cigarette cold in my fingers, I found myself musing upon an eldritch fancy indeed. For I thought, this is a haunted place, this manor of Mordance Hall.

Leonard Cline, The Dark Chamber (1927)

We boys used to overrun the place, and I can still recall my youthful terror not only at the morbid strangeness of this sinister vegetation, but at the eldritch atmosphere and odour of the dilapidated house.

H. P. Lovecraft, "The Shunned House" (1924)

Good God! What eldritch dream-world was this into which he had blundered?

H. P. Lovecraft, "The Colour Out of Space" (1927)

The Thing cannot be described—there is no language for such abysms of shrieking and immemorial lunacy, such eldritch contradictions of all matter, force, and cosmic order. A mountain walked or stumbled. God!

H. P. Lovecraft, "The Call of Cthulhu" (1926)

And yet I plodded on as if to some eldritch rendezvous—more and more assailed by bewildering fancies, compulsions, and pseudo-memories.

H. P. Lovecraft, "The Shadow out of Time" (1935)

Moon-madness? A touch of fever? I wish I could think so! But when I am alone after dark in the waste places where my wanderings take me, and hear across infinite voids the demon echoes of those screams and snarls, and that detestable crunching of bones, I shudder again at the memory of that eldritch night.

C. M. Eddy, Jr. & H. P. Lovecraft, "The Ghost-Eater" (1923)

Blake had reveled in the weird traditions and shuddering hints about the house and its former tenants. Such eldritch lore was an imaginative asset from whose enjoyment his physical state might not bar him.

C. M. Eddy, Jr. & H. P. Lovecraft, "Deaf, Dumb, and Blind" (1924)

Masters of the macabre like H. P. Lovecraft tried so hard (and so successfully) to put off actually introducing any of their eldritch horrors until the last moment, that the most dreadful thing about these stories is their endless tedium.

Damon Knight, *In Search of Wonder*

But Lovecraft preferred to write description rather than narration; he thought that the essential part of a story was its mood or atmosphere rather than its story-line or even its *dénouement*, which was sometimes given away at the very beginning of his tale; and so he peppered his tales with adjectives to heighten the mood. His choice of adjectives was not always the best, and some of them—like the ubiquitous *eldritch*—have been ridiculed by critics.

J. Vernon Shea, "On the Literary Influences Which Shaped Lovecraft's Works"

One could never guess what would trigger Stanley: Two boys talking in the back or an unusual display of ignorance could set off the scream. Now, the scream was no ordinary human scream. It was a cry from another species or world. An H. P. Lovecraft ghoul's eldritch howl or the blast Tarzan's Tantor the Elephant made.

Gore Vidal, *Palimpsest: A Memoir* (1995)

He felt an eery consternation, an eldrich horror.

Clark Ashton Smith, "Mother of Toads" (1937)

At the same time an irresistible drowsiness surged upon Gerard himself in spite of all his volition, in spite of the eldritch terrors and forebodings that still murmured in his brain.

Clark Ashton Smith, "A Rendezvous in Averoigne" (1930)

On the old lectern or reading-stand which he used for his heavier tomes, *The Testaments of Carnamagos*, in its covers of shagreen with hasps of human bone, lay open at the very page that had frightened him so unreasonably with its eldritch intimations.

Clark Ashton Smith, "The Treader of the Dust" (1935)

Then, towering to a terrible height, which the wrenchings of the rack had given him, he pointed his long forefinger, dark and sere as that of a mummy, at the king's crown; and simultaneously he uttered a foreign word that was shrill and eldritch as the crying of migrant fowl that pass over toward unknown shores in the night.

Clark Ashton Smith, "The Voyage of King Euvoran" (1933)

I would gladly have strangled the distant owl and the more distant dog, each of which, at irregular intervals, continued to emit its eldritch lament. Just as I would think that they had knocked off for good, one or the other of the eery sounds would break out through the night. And the miserable dog seemed to be coming gradually nearer!

Marion Brandon, "The Dark Castle" (1931)

There be many who revere the Devourer, though few have seen the full stature of this great power. It is a vision fraught with eldritch horror, and much sought by wizards of early times. One, Johannes of Madgeburg, wise in the lore of the ages, hath met success greatly in his efforts. He asserteth that the Devourer liveth in the Deep, and is not to be reached by any means, yet he hath been able to feel his breath and know his will. The secret is in a vaporous effluvium. For the Devourer hath power to manifest himself where there is moisture. His breath is the fog and the rain. Wherefore, many do account water the elemental, and do worship it in divers ways.

Kane, *Magic and the Black Arts*, as quoted in
Bertram Russell, "The Scourge of B'Moth" (1929)

Then did life become indeed but a dream, and the opium-visioned nightmares took on the semblances of events and places mentioned in the eldritch volumes that he read by day.

Robert Bloch, "Black Lotus" (1935)

A meager talent for sketching and crayon work led me to attempt crude picturizations involving the outlandish denizens of my nighted thoughts. The same somber trend of intellect which drew me in my art interested me in obscure realms of musical composition; the symphonic strains of the Planets Suite and the like were my favorites. My inner life soon became a ghoulish feast of eldritch, tantalizing horrors.

Robert Bloch, "The Shambler from the Stars" (1935)

There are some things that should not even be hinted at to sane minds, and the things that haunted him nightly were among them. In his visions these beings did not accost him and were seemingly unmindful of his presence; they continued to indulge in eldritch feastings in the charnel chambers or join in orgies without a name.

> Robert Bloch, "The Grinning Ghoul" (1936)

It has never been put on paper before—the true story of Edgar Gordon's death. As a matter of fact, nobody but myself knows that he *is* dead; for people have gradually forgotten about the strange dark genius whose eldritch tales were once so popular among fantasy lovers everywhere.

> Robert Bloch, "The Dark Demon" (1936)

Passing by the graveyard at night, a spot about which eldritch legends had clung for nearly three centuries, his drink-befuddled eyes must have given reality to the hazy phantoms of a superstitious mind.

> Henry Kuttner, "The Salem Horror" (1937)

"Still," she chuckled again, a mocking, eldritch cackle, and stared into the fire that woke red gleams in the amethysts on her hands, "I have been hostess at Witch House a long time; I may find it hard to forget my duties."

> Evangeline Walton, *Witch House* (1945)

How to describe such beauty? Her eyes were blue, wondrous, though not without a taint of fiendishness in them; an almost invisible veil slipped down from the neck, the shoulders, half-revealing, hoo boy, the gleaming breasts. And eldritch, eldritch beyond all song was that exquisite head and bust floating above me—and beautiful, dextrously beautiful beyond all singing, too. So might even Potiphar's wife, that ever-normal granary of fruitfulness, have shown herself tempting Joseph!

> James Blish & Judith Ann Lawrence, "Getting Along" (1972)

In those days the Faerie folk still dwelt upon earth, but even then a strangeness hung over their holdings, as if these wavered halfway between the mortal world and another; and places which might at a given time appear to be a simple lonely hill or lake or forest would at another time gleam forth in eldritch splendor. Hence those northern highlands known as the elf-hills were shunned by men.

> Poul Anderson, *The Broken Sword* (1954)

Kirby hesitated in the face of this awesome wonder but Quinlan dragged him forward into the stupendous opening which clearly led into an eldritch primal world.

> John Glasby, "The Ring of the Hyades"

He began to see phantom colors, shapes, things without name or form. He heard eldritch symphonies, ghost echoes, mad howling noises. A million impossible smells roiled through him. A thousand false pains and pressures tore at him, as if his whole body had been amputated.

Norman Spinrad, "Carcinoma Angels"

And inside none dared sleep, for sleep brought dreams like three-fold nightmare; they crouched trembling in the dark behind locked doors, while outside taloned *things* scratched at shutters and laughed, and eldritch lights slashed from the crest of the hill where the pillars stood, with none to see save that old man.

Gary Myers, "The Feast in the House of the Worm" (1970)

Forcing down a spasm of superstitious dread, Imaro recalled a tale he had heard from Pomphis, the Bambuti pygmy with whom he had shared fantastic adventures along the East Coast of Nyumbani. Bwala li Mwesu ... an eldritch, blasphemous ritual to the Mashataan once practiced by an inhuman race called the Kyaggath, one of many such which had dominated Nyumbani before the coming of the Sky Walkers. These fiendish creatures still survived, in myth if not reality ...

Charles R. Saunders, "The Pool of the Moon" (1976; ellipses in original)

And, of course, anti-Illuminati diatribes of all schools somberly agree that "accidents have a way of happening to those who find out too much about the Bavarian Illuminati." (Let's have that rising organ music again, and an eldritch laugh, like The Shadow's on the old radio series.)

Robert Anton Wilson, *Cosmic Trigger: The Final Secret of the Illuminati* (1977)

"I was walking on Lexington Avenue one morning around three A.M.," this drunk maundered on, "and I heard this URRRRRP, this horrible *eldritch laughter* just like in an H. P. Lovecraft story, and do you want to know what I think it was? A publisher and his lawyer had just figured out a new way to screw one of their writers."

Robert Anton Wilson, *The Universe Next Door* in the
Schrödinger's Cat Trilogy (1979)

The stranger, although dressed in the best clothing of the English upper class, carried a meager straw traveling case, which might contain deadly poison, venomous cobras or human heads to judge by the eldritch laugh which broke from his lips as he fought—visibly to all—to restrain an outright collapse into hysteria.

Robert Anton Wilson, *Masks of the Illuminati* (1981)

In each dream, Jones was dressed as a medieval wizard, with pointed hat and robes bearing the Order of Saint George with strange astrological glyphs, and he always led Sir John up a dark hill toward a crumbling Gothic building of indeterminate character midway between abbey and castle. This eldritch edifice was, of course (as Sir John knew even in the dream), a blend of various illustrations he had seen depicting Chapel Perilous of the Grail legend or the Dark Tower to which Childe Roland came.

Robert Anton Wilson, *Masks of the Illuminati* (1981)

Q: With what books was the library of Babcock Manor stocked by Sir John?
A: A prevarication of politics, a chronology of history, a gnome of mythology, a schiz of theology [including a serenity of Buddhists, a cosmology of Hindus, an inscrutability of Taoists and a war of Christians], an eldritch of Alhazreds, a fume of alchemists, a tree of Cabalists, a heresiarch of Brunos, a lot of Lulls, an ova of Bacons, a mystification of Rosycrosses, a silence of Sufis, an enoch of Dees, a wisdom of Gnostics and a small snivel of romances.

Robert Anton Wilson, *Masks of the Illuminati* (1981; brackets in original)

Adam, the gardener, had been tripping his brains out on LSD since the third week of the rains and the grounds had the eldritch and nameless appearance of the swamps of Yuggoth redesigned by Salvador Dali. If the damnable downpour did not cease soon, I feared that we all should become mad. I think I myself would have been sunk in lethargy and existential despair if it were not for my mescaline and XTC stashes.

Robert Anton Wilson, "The Horror on Howth Hill" (1990)

"For one who calls himself the Eldritch Lord of Evil, you look rather startled— 'thunderstruck' is the word!"

Gary Gygax, *Artifact of Evil* (1986)

They traveled through marine tunnels to the bottomless lakes near Sauk City, Wisconsin. There they colored the dreams of the Arkham House writers— producing many eldritch tomes bound in black Novolex.

Don Webb, "Metamorphosis No. 11" in *Uncle Ovid's Exercise Book* (1988)

elemental, *adj.* & *n.* Of or pertaining to one of the elements, particularly to one of the four classical elements—earth, air, fire, and water. Any of various non-human spirits held to inhabit the four elements. In the Rosicrucian conception, as established by Paracelsus, the major groups of the elementals and their respective elements, are: for fire, the salamanders; for earth, the gnomes; for water, the undines; for air, the sylphs. Many fairies and other spirits, demigods, etc. have also been considered elementals, including elves, fays, dwarves, trolls, kobolds, goblins, pixies, brownies, satyrs, fauns, nymphs, nixies, jinn, peris, and so forth. See the entries under the individual names of these various sorts of supernatural beings.

The Dwarfs and Elves of the Scandinavians; the Nymphs, Hamadryads, and Nature Spirits of the Greeks; the Fairies good and bad of the legends dear to our childish days; the host of Mermaids, Satyrs, Fauns, Sylphs, and Fays; the Forces intended to be attracted and propitiated by the Fetishes of the Negro-Race; are for the most part no other thing than the ill-understood manifestations of this great class, the Elementals.

S. L. MacGregor-Mathers, Introduction to *The Book of the Sacred Magic of Abra-Melin the Mage, as Delivered by Abraham the Jew unto His Son Lamech, A.D. 1458*

"These Hungarians believe in all sorts of rubbish: you remember the shop-woman at Pressburg warning us that no one ever landed here because it belonged to some sort of beings outside man's world! I suppose they believe in fairies and elementals, possibly demons too."

Algernon Blackwood, "The Willows"

But there are repulsive Elemental forms, as well, in addition to those mentioned by [Francis] Barrett, having, for instance, the appearance of huge insects, with heads of birds or of human beings. A gruesome theory, employed finely in fiction by Sheridan le Fanu, has been advanced, according to which the creatures seen by sufferers from delirium tremens, by opium-smokers and by other drug-slaves, are simply forms taken by the lowest class of Elements which the action of the poison has in some way rendered visible.

Sax Rohmer (Arthur Sarsfield Ward), *The Romance of Sorcery* (1917)

Branching away now and then were narrow, half-concealed roads that bored their way through solid, luxuriant masses of forest among whose primal trees whole armies of elemental spirits might well lurk.

H. P. Lovecraft, "The Whisperer in Darkness" (1930)

Narrow, half-hidden roads bore their way through solid, luxuriant masses of forest, among whose primal trees whole armies of elemental spirits lurk.

H. P. Lovecraft, "Vermont—A First Impression"

"There was a constant reference, too, in Wentworth's mutterings, to a Black-wood, by whom he evidently meant the writer Algernon Blackwood, a man who spent some time here in Canada, says Dr. Jamison. The doctor gave me one of this man's books, pointing out to me several strange stories of air elementals, stories remarkably similar in character to the curious Stillwater mystery, yet nothing so paradoxically definite and vague. I can refer you to the stories if you do not already know them."

August Derleth, "The Thing That Walked on the Wind" (1933)

"Elementals," I persisted, "—and you must believe this—yearn for life. They are cosmic ghouls, feeding on dead soul-bodies; but they long to lure a living man through the planes to them. Consider all legend—it's merely allegory. Stories of men disappearing, selling their souls to the devil, going to foreign worlds;

all are founded on the idea of Elementals seeking human prey and dragging men down to their plane."

Robert Bloch, "The Sorcerer's Jewel" (1939)

Elysian, elysian, *adj.* [< *Elysium*] Of, pertaining to, or resembling Elysium (q.v.), the Elysian Fields; hence, blissful, delightful, etc.

Amidst this elysian realm I dwelt not as a stranger, for each sight and sound was familiar to me; just as it had been for uncounted æons of eternity before, and would be for like eternities to come.

H. P. Lovecraft, "Beyond the Wall of Sleep" (1919)

"O Moonlit, Mound-mark'd Moor of *Death*,
Renew thy reign! Thy lethal breath
Is balm elysian to the soul
That sees the light and knows the whole."

H. P. Lovecraft, "Astrophobos" (1917)

Elysium, elysium, *pr.n* & *n.* In Greek mythology, the abode of the blessed in the afterlife. Also known as the Elysian Fields. Cf. **Elysian, Helusion.**

Beautiful beyond words was the marble sepulchre which stricken Musides carved for his beloved friend. None but Kalos himself could have fashioned such bas-reliefs, wherein were displayed all the splendours of Elysium.

H. P. Lovecraft, "The Tree" (1920)

The air is heavy with the noxious odors of fungi and the scent of damp, mouldy earth, but to me it is the aroma of Elysium.

C. M. Eddy, Jr. & H. P. Lovecraft, "The Loved Dead" (1923)

empusa (*pl.* **empusæ, empusas**), **empuse,** *n.* [< Gr *émpousa*] In Greek mythology, a lamia; a spectre, bugbear, hobgoblin. Among other conceptions, empusæ were believed to be ass-haunched and brazen-sandaled, or with one ass's foot and one brazen foot, and to be able to take the forms of a bitch, a cow, and a beautiful young woman. They would lie with men and vampirize them in their sleep.

Another miracle was performed by Apollonius in favour of a young man, named Menippus of Corinth, five and twenty years of age, for whom the prophet entertained a singular favour. This man conceived himself to be beloved by a rich and beautiful woman, who made advances to him, and to whom he was on the point of being contracted in marriage. Apollonius warned his young friend against the match in an enigmatical way, telling him that he nursed a serpent in his bosom. This, however, did not deter Menippus. All things were prepared; and the wedding table was spread. Apollonius, meanwhile, came among them, and prevented the calamity. He told the young man that the dishes before him, the wine he was drinking, the vessels of gold and silver that appeared around him, and the very guests themselves were unreal and illusory; and to prove his words, he caused them immediately to vanish. The bride alone was refractory. She prayed the philosopher not to torment her, and not to compel her to confess what she was. He was, however, inexorable. She at length owned that she was an empuse (a sort of vampire), and that she had determined to cherish and pamper Menippus, that she might in conclusion eat his flesh, and lap up his blood.

William Godwin, *Lives of the Necromancers; or, An Account of the Most Eminent Persons in Successive Ages Who Have Claimed for Themselves, or to Whom Has Been Imputed by Others, the Exercise of Magical Power* (1834)

We would tell of Haunting Old Women, and Knocking Ghosts, and Solitary Lean Hands, and Empusas on One Leg, and Ladies growing Longer and Longer, and Horrid Eyes meeting us through Keyholes, and Plaintive Heads, and Shrieking Statues, and shocking Anomalies of Shape, and Things which when seen drove people mad; and Indigestion knows what besides.

Leigh Hunt, "A Tale for a Chimney Corner" (1819)

APOLLONIUS

At last we left Babylon; and as we travelled by the light of the moon, we suddenly beheld an Empusa.

DAMIS

Aye, indeed! She leaped upon her iron hoof; she brayed like an ass; she galloped among the rocks. He shouted imprecations at her; she disappeared.

Gustave Flaubert (trans. Lafcadio Hearn), *The Temptation of Saint Anthony* (1882)

About his ankles, as he went to and fro, there clung lascivious empusæ with breasts that were furred like the bat; and serpent-bodied lamiæ minced and pirouetted before his eyes, like the dancers before the king.

Clark Ashton Smith, "The Witchcraft of Ulua" (1933)

energumen, *n.* [< LL *energūmenus* < Gr *energoúmenos*, worked-upon] One possessed by a demon or spirit; a dæmoniac.

Back and forth, in an irregular, drunken, zigzag course, from end to end and side to side of the harried realm, the giant strode without pause, like an energumen possessed by some implacable fiend of mischief and murder, leaving behind him, as a reaper his swath, an ever-lengthening zone of havoc, of rapine and carnage. And when the sun, blackened by the smoke of burning villages, had set luridly beyond the forest, men still saw him moving in the dusk, and heard still the portentous rumbling of his mad, stormy cachinnation.

Clark Ashton Smith, "The Colossus of Ylourgne" (1932)

Riding on Rosinante where the cars
With dismal unremitting clangors pass,
And people move like curbless energumens
Rowelled by fiends of fury back and forth,
Behold! Quixote comes, in battered mail,
Armgaunt, with eyes of some keen haggard hawk
Far from his eyrie.

> Clark Ashton Smith, "Don Quixote on Market Street" (1950)

Your idea for a new novel of cosmic fantasy is what the late H. S. Whitehead would have called a "honey-cooler," and strikes me as having infinite possibilities. I wonder if the old ecclesiastical word *energumen*, meaning a possessed person, would appeal to you as a title, or part of a title.

> Clark Ashton Smith, letter to Donald Wandrei (27 October 1948)

ensanguined, *ppl. adj.* Blood-stained.

Everybody shrieked when a large rat-like form suddenly jumped out from beneath the ensanguined bedclothes and scuttled across the floor to a fresh, open hole close by.

> H. P. Lovecraft, "The Dreams in the Witch House" (1932)

ephemeron (*pl.* **ephemera, ephemerons**), *n.* [< Gr *ephémeron*] (1) An insect that reputedly lives for only a single day. (2) A plant that reputedly lives for only a single day.

Titles: George Sterling, "Ephemera" (verse)

"Beauty's shadows are tricked up with time's colours which, being set to dry in the sun, are stained with the sun, scarce pleasing the sight ere they begin not to be worth the sight, not much unlike the herb ephemeron, which flourisheth in the morning and is withered before the sun setting."

> Robert Greene, *Pandosto, the Triumph of Time* (1588)

But how could I, an immortal, hope ever hereafter to feel a serious, an elevating and expansive passion for the ephemeron of an hour!

> William Godwin, *St. Leon: A Tale of the Sixteenth Century* (1799)

She had seen that the finger of Death was upon her bosom—that, like the ephemeron, she had been made perfect in loveliness only to die; but the terrors of the grave, to her, lay solely in a consideration which she revealed to me, one evening at twilight, by the banks of the River of Silence.

> Edgar Allan Poe, "Eleonora" (1841)

Man is the ephemeron of one cosmic moment; born to no purpose, unknown yesterday, and tomorrow so perfectly obliterated that MANĀ-YOOD-SUSHĀĪ will never recall whether or not he has ever existed.

> H. P. Lovecraft, letter to Frank Belknap Long (8 January 1924)

Epicure, epicure, *n.* A follower of the philosophy of Epicurus; one who believes that the highest good is pleasure, particularly the refined pleasure of the gourmet.

[. . .] who being demaunded of one what countryman he was, he answered, what countryman am I not? if I be in *Crete*, I can lye, if in *Greece* I can shift, if in *Italy* I can court it: if thou aske whose sonne I am also I aske thee whose sonne I am not. I can carous with *Alexander*, abstaine with *Romulus*, eate with the *Epicure*, fast with the *Stoyck*, sleepe with *Endimion*, watch with *Chrisippus*, using these speaches and other like.

> John Lyly, *Euphues: The Anatomy of Wit* (1578)

To an epicure in murder such as Williams, it would be taking away the very sting of the enjoyment if the poor child should be suffered to drink off the bitter cup of death without fully apprehending the misery of the situation.

> Thomas De Quincey, *On Murder Considered as One of the Fine Arts* (1854)

"Yes," he went on, "magic is justified of her children. There are many, I think, who eat dry crusts and drink water, with a joy infinitely sharper than anything within the experience of the 'practical' epicure."

> Arthur Machen, "The White People" (1899)

I think that we're fished for. It may be that we're highly esteemed by super-epicures somewhere. It makes me more cheerful when I think that we may be of some use after all.

> Charles Fort, *The Book of the Damned* (1919)

No one, I think, could be surprised to know that the famous Joris Karl Huysmans, an epicure in the byways of the occult, made many experiments in Spiritism, and séances were frequently held at No. 11 rue de Sèvres where he lived. Extraordinary manifestations took place, and upon one occasion at least the circle effected a materialization of General Boulanger, or an apparition of the General appeared to them.

> Montague Summers, *The History of Witchcraft and Demology* (1925)

Searchers after horror haunt strange, far places. For them are the catacombs of Ptolemais, and the carven mausolea of the nightmare countries. They climb to the moonlit towers of ruined Rhine castles, and falter down black cobwebbed steps beneath the scattered stones of forgotten cities in Asia. The haunted wood and the desolate mountain are their shrines, and they linger around the sinister monoliths on uninhabited islands. But the true epicure in the terrible, to whom a new thrill of unutterable ghastliness is the chief end and justification of existence, esteems most of all the ancient, lonely farmhouses of backwoods New England; for there the dark elements of strength, solitude, grotesqueness, and ignorance combine to form the perfection of the hideous.

> H. P. Lovecraft, "The Picture in the House" (1920)

Erebean, *adj.* [< *Erebus*] Of, pertaining to, or resembling Erebus (q.v.). [Not in *OED.*]

Not for the first time, there occurred to him the wish that Clément, the Archbishop, had delegated to someone else to investigate the Erebean turpitude of Azédarac.

Clark Ashton Smith, "The Holiness of Azédarac" (1931)

Erebus, *pr.n.* & *n.* [< L < Gr *Érebos*] The place of nether darkness through which departed souls must pass in order to reach Hades.

Titles: Aleister Crowley, "Erebus" in *White Stains: The Literary Remains of George Archibald Bishop, A Neuropath of the Second Empire* (1898)

> But hark! What hear I in the heavens? methinks
> The world's wall shakes, and it foundation shrinks.
> It seems even now that horrible Persephone
> Loosing Megar', Alecto and Tysiphone,
> Weary of reigning in black Erebus,
> Transports her hell between the heavens and us.

Josuah Sylvester, *Du Bartas his Divine Weeks and Workes* (1598)

Fainting and gasping, I looked at that unhallowed Erebus of titan toadstools, leprous fire, and slimy water, and saw the cloaked throngs forming a semicircle around the blazing pillar.

H. P. Lovecraft, "The Festival" (1923)

Approaching the doorway, the brothers beheld a gleaming of red fires within, like the eyes of dragons blinking through infernal murk. They felt sure that the place was an outpost of Erebus, and antechamber of the Pit; but nevertheless, they entered bravely, chanting loud exorcisms and brandishing their mighty crosses of hornbeam.

Clark Ashton Smith, "The Colossus of Ylourgne" (1932)

It had been swept clean of all detritus, and was like the interior of some Cyclopean conduit that might give upon a sub-Martian Erebus.

Clark Ashton Smith, "The Dweller in the Gulf" (1932)

An artist has the right to choose his own subject matter, even if he takes it from the nether pits of Limbo and Erebus.

Clark Ashton Smith, "The Hunters from Beyond" (1931)

> Know you the gulfs below,
> Where darkling Erebus on Erebus is driven
> Between the molecules—atom from atom riven,
> And tossing to and fro,
> Incessant, like the souls on Dante's wind of woe?

Clark Ashton Smith, "Interrogation" (1925)

It was as dark as the backdoor of Erebus.

> Robert E. Howard, "Lord of the Dead"

Whence do these horrors come? Out of what unspeakable Erebus of monstrous abortions in the depths of our own soul do they troop forth to make us dance our jig of loathing?

> John Cowper Powys,
> "My Philosophy up-to-date as Influenced by Living in Wales"

erudite, *adj.* [< L *ērudītus*] Having or displaying erudition or profound learning and knowledge.

The erudite reader, well versed in good-for-nothing lore, will perceive that the above Tale must have been suggested to the old Swiss by a little French anecdote, a circumstance said to have taken place at Paris.

> Washington Irving, note to
> "The Specter Bridegroom: A Traveler's Tale" (1820–21)

"The tone metaphysical is also a good one. If you know any big words this is your chance for them. Talk of the Ionic and Eleatic schools—of Archytas, Gorgias, and Alcmæon. Say something about objectivity and subjectivity. Be sure and abuse a man called Locke. Turn up your nose at things in general, and when you let slip any thing a little *too* absurd, you need not be at the trouble of scratching it out, but just add a foot-note and say that you are indebted for the above profound observation to the '*Kritik der reinen Vernunft*,' or to the '*Metaphysische Anfangsgründe der Naturwissenschaft*.' This will look erudite and—and—and frank."

> Edgar Allan Poe, "How to Write a Blackwood Article" (1838)

He had selected for the diversion of his mind and the delight of his eyes works of a suggestive charm, introducing him to an unfamiliar world, revealing to him traces of new possibilities, stirring the nervous system by erudite phantasies, complicated dreams of horror, visions of careless wickedness and cruelty.

> J.-K. Huysmans (trans. ?), *Against the Grain* (1931; orig. *À Rebours*)

I recall one very strange character who appeared during November—a dark, turbaned, and bushily bearded man with a laboured, unnatural voice, curiously expressionless face, clumsy hands covered with absurd white mittens, who gave a squalid West End address and called himself "Swami Chandraputra." This fellow was unbelievably erudite in occult lore and seemed profoundly and solemnly moved by the resemblance of the hieroglyphs on the scroll to certain signs and symbols of a forgotten elder world about which he professed vast intuitive knowledge.

> H. P. Lovecraft & Hazel Heald, "Out of the Æons" (1933)

He had all the earmarks of the lonely scholar who has devoted patient years to some line of erudite research. He was thin and bent, with a massive forehead and a mane of grizzled hair; and the pallor of the library was on his hollow, clean-shaven cheeks.

Clark Ashton Smith, "The Return of the Sorcerer" (1931)

"For a youth so erudite and clever, the question should be needless," answered Ulua, smiling obliquely.

Clark Ashton Smith, "The Witchcraft of Ulua" (1933)

But all the same she hung around our table, filling sugar basins and what not. We made our conversation especially erudite, each of us merrily spinning his favorite web of half understood intellectual jargon and half-baked private opinion. We were conscious of her presence, all right.

Fritz Leiber, "The Ship Sails at Midnight" (1950)

Before 1776 was over, Adam Smith quietly published *The Wealth of Nations* in Scotland and Adam Weishaupt, even more quietly, founded the Order of the Illuminati in Bavaria, which quickly infiltrated Freemasonic lodges throughout Europe and even in the American colonies; the Illuminati also established a branch at Harvard University, called Phi Beta Kappa, as you may read in Heckethorn's erudite and exhaustive *The Secret Societies of All Ages and Countries*. In England, Sir John Babcock and David Hartley and a few other radicals tried to persuade Parliament to abolish slavery entirely, importation of new slaves having been prohibited since 1772. But for a large part of the English reading public all these events were overshadowed by the Lady Maria Babcock scandal and the subsequent and bloodcurdling Beckersniff blasphemies.

Robert Anton Wilson, *Nature's God* (1991)

erudition, *n.* The state or quality of being erudite or profoundly learned and knowledgeable.

"Let me see. There was '*The Dead Alive*,' a capital thing!—the record of a gentleman's sensations when entombed before the breath was out of his body—full of taste, terror, sentiment, metaphysics, and erudition. You would have sworn that the writer had been born and brought up in a coffin."

Edgar Allan Poe, "How to Write a Blackwood Article" (1838)

As for the fragments of ostensible erudition which are scattered about my pages, hardly anything in them is not pure invention; there never was, naturally, any such book as that which I quote in "The Treasure of Abbot Thomas".

M. R. James, Preface to *Collected Ghost Stories* (1931)

"My race descends from a most notable scholar, mademoiselle, and it well may be the great Jurgen has bequeathed to me some flavor of his unique erudition. For that I certainly need not apologize—"

James Branch Cabell, *The High Place: A Comedy of Disenchantment* (1923)

She read Wilhelm Müller and the fantasies of Gustavo Adolfo Becquer in the original, and Baudelaire endlessly, and Eliphas Levy [*sic*] and those innumberable rhapsodies of Aleister Crowley, monstrous alike in erudition and obliquity. She seemed, in all her sensitive recognition of life, to hang suspended in a trance of horror.

Leonard Cline, The Dark Chamber (1927)

Algernon Harris was the young man's name and post-graduate degrees from Yale and Oxford set him distinctly apart from the undistinguished majority. But it is to his credit that he never paraded his erudition, nor succumbed to the impulse—almost irresistible in a young man with academic affiliations—to put a Ph.D. on the title page of his first book.

Frank Belknap Long, "The Horror from the Hills" (1930)

But Henricus Vanning himself seemed to have more than a surface smattering of erudition. His cultured allusions to various myth-sagas in my stories seemed to hint at deep knowledge and sincere research that peered beyond the blacker veils of human thought. He spoke quite fluently of his delvings into manicheism and primal cult-ceremonials.

Robert Bloch, "The Secret of Sebek" (1937)

Here was wit, erudition, literary criticism; here were the muddled, maudlin outpourings of a mind gone in drink and despair; here was the draft of a projected story, the fragments of a poem; here were a pitiful cry for deliverance and a pæan to living beauty; here were a dignified response to a dunning letter and an editorial pronunciamento to an admirer; here were love, hate, pride, anger, celestial serenity, abject penitence, authority, wonder, resolution, indecision, joy, and soul-sickening melancholia.

Robert Bloch, "The Man Who Collected Poe" (1951)

Borlsover sons for some reason always seemed to marry very ordinary women; which perhaps accounted for the fact that no Borlsover had been a genius, and only one Borlsover had been mad. But they were great champions of little causes, generous patrons of odd sciences, founders of querulous sects, trustworthy guides to the bypath meadows of erudition.

William Fryer Harvey, "The Beast with Five Fingers" (1919)

Esbat, Estbat, *n.* [?< OF *esbat*, play, sport, pastime, frolic < *s'esbattre, s'esbatre*, to play, sport, frolic, pass the time in joyful recreation. Miss Margaret Murray, *The Witch-Cult in Western Europe* (1921), cites Estebène de Cambrue (1567), as quoted in Pierre De Lancre's *Tableau de l'Inconstance des mauvais Anges* (1613): "*les petites assemblées qui se font pres des villes ou parroisses, où il n'y va que ceux du lieu, ils les appellent les esbats: & se font ores en vn lieu de ladicte paroisse, ores en vn autre, où on ne faict que sauter & folastrer, le Diable n'y estant auec tout son grand arroy comme aux grandes assembles.*"] According to Miss Margeret Murray, a periodic, local meeting of the Western Witch-cult, as opposed to the larger, less frequent **Sabbat** or **Sabbath** (q.v.). This distinction is not now generally accepted as valid by scholars. [Not in *OED*.]

> There were two kinds of assemblies; the one, known as the Sabbath, was the General Meeting of all the members of the religion; the other, to which I give— on the authority of Estebène de Cambrue—the name of Esbat, was only for the special and limited number who carried out the rites and practices of the cult, and was not for the general public.
>
> Miss Margaret Murray, *The Witch-Cult in Western Europe* (1921)

> The Esbat differed from the Sabbath by being primarily for business, whereas the Sabbath was purely religious. In both, feasting and dancing brought the pro- ceedings to a close. The business carried on at the Esbat was usually the practice of magic for the benefit of a client or for the harming of an enemy.
>
> Miss Margaret Murray, *The Witch-Cult in Western Europe* (1921)

> There was no fixed day or hour for the Esbat, and in this it differed from the Sab- bath, which was always at night. The Devil let his followers know the time, either by going to them himself or by sending a message by the officer. The message might be by word of mouth, or by some signal understood by the initiated.
>
> Miss Margaret Murray, *The Witch-Cult in Western Europe* (1921)

> In a small district the Chief himself would notify all members as to the place where the *Esbat* or weekly meeting would be held; but in a large district a mem- ber, well known to the whole coven, went from house to house with the infor- mation.
>
> Miss Margaret Murray, *The God of the Witches* (1931)

> Miss Murray, misled no doubt by the multiplicity of material, postulates two separate and distinct kinds of assemblies: The Sabbat, the General Meeting of all members of the religion; the Esbat "only for the special and limited number who carried out the rites and practices of the cult, and [which] was not for the general public. *The Witch-Cult in Western Europe*, p. 97. Görres had already pointed out that the smaller meetings were often known as Esbats. The idea of a "general public" at a witches' meeting is singular.
>
> Montague Summers, *The History of Witchcraft and Demology* (1925; brackets in original)

> I could see very little of the landscape—just a small, swampy valley of strange brown weed-stalks and dead fungi surrounded by scraggly, evilly twisted trees with bare boughs. But behind the village is a dismal-looking hill on whose sum- mit is a circle of great stones with another stone at the centre. That, without question, is the vile primordial thing V—— told me about at the N—— estbat.
>
> H. P. Lovecraft & William Lumley, "The Diary of Alonzo Typer" (1935)

I'm interested in the way you prefer human flesh. De gustibus non disputandum est—but I like mine well-done. I'm particularly fond of the canned brand sold by the Black Man of the Arkham witch-cult coven and prepared in the secret cannery at Innsmouth. It is prepared only from plump, healthy bourgeois specimens (usually those sacrificed as the Sabbats and Estbats in the forest behind Arkham), and is seasoned very highly with forbidden spices grown by non-human gardeners in the walled lamaseries of Leng. I don't care overmuch for vampire-blood, but share your taste for embalming-fluid. As for authors—of course, some are fairly plumpish, but they have an unpleasant flavour for all that. Probably because of the saturation of their tissues with alcohol.

H. P. Lovecraft, letter to Willis Conover (23 September 1936)

"Westcott is playing his last card to dominate the valley," he said. "He's called an Esbat, a meeting, and he intends a sacrifice. I knew it was coming ever since I saw that goat-head in Wagner's fist. The goat-head is used as an announcement for a coming event. Wagner was on his way to somebody with the sign when he was smashed in the head and killed. That's when I started thinking. There hasn't been an Esbat in this valley since old Captain Uriah Carrier died, and my dad told me all about him."

Herbert Gorman, *The Place Called Dagon* (1927)

The rock appeared as old as the ages. It seemed riven immutably into the earth. Yet it was unmistakably the Devil Stone and from its moist toad-like surface the Black Man had preached his blasphemous sermons in times past, had conducted the orgiastic liturgies of the Witches' Sabaoth and the Esbat.

Herbert Gorman, *The Place Called Dagon* (1927)

"They've got a coven *here*, Minnie and Roman, with Laura-Louise and the Fountains and the Gilmores and the Weeses; those parties with the flute and the chanting, those are *sabbaths* or *esbats* or whatever-they-are!"

Ira Levin, *Rosemary's Baby* (1967)

Belladonna would account for the dilation of the eyes, and nightshade was a traditional component of the flying ointment that diabolic witches wore to the Sabbat—or Esbat.

Marion Zimmer Bradley, *Heartlight* (1998)

For a moment Sally broke down completely, then finished her story in a wavering ragged voice: how she'd fallen down in a swoon with the witches' unguent on her hands—the Esbat afterward that seemed half dream, half nightmarish reality—how she'd awakened, naked, in the graveyard at dawn.

Marion Zimmer Bradley, *Heartlight* (1998)

Thus the archer Jean-Louis Pelletier conceived the plan of holding an *Estbat*—a rite kindred to those of Walpurgisnacht and Hallowmass but held at irregular times—to lure forth the Guardian of the Gate, in whose brief absence the archer would perhaps be able to dive into the ancient pool and traverse the gate.

Donald R. Burleson, "The Pool" (1987)

The archer told him that they would prepare the ceremonial sacrifice of a goat in the *Esbat*-rites to tempt the Guardian of the Gate forth from its sentry-post.

Donald R. Burleson, "The Pool" (1987)

F

fain, *adj.* & *adv.* Gladly or happily; wishful or desirous of.

Fain would the curious monk have receded from this horrible place; fain would he have retraced his steps and sought again his cell, fain would he have shut his eyes to the fearful scene; but he could not stir from the spot, he felt rooted there; and though he once succeeded in turning his eyes to the entrance of the vault, to his infinite surprise and dismay he could not discover where it lay, nor perceive any possible means of exit.

"The Monk of Horror; or, The Conclave of Corpses" (1798)

> In dreams I fain would flee the day—
> Too late, for I have lost the way.
>
> H. P. Lovecraft, "Astrophobos" (1917)

Gentle reader, the ugliness of that spectacle buggers description. Who can be a cringing pissing coward, yet vicious as a purple-assed mandril, alternating these deplorable conditions like vaudeville skits? Who can shit on a fallen adversary who, dying, eats the shit and screams with joy? Who can hang a weak passive and catch his sperm in mouth like a vicious dog? Gentle reader, I fain would spare you this, but my pen hath its will like the Ancient Mariner. Oh Christ what a scene is this!

William S. Burroughs, Naked Lunch (1955–59)

familiar, *adj.* & *n.* An attendant spirit or demon, often in animal form.

Titles: J. S. LeFanu, "The Familiar"; H. P. Lovecraft, "The Familiars" in *Fungi from Yuggoth*; August Derleth, "Lesandro's Familiar"

> Thanks gentle Duke: but where is *Pucel* now?
> I thinke her old Familiar is asleepe.
>
> William Shakespeare, King Henry VI, Part I (159-)

> This speedy and quicke appearance argues proofe
> Of your accustom'd diligence to me.
> Now ye Familiar Spirits, that are cull'd
> Out of the powerfull Regions vnder earth,
> Helpe me this once, that France may get the field.
>
> William Shakespeare, King Henry VI, Part I (159-)

The Druids that dwelt in the Isle of Man, which are famous for great conjurers, are reported to have been lousy with familiars. Had they but put their finger and their thumb into their neck, they could have plucked out a whole nest of them.

Thomas Nashe, "The Terrors of the Night; or, A Discourse of Apparitions" (1593)

"I have heard and seen men in love with Platonic superstition under the hot skies of Spain, where the air seems as if it was the breathing of kind spirits and the waters are bright enough for the dwelling; but here in this foggy island—in this old man's dark head and iron heart! I will see what familiar demon stoops to hold converse with such a sorcerer."

William Child Green, "Secrets of Cabalism; or,
Ravenstone and Alice of Huntingdon" (1809)

The witch's familiar or Astral Spirit is a demon, and as such the word will be used here. Other names signifying a familiar are bunn (generally a term of endearment), imp, likeness, spirit, devil, fiend, angel, maumet, puckrel, nigget.

Montague Summers, *A Popular History of Witchcraft* (1936)

In England the witch's familiar or Astral Spirit went under many names. He was called a bunn or bunting; a dandiprat—terms of endearment; imp; spirit; devil; fiend; fury; angel; little master; maumet; puckril; nigget, and (particularly in New England) spectre.

Montague Summers, *Witchcraft and Black Magic* (1945)

There was, too, the baffling problem of the messengers or intermediaries—the quasi-animals and queer hybrids which legend depicts as witches' familiars.

H. P. Lovecraft, "The Dreams in the Witch House" (1932)

"The demons of the five elements are his familiars," said the second. "The gross eyes of men have beheld them often, flying like birds about his tower, or crawling lizard-wise on the walls and pavements."

Clark Ashton Smith, "The Death of Malygris" (1933)

"By the black thorns of Taaran!" cried Fustules. "It is one of Malygris' familiars. I have heard of this viper—"

Clark Ashton Smith, "The Death of Malygris" (1933)

"Ay. None but a witch would save a witch from honest men, unless it were that witch's own familiar—a comely boy, springing from fiend knows where in the lonely hills."

Leslie Barringer, *Gerfalcon* (1927)

The seven cried aloud, and ran from the window to the inner rooms where the doctor's daughter, bent on uncovered knees, counselled the black toad, her familiar, and the divining cat slept by the wall. The familiar moved its head. The seven danced, rubbing the white wall with their thighs until the blood striped the thin symbols of fertility upon them. Hand in hand they danced among dark symbols, under the charts that marked the rise and fall of the satanic seasons, and their white dresses swung around them.

Dylan Thomas, "The School for Witches" (1936)

Ludvig was reputed to have dwelt there amidst a swarm of familiars and fearsomely invoked conjurations. Manuscripts still extant speak of him guardedly as being attended by "invisible companions" and "Star-sent servants."

Robert Bloch, "The Shambler from the Stars" (1935)

He was particularly interested in the old lore about "familiars"—the tiny creatures who were said to be emissaries of the devil, and were supposed to attend the witch or wizard in the form of a small animal—rat, cat, mole, or ousel. Sometimes they were represented as existing on the body of the warlock himself, or subsisting upon it for their nourishment.

Robert Bloch, "The Mannikin" (1936)

For Arkham was a queer place, once; abode of witch and warlock, familiar and fiend.

Robert Bloch, "The Creeper in the Crypt" (1937)

Ware sat up, mopping his pate with the top sheet, and stared at the cat with nearly neutral annoyance. Even for an Abyssinian, a big-boned breed, the familiar was grossly overweight; clearly an exclusive diet of human flesh was not a healthy regimen for a cat. Furthermore, Ware was not even sure it was necessary. It was prescribed only in Éliphas Lévi, who often made up such details as he went along.

James Blish, Black Easter; or, Faust Aleph-Null (1968)

Then there was an old Irish crone who taught him to call the toads. She could go out into the back yard and croon a toad out from under a stone and Audrey learned to do it too. He had his familiar toad that lived under a rock by the goldfish pool and came when he called it. And she taught him a curse to bring "the blinding worm" from rotten bread.

William S. Burroughs, The Wild Boys: A Book of the Dead (1968–69)

"Lady Desdea is beside herself with anxiety; she suspects that Madouc is moonstruck or possibly possessed by a familiar."

Jack Vance, Madouc (1990)

fantaisiste, *n.* [< Fr] A fantasist; a writer or artist who creates works of fantasy. [Not in *OED*.]

It was not any mere artist's interpretation that we saw; it was pandemonium itself, crystal clear in stark objectivity. That was it, by heaven! The man was not a fantaisiste or romanticist at all—he did not even try to give us the churning, prismatic ephemera of dreams, but coldly and sardonically reflected some stable, mechanistic, and well-established horror-world which he saw fully, brilliantly, squarely, and unfalteringly. God knows what that world can have been, or where he ever glimpsed the blasphemous shapes that loped and trotted and crawled through it; but whatever the baffling source of his images, one thing was plain. Pickman was in every sense—in conception and in execution—a thorough, painstaking, and almost scientific *realist*.

H. P. Lovecraft, "Pickman's Model" (1926)

Later on we see the stream divide, producing strange poets and fantaisistes of the Symbolist and Decadent schools whose dark interests really centre more in abnormalities of human thought and instinct than in the actual supernatural, and subtle story-tellers whose thrills are quite directly derived from the night-black wells of cosmic unreality.

H. P. Lovecraft, "Supernatural Horror in Literature" (1925–27)

The ghost stories you heard from other children form an interesting item. I never heard *oral* weird tales except from my grandfather—who, observing my tastes in reading, used to devise all sorts of impromptu original yarns about black woods, unfathomed caves, winged horrors (like the "night-gaunts" of my dreams, about which I used to tell him), old witches with sinister cauldrons, & "deep, low, moaning sounds". He obviously drew most of his imagery from the early gothic romances—Radcliffe, Lewis, Maturin, &c.—which he seemed to like better than Poe or other later fantaisistes. He was the only other person I knew—young or old—who cared for macabre & horrific fiction.

H. P. Lovecraft, letter to J. Vernon Shea (4 February 1934)

For sustained magic and subtle colour it is hard to touch Klarkash-Ton, High-Priest of Night's Tsathoggua. Poet—artist—fantaisiste—nobody else has yet produced such an exhaustless and exuberant stream of rich, maturely polished fantasy of every sort.

H. P. Lovecraft, letter to C. L. Moore (27 April 1935)

farnoth-fly, *n.* [< *Farnsworth* Wright, editor of *Weird Tales*] An obnoxious insect native to the planet Venus. [Not in *OED*.]

There was little visible decay, and I reflected that in this climate such a thing meant death not more than a day before. Soon the hateful farnoth-flies would begin to cluster about the corpse.

H. P. Lovecraft & Kenneth Sterling, "In the Walls of Eryx" (1936)

fastness, *n.* A strongly fortified place, a stronghold, castle, fort; a secure place to which one can retreat.

"And she sang of how subtle and bitter and bright was a beast brought forth, that was clad with the splendor and light of the cold far ends of the north, like a fleshly blossom more white than augmenting tempests that go, with thunder for weapon, to ravage the strait waste fastness of snow. She sang how that all men on earth said, whether its mistress at morn went forth or waited till night,—whether she strove through the foam and wreckage of shallow and firth, or couched in glad fields of corn, or fled from all human delight,—that thither it likewise would roam."

> James Branch Cabell, *Figures of Earth: A Comedy of Appearances* (1920)

His name, as given on the records, was Joe Slater, or Slaader, and his appearance was that of the typical denizen of the Catskill Mountain region; one of those strange, repellent scions of a primitive colonial peasant stock whose isolation for nearly three centuries in the hilly fastnesses of a little-travelled countryside has caused them to sink to a kind of barbaric degeneracy, rather than advance with their more fortunately placed brethren of the thickly settled districts. Among these odd folk, who correspond exactly to the decadent element of "white trash" in the South, law and morals are non-existent; and their general mental status is probably below that of any other section of the native American people.

> H. P. Lovecraft, "Beyond the Wall of Sleep" (1919)

faveolate, *adj.* Honeycombed.

Beyond the Zone of the Thirteen Faveolate Colossi lies Yuggoth, where dwell the denizens of many extraterrestrial realms. Yuggoth's black streets have known the tread of malformed paws and the touch of misshapen appendages, and unviseagable shapes creep among its lightless towers. But few of the creatures of the rim-world are as feared as that survival of Yuggoth's youth which remains in a pit beyond one of the cities. This survival few have seen, but the legends of the crustaceans tells of a city of green pyramids which hangs over a ledge far down in the dark. It is said that no mind can stand the sight of what occurs on that ledge at certain seasons.

> *Revelations of Glaaki,* as quoted in
> Ramsey Campbell, "The Mine on Yuggoth" (1964)

He glanced up at the names of groups above the ballroom door: the Titus Groans, the Faveolate Colossi. "OK, guys and gals, we've got a fabulously faveolate evening ahead for you," he muttered in faint parody.

> Ramsey Campbell, "Potential"

febrile, *adj.* [< Fr < L *febrīlis* < *febris*, fever] Of or pertaining to fever; characterized by fever; feverish.

"Merriment," replied Florian, "is a febrile passion. But content is quiet."

> James Branch Cabell, *The High Place: A Comedy of Disenchantment* (1923)

It is likely that he felt only vexation when, in 1804, the town council ordered him to fumigate the place with sulphur, tar, and gum camphor on account of the much-discussed deaths of four persons, presumably caused by the then diminishing fever epidemic. They said the place had a febrile smell.

H. P. Lovecraft, "The Shunned House" (1924)

Can it be possible that this planet has actually spawned such things; that human eyes have truly seen, as objective flesh, what man has hitherto known only in febrile phantasy and tenuous legend?

H. P. Lovecraft, "The Shadow over Innsmouth" (1931)

And mixed with the distant chant of the Sabbat and the whimpers of Brown Jenkin in the gulf below he thought he heard another and wilder whine from unknown depths. Joe Mazurewicz—the prayers against the Crawling Chaos now turning to an inexplicably triumphant shriek—worlds of sardonic actuality impinging on vortices of febrile dream—Iä! Shub-Niggurath! The Goat with a Thousand Young. . . .

H. P. Lovecraft, "The Dreams in the Witch House" (1932; ellipsis in original)

All the frantic eagerness hitherto frustrated by obstacles now took itself out in a kind of febrile speed, and I literally raced along the low-roofed, monstrously well-remembered aisles beyond the archway.

H. P. Lovecraft, "The Shadow out of Time" (1935)

Feeling an aroused concern, rather than any offense, I began to note, for the first time, the unwonted pallor of his face, and the bright, febrile luster of his eyes.

Clark Ashton Smith, "Genius Loci" (1932)

"What is your difficulty, febrile magician?"

Jack Vance, "Mazirian the Magician" in *The Dying Earth* (1950)

The goat was laid out upon the ground within a circle of black candles, and with much ceremonial chanting and many febrile intonings of the names of Azathoth and Yog-Sothoth, Jean-Louis Pelletier plunged a dagger into the goat's bowels, passing around clay bowls of the blood to drink, and sprinkling some of the sticky fluid upon the lichened stone rim of the pool.

Donald R. Burleson, "The Pool" (1987)

fell, *adj.* Deadly, dire, fierce, cruel.

I stood a few moments, to let the hearers have a chance to spread my announcement to those who couldn't hear, and so convey it to the furthest ranks, then I made a grand exhibition of extra posturing and gesturing, and shouted:

"Lo, I command the fell spirit that possesses the holy fountain to now disgorge into the skies all the infernal fires that still resmain in him, and straightway dissolve his spell and flee hence to the pit, there to lie bound a thousand years. By his own dread name I command it—BGWJJILLIGKKK!"

Mark Twain, *A Connecticut Yankee in King Arthur's Court* (1889)

Now in the time I tell of, there was trouble in Allathurion, for of an evening fell dreams were wont to come slipping through the tree trunks and into the peaceful village; and they assumed dominion of men's minds and led them in watches of the night, through the cindery plains of Hell.

Lord Dunsany, "The Fortress Unvanquishnable, Save for Sacnoth" (1908)

His speech dried up in his throat as, gazing wildly round, he saw how the Vicar beheld him with a look as fell, as venemous, and as cruel as is in the face of the death-adder.

E. R. Eddison, *A Fish Dinner in Memison* (1936–40)

There is one woman who in fell loveliness excels all the rest. Her poisonous charms are like a honeyed flower growing on the brink of hell.

H. P. Lovecraft & William Lumley, "The Diary of Alonzo Typer" (1935)

"The Paths of the Dead!" said Gimli. "It is a fell name; and little to the liking to the Men of Rohan, as I saw."

J. R. R. Tolkien, *The Return of the King in The Lord of the Rings* (1936–49)

Oromë loved the lands of Middle-earth, and he left them unwillingly and came last to Valinor; and often of old he passed back east over the mountains and returned with his host to the hills and the plains. He is a hunter of monsters and fell beasts, and he delights in horses and in hounds; and all trees he loves, for which reason he is called Aldaron, and by the Sindar Tauron, the Lord of Forests.

J. R. R. Tolkien, *The Silmarillion*

"I, SATAN MEKRATIG, can no longer bear
This deepest, last and bitterest of all
My fell damnations: That at last I know
I never wanted to be God at all;
And so, by winning all, All have I lost."

James Blish, *The Day after Judgment* (1971)

Let him that vizard keep unto his grave,
That vain usurping of an honour'd name;
We'll dance his masque as if it were the truth,
Enlist the poniards swift of Those who, sworn
To punctual vendetta never sleep,
Lest at the palest whisper of the name
Sweet Niccolò hath stol'n, one trice be lost
In bringing down a fell and soulless doom
Unutterable. . . .

Richard Wharfinger, *The Courier's Tragedy*, as quoted in
Thomas Pynchon, *The Crying of Lot 49* (1965; ellipsis in original)

Fescennine, fescennine, *adj.* & *n.* [< *Fescennia*, a city of ancient Etruria renowned for its obscene poetry; perhaps also associated with L *fascinum*, a phallic emblem worn as an amulet] Licentious, obscene, scurrilous; a song or verse of such a character.

Annianus, Sulpicius, Evenus, Menander, and many old poets besides, did *in scriptis prurire*, write Fescennines, Atellanes, and lascivious songs, *lætem materiam*; yet they had *in moribus censuram et severitatem*, they were chaste, severe, and upright livers.

> Robert Burton, *The Anatomy of Melancholy: What It Is, With All the Kinds,*
> *Causes, Symptomes, Prognostickes & Severall Cures of It* (1621)

"I must tell you I perceive, in honest sorrow, that with a desire for fescennine expression you combine a vulgar atheism and an iconoclastic desire to befoul the sacred ideas of the average man or woman, collectively scorned as the bourgeoisie—"

> James Branch Cabell, *The High Place: A Comedy of Disenchantment* (1923)

Balbutius went quite mad, & began to grin & sing an old Fescennine verse from his native Italian countryside.

> H. P. Lovecraft, letter to Bernard Austin Dwyer (4 November 1927)

Balbutius had gone mad and was grinning and simpering out an old Fescennine verse recalled from the Latin countryside of his boyhood.

> Frank Belknap Long, "The Horror from the Hills" (1930;
> adapted from a 1927 letter to Long by H. P. Lovecraft)

They joined in the singing of fescennine songs, they returned the bacchanalian jests that were flung by passers-by, they drank the wines that were proffered them by public urn-bearers, they tarried when the throng tarried, moved when it moved.

> Clark Ashton Smith, "The Planet of the Dead" (1930;
> aka "The Doom of Antarion")

Was there not something absurd about that stiff, twinkling archaic world—the mixture of prudery and sensuality, the stylised ardours of the groom and the conventional bashfulness of the bride, the religious sanction, the permitted salacities of Fescennine song, and the suggestion that everyone except the principals might be expected to be rather tipsy?

> C. S. Lewis, *That Hideous Strength: A Modern Fairy-Tale for Grown-Ups* (1943)

fescenninely, *adv.* In a fescennine (q.v.) manner.

Laying an affectionate hand on Valzain's shoulder, he hoisted aloft with the other that fescenninely graven quart goblet from which he was wont to drink only wine, eschewing the drugged and violent liquors often preferred by the sybarites of Umbri.

Clark Ashton Smith, "Morthylla" (1952)

fetish, fetich, fetiche, *n.* [< Fr *fétiche* < Portuguese *feitiço* < L *facticius,* artificial] An object superstitiously believed to possess magical or spiritual powers.

Later he had somewhat relaxed the severity of his pursuits, and had dabbled in the more frivolous subjects of palæontology and ethnology; he had a cabinet in his sitting-room whose drawers were stuffed with rude flint implements, and a charming fetish from the South Seas was the dominant note in the decorative scheme of the apartment.

Arthur Machen, "Adventure of the Missing Brother" in
The Three Impostors; or, The Transmutations (1894)

But there was a strange thing. There was a little bottle on the mantelpiece, a bottle of dark blue glass, and he trembled and shuddered before it, as if it were a fetish.

Arthur Machen, The Hill of Dreams (1897)

About his person he always carried two small bones wrapped around with a black string, which bones he really appeared to revere as fetiches.

Lafcadio Hearn, "The Last of the Voudoos"

I at least have not ever offended Æsred. Throughout the last some and twenty years, in the while that my more temerarious fellows have with untiring typewriters assailed and derided her notions, I have written on sedately in praise of monogamy in *Jurgen*, and of keeping up appearances in *Figures of Earth*, and of chastity in *Something About Eve*, and of moderation in *The High Place*, and of womanhood in *Domnei*, and of religion in *The Silver Stallion*: and indeed throughout the long building of the Biography I have at every instant upheld, in my own unpresuming way, all that Æsred endorses as the more comfortable fetishes for a man to believe in.

Branch Cabell, These Restless Heads: A Trilogy of Romantics (1931)

All these lived and moved in harmony, employed, happy, free labourers, protected by the most rigid laws. Man-eating, fetich-worship, slavery had been abolished, stamped out.

Joseph Conrad & Ford Madox Ford (Ford Madox Hueffer),
The Inheritors: An Extravagant Story (1901)

"Pah! Don't they stink! You, Makola! Take that herd over to the fetish" (the storehouse was in every station called the fetish, perhaps because of the spirit of civilization it contained) "and give them up some of the rubbish you keep there. I'd rather see it full of bone than full of rags."

Joseph Conrad, "An Outpost of Progress"

Florian had at last persuaded him of how untactful it would be for Hoprig to disrupt a simple and high-hearted faith that had thrived for so many hundred years, by appearing at Bellegarde in person. Florian had pointed out the attendant awkwardnesses, for the fetich no less than for the devotees. And Hoprig, upon reflection, had conceded that for a saint in the prime of life there were advantages in traveling incognito.

James Branch Cabell, *The High Place: A Comedy of Disenchantment* (1923)

The statuette, idol, fetish, or whatever it was, had been captured some months before in the wooded swamps south of New Orleans during a raid on a supposed voodoo meeting; and so singular and hideous were the rites connected with it, that the police could not but realise that they had stumbled on a dark cult totally unknown to them, and infinitely more diabolic than even the blackest of African voodoo circles.

H. P. Lovecraft, "The Call of Cthulhu" (1926)

But just now of prime significance was the fetish which this cult had cherished, and around which they danced when the aurora leaped high over the ice cliffs. It was, the professor stated, a very crude bas-relief of stone, comprising a hideous picture and some cryptic writing.

H. P. Lovecraft, "The Call of Cthulhu" (1926)

Another function of religion was the regulation of the calendar, born of a period when time and speed were regarded as prime fetiches in man's emotional life. Periods of alternate waking and sleeping, prolonged, abridged, and inverted as mood and convenience dictated, and timed by the tail-beats of Great Yig, the Serpent, corresponded very roughly to terrestrial days and nights; though Zamacona's sensations told him they must actually be almost twice as long. The year-unit, measured by Yig's annual shedding of his skin, was equal to about a year and a half of the outer world.

H. P. Lovecraft & Zealia Bishop, "The Mound" (1930)

Looking desultorily about, his attention had been drawn by a dull glimmering on one of the tables; and he had extricated the queer orb-like stone from its shadowy, crowded position between an ugly little Aztec idol, the fossil egg of a dinornis, and an obscene fetich of black wood from the Niger.

Clark Ashton Smith, "Ubbo-Sathla" (1932)

So peace was made with much pow-wow, and sworn to with many strange oaths and rituals—we swore only by Ymir, and an Æsir never broke that vow. But they swore by the elements, by the idol which sat in the fetish-hut where fires burned for ever and a withered crone slapped a leather-covered drum all night long, and by another being too terrible to be named.

Robert E. Howard, "The Valley of the Worm" (1934)

Here in the rear of the place he had relics of other days which made his commercial antiques seem bright and new by contrast. The centuried symbols of magic, alchemy, and the secret sciences fascinated Voorden; he had gathered unto himself a collection of statuettes, talismans, fetishes and other paraphernalia of wizardry that would have been hard to match.

> Robert Bloch, "The Sorcerer's Jewel" (1939)

When the mock grave, their great fetish, was destroyed, the central bonds which held their system together were broken.

> Mearle Prout, "The House of the Worm" (1933)

This greybeard, they said, had become a hermit, and had secreted his dwelling on the hill where the trees are thick and do not behave as trees, and now he spoke no more to men, but worshipped a curious fetish at night when red.

> Gary Myers, "The Feast in the House of the Worm" (1970)

"Ah, we are kindred spirits then. You see, I am not interested in personal gain either. I want the fetiche for the cause of chaos!"

> Paul Di Filippo, *Hottentots* (1994) in the *Steampunk Trilogy*

fetishism, fetichism, *n.* The worship of or belief in fetishes (q.v.).

The mental prostitute, Mrs. Eddy (for example), having invented the idea which ordinary people call "God," christened it "Mind," and then by affirming a set of propositions about "Mind," which are only true of "God," set all hysterical, dyspeptic, crazy Amurka by the ears. Personally, I don't object to people discussing the properties of four-sided triangles; but I draw the line when they use a well-known word, such as pig, or mental healer, or dung-heap, to denote the object of their paranoiac fetishism.

> Aleister Crowley, *777 vel Prolegomena Symbolica ad Systemam Sceptico-Mysticæ Viæ Explicandæ, Fundamentum Hieroglyphicum Sanctissimorum Scientiæ Summæ* (1907)

But before many questions were asked, it became manifest that something far deeper and older than negro fetichism was involved.

> H. P. Lovecraft, "The Call of Cthulhu" (1926)

flaff, *v.intr.* & *v.tr.* To flap, flutter.

> Cloud on hellish cloud
> They arch the zenith, and a dreadful wind
> Falls from them like the wind before the storm,
> And in the wind my riven garment streams
> And flutters in the face of all the void,
> Even as flows a flaffing spirit, lost
> On the pit's undying tempest.

> Clark Ashton Smith, *The Hashish-Eater; or, The Apocalypse of Evil* (1920)

Chill and sere,
Like the grass
Flaffing in a field of snow,
We shall know that nothing mattered,
As we tell our faded woe
Ere we pass.

Clark Ashton Smith, "We Shall Meet" (1923)

Baudelaire (as translated) has nothing better than "We Shall Meet." I don't like that "flaffing," though—it seems an absurd word *in itself*. I'd keep off the ultra-obsolete.

George Sterling, letter to Clark Ashton Smith (6 April 1923)

fœtid, fetid, *adj.* Characterized by a pronounced fœtor (q.v.); noisome and foul-smelling.

"Four thousand of them will live together in a space smaller than the last and lightest colonnade of your young banyan-tree, in order, doubtless, to increase the effects of fœtid air, artificial heat, unnatural habits, and impracticable exercise. The result of these judicious precautions is just what may be guessed. The most trifling complaint becomes immediately infectious, and, during the ravages of the pestilence, which this habit generates, ten thousand lives a-day are the customary sacrifice to the habit of living in cities."

Charles Maturin, *Melmoth the Wanderer: A Tale* (1820)

The eight corpses swung in their chains, a fetid, blackened, hideous, and indistinguishable mass.

Edgar Allan Poe, "Hop-Frog" (1849)

"Imagine some foul and putrid corpse that has lain rotting and decomposing in the grave, a jellylike mass of liquid corruption. Imagine such a corpse a prey to flames, devoured by the fire of burning brimstone and giving off dense choking fumes of nauseous loathsome decomposition. And then imagine this sickening stench, multiplied a millionfold and a millionfold again from the millions upon millions of fetid carcasses massed together in the reeking darkness, a huge and rotting human fungus."

James Joyce, A Portrait of the Artist as a Young Man (1904–14)

"I dreamed one night that I was swimming in a broad stagnant lagoon, tropical, covered with eddies of greenish scum, suspiring a thickly, sweetishly odorous vapor beneath the fierce sun. All around me were the coiling figures of gigantic reptiles among which I swam . . . without dread or revulsion. It was only in the morning when I awoke and remembered the dream that I felt the normal loathing toward that fetid bath."

Leonard Cline, *The Dark Chamber* (1927; ellipsis in original)

Then I went on and parted the close willows, going by intuition and by that guiding thread of sinister reek twined between the trees, fetid.

Leonard Cline, *The Dark Chamber* (1927)

When I opened the door into the elm-arched blackness a gust of insufferably fœtid wind almost flung me prostrate.

H. P. Lovecraft, "The Thing on the Doorstep" (1933)

My seat is the fœtid hollow of an aged grave; my desk is the back of a tomb-stone worn smooth by devastating centuries; my only light is that of the stars and a thin-edged moon, yet I can see as clearly as though it were mid-day.

C. M. Eddy, Jr. & H. P. Lovecraft, "The Loved Dead" (1923)

I stumbled by cave-riddled mountains
    That rise barren and bleak from the plain,
I have drunk of the frog-fœtid fountains
    That ooze down to the marsh and the main;
And in hot cursed tarns I have seen things I care not to gaze on again.

H. P. Lovecraft, "Nemesis" (1917)

Aloft the light of knowledge crawls,
Staining the crumbling city walls
Thro' which in troops ungainly squirm
The fœtid lizard and the worm.

H. P. Lovecraft, "Astrophobos" (1917)

As I had expected, there was no blood—only a black, tarry, fetid exudation, far from copious, which ceased in a few minutes and vanished utterly from my sword and from the *eighon*-wood.

Clark Ashton Smith, "The Testament of Athammaus" (1931)

Evil, ancient, soporous, the night hung about them. It was like the thick and fetid fur of bats: a material thing that choked the lungs, that deadened all the senses. It was silent as the slumber of dead worlds. . . . But out of that silence, after the lapse of apparent years, a twofold and familiar sound arose and over-took the fugitives: the sound of something that slithered over stone far down in the abyss: the sucking noise of a creature that withdrew its feet as if from a quagmire.

Clark Ashton Smith, "The Dweller in the Gulf" (1932; ellipsis in original)

Thou hast departed—and the dog and swine abide,
The fetid-fingered ghouls will delve, on many a morrow
In charnel, urn and grave: the sun shall lantern these,
Oblivious, till they too have faltered and have died,

And are no more than pestilential breath that flees
On air unwalled and wide.

> Clark Ashton Smith, "To George Sterling: A Valediction" (1926)

Then I went alone through the primordial twilight jungle until an over-powering fetid odor assailed my nostrils, and from the rank vegetation in front of me, Satha reared up his hideous head, swaying lethally from side to side, while his forked tongue jetted in and out, and his great yellow terrible eyes burned icily on me with all the evil wisdom of the black elder world that was when man was not.

> Robert E. Howard, "The Valley of the Worm"

"Thereat the great stone cried out as a live thing cries, and the king and his soldiers saw a black cloud spinning up from the floor, and out of the cloud blew a fetid wind, and out of the wind came a grisly shape which stretched forth fearsome paws and laid them on the king, who shriveled and died at their touch."

> Robert E. Howard, "The Fire of Asshurbanipal"

The vision of that fetid obscenity will come between me and the pleasures of the world as long as I remain in the world.

> Frank Belknap Long, "The Space Eaters" (1927)

[Later version: "The vision of that terrible, darkly shrouded shape will come between me and the pleasures of the world as long as I remain in the world."]
From the ceiling to the floor it towered, and it threw off drooling shafts of light. The light was slimy and unspeakable—a liquid light that dripped and dripped, like spittle, like the fetid mucous of loathsome slugs. And pierced by the shafts, whirling around and around, were the pages of Howard's story.

> Frank Belknap Long, "The Space Eaters" (1927)

[Later version: "From the ceiling to the floor it towerd, and it threw off blinding light. And pierced by the shafts, whirling around and around, were the pages of Howard's story."]

I cannot hope to convey the utter strangeness, the atmosphere of unearthliness that surrounded him, almost as palpable as the fetid tomb-stench that welled from his dark garments.

> Henry Kuttner, "The Secret of Kralitz" (1936)

All about him was a musty salt odor of sea decay, the fetid smell of useless ocean caves and holds of ancient ships.

> Robert Bloch & Henry Kuttner, "The Black Kiss" (1937)

As usual lately, my creativity was dampened by the depressing rain, the eldritch, unhallowed and Peter Lorre-like giggles of the gardener after his day's dose of

LSD took effect and the strange, fœtid and nameless fungi that have grown on the furniture since the maids got hooked on methamphetamines and stopped even pretending to clean up.

> Robert Anton Wilson, "The Horror on Howth Hill" (1990)

fœtidity, fetidity, *n.* The state or quality of being fœtid (q.v.).

The black interior of the temple yawned before us, and from it there surged an odor of long-imprisoned mustiness combined with a queer and unfamiliar fetidity.

> Clark Ashton Smith, "The Tale of Satampra Zeiros" (1929)

Try as I would, I could not throw off the thought that a nameless fetidity had me in its control at that moment, and was even now within the car bent upon my destruction.

> Bertram Russell, "The Scourge of B'Moth" (1929)

fœtidly, fetidly, *adv.* In a fœtid (q.v.) manner.

From these foothills the black, ruin-crusted slopes reared up starkly and hideously against the east, again reminding us of those strange Asian paintings of Nicholas Roerich; and when we thought of the damnable honeycombs inside them, and of the frightful amorphous entities that might have pushed their fœtidly squirming way even to the topmost hollow pinnacles, we could not face without panic the prospect of again sailing by those suggestive skyward cavemouths where the wind made sounds like an evil musical piping over a wide range.

> H. P. Lovecraft, *At the Mountains of Madness* (1931)

fœtor, fetor, *n.* A strong and offensive foul odor or stench.

Above the anthropomorphic patch of mould by the fireplace it rose; a subtle, sickish, almost luminous vapour which as it hung trembling in the dampness seemed to develop vague and shocking suggestions of form, gradually trailing off into nebulous decay and passing up into the blackness of the great chimney with a fœtor in its wake.

> H. P. Lovecraft, "The Shunned House" (1924)

Once in a while a wind, sweeping up out of Cold Spring Glen, would bring a touch of ineffable fœtor to the heavy night air; such a fœtor as all three of the watchers had smelled once before, when they stood above a dying thing that had passed for fifteen years and a half as a human being.

> H. P. Lovecraft, "The Dunwich Horror" (1928)

The curious new fœtor which had supplemented the nameless scent was excessively pungent here; so much so that it destroyed all trace of the other.

> H. P. Lovecraft, *At the Mountains of Madness* (1931)

At the same time I breathed an insupportable fetor, like a mingling of rancid serpent-stench with the moldiness of antique charnels and the fearsome reek of newly decaying carrion.

Clark Ashton Smith, "The Hunters from Beyond" (1931)

I seemed to read a nameless purpose in its yellow-slitted eyes, in the soundless moving of its oozy lips; and my soul recoiled with nausea and revulsion as I breathed its pestilential fetor.

Clark Ashton Smith, "The Hunters from Beyond" (1931)

Adompha, watching him curiously, was aware as never before of the stark evil and turpitude that flowed like an overwhelming fetor from Dwerulas' hunched body and twisted limbs.

Clark Ashton Smith, "The Garden of Adompha" (1937)

Like the clammy arms of specters, with death-chill fingers that clutched and caressed, the weird mists drew closer still about Pierre. They thickened in his nostrils and throat, they dripped in a heavy dew from his garments. They choked him with the fetor of rank waters and putrescent ooze . . . and a stench as of liquefying corpses that had risen somewhere to the surface amid the fen.

Clark Ashton Smith, "Mother of Toads" (1937; ellipsis in original)

> Things unseen,
> Whose charnel breath informs the tideless air
> With spreading pools of fetor, follow me
> Elusive past the ever-changing palms;
> And pittering moths with wide and ashen wings
> Flit on before, and insects ember-hued,
> Descending, hurtle through the gorgeous gloom
> And quench themselves on crumbling thickets.

Clark Ashton Smith, *The Hashish-Eater; or, The Apocalypse of Evil* (1920)

For an instant it loomed thus terribly menacing, the soul of all malignancy and horror, a cancerous cyclops oozing fetor.

Frank Belknap Long, "The Horror from the Hills" (1930)

The chimera lay sleeping on a pile of freshly turned clay, and it coughed in its sleep; and the fetor of its belching, wafting upwards, asphyxiated the gnats that swarmed about its head.

Charles G. Finney, *The Circus of Dr. Lao* (1934)

The gray surface of the rock was bedaubed with whitish streaks of fetor, and the shredded bits of the toad's eye.

Henry Kuttner, "Bells of Horror" (1939)

Subadar Ind'dni sniffed curiously. His nostrils twitched. He was familiar with the hundreds of fetors that polluted the Guff, but this stench was new. It was unique. He was astonished again.

Alfred Bester, Golem[100] (1980)

He reached into the urnlike vessel and pulled out, not cremated human ash and bone fragments as I half expected, but the dried leaves of some preserved plant. An intolerable fœtor seemed to billow forth as he disturbed the contents of the receptacle.

Harry S. Robbins, "The Smoker from the Shadows" (1990)

freaked, *ppl. adj.* [Coined by John Milton, perhaps after L *lūsus*, adorned.] Streaked or flecked in a variegated, capricious, and whimsical manner.

> Bring the rathe primrose that forsaken dies,
> The tufted crow-toe, and pale jessamine,
> The white pink, and the pansy freaked with jet,
> The glowing violet
> The musk-rose, and the well-attired woodbine,
> With cowslips wan that hang the pensive head,
> And every flower that sad embroidery wears:
> Bid amaranthus all his beauty shed,
> And daffadillies fill their cups with tears,
> To strew the laureate hearse where Lycid lies.

John Milton, Lycidas (1638)

> Yet there Life glows;
> Yet cherish'd beneath the shining Waste,
> The furry Nations harbour: tipt with Jet,
> Fair Ermines, spotless as the Snows they press;
> Sables, of glossy Black; and dark-embrown'd,
> Or beauteous freakt with many a mingled Hue,
> Thousands besides, the costly Pride of Courts.

James Thomson, "Winter" in The Seasons

> The very dawn was dashed with stormy dew
>   And freaked with fire as when God's hand would mar
> Palaces reared of tyrants, and the blue
>   Deep heaven was kindled round her thunderous car,
> That saw how swift a gathering glory grew
>   About him risen, ere clouds could blind or bar
> A splendor strong to burn and burst them through
>   And mix in one sheer light things near and far.

Algernon Charles Swinburne, "Song for the Centenary of Walter Savage Landor"

A ninefold garland wrought of song-flowers nine
Wound each with each in chance-inwoven accord
Here at your feet I lay as on a shrine
Whereof the holiest love that lives is lord.
With faint strange hues their leaves are freaked and scored:
The fable-flowering land wherein they grew
Hath dreams for stars, and grey romance for dew:
Perchance no flower thence plucked may flower anew.

Algernon Charles Swinburne, Locrine: A Tragedy

—It was as though a garland of red roses
Had fallen about the hood of some smug nun
When irresponsibly dropped as from the sun,
In fulth of numbers freaked with musical closes,
Upon Victoria's formal middle time
    His leaves of rhythm and rhyme.

Algernon Charles Swinburne, "A Singer Asleep"

    Illumined this wise on,
He threads securely the far intricacies,
    With brede from Heaven's wrought vesture overstrewn;
Swift Tellus' purfled tunic, girt upon
With the blown chlamys of her fluttering seas;
    And the freaked kirtle of the pearlèd moon:
Until he gain the structure's core, where stands—
    A toil of magic hands—
The unbodied spirit of the sorcerer,
    Most strangely rare,
    As is a vision remembered in the noon:
Unbodied, yet to mortal seeing clear,
Like sighs exhaled in eager atmosphere.

Francis Thompson, Sister Songs (1895)

Through the belt of trees beyond the brook shone a strange red light, the trunks and branches of the trees making a black lacework against it. It struck the creeping figures and gave them monstrous shadows, which caricatured their movements on the lit grass. It fell upon their faces, touching their whiteness with a ruddy tinge, accentuating the stains with which so many of them were freaked and maculated.

Ambrose Bierce, "Chickamauga" (1889)

It must be near daybreak, for the moon, nearly at full, is low in the west, showing blood-red through the mists with which the landscape is fantastically freaked.

Ambrose Bierce, "Visions of the Night" (1887)

I stood upon a hill. The setting sun
Was crimson with a curse and a portent,
And scarce his angry ray lit up the land
That lay below, whose lurid gloom appeared
Freaked with a moving mist, which, reeking up
From dim tarns hateful with some horrid ban,
Took shapes forbidden and without a name.

Ambrose Bierce, "A Vision of Doom"

I know the blooms
Of bluish fungus, freaked with mercury,
That bloat within the craters of the moon,
And in one still, selenic hour have shrunk
To pools of slime and fetor; and I know
What clammy blossoms, blanched and cavern-grown,
Are proffered to their gods in Uranus
By mole-eyed peoples; and the livid seed
of some black fruit a king in Saturn ate,
Which, cast upon his tinkling palace-floor,
Took root between the burnished flags, and now
Hath mounted and become a hellish tree,
Whose lithe and hairy branches, lined with mouths,
Net like a hundred ropes his lurching throne,
And strain at starting pillars.

Clark Ashton Smith, *The Hashish-Eater; or, The Apocalypse of Evil* (1920)

frisson, *n.* [< Fr, shudder, shiver, thrill] An emotional thrill, shudder. Victor Hugo famously credited Charles Baudelaire with adding the desired *nouveau frisson* (new or novel *frisson*) to modern literature; many uses bear reference to this statement.

> *The Ancient Mariner*, as also, in its measure, *Christabel*, is a "romantic" poem, impressing us by bold invention, and appealing to that taste for the supernatural, that long for *le frisson*, a shudder, to which the "romantic" school in Germany, and its derivations in England and France, directly ministered.
>
> Walter Pater, "Coleridge" (1865) in *Appreciations*

> Yesterday it was Realism that charmed one. One gained from it that *nouveau frisson* which it was its aim to produce. One analysed it, and wearied of it. At sunset came the *Luministe* in painting, and the *Symboliste* in poetry, and the spirit of mediævalism, that spirit which belongs not to time but to temperament, woke suddenly in Russia, and stirred us for a moment by the terrible fascination of pain.
>
> Oscar Wilde, "The Critic as Artist" (1891)

You have given me the *nouveau frisson* I am always looking for.

Oscar Wilde, letter to Edgar Saltus (September 1890)

Sporion stepped forward and explained with swift and various gesture that he and his friends were tired of the amusements, wearied with the poor pleasures offered by the civil world, and had invaded the Arcadian valley hoping to experience a new *frisson* in the destruction of some shepherd's or some satyr's naïveté, and the infusion of their venom among the dwellers of the woods.

Aubrey Beardsley, *The Story of Venus and Tannhäuser: A Romantic Novel* (1894–98)

I hope the yarn will afford *"un frisson nouveau."*

Clark Ashton Smith, letter to H. P. Lovecraft (c. 15–23 February 1931)

His girls had earned $46,000 during March, of which he took $23,000; after paying 10 percent to the Brotherhood for permission to operate without molestation by Banana-Nose Maldonado's soldiers, this left a tidy profit of $20,700, all of it tax free. Little Carmel, who stood five feet two and had the face of a mournful weasel, beamed as he completed his calculations; his emotion was as inexpressible, in normal terms, as that of a necrophile who had just broken into the town morgue. He had tried every possible sexual combination with his girls; none gave him the *frisson* of looking at a figure like that at the end of the month.

Robert Anton Wilson & Robert Shea,
The Eye in the Pyramid in *The Illuminatus! Trilogy* (1969–71)

A frisson had gone around the table at the mention of Voldemort's name.

J. K. Rowling, *Harry Potter and the Order of the Phœnix* (2003)

frore, *adj.* Very cold; frosty; frigorific.

Behind and below was only a darkness to which the men dared not return, and all about was a mounting wind which seemed to sweep down in black, frore gusts from interstellar space.

H. P. Lovecraft, "The Colour out of Space" (1927)

froreness, *n.* The state, condition, or quality of being frore (q.v.).

Scarce could he draw breath in the cold that was in the air; and the light of the huge ice-berg seared his eyeballs with an exceeding froreness.

Clark Ashton Smith, "The Coming of the White Worm" (1933)

fulgent, *adj.* Shining brightly or brilliantly; effulgent.

And they were surmounted by a mighty dome of glass, through which shone the sun and moon and stars and planets when it was clear, and from which were hung fulgent images of the sun and moon and stars and planets when it was not clear.

H. P. Lovecraft, "The Doom That Came to Sarnath" (1919)

fulvous, *adj.* Tawny, fulvid.

It was a minute anatomical and generally desciptive account of the large fulvous Ourang-Outang of the East Indian Islands.

Edgar Allan Poe, "The Murders in the Rue Morgue" (1841)

He was naked to the waist, and wore the fulvous hide of some long-haired animal which hung in filthy tatters to his knees.

Clark Ashton Smith, "The Testament of Athammaus" (1931)

Do not fear to use an uncommon word if it is the only one that exactly expresses your meaning, but do not use it merely to dazzle the reader. Clark Ashton Smith, in "The Testament of Athammaus," gained nothing by speaking of a "fulvous hide" when "tawny hide" would have done just as well.

L. Sprague de Camp & Catherine Crook de Camp, Science Fiction Handbook, Revised:
A Guide to Writing Imaginative Literature (1953/1975)

funebrial, *adj.* Of, pertaining to, or suggestive of a funeral or tomb; funereal; dark, dismal, and gloom-ridden.

Our days were spent in roaming through the ruins of lone and immemorial cities, or in the vast and shadowy fanes from whose awful and everlasting glooms of elder mystery, the simulachres of century-forgotten gods looked forth with unalterable eyes on the hopeless heavens, and saw but night and oblivion. Or, wandering through ashen fields of perennial autumn, we found the flowers of wan funebrial immortelles, that wept with a melancholy dew by the flowing silence of Acherontic waters.

Clark Ashton Smith, "From the Crypts of Memory" (1917)

funereal, *adj.* Of, pertaining to, or suggestive of a funeral or tomb; dark, dismal, gloom-ridden.

> This is the desert, this the solitude:
> How populous, how vital, is the grave!
> This is creation's melancholy vault,
> The vale funereal, the sad cypress gloom;
> The land of apparitions, empty shades!
> All, all on earth is shadow, all beyond
> Is substance: the reverse is folly's creed:
> How solid all, where change shall be no more!

Edward Young, The Complaint, and the Consolation; or, Night Thoughts (1742)

> Thine eyes, in Heaven of heart enshrined
>   Then desolately fall,
> O God! on my funereal mind
>   Like starlight on a pall—

Edgar Allan Poe, "To ——" (1829)

Never did tombs look so ghastly white; never did cypress, or yew, or juniper so seem the embodiment of funereal gloom; never did tree or grass wave or rustle so ominously; never did bough creak so mysteriously; and never did the faraway howling of dogs send such a woeful presage through the night.

Bram Stoker, *Dracula* (1897)

Then Guivric passed through this door likewise; and so, with glowing feet and with an odor of funereal spices, Guivric came into the room in which was the Sylan.

James Branch Cabell, *The Silver Stallion: A Comedy of Redemption* (1925)

A team of horses passed from Finglas with toiling plodding tread, dragging through the funereal silence a creaking waggon on which lay a granite block.

James Joyce, *Ulysses* (1914–21)

There was something menacing and uncomfortable in the funereal stillness, in the muffled, subtle trickle of distant brooks, and in the crowding green peaks and black-wooded precipices that choked the narrow horizon.

H. P. Lovecraft, "The Whisperer in Darkness" (1930)

He fell through Erebus-like darkness, for what seemed an immense distance, before he struck bottom. Lying half stunned in a shallow, fetid pool, he heard the funereal thud of the heavy slab as it slid back into place far above him.

Clark Ashton Smith, "The Colossus of Ylourgne" (1932)

Now the necropolis yawned before Xanlicha, and her path entered the cavernous gloom of far-vaulted funereal trees, as if passing into monstrous and shadowy mouths that were tusked with white monuments. The air grew dank and noisome, as if filled with the breathings of open crypts.

Clark Ashton Smith, "The Death of Ilalotha" (1937)

fungoid, *adj.* Of, pertaining to, or resembling a fungus or fungi.

It was just past five, with the bloated, fungoid moon sinking in the west, when I staggered into camp—hatless, tattered, features scratched and ensanguined, and without my electric torch.

H. P. Lovecraft, "The Shadow out of Time" (1935)

The dæmon wind died down, and the bloated, fungoid moon sank reddeningly in the west.

H. P. Lovecraft, "The Shadow out of Time" (1935)

The oddly unnatural face disclosed by the match's glow gave even this common cigarette an indefinable strangeness. Its newly-lit point pulsed in a feverish rhythm curiously unlike the puffs on the normal smoker, and when it blazed brightest one could see the whole white cylinder protruding like a fungoid excrescence from the thin, pallid lips. The smoke, when glimpsed, seemed to weave fantastic designs; and a long ash appeared with anomalous rapidity.

H. P. Lovecraft, "Cigarette Characterization" (1934)

The darkness crept down the pedestal that supported the crucible; it spread out like a fungoid stain across the onyx floor.

Henry Kuttner, "The Jest of Droom-avista" (1937)

fungous, *adj.* Of, pertaining to, or resembling a fungus or fungi; covered with or characterized by a fungus or fungi.

I retired early, being very sleepy, but was harassed by dreams of the most horrible sort. I seemed to be looking down from an immense height upon a twilit grotto, knee-deep with filth, where a white-bearded dæmon swineherd drove about with his staff a flock of fungous, flabby beasts whose appearance filled me with unutterable loathing.

H. P. Lovecraft, "The Rats in the Walls" (1923)

There were hellish forms with streaming hair, and lean rubbery things. Slavering, dog-faced throwbacks that mocked the human form. Fungous, flabby beasts with mould-caked bodies. Great Cthulhu bubbling up from a chasm of water below, all gelid tentacles and vaginal slit for a face.

Michael Slade, *Ghoul* (1987)

fusty, *adj.* Musty.

My mind shuddered, its very fabric soiled, at the hellish implications of his apparently harmless words; however, I allowed him to precede me (again with that hellish taper of corpse-fat, whose sickly coil of filthy vapour tainted my quivering nostrils) out of the library and into the darkness of the outer hall; thereupon, he led me up a rickety staircase fashioned (by *whose* fingers my frozen brain could not imagine) of some unutturably hideous wood (or *was* it wood?), which teetered over the yawning edge of an ink-black pit, above which we wound our slow and tortuous way, at every step my mind quailing at the thought of what might await me above; we proceeded upward, however, while the wind screamed and whooped outside and the thunder rocked and rolled like the mad laughter of an insane deity, while darkness closed about us, clammy, noisome darkness tainted with the charnel-stench of things long dead and better left unnamed; then my eldritch host, reaching the worm-rotted landing of the hideous staircase, gestured to a scarred and slime encrusted door, which, as I watched with growing horror, began slowly to open, its hinges groaning, as the sound of a damned soul crying for succor from the depths of hell's blackest pit, revealing behind it a stygian chamber whose infernal darkness the oily taper could not penetrate, and with a thrill of terror I realized that this foul cell was intended by my host to be my resting place; feeling then his gnarled talon gripping my arm, and hearing these perverted syllables escape his fusty lips—"Here's the guest room; hope you'll be comfortable."—

> H. P. Lowcraft (Lin Carter & Dave Foley), "The Slitherer from the Slime"

Futurism, futurism, *n.* An early twentieth-century *avant-garde* art movement related to Dada and Cubism, with branches in Italy, Russia, and the Ukraine. In painting, Futurism employed techniques resembling those of Cubism, such as abstraction and the simultaneous presentation of objects from viewpoints and at different stages of motion.

> In comparison with the effected futurism of the other pictures in the studio, "Our Lady of the Poppies," beyond question was a great painting.
>
> Sax Rohmer (Arthur Sarsfield Ward), *The Yellow Claw* (1915)

> And when the shiftings of the Metal Hordes permitted, we saw that all the flat floor of the valley was stripped and checkered, stippled and tesselated with every color, patterned with enormous lozenges and squares, rhomboids and parallelo-grams, pentagons and hexagons and diamonds, lunettes, circles and spirals; har-lequined yet harmonious; instinct with a grotesque suggestion of a super-Futurism. But always was this patterning ordered, always *coherent!* As though it were a page on which was spelled some untranslatable other world message! Fourth Dimensional revelations by some Euclidean deity! Commandments traced by some mathematical God!
>
> A. Merritt, *The Metal Monster* (1920)

> The bas-relief was a rough rectangle less than an inch thick and about five by six inches in area; obviously of modern origin. Its designs, however, were far from modern in atmosphere and suggestion; for although the vagaries of cubism and futurism are many and wild, they do not often reproduce that cryptic regularity which lurks in prehistoric writing.
>
> H. P. Lovecraft, "The Call of Cthulhu" (1926)

> Without knowing what futurism is like, Johansen achieved something very close to it when he spoke of the city; for instead of describing any definite structure or building, he dwells only on broad impressions of vast angles and stone sur-faces—surfaces too great to belong to any thing right or proper for this earth, and impious with horrible images and hieroglyphs.
>
> H. P. Lovecraft, "The Call of Cthulhu" (1926)

Futurist, futurist, *n.* An adherent of Futurism (q.v.).

> There is a quality in the scene as if a futurist with a considerable knowledge of modern chemical and physical speculation and some obscure theological animus had repainted the designs of a pre-Raphaelite.
>
> H. G. Wells, *The Undying Fire: A Novel Based on the Book of Job* (1919)

With the loaded brush in his fingers, Sarkis could only stand and stare, held in the same hypnotic thrall that had swept him beyond fear or wonder on the mountain. Once more he beheld the gradual, somnolent waving of the arabesque feelers; again he heard the dreamy monotonous hum that resolved itself into longdrawn vocables, inviting him to go with the visitants. Again, on the moonfish disks, were depicted scenes that would have been the despair of a futurist.

Clark Ashton Smith, "A Star-Change" (1932)

futuristic, *adj.* Of, pertaining to, or resembling Futurism (q.v.).

Then the frieze appeared to have an open street for background, with a confused, ever-changing multitude of other faces and forms, of vehicles and sections of buildings, all jumbled together as in some old-time futuristic painting.

Clark Ashton Smith, "The Plutonian Drug" (1932)

"They are riding the seas in bark canoes and enormous steamships; they are painting bison and mammoths on the walls of dismal caves and covering huge canvases with queer futuristic designs."

Frank Belknap Long, "The Hounds of Tindalos" (1929)

G

gaud, *n.* A piece of jewelry or finery, especially with connotations of showiness and gaudiness; a trinket or ornament.

And when Iranon had wept over the grave of Romnod and strown it with green budding branches, such as Romnod used to love, he put aside his silks and gauds and went forgotten out of Oonai the city of lutes and dancing clad only in the ragged purple in which he had come, and garlanded with fresh vines from the mountains.

> H. P. Lovecraft, "The Quest of Iranon" (1921)

He shook his head and muttered, "Gauds and bright trappings are dust of vanity and fade before the march of the years, but the edge of slaughter is not dulled, and the scent of fresh-spilled blood is good to an old man's nostrils."

> Robert E. Howard, "Marchers of Valhalla"

Around her wrists she placed gauds of silver and bright stones.

> Charles G. Finney, *The Circus of Dr. Lao* (1934)

"The gems and ornaments of this world and the jewels and gauds of the world of demons cannot tempt or corrupt me. My purpose in coming here is to destroy an evil thing."

> Fritz Leiber, "The Jewels in the Forest" (1939)

gelatinous, *adj.* Of, pertaining to, or resembling gelatin or jelly.

In the first place, the voice seemed to reach our ears—at least mine—from a vast distance, or from some deep cavern within the earth. In the second place, it impressed me (I fear, indeed, that it will be impossible to make myself comprehended) as gelatinous or glutinous matters impress the sense of touch.

> Edgar Allan Poe, "The Facts in the Case of M. Valdemar" (1845)

Shall I say that the voice was deep; hollow; gelatinous; remote; unearthly; inhuman; disembodied? What shall I say?

> H. P. Lovecraft, "The Statement of Randolph Carter" (1919)

I heard voices, and yowls, and echoes, but above all there gently rose that impious, insidious scurrying; gently rising, rising, as a stiff bloated corpse gently rises above an oily river that flow under endless onyx bridges to a black, putrid sea. Something bumped into me—something soft and plump. It must have been the rats; the viscous, gelatinous, ravenous army that feast on the dead and the living.

> H. P. Lovecraft, "The Rats in the Walls" (1923)

259

He dreamed of Salem, and of a dimly glimpsed, gelatinous black thing that hurtled with frightful speed through the streets, a thing like an incredibly huge, jet black amœba that pursued and engulfed men and women who shrieked and fled vainly.

Henry Kuttner, "The Salem Horror" (1937)

For a moment he was back in the brown canals of Mars in the grip of a giant clam, which takes a week to satisfy its consuming sex habit and spits out its unfortunate victim covered with its discharge like a gelatinous pearl on the dry red sands—

William S. Burroughs, The Ticket That Exploded (1957–61)

Found himself choking as unknown bodies tear his insides apart—Wafted by currents of glowing halves shifting mist in electric waves—gelatinous rectal swamps fermenting in darkness—

William S. Burroughs, The Ticket That Exploded (1957–61)

Genie (*pl.* **Genii, Genies**), *n.* [< Fr *génie* < Ar *jinnî*; influenced by *genius*] In Arabian folklore, a spirit.

Genn, or *Ginn,* in the Arabic, signifies a Genius or Demon, a being of a higher order, and formed of more subtle matter than man. According to Oriental mythology, the Genii governed the world long before the creation of Adam. The Mahometans regarded them as an intermediate race between angels and men, and capable of salvation; whence Mahomet pretended a commission to convert them. Consonant to this, we read that, *when the* Servant of God *stood up to invoke him, it wanted little but that the* Genii *had pressed on him in crowds, to hear him rehearse the Koran.*—D'HERBELOT, p. 375. *Al Koran,* chapter 72. It is asserted, and not without plausible reasons, that the words *Genn, Ginn—Genius, Genie, Gian, Gigas, Giant, Géant*—proceed from the same themes, viz. [*Gê*], *the earth,* and [*gáô*], *to produce;* as if these supernatural agents had been an early production of the earth, long before Adam was modelled out from a lump of it. The [*Ôntes*] and [*Éôntes*] of Plato bear a close analogy to these supposed intermediate creatures between God and man. From these premises arose the consequence that, boasting a higher order, formed of more subtle matter, and possessed of much greater knowledge, than man, they lorded over the planet, and invisibly governed it with superior intellect. From this last circumstance they obtained in Greece the title of [*Daímones*], Demons, from [*dáêmôn*], *sciens,* knowing. The Hebrew word, [NPhLIM], Nephilim (Gen. vi, 4), translated by *Gigantes,* giants, claiming the same etymon with [*nephélê*], a cloud, seems also to indicate that these intellectual beings inhabited the void expanse of the terrestrial atmosphere. Hence the very ancient fable of men of enormous strength and size revolting against the gods, and all the mythological lore relating to that mighty conflict; unless we trace the origin of this important event to the ambition of Satan, his revolt against the Almighty, and his fall with the angels.

Samuel Henley, note to William Beckford,
The History of the Caliph Vathek: An Arabian Tale (1786)

"A wild but deeply-fixed conviction—a wandering image of preternatural power, overshadowed her mind while she thought of Melmoth;—and this image, which had caused her so much terror and inquietude in her early hours of love, now formed her only resource against the hour of inconceivable suffering; as those unfortunate females in the Eastern Tales, whose beauty has attracted the fearful passion of some evil genie, are supposed to depend, at their nuptial hour, on the presence of the seducing spirit, to tear from the arms of the agonised parent, and the distracted bridegroom, the victim whom he has reserved for himself, and whose wild devotion to him gives a dignity to the union so unhallowed and unnatural."

Charles Maturin, Melmoth the Wanderer: A Tale (1820)

Now there are fine tales in the volumes of the Magi—in the iron-bound, melancholy volumes of the Magi. Therein, I say, are glorious histories of the Heaven, and of the Earth, and of the mighty sea—and of the Genii that overruled the sea, and the earth, and the lofty heaven. There was much lore too in the sayings which were said by the Sibyls; and holy, holy things were heard of old by the dim leaves that trembled around Dodona—but, as Allah liveth, that fable which the Demon told me as he sat by my side in the shadow of the tomb, I hold to be the most wonderful of all!

Edgar Allan Poe, "Silence—A Fable" (1838)

A brief examination convinced me that the contents were less taking than the title. Rasselas looked dull to my trifling taste. I saw nothing about fairies, nothing about genii; no bright variety seemed spread over the closely-printed pages.

Charlotte Brontë, Jane Eyre: An Autobiography (1847)

Standing on the same mounts of vision where they stood, listening to the same gurgling melody that broke from their enchanted fountains, yes, plunging into their rayless caverns of sorcery, and imprisoned with their genie in the unutterable silence of the fathomless sea, have I dearly bought the right to come to men with the chart of my wanderings in my hands, and unfold to them the foundations of the fabric of Oriental story.

Fitz Hugh Ludlow, The Hasheesh Eater:
Being Passages from the Life of a Pythagorean (1857)

As I walked cautiously in the blackness, the draught grew stronger and more offensive, till at length I could regard it as nothing less than a tangible stream of detestable vapour pouring out of some aperture like the smoke of the genie from the fisherman's jar in the Eastern tale.

H. P. Lovecraft & Harry Houdini, "Under the Pyramids" (1924)

Beyond the city ramparts, as if wrought by black magic or the toil of genii, another city had reared, and its high towers were moving swiftly forward beneath the rubescent dome of the burning cloud!

Clark Ashton Smith, "Beyond the Singing Flame" (1931)

A strange heaviness had stilled all the air; and great coppery clouds were piled like towering, many-domed palaces of genii on the desert hills.

> Clark Ashton Smith, "The Witchcraft of Ulua" (1933)

In this process the magician had employed the gums of infernal plants, and had repeatedly invoked the curious powers of certain underground genii, as was his wont on such occasions.

> Clark Ashton Smith, "The Garden of Adompha" (1937)

Swelling and towering swiftly, like a genie loosed from one of Solomon's bottle's, the cloud rose on the planet's rim. A rusty and colossal column, it strode above the dead plain, through a sky that was dark as the brine of desert seas that have ebbed down to desert pools.

> Clark Ashton Smith, "The Dweller in the Gulf" (1932)

Genius (*pl.* **Genii, Geniuses**), *n.* A spirit; in particular, a tutelary spirit, a guardian angel, dæmon; a genie or jinn.

> There is none but he,
> Whose being I doe feare: and vnder him,
> My *Genius* is rebuk'd, as it is said
> Mark Anthonies was by Cæsar.
>
> William Shakespeare, *The Tragedie of Macbeth* (1606)

In truth, the Baronet felt, what he would not willingly have acknowledged, that his genius stood rebuked before that of the Antiquary.

> Sir Walter Scott, *The Antiquary* (1816)

"It was his guiding Genius (*Dämon*) that inspired him; he must go forth and meet his Destiny."

> Thomas Carlyle, *Sartor Resartus: The Life and Opinions of Herr Teufelsdröckh* (1831)

Could he, for an instant, have supposed that, in my admonisher at Eton—in the destroyer of my honor at Oxford,—in him who thwarted my ambition at Rome, my revenge at Paris, my passionate love at Naples, or what he falsely termed my avarice in Egypt,—that in this, my arch-enemy and evil genius, I could fail to recognise the William Wilson of my school-boy days,—the namesake, the companion, the rival,—the hated and dreaded rival at Dr. Bransby's?

> Edgar Allan Poe, "William Wilson" (1839)

By gradations, still more imperceptible, this cloud assumes shape, as did the vapor from the bottle out of which arose the genius in the Arabian Nights. But out of this *our* cloud upon the precipice's edge, there grows into palpability, a shape, far more terrible than any genius or any demon of a tale, and yet it is but a thought, although a fearful one, and one which chills the very marrows of our bones with the fierceness of the delight of its horror.

> Edgar Allan Poe, "The Imp of the Perverse" (1845)

"This morning, when I cam down, about half-an-hour before noon, Mr. Earnshaw was sitting by the fire, deadly sick; his evil genius, almost as gaunt and ghastly, leant against the chimney."

Emily Brontë, *Wuthering Heights: A Novel* (1847)

"Having become a member of the Secret Society as directed by the writer of the letter I have just read, and having obtained the secrets hinted at in the mystic directions, my next desire was to find a secluded spot where, without interruption, I could prepare for publication what I had gathered surreptitiously in the lodges of the fraternity I designed to betray. This I entitled "My Confession." Alas! why did my evil genius prompt me to write it? Why did not some kind angel withhold my hand from the rash and wicked deed?"

John Uri Lloyd, *Etidorhpa; or, The End of Earth: The Strange History of a Mysterious Being and the Account of a Remarkable Journey* (1894)

The rays seemed to spring upward from the earth. Now they were like countless lances of light borne by marching armies of Titans; now they crossed and angled and flew as though they were clouds of javelins hurled by battling swarms of the Genii of Light; and now they stood upright while through them, thrusting them aside, bending them passed vast, vague shapes like mountains forming and dissolving; like darkening monsters of some world of light pushing through thick forests of slender, high-reaching trees of cold flame; shifting shadows of monstrous chimeræ slipping through jungles of bamboo with trunks of diamond fire; phantasmal leviathans swimming through brakes of giant reeds of radiance rising from the sparkling ooze of a sea of star shine!

A. Merritt, *The Metal Monster* (1920)

> Of late I climb'd a lonely height
> And watch'd the moon-streak'd clouds in flight,
> Whose forms fantastic reel'd and whirl'd
> Like genii of a spectral world.

H. P. Lovecraft, "Clouds" in "A Cycle of Verse" (1918)

I alone, it would seem, among the living, have guessed the secret of Chapman's death, and the death of Avis and Amberville; and no one else, apparently, has felt the malign genius of the meadow.

Clark Ashton Smith, "Genius Loci" (1932)

> The wicked God
> The wicked Demon
> The Demon of the Desert
> The Demon of the Mountain
> The Demon of the Sea
> The Demon of the Marsh
> The wicked Genius

The Enormous Larvæ
The wicked Winds
The Demon that seizeth the body
The Demon that rendeth the body
SPIRIT OF THE SKY, REMEMBER!
SPIRIT OF THE EARTH, REMEMBER!

Abdul Alhazred (trans. "Simon"), Necronomicon (1977)

genius loci (*pl.* **genii locorum**), *n.* [< L] The minor deity or spirit associated with a particular place; the pervading spirit or atmosphere of a particular place.

Titles: Clark Ashton Smith, "Genius Loci"

A large old-fashioned oaken table was covered with a profusion of papers, parchments, books, and nondescript trinkets and gewgaws, which seemed to have little to recommend them besides rust and the antiquity which it indicates. In the midst of this wreck of ancient books and utensils, with a gravity equal to Marius among the ruins of Carthage, sat a large black cat, which to a superstitious eye might have presented the *genius loci*, the tutelar demon of the apartment.

Sir Walter Scott, The Antiquary (1816)

The Genius Loci, the *tutela* of Nightmare Abbey, the spirit of black melancholy, began to set his seal on her pallescent countenance.

Thomas Love Peacock, Nightmare Abbey (1817)

"The place has an entity of its own—an indwelling personality. It's there, like the soul in a human body, but I can't pin it down or touch it. You know that I'm not superstitious—but, on the other hand, I'm not a bigoted materialist, either; and I've run across some odd phenomena in my time. That meadow, perhaps, is inhabited by what the ancients called a *Genius Loci*."

Clark Ashton Smith, "Genius Loci" (1932)

"I think another place would be better. Atmosphere is extremely important, and we need solitude—someplace free of distractions and conflicting auræ. Dreams are influenced by the dreamer's surroundings, and the *genius loci* of Enseljos is not conducive to the tone of dream you seek. I think the Old City is evocative of the mood you desire, and one of its abandoned temples should retain sufficient occult magnetism to facilitate communion with the dark muse."

Karl Edward Wagner, "The Dark Muse" (1975)

It seems that in this place, this far-flung realm, Dr. N— has discovered an ancient and long-sought artifact, a marginal but astonishing entry in that unspeakably voluminous journal of creation. Soon after landfall, Mr. Gray finds himself verifying the truth of the archæologist's claims: that the island has been strangely molded in all its parts, and within its shores every manifestation of plant or mineral or anything whatever appears to have fallen at the mercy of some shaping force of demonic temperament, a genius loci which has sculpted its nightmares out of the atoms of the local earth.

Thomas Ligotti, "Nethescurial" (1991)

ghast, *n.* [backformation < *ghastly* < OE *gǽstan,* to terrify] A fabulous creature that inhabits the Dreamlands of H. P. Lovecraft. [Not in *OED.*]

They must beware, however, of a large cave near the cemetery; for this is the mouth of the vaults of Zin, and the vindictive ghasts are always on watch there murderously for those denizens of the upper abyss who hunt and prey on them. The ghasts try to come out when the gugs sleep, and they attack ghouls as readily as gugs, for they cannot discriminate. They are very primitive, and eat one another. The gugs have a sentry at a narrow place in the vaults of Zin, but he is often drowsy and is sometimes surprised by a party of ghasts. Though ghasts cannot live in real light, they can endure the grey twilight of the abyss for hours.

H. P. Lovecraft, *The Dream-Quest of Unknown Kadath* (1926–27)

ghost-light, *n.* An *ignis fatuus,* will-o'-the-wisp; a corpse-candle.

Oh, the white flame of limbs in dusky air,
The furnace of thy great grey eyes on me
Turned till I shudder. Darkness on the sea,
And wan ghost-lights are flickering everywhere
So that the world is ghastly.

Aleister Crowley, "At Kiel" in *White Stains: The Literary Remains of*
George Archibald Bishop, A Neuropath of the Second Empire (1898)

"Yes," he answered, "it's the blue ghost-light—and that is the mound."

H. P. Lovecraft & Zealia Bishop, "The Mound" (1930)

ghoul, goul, goule, ghool, ghole, gowl, *n.* [< Ar *ghûl* < a root meaning "to seize"] In Arabian folklore, a creature that robs graves and devours human corpses.

Ghoul, or *ghul,* in Arabic, signifies any terrifying object, which deprives people of the use of their senses. Hence it became the appellative of that species of monster which was supposed to haunt forests, cemeteries, and other lonely places; and believed not only to tear in pieces the living, but to dig up and devour the dead.—RICHARDSON's *Dissertation on the Languages, etc., of Eastern Nations,* pp. 174, 274.

That kind of insanity called by the Arabians *Kutrub* (a word signifying not only a *wolf,* but likewise a *male Ghoul*), which incites such as are afflicted with it to roam howling amidst those melancholy haunts, may cast some light on the nature of the possession recorded by St. Mark., ch. V, 1, etc.

Samuel Henley, note to William Beckford,
The History of the Caliph Vathek: An Arabian Tale (1786)

It appears that "Ghool" is, properly speaking, a name only given to a *female* demon of the kind above described: the male is called "Kutrub."

> Edward William Lane, note to *The Arabian Nights Entertainments;*
> *or, The Thousand and One Nights* (1838–40)

"Ghooleh" is the feminine of "Ghool."

> Edward William Lane, note to *The Arabian Nights Entertainments; or,*
> *The Thousand and One Nights* (1838–40)

And now in conjunction therewith consider this other: "It is the Night of the World, and still long till it be Day: we wander amid the glimmer of smoking ruins, and the Sun and the Stars of Heaven are as if blotted out for a season; and two immeasurable Phantoms, HYPOCRISY and ATHEISM, with the Gowl, SENSUALITY, stalk abroad over the Earth, and call it theirs: well at ease are the Sleepers for whom Existence is a shallow Dream."

> Thomas Carlyle, *Sartor Resartus: The Life and Opinions of Herr Teufelsdröckh* (1831)

Nisida saw that the Grand Vizier was in haste to depart,—not through any ridiculous fears on his part, because he was too enlightened to believe in the fearful tales of mermaids, genii, gholes, vampires, and other evil spirits by which the island was said to be haunted:—but because his renegadism had been of so recent a date, that he dared not, powerful and exalted as he was, afford the least ground for suspecting that the light of Christianity triumphed in his soul over the dark barbarism of his assumed creed.

> G. W. M. Reynolds, *Wagner, the Wehr-Wolf: A Romance* (1846)

Ghoul! Chewer of corpses!

> James Joyce, *Ulysses* (1914–21)

Now I ride with the mocking and friendly ghouls on the night-wind, and play by day amongst the catacombs of Nephren-Ka in the sealed and unknown valley of Hadoth by the Nile. I know that light is not for me, save that of the moon over the rock tombs of Neb, nor any gaiety save the unnamed feasts of Nitokris beneath the Great Pyramid; yet in my new wildness and freedom I almost welcome the bitterness of alienage.

> H. P. Lovecraft, "The Outsider" (1921)

A phrase from some book flashed through my head. "Ghoul—Chewer of Corpses."

> Robert Bloch, "The Brood of Bubastis" (1937)

gibber, *v.intr.* & *v.tr.* To prattle and chatter rapidly, inarticulately, and unintelligibly; to jabber, gabble, etc. A rather common activity on the part of madmen, as well as of ghosts, goblins, and other fantastic creatures.

In the most high and palmy state of Rome,

A little ere the mightiest *Iulius* fell
The graues stood tennatlesse, and the sheeted dead
Did squeake and gibber in the Roman streets
As starres with traines of fier, and dewes of blood
Disasters in the sunne; and the moist starre,
Vpon whose influence *Neptunes* Empier stands,
Was sicke almost to doomesday with eclipse.
And euen the like precurse of feare euents
As harbindgers preceeding still the fates
And prologue to the *Omen* comming on
Haue heauen and earth together demonstrated
Vnto our Climatures and countrymen.

William Shakespeare, *The Tragedy of Hamlet, Prince of Denmark* (1602)

Old tales and legends are not quite forgot.
Still Superstition hovers o'er the spot,
And tells how here, the wan and restless sprite,
By some way-wilder'd peasant seen at night,
Gibbers and shrieks, among the ruins drear;
And how the friar's lanthorn will appear
Gleaming among the woods, with fearful ray,
And from the church-yard take its wavering way,
To the dim arches of Saint Monica.

Charlotte Smith, "Saint Monica" (1807)

The word Gibber has been also objected to; but besides that it appears to me very expressive, I have for its use the example of Shakspeare: "—the sheeted dead / Did squeal and *gibber* in the streets of Rome." *Hamlet.*

Charlotte Smith, note to "Saint Monica" (1807)

"Few would covet to rule over gibbering ghosts, and howling winds, and raging currents. My throne is a cloud, my sceptre a meteor, my realm is only peopled with fantasies; but I must either cease to be, or continue to be the mightiest as well as the most miserable of beings."

Sir Walter Scott, *The Pirate* (1821)

"And when you've learned to squeak, my man,
    And caught the double sob,
You're pretty much where you began:
Just try and gibber if you can!
    That's something *like* a job!

"*I've* tried it, and can only say
    I'm sure you couldn't do it, e-
ven if you practised night and day,

Unless you have a turn that way,
    And natural ingenuity.

"Shakspeare I think it is who treats
    Of Ghosts, in days of old,
Who 'gibbered in the Roman streets,'
Dressed, if you recollect, in sheets—
    They must have found it cold."

Lewis Carroll, Phantasmagoria (1869)

Sublimely in the air above me, in front, beside me, on either hand, and behind my back, a wilderness of insane faces gnashed at me, glared, gibbered, howled, laughed horribly, hissed and cursed.

Fitz Hugh Ludlow, The Hasheesh Eater:
Being Passages from the Life of a Pythagorean (1857)

"Here he is strong and stark, and full of joy and love; but otherwhere he would be but a gibbering ghost drifting down the wind of night."

William Morris, The Story of the Glittering Plain, Which Has Been
Also Called the Land of Living Men or the Acre of the Undying (1890)

What spectres stood beside me then!—what horrid voices shouted in my ears!—how strange and loathly the half-formed creatures that followed me and mouthed at me, gibbering in uncouth speech scarcely intelligible!—how the murdered man Silvion came and looked at me as at some foul thing!—how Pauline, fair and pale, with a dying sweetness in her smile drifted by me, finely fairy-like as a fleecy cloud in summer-time!—and, ah God! how the soft large eyes of Heloise beamed piteous wonder and reproach upon me like bland stars shining solemnly on a criminal in his cell!

Marie Corelli (Mary Mackay), Wormwood: A Drama of Paris (1890)

"Remember we have to deal not only with the spectral lumber left here by your scarlet aunt, but as well with the supererogatory curse of that hell-cat Torrevieja. Come on! let's get inside before the hour arrives for the sheeted dead to squeak and gibber in these lonely halls. Light your pipes, your tobacco is a sure protection against 'your whoreson dead bodies'; light up and move on."

Ralph Adams Cram, "No. 252 Rue M. le Prince" (1895)

It will be an expression of mine that there is a godness in this idiocy. But, no matter what sometimes my opinion may be, I am not now writing that God is an Idiot. Maybe he, or it, drools comets and gibbers earthquakes, but the scale would have to be considered at least super-idiocy.

Charles Fort, Lo! (1931)

He tried to speak, but gibbered meaningless syllables.

Arthur Machen, The Green Round (1932)

In the still night were flames seen, and flying forms dim in the moonlit air; and in moonless nights unstarred, moans heard and gibbering accents: prodigies beside their beds, and ridings in the sky, and fleshless fingers plucking at Juss unseen when he went forth to make question of the night.

E. R. Eddison, *The Worm Ouroboros* (1922)

"Silence, you foul-mouthed, pompous, brainless, wind-bag! You . . . you . . . foul gibbering Son of a Fairy!" sputtered Master Nathaniel.

Hope Mirrlees, *Lud-in-the-Mist* (1926; ellipses in original)

Slowly, amidst the distorted horrors of that indescribable scene, she began to churn the lethal waters; whilst on the masonry of that charnel shore that was not of earth the titan Thing from the stars slavered and gibbered like Polypheme cursing the fleeing ship of Odysseus.

H. P. Lovecraft, "The Call of Cthulhu" (1926)

I knew something of the old hermit-like man who had lived in his great dark house on the hill; indeed, I had once witnessed one of his strange seizures, and I had been appalled at the writhings, howlings and yammerings of the wretch, who had groveled on the earth like a wounded snake gibbering terrible curses and black blasphemies until his voice broke in a wordless screaming which spattered his lips with foam.

Robert E. Howard, "Dig Me No Grave"

Gollum would not move. He stood shaking and gibbering to himself, until with a rush the wind came upon them, hissing and snarling over the marshes.

J. R. R. Tolkien, *The Two Towers in The Lord of the Rings* (1936–49)

Now, as I hesitated upon the door-step, a million idiot voices gibbered an invitation to enter that mortal mind could not withstand.

Robert Bloch, "The Secret in the Tomb" (1934)

The stars rocked in red anguish; the cold wind gibbered in my ears. I crouched in my chair, with my eyes riveted on that astounding scene in the corner.

Robert Bloch, "The Shambler from the Stars" (1935)

"The superman!" he jeered. "Nietzsche—Nietzsche and Gobineau! Was it your shades that gibbered around my nuptial couch?"

Stanley Weinbaum, *The New Adam* (193-)

You know how old people lose all shame about eating, and it makes you puke to watch them? Old junkies are the same about junk. They gibber and squeal at the sight of it. The spit hangs off their chin, and their stomach rumbles and all their guts grind in peristalsis while they cook up, dissolving the body's decent skin, you expect any moment a great blob of protoplasm will flop right out and surround the junk. Really disgust you to see it.

William S. Burroughs, *Naked Lunch* (1955–59)

Young junkies return it to the white reader and one day I would wake up as Bill covered with ice and burning crotch—drop my shorts and comes gibbering up me with a corkscrew motion—

William S. Burroughs, *The Soft Machine* (1957–60)

He is carefully scraping out the inside of each persimmon-colored mushroom cup and shredding the rest. Dispossessed elves run around up on the roof, gibbering. He now has a growing heap of orange-grey fungus, which he proceeds to add in fistfuls to a pot of steaming water.

Thomas Pynchon, *Gravity's Rainbow* (1973)

Almost certainly any other man would have gone to the end of his days in this gibbering state of frightened madness.

Karl Edward Wagner, "The Dark Muse" (1975)

"Off with their heads! Off with their heads!" God seemed to be gibbering most of the time, like the Red Queen in *Alice*. Does He really kill us for His sport?

Robert Anton Wilson, *Masks of the Illuminati* (1981)

I walked past the various mirrors. The Things locked in them gibbered and writhed. I showed them my teeth and they writhed away.

Roger Zelazny, *A Night in the Lonesome October* (1993)

gibber, *n.* Rapid and inarticulate chatter.

The roar of the alien forest had risen to a howl—an eldritch gibber which sang in our ears and drew at our brains as we toiled.

Mearle Prout, "The House of the Worm" (1933)

gibbous, *adj.* [< LL *gibbosus*, hunchbacked < L *gibbus*, hump] Convex, protuberant, rounded; (of the moon or a planet) more than half but less than fully illuminated, more than half full; (of a person or animal) hunchbacked or humpbacked; (of a body part) hump-shaped.

a. General:

And if will yet insist, and urge the question farther still upon me, I shall be enforced unto divers of the like nature, wherein perhaps I shall receive no greater satisfaction. I shall demand how the Camels of *Bactria* came to have two bunches on their backs, whereas the Camels of *Arabia* in all relations have but one? How Oxen in some Countries began and continue gibbous or bunchback'd? what way those many different shapes, colours, hairs, and natures of Dogs came in? how they of some Countries became depilous, and without any hair at all, whereas some sorts in excess abound therewith?

Sir Thomas Browne, *Pseudodoxia Epidemica; or, Enquiries into Very Many Received Tenents and Commonly Presumed Truths* (1646)

I abhor flies—to see them stare upon me
Out of their little faces of gibbous eyes;
To feel the dry cool skin of their bodies alight
Perching upon my lips!—O yea, a dream,
A dream of impious obscene Satan, this
Monstrous frenzy of life, the Indian being!

> Lascelles Abercrombie, *The Sale of St. Thomas*

—A farternoiser for his tuckish armenities. Ouhr Former who erred in having down to gibbous disdag our darling breed.

> James Joyce, *Finnegans Wake* (1922–39)

The aperture was black with a darkness almost material. That tenebrousness was indeed a *positive quality*; for it obscured such parts of the inner walls as ought to have been revealed, and actually burst forth like smoke from its æon-long imprisonment, visibly darkening the sun as it slunk away into the shrunken and gibbous sky on flapping membraneous wings.

> H. P. Lovecraft, "The Call of Cthulhu" (1926)

As drear and barren as the glooms of Death,
It lies, a windless land of livid dawns,
Nude to a desolate firmament, with hills
That seem the gibbous bones of the mummied Earth,
And plains whose hollow face is rivelled deep
With gullies twisting like a serpent's track.

> Clark Ashton Smith, "Medusa" (1911)

Where hills made gibbous shadows in the moon,
They heard the eldritch laughters of the wind,
Seeming the mirth of doom; and 'neath their gaze
Gaunt valleys deepened like an old despair.

> Clark Ashton Smith, "Saturn" (1912)

This shadow was not the shadow of man, nor ape, nor any known beast: the head was too grotesquely elongated, the squat body too gibbous; and I was unable to determine whether the shadow possessed five legs, or whether what appeared to be the fifth was merely a tail.

> Clark Ashton Smith, "The Abominations of Yondo" (1925)

b. Of the moon, etc.:

In examining the boundary between light and darkness (in the crescent or gibbous moon) where this boundary crosses any of the dark places, the line of division is found to be rough and jagged; but, were these dark places liquid, it would evidently be seen.

> Edgar Allan Poe, note to "The Unparalleled Adventure of One Hans Pfaall" (1835)

Very soon I saw the full circle of the earth, slightly gibbous, like the moon when she nears her full, but very great; and the silvery shape of America was now in the noonday blaze, wherein (as it seemed) little England had been basking but a few minutes ago.

H. G. Wells, "Under the Knife" (1896)

> But Fancy is unsatisfied, and soon
> She seeks the silence of a vaster night,
> Where powers of wizardry, with faltering sight
> (Whenas the hours creep farthest from the noon)
> Seek by the glow-worm's lantern cold and dull
> A crimson spider hidden in a skull,
> Or search for mottled vines with berries white,
> Where waters mutter to the gibbous moon.

George Sterling, "A Wine of Wizardry" (1907)

A storm was gathering around the peaks of the range, and weirdly shaped clouds scudded horribly across the blurred patch of celestial light which marked a gibbous moon's attempts to shine through many layers of cirro-stratus vapours.

H. P. Lovecraft, "The Transition of Juan Romero" (1919)

Here is a lesson in scientific accuracy for fiction writers. I have just looked up the moon's phases for October, 1894, to find when a gibbous moon was visible at 2. a.m., and have changed the dates to fit!

H. P. Lovecraft, note to "The Transition of Juan Romero" (1919)

I know not why my dreams were so wild that night; but ere the waning and fantastically gibbous moon had risen far above the eastern plain, I was awake in a cold perspiration, determined to sleep no more.

H. P. Lovecraft, "Dagon" (1917)

It is at night, especially when the moon is gibbous and waning, that I see the thing.

H. P. Lovecraft, "Dagon" (1917)

However this may be, it is certain that they worshipped a sea-green stone idol chiselled in the likeness of Bokrug, the great water-lizard; before which they danced horribly when the moon was gibbous.

H. P. Lovecraft, "The Doom That Came to Sarnath" (1919)

And it was the high-priest Gnai-Kah who first saw the shadows that descended from the gibbous moon into the lake, and the damnable green mists that arose from the lake to meet the moon and to shroud in a sinister haze the towers and the domes of fated Sarnath.

H. P. Lovecraft, "The Doom That Came to Sarnath" (1919)

It was on the evening of July 11th, when a gibbous moon flooded the mysterious hillocks with a curious pallor.

H. P. Lovecraft, "The Shadow out of Time" (1935)

> One midnight, redolent of ill,
> I saw that lake, asleep and still;
> While in the lurid sky there rode
> A gibbous moon that glow'd and glow'd.

H. P. Lovecraft, "The Nightmare Lake" (1919)

A red moon, ominous and gibbous, had declined above the crags; and the shadows of the cedars were elongated in the moon; and they wavered in the gale like the blown cloaks of enchanters.

Clark Ashton Smith, "The Double Shadow" (1932)

And Gaspard, fleeing headlong beneath the gibbous moon toward Vyones, and fearing to hear the tread of a colossal pursuer at any moment, had thought it more than useless to give warning in such towns and villages as lay upon his line of flight. Where, indeed—even if warned—could men hope to hide themselves from the awful thing, begotten by Hell on the ravished charnel, that would walk forth like the Anakim to visit its roaring wrath on a trampled world?

Clark Ashton Smith, "The Colossus of Ylourgne" (1932)

He could see but dimly, for all the torches in the courtyard, save one, had burnt out or been extinguished; and the low gibbous moon had not yet climbed the wall.

Clark Ashton Smith, "The Black Abbot of Puthuum" (1935)

They could see plainly enough in the weird twilight, strengthened as it was by the glimmering of the two moons, one of which was crescent and the other gibbous.

Clark Ashton Smith, "The Amazing Planet" (1931)

> Vast wings were flapping in the still night air;
> I saw great shadows across a gibbous moon;
> The mandrakes moaned along the black lagoon,
> And in the sky, there hung a baleful glare.

Donald Wandrei, "The Creatures" in *Sonnets of the Midnight Hours* (1928)

The waxing gibbous moon had set, and the stars at the top of the black heavens were still diamond sharp.

Fritz Leiber, *Our Lady of Darkness* (1977)

> Beyond yon gibbous, crumbling moon,
> Beneath some mausoleum's skull-white ruin;
> Or out past the dread-filled fields of night,
> Where blood-dripped stars blur in endless flight?

Emil Petaja, "Cthulhu Done It"

Darkness clamped down. The wind had resumed, and strengthened hourly. Orange flames streamed along the ground; sparks flew off like meteors and were as swiftly snuffed. Overhead lay a blackness where the gibbous moon was seen in rare glimpses, racing among monstrous cloud shapes. The night was full of whistlings, rustlings, and croakings.

Poul Anderson, Three Hearts and Three Lions (1953)

The sun burned bloodily to darkness. A gibbous moon swept through clouds blown on a sharp wind. There would be storm tonight; the long fall of elven-welcome was past and winter came striding.

Poul Anderson, The Broken Sword (1954)

The church itself was lit by the gibbous moon which swung high in the gulfs of space, and the tottering gravestones, overgrown with repulsively decaying vegetation, cast curious shadows over the fungus-strewn grass.

Ramsey Campbell, "The Church in High Street" (1962)

The grass was green, long and wild, rising to nighted hills of grey and purple, silvered a little by a gibbous moon.

Brian Lumley, "The House of the Temple" (1981)

"And yesternight at midnight we looked eastward from the jasper terraces of Kiran, and saw the thousand gilded spires of Thran melt beneath the gibbous moon."

Gary Myers, "The Snout in the Alcove" (1977)

The temperature fell quickly and with the rising of the gibbous moon a wind sprang up from the north, piping and murmuring among the sandhills, adding a weird cacophony to the night.

John S. Glasby, "The Brooding City"

A rising gibbous moon cast its sickly light over us as we emerged from the club. Tillinghast found himself carrying his moustache cup, which he pocketed after two or three attempts.

Harry S. Robbins, "The Smoker from the Shadows" (1990)

glame stone, *n.* [< Welsh *glain neidr, glein neidyr, glain naidr,* adder-stone] See quotation. [Not in *OED*.]

And she could do what they called the shib-show, which was a very wonderful enchantment. She would tell the great lord, her father, that she wanted to go into the woods to gather flowers, so he let her go, and she and her maid went into the woods where nobody came, and the maid would keep watch. Then the lady would lie down under the trees and begin to sing a particular song, and she stretched out her arms, and from every part of the wood great serpents would come, hissing and gliding in and out among the trees, and shooting out their forked tongues as they crawled up to the lady. And they all came to her, and twisted round her, round her body, and her arms, and her neck, till she was covered with writhing serpents, and there was only her head to be seen. And she whispered to them, and she sang to them, and they writhed round and round, faster and faster, till she told them to go. And they all went away directly, back to their holes, and on the lady's breast there would be a most curious, beautiful stone, shaped something like an egg, and coloured dark blue and yellow, and red, and green, marked like a serpent's scales. It was called a glame stone, and with it one could do all sorts of wonderful things, and nurse said her great-grandmother had seen a glame stone with her own eyes, and it was for all the world shiny and scaly like a snake.

> Arthur Machen, "The White People" (1899)

glamour, glamor, *n.* [< *grammar*; cf. gramarye, grimoire] A charm, spell, enchantment, especially one that creates an alluring illusion; an aura of romance and excitement.

Usage: In contrast to such pairs as colour-color, honour-honor, labour-labor, etc., both British and American usage favor the spelling *glamour*; some authorities, however, accept both spellings.

Titles: Algernon Blackwood, "The Glamour of the Snow"; Seabury Quinn, "Glamour"; Thomas Ligotti, "The Glamour"

> This species of witchcraft is well known in Scotland as the *glamour*, or *deceptio visus* [visual deception], and was supposed to be a special attribute of the race of Gipsies.
>
> Sir Walter Scott, *Letters on Demonology and Witchcraft,*
> *Addressed to J. G. Lockheart, Esq.* (1830)

> They had lingered at the corner of a street on the north side of the Strand, enjoying the contrasts and the glamour of the scene.
>
> Arthur Machen, "Incident of the Private Bar" in
> *The Three Impostors; or, The Transmutations* (1894)

> I have spoken of systems of thoroughfare, and I assure you that walking alone through these silent places I felt fantasy growing on me, and some glamour of the infinite.
>
> Arthur Machen, "Novel of the Iron Maid" in
> *The Three Impostors; or, The Transmutations* (1894)

> I was firmly convinced that awful and incredible as was the thing I had seen the night before, yet it was no illusion, no glamour of bewildered sense, and in the course of the evening I again went to the doctor's house.
>
> Arthur Machen, "Novel of the White Powder" in
> *The Three Impostors; or, The Transmutations* (1894)

> But all the afternoon his eyes had looked on glamour; he had strayed in fairyland.
>
> Arthur Machen, *The Hill of Dreams* (1897)

And look she did, all a-glamor, and cried out:
"You great, yellow giant-thing of a man!"

Jack London, *The Star Rover* (1915)

The witches too not unseldom appear to be metamorphosed into animals, especially cats. And this is merely glamour, a trick of the devil, who, Saint Thomas tells us, can entirely confuse and cheat the senses, so that a witch is persuaded she is changed into a cat, and those of her society see her as a cat, whereas it is all illusion.

Montague Summers, *A Popular History of Witchcraft* (1936)

It may be urged against my use of the word incomparable that in the burglary business the name of Slith stands paramount and alone; and of this I am not ignorant; but Slith is a classic, and lived long ago, and knew nothing at all of modern competition; besides which the surprising nature of his doom has possibly cast a glamour upon Slith that exaggerates in our eyes his undoubted merits.

Lord Dunsany, "How Nuth Would have Practised His Art
upon the Gnoles" (1912)

Pan might come down now at high noon to bask in the lawn; or wander anywhere, and take no precautions as to casting glamors against visibility or the like.

Kenneth Morris, "A Wild God's Whim" (1917)

Long I looked—and turned away saddened. Knowing even as I did what the irised curtain had hidden, still it was as though some thing of supernal beauty and wonder had been swept away, never to be replaced; a glamour gone for ever; a work of the high gods destroyed.

A. Merritt, *The Moon Pool* (1919)

Up rushed the spheres of glamour; they touched the surface of the wan sea. They opened.

A. Merritt, *The Ship of Ishtar* (1924)

Though I had seen it by day, I wished to study the alleys and bazaars in the dusk, when rich shadows and mellow gleams of light would add to their glamour and fantastic illusion.

H. P. Lovecraft & Harry Houdini, "Under the Pyramids" (1924)

In my sleeping brain there took shape a melodrama of sinister hatred and pursuit, and I saw the black soul of Egypt singling me out and calling me in inaudible whispers; calling and luring me, leading me on with the glitter and glamour of a Saracenic surface, but ever pulling me down to the age-mad catacombs and horrors of its dead and abysmal pharaonic heart.

H. P. Lovecraft & Harry Houdini, "Under the Pyramids" (1924)

I thought I'd caught your system to perfection—indeed, I really don't think the Yankee destroyers leave the *u* out of *glamour*, any more than they leave it out of *amour*.

> H. P. Lovecraft, letter to James Ferdinand Morton (12 December 1929)

It came to him, for an instant, that all this was a questionable enchantment, a glamor wrought by the witch's wine.

> Clark Ashton Smith, "Mother of Toads" (1937)

Like some delaying sunset, brave with gold,
The glamors and the perils shared of old
Outsoar the shrunken empire of the mould.

> Clark Ashton Smith, "Lament for Vixeela" (c. 1953–54)

Your supple youth and loveliness
A glamor left upon the air:
Whether to curse, whether to bless,
You wrought a stronger magic there
With your lithe youth and loveliness.

> Clark Ashton Smith, "Witch-Dance" (1939)

O young and dear and tender sorceress!
Your delicate, slim hands
Reweave the glamors of Hellenic lands
To enchant the noon or night—
With many a soft caress
Restore the lost and lyrical delight.

> Clark Ashton Smith, "Ode"

Strange, that my wandering feet,
In all the years, have never known this place,
Where beauty, with a glamor wild and sweet,
Awaits the final witchcraft of your face.

> Clark Ashton Smith, "Future Pastoral" (1942)

Woe, woe unto Bel Yarnak! Fallen forever are the shining silver towers, lost the magic, soiled the glamor.

> Henry Kuttner, "The Jest of Droom-avista" (1939)

So Glyneth indulged himself with romantic excesses, and at times wondered if someone had cast a glamour upon her. Dame Flora became vaguely worried because her darling Glyneth had not gone out to climb trees or jump fences.

> Jack Vance, *The Green Pearl* (1985)

Belief in Verey's letter was impossible to resist: though the dwarf and the alleged "Oriental" in black and even the bat-winged Things that tittered were all glamours, phantasms, illusions, yet the force, the malign intelligence, behind these phenomena was something humanity had confronted from before the dawn of history and could not, ever, escape.

Robert Anton Wilson, *Masks of the Illuminati* (1981)

glamour, glamor, *v.tr.* To affect with a glamour (q.v.).

"Wait, O Queen," I answered, "thou hast not seen all." And, as I spoke, the serpent seemed to break in fragments, and from each fragment grew a new serpent. And these, too, broke in fragments and bred others, till in a little while the place, to their glamoured sight, was a seething sea of snakes, that crawled, hissed, and knotted themselves in knots. Then I made a sign, and the serpents gathered themselves round me, and seemed slowly to twine themselves about my body and my limbs, till, save my face, I was wreathed thick with hissing snakes.

H. Rider Haggard, note to *Cleopatra: Being an Account of the Fall and Vengeance of Harmachis, the Royal Egyptian, as Set Forth by His Own Hand* (1889)

My remarks must have glamored her mind, for her eyes continued to sparkle, and mine was half a guess that she was leading me on.

Jack London, *The Star Rover* (1915)

> Other will make libation, chant thy litanies. . . .
> But, when the glamored moons on inmost Stygia glare
> And quenchlessly the demon-calling altars flare,
> I shall go forth to madder gods and mysteries.

Clark Ashton Smith, "Farewell to Eros" (1937; ellipsis in original)

glibber, *v.intr., v.tr.,* & *n.* [? portmanteau of *glib* + *gibber*] To communicate in the manner of H. P. Lovecraft's ghouls; the utterance of a ghoul. Cf. **meep.** [Not in *OED*.]

A man he had known in Boston—a painter of strange pictures with a secret studio in an ancient and unhallowed alley near a graveyard—had actually made friends with the ghouls and had taught him to understand the simpler part of their disgusting meeping and glibbering.

H. P. Lovecraft, *The Dream-Quest of Unknown Kadath* (1927)

Sound travels slowly, so that it was some time before he heard an answering glibber.

H. P. Lovecraft, *The Dream-Quest of Unknown Kadath* (1927)

Golgotha, *pr.n.* & *n.* [< Gr *Golgothá* < Hb GVLGLThA, a skull] The proper name of the place where Jesus was crucified. Hence, a graveyard, cemetery; a charnel-house.

Think this:—this earth is the only grave and Golgotha wherein all things that live must rot; 't is but the draught wherein the heavenly bodies discharge their corruption; the very muck-hill on which the sublunary orbs cast their excrements: man is the slime of this dung pit, and princes are the governors of these men; for, for our souls, they are as free as emperors, all of one piece; there goes but a pair of sheers betwixt an emperor and the son of a bagpiper; only the dyeing, dressing, pressing, glossing, makes the difference.

John Marston, The Malcontent (1603)

A wilderness of filthy desolation walled in by dismal factories; a Golgotha of foul bones and refuse; a great grave-yard for worn-out pots and kettles and smashed glasses, and rotten vegetables and animal filth, and shattered household utensils and abominations unutterable.

Lafcadio Hearn, "Les Chiffoniers"

Her breasts are Golgotha to me!
Her lips, his dripping hands and feet!
Her secret-cinctured armoury
Of pleasures seems—how utter sweet!—
The gaping spear-wound in his side
Wherein I smote the Crucified!

Aleister Crowley, "La Juive" in White Stains: The Literary Remains of George Archibald Bishop, A Neuropath of the Second Empire (1898)

None of these colloquies were ever ocularly witnessed, since the windows were always heavily draped. Once, though, during a discourse in an unknown tongue, a shadow was seen on the curtain which startled Weeden exceedingly; reminding him of one of the puppets in a show he had seen in the autumn of 1764 in Hacher's Hall, when a man from Germantown, Pennsylvania, had given a clever mechanical spectacle advertised as a "View of the Famous City of Jerusalem, in which are represented Jerusalem, the Temple of Solomon, his Royal Throne, the noted Towers, and Hills, likewise the Sufferings of Our Saviour from the Garden of Gethsemane to the Cross on the Hill of Golgotha; an artful piece of Statuary, Worthy to be seen by the Curious."

H. P. Lovecraft, The Case of Charles Dexter Ward (1927)

I have indeed only to be aware of really enjoying myself when lo! some jumping-Jack-devil, with a spurt of blue fire leaps out of his box. The mere fact of having been given the miraculous privilege of life seems enough in itself to draw forth, out of some world-Golgotha or other, Larvæ and Lemurs, Were-wolves and Vampires, whose insane necrophiliast lust scents the hidden death in our vital extravagances.

John Cowper Powys,
"My Philosophy up-to-date as Influenced by Living in Wales"

gn'ag (*pl.* **gn'agn**), *n.* See quotations. [Not in *OED*.]

Zamacona and T'la-yub were tried before three *gn'agn* of the supreme tribunal in the gold-and-copper palace behind the gardened and fountained park, and the Spaniard was given his liberty because of the vital outer-world information he still had to impart.

> H. P. Lovecraft & Zealia Bishop, "The Mound" (1930)

Zamacona had felt that there was an element of irony in the parting words of the chief *gn'ag*—an assurance that all of his *gyaa-yothn*, including the one which had rebelled, would be returned to him.

> H. P. Lovecraft & Zealia Bishop, "The Mound" (1930)

Gorgo, *pr.n.* An appellation of Hecate, goddess of witchcraft. See under **Mormo**.

GORGO—dim. of Demogorgon, Greek name of the devil

> Anton Szandor LaVey (Howard Stanton Levey), *The Satanic Bible* (1969)

[Presumably a solecism, as it appears to confound Gorgo with Gorgon, an abbreviated form of Demogorgon; but the Gr nominative is identical (*Gorgó*).]

Gorgon (*pl.* **Gorgons, Gorgones**), *n.* [< Gr < *gorgó* (root: *gorgon-*), terrible] In Greek mythology, one of the three daughters of Ceto and Phorcys, who had brazen claws, serpents for hair, and a petrifying gaze. Two of them, Euryale and Stheno, were immortal; the third, Medusa, was slain by Perseus. Also, a synonym for **Catoblepas**.

> But then he told Pamela—not so much because she should know it as because he would tell it—the wonderful act Zelmane had performed, which Gynecia likewise spake of, both in such extremity of praising as was easy to be seen the construction of their speech might best be made by the grammar rules of affection. Basilius told with what a gallant grace she ran with the lion's head in her hand, like another Pallas with the spoils of Gorgon.

> Sir Philip Sidney, *The Countess of Pembroke's Arcadia* (1580)

> Unable to obtain the companionship of men, I at last sought that of wild beasts and reptiles—of the gods of ancient mythology, and the monsters of fairydom; but, all to no purpose. The crocodiles buried themselves in the mid-current of the Nile, as I stealthily approached its banks. I unavailingly chased the terrified speed of tigers and anacondas through the stifling heat of the jungles of Bengal. Memnon arose from his throne, and hid himself in the clouds, when he saw me kneeling at his granite feet. I followed in vain the sublime flight of Odin over the polar snows and ice-islands of both hemispheres. Satyrs hid from me; dragons and gorgons avoided me. The very ants and insects disappeared from my presence, taking refuge in dead trunks, and in the bowels of the earth.

> "The Hasheesh Eater" (1856)

The sweet lips that even at their sweetest could never lose their delicate cruelty, had no sweetness now. They were drawn into a square—inhuman as that of Medusa; in her eyes were the fires of the pit, and her hair seemed to writhe like the serpent locks of that Gorgon whose mouth she had borrowed; all her beauty was transformed into a nameless thing—hideous, inhuman, blasting!

A. Merritt, *The Moon Pool* (1919)

The hideous hopping figure became rigid; its face of a fallen angel staring at that flare. Its gaze dropped from it to its body. Graydon, every nerve at breaking point, watched incredulity change to truly demonic rage—the eyes glared like blue hell flames, the mouth became an open square from which slaver dripped, the face writhed into a Gorgon mask.

A. Merritt, *The Face in the Abyss* (1924)

The blasphemous thing held me like a magnet. I was helpless, and did not wonder at the myth of the gorgon's glance which turned all beholders to stone.

H. P. Lovecraft & Zealia Bishop, "Medusa's Coil" (1930)

Grimalkin, grimalkin, *pr.n.* & *n.* [< *grey* + *malkin,* diminutive of Matilda] A cat, particularly an old, grey, female cat.

> So (Poets sing)
> *Grimalkin* to Domestick Vermin sworn
> An everlasting Foe, with watchful Eye,
> Lyes nightly brooding o'er a chinky gap,
> Protending her fell Claws, to thoughtless Mice
> Sure Ruin.

John Philips, "The Splendid Shilling: An Imitation of Milton" (1701)

This could not be, however; he was not there; for, while Hepzibah was looking, a strange Grimalkin stole forth from the very spot, and picked his way across the garden.

Nathaniel Hawthorne, *The House of the Seven Gables* (1850–51)

> Vain, fruitless hope!—The wearied sentinel
>   At eve may overlook the crouching foe,
> Till, ere his hand can sound the alarum-bell,
>   He sinks beneath the unexpected blow;
> Before the whiskers of Grimalkin fell,
>   When slumb'ring on her post, the mouse may go—
> But woman, wakeful woman, 's never weary,
> —Above all, when she waits to thump her deary.

Thomas Ingoldsby (Richard Harris Barham),
"The Ghost" in *The Ingoldsby Legends* (1840)

Two benches, shaped in sections of a circle, nearly enclosed the hearth; on one of these I stretched myself, and Grimalkin mounted the other.

         Emily Brontë, *Wuthering Heights: A Novel* (1847)

Very quietly therefore did Randolph Carter steal to the edge of the wood and send the cry of the cat over the starlit fields. And a great grimalkin in a nearby cottage took up the burden and relayed it across leagues of rolling meadow to warriors large and small, black, grey, tiger, white, yellow, and mixed; and it echoed through Nir and beyond the Skai even into Ulthar, and Ulthar's numerous cats called in chorus and fell into a line of march.

     H. P. Lovecraft, *The Dream-Quest of Unknown Kadath* (1926–27)

gug, *n.* A fabulous creature that inhabits H. P. Lovecraft's Dreamlands. [Not in *OED*.]

The gugs, hairy and gigantic, once reared stone circles in that wood and made strange sacrifices to the Other Gods and the crawling chaos Nyarlathotep, until one night an abomination of theirs reached the ears of earth's gods and they were banished to caverns below. Only a great trap-door of stone with an iron ring connects the abyss of the earth-ghouls with the enchanted wood, and this the gugs are afraid to open because of a curse.

     H. P. Lovecraft, *The Dream-Quest of Unknown Kadath* (1926–27)

gyaa-yoth (*pl. **gyaa-yothn***), *n.* See quotations. [Not in *OED*.]

The party observed Zamacona's fright, and hastened to reassure him as much as possible. The beasts or *gyaa-yothn*, they explained, surely were curious things; but were really very harmless. The flesh they ate was not that of intelligent people of the master-race, but merely that of a special slave-class which had for the most part ceased to be thoroughly human, and which indeed was the principal meat stock of K'n-yan. They—or their principal ancestral element—had first been found in a wild state amidst the Cyclopean ruins of the deserted red-litten world of Yoth which lay below the blue-litten world of K'n-yan.

     H. P. Lovecraft & Zealia Bishop, "The Mound" (1930)

It argues well for the intrepid fire of those Renaissance Spaniards who conquered half the unknown world, that Pánfilo de Zamacona y Nuñez actually mounted one of the morbid beasts of Tsath and fell into place beside the leader of the cavalcade—the man named Gll'-Hthaa-Ynn, who had been most active in the previous exchange of information. It was a repulsive business; but after all, the seat was very easy, and the gait of the clumsy *gyaa-yoth* surprisingly even and regular. No saddle was necessary, and the animal appeared to require no guidance whatever.

     H. P. Lovecraft & Zealia Bishop, "The Mound" (1930)

H

Halcyon, halcyon, *n.* & *adj.* [< Gr *alkyón*, a kingfisher] The kingfisher, fabled to charm the wind and sea to calm, for a period about two weeks long, around the time of the winter solstice, so that it could float its nest on the water in peace. Hence, characterized by calm, peacefulness, and tranquility, as halcyon days.

> And if great things by smaller may be ghuest,
> So, in the mid'st of Neptunes angrie tide,
> Our Britan Island, like the weedie nest
> Of true Halcyon, on the waves doth ride,
> And softly sayling, skornes the waters pride:
> While all the rest, drown'd on the continent,
> And tost in bloodie waves, their wounds lament,
> And stand, to see our peace, as struck with woonderment.
>
> Giles Fletcher, *Christ's Triumph after Death* (1610)

> Speed, Halcyon, speed, and here construct thy nest:
> Brood on these waves, and charm the winds to rest!
>
> M. G. Lewis, *The Isle of Devils: A Metrical Tale* (1816)

For as Jove, during the winter season, gives twice seven days of warmth, men have called this clement and temperate time the nurse of the beautiful Halcyon.

> Simonides (fragment), as quoted in Edgar Allan Poe, "Berenice" (1835)

And at length the period of our nuptials was approaching, when, upon an afternoon in the winter of the year,—one of those unseasonably warm, calm, and misty days which are the nurse of the beautiful Halcyon,—I sat, (and sat, as I thought, alone,) in the inner apartment of the library.

> Edgar Allan Poe, "Berenice" (1835)

> He cried: "There was no rest for me,
> I could not bear their mockery;
> So, in the sapphire-coloured day,
> I passed my lonely antique way
> With halcyon feet by seas of rose,
> Against whose foam the ilex grows,
> To Nyssa, where with golden strings
> Bacchus his laden leopard flings."
>
> Samuel Loveman, *The Hermaphrodite* (1922)

283

> The avenues lur'd me
> With vistas sublime;
> Tall arches assur'd me
> That once on a time
> I had wander'd in rapture beneath them, and bask'd in the Hal-
> cyon clime.
>
> H. P. Lovecraft, "The City"

halcyonian, *adj.* Halcyon.

On marble cliffs above the halcyonian seas, are ancient woods of cedar illumed by scarlet orchids.

> Clark Ashton Smith, "The Land of Fruitful Palms"

Hallowmas, Hallowmass, *n.* All Hallows' Day or All Saints' Day, November 1.

"I had to save myself—I had to, Dan! She'd have got me for good at Hallow-mass—they hold a Sabbat up there beyond Chesuncook, and the sacrifice would have clinched things."

> H. P. Lovecraft, "The Thing on the Doorstep" (1933)

When he heard the hushed Arkham whispers about Keziah's persistent presence in the old house and the narrow streets, about the irregular tooth-marks left on certain sleepers in that and other houses, about the childish cries heard near May-Eve, and Hallowmass, about the stench often noted in the old house's attic just after those dreaded seasons, and about the small, furry, sharp-toothed thing which haunted the mouldering structure and the town and nuzzled people curi-ously in the black hours before dawn, he resolved to live in the place at any cost.

> H. P. Lovecraft, "The Dreams in the Witch House" (1932)

Indeed, there were always vague local tales of unexplained stenches upstairs in the Witch House just after May-Eve and Hallowmass.

> H. P. Lovecraft, "The Dreams in the Witch House" (1932)

hashish, hasheesh, hashiesh, hascheesh, hashsheesh, haschisch, hasch-ish, etc., *n.* [< Ar *hashísh,* grass, hay, herb, hemp, hashish] A slightly acrid gum resin produced by the flowering tops of the female hemp or cannabis plant, which may be purified and used as an intoxicant. Found in such compounds as **hashish-crazed, hashish-dream, hashish-drunk, hashish-eater, hashish eternity, hashish guzzler, hashish land, hashish-mænad, hashish party, hashish pipe, hashish vision,** etc.

Titles: John Greenleaf Whittier, "The Haschish" (verse); "The Hasheesh Eater"; Fitz Hugh Ludlow, "The Apocalypse of Hasheesh" (non-fiction), *The Hasheesh Eater: Being Passages from the Life of a Pythagorean* (non-fiction); Thomas Bailey Al-drich, "Hascheesh" (verse); Aleister Crowley (as Oliver Haddo), "The Psychology of Hashish" (non-fiction); Lord Dunsany, "The Hashish Man," *The Hashish Man and Other Stories* (collection); Clark Ashton Smith, *The Hashish-Eater; or, The Apocalypse of Evil* (verse), "In a Hashish Dream" (fragment); Frank Belknap Long, "The Hashish Eater" (verse); E. Hoffman Price, "Hasheesh Wisdom"; Robert E. Howard, "Hashish Land" (non-fiction)

a. General:

> Of all that Orient lands can vaunt
>> Of marvels with our own competing,
> The strangest is the Haschish plant,
>> And what will follow on its eating.
>
> John Greenleaf Whittier, "The Haschish" (c. 1853)

"It is hasheesh," I said, looking at it as if I saw an afreet or a ghoul.

> "The Hasheesh Eater" (1856)

I allude to various chemical and botanical compounds; for instance, those plants which furnish a large percentage of the chemical principles Narcotine, Morphia and others of the same general characteristics, as Opium, Beng and Hemp, the preperations of the delightful but dangerous ——, the equally fascinating decoctions of ——, not forgetting Hasheesh, that accursed drug, beneath whose sway millions in the Orient have sunk into untimely but rainbow-tinted graves, and which, in western lands, has made hundreds of howling maniacs and transformed scores of strong men into the most loathly, driveling idiots.

> Paschal Beverly Randolph, *Ravalette: The Rosicrucian's Story* (1863)

Plants also have like mystical properties in a most wonderful degree, and the secrets of the herbs of dreams and enchantments are only lost to European science and, useless to say, are unknown to it, except in a few marked instances, such as opium and hashish. Yet, the psychical effects of even these few upon the human system are regarded as evidences of a temporary mental disorder.

> H. P. Blavatsky, *Isis Unveiled: A Master-Key to the Mysteries of Ancient and Modern Science and Theology* (1877)

There was opium of course; but he was one of those on whom opium has little exciting influence, and so far as it had any, it only made his visions more incoherent. Haschish was in this respect still worse. It was not to be thought of, that one should resort, for the sake of dreams, to raw meat, like Dryden and Fuseli; or to other indigestible food, like Mrs. Radcliffe.

> Thomas Wentworth Higginson, "The Monarch of Dreams" (1887)

And, doubtless, this understanding of the artificer of the artist varies in an almost infinite chain of *nuances*: there have been artists, perhaps, who have worked like men under the influence of haschish, who have opened their mouths and prophesied, and then recovering from the possession have sat up and stared, and asked where they were, and what they had been doing.

Arthur Machen, *Hieroglyphics: A Note upon Ecstasy in Literature* (1902)

"Go on, please," he said. "I quite understand. I know something myself of the hashish laughter."

Algernon Blackwood, "A Psychical Invasion" (1908)

> Death! Death!
> It is a year to-night. I arrayed her first
> In yon gold ornaments—My brain is sick!
> I want coffee—or hashish—No! That is for her!
> I must be very clear and calm, very clear, very calm,
> How I must be ill—

Aleister Crowley, "The God-Eater: A Tragedy of Satire" (1903)

And indeed the brains of them all were awhirl. As Eliphaz Levi says, evil ceremonies are a true intellectual poison; they do invoke the powers of hallucination and madness as surely as does hashish. And who dare call the phantoms of delirium "unreal?" They are real enough to kill a man, to ruin a life, to push a soul to every kind of crime, and there are not many "real" "material" things that have such weight in work.

Aleister Crowley, *Moonchild* (1917; aka *The Butterfly-Net* or *The Net*)

Still, perhaps with a little help from Hashish, one can imagine a Merchant Prince or a Banker being intelligent, or even, in a weak moment, human; and this is not the case with officials.

Aleister Crowley, *Magick without Tears* (1944)

> Hashsheesh nor opium are worth not thy caresses,
> Sweeter than opium to still the spirit's drouth
> Thine unassuaged mouth;
> Him that hath known thy love no mortal grief distresses;
> Sweeter thy kisses are than incense which oppresses
> The breezes of the South . . .

David Park Barnitz, "Song of India" in *The Book of Jade* (1901; ellipsis in original)

These proud Turks died stolidly, many of them: in streets of Kassim-pacha, in crowded Taxim on the heights of Pera, and under the arcades of Sultan-Selim, I have seen the open-air barber's razor with his bones, and with him the skull of the faithful half-shaved, and the two-hours' narghile with traces of tembaki and haschish still in the bowl.

M. P. Shiel, *The Purple Cloud* (1901)

Among these is Baudelaire. With nothing but haschisch for ladder the ascent was effected; he was there, living in uninterrupted delights, listening to harmonies no mortal ever heard before, contemplating landscapes of amber and emerald, perspectives the colour of dream, and with them, perhaps, the lost arcana, the secrets of the enigmæ of the universe, the science that Plutonian cataclysms engulfed, the recitals of the genesis and metamorphosis of the supernal, the chronicles of the forgotten relations of nature and man.

Edgar Saltus, "The Quest of Paradise" in *The Pomps of Satan* (1904)

Even a drug may thus delude and cheat—
One word, "assassin", is a proof of it.
Muffle your brain with hashish: and the beat
Of clock falls slow as echo in the night
In some primæval cavern hidden from sight—
Stalactite whispering to stalagmite.

Walter de la Mare, *Winged Chariot*

And he said, "Yes; I do it with hashish. I know Bethmoora well." And he took out of his pocket a small box full of some black stuff that looked like tar, but had a stranger smell. He warned me not to touch it with my finger, as the stain remained for days. "I got it from a gipsy," he said. "He had a lot of it, as it had killed his father."

Lord Dunsany, "The Hashish Man" (1910)

"It was about the time that I got the hashish from the gipsy, who had a quantity that he did not want. It takes one literally out of oneself. It is like wings. You swoop over distant countries and into other worlds. Once I found out the secret of the universe. I have forgotten what it was, but I know that the Creator does not take Creation seriously, for I remember that He sat in Space with all His work in front of Him and laughed."

Lord Dunsany, "The Hashish Man" (1910)

"Bayard Taylor's book," he said dully. "Yes! . . . I know of what my brain sought to remind me—Taylor's account of his experience under hashish. Mr Smith, someone doped me with hashish!"

Sax Rohmer (Arthur Sarsfield Ward), *The Mystery of Dr. Fu-Manchu* (1913;
aka *The Insidious Dr. Fu-Manchu*) (ellipsis in original)

"Mr West's statements," I said, "ran closely parallel with portions of Moreau's book on *Hashish Hallucinations*. Only Fu-Manchu, I think, would have thought of employing Indian hemp. I doubt, though, if it was the pure *Cannabis indica*. At any rate, it acted as an opiate—"

Sax Rohmer (Arthur Sarsfield Ward),
The Mystery of Dr. Fu-Manchu (1913; aka *The Insidious Dr. Fu-Manchu*)

"I have sampled every so-called 'vice,' including every known drug. Always, however, with an object in view. Mere purposeless debauchery is not in my character. My art, to which you have so kindly referred, must always come first. Sometimes it demands that I sleep with a Negress, that I take opium or hashish; sometimes it dictates rigid asceticism, and I tell you, my friend, that if such an instruction came again tomorrow, as it has often come in the past, I could, without the slightest effort, lead a life of complete abstinence from drink, drugs and women for an indefinite period."

H. R. Wakefield, "'He Cometh and He Passeth By!'" (1928)

There is chloroform in the collection. The odor of it sometimes seeps through every hall and closet, and I pace the floor tense with anxiety, and when next Sally comes creeping through the eternal gloom to summon me I perceive raw burns scarring red the sunken plaster cheeks of Richard Pride. Ether is here; it serves on occasion to put Pride to sleep when he is exhausted. There are bottles of paregoric and an abundance of morphine, store of cocaine and a flask of tincture of cannabis indica, and pounds of opium; and there are packages of those curious hashish cigarettes from Mexico. But eventually after some tests Richard Pride finds most suitable the drug hyoscine hydrobromide, the twilight-sleep anesthetic of the obstetrical hospital, which he swallows in the powerful hypodermic dose of a hundredth of a grain.

Leonard Cline, *The Dark Chamber* (1927)

Whence he had come, no one could tell. One night he had burst wildly into Sheehan's, foaming at the mouth and screaming for whiskey and hasheesh; and having been supplied in exchange for a promise to perform odd jobs, had hung about ever since, mopping floors, cleaning cuspidors and glasses, and attending to an hundred similar menial duties in exchange for the drink and drugs which were necessary to keep him alive and sane.

H. P. Lovecraft, "Old Bugs: An Extemporaneous Sob Story by Marcus Lollius, Proconsul of Gaul" (1919)

The disposition of Old Bugs was as odd as his aspect. Ordinarily he was true to the derelict type—ready to do anything for a nickel or a dose of whiskey or hasheesh—but at rare intervals he shewed the traits which earned him his name.

H. P. Lovecraft, "Old Bugs: An Extemporaneous Sob Story by Marcus Lollius, Proconsul of Gaul" (1919)

Hasheesh helped a great deal, and once sent him to a part of space where form does not exist, but where glowing gases study the secrets of existence. And a violet-coloured gas told him that this part of space was outside what he had called infinity.

H. P. Lovecraft, "Celephaïs" (1920)

It had left him in the sort of psychic muddlement that follows a debauch of hashish.

Clark Ashton Smith, "Ubbo-Sathla" (1932)

Below the bridge, about the pavilion, and around the whole edifice above, were gardens of trees and flowers that caused Alvor to recall the things he had seen during his one experiment with hashish. The foliation of the trees was either very fine and hair-like, or else it consisted of huge, semi-globular and discoid forms depending from horizontal branches and suggesting a novel union of fruit and leaf. Almost all colors, even green, were shown in the bark and foliage of these trees. The flowers were mainly similar to those Alvor had seen from the pavilion, but there were others of a short, puffy-stemmed variety, with no trace of leaves, and with malignant purple-black heads full of crimson mouths, which swayed a little even when there was no wind. There were oval pools and meandering streams of a dark water with irisated glints all through this garden, which, with the columnar edifice, occupied the middle of a small plateau.

Clark Ashton Smith, "The Monster of the Prophecy" (1929)

They were a philosophical race, much given to dreaming, and were universally addicted to the use of a strange drug, known as *gnultan*, the juice of a Martian weed. This drug was more powerful than opium or hashish, and gave rise to even wilder visions, but its effects were physically harmless. Its use had spread among human beings, till a law was passed forbidding its importation.

Clark Ashton Smith, "An Adventure in Futurity" (1930)

"I've monkeyed with hashish and peyote beans in my time," said Morris, "but I'll admit that I never saw anything like this."

Clark Ashton Smith, "The Dimension of Chance" (1932)

High in the heavens, above all the other growths, there towered two incredibly elongated boles such as might be seen in the delirium of hashish; and about them a medley of lesser forms, no two of which displayed the same habit, leaned and crawled and squatted or massed themselves in monstrous tangles.

Clark Ashton Smith, "The Dimension of Chance" (1932)

The first effects of hashish, like those of opium, are often disappointing to the Occidental: mere drowsiness, or trivial dreams, and slight half-conscious hallucinations are likely to be the only result. The dose must be repeated, the nerves must absorb a residuum of the drug, before their derangement can give rise to that marvellous and baroque efflorescence of visionary images and sensations for which these opiates are dear to the Oriental.

Clark Ashton Smith, "In a Hashish-Dream"

I shall say only that I succeeded in demonstrating, through the graphic device that I had invented, the direct influence of narcotics on the pineal gland, and the temporary activating of that gland as a sort of optic organ. The reactions recorded by this instrument while I was enduring the effect of hashish were unusually strong, and markedly similar to those which the graph had detected in the human eye during the reception of sight-images. Thus was confirmed my thesis of an objective world behind the teeming phantasmagoria evoked by drugs.

Clark Ashton Smith, "Double Cosmos" (1940)

Opium poppies' brew
Nor hasheesh from far India's mystic land
Have not such properties, nor can command
Visions of more fantastic form and hue.

Clark Ashton Smith, "The Potion of Dreams"

Don't worry about my experimenting with hashish. Life is enough of a nightmare without drugs and I feel content to take the effects on hearsay.

Clark Ashton Smith, letter to George Sterling (10 July, 1920)

No, I shouldn't advise you to tamper with hasheesh. The reaction is terrible, especially in those of a nervous temperament. I have never taken it myself, but I know several people who have. My friend George Sterling had a lot of the stuff in his possession at one time.

Clark Ashton Smith, letter to Frank Belknap Long (7 July, 1923)

If the dread being behind the screen had discovered the secret of breaking hashish's terrible power, what other monstrous secrets had he discovered and what unthinkable dominance was his? The suggestion of evil crawled serpent-like through my mind.

Robert E. Howard, *Skull-Face* (1929)

"Like an octopus his tentacles stretch to the high places of civilization and the far corners of the world. And his main weapon is—dope! He has flooded Europe and no doubt America with opium and hashish, and in spite of all effort it has been impossible to discover the break in the barriers through which the hellish stuff is coming. With this he ensnares and enslaves men and women.

Robert E. Howard, *Skull-Face* (1929)

"You are not real!" he shrieked, throwing out his hand as if to ward off a dreadful apparition. "You are a dream of the *hashish*! No, no! There is blood on the floor! You were dead—they told me you had been given to the ape! But you have come back to slay me! You are a fiend! A devil, as men say! Help! Help! Guard! To me!"

Robert E. Howard, *Three-Bladed Doom* (1934)

"I would take hashish, opium, all manner of drugs. I would emulate the sages of the East. And then perhaps I would apprehend—"

Frank Belknap Long, "The Hounds of Tindalos" (1929)

Hayward took the pellet from me rather hastily, watching my face. "That was the beginning," he said after a pause. "It's a drug. Yes," he went on at our startled expressions. "I've been taking it. Oh, it's not hashish or opium—I wish it were! It's far worse—I got the formula from Ludvig Prinn's *De Vermis Mysteriis.*"

Henry Kuttner, "The Invaders" (1939)

To my horror, I found myself standing on the edge of a frightful precipice looking down into a chasm thousands of feet deep, filled with the steam and smoke of a hundred geysers and bubbling lava pools. Surely, I thought, the mad Arab, Abdul Hashish, must have had such a spot in mind when he wrote of the hellish valley of Oopadoop in that frightful book the forbidden *Pentechnicon.*

Arthur C. Clarke, "At the Mountains of Murkiness; or, From Lovecraft to Leacock" (1940)

When I had been at Cambridge, the decadent verse of Ariel Prescott had enjoyed a mild vogue among the undergraduates—those of them given to sampling hashish and studying occultism and Theosophy, at any rate. I had looked into her work and found it to be puerile pseudo-Swinburne, seasoned with the dark perversities of *Maldoror.*

Lin Carter, "Dreams in the House of Weir" (1980)

"We don't just have beer, pot, hashish, and sisters. There're other attractions."

Philip José Farmer, "The Freshman" (1979)

b. In **hashish-eater:**

"It sounds like the ravings of a hashish-eater, or the recollection of a most unpleasant dream," I volunteered.

Seabury Quinn, "The Man in Crescent Terrace" (1946)

It was crazy as a hasheesh-eater's dream, a scene straight out of the *Arabian Nights* with overtones of the Left Bank.

Seabury Quinn, "Masked Ball" (1947)

Words cannot describe the utter, supernal loveliness of those formations known as the Diamond Lake and Oriental Room—they are not of this earth, but are sheer fragments of the narcotic rhapsodies of hasheesh-eaters, and the inspired visions of those few rare artists in words and colours who have had glimpses of realms beyond starry space.

H. P. Lovecraft, "A Descent to Avernus" (1929)

Al Hakim answered not; he sat with hands folded, his gaze detached and impersonal as that of a hashish eater.

Robert E. Howard, "Hawks over Egypt"

I thought of drugs; he looked like a typical addict. But his eyes were not the feverish globes of fire which characterize the hashish-eater, and opium had not
wasted his physique.

> Robert Bloch, "The Dark Demon" (1936)

c. In other compounds or as modifier:

Almost through the very same symbols as De Quincey, a hasheesh-mænad
friend of mine also saw it, as this book relates, and the vision is accessible to all
of the same temperament and degree of exaltation.

> Fitz Hugh Ludlow, *The Hasheesh Eater:*
> *Being Passages from the Life of a Pythagorean* (1857)

On the pages of Gibbon the palaces and lawns of Nicomedia were illustrated
with a hasheesh tint and a hasheesh reality; and journeying with old Dan Chaucer, I drank in a delicious landscape of revery along all the road to Canterbury.

> Fitz Hugh Ludlow, *The Hasheesh Eater:*
> *Being Passages from the Life of a Pythagorean* (1857)

[Clark Ashton] Smith's drawings & paintings range from realistic subjects with
an aura of strangeness about them to the very peaks & depths of livid nightmare, hashish-ecstasy, & polychromatic madness.

> H. P. Lovecraft, letter to Elizabeth Toldridge (21 February 1929)

The moonlit plain seemed to shift and waver before him, but was interminable
as the landscape of a hashish-dream.

> Clark Ashton Smith, "The Monster of the Prophecy" (1929)

Flying in the jungle was like moving in a hashish eternity. There was no end to it
and no change—it simply went on and on through a world without limits or horizons.

> Clark Ashton Smith, "The Immeasurable Horror" (1930)

Please, dear editor, will you kindly enlighten our abysmal ignorance, as to the
brand of dope Clark Ashton Smith uses? "The Eternal World" is certainly an
excellent revelation of a hashish guzzler's mental processes—of all the imbecilic
drivel!!!

> C. Ferry & B. Rogers, letter to the editor of *Wonder Stories* (December 1933)

The horror first took concrete form amid that most unconcrete of all things—a
hashish dream. I was off on a timeless, spaceless journey through the strange
lands that belong to this state of being, a million miles away from Earth and all
things earthly; yet I became cognizant that something was reaching across the
unknown voids—something that tore ruthlessly at the separating curtains of my
illusions and intruded itself into my visions.

> Robert E. Howard, *Skull-Face* (1929)

Cannabis indica formed one of the ingredients of the mixture in the brazier; that has been ascertained by analysis. It was the presence of this Indian drug which led so many to believe that the later entries in Edmond's diary were evolved from nothing more tangible than the fantasies of an opium or hashish dream, directed along the curious channels they took merely because of the students' preoccupation with those things at the time.

Henry Kuttner, "Hydra" (1939)

One is inclined to believe that the anomalous mixture of drugs in the brazier continued to exert its influence on the minds of the two students, for certainly Ludwig's experiences, as recorded by Edmond, seem like a continuation of the original hashish dream.

Henry Kuttner, "Hydra" (1939)

From the vast desert of Arabia had come intriguing tales as old as time; furtive fables of mystic Irem, city of ancient dread, and the lost legends of vanished empires. He had spoken to the dreaming dervishes whose hashish visions revealed secrets of forgotten days, and had explored certain reputedly ghoul-ridden tombs and burrows in the ruins of an older Damascus than recorded history knows.

Robert Bloch, "Fane of the Black Pharaoh" (1937)

"Odd sort of fellow. Looks like a Russian Tartar—he brags that his grandmother was the niece of a Mongol Incarnate God, and likes to fancy himself psychic. Used to stage hashish parties in Greenwich Village to try to open the way into other realms—dimensions or psychic planes adjoining ours, but invisible."

Evangeline Walton, *Witch House* (1945)

The being was affecting my very thought-processes—and even as I stood before the cone, the insect-creature was pouring its memories into me. For as the landscape melted about me, I began to experience visions. I seemed to float above scenes like those of a hashish-dream—in a body such as that of the horror from the cone.

Ramsey Campbell, "The Insects from Shaggai" (1964)

The invocations grew wilder and more frantic. Sade and Masoch were brought into the chapel to assist with demoniac mucis performed on a tom-tom and an ancient Greek pipe, they ate hashish cakes before the invocation now and she couldn't remember afterward exactly what had happened, the voice of the male called upward to her, "Mother! Creator! Ruler! Come to me! [IÔ ERIS]! Come to me! [IÔ ERIS ERIS]! Come to me! Ave, Discordia! Ave, Magna Mater! Venerandum, vente, vente!

[IÔ ERIS ELANDROS]! [IÔ ERIS ELEPROLIS]!

Thou bornless ever reborn one! Thou deathless ever-dying one! Come to me as Isis and Artemis and Aphrodite, come as Helen, as Hera, come especially as Eris!"

    Robert Anton Wilson & Robert Shea, *Leviathan* in *The Illuminatus! Trilogy* (1969–71)

*As he chanted this blasphemous and nameless invocation, the mad Arab began to metamorphose before our very eyes, growing, swelling, becoming like unto a huge bowl of green yogurt, then changing into a jellyfish with a million bloodshot eyes, then becoming a pit bull with AIDS, then a Republican attorney general, a werewolf, every fearsome creature of nightmare and horror imaginable by a hashish-crazed brain, **for all these horrific visions were, I now realized, individual aspects of the multiple monstrosity that was Cthulhu, the Interstellar Banker, source of all evil and conspiracy, inventor of punk rock, Eater of Souls, the Thing in the center of the Pentagon!!!***

    Robert Anton Wilson, "The Horror on Howth Hill" (1990)

Heliogabalian, Heliogabalan, *adj.* [< L *Heliogabalus* < *Elah-Gabal,* a Syrio-Phœnician sun-deity] Of, pertaining to, or resembling the Roman Emperor (218–222 CE) Heliogabalus (Varius Avitus Bassianus), renowned for profligacy and perversity.

If this high-class journal may be believed, His Majesty is one of the most Heliogabalian profligates that ever disgraced an autocratic throne!

    W. S. Gilbert, *Utopia Limited; or, The Flowers of Progress* (1893)

Good idea, your going there, but don't get in his Bohemian, near-Oscar-Wilde sort of circles! Gawd, how I hate that swinish Heliogabalan type!

    H. P. Lovecraft, letter to Samuel Loveman (29 April 1923)

hemp, *n.* The cannabis plant, particularly when considered as a producer of fiber, such as that used to make rope for hangings, or other useful material. Found in compounds such as **hempseed, hemp-eater, hemp-maddened**.

Cummin and hempseed sowne with curssing and opprobrious words grow the faster.

    Reginald Scot, *The Discoverie of Witchcraft* (1584)

Steal out unperceived and sow a handful of hemp-seed, harrowing it with anything you can conveniently draw after you. Repeat now and then, "Hemp-seed, I saw thee, hemp-seed, I saw thee; and him (or her) that is to be my true-love, come after me and pou thee." Look over your left shoulder, and you will see the appearance of the person invoked in the attitude of pulling hemp. Some traditions say, "come after me and shaw thee," that is, show thyself; in which case it simply appears. Others omit the harrowing, and say, "come after me and harrow thee."

    Robert Burns, note to "Halloween"

We passed the greater part of the night in a delightful stream of that somnolent and half-mystic talk which Prince Zaleski alone could initiate and sustain, during which he repeatedly pressed on me a concoction of Indian hemp resembling *hashish*, prepared by his own hands, and quite innocuous.

M. P. Shiel, "The Race of Orven"

"Either bamboo will greet his feet or hemp adorn his neck," persisted the other, with a significant movement of his hands in the proximity of his throat.

Ernest Bramah, *Kai Lung's Golden Hours* (1922)

Hemp, hemp, hurray! says the captain in the moonlight.

James Joyce, *Finnegans Wake* (1922–39)

And the third sorcerer huddled over a small fire wherein burned cypress branches and broken crucifixes and portions of a gibbet. In his hand was a skull filled with dark wine which had been seasoned with hemp and with the fat of a girl child and with poppy seed: and his familiar, in the shape of a large dun-colored cat, was lapping up that bitter drink.

James Branch Cabell, *Something About Eve: A Comedy of Fig-Leaves* (1927)

In the main corridor we found the night watchman strangled to death—a bit of East Indian hemp still knotted around his neck—and realised that despite all precautions some darkly evil intruder or intruders had gained access to the place.

H. P. Lovecraft & Hazel Heald, "Out of the Æons" (1933)

"Their followers were called Assassins. They were hemp-eaters, *hashish* addicts, and their terrorist methods made the Shaykhs feared all over Western Asia."

Robert E. Howard, *Three-Bladed Doom* (1934)

He detached a force of a hundred men to steal through the gardens that lay on the east side of the town and charge the orchard from the east at an auspicious moment, while he led three hundred hemp-maddened fanatics straight down the street, against the southwestern angle of the orchard-wall.

Robert E. Howard, *Three-Bladed Doom* (1934)

Though my cousin had no objection to showing me about the extensive laboratory, he required the utmost solitude when he was conducting his experiments. Nor had he any intention of setting down exactly what drugs he had recourse to—though I had reason to believe that *Cannabis indica*, or Indian hemp, commonly known as hashish, was one of them—in the punishment he inflicted on his body in pursuit of his wild dream to recapture his ancestral and hereditary memory, a goal he sought daily and often nightly, as well, without surcease, so much so that I saw him with increasing rarity, though he sat for a long time with me on the night I finally gave him the transcript of his notes tracing the course of his life through his recaptured memory, going over each page with me, making certain small corrections and additions, striking out a few passages here and there, and, in general, improving the narrative as I had transcribed it.

August Derleth (as H. P. Lovecraft & August Derleth), "The Ancestor" (1957)

There was a sudden halloo, and the rush of a great hemped spiderwebbing dropping down over his huge body.

John Jakes, "The Barge of Souls" (1967) in *Brak the Barbarian*

heptagram, *n.* A seven-pointed star. [Not in *OED*.]

> Trifle not with charm or spell,
> Heptagram or pentacle,
> Leave in silence, long unsaid,
> All the words that wake the dead.

Clark Ashton Smith, "Canticle" (1927)

Hesperean, *adj.* Hesperian, Hesperidean (q.v.). [Not in *OED*.]

> It was a jasmine bower, all bestrown
> With golden moss. His every sense had grown
> Ethereal for pleasure; 'bove his head
> Flew a delight half-graspable; his tread
> Was Hesperean; to his capable ears
> Silence was music from the holy spheres;
> A dewy luxury was in his eyes;
> The little flowers felt his pleasant sighs
> And stirr'd them faintly.

John Keats, *Endymion: A Poetic Romance* (1817–18)

> Hast thou forgot the tale of kisses told
> By summer waters calm as sleep,
> When Hesperèan sunsets touched thy hair
> From islands lost and fair?

Clark Ashton Smith, "Alienage" (1923)

Hesperian, hesperian, *adj.* Of or pertaining to the west, where the sun sets, or to the Hesperides (q.v.).

Titles: Clark Ashton Smith, "Hesperian Fall" (verse)

"In thy yearning hast thou divined what no mortal else, saving only a few whom the world rejects, remembereth; *that the Gods were never dead*, but only sleeping the sleep and dreaming the dreams of Gods in lotos-filled Hesperian gardens beyond the golden sunset."

H. P. Lovecraft & Anna Helen Crofts, "Poetry and the Gods" (1920)

I have in literal truth built altars to Pan, Apollo, and Athena, and have watched for dryads and satyrs in the woods and fields at dusk. Once I firmly thought I beheld some of the sylvan creatures dancing under autumnal oaks; a kind of "religious experience" as true in its way as the subjective ecstasies of a Christian. If a Christian tell me he has *felt* the reality of his Jesus or Jehveh, I can reply that I have *seen* the hoofed Pan and the sisters of the Hesperian Phaëthusa.

H. P. Lovecraft, "A Confession of Unfaith" (1922)

> Rich as the pyre of some Hesperian queen,
> Feeding the ultimate sunset with sad fires,
> Is this, where beauty with her doom conspires
> To tell in flame what death and beauty mean.

Clark Ashton Smith, "Autumn Orchards" (1923)

> Men say the gods have flown;
> The Golden Age is but a fading story,
> And Greece was transitory:
> Yet on this hill hesperian we have known
> The ancient madness and the ancient glory.

Clark Ashton Smith, "Bacchante" (1939)

> Thy purple eyes, Valerian,
>   Have known the fungi of the moon,
> Have travelled lands Hesperian,
>   Have seen the blood-red plenilune.

Donald Wandrei, "Valerian" (1928)

hesternal, *adj.* [< L *hesternus*] Pertaining to yesterday or the past.

> It seemed the hueless ashes of the day
> And darkened glories filled that glooming world:
> The spectrum of hesternal suns was furled
> In immemorial valleys vast and grey.

Clark Ashton Smith, "The Nameless Wraith" (1948)

heteroclitic, *adj.* Deviating from ordinary forms or rules, as an irregularly inflected word.

The continents and seas and isles on this map were not those of the world I knew; and their names were written in heteroclitic runes of a lost alphabet.

Clark Ashton Smith, "The Uncharted Isle" (1930)

They passed through several pavilions and winding colonnades, and reached the circular wall at the core of the edifice. Here a high narrow door, engraved with heteroclitic ciphers, gave admission to a huge room without windows, lit by a yellow glow whose cause was not ascertainable.

Clark Ashton Smith, "The Monster of the Prophecy" (1929)

hieratic, *n.* Associated with priests or the priesthood, sacerdotal; of or pertaining to a simplified, cursive form of ancient Egyptian hieroglyphics; (of a work of art) stylized, adhering to a fixed form.

"Hziulquoigmnzhah! Zhothaqquah!" said Eibon with oracular solemnity and sonority. Then, after a pause of hieratic length: "*Iqhui dlosh odhqlongh!*"

Clark Ashton Smith, "The Door to Saturn" (1930)

The young walking-sticks gather daily to worship—they make those enigmatic signs which I have never understood, and they move in swift gyrations about the vessel, as in the measures of a hieratic dance.

Clark Ashton Smith, "Master of the Asteroid" (1932)

The real people are giants, too; but they move slowly, with solemn, hieratic paces. Their bodies are nude and swart, and their limbs are those of caryatides—massive enough, it would seem, to uphold the roofs and lintels of their own buildings.

Clark Ashton Smith, "The City of the Singing Flame" (1931)

hierophant, *n.* A high priest or initiate into sacred mysteries and arcana.

Titles: Margaret St. Clair, "The Hierophants"

Like Schelling in time to come, he maintained the necessity of a special organ for the apprehension of philosophy, without perceiving that he thereby proclaimed philosophy bankrupt, and placed himself on the level of the Oriental hierophants, with whose sublime quackeries the modest sage could not hope to contend.

Richard Garnett, "The City of the Philosophers" (1888)

Other ugly reports concerned my intimacy with leaders of occultist groups, and scholars suspected of connexion with nameless bands of abhorrent elder-world hierophants.

H. P. Lovecraft, "The Shadow out of Time" (1935)

This cult, led by the arch-hierophants of Bubastis, Anubis, and Sebek, viewed their gods as the representatives of actual Hidden Beings—monstrous beast-men who shambled on Earth in primal days.

Robert Bloch, "Fane of the Black Pharaoh" (1937)

hierophantic, *adj.* Of, pertaining to, or resembling a hierophant or the teaching of hierophants.

"Of the choral hymns there sung, the hierophantic ritual, liturgies, pæans, the gorgeous symbolisms—of the wealth there represented, the culture, art, self-sacrifice—of the mingling of all the tongues of Europe—I shall not speak; nor shall I repeat names which you would at once recognize as familiar to you—

though I may, perhaps, mention that the 'Morris,' whose name appears on the papyrus sent to me is a well-known *littérateur* of that name."

M. P. Shiel, "The S.S." (1895)

high relief, *n.* A relief in which figures project at a ration greater than one half of their true proportions; alto-relievo. A relatively rare art form in fantasy and weird fiction.

The walls were of black obsidian stone, and upon all save that which had windows were huge devilish faces, antic grotesco-work, cut in high relief, thirteen, with their tongues out, and upon each tongue's tip a lamp; and the goggling eyes of them were looking-glass artificially cut in facets to disperse the beams of the lamplight in bushes of radiance, so that the hall was filled with light that shifted and glittered ever as the beholder moved his head.

E. R. Eddison, *A Fish Dinner in Memison* (1936–40)

The material seemed to be predominantly gold, though a weird lighter lustrousness hinted at some strange alloy with an equally beautiful and scarcely identifiable metal. Its condition was almost perfect, and one could have spent hours in studying the striking and puzzlingly untraditional designs—some simply geometrical, and some plainly marine—chased or moulded in high relief on its surface with a craftsmanship of incredible skill and grace.

H. P. Lovecraft, "The Shadow over Innsmouth" (1931)

Double doors of green bronze stood open against the wall, and portrayed in high relief the primal allegory of Nodens, the Lord of the Great Abyss: an anthropomorphic god with a beard of tentacles, now hunting winged octopi with a trident, now enthroned in a scallop shell.

Gary Myers & Marc Laidlaw, "The Summons of Nuguth-Yug" (1981)

hippocephalic, *adj.* Having a horse's head; horse-headed.

Great polypous horrors slid darkly past, and unseen bat-wings beat multitudinous around him, but still he clung to the unwholesome mane of that loathly and hippocephalic scaled bird.

H. P. Lovecraft, *The Dream-Quest of Unknown Kadath* (1926–27)

hippogriff, hippogrif, hippogryph, hippogriffin, *n.* A fabulous creature with the body and hindquarters of a horse, and the head, wings and foreclaws of a griffin.

> So saying he caught him up, and without wing
> Of hippogrif bore through the air sublime
> Over the wilderness and o'er the plain; [. . .]

John Milton, *Paradise Regained* (1671)

All in that city was of ancient device; the carving on the houses, which, when age had broken it remained unrepaired, was of the remotest times, and everywhere were represented in stone beasts that have long since passed away from Earth—the dragon, the griffin, and the hippogriffin, and the different species of gargoyle.

Lord Dunsany, "Idle Days on the Yann" (1910)

"The hippogriff?" said Lord Brandoch Daha. "What else is it than the emblem of our greatness? A thousand years ago they nested on Neverdale Hause, and there abide unto this day in the rocks the prints of their hooves and talons. He that rode it was a forefather of mine and of Lord Juss."

E. R. Eddison, *The Worm Ouroboros* (1922)

The odours occasionally wafted from the laboratory were likewise exceedingly strange. Sometimes they were very noxious, but more often they were aromatic, with a haunting, elusive quality which seemed to have the power of inducing fantastic images. People who smelled them had a tendency to glimpse momentary mirages of enormous vistas, with strange hills or endless avenues of sphinxes and hippogriffs stretching off into infinite distance.

H. P. Lovecraft, *The Case of Charles Dexter Ward* (1927)

> But I am gone,
> For at my call a hippogriff hath come,
> And firm between his thunder-beating wings,
> I mount the sheer cerulean walls of noon,
> And see the earth, a spurnèd pebble, fall
> Lost in the fields of nether stars—and seek
> A planet where the outwearied wings of time
> Might pause and furl for respite, or the plumes
> Of death be stayed, and loiter in reprieve
> Above some deathless lily; for therein
> Beauty hath found an avatar of flowers—
> Blossoms that clothe it as a colored flame
> From peak to peak, from pole to sullen pole,
> And turn the skies to perfume.

Clark Ashton Smith, *The Hashish-Eater; or, The Apocalypse of Evil* (1920)

> O, dark as Satan's nightmare, or the fruit
> Of Belial's rape on hell's black hippogriff!

Clark Ashton Smith, "The Ghoul and the Seraph" (1919)

"Oh hurry up," Ron moaned, beside Harry, "I could eat a hippogriff."

J. K. Rowling, *Harry Potter and the Goblet of Fire* (2000)

hoary, *adj.* White or grey with age; extremely old or ancient; canescent or pubescent with greyish hair.

No hoary falsehood shall be a truth to me—no cult or dogma shall encramp my pen.

Ragnar Redbeard, Might Is Right (1896)

No hoary falsehood shall be a truth to me; no stifling dogma shall encramp my pen!

Anton Szandor LaVey (Howard Stanton Levey), The Satanic Bible (1969)

Pointing to a chair, table, and pile of books, the old man now left the room; and when I sat down to read I saw that the books were hoary and mouldy, and that they included old Morryster's wild *Marvells of Science,* the terrible *Saducismus Triumphatus* of Joseph Glanvill, published in 1681, the shocking *Dæmonolatreia* of Remigius, printed in 1595 at Lyons, and worst of all, the unmentionable *Necronomicon* of the mad Arab Abdul Alhazred, in Olaus Wormius' forbidden Latin translation; a book which I had never seen, but of which I had heard monstrous things whispered.

H. P. Lovecraft, "The Festival" (1923)

> I have plung'd like a deer thro' the arches
>   Of the hoary primordial grove,
> Where the oaks feel the presence that marches
>   And stalks on where no spirit dares rove;
> And I flee from a thing that surrounds me, and leers thro' dead branches above.

H. P. Lovecraft, "Nemesis" (1917)

It was older than secret Egypt, more hoary than sea-doomed Atlantis, more ancient than time-forgotten Mu.

Robert Bloch, "The Faceless God" (1936)

horrent, *adj.* Covered with bristles, bristling; standing erect, as hair.

> The *Stygian* Council thus dissolv'd; and forth
> In order came the grand infernal Peers:
> Midst came thir mighty Paramount, and seem'd
> Alone th' Antagonist of Heav'n, nor less
> Than Hell's dread Emperor with pomp Supreme,
> And God-like imitated State; him round
> A Globe of fiery Seraphim inclos'd
> With bright imblazonry, and horrent Arms.

John Milton, Paradise Lost (1667)

After an hour or two of progression along the yielding ashy thoroughfare, amid the vegetation that was more horrent than ever with knives and caltrops, the travellers began to remember that they were hungry.

Clark Ashton Smith, "The Door to Saturn" (1930)

horrible, *adj.* Inspiring horror, horrifying.

The almost expiring light flashed faintly upon the walls of the passage, shewing the recess more horrible. Across the hall, the greater part of which was concealed in shadow, the feeble ray spread a tremulous gleam, exhibiting the chasm in the roof, while many nameless objects were seen imperfectly through the dusk.

Ann Radcliffe, *The Romance of the Forest, Interspersed with Some Pieces of Poetry* (1791)

Yet the old-time fairy tale, having served for generations, may now be classed as "historical" in the children's library; for the time has come for a series of newer "wonder tales" in which the stereotyped genie, dwarf and fairy are eliminated, together with all the horrible and bloodcurdling incident devised by their authors to point a fearsome moral to each tale.

L. Frank Baum, *The Wonderful Wizard of Oz* (1899)

"I have obtained many books, famed as being horrible, but they all lack something, or at best have only a temporary effect. *The Monk* in reality does not belong to the class; *Melmoth* is more properly an adventure novel; *The Vampyre* is as good as its progeny *Dracula*, but vampires are becoming common; *Frankenstein* is famous mainly because it was one of the first Gothic romances; Benson is often too definite; Poe is the master, of course, though Lovecraft is now writing terrific tales."

Donald Wandrei, "The Shadow of a Nightmare" (1929)

horrid, *adj.* Bristling, rough, shagged; inspiring horror, horrifying.

Titles: Marquis of Grosse, *Horrid Mysteries*

a. Bristling, etc.:

> From Godfrey's camp a grove a little way,
>   Amid the valleys deep, grows out of sight,
> Thick with old trees, whose horrid arms display
>   An ugly shade, like everlasting night:
> There, when the sun spreads forth his clearest ray,
>   Dim, thick, uncertain, gloomy seems the light;
> As when, in ev'ning, day and darkness strive
> Which should his foe from our horizon drive.

Torquato Tasso (trans. Edward Fairfax), *Jerusalem Delivered* (1640)

b. Horrifying, etc.:

"Dear creature! how much I am obliged to you; and when you have finished Udolpho, we will read the Italian together; and I have made out a list of ten or twelve more of the same kind for you."

"Have you, indeed! How glad I am!—What are they all?"

"I will read you their names directly; here they are, in my pocket-book. Castle of Wolfenbach, Clermont, Mysterious Warnings, Necromancer of the Black Forest, Midnight Bell, Orphan of the Rhine, and Horrid Mysteries. Those will last us some time."

"Yes, pretty well; but are they are all horrid, are you sure they are all horrid?"

Jane Austen, Northanger Abbey (1803)

It began with an ill omen! I might have foreseen that some deed of horrid circumstance was at hand.

William Godwin the Younger, "The Executioner" (1832)

horripilant, *adj.* Causing or inducing horripilation (q.v.).

The sentence "*It is a very strange affair,*" would be the very one naturally suggested under the circumstances, and had happily been selected as the most fitting one to afford exercise to the ventriloquist employed; and this apparent echoing of an unspoken thought would add additional piquancy to the scene and materially assist in piling up the horripilant.

Paschal Beverly Randolph, Ravalette: The Rosicrucian's Story (1863)

horripilate, *v.intr.* To undergo horripilation (q.v.).

"Harken, therefore, O matchless artificer! It is now our will that thou make for us a vase having the tint and the aspect of living flesh, but—mark well our desire!—*of flesh made to creep by the utterance of such words as poets utter—flesh moved by an Idea, flesh horripilated by a Thought!* Obey, and answer not! We have spoken."

Lafcadio Hearn, "The Tale of the Porcelain-God" in Some Chinese Ghosts

horripilation, *n.* [< LL] A bristling of the body hair, as from cold or fear.

Then he saw that almost the whole inner wall of the castle, giving on the court-yard, had been removed. It was the tearing-down of the prodigious blocks, no doubt through an extrahuman labor levied by sorcery, that he had heard during his ascent from the subterrene vaults. His blood curdled; he felt an actual horripilation, as he realized the purpose for which the wall had been demolished.

Clark Ashton Smith, "The Colossus of Ylourgne" (1932)

Just then a beam of violet-tinged light sprang past him. Gord felt the hair on the back of his neck rise in horripilation at the nearness of the ray.

Gary Gygax, "The Five Dragon Bowl" in Night Arrant (1987)

houri, *n.* [< Fr < Persian < Ar, "black-eyed like a gazelle," referring to the conventionally dilated pupils of beautiful women.] One of the virginal nymphs reported to inhabit the Islamic paradise, whom the faithful have the privilege of depucelating.

> The virgins of Paradise, called, from their large black eyes, *Hur al oyun.* An intercourse with these, according to the institutions of Mahomet, is to constitute the principal felicity of the faithful. Not formed of clay, like mortal women, they are deemed in the highest degree beautiful, and exempt from every inconvenience incident to the sex.—*Al Koran; passim.*
>
> > Samuel Henley, note to William Beckford,
> > *The History of the Caliph Vathek: An Arabian Tale* (1786)

> Tell me not of Houris' eyes;—
> > Far from me their dangerous glow,
> If those looks that light the skies
> > Wound like some that burn below.
>
> > Thomas Moore, *Lalla Rookh* (1817)

> But the skies that angel trod,
> > Where deeps thoughts are a duty—
> Where Love's a grown-up God—
> > Where the Houri glances are
> Imbued with all the beauty
> > Which we worship in a star.
>
> > Edgar Allan Poe, "Israfel" (1831)

And at such moments was her beauty—in my heated fancy thus it appeared perhaps—the beauty of beings either above or apart from the earth—the beauty of the fabulous Houri of the Turk.

> > Edgar Allan Poe, "Ligeia" (1838)

The girl was gone, even as I told myself that she was an houri, and that I, though a Christian, had been consigned by some error to the paradise of Mohammed.

> > Sax Rohmer (Arthur Sarsfield Ward),
> > *The Mystery of Dr. Fu-Manchu* (1913; aka *The Insidious Dr. Fu-Manchu*)

"And I tell you, pleasure and pain have nothing to do with heaven or hell. Pleasure and pain—Bah! What is your theologian's ecstasy but Mahomet's houri in the dark?"

> > H. G. Wells, *The Island of Dr. Moreau* (1896)

An incompleted Saturnalia filled the towers. I saw that some had gilded their bodies and that some had painted their breasts and cheeks and that others had hung themselves with ornaments so that their thighs glittered and their hair shone like lanterns. Nuns and Messalinas, virgins and houris, they sprawled nude and multitudinous about me. Decorated with paints and gems, their eyes swimming in lecherous dreams they lay upon the thousands of couches exhaling the perfumes of lust.

> Ben Hecht, *The Kingdom of Evil: A Continuation of the*
> *Journal of Fantazius Mallare* (1924)

Waking, I deemed perforce that I had died and was in a sequestered nook of Paradise. For surely the sward on which I lay, and the waving verdure about me, were lovelier than those of earth; and the face that leaned above me was that of the youngest and most compassionate houri.

> Clark Ashton Smith, "Told in the Desert" (1930)

The ecstasy heightened, and he heard a singing that appeared to emanate from the mouths of the blossoms: a singing as of houris, that turned his blood to a golden philtre-brew.

> Clark Ashton Smith, "Vulthoom" (1933)

"On Mount Alamut, in Persia, the first Shaykh, Hassan ibn Sabah, built his great castle-city, with its hidden gardens where his followers were permitted to taste the joys of paradise where dancing girls fair as *houris* flitted among the blossoms and the dreams of *hashish* gilded all with rapture."

> Robert E. Howard, *Three-Bladed Doom* (1934)

> Great wealth have I, a kingdom own, with palaces for pleasure,
> Jades exquisite, delicately carved ivory,
> And polished ebony,
> And lissome houris, gems and gold in many a measure,
> But what is there in wealth? In treasure what but treasure?
> Things of small worth to me.
>
> Donald Wandrei, "Somewhere Past Ispahan"

Hydra (*pl.* **Hydras, Hydræ**), *n.* [< L < Gr *hýdra*] In Græco-Roman mythology, a monstrous serpent with many heads (variously numbered at seven, nine, fifty, one hundred, or ten thousand); whenever one head is severed, two more grow in its place. Also, a small freshwater polyp with a tubular body and a mouth surrounded by a circle of tentacles, named after the mythical monster because each part of a divided specimen will regenerate into a complete animal.

Titles: Henry Kuttner, "Hydra" (1939)

> I will aske him for my Place againe, he shall tell
> me, I am a drunkard: had I as many mouthes as *Hydra*,
> such an answer would stop them all.
>
> William Shakespeare, *The Tragedy of Othello, the Moor of Venice* (160-)

Often tymes herde Manuel tell of the fayrness of this Queene of *Furies* and *Goblins* and *Hydræs*, insomuch that he was enamoured of hyr, though he neuer sawe hyr: then by this Connynge made he a Hole in the fyer, and went ouer to hyr, and when he had spoke with hyr, he shewed hyr his mynde.

> *The Terrible and Marvellous History of Manuel Pig-Tender*
> *That Afterwards Was Named Manuel the Redeemer*
> (an anonymous sixteenth-century English chapbook redaction of *Les Gestes de Manuel*),
> as quoted in James Branch Cabell, *Figures of Earth: A Comedy of Appearances* (1920)

> And overside, when leap the startled waves
> And crimson bubbles rise from battle-wrecks,
> Unresting hydras wrought of bloody light
> Dip to the ocean's phosphorescent caves.
>
> George Sterling, "A Wine of Wizardry" (1907)

"Beside them the venomous red trees raised themselves like the heads of hydras guarding nests of gigantic, jeweled and sleeping worms!"

> A. Merritt, "The People of the Pit" (1918)

Age-old horror is a hydra with a thousand heads, and the cults of darkness are rooted in blasphemies deeper than the well of Democritus.

> H. P. Lovecraft, "The Horror at Red Hook" (1925)

A tide of profound alarm and panic, due in part to the immemorial human aversion toward the unknown, swept immediately upon the nation; and immense, formless, exaggerated fears were bred like shadowy hydras in the dark minds of men.

> Clark Ashton Smith, "Seedling of Mars" (1931)

"These and others—some of such aspect that only delirious castaways have ever seen them and lived. These are the sources of the legendary hydras and harpies, Medusa and mermaids, Scylla and Circe, which have terrified human beings from the dawn of civilization, and before."

> James Wade, "The Deep Ones" (1969)

hydrophiinæ (*pl.*), *n.* Sea snakes of the subfamily *hydrophiinæ*. (Cf. the title of Gantley's *Hydrophinnæ*, first introduced by Carl Jacobi in "The Aquarium.") [Not in *OED*.]

The sun was incandescent in the white sky. The sea was calm, greasy, unbroken except for the slow, patient black fins that had been following the boat for days. But something else, during the night, had joined the sharks in their hellish pursuit. Sea snakes, hydrophiinæ, wriggling out of nowhere, had come to haunt the dory, gliding in circles round and round, venomous, vivid, vindictive.

> Hugh B. Cave, "Stragella" (1932)

hypostyle, *n.* A building whose roof or ceiling is supported by rows of columns.

Down limitless reaches of sunless pavement a spark of light flickered in the malodorous wind, and I drew behind the enormous circumference of a Cyclopic column that I might escape for a while the horror that was stalking million-footed toward me through gigantic hypostyles of inhuman dread and phobic antiquity.

H. P. Lovecraft & Harry Houdini, "Under the Pyramids" (1924)

I

ichor, *n.* [< L *ichor* < Gr *ikhōr*] In Græco-Roman mythology, the fluid that flows in the veins of the gods in lieu of blood; the blood or equivalent bodily fluid of various fabulous creatures; a watery, acidic discharge that issues from various wounds and sores; any foul and noxious fluid.

Titles: Esther M. Friesner, "Love's Eldritch Ichor"

But we aren't through yet, no, we haven't had the fancy words. Eldritch. Tenebrous. Smaragds and chalcedony. Mayhap. It can't be maybe, it can't be perhaps; it has to be mayhap, unless it's perchance. And then comes the final test, the infallible touchstone of the seventh-rate: Ichor. You know ichor. It oozes out of several tentacles, and beslimes tessellated pavements, and bespatters bejeweled courtiers, and bores the bejesus out of everybody.

> Ursula K. LeGuin, "From Elfland to Poughkeepsie" (1973)

The first indication of revival was afforded by a partial descent of the iris. It was observed, as especially remarkable, that this lowering of the pupil was accompanied by the profuse out-flowing of a yellowish ichor (from beneath the lids) of a pungent and highly offensive odor.

> Edgar Allan Poe, "The Facts in the Case of M. Valdemar" (1845)

We felt and knew that they were living, actual realities, a genuine and horrid trinity of facts, and not a mere optical illusion, or the result of a play upon our fancies, mesmeric or otherwise. This opinion was confirmed by the most positive and blasting testimony, for, as they solemnly, demoniacally marched about the center of that symbolic chart, they left a trailing streak of greenish—*dead, hard, greenish* ichor, or pus, behind them at each revolution, and a few drops of this fell upon the Baron's carpet.

> Paschal Beverly Randolph, *Ravalette: The Rosicrucian's Story* (1863)

"To attain to anything, he must needs screw the head up into the atmosphere of the future, while feet and hands drip dark ichors of despair from the crucifying cross of the crude present—*a horrid strain!*"

> M. P. Shiel, "The Race of Orven"

> Lightly and dull fell each proud head,
>   Spiked keen without avail,
> Till swam my uncontented blade
>   With ichor green and pale.

> Walter de la Mare, "The Massacre"

The tickle of her hair against his eyelids stirred his blood to ichor.

> E. R. Eddison, *A Fish Dinner in Memison* (1936–40)

Our lanterns disclosed the top of a flight of stone steps, dripping with some detestable ichor of the inner earth, and bordered by moist walls encrusted with nitre.

> H. P. Lovecraft, "The Statement of Randolph Carter" (1919)

Dying almost-humans screamed, and cats spit and yowled and roared, but the toad-things made never a sound as their stinking green ichor oozed fatally upon that porous earth with the obscene fungi.

> H. P. Lovecraft, *The Dream-Quest of Unknown Kadath* (1926–27)

As I turned up the stinking black earth in front of the fireplace, my spade causing a viscous yellow ichor to ooze from the white fungi which it severed, I trembled at the dubious thoughts of what I might uncover.

> H. P. Lovecraft, "The Shunned House" (1924)

The thing that lay half-bent on its side in a fœtid pool of greenish-yellow ichor and tarry stickiness was almost nine feet tall, and the dog had torn off all the clothing and some skin.

> H. P. Lovecraft, "The Dunwich Horror" (1928)

Of genuine blood there was none; only the fœtid greenish-yellow ichor which trickled along the painted floor beyond the radius of the stickiness, and left a curious discolouration behind it.

> H. P. Lovecraft, "The Dunwich Horror" (1928)

Close contact with the utterly bizarre is often more terrifying than inspiring, and it did not cheer me to think that this very bit of dusty road was the place where those monstrous tracks and that fœtid green ichor had been found after moonless nights of fear and death.

> H. P. Lovecraft, "The Whisperer in Darkness" (1930)

Their noisome dark-green ichor formed a large, spreading pool; but its stench was half overshadowed by that newer and stranger stench, here more pungent than at any other point along our route.

> H. P. Lovecraft, *At the Mountains of Madness* (1931)

Their blood was a sort of deep-greenish ichor of great thickness.

> H. P. Lovecraft, "The Shadow out of Time" (1935)

Thy clear brow, Zara, rests so fair
I cannot think death lingers there;
Thy lip as from thy blood is red,
Nor hints of ichors of the dead:

> Canst thou, whom love so late consum'd,
> Lie prey to worms—dissolv'd, entomb'd?
>
> H. P. Lovecraft, "To Zara" (1922)

Disregarding the moon-powder, the coals of star-fire, the jellies made from the brains of gorgons, the ichor of salamanders, the dust of lethal fungi, the marrow of sphinxes, and other equally quaint and pernicious matters, the magician soon found the essences that he required.

> Clark Ashton Smith, "The Flower-Women" (1933)

Consummately, and with never-failing success, the magician had joined them to the half-vegetable, half-animate stocks, on which they lived and grew thereafter, drawing an ichor-like sap.

> Clark Ashton Smith, "The Garden of Adompha" (1937)

A mad ichor mounted in his blood, before him hovered the vague images of pleasures he had never known or suspected; pleasures in which he would pass far beyond the ordained limits of mortal sensations.

> Clark Ashton Smith, "The Garden of Adompha" (1937)

And with equal horror and curiosity I wondered what the stroke of justice would reveal, and what noisome, mephitic ichor would befoul the impartial sword in lieu of honest blood.

> Clark Ashton Smith, "The Testament of Athammaus" (1931)

Abhorrent was the bowl—which, like the leaves, was legended to renew itself at intervals of a thousand years. It smouldered with sullen ruby at the base; it lightened into zones of dragon's-blood, into belts of the rose of infernal sunset, on the full, swelling sides; and it flamed at the rim to a hot yellowish nacarat red, like the ichor of salamanders.

> Clark Ashton Smith, "The Demon of the Flower" (1931)

He was starkly nude, and his chest and arms were covered with a peculiar bluish pus or ichor.

> Frank Belknap Long, "The Hounds of Tindalos" (1929)

The swollen blossom was rent and gashed in numberless places before the emperor became aware of it. It was too late then, for great yellow drops of sickening ichor slowly coursed down the drooping vines and the bloom itself was purpling fast.

> Robert H. Barlow, "The Flower God" in *Annals of the Jinns*

A dreadful metamorphosis was overtaking it. It seemed to be losing its outline, to sprawl down until it wriggled rather than crawled along the sand. Then I knew! In the space of seconds it was reversing the entire evolutionary upsurge of the human species! It squirmed there like a snake, losing its resemblance to anything human as I watched, sick and shuddering. It melted and shrank and shriveled until there was nothing left but a loathsome foul ichor that was spreading in a black puddle of odious black slime.

Henry Kuttner, "The Invaders" (1939)

Hartley suddenly remembered his automatic and clawed it out, fired point blank at the creature as it came at him. There was a croaking snarl of rage, and the loose slit-mouth worked hideously; a little stream of foul black ichor began to trickle slowly from a wound on the wattled, pouchy throat of the thing.

Henry Kuttner, "The Frog" (1939)

At the fifty-foot level I forced myself to stop and wait. The water below was clear and no inchoate ichor rose about me.

Robert Bloch, "Terror in Cut-Throat Cove" (1958)

The bronze statue of a masturbating boy yielded a drop of phosphorescent black ichor—"That is where the Black Fruit comes from—Then it is grafted into the vines and it must ripen in the jars until it is ready"—There were other statues of silver and gold and porcelain all yielding the slow fruit of time—

William S. Burroughs, *The Ticket That Exploded* (1957–61)

And then—Good God!—what dream-world was this into which I had blundered? Out of that roughly yet inarguably shaped stone, with a feeble mewling and scratching, came—merciful Heavens! How can I go on? Polymorphous, perverse, partly dextrose, partly levulose, oozing a blasphemous ichor, it enfolded me, and for a while—blessed release!—my horror overcame me and I knew no more.

James Blish & Judith Ann Lawrence, "Getting Along" (1972)

Swallowing the instrument of its own destruction, the Hellarms began to writhe, crash about the pool even more wildly. Poisonous ichor gushed from its suddenly opened mouth, deep inside which the fragment of Sea-Stone was now lodged, choking and cutting, choking and cutting—

John Jakes, "The Girl in the Gem" (1965)

I rushed in, bringing my vorpal blade just beneath the skull. A good gash, the room filled with the fetid odour of its ichor.

Don Webb, "Metamorphosis No. 90" in *Uncle Ovid's Exercise Book* (1988)

ichorous, *adj.* Of, pertaining to, resembling, or characterized by ichor (q.v.).

> My healthy sperm begets the Son of God
> Winged with the dawn and with the star-stream shod!
> Not on your purulence and ichorous itch,
> O English girl, half baby and half bitch,
> But on the glorious body and soul of her

> Of whom I am the Lord and worshipper,
> The brave gay cleanly maiden whose embrace
> Flushes with shameless fervour the fair face,
> Fills the whole leaping heaven with the light
> Till all the world is drunken with delight.
>
> Aleister Crowley, *The World's Tragedy* (1908)

I screamed and fled from it, but the faces and the feelers flowed forth to envelop me in ichorous essence, so that I drowned in the bubbling blackness of its being. I was consumed by it.

Robert Bloch, "Terror in Cut-Throat Cove" (1958)

The water made his wrist itch and burn and he saw there the broad raw ichorous streak the iron had put on him.

Fred Chappell, *Dagon* (1968)

ichthyic, *adj.* [< Gr *ichthyïkós* < *ichthýs,* fish] Of, pertaining to, or resembling a fish or fishes.

Titles: Kermit Marsh III, "Derleth's Use of the Terms 'Ichthyic' and 'Batrachian'"

"You have gone from island to island, and you will have seen certainly that in some areas there is a marked emphasis on the batrachian motif, or the ichthyic motif—it matters little, save that we have reason to believe one island at least to be either the focal point or near the focal point of the occurrence of artifacts and works of art stressing the batrachian."

August Derleth, "The Black Island" (1952) in *The Trail of Cthulhu*

"Quite literally! I mean, they *looked* fishy. Or maybe froggy? Protuberant lips, wide-mouthed, scaly-skinned, popeyed—you name it. To use Father Nicholls' own expression, 'ichthyic.'"

Brian Lumley, "Dagon's Bell" (1988)

"No, don't interrupt me! I knew it as soon as I saw her at the university; the signs are unmistakable, though not far advanced yet: the bulging, ichthyic eyes, the rough skin around the neck where incipient gill-openings will gradually develop with age."

James Wade, "The Deep Ones" (1969)

illimitable, *adj.* Unable to be limited or bounded; limitless or without limit.

And now was acknowledged the presence of the Red Death. He had come like a thief in the night. And one by one dropped the revelers in the blood-bedewed halls of their revel, and died each in the despairing posture of his fall. And the life of the ebony clock went out with that of the last of the gay. And the flames of the tripods expired. And Darkness and Decay and the Red Death held illimitable dominion over all.

Edgar Allan Poe, "The Masque of the Red Death" (1842)

"What I had told him of the ritual of Khalk'ru was nothing but the second law of thermodynamics expressed in terms of anthropomorphism. Life *was* an intrusion upon Chaos, using that word to describe the unformed, primal state of the universe. An invasion. An accident. In time all energy would be changed to static heat, impotent to give birth to any life whatsoever. The dead universes would float lifelessly in the illimitable void. The void *was* eternal, life was not. Therefore the void *would* absorb it. Suns, worlds, gods, men, all things animate, would return to the void. Go back to Chaos. Back to Nothingness."

A. Merritt, *Dwellers in the Mirage* (1932)

Then, as I playfully shook him and turned him around, I felt the strangling tendrils of a cancerous horror whose roots reached into illimitable pasts and fathomless abysms of the night that broods beyond time.

H. P. Lovecraft, "The Lurking Fear" (1922)

Then there came a sound from that inky, boundless, farther distance that I thought I knew; and I saw my old black cat dart past me like a winged Egyptian god, straight into the illimitable gulf of the unknown.

H. P. Lovecraft, "The Rats in the Walls" (1923)

He saw now, in the brooding shadows of that which had been first a vortex of power and then an illimitable void, a sweep of creation that dizzied his senses.

H. P. Lovecraft & E. Hoffmann Price,
"Through the Gates of the Silver Key" (1932–33)

There was a sense of fading time and space—a sensation of being whirled over illimitable gulfs, with cosmic winds blowing against me—then I looked upon churning clouds, unreal and luminous, which crystallized into a strange landscape—familiar, and yet fantastically unfamiliar. Vast treeless plains swept away to merge with hazy horizons. In the distance, to the south, a great black cyclopean city reared its spires against the evening sky, and beyond it shone the blue waters of a placid sea.

Robert E. Howard, "Marchers of Valhalla"

There was nothing in all Space except an illimitable expanse of dust that stretched on and on in every direction; only this, and Antares.

Donald Wandrei, "The Red Brain" (1926)

As he looked he seemed to see something in that black pit of horror—something that was staring at him from illimitable gulfs beyond—something

with great flaming eyes that bored into his being with a fury greater than the
fires that were consuming him.

Robert Bloch, "The Faceless God" (1936)

illume, *v.tr.* & *v.intr.* [< *illumine*] To illumine, illuminate.

> To work an angel's ruin,—to behold
> As white a page as virtue e'er unroll'd
> Blacken, beneath his touch, into a scroll
> Of damning sins, seal'd with a burning soul—
> This is his triumph; this the joy accursed,
> That ranks him among demons all but first!
> This gives the victim, that before him lies
> Blighted and lost, a glory in his eyes,
> A light like that with which hell-fire illumes
> The ghastly, writhing wretch whom it consumes!

Thomas Moore, "The Veiled Prophet of Khorassan" in Lalla Rookh (1817)

> Bow down: I am the emperor of dreams;
> I crown me with the million-colored sun
> Of secret worlds incredible, and take
> Their trailing skies for vestment when I soar,
> Throned on the mounting zenith, and illume
> The spaceward-flown horizon infinite.

Clark Ashton Smith, The Hashish-Eater; or, The Apocalypse of Evil (1920)

immarcescible, *adj.* Unfading, everlasting, or eternal.

> Now let the loathlier vultures of the soul convene:
> They have no wings to follow thee, whose flight is furled
> Upon oblivion's nadir, or some lost demesne
> Of the pagan dead, vaulted with perfume and with fire,
> Where blossoms immarcescible in vespertine
> Strange amber air suspire.

Clark Ashton Smith, "To George Sterling: A Valediction" (1926)

Strange pleasures are known to him who flaunts the immarcescible purple of
poetry before the color-blind.

Clark Ashton Smith, "Epigrams and Apothegms"

> To flaunt
> Before the blind an immarcescible purple
> Won from the murex of Uranian seas,
> And fire-plucked vermeil of Vulcan, worn against
> These aguish mists and wintry shadows!

Clark Ashton Smith, "Soliloquy in an Ebon Tower" (1951)

immemorial, *adj.* Beyond memory; unable to be remembered; ancient beyond the limits of memory, history, or tradition; indefinitely old.

> So waste not thou, but come; for all the vales
> Await thee; azure pillars of the hearth
> Arise to thee; the children call, and I,
> Thy shepherd, pipe, and sweet is every sound,
> Sweeter thy voice, but every sound is sweet;
> Myriads of rivulets hurrying thro' the lawn,
> The moan of doves in immemorial elms,
> And murmuring of unnumerable bees.

> Alfred, Lord Tennyson, *The Princess: A Medley* (1850)

> The skies they were ashen and sober;
> The leaves they were crispèd and sere—
> The leaves they were withering and sere:
> It was night, in the lonesome October
> Of my most immemorial year:
> It was hard by the dim lake of Auber,
> In the misty mid region of Weir:—
> It was down by the dank tarn of Auber,
> In the ghoul-haunted woodland of Weir.

> Edgar Allan Poe, "Ulalume—A Ballad" (1847)

He also rowed out twice to the ill-regarded island in the river, and made a sketch of the singular angles described by the moss-grown rows of grey standing stones whose origin was so obscure and immemorial.

> H. P. Lovecraft, "The Dreams in the Witch House" (1932)

Never before, if my mad dreams held anything of truth, had human feet pressed upon those immemorial pavements.

> H. P. Lovecraft, "The Shadow out of Time" (1935)

I dared not stop, for behind me now I heard the gibber of frightful and immemorial things that had held lordship of the desert for ages, and would not abide the intrusion of life: I knew the cups of a green and awful madness that they bore with their bony white hands.

> Clark Ashton Smith, "In a Hashish-Dream"

Then began another lengthy journey through endless labyrinthine caverns and charnel vaults. On and on he wandered, through cave and crypt, tunnel and abyss-burrowed pit; all cloaked in the blackness of immemorial night.

> Robert Bloch, "The Grinning Ghoul" (1936)

"We giants have watched the frantic history of your race. We recall when mankind aborted from its womb, pretending to be adult instead of misbegotten fetus. To man these few centuries are time immemorial; to our race a nostalgic yesterday."

Karl Edward Wagner, "Two Suns Setting" (1975)

immensurable, *adj.* Immeasurable.

As I have said before, there is no author but yourself who seems to have glimpsed fully those tenebrous wastes, immensurable gulfs, grey topless pinnacles, crumbling corpses of forgotten cities, slimy, stagnant, cypress-bordered rivers, & alien, indefinable, antiquity-ridden gardens of strange decay, with which my own dreams have been crowded since earliest childhood. I read your work as the record of the only other human eye which has seen the things I have seen in far planets.

H. P. Lovecraft, letter to Clark Ashton Smith (25 March 1923)

At the moment, unhappily, he had no event to cast a horoscope either from or toward—only a pervasive, immensurable fog of rising evil.

James Blish, *Black Easter; or, Faust Aleph-Null* (1968)

immundane, *adj.* Not mundane. [Not in *OED.*]

I have frequently wondered if the majority of mankind ever pause to reflect upon the occasionally titanic significance of dreams, and of the obscure world to which they belong. Whilst the greater number of our nocturnal visions are perhaps no more than faint and fantastic reflections of our waking experiences—Freud to the contrary with his puerile symbolism—there are still a certain remainder whose immundane and ethereal character permits of no ordinary interpretation, and whose vaguely exciting and disquieting effect suggests possible minute glimpses into a sphere of mental existence no less important than physical life, yet separated from that life by an all but impassable barrier.

H. P. Lovecraft, "Beyond the Wall of Sleep" (1919)

> When, in midst of this immundane dreaming
> Come effulgent the first rays of light,
> Bringing back my rapt soul with their beaming,
> Lending splendour to all within sight;
> And I wake to the sunrise at dawning, fit close to the dusk's mad delight.

Alfred Galpin, "Selenaio-Phantasma" (1918)

immure, *v.tr.* To enclose within walls; to imprison or incarcerate; to inter within a wall.

"A low door at the end presented a frightful perspective. At sight of it I cried aloud, 'You will not immure me? You will not plunge me in that horrible dungeon, to be withered by damps, and devoured by reptiles?'"

Charles Maturin, *Melmoth the Wanderer: A Tale* (1820)

It was more than a mirror—it was a gate; a trap; a link with spatial recesses not meant for the denizens of our visible universe, and realizable only in terms of the most intricate non-Euclidean mathematics. *And in some outrageous fashion Robert Grandison had passed out of our ken into the glass and was there immured, waiting for release.*

Henry S. Whitehead & H. P. Lovecraft, "The Trap" (1931)

imp, *n.* (1) A grafted shoot or scion. (2) An offspring, child, progeny, scion, or heir. (3) A small demon, devil, or fairy, particularly a mischievous one, or one employed as a familiar by a witch or wizard. (4) A mischievous and playful child.

Titles: Edgar Allan Poe, "The Imp of the Perverse"; Robert Louis Stevenson, "The Bottle Imp"; Walter de la Mare, "The Imp Within" (verse)

These familiar spirits often assumed the form of animals, and a black dog or cat was considered as a figure in which the attendant devil was secretly hidden. These subordinate devils were called Imps. Impure and carnal ideas were mingled with these theories. The witches were said to have preternatural teats from which their familiars sucked their blood.

William Godwin, Lives of the Necromancers; or, An Account of the Most Eminent Persons in Successive Ages Who Have Claimed for Themselves, or to Whom Has Been Imputed by Others, the Exercise of Magical Power (1834)

"Interspersed between them were the stuffed figures of animals I knew not then the names of,—an alligator,—some gigantic bones, which I took for those of Sampson, but which turned out to be fragments of those of the Mammoth,—and antlers, which in my terror I believed to be those of the devil, but afterwards learned to be those of an Elk. Then I saw figures smaller, but not less horrible,—human and brute abortions, in all their states of anomalous and deformed construction, not preserved in spirits, but standing in the ghastly nakedness of their white diminutive bones; these I conceived to be the attendant imps of some infernal ceremony, which the grand wizard, who now burst on my sight, was to preside over."

Charles Maturin, Melmoth the Wanderer: A Tale (1820)

Had I not been thus prolix, you might either have misunderstood me altogether, or, with the rabble, have fancied me mad. As it is, you will easily perceive tha I am one of the many uncounted victims of the Imp of the Perverse.

Edgar Allan Poe, "The Imp of the Perverse" (1845)

It must have been some imp of the perverse—or some sardonic pull from dark, hidden, sources—which made me change my plans as I did.

H. P. Lovecraft, "The Shadow over Innsmouth" (1931)

The wood, it seemed, was full of execrably sighing voices, and weird whimpers and little moanings as of imp-children astray from Satanic dams.

> Clark Ashton Smith, "The Death of Malygris" (1933)

What imp of perversity had caused him to select that particular phrase among all the thousands of popular song lyrics?

> Donald Wandrei, *The Web of Easter Island* (1929–31)

Only a few hours ago he had worn it, and caught a small goblin-imp. How it squeaked! He still had a bone or two left to gnaw, but he wanted something softer.

> J. R. R. Tolkien, *The Hobbit; or, There and Back Again* (1930–36)

There was some perverse imp of burning compulsion within us which made us turn the light from our torches downward, down into that great abyss at our feet.

> John S. Glasby, "The Brooding City"

The mirror was an antique dating from the 1850s. Its hardwood frame—now jet-black from the grime of so many years—was carved with scenes from the stories of Edgar Allan Poe. Frozen in oak was the tomb broken open in "Berenice" to reveal the corpse of a woman with all her teeth lovingly pulled out; "The House Of Usher" with its eye-like windows and pervading sense of evil twinship, incest, and decay; "The Pit and the Pendulum'"; "The Tell-Tale Heart". For Here in this basement room were all the victims of "The Imp Of The Perverse".

> Michael Slade, *Ghoul* (1987)

Of course, the imp of perversity in *your* thoughts is only one of the many offspring of the imp of the *diverse*.

> Thomas Ligotti, "The Chymist"

impious, *adj.* Blasphemous (q.v.).

impiously, *adv.* Blasphemously (q.v.).

Such is the end of too many great New-England lines—to think of these indescribable creatures; ragged, guttural-voiced, unkempt, sinister-featured, impiously aged, & almost witch-like in their eery expression; and of their fastidiously elegant grandfather who demanded the best French wall paper, the finest brass latches, the choicest carved mantels, cornices, & wainscoting, & the most delicate silver, china, & ornaments that Europe & America could afford.

> H. P. Lovecraft, letter to Samuel Loveman (29 April 1923)

incarn, *v. t.* & *v.intr.* To cover with flesh; to grow covered with flesh; to incarnate, to become embodied in flesh.

"Great Chaugnar is a terrible god, an utterly cosmic and unanthropomorphic god. It is akin to the fire mists and the primordial ooze, and before it incarned itself in Time it contained within itself the past, the present and the future. Nothing was and nothing will be, but all things are. And Chaugnar Faugn was once the sum of all things that are."

Frank Belknap Long, "The Horror from the Hills" (1930)

It was not cold that made him tremble as he sat there in his chair; it was not fever that caused his eyes to flame like jewel-incarned fires.

Robert Bloch, "The Shambler from the Stars" (1935)

incubus (*pl.* **incubi, incubuses**), *n.* [< L, one who lies on top of one] (1) A nightmare, envisioned as an old hag who sits upon the sleeper's chest. (2) A demon or devil that has taken on the form of a male human being in order to lie upon and engage in sexual intercourse with a woman. (3) Any oppressive or nightmarish burden that weighs upon one. Cf. **succubus**.

Titles: Clark Ashton Smith, "The Incubus of Time" (verse); Donald Wandrei, "Incubus" (verse)

In th'olde dayes of the Kyng Arthour,
Of which that Britons speken greet honour,
Al was this land fulfild of fayerye.
The elf-queene, with hir joly compaignye,
Daunced ful ofte in many a grene mede.
This was the olde opinion, as I rede;
I speke of manye hundred yeres ago.
But now kan no man se none elves mo,
For now the grete charitee and prayeres
Of lymytours and othere holy freres,
That serchen every lond and every streem,
As thikke as motes in the sonne-beem,
Blessynge halles, chambres, kichenes, boures,
Citees, burghes, castels, hye toures,
Thropes, bernes, shipnes, dayeryes—
This maketh that ther ben no fayeryes.
For ther as wont to walken was an elf,
Ther walketh now the lymytour hymself
In undermeles and in morwenynges,
And seyth his matyns and his hooly thynges
As he gooth in his lymytacioun.
Wommen may go now now saufly up and doun.
In every bussh or under every tree
Ther is noon oother incubus but he,
And he ne wol don them but dishonour.

Geoffrey Chaucer, "The Wife of Bath's Tale" in *The Canterbury Tales*

This we see verified in sleepers, which by reason of humours and concourse of vapours troubling the phantasy, imagine many times absurd and prodigious things, and in such as are troubled with *incubus*, or witch-ridden (as we call it); if they lie on their backs, they suppose an old woman rides and sits so hard upon them that they are almost stifled for want of breath; when there is nothing offends but a concourse of bad humours, which trouble the phantasy.

> Robert Burton, *The Anatomy of Melancholy: What It Is, With All the Kinds, Causes, Symptomes, Prognostickes & Severall Cures of It* (1621)

> So spake the old serpent doubting, and from all
> With clamour was assured their utmost aid
> At his command; when from amidst them rose
> Belial the dissolutest spirit that fell,
> The sensualest, and after Asmodai
> The fleshliest incubus, and thus advised.

> John Milton, *Paradise Regained* (1671)

BERTHA: Out, hunchback!
ARNOLD: I was born so, mother!
BERTHA   Out,
Thou incubus! Thou nightmare! Of seven sons,
The sole abortion!

> George Gordon, Lord Byron, *The Deformed Transformed: A Drama* (1821–22)

The opium-eater loses none of his moral sensibilities or aspirations; he wishes and longs as earnestly as ever to realize what he believes possible and feels to be exacted by duty; but his intellectual apprehension of what is possible greatly outruns his power, not of execution only, but even of power to attempt. He lies under the weight of incubus and nightmare; he lies in sight of all that he would fain perform, just as a man forcibly confined to his bed by the mortal languor of a relaxing disease, who is compelled to witness injury or outrage offered to some object of his tenderest love: he curses the spells which chain him down from motion; he would lay down his life if he might but get up and walk; but he is powerless as an infant and cannot even attempt to rise.

> Thomas De Quincey, *Confessions of an English Opium-Eater: Being an Extract from the Life of a Scholar* (1821)

> He snores, 'tis true, but he snores no more
> As he's aye been accustom'd to snore before,
> And as men of his kidney are wont to snore;—
> (Sir Thopas's weight is sixteen stone four;)
> He draws his breath like a man distress'd
> By pain or grief, or like one oppress'd
> By some ugly old Incubus perch'd on his breast.

> Thomas Ingoldsby (Richard Harris Barham),
> "The Witches' Frolic" in *The Ingoldsby Legends* (1840)

An irrepressible tremour gradually pervaded my frame; and, at length, there sat upon my very heart an incubus of utterly causeless alarm.

Edgar Allan Poe, "The Fall of the House of Usher" (1839)

During the epoch of his residence at G———n it really appeared that the demon of the *dolce far niente* lay like an incubus upon the university.

Edgar Allan Poe, "Mystification" (1837)

He had seen many ghosts in his time, and witches and enchanters, and once he was lost in a fierce storm at midnight in the mountains, and by the glare of the lightning had seen the Wild Huntsman rage on a blast with his specter dogs chasing after him through the driving cloud-rack. Also he had seen an incubus once, and several times he had seen the great bat that sucks the blood from the necks of people while they are asleep, fanning them softly with its wings and so keeping them drowsy till they die.

Mark Twain, "The Mysterious Stranger" (1898)

It was an awakening, which, for torture, had no parallel in all the stupendous domain of sleeping incubus.

Fitz Hugh Ludlow, *The Hasheesh Eater:*
Being Passages from the Life of a Pythagorean (1857)

"A powerful and little-known anæsthetic—the means by which all their murders have been accomplished—was now produced. A cloth, saturated with the fluid, was placed on my mouth and nostrils. I was stifled. Sense failed. The incubus of the universe blackened down upon my brain. How I tugged at the mandrakes of speech! was a locked pugilist with language!"

M. P. Shiel, "The S.S." (1895)

She spoke pleadingly, as imploring to be released from some awful incubus which it was impossible to explain.

Charles Willing Beale, *The Ghost of Guir House* (1897)

The incubus (the word derives from post-classical Latin and literally means *one who lies upon* anything) is the demon who assumes a male form, the succubus or succuba (from late Latin, literally meaning *one who lies under* anything, a harlot) is the demon when assuming a female form, and the famous Dominican Charles Réné Billuart in his *Treatise upon the Angelic Hosts* explicitly informs us: "The same evil spirit may serve as a succubus to a man, and as an incubus to a woman."

Montague Summers, *A Popular History of Witchcraft* (1936)

Horror-breeding hints and noisome intuitions invaded my brain. More and more the atmosphere of that house enveloped and stifled me with poisonous, miasmal mystery; and I felt everywhere the invisible brooding of malignant incubi.

Clark Ashton Smith, "The Return of the Sorcerer" (1931)

I remember no dreams—only the vast, incubus-like oppression that persisted even in the depth of slumber, as if to drag me down with its formless, ever-clinging weight into gulfs beyond the reach of created light or the fathoming of organized entity.

> Clark Ashton Smith, "The Hunters from Beyond" (1931)

It seemed that an incubus smothered him, weighing upon all his limbs and body.

> Clark Ashton Smith, "Mother of Toads" (1937)

A brooding sense of inimical volition, a vast and freezing malignity, seemed to pervade the air and to settle upon Quanga like an incubus.

> Clark Ashton Smith, "The Ice-Demon" (1932)

But, even as the faint, distorted shadows of slumber often tinge one's waking hours, it may have contributed to the nameless mood in which I found myself: a mood in which I felt the unhuman alienage of our surroundings and the black, fathomless antiquity of the ruins like an almost unbearable oppression. The feeling seemed to be made of a million spectral adumbrations that oozed unseen but palpable from the great, unearthly architecture; that weighed upon me like tomb-born incubi. I appeared to move, not in the open air, but in the smothering gloom of sealed sepulchral vaults; to choke with a death-fraught atmosphere, with the miasmata of æon-old corruption.

> Clark Ashton Smith, "The Vaults of Yoh-Vombis" (1931)

Down, down, I appeared to go, in the bottomless and phantom hell that was impinging upon reality. Death, decay, malignity, madness, gathered in the air and pressed me down like Satanic incubi in that ecstatic horror of descent. I felt that there were a thousand forms, a thousand faces about me, summoned from the gulfs of perdition.

> Clark Ashton Smith, "The Devotee of Evil" (1930)

With a suspiration of relief that seemed to lift a horrid incubus from his bosom, he decided that his first conjecture had been correct.

> Clark Ashton Smith, "The Treader of the Dust" (1935)

Now, as he sat there in a state half terror, half stupor, his eyes were drawn to the wizard volume before him: the writings of that evil sage and seer, Carnamagos, which had been recovered a thousand years agone from some Græco-Bactrian tomb, and transcribed by an apostate monk in the original Greek, in the blood of an incubus-begotten monster. In that volume were the chronicles of great sorcerers of old, and the histories of demons earthly and ultra-cosmic, and the veritable spells by which the demons could be called up and controlled and dismissed.

> Clark Ashton Smith, "The Treader of the Dust" (1935)

Again he felt the impulse of flight: but his body was a dry dead incubus that refused to obey his volitions.

Clark Ashton Smith, "The Treader of the Dust" (1935)

The emperor's heart was crushed within him by the trampling of such calamities, and despair weighed upon him like a foul incubus on the shoulders of a man lost in some land of accursed night.

Clark Ashton Smith, "The Dark Eidolon" (1932)

> Briefly, in desert hermitages,
> I have lain down in my despair,
> Dreaming to sleep as slept the sages:
> But unseen lust oppressed the air,
> And crimson dreams of incubi,
> And thirst of anthropophagi.

Clark Ashton Smith, "The Outer Land" (1935)

"You either lie, Dolores Haze, or it was an incubus."

Vladimir Nabokov, *Lolita* (1954)

His favorites were the Abominations like Humwawa, whose face is a mass of entrails and who rides on a whispering south wind. Pazuzu, Lord of Fevers and Plagues, and especially Gelal and Lilit, who invade the beds of men, because he did sometimes experience a vivid sexual visitation he hoped was an incubus. He knew that the horror of these demon lovers was a gloomy Christian thing.

William S. Burroughs, *The Place of Dead Roads* (1977–83)

As Azathoth rules now as he did in his bivalvular shape, his name subdues all, from the incubi which haunt Tond to the servants of Y'golonac. Few can resist the power of the name Azathoth, and even the haunters of the blackest night of Yuggoth cannot battle the power of N———, *his other name.*

Abdul Alhazred, *Necronomicon*, as quoted in
Ramsey Campbell, "The Mine on Yuggoth" (1964)

incunabula (*pl., sing.* **incunabulum**), *n.* [< L *incūnābula*, swaddling clothes]
Books produced while the art of printing remained in its "infancy," i.e., before
c. 1500 CE.

Uneasy, uncertain, and unnerved, I retreated into the shadows of the bookshelves at the farther end of the room, and idly scanned the titles of a row of ancient tomes. Here was the *Chiromancy* of Robert Flud, the *Directorium Inquisitorum*, a rare and curious book in quarto Gothic that was the manual of a forgotten church; and betwixt and between the volumes of pseudo-scientific inquiry, theological speculation, and sundry incunabula I found titles that arrested and appalled me. *De Vermis Mysteriis* and the *Liber Eibon*, treatises on demonology, on witchcraft, on sorcery mouldered in crumbling binding. The books were old, but the books were not dusty. They had been read—

Robert Bloch, "The Man Who Collected Poe" (1951)

inenarrable, *adj.* Unable to be narrated; ineffable, indescribable, unspeakable.

What rumour or legend has drawn them from outland realms and ulterior planets to that place of inenarrable danger and destruction?

Clark Ashton Smith, "The City of the Singing Flame" (1931)

The vestal moon, the violating sun,
For him were made Love's metamorphoses;
Till, flown from these, as from the forms of old,
The god was gone in worlds beyond access,
With flame-ensculptured bosom found of none,
And eyes too bright with inenarrable gold.

Christophe des Laurières (Clark Ashton Smith), "Heliogabalus" (1919)

infandous, *adj.* [< L *infandus* < *in*, not + *fandus*, gerundive of *fārī*, to speak] Unutterable, unspeakable, nefandous.

The horrendous desolations that have come upon mankind, by the Irruptions of the old *Barbarians* upon the *Roman* World, and then of the *Saracens*, and since, of the *Turks*, were such *woes* as men had never seen before. The Infandous *Blindness* and *Vileness* which then came upon mankind, and the Monstrous *Croisadoes* which thereupon carried the *Roman* World by Millions together unto the Shambles; were also such *woes* as had never yet had a Parallel. And yet these were some of the things here intended, when it was said, *Wo! For the Devil is come down in great Wrath, having but a short time.*

Cotton Mather, *The Wonders of the Invisible World* (1692)

Unwholesome recollections of things in the *Necronomicon* and the Black Book welled up, and he found himself swaying to infandous rhythms said to pertain to the blackest ceremonies of the Sabbat and to have an origin outside the time and space we comprehend.

H. P. Lovecraft, "The Dreams in the Witch House" (1932)

Inferno, inferno, *pr.n.* & *n.* Hell or the infernal regions; a place of great suffering or death; a place of intense and uncontrolled fire. Used by Dante as the title of the first part of *The Divine Comedy.*

Titles: Clark Ashton Smith, "Inferno" (verse)

More than ever that day the suburb had oppressed him; insignificant, detestable, repulsive to body and mind, it was the only hell that a vulgar age could conceive or make, an inferno created not by Dante but by the jerry-builder.

Arthur Machen, *The Hill of Dreams* (1897)

I beheld such a sight as I had never beheld before, and which no living person can have seen save in the delirium of fever or the inferno of opium.

H. P. Lovecraft & Winifred Virginia Jackson, "The Crawling Chaos" (1920–21)

Fantastic images rose in his mind: it was like the last glimmering of hell-fire in some extinct inferno; like the drowning of nebulæ in voids beneath the universe.

Clark Ashton Smith, "The Dweller in the Gulf" (1932)

The *Cardigan* had foundered in the typhoon off the Mergui Archipelago. For twelve hours she had heaved and groaned through an inferno of swirling seas. Then she had gone under.

Hugh B. Cave, "Stragella" (1932)

His nocturnal flights always ended with the passage of a vast procession of these monstrosities through a cavern still farther beneath—a journey which he would view from a ledge above. Shuddery glimpses into the realms below led him to recall tales of the *Inferno*, and he would cry out in his sleep. As he watched that demon procession from the brink, he would suddenly lose his footing and be precipitated into the charnel swarm below.

Robert Bloch, "The Grinning Ghoul" (1936)

We spent hours on composing scenes from an imaginary Inferno; constructing bat-winged figures that flew against bizarre, other-worldly backgrounds of fire, and great malignant demons that squatted and brooded on jagged peaks over-looking the Fiery Pit.

Robert Bloch, "The Sorcerer's Jewel" (1939)

innominable, *adj.* That cannot be named; nameless, unnameable, unspeakable.

Forthwith I would try to escape,—(feeling at every step a sensation *as of wad-ing*),—and would sometimes succeed in struggling half-way across the room;—but there I would always find myself brought to a standstill,—paralyzed by some innominable opposition.

Lafcadio Hearn, "Nightmare-Touch" in *Shadowings* (1900)

Was there not some elusive change, too subtle to be named or defined, had time and the grave not taken something away—an innominable something that his magic had not wholly restored?

Clark Ashton Smith, "The Last Incantation" (1929)

In the oblique rays, the elongated webs of shadow wrought by the dying after-noon, the forest seemed to attend with bated breath the noisome and furtive passing of innominable things.

Clark Ashton Smith, "The Holiness of Azédarac" (1931)

Gazing, I lost myself in reveries that I could not recall afterward, but which left behind them the same tantalizing sense of innominable delight which forgotten nocturnal dreams may sometimes leave.

> Clark Ashton Smith, "The End of the Story" (1929)

More and more, I felt an imperative conviction of some peril that threatened them both—some hideous and innominable thing to whose power, perhaps, they had already yielded.

> Clark Ashton Smith, "Genius Loci" (1932)

The chill of ancient death was upon me; it hung in the web of timeless twilight along those irrecognizable ways, around those innominable houses; and it followed me as I went.

> Clark Ashton Smith, "The Gorgon" (1930)

innominate, *ppl. adj.* Unnamed, having no name, anonymous; nameless, unnameable, unspeakable.

Then, from a dimension that must be a little lower than all others, a little nearer the ultimate nadir of hell, I called the innominate beings who posed for this new figure-piece.

> Clark Ashton Smith, "The Hunters from Beyond" (1931)

He saw the bones of men that were piled in repugnant confusion with those of fell monsters, and the riven sarcophagi from which protruded the half-decayed members of innominate beings; members which were neither heads nor hands nor feet.

> Clark Ashton Smith, "The Last Hieroglyph" (1934)

And though it was but an image and without even the semblance of life, she felt unmistakably the presence of something alive in the temple, something so alien and innominate that instinctively she drew away.

> C. L. Moore, "Black God's Kiss" (1934)

I dreamed a dream: a million-colored rose unfolded to my view. Standing on an empty plain beneath an empty sky, I watched both the plain and the sky gradually disappear, and I myself became concentred only to one enormous eye that could see in any direction, an eye that also had the power somehow to apprehend sound, an essence of audient vision somehow suspended in pure space. But somehow I knew that I lay at the bottom of some innominate abyss.

> Donald Sidney-Fryer, "A Vision of Strange Splendor"

instinct, *adj.* Deeply filled, imbued, permeated with.

Before use stood a monstrous shape, a geometric prodigy. A shining angled pillar that, though rigid, immobile, seemed to crouch, be instinct with living force striving to be unleashed. Two great globes surmounted it—like the heads of some two-faced Janus of an alien world.

A. Merritt, The Metal Monster (1920)

This thing, which seemed instinct with a fearsome and unnatural malignancy, was of a somewhat bloated corpulence, and squatted evilly on a rectangular block or pedestal covered with undecipherable characters.

H. P. Lovecraft, "The Call of Cthulhu" (1926)

It was crawling towards him, and in the pale glow of the flashlight the man say a frightful gargoyle face thrust into his own. It was the passionless, death's-head skull of a long-dead corpse, instinct with hellish life; and the glazed eyes swollen and bulbous betrayed the thing's blindness. It made a faint groaning sound as it crawled towards Masson, stretching its ragged and granulated lips in a grin of dreadful horror.

Henry Kuttner, "The Graveyard Rats" (1936)

invultuation, invultation, *n.* The creation of a waxen image of a person for the purpose of performing witchcraft or sorcery.

They designed an invultuation against Malygris that would break the power of the dead necromancer by rendering evident to all the mere fact of his death. Employing an unlawful Atlantean science, Maranapion had created living plasm with all the attributes of human flesh, and had caused it to grow and flourish, fed with blood. Then he and his assistants, uniting their wills and convoking the forces that were blasphemy to summon, had compelled the shapeless, palpitating mass to put forth the limbs and members of a new-born child; and had formed it ultimately, after all the changes that man would undergo between birth and senescence, into an image of Malygris.

Clark Ashton Smith, "The Death of Malygris" (1933)

Others still, among whom were certain rival astrologers and enchanters, said that Nathaire had retired from the public view merely that he might commune without interruption with various coadjutive demons; and thus might weave, unmolested, the black spells of a supreme and lycanthropic malice. These spells, they hinted, would in due time be visited upon Vyones and perhaps upon the entire region of Averoigne; and would no doubt take the form of a fearsome pestilence, or a wholesale invultuation, or a realm-wide incursion of succubi and incubi.

Clark Ashton Smith, "The Colossus of Ylourgne" (1932)

The impulse was immediate, overwhelming, ineluctable; and even if I had so desired, I could no more have fought against it than if I had been the victim of some sorcerer's invultuation.

Clark Ashton Smith, "The End of the Story" (1929)

From certain curious flavors detected more than once in his food and drink, he suspected that the love-potions for which she had become infamous were being administered to him; but beyond a light, and passing qualmishness, he experienced no ill effect whatever; and he was wholly ignorant of the spells woven against him in secret, and the thrice-lethal invultuations that were designed to wound his heart and senses.

Clark Ashton Smith, "The Witchcraft of Ulua" (1933)

Ilalotha, the queen knew, had loved Thulos to the point of frenzy, and had grieved inconsolably after his desertion of her. People said that she had wrought various ineffectual spells to bring him back; that she had vainly invoked demons and sacrificed to them, and had made futile invultuations and death-charms against Xantlicha.

Clark Ashton Smith, "The Death of Ilalotha" (1937)

Iram, *n.* See under **Irem**.

Irem, Iram, Irim, *pr.n.* In Arabian mythology, the ancient city Ubar, lost under the desert sand, but occasionally glimpsed by a sole traveller as the shifting dunes temporarily uncover it; known as the Atlantis of the Sands. (Discovered in 1992.) [Not in *OED*.]

> Iram indeed is gone with all his Rose,
> And Jamshyd's Sev'n-ring'd Cup where no one knows;
>   But still a Ruby kindles in the Vine,
> And many a Garden by the Water blows.

Omar Khayyám (trans. Edward FitzGerald), *The Rubáiyát of Omar Khayyám*

Shedad, who made the delicious gardens of Irim, in imitation of Paradise, and was destroyed by lightning the first time he attempted to enter them.

Thomas Moore, note to *Lalla Rookh* (1817)

Though the heart she had to offer to the King of Bucharia might be cold and broken, it should at least be pure; and she must only endeavor to forget the short dream of happiness she had enjoyed,—like that Arabian shepherd, who, in wandering into the wilderness, caught a glimpse of the Gardens of Irim, and then lost them again for ever!

Thomas Moore, *Lalla Rookh* (1817)

> Of that far golden Irem I am dreaming,
> Whence for few kisses I did follow thee;
>   Fair is that spot to see,
>
> With far-off waving palms and towers gleaming;
> Great deserts round that isle of blissful seeming
>   Lie stretching endlessly.

David Park Barnitz, "Hélas" in *The Book of Jade* (1901)

"We came out of the cleft and into a garden. The Gardens of Many-Columned Iram, lost in the desert because they were too beautiful, must have been like that place."

A. Merritt, "Through the Dragon Glass" (1917)

A hundred yards beneath us stretched gardens that must have been like those of many-columned Iram, which the ancient Addite King had built for his pleasure ages before the deluge, and which Allah, so the Arab legend tells, took and hid from man, within the Sahara, beyond all hope of finding—jealous because they were more beautiful than his in paradise.

A. Merritt, *The Moon Pool* (1919)

Emaciated priests, displayed as reptiles in ornate robes, cursed the upper air and all who breathed it; and one terrible final scene shewed a primitive-looking man, perhaps a pioneer of ancient Irem, the City of Pillars, torn to pieces by members of the elder race.

H. P. Lovecraft, "The Nameless City" (1921)

Of the cult, he said that he thought the centre lay amid the pathless deserts of Arabia, where Irem, the City of Pillars, dreams hidden and untouched.

H. P. Lovecraft, "The Call of Cthulhu" (1926)

"Be careful, you ——! There are powers against your powers—I didn't go to China for nothing, and there are things in Alhazred's *Azif* which weren't known in Atlantis! We've both meddled in dangerous things, but you needn't think you know all my resources. How about the Nemesis of Flame? I talked in Yemen with an old man who had come back alive from the Crimson Desert—he had seen Irem, the City of Pillars, and had worshipped at the underground shrines of Nug and Yeb—Iä! Shub-Niggurath!"

H. P. Lovecraft & Adolphe de Castro, "The Last Test" (1927)

You & young Derleth present interesting stages of relative sophistication. He thinks your world artificial & Baudelairian, whilst I am such a naive old gentleman that even he & Sauk City are blasé, & fin de siecle by comparison! Then at the other end, you find Manhattan far gone in diabolism, Manhattan takes hints from a cryptical Paris, Paris shudders at Constantinople, Constantinople looks back to Imperial Rome & Alexandria & Antioch, they look back to Babylon, Babylon looks back to Irem, the City of Pillars, Irem looks back to sunken R'lyeh, & R'lyeh fears to mention the hellish N'gha-G'un, on that dark star whence the people of R'lyeh came to earth.

H. P. Lovecraft, letter to Donald Wandrei (1 December 1930)

Irem would be a splendid theme for a story. Do you know of the present-day tradition among the Arabs, that the city still exists in the desert, though invisible, and is occasionally vouchsafed as a brief vision to some favored mortal? One might make a modern tale out of this.

Clark Ashton Smith, letter to H. P. Lovecraft (c. 16 November 1930)

iridescence, *n.* The state or property of being iridescent (q.v.); an iridescent formation.

Not the least remarkable point in the matter is the fact that a large number of people in the neighbourhood dreamed singularly vivid dreams of Plattner during the period of excitement before his return, and that these dreams had a curious uniformity. In almost all of them Plattner was seen, sometimes singly, somtimes in company, wandering through a coruscating iridescence.

H. G. Wells, "The Plattner Story" (1896)

Across my line of vision, moving stately over the sea, floated a half globe, luminous, diaphanous, its iridescence melting into turquoise, thence to amethyst, to orange, to scarlet shot with rose, to vermilion, a translucent green, thence back into the iridescence; behind it four others, and the least of them ten feet in diameter, and the largest no less than thirty. They drifted past like bubbles blown from froth of rainbows by pipes in mouths of Titans' young. Then from the base of one arose a tangle of shimmering strands, long, slender whip lashes that played about and sank slowly again beneath the crimson surface.

A. Merritt, *The Moon Pool* (1919)

We were slowly gliding toward something that looked like nothing so much as a huge and shimmering bubble of mingled sapphire and turquoise, swimming up from and two-thirds above and the balance still hidden within earth. It seemed to draw to itself the light, sending it back with gleamings of the gray-blue of the star-sapphire, with pellucid azures and lazulis like clouded jades, with glistening peacock iridescences and tender, milky blues of tropic shallows.

A. Merrit, *The Metal Monster* (1920)

It was a sun yellow isle, high and rounded, and splashed with craters of color like nests of rainbows. Save for these pansied dapplings, the island curved all glowing topaz, from its base in immense panaches of ostrich plumes dyed golden amber. Over and about that golden isle shot flashes of iridescences from what seemed luminous flying flowers.

A. Merritt, *The Ship of Ishtar* (1924)

It was truly an awful moment; with terror in that ancient and accursed house itself, four monstrous sets of fragments—two from the house and two from the well—in the woodshed behind, and that shaft of unknown and unholy iridescence from the slimy depths in front.

H. P. Lovecraft, "The Colour out of Space" (1927)

iridescent, *adj.* [< L *iris* (root: *irid-*), a rainbow] Characterized by a lustrous, rainbow-like play of colors; opalescent, nacreous, pearlescent.

He thinned away and thinned away until he was a soap-bubble, except that he kept his shape. You could see the bushes through him as clearly as you see things through a soap-bubble, and all over him played and flashed the delicate iridescent colors of the bubble, and along with them was that thing shaped like a window-sash which you always see on the globe of the bubble.

Mark Twain, "The Mysterious Stranger" (1898)

As vultures swoop down upon the dying, there came sailing swiftly to where the dead men floated, dozens of the luminous globes. Their slender, varicoloured tentacles whipped out; the giant iridescent bubbles *climbed* over the cadavers. And as they touched them there was the swift dissolution, the melting away into putrescence of flesh and bone that I had witnessed when the dart touched fruit that time I had saved Rador—and upon this the Medusæ gorged; pulsing lambently; their wondrous colours shifting, changing, growing stronger; elfin moons now indeed, but satellites whose glimmering beauty was fed by death; alembics of enchantment whose glorious hues were sucked from horror.

A. Merritt, *The Moon Pool* (1919)

Here and to the southward the neighbourhood became better, flowering at last into a marvellous group of early mansions; but still the little ancient lanes led off down the precipice to the west, spectral in their many-gabled archaism and dipping to a riot of iridescent decay where the wicked old waterfront recalls its proud East India days amidst polyglot vice and squalor, rotting wharves, and blear-eyed ship-chandleries, with such surviving alley names as Packet, Bullion, Gold, Silver, Coin, Doubloon, Sovereign, Guilder, Dollar, Dime, and Cent.

H. P. Lovecraft, *The Case of Charles Dexter Ward* (1927)

Then, like the bursting of a bubble, the great jewel vanished in a rainbow burst of iridescent gleams, and the ebony table-top lay bare and deserted—as bare, Conan somehow knew, as the marble couch in the chamber above, where the body of that strange transcosmic being called Yag-kosha and Yogah had lain.

Robert E. Howard, "The Tower of the Elephant" (1933)

The serpent glanced down at himself and sent one or two long, sliding ripples gliding along his iridescent body. The angel shape that hung in the air about him gradually faded, and the beauty deepened as it focused itself more strongly in the flesh he wore.

C. L. Moore, "Fruit of Knowledge" (1940)

Traffickers in the Black Meat, flesh of the giant aquatic black centipede—sometimes attaining a length of six feet—found in a lane of black rocks and iridescent, brown lagoons, exhibit paralyzed crustaceans in camouflage packets of the Plaza visible only to the Meat Eaters.

William S. Burroughs, *Naked Lunch* (1955–59)

As he passed over a bridge a green newt boy surfaced in a canal smiled and mas-
turbated quickly ejaculating an iridescent fluid that glinted in the clear light—He
twisted with a mocking laugh and dove out of sight in the black water—

> William S. Burroughs, *The Ticket That Exploded* (1957–61)

Some boy surfaced in the canal—Iridescent harbor glinted in the stellar light—
mocking laugh of absent tenants—ghost riots along the canal and found himself
in a garage—

> William S. Burroughs, *The Ticket That Exploded* (1957–61)

The principal weapon of Minraud is of course heat—In the center of all their
cities stand The Ovens where those who disobey the control brains are brought
for total disposal—A conical structure of iridescent metal shimmering heat from
the molten core of a planet where lead melts at noon—

> William S. Burroughs, *Nova Express* (1961–63)

Israfil, Israfel, Isráfeel, *pr.n.* In Arabian mythology, an archangel possessed of
a splendid voice, who will blow the trumpet on Resurrection Day. [Not in
OED.]

Titles: Edgar Allan Poe, "Israfel" (verse); Walter de la Mare, "Israfel" (verse)

> "And thou—" but ha!—he answers not—
>   Good Heaven!—and does she go alone?
> She now has reach'd that dismal spot,
>   Where, some hours since, his voice's tone
> Had come to soothe her fears and ills,
> Sweet as the angel ISRAFIL'S,
> When every leaf on Eden's tree
> Is trembling to his minstrelsy—
> Yet now—oh, now, he is not nigh.—

> Thomas Moore, "The Fire-Worshippers" in *Lalla Rookh* (1817)

> In Heaven a spirit doth dwell,
>   "Whose heart-strings are a lute;"
> None sing so wildly well
> As the angel Israfel,
> And the giddy stars (so legends tell)
> Ceasing their hymns, attend the spell
>   Of his voice, all mute.

> Edgar Allan Poe, "Israfel" (1831)

> Gods, what a spectacle! The angels lean
> Out of high Heaven to view the sorry scene,
> And Israfel, "whose heart-strings are a lute,"
> Though now compassion makes their music mute,

Among the weeping company appears,
Pearls in his eyes and cotton in his ears.

Ambrose Bierce, "An Anarchist" (1900)

I caught a glimpse of luminous immensities on the verge of which we flew; of depths inconceivable, and flitting through the incredible spaces—gigantic shadows as of the wings of Israfel, which are so wide, say the Arabs, the world can cower under them as a nestling—and then—again the living blackness!

A. Merritt, *The Moon Pool* (1919)

There (thought I) lie scenes of pleasure,
    Where the free and blessed dwell,
And each moment hears a treasure
    Freighted with a lotus-spell,
And there floats a liquid measure
    From the lute of Israfel.

H. P. Lovecraft, "Astrophobos" (1917)

Clang-g-g—clang-g-g—thundering, fantastic music, such as might issue from the throat of a god, or from the heart-strings of the dark angel Israfel—

Henry Kuttner, "Bells of Horror" (1939)

ivory gate, gate of ivory, *n.* In Græco-Roman mythology, the gate through which false dreams come to men from the cave of Hypnos or Somnus, the god of sleep.

Titles: Thomas Lovell Beddoes, *The Ivory Gate* (verse collection)

Dreamer of dreams, born out of my due time,
Why should I strive to set the crooked straight?
Let it suffice me that my murmuring rime,
Beats with light wing against the ivory gate,
Telling a tale not too importunate
To those who in the sleepy region stay,
Lulled by the singer of an empty day.

William Morris, *The Earthly Paradise* (1896)

But some of us awake in the night with strange phantasms of enchanted hills and gardens, of fountains that sing in the sun, of golden cliffs overhanging murmuring seas, of plains that stretch down to sleeping cities of bronze and stone, and of shadowy companies of heroes that ride caparisoned white horses along the edges of thick forests; and then we know that we have looked back through the ivory gates into that world of wonder which was ours before we were wise and unhappy.

H. P. Lovecraft, "Celephaïs" (1920)

J

jibber, *v.intr.* To prattle and chatter rapidly, inarticulately, and unintelligibly; to jabber, gabble, gibber, etc.

> "Help me, daughter divine, for my Dæmon has deserted me, or if he comes at all it is but to jibber and to mock."
>
> H. Rider Haggard, *Wisdom's Daughter: The Life and Love Story of She-Who-Must-Be-Obeyed* (1923)

jounce, *v.tr.* To jolt, shake, bounce.

> He had, it seems, planned in vain when choosing the stoutest coffin for the platform; for no sooner was his full bulk again upon it than the rotting lid gave way, jouncing him two feet down on a surface which even he did not care to imagine.
>
> H. P. Lovecraft, "In the Vault" (1925)

> Kothar was aware that the emperor and his nobles, surrounded by guests and guardsmen, were pressing closer as he thumped and was jounced down the slanted steps to the main deck.
>
> Gardner F. Fox, "The Helix from Beyond" in *Kothar of the Magic Sword* (1969)

K

ka, **ka**, *n*. [< Ancient Egyptian] In Ancient Egyptian mythology and religion, one of the seven parts of a person, the *ka* is an astral double which frequently hovers near the deceased's body after death, and which is sometimes offered food by his relatives and friends. [Blavatsky antedates *OED* by 15 years.]

Titles: Dennis Wheatley, *The Ka of Gifford Hillary*

In the Egyptian notions, as in those of all other faiths founded on philosophy, man was not merely, as with the Christians, a union of soul and body; he was a trinity when spirit was added to it. Besides, that doctrine made him consist of *kha*—body; *khaba*—astral form, or shadow; *ka*—animal soul or life-principle; *ba*—the higher soul; and *akh*—terrestrial intelligence. They had also a sixth principle named *sah*—or mummy; but the functions of the one commenced only after the death of the body.

> H. P. Blavatsky, *Isis Unveiled: A Master-Key to the Mysteries of Ancient and Modern Science and Theology* (1877)

Then Satni played a game of chess with Noferkephtah, while the *Kas*, the Shadows, the Doubles of Ahouri, and the large-eyed boy looked on.

> Lafcadio Hearn, "The Book of Thoth" in *Stray Leaves from Strange Literature* (1884)

"Have you never heard of the Egyptians, a very wise people who, as I remember, declared that man has a *Ka* or Double, a second self, that can either dwell in his statue or be sent afar?"

> H. Rider Haggard, *She and Allan* (1920)

"The Ba was the soul—as distinct from the Ka, the double, or astral body. There was also the winged Ish, the spirit that dwelled in the abode of the gods."

> Victor Rousseau, "The Curse of Amen-Ra" (1932)

Connected with each tomb was a chapel in which priests and relatives offered food and prayer to the hovering *ka* or vital principle of the deceased.

> H. P. Lovecraft & Harry Houdini, "Under the Pyramids" (1924)

All these people thought of was death and the dead. They conceived of a literal resurrection of the body which made them mummify it with desperate care, and preserve all the vital organs in canopic jars near the corpse; whilst besides the body they believed in two other elements, the soul, which after its weighing and approval by Osiris dwelt in the land of the blest, and the obscure and portentous ka or life-principle which wandered about the upper and lower worlds in a horrible way, demanding occasional access to the preserved body, consuming the food offerings brought by priests and pious relatives to the mortuary chapel, and sometimes—as men whispered—taking its body or the wooden double always buried beside it and stalking noxiously abroad on errands peculiarly repellent.

H. P. Lovecraft & Harry Houdini, "Under the Pyramids" (1924)

"Tonight I did a dangerous thing, since there was no other way. Drinking the juice of the purple *dedaim*, which induces profound trance, I projected my ka into his elemental-guarded chamber. The elementals knew my presence, they gathered about me in shapes of fire and shadow, menacing me unspeakably."

Clark Ashton Smith, "The Master of the Crabs" (1947)

It is true that I can call
Both lich and ka, though not the soul, which roams
In regions past my scope, and can constrain
The genii of the several elements
To toil my mandate.

Clark Ashton Smith, *The Dead Will Cuckold You* (1951)

Whether he had been physically transported through the endless gulfs of space to the Hyades—or it had merely been some intangible part of him, perhaps that which the various religions called the *soul*, or *ka*—he did not know. But of one thing he was certain.

John Glasby, "The Ring of the Hyades"

Lying back, throwing aside the wrapping, she stretched out upon the rotting remains of the dead sorcerer. She understood now the reason for the cold, it was to hold her flesh in eternal ice while her *ka* went searching for the barbarian. Without its spirit, the flesh might putrefy; the cold would prevent this, would keep her body as it was now, while her spirit was still inside it.

Gardner F. Fox, *Kothar and the Wizard Slayer* (1970)

kadishtu, *adj.* [< Akkadian *qadishtu*; cognate with Hb *qadesh*, holy, holy one; also the term for a temple prostitute: masc. *qadesh* (*pl. qadeshim*), fem. *qadeshah* (*pl. qadeshoth*).] Literally, a "holy one"; a title of the priestess of Ishtar in the Babylonian religion; also, a priestess of Ishtar serving as a temple prostitute. [Not in *OED*.]

She dropped to her knees; crossed her hands, palms outward, over her forehead. She leaped to her feet; ran to the closed door of the cabin.

"*Kadishtu!*" She struck it with clenched hands. "Holy One—a messenger from Nabu!"

A. Merritt, *The Ship of Ishtar* (1923)

"High Priestess of Ishtar at her Great House in Uruk was Zarpanit. *Kadishtu*, Holy One, was she. And I, Sharane, who come from Babylon, was closest to her; her priestess; loved by her even as she was loved by Ishtar."

A. Merritt, *The Ship of Ishtar* (1923)

"Ya na kadishtu nilgh'ri . . . stell'bsna kn'aa Nyogtha . . . k'yarnak phlegethor. . ."

Henry Kuttner, "The Salem Horror" (1936; ellipses in original)

"Ya na kadishtu nilgh'ri stell'bsna Nyogtha,
K'yarnak phlegethor l'ebumna syha'h n'ghft,
Ya hai kadishtu ep r'luh-eeh Nyogtha eeh,
S'uhn-ngh athg li'hee orr'e syha'h."

Joachim Feery, *Notes on the* Necronomicon, as quoted in
Brian Lumley, *The Burrowers Beneath* (1974)

If thou recitest the above Ritual of Summoning thrice, and if upon each Adjuration thou completest thou drawest upon the floor with the Scimitar of Barzai the Kadishtu Symbol before the sepulchre, the Apparition will slowly form above the tomb, taking on flesh and substance and shaping itself slowly as a thing of mist of Vapour, drawing betimes at need upon the vital force of thine acolyte.

Abdul Alhazred (trans. John Dee), *Necronomicon*, as given by Lin Carter

Summon *Nyogtha* if thou must, but at thy peril, and have to hand the proper instruments to enforce the Dismissal, whereof I have found most potent and powerful the Vach-Viraj incantation, which is to say, in the primal Senzar, known to Sorcerers and by all Men else forgot, *Ya na kadishtu nilgh're stell'hsna kn'aa Nyogtha, k'yarnak phlegethor, ka gna ril'krii, pishtao, ghaah-gr'ng, Iä! Nyogtha!;* the which, nine times repeated with Sirius in the ascendant, driveth Him from hence unto His noisome lair.

Abdul Alhazred (trans. John Dee), *Necronomicon*, as given by Lin Carter

"Na kadish iom-thaa kadishtu," he intoned in ritual blessing. The language was supposedly in the lost tongue of the Lemurians, but Brother Ahriman, at least, had his doubts. Privately, he considered it to be mere gibberish.

Lin Carter, *The Nemesis of Evil* (1978)

"Open to me now, oh Lord," he screamed with a voice which no longer seemed his own. "Phlegethor k'yarnak, Cyäegha kn'aa stell'hsna, kadishtu na Ya!"

Eddy C. Bertin, "Darkness, My Name Is" (1975)

A voice close to me ripped the silence. "Iä Nyogtha! Erikthnar l'hor kadishtu . . . Iä Nyogtha! Ygnaiih Nyogtha k'yarnak!"

Steve Berman, "Path of Corruption" (ellipsis in original)

kallikanzaros (*pl.* *kallikanzaroi, kallikanzari*), **callicantzaros** (*pl.* **callicantzari**), *n.* [< Gr *kallikántzaros* < *kalós,* beautiful + *kéntauros,* centaur] In Greek folklore, a fabulous creature, half-human, half-goat, horse, wolf, etc. [Not in *OED.*]

It was of no use to demonstrate to such opponents that the Vermont myths differed but little in essence from those universal legends of natural personification which filled the ancient world with fauns and dryads and satyrs, suggested the *kallikanzari* of modern Greece, and gave to wild Wales and Ireland their dark hints of strange, small, and terrible hidden races of troglodytes and burrowers.

> H. P. Lovecraft, "The Whisperer in Darkness" (1930)

No, I will not speak of these things—nor even *hint* that an Arcadian ancestress of that Byzantine progenitress was once held for nearly three days in the clutches of the dreaded *Kallikanzari* in the dreadful season betwixt Christmas and Epiphany.

> H. P. Lovecraft, letter to Frank Belknap Long (December 1927)

kalpa, **kalpa,** *n.* [< Skr] A period of 4,320,000,000 years; an indefinitely long period; an æon.

For a long time, I waited, passively, with a sense of growing content. I had no longer that feeling of unutterable loneliness; but felt, rather, that I was less alone, then I had been for kalpas of years.

> William Hope Hodgson, *The House on the Borderland* (1908)

Then in the slow creeping course of eternity the utmost cycle of the cosmos churned itself into another futile completion, and all things became again as they were unreckoned kalpas before.

> H. P. Lovecraft, *The Dream-Quest of Unknown Kadath* (1926–27)

Centuries, æons, *kalpas* of time, were going by in the strange night.

> Clark Ashton Smith, "The Letter from Mohaun Los" (1931;
> aka "Flight into Super-Time")

He had thought to feel the overwhelming vertigo of unbottomed and undirectioned space. Instead, there was a weird sense of circumspection by the ambient night and emptiness, together with a sense of cyclic repetition, as if all that was happening had happened many times before and must recur often through endless future kalpas.

> Clark Ashton Smith, "Phœnix" (1953)

O world, thou shalt abide and be, for some brief travail of the sun,
The form and name of my distress, an image of the weariness
That shall survive thy kalpas done, the doom that is eternity.

> Clark Ashton Smith, "Apostrophe" (1926)

ken, *n.* The range or reach of sight, knowledge, understanding, cognizance.

But how could he close his ears to that horn which poured sleep into them as the sirens of old poured with their songs fatal fascinations into the ears of sailors strayed within their ken?

A. Merritt, The Ship of Ishtar (1924)

But I do not fear him now, for I suspect that he has known horrors beyond my ken. Now I fear *for* him.

H. P. Lovecraft, "The Statement of Randolph Carter" (1919)

> Alone in space, I view'd a feeble fleck
> Of silvern light, marking the narrow ken
> Which mortals call the boundless universe.

H. P. Lovecraft, "Aletheia Phrikodes" in
"The Poe-et's Nightmare: A Fable" (1916)

It was as if the monolith had been reared by alien hands, in an age distant and apart from human ken.

Robert E. Howard, "The Black Stone" (1931)

"Demons of the worlds beyond our ken! You who dwell where no man's eyes may see, where no man's limbs may go except that it be your will—heed me! Open wide your senses, hear my words!"

Gardner F. Fox, Kyrik: Warlock Warrior (1975)

ken, *v.tr.* To know, understand, perceive; to see.

> And through the drifts the snowy clifts
> Did send a dismal sheen:
> Nor shapes of men nor beasts we ken—
> The ice was all between.

S. T. Coleridge, "The Rime of the Ancient Mariner" (1798)

"Before the White Man came to this country, there was an Injun settlement where Marblehead stands today. It was shunned by all the neighboring Red Men, the Narragansett and the Pequots, since the tribe in question—the Miskatonicks—had a reputation as bein' unclean and unwholesome. Ye ken, the waters off Marblehead shore were just a-swarmin' with strange creatures—in fact, new ones seemed to be born daily—and the local Injuns were tainted through intimate contact with the queer beasts."

Paul Di Filippo, Hottentots (1994) in the Steampunk Trilogy

Khem, *n.* Ancient Egypt. [Not in *OED*.]

Of the Shining Trapazohedron he speaks often, calling it a window on all time and space, and tracing its history from the days it was fashioned on dark Yuggoth, before ever the Old Ones brought it to earth. It was treasured and placed in its curious box by the crinoid things of Antarctica, salvaged from their ruins by the serpent-men of Valusia, and peered at æons later in Lemuria by the first human beings. It crossed strange lands and stranger seas, and sank with Atlantis before a Minoan fisher meshed it in his net and sold it to swarthy merchants from nighted Khem. The Pharaoh Nephren-Ka built around it a temple with a windowless crypt, and did that which caused his name to be stricken from all monuments and records.

H. P. Lovecraft, "The Haunter of the Dark" (1935)

Incidentally, Commoriom seems to be a fruitful field for archæologic labour: I have retrieved therefrom various graven entities, including what is undoubtedly a representation, in some sort of prehistoric bone or ivory, of the woman-breasted cat-goddess, Phauz, whom the Hyperboreans worshipped æons before Bast was set up in Khem.

Clark Ashton Smith, letter to R. H. Barlow (November 1935)

Kobold, Kobbold, Kobald, *pr.n.* [Etymology unknown, but cf. Dutch *kabouter*; a connection with Gr *kobalos*, knave, has been suggested, but this seems unlikely.] In German folklore, either (1) a household spirit similar to the Scottish brownie; or (2) one of a goblin- or gnome-like race of beings which were believed to inhabit mines and other underground sites. The element *cobalt* takes its name from a variant form of the word *Kobold*.

The Kobolds were a species of gnomes, who haunted the dark and solitary places, and were often seen in the mines, where they seemed to imitate the labours of the miners, and sometimes took pleasure in frustrating their objects, and rendering their toil unfruitful. Sometimes they were malignant, especially if neglected or insulted; but sometimes also they were indulgent to individuals whom they took under their protection.

Sir Walter Scott, *Letters on Demonology and Witchcraft,*
Addressed to J. G. Lockheart, Esq. (1830)

From behind a rock a peal of harsh, grating laughter, full of evil humor, rang, through my ears, and, looking round, I saw a queer, goblin creature, with a great head and ridiculous features, just such as those described, in German histories and travels, as Kobolds.

George MacDonald, *Phantastes: A Faerie Romance for Men and Women* (1858)

Now in these subterranean caverns lived a strange race of beings, called by some gnomes, by some kobolds, by some goblins. There was a legend current in the country that at one time they lived above ground, and were very like other people.

George MacDonald, *The Princess and the Goblin* (1872)

They looked like kobolds from some magic mine—gnomes of the hills in conclave.

Rudyard Kipling, *Kim* (1901)

With the same startling abruptness there stood erect where but a moment before they had seethed a little figure, grotesque; a weirdly humorous, a vaguely terrifying foot-high shape, squared and angled and pointed and *animate*—as though a child should build from nursery blocks a fantastic shape which abruptly is filled with throbbing life! A troll from the kindergarten! A kobold of the toys!

A. Merritt, *The Metal Monster* (1920)

Prior to the Druids, & to the Aryan races which evolved them, Western Europe was undoubtedly inhabited by a squat Mongoloid race whose last living vestiges are the Lapps. This is the race which bequeathed the hideous witch-cult to posterity, & which lingers in popular folklore in the form of gnomes & kobolds, evil fairies & the "little people".

H. P. Lovecraft, letter to Elizabeth Toldridge (8 March 1929)

Thou art gnurled
And black as any Kobold from the mines
Where demons delve for orichalch and steel
To forge the infernal racks!

Clark Ashton Smith, "The Ghoul and the Seraph" (1919)

"O great spawn of the dank and dripping walls of Koboldom, they crave to see thy twilit grotto, bathed all in ruby hues. Yet they have killed thy kin and know not thou lurketh, awaiting their approach. They crave to plunder of thy hall, yet crush thy tiny minions 'neath their feet! I have heard them run shrieking from thy brothers, yet they come to steal thy bounty. O great and mighty spider-king, borne on the web that man calls fate, the Kobolds dance a saraband this night, and Arachne calls across the fierce Simoon. O thou who walkest in octaves and guardest the vaults of Crœsus, come forth this night, for I would grant thee audience."

Anton Szandor LaVey (Howard Stanton Levey), "The Ceremony of the Avoosal"

Kraken, kraken *pr.n* & *n*. In Scandinavian mythology, an enormous sea monster resembling a gigantic octopus or squid.

The kraken, that hugest of living things, was still supposed to cumber the recesses of the Northern Ocean; and often, when some fog-bank covered the sea at a distance, the eye of the experienced boatmen saw the horns of the monstrous leviathan welking and waving amidst the wreaths of mist, and bore away with all press of oar and sail, lest the sudden suction, occasioned by the sinking of the monstrous mass to the bottom, should drag within the grasp of its multifarious feelers his own frail skiff.

Sir Walter Scott, *The Pirate* (1821)

At times we gasped for breath at an elevation beyond the albatross—at times became dizzy with the velocity of our descent into some watery hell, where the air grew stagnant, and no sound disturbed the slumbers of the kraken.

Edgar Allan Poe, "MS. Found in a Bottle" (1833)

Below the thunders of the upper deep,
Far, far beneath in the abysmal sea,
His ancient, dreamless, uninvaded sleep
The Kraken sleepeth: faintest sunlights flee
About his shadowy sides; above him swell
Huge sponges of millennial growth and height;
And far away into the sickly light,
From many a wondrous grot and secret cell
Unnumbered and enormous polypi
Winnow with giant arms the slumbering green.
There hath he lain for ages, and will lie
Battening upon huge sea-worms in his sleep,
Until the latter fire shall heat the deep;
Then once by man and angels to be seen,
In roaring he shall rise and on the surface die.

Alfred, Lord Tennyson, "The Kraken" (1830)

"Don't you know what this is?" he asked me. "It's the Kraken—that super-wise, malignant and mythical sea-monster of the old Norsemen. See, its tentacles are not eight but twelve. Never was it pictured with less than ten. It symbolized the principle that is inimical to Life—not Death precisely, more accurately annihilation. The Kraken—and here in Mongolia!"

A. Merritt, Dwellers in the Mirage (1932)

"It is a human element—a woman or man or child—who is *en rapport* with the Being evoked. Of such was the Pythoness at Delphi, who upon her tripod threw herself open to the God and spoke with his voice. Of such were the Priestesses of Isis of the Egyptians, and of Ishtar of the Babylonians—themselves the one and the same. Of such was the Priestess of Hecate, Goddess of Hell, whose secret rites were lost until I rediscovered them. Of such was the warrior-king who was Priest of tentacled Khalk-ru, the Kraken God of the Uighurs, and of such was that strange priest at whose summoning came the Black God of the Scyths, in the form of a monstrous frog—"

A. Merritt, *Creep, Shadow!* (1934; aka *Creep, Shadow, Creep!*)

The boat began to shoot with plummet-like speed toward the cliffs, the sea foaming and streaming all around as though some kraken were dragging us to its caverned lair. Borne like a leaf on a cataract, we toiled vainly with straining oars against the ineluctable current.

Clark Ashton Smith, "The Master of the Crabs" (1947)

"I have told you what she wants—what all these hybrid horrors raven for. She will reveal herself to you in slumber, you will do her bidding. She will take you down into the deep, and show you the kraken-fouled gulfs where these things bide. You will go willingly, and that will be your doom."

Robert Bloch & Henry Kuttner, "The Black Kiss" (1937)

Kraken! The vast beast of the sea deeps that dwelt in sea caverns and the long-forgotten ruins that dot the floor of the Outer Sea. A creature large enough to attack a ship, a being of a hundred thick tentacles each able to shatter the mast of a large ship.

Gardner F. Fox, *Kothar and the Wizard Slayer* (1970)

kylix (*pl.* **kylikes**), *n.* [< Gr *kýlix*] A shallow, tall-stemmed cup.

On one side of the door stood a rack of savage whips, above which were some shelves bearing empty rows of shallow pedestalled cups of lead shaped like Grecian kylikes. On the other side was the table; with a powerful Argand lamp, a pad and pencil, and two of the stoppered lekythoi from the shelves outside set down at irregular places as if temporarily or in haste.

H. P. Lovecraft, *The Case of Charles Dexter Ward* (1927)

Behind the harpsichord and under the window there was a low glass cabinet which contained two or three classical pieces. There was a rhyton in the form of a human head, a black-figure kylix on one side, a small red-figure amphora on the other.

John Fowles, *The Magus* (1965)

L

lacuna (*pl.* **lacunæ, lacunas**), *n.* [< L *lacūna*, a hole, pit] An empty or blank spot in a text.

> I like the idea of reprinting old weird classics—it is surprising to discover how many person have failed to read certain noted standbys. I have many such lacunæ—for example, I have never read F. Marion Crawford's "Upper Berth", which you are about to use, much to my gratification.
>
> H. P. Lovecraft, letter to *Weird Tales* (October 1923)

> The reader will note certain lacunæ, due to passages written in an alphabet which neither I nor any scholar of my acquaintance can transliterate. These passages seem to form an integral part of the narrative, and they occur mainly toward the end, as if the writer had turned more and more to a language remembered from his ancient avatar.
>
> Clark Ashton Smith, "The Chain of Aforgomon" (1934)

lamia (*pl.* **lamiæ, lamias**), *n.* In Greek mythology, a vampiric monster with the head and breast of a woman and the body and tail of a serpent; in Roman mythology, an evil witch or sorceress that sucks the blood of children.

Titles: John Keats, *Lamia* (verse); Otis Adelbert Kline, *Lord of the Lamia*; Clark Ashton Smith, "Lamia" (verse); Manley Wade Wellman, *Lamia*

> This word *Lamia* hath many significations, being taken sometimes for a beast of *Lybia*, sometimes for a fish, and sometimes for a Spectre or apparition of women called Phairies. And from hence some have ignorantly affirmed, that either there were no such beasts at all, or else that it was a compounded monster of a beast and a fish, whose opinions I will briefly set down. *Aristophanes* affirmeth, that he heard one say, that he saw a great wilde beast having severall parts resembling outwardly an Oxe, and inwardly a Mule, and a beautifull woman, which he called afterwards *Empusa*.
>
> Edward Topsell, *The Historie of Foure-Footed Beastes* (1607)

> Philostratus, in his fourth book *de vita Apollonii*, hath a memorable instance in this kind, which I may not omit, of one Menippus Lycius, a young man twenty-five years of age, that going between Cenchreas and Corinth, met such a phantasm in the habit of a fair gentlewoman, which, taking him by the hand, carried him home to her house in the suburbs of Corinth, and told him she was a Phœnician by birth, and if he would tarry with her, "he should hear her sing and play, and drink such wine as never any drank, and no man should molest him;

but she being fair and lovely would live and die with him, that was fair and lovely to behold." The young man, a philosopher, otherwise staid and discreet, able to moderate his passions, though not this of love, tarried with her awhile to his great content, and at last married her, to whose wedding, amongst other guests, came Apollonius, who, by some probable conjectures, found her out to be a serpent, a lamia, and that all her furniture was like Tantalus' gold described by Homer, no substance, but mere illusions. When she saw herself descried, she wept, and desired Apollonius to be silent, but he would not be moved, and thereupon she, plate, house, and all that was in it, vanished in an instant: "many thousands took notice of this fact, for it was in the midst of Greece."

Robert Burton, *The Anatomy of Melancholy: What It Is, With All the Kinds, Causes, Symptomes, Prognostickes & Severall Cures of It* (1621)

Ah . . . my sister, the Lamia, lives in Corinth with her paramour Lycius! She lives in a Numidian ivory with portals of black sardonyx and a pavement of constellated gold. Her pools are pure chalcedony and her labyrinth is lighted by a single chrysoberyl. Her chariot is drawn by two Nysæan tigers with eyes like Attic emeralds. Each night veiled, white eidolons enter her chamber with sweet voices, sinful gestures and subtle perfumes. These are the beings that concert with my sister to do evil. Our father she turned into a winged phantom that haunts Cenchreas, our mother she stifled with a monstrous word that is known only to the malignant divinities of the Massagetæ, and me—O horror! horror!—

Samuel Loveman, "The Sphinx: A Conversation" (ellipsis in original)

It would be too hideous if they knew that the one-time heiress of Riverside— the accursed gorgon or lamia whose hateful crinkly coil of serpent-hair must even now be brooding and twining vampirically around an artist's skeleton in a lime-packed grave beneath a charred foundation—was faintly, subtly, yet to the eyes of genius unmistakably the scion of Zimbabwe's most primal grovellers. No wonder she owned a link with that old witch-woman Sophonisba—for, though in deceitfully slight proportion, Marceline was a negress.

H. P. Lovecraft & Zealia Bishop, "Medusa's Coil" (1930)

"I have written books—many books—describing dozens of instances of possession, of return, of immolation, of divination, and of transformation. I have confirmed the reality of the concubitis dæmonum; have proved incontestably the existence of vampires, succubi and lamias, and I have slipped not too unwillingly, into the warm and clinging arms of women five centuries dead."

Frank Belknap Long, "The Horror from the Hills" (1930)

"Foul vampire! accursed lamia! she-serpent of hell!" thundered the abbot suddenly, as he crossed the threshold of the room, raising the aspergillum aloft.

Clark Ashton Smith, "The End of the Story" (1929)

Men said, however, that malign goblins, tall as giants and humped like camels, had oftentimes beset the wayfarers through Izdrel; that fair but ill-meaning lamiæ had lured them to an eldritch death.

Clark Ashton Smith, "The Black Abbot of Puthuum" (1935)

In the end, she had died of sheer chagrin and despair, or perhaps had slain herself with some undetected poison.... . But, as was commonly believed in Tasuun, a witch dying thus, with unslaked desires and frustrate cantraips, could turn herself into a lamia or vampire and procure thereby the consummation of all her sorceries. . . .

Clark Ashton Smith, "The Death of Ilalotha" (1937; ellipses in original)

Night after night his disgust and weariness sloughed away from him, in a fascination fed by the spectral milieu, the environing silence of the dead, his withdrawal and separation from the carnal, garish city. By degrees, by alternations of unbelief and belief, he came to accept her as the actual lamia. The hunger that he sensed in her could be only the lamia's hunger; her beauty that of a being no longer human.

Clark Ashton Smith, "Morthylla" (1952)

Now they come,
A Sabbath of abominable shapes,
Led by the fiends and lamiæ of worlds
That owned my sway aforetime!

Clark Ashton Smith, *The Hashish-Eater; or, The Apocalypse of Evil* (1920)

Though we distill
Quintessences of hemlock or nepenthe,
We cannot slay the small, the subtle serpents,
Whose mother is the lamia Melancholy
That feeds upon our breath and sucks our veins,
Stifling us with her velvet volumes.

Clark Ashton Smith, "Soliloquy in an Ebon Tower" (1951)

I had been seated in the study, pondering upon a maggot-eaten volume of Heirarchus' *Occultus*, when without warning, I felt a tremendous urge keening through my weary brain. It beckoned and allured with unutterable promise, like the mating-cry of the lamia of old; yet at the same time it held an inexorable power whose potence could not be defied or denied.

Robert Bloch, "The Secret in the Tomb" (1934)

When the fat man stepped in front of me, blocking my way with his bulk, she nearly (yet not quite) embraced me, coming so close it seemed almost magical that we did not touch, her long-fingered hands moving at the opening of my

cloak with the desire to stroke my chest, but never quite doing so, so that I felt I
was about to fall prey to some blood-drinking ghost, a succubus or lamia.

Gene Wolfe, The Shadow of the Torturer (1980)

Lammas, *pr.n.* [< OE *hláfmæsse* < *hláf,* loaf, bread + *mæsse,* mass; folk etymol-
ogy as if *lamb* + *mass*;] The first of August, on which a harvest festival is held.

He who would be a Master of the Runes and possessor of Life eternaille must
consecrate to Crom Cruach on Lammas Night yᵉ Flesh of an infant newborn
and eat thereof. Nor is the consecration to be made by those faint of heart or
doubting in their souls, for Crom Cruach knows all, Crom Cruach sees all, Crom
Cruach is all. *Iä! Crom Cruach!*

Abdul Alhazred (trans. John Dee), Necronomicon, as quoted in
Brian McNaughton, Satan's Mistress (1978)

He would simply have to wait—and pray, of course—pray that nothing went
wrong when the birth came. He hoped it would not come tomorrow, on Lammas Eve; he hoped, for Freirs' sake, that the birth proved a successful one.

T. E. D. Klein, The Ceremonies (1984)

Larva (*pl.* **Larvæ**), **Larve,** *n.* [< L] In Roman mythology, a ghost, spirit, goblin,
dæmon, devil; in particular, a ghost that returns to haunt the living.

The parson never openly professes his belief in ghosts, but I have remarked that
he has a suspicious way of pressing great names into the defense of supernatural
doctrines, and making philosophers and saints fight for him. He expatiates at
large on the opinion of the ancient philosophers about larves, or nocturnal
phantoms, the spirits of the wicked, which wandered like exiles about the earth;
and about those spiritual beings which abode in the air, but descended occasionally to earth, and mingled among mortals, acting as agents between them
and the gods.

Washington Irving, Bracebridge Hall; or, The Humorists: A Medley (1822)

"Time flies—I may starve—starve! if you are not quick! Go—go! Yet stay—it is
horrible to be alone!—the air is like a charnel—and the scorpions—ha! and the
pale larvæ! Oh! stay, stay!"

Sir Edward Bulwer-Lytton, The Last Days of Pompeii (1834)

Nothing now was left but the Shadow, and on that my eyes were intently fixed,
till again eyes grew out of the Shadow—malignant, serpent eyes. And the bubbles of light again rose and fell, and in their disordered, irregular, turbulent
maze, mingled with the wan moonlight. And now from these globules themselves as from the shell of an egg, monstrous things burst out; the air grew filled
with them; larvæ so bloodless and so hideous that I can in no way describe them
except to remind the reader of the swarming life which the solar microscope
brings before his eyes in a drop of water—things transparent, supple, agile,

chasing each other, devouring each other—forms like nought ever beheld by the naked eye.

Sir Edward Bulwer-Lytton, "The Haunted and the Haunters; or, The House and the Brain" (1857)

FALLEN ONE!—I see before thee, Evil and Death, and Woe! Thou to have relinquished Adon-Ai, for the nameless Terror—the heavenly stars, for those fearful eyes! Thou, at the last to be the victim of the Larva of the dreary Threshold, that, in thy first novitiate, fled, withered and shrivelled, from thy kingly brow! When, at the primary grades of initiation, the pupil I took from thee on the shores of the changed Parthenopé, fell senseless and cowering before that Phantom-Darkness. I knew that his spirit was not formed to front the worlds beyond; for FEAR is the attraction of man to earthiest earth; and while he fears, he cannot soar.

Sir Edward Bulwer-Lytton, *Zanoni: A Rosicrucian Tale* (1842)

That which is indeed spiritual is not all the product of dead men, but much of it proceeds from the Larvæ and inhabitants of the spaces between the rolling globes.

Paschal Beverly Randolph, *Ravalette: The Rosicrucian's Story* (1863)

> What larve, what specter is this
> Thrilling the wilderness to life
> As with the bodily shape of Fear?

William Ernest Henley, "Space and Dread and the Dark"

Never before had he known what shapeless black things lurk and caper and flounder all through the æther, leering and grinning at such voyagers as may pass, and sometimes feeling about with slimy paws when some moving object excites their curiosity. These are the nameless larvæ of the Other Gods, and like them are blind and without mind, and possessed of singular hungers and thirsts.

H. P. Lovecraft, *The Dream-Quest of Unknown Kadath* (1926–27)

But Amalzain, riding swiftly toward Sabmon's hermitage, was haunted still by leprous larvæ that rose before him, posturing foully on the dun sands; and he heard the desirous moaning of succubi under the hooves of his horse.

Clark Ashton Smith, "The Witchcraft of Ulua" (1933)

> Know you the gulfs within?
> The larvæ, the minotaurs of labyrinths undared?
> The somber foam of seas by cryptic sirens shared?
> The pestilence and sin
> Borne by the flapping shroud of liches met within?

Clark Ashton Smith, "Interrogation" (1925)

Incubus, my cousin, come,
Drawn from out the night you haunt,
From the hollow mist and murk
Where discarnate larvæ lurk,
By the word of masterdom.

Clark Ashton Smith, The Dead Will Cuckold You (1951)

Know that salt absorbs the evil effluvia of the larvæ, and is useful to cleanse the tools with.

Abdul Alhazred (trans. "Simon"), Necronomicon (1977)

And remember that thou purify thy temple with the branches of cypress and of pine, and no evil spirit which haunteth buildings will cause habitation to be set up therein, and no larvæ will breed, as they do in many unclean places. The larvæ are enormous, twice as large as a man, but do breed on his excretions, and even, it is said, upon his breath, and grow to terrible height, and do not leave him until the Priest or some magician cut him off with the copper dagger, saying the name of ISHTAR seven times seven times, aloud, in a sharp voice.

Abdul Alhazred (trans. "Simon"), Necronomicon (1977)

Lascar, *n.* An East Indian sailor.

Ratcliffe Highway is a public thoroughfare in a most chaotic quarter of eastern, or nautical, London; and at this time (*viz.*, in 1812), when no adequate police existed except the *detective* police of Bow Street—admirable for its own peculiar purposes but utterly incommensurable to the general service of the capital—it was a most dangerous quarter. Every third man at the least might be set down as a foreigner. Lascars, Chinese, Moors, Negroes, were met at every step.

Thomas De Quincey, On Murder Considered as One of the Fine Arts (1854)

During a walk through a narrow lane near the Gothenburg dock, a bundle of papers falling from an attic window had knocked him down. Two Lascar sailors at once helped him to his feet, but before the ambulance could reach him he was dead.

H. P. Lovecraft, "The Call of Cthulhu" (1926)

From this last post he retired to his home in a suburb of Boston and began to live out his last years in an almost reclusive fashion; I write "almost," because he broke his seclusion from time to time to make strange secretive trips into all corners of the world, on one of which—while poking about certain unsavory districts of Limehouse, in London—he had met his death—a sudden riot of what appeared to be lascars and dacoits from ships in dock involving him and dissipating as suddenly as it had begun, leaving him dead.

August Derleth, "The Gorge beyond Salapunco" (1949) in The Trail of Cthulhu

I stepped out and faced one of them. He met my eyes questioningly for a moment, held my gaze, and looked away. A lascar, I judged him, but oddly deformed, with a curiously suggestive head, foreshortened, with little brow, and repellantly wide-mouthed, with scarcely a chin at all, but a sloping fold of skin that vanished into his neck.

> August Derleth, "The Black Island" (1952) in *The Trail of Cthulhu*

lekythos (*pl.* **lekythoi**), *n.* [< Gr *lékythos*] A narrow-necked Grecian oil-jug.

Some of the upper levels were wholly vacant, but most of the space was filled with small odd-looking leaden jars of two general types; one tall and without handles like a Grecian lekythos or oil-jug, and the other with a single handle and proportioned like a Phaleron jug. All had metal stoppers, and were covered with peculiar-looking symbols moulded in low relief. In a moment the doctor noticed that these jugs were classified with great rigidity; all the lekythoi being on one side of the room with a large wooden sign reading "Custodes" above them, and all the Phalerons on the other, correspondingly labelled with a sign reading "Materia".

> H. P. Lovecraft, *The Case of Charles Dexter Ward* (1927)

Lemur (*pl.* **Lemures, Lemurs**), **Lemure,** *n.* [< L] In Roman religion and mythology, a ghost, spirit, dæmon, devil; in particular, a maleficent ghost that returns to haunt the living. The name has also been given to a family of nocturnal, large-eyed, arboreal primates native to Madagascar and the East Indies after the native belief that they are the ghosts of human beings. A lost continent, placed in the Indian Ocean, was hypothesized in order to account for the presence of lemurs in both African and Indian sites. This continent was first christened Lemuria by Phillip L. Sclater and adopted by Ernst Hæckel, who posited it as the area in which human beings evolved from apes. It has since been adopted by Theosophists and other occultists, who have frequently confounded it with James Churchward's lost continent Mu, which is placed in the Pacific Ocean.

> Pale-sheeted ghosts, with gory locks, upstarting from their tombs—
> All fantasies and images that flit in midnight glooms—
> Hags, goblins, demons, lemures, have made me all aghast,—
> But nothing like that GRIMLY ONE who stood beside the mast!
>
> Thomas Hood, "The Demon-Ship"

So still lay the figure, and so dim was its outline, that any other than Arbaces might have felt a superstitious fear, lest he beheld one of those grim *lemures*, who, above all other spots, haunted the threshold of the homes they formerly possessed.

> Sir Edward Bulwer-Lytton, *The Last Days of Pompeii* (1834)

Forasmuch as it is ordained of God that all flesh hath spirit and thereby taketh on spiritual powers, so, also, the spirit hath powers of the flesh, even when it is gone out of the flesh and liveth as a thing apart, as many a violence performed by wraith and lemure showeth. And there be who say that man is not single in this, but the beasts have the like evil inducement, and—

Denneker, *Meditations*, as quoted in
Ambrose Bierce, "Staley Fleming's Hallucination" (1906)

"Lemur, who are you? No. What bogeyman's trick is this?"

James Joyce, *Ulysses* (1914–21)

What was this subtle thing that ate into one's marrow? I had read of banshees, lemures and leprechauns; they were the ghosts and fairies of ignorance but they were not like this.

Austin Hall & Homer Eon Flint, *The Blind Spot* (1921)

Together with my companions and our chief Javan, I entered the palace of the king. And Ahab sat beneath a dais of silver on a milk-white peristyle, paven with agate, and sculptured with glittering friezes of satyrs, fauns, griffins, harpies, lemures, apes and peacocks in Assyrian gold.

Samuel Loveman, "The Sphinx: A Conversation"

In an instant every moving entity was electrified; and forming at once into a ceremonial procession, the nightmare horde slithered away in quest of the sound—goat, satyr, and ægipan, incubus, succuba, and lemur, twisted toad and shapeless elemental, dog-faced howler and silent stutterer in darkness—all led by the abominable naked phosphorescent thing that had squatted on the carved golden throne, and that now strode insolently bearing in its arms the glassy-eyed corpse of the corpulent old man.

H. P. Lovecraft, "The Horror at Red Hook" (1925)

"The blood is the life, you know. Even the lemurs and elementals that are older than the earth will come when the blood of men or beasts is offered under the right conditions."

H. P. Lovecraft & Hazel Heald, "The Horror in the Museum" (1932)

And then the idea of taking such news to Pride filled me with dismay. I had never seen him angry, and rage in that enormous body, behind the lemur face, in the crawling hands, would be terrible to see.

Leonard Cline, *The Dark Chamber* (1927)

Love needs no stranger dream: your face calls back
The feet that flying Lemures have drawn
To years beyond the darkness and the dawn;
And thrusts afar the impending Zodiac.

Clark Ashton Smith, "No Stranger Dream" (1948)

> Call up the lordly dæmon that in Cimmeria dwells
> Amid the vaults untrodden, long-sealed with lethal spells,
> Amid the untouched waters of Lemur-warded wells.
>
> Clark Ashton Smith, "Pour Chercher du Nouveau" (1949)

lemurian, *adj.* Of or pertaining to Lemures (q.v.). [This sense not in *OED*.]

Around me on every side, sepulchral sentinels guarding unkempt graves, the tilting, decrepit headstones lie half-hidden in masses of nauseous, rotting vegetation. Above the rest, silhouetted against the livid sky, an august monument lifts its austere, tapering spire like the spectral chieftain of a lemurian horde.

> C. M. Eddy, Jr. & H. P. Lovecraft, "The Loved Dead" (1923)

lepidodendron (*pl.* **lepidodendra**), *n.* [< Gr, wing + tree] Any of a genus of vast, arborescent plants that throve in the Carboniferous period. [Not in *OED*.]

When I stood just within the opening, the corpse fifty yards away was exactly in line with a particular lepidodendron in the far-off forest. Now it occurred to me that this sighting might not have been of sufficient accuracy—the distance of the corpse making its difference of direction in relation to the horizon comparatively slight when viewed from the openings next to that of my first ingress. Moreover, the tree did not differ as distinctly as it might from other lepidodendra on the horizon.

> H. P. Lovecraft & Kenneth Sterling, "In the Walls of Eryx" (1936)

leprous, *adj.* Afflicted with leprosy; of or pertaining to leprosy; resembling leprosy or the effects of leprosy; characterized by loose, flaky scales; white, pale, pallid.

> Spawn, weeds and filth, a leprous scum,
> Made the running rivulet thick and dumb
> And at its outlet flags huge as stakes
> Dammed it up with roots knotted like water snakes.
>
> Percy Bysshe Shelley, *The Sensitive-Plant* (1820)

"I repelled him and his drink, which I had not a doubt was some magical drug, with horror unutterable; and losing all other fears in the overwhelming one of becoming a slave of Satan, and a victim of one of his agents, as I believed this extraordinary figure, I called on the name of the Saviour and the saints, and, crossing myself at every sentence, exclaimed, 'No, tempter, keep your infernal potions for the leprous lips of your imps, or swallow them yourself.'"

> Charles Maturin, *Melmoth the Wanderer: A Tale* (1820)

On every side monotonous grey streets, each house the replica of its neighbour, to the east an unexplored wilderness, north and west and south the brickfields and market-gardens, everywhere the ruins of the country, the tracks where sweet lanes had been, gangrened stumps of trees, the relics of hedges, here and there an oak stripped of its bark, white and haggard and leprous, like a corpse.

Arthur Machen, *The Hill of Dreams* (1897)

For if there is a landscape of sadness, there is certainly also a landscape of a horror of darkness and evil; and that black and oily depth, overshadowed with twisted woods, with its growth of foul weeds and its dead trees and leprous boughs was assuredly potent in terror.

Arthur Machen, "The Children of the Pool" (1935)

> Nay! for all the world-decay
> Rots from sapphirine to grey.
> All the leprous lichen clings
> Round the comeliness of things.

Aleister Crowley, *The World's Tragedy* (1908)

O Thou leprous claws of the ghoul, that coaxest the babe from its chaste cradle! I adore Thee, Evoe! I adore Thee, IAO!

J. F. C. Fuller, *The Treasure House of Images* (1913)

"Every sense of the flesh is tortured and every faculty of the soul therewith: the eyes with impenetrable utter darkness, the nose with noisome odours, the ears with yells and howls and execrations, the taste with foul matter, leprous corruption, nameless suffocating filth, the touch with redhot goads and spikes, with cruel tongues of flame."

James Joyce, *A Portrait of the Artist as a Young Man* (1904–14)

Bag of corpsegas in foul brine. A quiver of minnows, fat of a spongy titbit, flash through the slits of his buttoned trouserfly. God becomes man becomes fish becomes barnacle goose becomes featherbed mountain. Dead breaths I living breathe, tread dead dust, devour a urinous offal from all dead. Hauled stark over the gunwale he breathes upward the stench of his green grave, his leprous nosehole snoring to the sun.

James Joyce, *Ulysses* (1914–21)

The thing came abruptly and unannounced; a dæmon, rat-like scurrying from pits remote and unimaginable, a hellish panting and stifled grunting, and then from that opening beneath the chimney a burst of multitudinous and leprous life—a loathsome night-spawned flood of organic corruption more devastatingly hideous than the blackest conjurations of mortal madness and morbidity. Seething, stewing, surging, bubbling like serpents' slime it rolled up and out of that yawning hole, spreading like a septic contagion and streaming from the cellar at every point of egress—streaming out to scatter through the accursed midnight forests and strew fear, madness, and death.

H. P. Lovecraft, "The Lurking Fear" (1922)

A black rift began to yawn, and at length—when I had pushed away every fragment small enough to budge—the leprous moonlight blazed on an aperture of
ample width to admit me.

> H. P. Lovecraft, "The Shadow out of Time" (1935)

The moon, slightly past full, shone from a clear sky and drenched the ancient
sands with a white, leprous radiance which seemed to me somehow infinitely
evil.

> H. P. Lovecraft, "The Shadow out of Time" (1935)

> White leprous marble in the light
> Shews sculptures that repel and fright,
> And many a temple hints the sin
> And blasphemy that reign within.

> H. P. Lovecraft, "Astrophobos" (1917)

> It was the city I had known before;
> The ancient, leprous town where mongrel throngs
> Chant to strange gods, and beat unhallowed gongs
> In crypts beneath foul alleys near the shore.

> H. P. Lovecraft, "The Courtyard" in *Fungi from Yuggoth* (1929–30)

Day by day, through the middle summer, the fisher-folk went forth in their
coracles of elk-hide and willow, casting their seines. But in the seines they drew
dead fishes, blasted as if by fire or extreme cold; and they drew living monsters,
such as their eldest captains had never beheld: things triple-headed and tailed
and finned with horror; black, shapeless things that turned to a liquid foulness
and ran from the net; or headless things like bloated moons with green, frozen
rays about them; or things leprous-eyed and bearded with stiffly-oozing slime.

> Clark Ashton Smith, "The Coming of the White Worm" (1933)

Through blackening blurs of shadow, the men watched them as they seethed up
and down on the pyramid like a leprous, living frieze.

> Clark Ashton Smith, "The Dweller in the Gulf" (1932)

Anthropoid, leprous shadows loping down colossal black basaltic corridors of
pulsing, inhuman night. Mowing slavering abominations of an Elder World
squatting on a lone bare hill in a grisly ring, howling brain-shattering incantations to a hag-moon. Titanic shapes of blasphemy and gibbering madness growing out of the night and silence of a midnight oak forest. Age-forgotten gods
that ground writhing howling naked humans between their brutish jaws.

> Robert E. Howard, "The Temple of Abomination"

For a long time he kept on through the thick darkness, ever pressing toward the
forest ahead, and it was only when he had gone more than half way that the

darkness lightened dimly when a huge blood-red sun swept up from the eastern sky and cast a vivid, leprous glow on the land.

Donald Wandrei, "A Fragment of a Dream" (1926)

Dreadful as the Dead Marshes had been, and the arid moors of the Noman-Lands, more loathsome far was the country that the crawling day now slowly unveiled to his shrinking eyes. Even to the Mere of Dead Faces some haggard phantom of green spring could come; but here neither spring nor summer would ever come again. Here nothing lived, not even the leprous growths that feed on rottenness. The gasping pools were choked with ash and crawling muds, sickly white and grey, as if the mountains had vomited the filth of their entrails upon the lands about. High mounds of crushed and powdered rock, great cones of earth fire-blasted and poison-stained, stood like an obscene graveyard in endless rows, slowly revealed in the reluctant light.

J. R. R. Tolkien, *The Two Towers* in *The Lord of the Rings* (1936–49)

I learned of the fungoid, inhuman beings that dwell on far cold Yuggoth, of the cyclopean shapes that attend unsleeping Cthulhu in his submarine city, of the strange pleasures that the followers of leprous, subterranean Yog-Sothoth may possess, and I learned, too, of the unbelievable manner in which Iod, the Source, is worshiped beyond the outer galaxies.

Henry Kuttner, "The Secret of Kralitz" (1936)

As it was, a scream of utter horror ripped from my throat as I saw, through a spinning whirlpool of darkness, a squamous, glowing ball covered with squirming, snake-like tentacles—translucent, ivory flesh, leprous and hideous—a great faceted eye that held the cold stare of the Midgard serpent.

Henry Kuttner, "The Invaders" (1939)

A rat was approaching—the monster he had already glimpsed. Grey and leprous and hideous it crept forward with its orange teeth bared, and in its wake came the blind dead thing, groaning as it crawled.

Henry Kuttner, "The Graveyard Rats" (1936)

If I had but known the terrible events that were to follow, if I could only have had a foresight into the future that September day, I swear I would have avoided the book like a leprous thing, would have shunned that wretched antique store and the very street it stood on like places accursed.

Carl Jacobi, "Revelations in Black" (1933)

Edgar Henquist Gordon, sitting there in the wan lunar light of the moon; sitting at the wide window with eyes that equaled the leprous moonlight in the dreadful intensity of their pallid glow. . . .

Robert Bloch, "The Dark Demon" (1936; ellipsis in original)

He helped me stagger toward the old stairs, through the leprous dark.

> Robert Barbour Johnson, "The Silver Coffin" (1939)

As I passed through Berkeley, I remembered the horrible stories which were told about the town—about the leprous, bloated toad-monster which had been kept in a dungeon, and about the Witch of Berkeley, off whose coffin the chains had inexplicably fallen before the corpse stepped forth.

> Ramsey Campbell, "The Room in the Castle" (1964)

There was a spiraling, thickening cloud of pallid vapor obscuring it and from within that congealing, leprous mist came the sound of huge bubbles breaking the oily surface.

> John S. Glasby, "The Brooding City"

leprously, *adv.* In a leprous (q.v.) manner.

> The quicksand took it. Its huge hindquarters, black and glistening, corded with muscle, disappeared almost immediately, and then the distended, leprously white belly.
>
> Henry Kuttner, "The Frog" (1939)

lethiferous, *adj.* [< L *lētifer, lēthifer* < *lētum, lēthum,* death + *ferre,* to bear] Bringing death or destruction; deadly.

> I have seen the hoary, sky-confronting walls of Macchu Pichu amid the desolate Andes, and the teocallis that are buried in the Mexican jungles. And I have seen the frozen, giant-builded battlements of Uogam on the glacial tundras of the nightward hemisphere of Venus. But these were as things of yesteryear, bearing at least the memory or the intimation of life, compared with the awesome and lethiferous antiquity, the cycle-enduring doom of a petrified sterility, that seemed to invest Yoh-Vombis.
>
> Clark Ashton Smith, "The Vaults of Yoh-Vombis" (1931)

libation, *n.* The act of pouring out a liquid, usually a liquor, as a sacrifice or religious ceremony in honor of a deity; hence, jocularly, a serving of a liquor.

> La Motte seemed anxious to prevent thought, by assuming a fictitious and unnatural gaiety: he laughed and talked, and threw off frequent bumpers of wine: it was the mirth of desperation. Madame became alarmed, and would have restrained him, but he persisted in his libations to Bacchus till reflection seemed to be almost overcome.
>
> Ann Radcliffe, *The Romance of the Forest, Interspersed with Some Pieces of Poetry* (1791)

> I noted that he was white and shaken and called to one to bring him wine. He drank of it thankfully, not forgetting first to pour a libation at my feet, or rather at those of the goddess to whom I was so near.
>
> H. Rider Haggard, *Wisdom's Daughter: The Life and Love Story of She-Who-Must-Be-Obeyed* (1923)

"Here, O Youth—a libation! Wine of the cosmos—nectar of the starry spaces—Linos—Iacchus—Ialmenos—Zagreus—Dionysos—Atys—Hylas— sprung from Apollo and slain by the hounds of Argos—seed of Psamathë— child of the sun—Evoë! Evoë!"

> Adolphe de Castro & H. P. Lovecraft, "The Electric Executioner" (1929)

The entrance of the vault was guarded by earth-demons that obeyed the arch-sorcerer, Maranapion, who had long been the king's councillor. These demons would have torn limb from limb any who came unprepared to offer them a libation of fresh blood.

> Clark Ashton Smith, "The Death of Malygris" (1933)

lich, *n.* [< OE *lic*, body, corpse] A dead body, corpse, cadaver; in particular, one animated through magical or supernatural means.

Titles: Frank Belknap Long, "The Desert Lich"

For by death is wrought greater change than hath been shown. Whereas in general the spirit that removed cometh back upon occasion, and is sometimes seen of those in flesh (appearing in the form of the body it bore) yet it hath happened that the veritable body without the spirit hath walked. And it is attested of those encountering who have lived to speak thereon that a lich so raised up hath no natural affection, nor remembrance thereof, but only hate. Also, it is known that some spirits which in life were benign become by death evil altogether.

> Hali (whom God rest), as quoted in Ambrose Bierce,
> "The Death of Halpin Frayser" (1891)

"I will not change souls with that bullet-ridden lich in the madhouse!"

> H. P. Lovecraft, "The Thing on the Doorstep" (1933)

"Behold, it is only the lich of an old man after all, and one that has cheated the worm of his due provender overlong."

> Clark Ashton Smith, "The Death of Malygris" (1933)

Here he lay sleepless, with the curse of Ulua still upon him; for it seemed that the dry, dusty liches of desert tombs reclined at his side; and bony fingers wooed him toward the unfathomable sand-pits from which they had risen.

> Clark Ashton Smith, "The Witchcraft of Ulua" (1933)

The tales they told were both vague and frightful, and were of varying import; some said that this country was a desolation peopled only by the liches of the dead and by loathly phantoms; others, that it was subject to the ghouls and af-rits, who devoured the dead and would suffer no living mortal to trespass upon their dominions; and still others spoke of things all too hideous to be described, and of dire necromancies that prevailed even as the might of emperors doth prevail in more usually ordered lands.

> Clark Ashton Smith, "A Tale of Sir John Maundeville" (1930)

These also they raised up from death; and Mmatmuor bestrode the withered charger; and the two magicians rode on in state, like errant emperors, with a lich and a skeleton to attend them. Other bones and charnel remnants of men and beasts, to which they came anon, were duly resurrected in like fashion; so that they gathered to themselves an ever-swelling train in their progress through Cincor.

Clark Ashton Smith, "The Empire of the Necromancers" (1932)

"If I must battle devils or liches, leave me my hearing and my courage."

Fritz Leiber & Harry Otto Fischer, "The Lords of Quarmall" (1936/1961)

Michael Hayward was a writer—a unique one. Very few writers could create the strange atmosphere of eldritch horror that Hayward put into his fantastic tales of mystery. He had imitators—all great writers have—but none attained the stark and dreadful illusion of reality with which he invested his oftentimes shocking fantasies. He went far beyond the bounds of human experience and familiar superstition, delving into uncanny fields of unearthliness. Blackwood's vampiric elementals, M. R. James' loathsome liches—even the black horror of de Maupassant's "Horla" and Bierce's "Damned Thing"—paled by comparison.

Henry Kuttner, "The Invaders" (1939)

There was a sickening crunch; then dead flesh yielded before my hand as I seized the now faceless lich in my arms and cast it into fragments upon the bone-covered floor.

Robert Bloch, "The Secret in the Tomb" (1934)

"We burned the lich to make sure it would not walk again, and thereafter the folk had peace."

Poul Anderson, "The Tale of Hauk" (1977)

"They stipulate that for every square ell of soil two and one quarter million men have died and laid down their dust, thus creating a dank and ubiquitous mantle of lich-mold, upon which it is sacrilege to walk. The argument has a superficial plausibility, but consider: the dust of one desiccated corpse, spread over a square ell, affords a layer one thirty-third of an inch in depth. The total therefore represents almost one mile of compacted corpse-dust mantling the earth's surface, which is manifestly absurd."

Jack Vance, *The Eyes of the Overworld* (1966)

Tristram was caught in the crowd, borne irresistibly, apples be ripe, through the town, home of a swan, and nuts be brown, and a lexicographer, petticoats up, *Lich* meaning a corpse in Middle English, and trousers down, how inappropriately named—Lichfield—tonight

Anthony Burgess, *The Wanting Seed* (1962)

Kothar was fleeing from the thought of Red Lori, the sorceress who hated him and whom he had imprisoned in the tomb of Kalikalides and sealed therein with solid silver along the edges of the mausoleum door. He had ridden away, leaving her a prisoner with the lich of dead Kalikalides, and Kothar felt vaguely uneasy about the whole thing.

> Gardner F. Fox, Kothar and the Demon Queen (1970)

A vaguely terrible picture was presented to the warily watching Mary Allen, as James Phipps' widow made her way with that half-paralytic gait which seemed to be characteristic of all the Phipps family, between the dark houses under a lich-pale moon.

> Ramsey Campbell, "The Horror from the Bridge" (1964)

Revealed in the torchlight jutted an immense throne of hewn stone, upon which its skeletal king still reposed in sepulchral majesty. In the cool aridity of the cavern, the lich had outlasted centuries. Tatter of desiccated flesh held the skeleton together in leathery articulation.

> Karl Edward Wagner, "Two Suns Setting" (1975)

It was a lich's face—desiccated flesh tight over its skull. Filthy strands of hair were matted over its scalp, tattered lips were drawn away from broken yellowed teeth, and, sunken in their sockets, eyes that should be dead were bright with hideous life.

> Karl Edward Wagner, "Sticks" (1974)

Angobard would have left this dead wit in peace, but he wished neither to share the tomb nor to search the dangerous cliffs in darkness for another. Already the red wolves of the hills were tuning up a chilling antiphony, so over the side went the desiccated lich, but not without a brief prayer to Uaal for its eternal rest.

> Brian McNaughton, "Reunion in Cephalune" (1997)

litten, *ppl.adj.* [< *light*, a pseudo-archaic past participle formed by analogy with bitten, smitten, written, etc.] Lit or lighted. Frequently found in compounds, such as: **amber-litten, aurora-litten, black-litten, blue-litten, crimson-litten, dim-litten, emerald-litten, gas-litten, gray-litten, green-litten, half-litten, moon-litten, morning-litten, phosphor-litten, red-litten, rosy-litten, star-litten, sun-litten, unlitten, violet-litten, yellow-litten**. This pseudo-archaic form was coined by Edgar Allan Poe, who seems, however, to have removed or replaced it in the final versions of most of those texts in which he had used it.

a. Alone:

And therewith he swung merrily into the litten hall.

> William Morris, The Wood Beyond the World (1894)

The Kings of the Nations our Lord hath smitten,
　　His shoe hath He cast o'er the Gods of them,
But a lamp for our feet the Lord hath litten,
　　Wonders hath wrought in the Land of Khem.

H. Rider Haggard & Andrew Lang, The World's Desire (1890)

What surety that thy sons attain
　　The litten council of thy Lords,
　　And thunder of seraphic chords
To music not of Time and Pain?

George Sterling, The Testimony of the Suns (1902)

When, mid the hyacinth deep that girds the sky,
　　You saw, O brother, ere your eyes grew dim,
　　In wrath and loneliness the sight of Him,
Amid his bow'd and litten hierarchy:
Heard songs that fell from lips half-strange with years,
　　Outcast and ruin'd, beautiful in flame,
　　　　You—with the lost among the damnèd few,
　　　　The fallen rebel crew—
　　Hearing the flattery that fawned His name,
Turn'd back to hell a face that shone with tears.

Samuel Loveman, "To Satan" (1923)

Opiate oceans poured there, litten by suns that the eye may never behold and having in their whirlpools strange dolphins and sea-nymphs of unrememberable deeps.

H. P. Lovecraft, "Azathoth" (1922)

Atal was far below, and planning what he should do when he reached to the place, when curiously he noticed that the light had grown strong, as if the cloudless peak and moonlit meeting-place of the gods were very near. And as he scrambled on toward the bulging cliff and litten sky he felt fears more shocking than any he had known before.

H. P. Lovecraft, "The Other Gods" (1921)

As the steps and the passage grew broader, I heard another sound, the thin, whining mockery of a feeble flute; and suddenly there spread out before me the boundless vista of an inner world—a vast fungous shore litten by a belching column of sick greenish flame and washed by a wide oily river that flowed from abysses frightful and unsuspected to join the blackest gulfs of immemorial ocean.

H. P. Lovecraft, "The Festival" (1923)

Then he saw a sort of grey phosphorescence about, and guessed they were coming even to that inner world of subterrene horror of which dim legends tell, and which is litten only by the pale death-fire wherewith reeks the ghoulish air and the primal mists of the pits at earth's core.

H. P. Lovecraft, *The Dream-Quest of Unknown Kadath* (1927)

My hope was well-founded, for within a few minutes I descried a glimmering light through the forest boughs, and came suddenly to an open glade, where, on a gentle eminence, a large building loomed, with several litten windows in the lower story, and a top that was well-nigh indistinguishable against the bulks of driven cloud.

Clark Ashton Smith, "The End of the Story" (1929)

At the end of the hall, we entered a room that was similarly litten, and whose furniture was more than reminiscent of the classic.

Clark Ashton Smith, "The Gorgon" (1930)

Now, in the litten air, a voice began to speak: a voice that was toneless, deliberate—and disembodied.

Clark Ashton Smith, "The Maze of Maal Dweb" (1932)

Both became silent, feeling a sort of awe before the vastness of the cavern-world whose litten corridors reached away on every hand.

Clark Ashton Smith, "Vulthoom" (1933)

To one standing in the ice-bound valley below the observatory, it would have seemed that the tower's litten window was a yellow eye that stared back from the dead earth to that crimson eye of the dead sun.

Clark Ashton Smith, "Phœnix" (1953)

He heard no sound from the evening city; nor could he see aught but close-encroaching darkness beyond the windows that should have gazed on a litten street. Also, it seemed that the stairs had changed and lengthened, giving no more on the courtyard of the tenement, but plunging deviously into an unsuspected region of stifling vaults and foul, dismal, nitrous corridors.

Clark Ashton Smith, "The Last Hieroglyph" (1934)

> In gulfs depressed nor in the gulfs exalted
> Shall shade nor lightening of her flame be found;
> In space that litten orbits gird around,
> Nor in the bottomless abyss unvaulted
> Of unenvironed, all-outlying night.

Clark Ashton Smith, "Lament of the Stars"

b. In compounds, or with modifier:

[. . .]
Bright beings! that ponder,
   With half closing eyes,
On the stars which your wonder
   Hath drawn from the skies,
Till they glance thro' the shade, and
   Come down to your brow
Like—eyes of the maiden
   Who calls on you now—
Arise! from your dreaming
   In violet bowers,
To duty beseeming
   These star-litten hours—
And shake from your tresses
   Encumber'd with dew
The breath of those kisses
   That cumber them too—
(O! how, without you, Love!
   Could angels be blest?)
Those kisses of true love
   That lull'd ye to rest!
Edgar Allan Poe, "Al Aaraaf" (1829)

And travellers within that valley,
   Through the red-litten windows, see
Vast forms that move fantastically
   To a discordant melody;
While, like a rapid ghastly river,
   Through the pale door,
A hideous throng rush out forever,
   And laugh—but smile no more.

      Edgar Allan Poe, "The Haunted Palace" (1839)
[Altered to "encrimsoned" in the latest surviving manuscript version.]

I lingered behind, for the black rift in the green-litten snow was frightful, and I thought I had heard the reverberations of a disquieting wail as my companions vanished; but my power to linger was slight.

      H. P. Lovecraft, "Nyarlathotep" (1920)

And as I ran along the shore, crushing sleeping flowers with heedless feet and maddened ever by the fear of unknown things and the lure of the dead faces, I saw that the garden had no end under that moon; for where by day the walls were, there stretched now only new vistas of trees and paths, flowers and shrubs, stone idols and pagodas, and bendings of the yellow-litten stream past grassy banks and under grotesque bridges of marble.

H. P. Lovecraft, "What the Moon Brings" (1922)

There my eyes dilated again with a wild wonder as great as if I had not just turned from a scene beyond the pale of Nature, for on the ghastly red-litten plain was moving a procession of beings in such a manner as none ever saw before save in nightmares.

H. P. Lovecraft, "The Moon-Bog" (1921)

After that I recall running, spade in hand; a hideous run across moon-litten, mound-marked meadows and through diseased, precipitous abysses of haunted hillside forest; leaping, screaming, panting, bounding toward the terrible Martense mansion.

H. P. Lovecraft, "The Lurking Fear" (1922)

And when I saw on the dim-litten moor a wide nebulous shadow sweeping from mound to mound, I shut my eyes and threw myself face down upon the ground.

H. P. Lovecraft, "The Hound" (1922)

Out they swarmed, from hidden burrow and honeycombed tree, till the whole dim-litten region was alive with them.

H. P. Lovecraft, *The Dream-Quest of Unknown Kadath* (1926–27)

Finally, after an unguessed span of hours or days, the great stone door swung wide again and Carter was shoved down the stairs and out into the red-litten streets of that fearsome city.

H. P. Lovecraft, *The Dream-Quest of Unknown Kadath* (1926–27)

He was now on a dim-litten plain whose sole topographical features were great boulders and the entrances of burrows.

H. P. Lovecraft, *The Dream-Quest of Unknown Kadath* (1926–27)

It made him think of a frightful red-litten city and of the revolting procession that once filed through it; of that, and of an awful climb through lunar countryside beyond, before the rescuing rush of earth's friendly cats.

H. P. Lovecraft, *The Dream-Quest of Unknown Kadath* (1926–27)

But always he succeeded in avoiding discovery, so that in a short time he had found a spot behind a titan pillar whence he could watch the whole green-litten scene of action.

H. P. Lovecraft, *The Dream-Quest of Unknown Kadath* (1926–27)

"You know they were here long before the fabulous epoch of Cthulhu was over, and remember all about sunken R'lyeh when it was above the waters. They've been inside the earth, too—there are openings which human beings know nothing of—some of them in these very Vermont hills—and great worlds of unknown life down there; blue-litten K'n-yan, red-litten Yoth, and black, lightless N'kai. It's from N'kai that frightful Tsathoggua came—you know, the amorphous, toad-like god-creature mentioned in the Pnakotic Manuscripts and the *Necronomicon* and the Commoriom myth-cycle preserved by the Atlantean high-priest Klarkash-Ton.

H. P. Lovecraft, "The Whisperer in Darkness" (1930)

As he bathed and changed clothes he tried to recall what he had dreamed after the scene in the violet-litten space, but nothing definite would crystallize in his mind.

H. P. Lovecraft, "The Dreams in the Witch House" (1932)

Gilman wondered, too, whether he could trust his instinct to take him back to the right part of space. How could he be sure he would not land on that green-litten hillside of a far planet, on the tessellated terrace above the city of tentacled monsters somewhere beyond the galaxy, or in the spiral black vortices of that ultimate void of Chaos wherein reigns the mindless dæmon-sultan Azathoth?

H. P. Lovecraft, "The Dreams in the Witch House" (1932)

About that "interplanetary" idea of mine—it would begin as a dream-phenomenon creeping on the victim in the form of recurrent nightmares, as a result of his concentration of mind on some dim trans-galactic world. Eventually it would enmesh him totally—leaving his body to vegetate in a coma in some madhouse whilst his mind roamed desolate & unbodied for ever above the half-litten stones of an æon-dead civilisation of alien Things on a world that was in decay before the solar system evolved from its primal nebula.

H. P. Lovecraft, letter to Clark Ashton Smith (19 December 1929)

The first real planet to be discovered since 1846, & only the *third* in the history of the human race! One wonders what it is like, & what dim-litten fungi may sprout coldly on its frozen surface! I think I shall suggest its being named *Yuggoth!*

H. P. Lovecraft, letter to Elizabeth Toldridge (1 April 1930)

Beside him, a strange, unearthly being was closing the panel-like door through which he had been drawn from the emerald-litten vault; and beyond this being, there were two others of the same type, one of whom was holding Howard's garments in his arms.

Clark Ashton Smith, "The Immortals of Mercury" (1932)

Here there was no rustling of serpent or lizard, and naught but their own voices and the shuffling of the camels to break the silence that lay upon all things like a mute malediction. Sometimes, on the desiccated tors above them, against the darkly litten sky, they saw the boughs of century-withered cacti, or the boles of trees that immemorial fires had blasted.

Clark Ashton Smith, "The Weaver in the Vault" (1933)

Upon the shadowy heavens half-revealed,
I show their planets turned,
Whose strange ephemeræ,
On adamantine tablets deeply written,
In cities long unlitten,
Have left their history
And lore beyond redemption or surmise.

Clark Ashton Smith, "The Song of a Comet" (1912)

And I see,
In gardens of a crimson-litten world
The sacred flow'r with lips of purple flesh,
And silver-lashed, vermilion-lidded eyes
Of torpid azure; whom his furtive priests
At moonless eve in terror seek to slay,
With bubbling grails of sacrificial blood
That hide a hueless poison.

Clark Ashton Smith, *The Hashish-Eater; or, The Apocalypse of Evil* (1920)

Love, will you look with me
Upon the phosphor-litten labour of the worm—
Time's minister, who toils for his appointed term,
And has for fee
All superannuate loves, and all the loves to be?

Clark Ashton Smith, "Interrogation" (1925)

Love, could we have only found
The forgotten road that runs
Under all the sunken suns
To that time estrangèd ground,
Surely, love were proven there
More than long and lone despair;
Holden and felicitous,
Love were fortunate to us;
And we too might ever dwell,
Deathless and impossible,
In those amber-litten leas,
Circled all with euphrasies.

Clark Ashton Smith, "Fantaisie d'Antan" (1927)

> Wake not, dread ruin that the tides caress,
> Thou weed-grown mass of thronged decaying spires,
> Dim, phosphor-litten with putrescent fires—
> Sleep on, thou whelmed, accurst necropolis!
> Too soon shall from thy cyclopean fane,
> Cthulhu wake to walk the earth again!
>
> Lin Carter, "Lost R'lyeh" in *Dreams from R'lyeh*

> Now, till the light of morning-litten east
> Bids them return to the unbottomed slime,
> Freely they roam the darkling earth a time
> And from fresh grave abominably feast.
>
> Lin Carter, "Spawn of the Black Goat" in *Dreams from R'lyeh*

Down green-litten echo-y hallways we chased hordes of scaly, hooved brutes which, as they fled, deafened us with the trumpetings of their brazen, funiculate mouths.

Michael Shea, *The Mines of Behemoth* (1997)

lotos, *n.* [< L < Gr *lótós*; an etymological spelling of *lotus.*] A lotus.

Titles: Tennyson, "The Lotos-Eaters" (verse)

> And them amongst the wicked Lotos grew,
> Wicked, for holding guilefully away
> *Ulysses* men, whom rapt with sweetenes new,
> Taking to hoste, it quite from him did stay,
> And eke those trees, in whose transformed hew
> The Sunnes sad daughters waylde the rash decay
> Of *Phaeton,* whose limbs with lightening rent,
> They gathering up, with sweete teares did lament.
>
> Edmund Spenser, *Virgils Gnat* (1590)

I avow that that lonesome room—gloomy in its lunar bath of soft perfumed light—shrouded in the sullen voluptuousness of plushy, narcotic-breathing draperies—pervaded by the mysterious spirit of its brooding occupant—grew more and more on my fantasy, till the remembrance had for me all the cool refreshment shed by a midsummer-night's dream in the dewy deeps of some Perrhæbian grove of cornel and lotos and ruby stars of the asphodel.

M. P. Shiel, "The S.S." (1895)

The electric lights were sparkling among the trees, and the new moon shone in the sky above the Lethal Chamber. It was tiresome waiting in the square; I wandered from the Marble Arch to the artillery stables, and back again to the lotos fountain.

Robert W. Chambers, "The Repairer of Reputations" (1895)

"Long have we dreamed in lotos-gardens beyond the West, and spoken only through our dreams; but the time approaches when our voices shall not be silent."

H. P. Lovecraft & Anna Helen Crofts, "Poetry and the Gods" (1920)

"My wealth is in little memories and dreams, and in hopes that I sing in gardens when the moon is tender and the west wind stirs the lotos-buds."

H. P. Lovecraft, "The Quest of Iranon" (1921)

There would be walks, and bridges arching over
Warm lotos-pools reflecting temple eaves,
And cherry trees with delicate boughs and leaves
Against a pink sky where the herons hover.

H. P. Lovecraft, "The Gardens of Yin" in *Fungi from Yuggoth* (1929–30)

Thy body is a secret Eden
Fed with lethean springs,
And the touch of thy flesh of like to the savor of lotos.

Clark Ashton Smith, "A Psalm to the Best Beloved" (1921)

What knowest *thou* of Paradise, where grow
The gardens of the manna-laden myrrh,
And lotos never known to Ulysses,
Whose fruit provides our long and sateless banquet?

Clark Ashton Smith, "The Ghoul and the Seraph" (1919)

His fingers groped toward the girl with strangling motions. "Poison—dope—the black lotos—"

Robert E. Howard, "Lord of the Dead"

lucent, *adj.* Shining, luminous, giving off light; clear, transparent, translucent.

It scarcely seemed possible that the symmetry of tree and lawn and lucent pool could have been one of nature's accidents.

Robert W. Chambers, "The Maker of Moons" (1896)

Methought a fire-mist drap'd with lucent fold
The well-remember'd features of the grove
Whilst whirling ether bore in eddying streams
The hot, unfinish'd stuff of nascent worlds
Hither and thither thro' infinities
Of light and darkness, strangely intermix'd;
Wherein all entity had consciousness,
Without th' accustom'd outward shape of life.

H. P. Lovecraft, "Aletheia Phrikodes" in
"The Poe-et's Nightmare: A Fable" (1916)

He advanced through an interminable nightmare where time prolonged itself upon itself; a vortex of impalpable flame, cold fire of a color unlike any color of earth, reeling miles down a sunken gallery of endless dimensions, floors that swam free in mushroomed space, mockery of lucent green surfaces that closed him in yet opened upon the borderlands to far immensities of hyper-regions beyond comprehension.

Donald Wandrei, *The Web of Easter Island* (1929–31)

The Garden was like a vast, half-sentient entity all around her, pulsing subtly with the pulse of the lucent air. Had God drawn from this immense and throbbing fecundity all the life which peopled Eden?

C. L. Moore, "Fruit of Knowledge" (1940)

Luciferian, Luciferean, *adj.* & *n.* Of, pertaining to, or resembling Lucifer; such an individual.

It was man's face and the face of a fallen angel's in one; Luciferean; imperious; ruthless—and beautiful. Upon its broad brows power was enthroned—power which could have been godlike in beneficence, had it so willed, but which had chosen instead the lot of Satan.

A. Merritt, *The Face in the Abyss* (1923)

There are, in addition, at least two lines of rather more positive evidence; one of which comes through my researches in Danish annals concerning the sorcerer, Axel Holm. Such a person, indeed, left many traces in folklore and written records; and diligent library sessions, plus conferences with various learned Danes, have shed much more light on his evil fame. At present I need say only that the Copenhagen glass-blower—born in 1612—was a notorious Luciferian whose pursuits and final vanishing formed a matter of awed debate over two centuries ago.

Henry S. Whitehead & H. P. Lovecraft, "The Trap" (1931)

A Luciferean butler took my hat, handed me a goblet of cherry brandy.

Robert Bloch, "The Secret of Sebek" (1937)

luctation, *n.* A struggle, effort, endeavor.

He remembered his youthful luctations against poverty, his desire for that wealth and leisure which alone makes possible the pursuit of every chimera; and his slow but accelerative progress when once he had acquired a modicum of capital and had gone into business for himself as an importer of Oriental rugs.

Clark Ashton Smith, "An Offering to the Moon" (1930)

lucubration, *n.* [< *lucubrate*, literally "to work by artificial light"] Nocturnal study and meditation; hence, the resulting literary works, with connotations of over-elaborateness, etc.

Titles: H. P. Lovecraft, "Lovecraftian Lucubrations" (non-fiction)

"What!" exclaimed she; "must I lose, then, my tower! my mutes! my negresses! my mummies! and, worse than all, the laboratory, the favourite resort of my nightly lucubrations, without knowing, at least, if my hare-brained son will complete his adventure? No!"

William Beckford, The History of the Caliph Vathek: An Arabian Tale (1786)

lugubrious, *adj.* Mournful, sorrowful, doleful, dismal, gloomy; in particular, exaggeratedly so.

No reply came in response to his call. Naught followed but a dead silence. . . . that stillness which, in the domain of sounds, usually denotes death. In the presence of a corpse, as in the lugubrious stillness of a tomb, such silence acquires a mysterious power, which strikes the sensitive soul with a nameless terror. . . .

H. P. Blavatsky, "The Ensouled Violin" (1880; ellipses in original)

The booming of the river had everything its own way then: it filled the air with deep murmurs, more musical than the wind noises, but infinitely more monotonous. The wind held many notes, rising, falling, always beating out some sort of great elemental tune; whereas the river's song lay between three notes at most— dull pedal notes, that held a lugubrious quality foreign to the wind, and somehow seemed to me, in my then nervous state, to sound wonderfully well the music of doom.

Algernon Blackwood, "The Willows"

Then came a halt in the gasping, and the dog raised its head in a long, lugubrious howl.

H. P. Lovecraft, "The Dunwich Horror" (1928)

As the organ wheezed into *Beautiful Isle of Somewhere* the Methodist church choir added their lugubrious voices to the gruesome cacophony, and everyone looked piously at Deacon Leavitt—everyone, that is, except crazy Johnny Dow, who kept his eyes glued to the still form beneath the glass of the coffin.

H. P. Lovecraft & Hazel Heald, "The Horror in the Burying-Ground" (1933–35)

lupanar, *n.* [< L *lupānar*] A brothel, bordello, whorehouse.

That they might enjoy death more speedily, the virgins of Miletus strangled themselves with their girdles. At Syracuse the philosopher Hegesias preached so eloquently upon death that men deserted the lupanars to go hang themselves in the fields. The patricians of Rome sought for death as a new form of debauch.

Gustave Flaubert (trans. Lafcadio Hearn), The Temptation of Saint Anthony (1882)

> Or did you while the earthen skiffs dropped down the gray Nilotic flats
> At twilight, and the flickering bats flew round the temple's triple glyphs,
> Steal to the border of the bar and swim across the silent lake

And slink into the vault and make the Pyramid your lúpanar,
Till from each black sarcophagus rose up the painted swathéd dead?

Oscar Wilde, "The Sphinx" (1894)

"Songs of the frantic lupanar delirium of the madhouse. Not extreme wickedness, but the insensate, the unintelligible, the lunatic passion and idea, the desire
that must come from some other sphere that we cannot even faintly imagine.
Look for yourself; it is easy."

Arthur Machen, "Psychology" in *Ornaments of Jade* (1897)

In her loose lusts I find again
The memory of that dream gone by;
Her kisses waken in my brain
The picture of that infamy,
The low dark hill, the storm, the star
That lit my bestial lupanar!

Aleister Crowley, "La Juive" in *White Stains: The Literary Remains of
George Archibald Bishop, A Neuropath of the Second Empire* (1898)

How she gasps and stares about her! How she shivers! Are the hosts
Of her lovers there to haunt her, life's lupanar thick with ghosts?

Aleister Crowley, "The Stone of the Philosophers" in
Konx Om Pax: Essays in Light (1907)

The Pantheon had become a lupanar of divinities that presided over birth, and
whose rites were obscene; an abattoir of gods that presided over death, and
whose worship was gore. To please them was easy. Blood and debauchery was
all that was required.

Edgar Saltus, *Imperial Purple* (1891)

Meanwhile, though the Pantheon was obviously but a lupanar, the people clung
piously to creeds that justified every disorder, tenaciously to gods that sanctified
every vice, and fervently to Cæsars that incarnated them all.

Edgar Saltus, *Historia Amoris: A History of Love Ancient and Modern* (1906)

Keeping as far as we could from the public places, where most of the police
were gathered around taverns and the cheaper lupanars, we circled across Uz-
uldaroum and found, at some distance from Leniqua's fane, a road that ran
countryward.

Clark Ashton Smith, "The Theft of the Thirty-Nine Girdles" (1957)

Without impulses, other than that of an urgent desire for solitude, he turned his
steps toward the suburb, avoiding the neighborhood of taverns and lupanars.

Clark Ashton Smith, "Morthylla" (1952)

lupine, *adj.* Of, pertaining to, or resembling a wolf.

> The eyes turned from my direction to the bed, and gazed gluttonously on the spectral sleeping form there. Then the head tilted back, and from that demon throat came the most shocking ululation I have ever heard; a thick, nauseous, lupine howl that made my heart stand still.
>
> C. M. Eddy, Jr. & H. P. Lovecraft, "The Ghost-Eater" (1923)

lurid, *adj.* [< L *lūridus,* pale < *luror,* pallor] (1) Ghastly pale, gloomy, dismal, wan. (2) Shining or glowing as with the glare of fire seen through a haze of smoke or cloud.

> How wonderful is Death,
> Death and his brother Sleep!
> One, pale as yonder waning moon
> With lips of lurid blue;
> The other, rosy as the morn
> When throned on ocean's wave
> It blushes o'er the world:
> Yet both so passing wonderful!
>
> Percy Bysshe Shelley, *Queen Mab: A Philosophical Poem* (1813)

> The ceiling of cloud was no longer steely gray. It was becoming lurid, tinged with a sinister red which slowly deepened as he looked.
>
> A. Merritt, *The Face in the Abyss* (1923)

> Far off at its end the pillars spread to mark a vast round plaza, and in that open circle there loomed gigantic under the lurid night clouds a pair of monstrous things.
>
> H. P. Lovecraft, *The Dream-Quest of Unknown Kadath* (1926–27)

M

Maelstrom, maelstrom, Maelström, maelström, *pr.n.* & *n.* [< Dutch *mael-strom* (now *maalstroom*), whirlpool < *malen*, to grind + *strom*, stream; in G form *Mahlstrom*.] A famous whirlpool off the coast of Norway; hence, any especially powerful whirlpool or vortex.

Titles: Edgar Allan Poe, "A Descent into the Maelström" (Poe appears to be unique in adding an umlaut to the spelling); August Derleth & Mark Schorer, "Spawn of the Maelstrom"

> Kircher and others imagine that in the centre of the channel of the Maelström is an abyss penetrating the globe, and issuing in some very remote part—the Gulf of Bothnia being somewhat decidedly named in one instance.
>
> Edgar Allan Poe, "A Descent into the Maelström" (1841)

> We came to the fearful hollow where once had wallowed the monsters of the earth: it was indeed, as I had beheld it in my dream, a lovely lake. I gazed into its pellucid depths. A whirlpool had swept out the soil in which the abortions bur-rowed, and at the bottom lay visible the whole horrid brood: a dim greenish light pervaded the crystalline water, and revealed every hideous form beneath it. Coiled in spires, folded in layers, knotted on themselves, or "extended long and large," they weltered in motionless heaps—shapes more fantastic in ghoulish, blasting dismay, than ever wine-sodden brain of exhausted poet fevered into misbeing. He who dived in the swirling Maelstrom saw none to compare with them in horror, tentacular convolutions, tumid bulges, glaring orbs of sepian de-formity, would have looked to him innocence beside such incarnations of hate-fulness—every head the wicked flower that, bursting from an abominable stalk, perfected its evil significance.
>
> George MacDonald, *Lilith: A Romance* (1895)

> The baronet had consumed his vitality in the life-long attempt to sound the too fervid Maelstrom of Oriental research, and his mind had perhaps caught from his studies a tinge of their morbidness, their esotericism, their insanity.
>
> M. P. Shiel, "The Stone of the Edmundsbury Monks" (1895)

> "*No—it wasn't that way at all.* It was everywhere—a gelatin—a slime—yet it had shapes, a thousand shapes of horror beyond all memory. There were eyes—and a blemish. It was the pit—the maelstrom—the ultimate abomination. Carter, *it was the unnamable!*"
>
> H. P. Lovecraft, "The Unnamable" (1923)

On the morning of the 29th Gilman awaked into a maelstrom of horror.

> H. P. Lovecraft, "The Dreams in the Witch House" (1932)

And under a ghastly moon there gleamed sights I can never describe, sights I can never forget; deserts of corpse-like clay and jungles of ruin and decadence where once stretched the populous plains and villages of my native land, and maelstroms of frothing ocean where once rose the mighty temples of my forefathers.

> H. P. Lovecraft & Winifred Virginia Jackson, "The Crawling Chaos" (1920–21)

There was a sense of abysmal falling, a suction as of ineluctable winds, of maelstroms that bore him down through fleet unstable visions of his own past life into antenatal years and dimensions.

> Clark Ashton Smith, "Ubbo-Sathla" (1932)

"I will have a tale," answered the other in a voice which betrayed no emotion, just as his dark face, schooled to immobility, showed no evidence of the maelstrom in his soul.

> Robert E. Howard, "Worms of the Earth" (1930)

Bran leaped into the saddle, wild for the clean heather and the cold blue hills of the north where he could plunge his sword into clean slaughter and his sickened soul into the red maelstrom of battle, and forget the horror which lurked below the fens of the west.

> Robert E. Howard, "Worms of the Earth" (1930)

Then the sands were troubled, and a whirling and dancing of mist-motes blinded the Sindara. Out of the maelstrom the god spoke thinly, and his voice was like the tinkling of countless tiny crystal goblets.

> Henry Kuttner, "The Eater of Souls" (1937)

There was a maelstrom of dust and flying shale on the slope above.

> Henry Kuttner, "Bells of Horror" (1939)

Mænad (*pl.* **Mænades, Mænads**), **Menad** (*pl.* **Menades, Menads**), **Mœnad** (*pl.* **Mœnades, Mœnads**) *n.* A female member of the orgiastic cult of Dionysus or Bacchus; a Bacchante, Bacchanal, Thyiad; a frenzied woman.

> Now down the lines of tasselled pines the yearning whispers wake—
> Pitys of old thy love behold. Come in for Hermes' sake!
> How long since that so-Boston boot with reeling Mænads ran?
> *Numen adest!* Let be the rest. Pipe and we pray, O Pan.
>
> Rudyard Kipling, "Pan in Vermont"

Behold! floating between the long lines of the flame-clad guardians of that hall, attended by her subject gods, her mænads and her maidens, a shape of naked loveliness, came Aphrodite of the Greeks.

H. Rider Haggard, *Wisdom's Daughter: The Life and Love Story of
She-Who-Must-Be-Obeyed* (1923)

> And I rave; and I rape and I rip and I rend
> Everlasting, world without end,
> Mannikin, maiden, mænad, man,
> In the might of Pan.
> Io Pan! Io Pan Pan! Pan! Io Pan!

Aleister Crowley, "Hymn to Pan"

I thought of the mœnads and Bacchus; I saw them through the vivid eyes of
Euripides and Swinburne. And still unsatisfied, I craved for stranger symbols
yet. I became a Witch-Doctor presiding over a cannibal feast, driving the yellow
mob of murderers into a fiercer Comus-rout, as the maddening beat of the tom-
tom and the sinister scream of the bull-roarer destroy every human quality in the
worshippers and make them elemental energies; Valkyrie-vampires surging and
shrieking on the summit of the storm.

Aleister Crowley, *The Diary of a Drug Fiend* (1922)

Our younger generation now glorify fornication, adultery, & sodomy. Next will
come a worship of incest—with brothers & sisters, parents & children, glorying
in a warmer tie now despised by "old-fashioned prejudice"—the frenzied
mænad & the goat of the Sabbat.

H. P. Lovecraft, letter to Donald Wandrei (27 February 1933)

In the music room I found a skirling lecherous theme in the macabre key of B-
minor and accompanied it with corybant arpeggios and drumming chords in an
orgiastic rhythm. And Janet was mad and danced, whirling and leaping and posturing, and singing shrilly and calling, mænad through the dim halls where the
luster of sunset lay a blotch of gangrene on the silence.

Leonard Cline, *The Dark Chamber* (1927)

At twilight, Pan piped across the hills, and reedy notes floated on the wind to
the temple of Aphrodite, and wild melodies from the pagan piper drifted down
the hillsides calling mænad and centaur and satyr, while the trembling maidens
waited.

Donald Wandrei, "Paphos" (1927)

mantic, *adj.* Of or pertaining to divination or prophecy; of or pertaining to a
diviner or prophet; of or pertaining to an act of divining or prophesying; pro-
phetic, sibylline, vatic.

> Unseen, unheard, amid the dell
> Lie all the winds that mantic trees

Have lulled with crystal warlockries
And bound about with Merlin-spell.

> Clark Ashton Smith, "Twilight on the Snow" (1922)

To mantic mutterings, brief and low,
    My palaces shall lift amain,
    My bowers bloom; I will regain
    The lips whereon my lips have lain
In rose-red twilights long ago.

> Clark Ashton Smith, "Song of the Necromancer" (1937)

I noted that his library on occultism had been greatly augmented since his first interest in it, during college. The walls were solidly shelved with books bearing unmistakable earmarks of the mantic arts. The skull on the mantel was a rather affected touch, I thought, though there was a genuine note of weirdness in some of the paintings and tapestries.

> Robert Bloch, "The Brood of Bubastis" (1937)

manticore, mantichore, mantichor, manticora, mantichora, martichora, martichoras, menticore, mantiger, martegre, mantissera, *n.* [< Middle English *manticores* < L *mantichora* < Gr *mantikhóras, martikhóras, martiokhóras* < Old Iranian *martīya-xʷara*, man-eater] A fabulous monster with the body of a lion (sometimes with crocodile scales rather than fur), the tail of a scorpion, the head of a man, two or three rows of teeth, and, sometimes, dragon's wings.

Titles: Clark Ashton Smith, "A Hunter Meets the Martichoras" in "Experiments in Haiku: Strange Miniatures"

The mantycors of the montayns
Myght fede them on thy braynes!

> John Skelton, *Philip Sparrow*

I saw some *Menticores*, a most strange sort of Creatures, which have the Body of a Lyon, red Hair, a Face and Ears like a man's, three Rows of Teeth which close together, as if you join'd your hand with your fingers between each other; they have a Sting in their Tails like a Scorpions, and a very melodious Voice.

> François Rabelais (trans. Sir Thomas Urquhart & Pierre Le Motteux),
> *The Lives, Heroick Deeds, and Sayings of Gargantua and His Son Pantagruel* (1653/1694)

And his horror augments upon beholding:
THE MARTICHORAS
a gigantic red lion, with human face, and three rows of teeth.
    The gleam of my scarlet hair mingles with the reflection of the great sands. I breathe through my nostrils the terror of solitudes. I spit forth plague. I devour armies when they venture into the deserts.

My claws are twisted like screws, my teeth sharpened like saws; and my curving tail bristles with darts which I cast to right and left, before and behind!
    —See! see!

The Martichoras shoots forth the keen bristles of his tail, which irradiate in all directions like a volley of arrows. Drops of blood rain down, spattering upon the foliage.

> Gustave Flaubert (trans. Lafcadio Hearn), *The Temptation of Saint Anthony* (1882)

The beeste Mantichora, whych is as muche as to saye devorer of menne, rennith as I herde tell, on the skirt of the mowntaynes below the snow feldes. These be monstrous bestes, ghastlie and ful of horrour, enemies to mankinde, of a red coloure, with ij rowes of huge grete tethe in their mouthes. It hath the head of a man, his eyen like a ghoot, and the bodie of a lyon lancing owt sharpe prickles fro behinde. And hys tayl is the tail of a scorpioun. And is more delyverer to goo than is fowle to flee. And hys voys is as the roaryng of x lyons.

> Gro, untitled MS., as quoted in E. R. Eddison, *The Worm Ouroboros* (1922)

"Seest thou where the Barriers end in the east against yonder monstrous pyramid of tumbled crags and hanging glaciers that shuts out our prospect east-away? Menksur men call it, but in heaven it hath a more dreadful name: Ela Mantissera, which is to say, the Bed of the Mantichores. O Brandoch Daha, I will climb with thee what unscaled cliff thou list, and I will fight with thee against the most grisfullest beasts that ever grazed by the Tartarian streams. But both these things in one moment of time, that were a rash part and a foolish."

> E. R. Eddison, *The Worm Ouroboros* (1922)

So you've read "Ouroboros"! Didn't you find it magnificently poetic? The "Mercurian" setting was of course a mere surface gesture, the tale itself being preëminently terrestrial, with mediæval wonder as the keynote. Some of the pictures are unforgettable—I can still see Koshtra Pivrarcha towering up snow-clad & mysterious . . . . . and God! Those *Mantichores!* . . . . take 'em away! . . . .

> H. P. Lovecraft, letter to Donald Wandrei
> (27 September 1927) (ellipses as in original)

Through his three rows of teeth
The martichoras roared
Against my broken sword.

> Clark Ashton Smith, "A Hunter Meets the Martichoras" in
> "Experiments in Haiku: Strange Miniatures"

materialize, materialise, *v.intr.* & *v.tr.* To assume or cause to assume a material form; to enter or cause to enter the material plane from another plane, such as the astral or ethereal; to enter or cause to enter the three-dimensional space-time continuum from another dimension or universe.

The Dimensionists were to come in swarms, to materialise, to devour like locusts, to be all the more irresistible because indistinguishable. They were to come like snow in the night: in the morning one would look out and find the world white; they were to come as the gray hairs come, to sap the strength of us as the years sap the strength of the muscles. As to methods, we should be treated as we ourselves treat the inferior races.

> Joseph Conrad & Ford Madox Ford (Ford Madox Hueffer),
> *The Inheritors: An Extravagant Story* (1901)

Too late—cannot help self—black paws materialise—am dragged away toward the cellar. . . .

> H. P. Lovecraft & William Lumley,
> "The Diary of Alonzo Typer" (1935; ellipsis in original)

maunder, *v.intr.* To wonder aimlessly; to speak incoherently and aimlessly.

But just now his mind was in a pitiable state; for he was mumbling wild extravagances about his wife, about black magic, about old Ephraim, and about some revelation which would convince even me. He repeated names which I recognised from bygone browsings in forbidden volumes, and at times made me shudder with a certain thread of mythological consistency—of convincing coherence—which ran through his maundering.

> H. P. Lovecraft, "The Thing on the Doorstep" (1933)

For more than a year rumors had crept snakily out of the black alleys and crumbling doorways behind which the mysterious yellow people moved phantom-like and inscrutable. Scarcely rumors, either; that was a term too concrete and definite to be applied to the maunderings of dope-fiends, the ravings of madmen, the whimpers of dying men—disconnected whispers that died on the midnight wind. Yet through these disjointed mutterings had wound a dread name, fearsomely repeated, in shuddering whispers: "*Erlik Khan!*"

> Robert E. Howard, "Lord of the Dead"

mausolean, *adj.* Of, pertaining to, or resembling a mausoleum.

> Shall augury his goal impart,
>   Or mind his hidden steps retrace
>   To mausolean pits of space
> Where throbs the Hydra's crimson heart?

> George Sterling, *The Testimony of the Suns* (1902)

Over the valley's rim a wan, waning crescent moon peered through the noisome vapours that seemed to emanate from unheard-of catacombs, and by its feeble, wavering beams I could distinguish a repellent array of antique slabs, urns, cenotaphs, and mausolean facades; all crumbling, moss-grown, and moisture-stained, and partly concealed by the gross luxuriance of the unhealthy vegetation.

> H. P. Lovecraft, "The Statement of Randolph Carter" (1919)

At a single step they passed into mausolean silence. Around them the lamplight fell unshaken on caryatids of black marble, on mosaics of precious gems, on fabulous metals and many-stories tapestries; and a tideless perfume weighed upon the air like a balsam of death.

> Clark Ashton Smith, "The Death of Malygris" (1933)

Medusæan, Medusean, Medusian, *adj.* [< L *Medúsæus* < *Medúsa* < Gr *Médousa*] Of, pertaining to, or resembling the gorgon Medusa; petrifying.

For an instant, the supreme evil which Averaud had worshiped so madly, which he had summoned from the vaults of incalculable space, had made him one with itself; and passing, it had left him petrified into an image of its own essence. The form that I touched was harder than marble; and I knew that it would endure to all time as a testimony of the infinite Medusean power that is death and corruption and darkness.

> Clark Ashton Smith, "The Devotee of Evil" (1930)

As he ruminated in growing dread, Carteret and his guide proceeded. Now that he had looked, a Medusian fascination held the man's eyes to the wall.

> Robert Bloch, "Fane of the Black Pharaoh" (1937)

meep, *v.intr., v.tr.,* & *n.* [? onomatopoietic] To communicate in the manner of H. P. Lovecraft's ghouls; the utterance of a ghoul. [Not in *OED*.]

As he pondered he was struck by a flying bone so heavy that it must have been a skull, and therefore realising his nearness to the fateful crag he sent up as best he might that meeping cry which is the call of the ghoul.

> H. P. Lovecraft, *The Dream-Quest of Unknown Kadath* (1926–27)

Javelins began to fly from both sides, and the swelling meeps of the ghouls and the bestial howls of the almost-humans gradually joined the hellish whine of the flutes to form a frantick and indescribable chaos of dæmon cacophony.

> H. P. Lovecraft, *The Dream-Quest of Unknown Kadath* (1926–27)

Memnon, *pr.n.* In Græco-Roman mythology, a demi-god, son of Tithonus and Eos, King of Æthiopia; the statue of Memnon at Thebes in Egypt was said to give forth a musical sound at dawn. [Not in *OED*.]

Titles: Clark Ashton Smith, "Echo of Memnon" (verse), "The Memnons of the Night," "Memnon at Midnight" (verse); Many Wade Wellman, "Memnon" (verse)

> Regal his shape majestic, a vast shade
> In midst of his own brightness, like the bulk
> Of Memnon's image at the set of sun
> To one who travels from the dusking East:
> Sighs, too, as mournful as that Memnon's harp

He utter'd, while his hands contemplative
He press'd together, and in silence stood.

John Keats, Hyperion: A Fragment (1818–19)

Perchance we may listen to some such prophecy as this: There is a land, oh dreamer, on which the sun rises in music, and his rays are heard sounding symphony to the greeting of Memnon.

Fitz Hugh Ludlow, The Hasheesh Eater:
Being Passages from the Life of a Pythagorean (1857)

Still from his chair of porphyry gaunt Memnon strains his lidless eyes
Across the empty land, and cries each yellow morning unto thee.

Oscar Wilde, "The Sphinx" (1894)

He heard, somewhere, the continuous throbbing of a great drum, with desultory bursts of far music, inconceivably sweet, like the tones of an æolian harp. He knew it for the sunrise melody of Memnon's statue, and thought he stood in the Nileside reeds hearing with exalted sense that immortal anthem through the silence of the centuries.

Ambrose Bierce, "The Man and the Snake" (1890)

As the singer ceased, there came a sound in the wind blowing from far Egypt, where at night Aurora mourns by the Nile for her slain son Memnon.

H. P. Lovecraft & Anna Helen Crofts, "Poetry and the Gods" (1920)

Then suddenly above the desert's far rim came the blazing edge of the sun, seen through the tiny sandstorm which was passing away, and in my fevered state I fancied that from some remote depth there came a crash of musical metal to hail the fiery disc as Memnon hails it from the banks of the Nile.

H. P. Lovecraft, "The Nameless City" (1921)

And as the wind died away I was plunged into the ghoul-peopled blackness of earth's bowels; for behind the last of the creatures the great brazen door clanged shut with a deafening peal of metallic music whose reverberations swelled out to the distant world to hail the rising sun as Memnon hails it from the banks of the Nile.

H. P. Lovecraft, "The Nameless City" (1921)

Dark with defeat, gigantically dumb,
Like Memnons morningless, that have survived
The dawn-voiced vibrant sun's last silencing,
The Titans waited.

Clark Ashton Smith, "The Titans in Tartarus" (1912)

Memnonian, *adj.* Of, pertaining to, or resembling Memnon (q.v.).

I remember only the impression of shadowy, flickering space, of a vault that was lost in the azure of infinity, of colossal and Memnonian statues that looked down from Himalaya-like altitudes; and, above all, the dazzling jet of flame that aspired from a pit in the pavement and rose into the air like the visible rapture of gods.

Clark Ashton Smith, "Beyond the Singing Flame" (1931)

Mephistophelian, *adj.* Of, pertaining to, or resembling Mephistopheles.

Professor Gibberne, as many people know, is my neighbour in Folkestone. Unless my memory plays me a trick, his portrait at various ages has already appeared in *The Strand Magazine*—I think late in 1899; but I am unable to look it up because I have lent that volume to some one who has never sent it back. The reader may, perhaps, recall the high forehead and the singularly long black eyebrows that give such a Mephistophelian touch to his face.

H. G. Wells, "The New Accelerator" (1901)

It is not a single voice, but many! * * * Lecherous buzzing of bestial blowflies . . . Satanic humming of libidinous bees . . . sibilant hissing of obscene reptiles . . . a whispering chorus no human throat could sing! It is gaining in volume . . . the room rings with demoniacal chanting; tuneless, toneless, and grotesquely grim . . . a diabolical choir rehearsing unholy litanies . . . pæans of Mephistophelian misery set to music of wailing souls . . . a hideous crescendo of pagan pandemonium * * *

C. M. Eddy, Jr. & H. P. Lovecraft, "Deaf, Dumb, and Blind" (1924; ellipses in original)

mephitic, *adj.* Of or pertaining to mephitis (q.v.); foul-smelling, fœtid, noisome, malodorous.

One disgusting canvas seemed to depict a vast cross-section of Beacon-Hill, with ant-like armies of the mephitic monsters squeezing themselves through burrows that honeycombed the ground.

H. P. Lovecraft, "Pickman's Model" (1926)

Of course there was nothing which can be proved as being outside the order of Nature. The possible causes of such an event are many. No one can speak with certainty of the obscure chemical processes arising in a vast, ancient, ill-aired, and long-deserted building of heterogeneous contents. Mephitic vapours— spontaneous combustion—pressure of gases born of long decay—any one of numberless phenomena might be responsible.

H. P. Lovecraft, "The Haunter of the Dark" (1935)

Mephitic odors as of brimstone and burning flesh had floated across the valley; and even by day, when the noises were silent and the lights no longer flared, a thin haze of hell-blue vapor hung upon the battlements.

Clark Ashton Smith, "The Colossus of Ylourgne" (1932)

Like pygmies lost in some shattered fortalice of the giants, we stumbled onward, strangling in mephitic and metallic vapours, reeling with weariness, dizzy with the heat that emanated everywhere to surge upon us in buffeting waves.

> Clark Ashton Smith, "Beyond the Singing Flame" (1931)

The room was lighted by braziers set in a thousand stations; their glow bathed the enormous burrow with fiery luminance. Captain Carteret, his head reeling from the heat and mephitic miasma of the place, was thus able to see the entire extent of this incredible cavern.

> Robert Bloch, "Fane of the Black Pharaoh" (1937)

"I stayed in that crater all night. I accustomed myself to the mephitic stench."

> John Fowles, *The Magus* (1965)

No, death wasn't the ultimate horror. For, while I had crouched and watched the last living remnants of Innsmouth's abysmal evolution stream out of that shattered portal, I realised with a shock that all of the slippery, sub-human life-forms—*all of them*—were *female* ... If I hadn't escaped that God-forsaken swamp ... oh, Jesus, if those mephitic-ridden [*sic*: mephitis-ridden?] hags had ever taken me alive!

> David Sutton, "Innsmouth Gold" (1994; ellipses in original)

mephitical, *adj.* Mephitic (q.v.).

mephitis, *n.* [< L *mephītis*] A noxious, foul, and offensive exhalation or stench such as that given off by decomposing substances.

But he climbed steadily, pausing only at long intervals to regain his breath as best he could in the dead, mephitis-burdened air.

> Clark Ashton Smith, "The Colossus of Ylourgne" (1932)

mésalliance, mesalliance, *n.* A marriage between individuals of differing social rank or position; a misalliance.

Twelve years after succeeding to his title he married the daughter of his gamekeeper, a person said to be of gypsy extraction, but before his son was born joined the navy as a common sailor, completing the general disgust which his habits and mesalliance had begun.

> H. P. Lovecraft, "Facts Concerning the Late Arthur Jermyn
> and His Family" (1920)

miasma (*pl.* **miasmata, miasmas**), *n.* [< Gr < *miaínein*, to pollute] An atmosphere made noxious and noisome by toxic particles or effluvia.

Johansen and his men landed at a sloping mud-bank on this monstrous Acropolis, and clambered slipperily up over titan oozy blocks which could have been no mortal staircase. The very sun of heaven seemed distorted when viewed through the polarising miasma welling out from this sea-soaked perversion, and twisted menace and suspence lurked leeringly in those crazily elusive angles of carven rock where a second glance shewed concavity after the first shewed convexity.

H. P. Lovecraft, "The Call of Cthulhu" (1926)

A harsh laugh escaped the professor. "Entirely natural phenomena, my boy! There's a mineral deposit under that grotesque slab in the woods; it gives off light and also a miasma that is productive of hallucinations. It's as simple as that."

August Derleth, "The Dweller in Darkness" (1944)

It was as if a miasma of fear had welled up from the cellars far below.

Fritz Leiber, "Thieves' House" (1943)

Slowly I turned, expecting to see a corpse weltering in a miasma of filth, and saw—a man calmly sleeping!

Mearle Prout, "The House of the Worm" (1933)

Involuntarily his glance moved aside, rested on the tombs and monuments that dotted the old graveyard. No one had been buried there for over a century, and the lichen-stained tombstones, with their winged skulls, fat-cheeked cherubs, and funeral urns, seemed to breathe out an indefinable miasma of antiquity.

Henry Kuttner, "The Salem Horror" (1937)

Illinois and Missouri, miasma of mound-building peoples, groveling worship of the Food Source, cruel and ugly festivals, dead-end horror of the Centipede God reaches from Moundville to the lunar deserts of coastal Peru.

William S. Burroughs, *Naked Lunch* (1955–59)

"The hot sun," he mumbled again, half to himself. "And the honeysuckle. Almost a miasma. Nauseating, untinuntil you get used to it. June has suffered in exactly the same way."

Brian Lumley, "Dagon's Bell" (1988)

Or again it could be David's summer "miasma"—an allergy, perhaps.

Brian Lumley, "Dagon's Bell" (1988)

"I thought I had the—the 'miasma'—on the run. *Hah!*" he gave a bitter snort. "A 'summer miasma,' I called it. Blind, blind!"

Brian Lumley, "Dagon's Bell" (1988)

It blew full into my face, jetting up like some noxious, invisible geyser, a pressured stench of time and ocean, darkness and damp, and alien things. And I knew it at once: that tainted odour I had first detected in the summer, which David had naively termed "a miasma."

Brian Lumley, "Dagon's Bell" (1988)

Admittedly, my mind was much disordered by grief and bitterness then, but I was struck by the unwholesomeness of a dank and gloomy house that seemed to exude a thicker miasma than the graveyard around it.

Brian McNaughton, "The Doctor's Tale" (1997)

miasmal, *adj.* Characterized by a miasma (q.v.); miasmatic or miasmic.

The removal of the slab revealed a black aperture, from which rushed an effluence of miasmal gases so nauseous that we started back in horror.

H. P. Lovecraft, "The Statement of Randolph Carter" (1919)

This jungle is a pestilential place—steaming with miasmal vapours. All the lakes look stagnant. In one spot we came upon a trace of Cyclopean ruins which made even the Gallas run past in a wide circle. They say these megaliths are older than man, and that they used to be a haunt or outpost of "The Fishers from Outside"—whatever that means—and of the evil gods Tsadogwa and Clulu.

H. P. Lovecraft & Hazel Heald, "Winged Death" (1933)

During the summer months the smell of shit and coal gas permeated the city, bubbling up from the river's murky depths to cover the oily iridescent surface with miasmal mists. I liked this smell myself, but there was talk of sealing it in and mutters of revolt from the peasantry: "My teenage daughters is cunt deep in shit. Is this the American way of life?"

William S. Burroughs, *Cobble Stone Gardens* (1976)

miasmatic, *adj.* Characterized by miasma (q.v.); miasmal, miasmic.

Even now—now, after years—I thrill intensely to recall the dread remembrance; but to live through it, to breathe daily the mawkish, miasmatic atmosphere, all vapid with the suffocating death—ah, it was terror too deep, nausea too foul, for mortal bearing.

M. P. Shiel, "The S.S." (1895)

miasmic, *adj.* Characterized by miasma (q.v.); miasmal, miasmatic.

My Uncle Asa stood there; from behind him on all sides came an overpowering smell, as of fish or frogs, a thick miasmic odour of stagnant water so powerful that it brought me close to nausea.

August Derleth, "The Sandwin Compact" (1940) in *The Mask of Cthulhu*

Thus horror came to Monk's Hollow. Like a foul breath of corruption from the generations of decadence in which the witch-town had brooded, a miasmic exhalation from the grave of Persis Winthorp lay like an ominous pall over the town.

Henry Kuttner, "The Frog" (1939)

Mi-Go, Migo, *n.* [< Nepalese] The Abominable Snowman of the Himalayas. [Not in *OED*.]

During the Jurassic age the Old Ones met fresh adversity in the form of a new invasion from outer space—this time by half-fungous, half-crustacean creatures from a planet identifiable as the remote and recently discovered Pluto; creatures undoubtedly the same as those figuring in certain whispered hill legends of the north, and remembered in the Himalayas as the Mi-Go, or Abominable Snow-Men.

H. P. Lovecraft, *At the Mountains of Madness* (1931)

By the way, though strange as it may seem, I did *not* invent the Mi-go or Abominable Snow Men. This is genuine Nepalese folklore surrounding the Himalayas, and I picked it up in most unscholarly fashion from the newspaper and magazine articles exploiting one or another of the attempts on Mt. Everest.

H. P. Lovecraft, letter to Fritz Leiber (18 November 1936)

"Yeti," of course, is only a convenient term; the proper scientific nomenclature is *Gigantanthropus correctus*. They have been called many names, in many cultures: *Sisimite* (Guatemala), *Almas* (Central Asia), *Dzu-Teh* (Indonesia and Szechwan), *Didi* and *Mapinquary* (S. America), *Mi-Go* (Lovecraft) and *Mangani* (Tarzan). *Yeti* is what the Nepalese of the Himalayas call them, and we find it more dignified than the epithet, "Abominable Snowman," or the Native American *Sasquatch* (literally, "Raping Demon"). We especially resent the popular racist term "Bigfoot," which is not even particularly accurate.

The SubGenius Foundation, *Revelation X* (1994)

Miltonic, *adj.* Of or pertaining to John Milton or his works; in particular, to *Paradise Lost*, and hence, hellish or infernal; Miltonian.

In another instant I was knocked from my gruesome bench by the devilish threshing of some unseen entity of titanic size but undetermined nature; knocked sprawling on the root-clutched mould of that abhorrent graveyard, while from the tomb came such a stifled uproar of gasping and whirring that my fancy peopled the rayless gloom with Miltonic legions of the misshapen damned.

H. P. Lovecraft, "The Unnamable" (1923)

minuscule, *n.* A letter in a small, lower-case cursive script derived from the uncial (q.v.).

Then there were the mysteries and coincidences of the Orne and Hutchinson letters, and the problem of the Curwen penmanship and of what the detectives brought to light about Dr. Allen; these things, and the terrible message in mediæval minuscules found in Willet's pocket when he gained consciousness after his shocking experience.

H. P. Lovecraft, *The Case of Charles Dexter Ward* (1927)

mole, *n.* An artificial structure serving as a pier or breakwater.

In about a week the desiderate ship put in by the black mole and tall lighthouse, and Carter was glad to see that she was a barque of wholesome men, with pointed sides and yellow lateen sails and a grey captain in silken robes.

H. P. Lovecraft, The Dream-Quest of Unknown Kadath (1926–27)

moonquake, *n.* [< *moon* + earth*quake*] An earthquake-like tremor of the moon's surface. [Smith antedates *OED* by 20 years.]

> And I read
> Upon the tongue of a forgotten sphinx,
> The annulling word a spiteful demon wrote
> In gall of slain chimeras; and I know
> What pentacles the lunar wizards use,
> That once allured the gulf-returning roc,
> With ten great wings of furlèd storm, to pause
> Midmost an alabaster mount; and there,
> With boulder-weighted webs of dragons' gut
> Uplift by cranes a captive giant built,
> They wound the monstrous, moonquake-throbbing bird,
> And plucked from off his saber-taloned feet
> Uranian sapphires fast in frozen blood,
> And amethysts from Mars.

Clark Ashton Smith, The Hashish-Eater; or, The Apocalypse of Evil (1920)

moonstruck, moon-struck, *ppl. adj.* Insane, crazed, mad, as though under the influence of the moon.

> Immediately a place
> Before his eyes appear'd, sad, noisome, dark,
> A Lazar-house it seem'd, wherein were laid
> Numbers of all diseas'd, all maladies
> Of ghastly Spasm, or racking torture, qualms
> Of heart-sick Agony, all feverous kinds,
> Convulsions, Epilepsies, fierce Catarrhs,
> Intestine Stone and Ulcer, Colic pangs,
> Dæmoniac Frenzy, moping Melancholy
> And Moon-struck madness, pining Atrophy,
> Marasmus, and wide-wasting Pestilence,
> Dropsies, and Asthmas, and Joint-racking Rheums.

John Milton, Paradise Lost (1667)

> O Hunter, snare me his shadow!
>   O Nightingale, catch me his strain!
> Else moonstruck with music and madness
>   I track him in vain!

Oscar Wilde, "In the Forest"

—Hark to the fellow! . . But riddle me this, now, in the name of Œdipus! who wants to hear about your moonstruck theories?

> John Charteris, *Ashtaroth's Lackey*, as quoted in
> James Branch Cabell, *Beyond Life: Dizain des Démiurges* (1919; ellipsis as in original)

"They say that I am moonstruck," Demetrios answered; "but I will tell you a secret. There is a wisdom lies beyond the moon, and it is because of this that the stars are glad and admirable."

> James Branch Cabell, *Domnei: A Comedy of Woman Worship* (1910–12)

"No woman likes playing second fiddle, even in the moonstruck brain of a poet."

> James Branch Cabell, *Something About Eve: A Comedy of Fig-Leaves* (1927)

"There ought to be some excuse for offering a new drink—though it won't take much planning to fool those moonstruck nincompoops."

> H. P. Lovecraft & Hazel Heald, "The Man of Stone" (1932)

> This is the hour when moonstruck poets know
> What fungi sprout in Yuggoth, and what scents
> And tints of flowers fill Nithon's continents,
> Such as in no poor earthly garden blow.

> H. P. Lovecraft, "Star-Winds" in *Fungi from Yuggoth* (1929–30)

Children will always be afraid of the dark, and men with minds sensitive to hereditary impulse will always tremble at the thought of the hidden and fathomless worlds of strange life which may pulsate in the gulfs beyond the stars, or press hideously upon our own globe in unholy dimensions which only the dead and the moonstruck can glimpse.

> H. P. Lovecraft, "Supernatural Horror in Literature" (1925–27)

> Leave them to enchantment where you left them lingering
>   Moonstruck, voiceless, yet their sorceress-eyes agleam,
>   Waiting, watching till I come and join them where,
>   Lost amid their dreamlands, you captured phantoms dream.

> Donald Wandrei, "On Some Drawings" (1928)

"Madam, I was as moonstruck as Quixote on that occasion."

> Robert Anton Wilson, *The Widow's Son* (1985)

Mormo, *pr.n.* [< Gr, *Mormô*] An appellation of Hecate, goddess of witchcraft. [Not in *OED*.]

The worship of Hecate, the moon, sender of midnight phantoms, lent itself especially to the magicians rites, as may be seen from this formula to evoke her: "O friend and companion of night, thou who rejoicest in the baying of dogs and spilt blood, who wanderest in the midst of shades among the tombs, who longest for blood and bringest terror to mortals, Gorgo, Mormo, thousand-faced moon, look favorably on our sacrifices!"

Sir Edward Burnett Tylor, "Magic" in the Encyclopædia Britannica
(9th edition; 1875–1889)

Hecate in vengeance sent spectres and ghostly phantoms which filled men's hearts with hideous fear and drove them to madness and despair. These were the [epōpídes], the silent watchers of the night. Other of her train were the [Empoúsai] (Empusas), monstrous hobgoblins with the feet of donkeys, who might, on a sudden, take a thousand forms to scare belated travellers; the [Kerkōpis] (Cercopis), a poltergeist, who haunted four crossways; and, the most dreaded of all, [Mormó] (Mormo), a foul and loathly ghoul.

Montague Summers, The Geography of Witchcraft (1926)

Probably the invocation which Eusebius omitted, is that we find in the *Philosophumena* of S. Hippolytus. "Come, infernal, terrestrial, and heavenly Bombo, goddess of the broad roadways, of the cross-road, thou who goest to and fro at night, torch in hand, enemy of the day, friend and lover of darkness, thou who dost rejoice when the bitches are howling and warm blood is spilled, thou who art walking amid the phantom and in the place of tombs, thou whose thirst is blood, thou who dost strike chill fear into mortal heart, Gorgo, Mormo, Moon of a thousand forms, cast a propitious eye upon our sacrifice."

Montague Summers, The Geography of Witchcraft (1926)

Manuel cried aloud: "Now be propitious, infernal, terrestrial and celestial Bombo! Lady of highways, patroness of crossroads, thou who bearest the light! Thou who dost labor always in obscurity, thou enemy of the day, thou friend and companion of darkness! Thou rejoicing in the barking of dogs and in shed blood, thus do I honor thee."

Manuel did as Helmas had directed, and for an instant the screamings were pitiable, but the fire ended these speedily.

Then Manuel cried, again: "O thou who wanderest amid shadows and over tombs, and dost tether even the strong sea! O whimsical sister of the blighting sun, and fickle mistress of old death! O Gorgo, Mormo, lady of a thousand forms and qualities! now view with a propitious eye my sacrifice!"

James Branch Cabell, Figures of Earth: A Comedy of Appearances (1920)

INVOCATION—The words used by Manuel to call Freydis forth from the fire are those of an old invocation to Hecate, a moon goddess who possessed all the attributes of the ancient and medieval witches. The spell was uttered in a grove of laurel boughs, at the time of the full moon, over a small statue of the root of the wild rue anointed with a paste made of myrrh, storax, incense, and the crushed bodies of lizards. It would seem that Mr. Cabell has made some slight changes in the words of the invocation, but these do not in the least change its sense. Bombo, Gorgo, and Mormo occur in the original invocation and are obviously appellations of Hecate.

John Philips Cranwell & James P. Cover, *Notes on* Figures of Earth (1929)

Then, too, he did not relish the Greek inscription on the wall above the pulpit; an ancient incantation which he had once stumbled upon in Dublin college days, and which read, literally translated,

"O friend and companion of night, thou who rejoicest in the baying of dogs and spilt blood, who wanderest in the midst of shades among the tombs, who longest for blood and bringest terror to mortals, Gorgo, Mormo, thousand-faced moon, look favorably on our sacrifices!"

H. P. Lovecraft, "The Horror at Red Hook" (1925)

Vaguely he was conscious of chanted horrors and shocking croakings afar off. Now and then a wail or whine of ceremonial devotion would float to him through the black arcade, whilst eventually there rose the dreadful Greek incantation whose text he had read above the pulpit of that dance-hall church.

"O friend and companion of night, thou who rejoicest in the baying of dogs (*here a hideous howl burst forth*) and spilt blood (*here nameless sounds vied with morbid shriekings*), who wanderest in the midst of shades among the tombs (*here a whistling sigh occurred*), who longest for blood and bringest terror to mortals (*short, sharp cries from myriad throats*), Gorgo (*repeated as response*), Mormo (*repeated with ecstasy*), thousand-faced moon (*sighs and flute notes*), look favourably on our sacrifices!"

H. P. Lovecraft, "The Horror at Red Hook" (1925)

"Every god and entity has had its worshippers, from black Pharol to the least of the Aliens whose powers are more than human. And these cults intermingle in a very curious way, so that we find traces of a forgotten worship cropping up in far later times. When the Romans worshipped the Magna Mater in Italy's dark forests, for instance, why do you suppose they incorporated into their ritual the mystic adoration, 'Gorgo, Mormo, *thousand-faced* moon'? The implication is clear."

Henry Kuttner, "Hydra" (1939)

O friend and companion of night thou who rejoiceth in the baying of dogs and spilt blood, ye who wandereth in ye midst of shades among ye tombs, who longeth for blood and who bringeth terror to mortals, Hastur and Mormo, thousand-faced moon, look with favour on our sacrifices.

The Sussex Manuscript (*Cultus Maleficarum*), as given by Fred L. Pelton (1946)

Then, to Leakey's horror, the crowd began: "Astarte—Ashtaroth—Magna Mater . . . *Ia! Shub-Niggurath!* Gorgo, Mormo, thousand-faced moon, look favorably on our sacrifices . . . Ram with a Thousand Ewes, fill us with thy seed that more may come to worship at thy shrine . . . *Gof'nn hupadgh Shub-Niggurath . . .*"

Ramsey Campbell, "The Moon-Lens" (1964; ellipses in original)

MORMO—(*Greek*) King of the Ghouls, consort of Hecate.

Anton Szandor LaVey (Howard Stanton Levey), *The Satanic Bible* (1969)
[Perhaps LaVey misunderstood Montague Summers' *The Geography of Witchcraft*.]

O friend and companion of the Night, thou who rejoicest in the bayings of dogs and spilt blood, who wanderest amidst the shades, among the tombs, who longest for blood and bringest terror to mortals: Gorgo, Mormo, Thousand-faced Moon—Look favorably upon our sacrifices.

Michael A. Aquino (& Mohammed), "The Celebration of Death"

Morphean, *adj.* [< L < Gr, *morphé,* form, shape] Of or pertaining to Morpheus, god of dreams; of or pertaining to dreams or sleep.

"One never seems, in fact, to use one's mouth,—you never actually eat anything, you may also notice, in dreams, even though food is very often at hand. I suppose it is because all dream food is akin to the pomegranates Persephone, so that if you taste it you cannot ever return again to the workaday world. . . . But why, I wonder, are we having the same dream?—it rather savors of Morphean parsimony, don't you think, thus to make one nightmare serve for two people?"

James Branch Cabell, *The Cream of the Jest: A Comedy of Evasion*
(1911–15; ellipsis in origin.)

To parallel your Morphean achievement of last Sunday, I can cite my own performance of last night—when, gorged with a Thansgiving feast of the utmost peril to my 140-lb. standard, I was overcome by drowsiness at 5 p.m., & continued in a somnolent state till ten this morning! My dreams occasionally approach'd the phantastical in character, tho' falling somewhat short of coherence.

H. P. Lovecraft, letter to Donald Wandrei (24 November 1927)

mortuary, *adj.* [< L *mortuārius*] Of or pertaining to the dead or to the burial of the dead.

Sophie and others who saw the body were most startled by its utter lifelikeness, and the mortuary virtuoso made doubly sure of his job by repeating certain injections at stated intervals.

H. P. Lovecraft & Hazel Heald, "The Horror in the Burying-Ground" (1933–35)

And now, with what would seem to an outsider the acme of gruesome unconscious comedy, the whole funeral mummery of the afternoon was listlessly repeated. Again the organ wheezed, again the choir screeched and scraped, again a droning incantation arose, and again the morbidly curious spectators filed past a macabre object—this time a dual array of mortuary repose.

H. P. Lovecraft & Hazel Heald, "The Horror in the Burying-Ground" (1933–35)

The leather was greasy and blackened as if from long years of mortuary use.

Clark Ashton Smith, "The Charnel God" (1932)

All around him the mortuary silence seemed to burn and quiver with a thousand memories of Ilalotha, together with those expectations to which he had given as yet no formal image. . . .

> Clark Ashton Smith, "The Death of Ilalotha" (1937; ellipsis in original)

No one save a sorcerer would have access to the ancient manuscripts bound in Ethiopian skin, or burn such rich and aphrodisiac incense in an enshrined skull. Who else would fill the mercifully cloaking darkness of the room with curious relics, mortuary souvenirs from ravished graves, or worm-demolished scrolls of primal dread?

> Robert Bloch, "The Suicide in the Study" (1935)

Musæan, *adj.* Of, pertaining to, or resembling the fifth-century Greek poet Musæus, author of a poem concerning Hero and Leander. [Not in *OED*.]

Before the laurel-draped mouth of the Corycian cave sat in a row six noble forms with the aspect of mortals, but the countenances of Gods. These the dreamer recognised from images of them which she had beheld, and she knew they were none else than the divine Mæonides, the Avernian Dante, the more than mortal Shakespeare, the chaos-exploring Milton, the cosmic Goethe, and the Musæan Keats.

> H. P. Lovecraft & Anna Helen Crofts, "Poetry and the Gods" (1920)

Mussulman (*pl.* **Mussulmans, Mussulmen**), *n.* A Muslim, Moslem.

Usage: Considering that this word is etymologically unrelated to the English word "man," the plural "Mussulmans" should be preferred over "Mussulmen."

The Duc knew it to be a ruby; but from it there poured a light so intense, so still, so terrible, Persia never worshipped such—Gheber never imagined such—Mussulman never dreamed such when, drugged with opium, he has tottered to a bed of poppies, his back to the flowers, and his face to the God Apollo.

> Edgar Allan Poe, "The Duc de L'Omelette" (1832)

At one time, I formed a juvenile collection of Oriental pottery and objets d'art, announcing myself as a devout Mussulman and assuming the pseudonym of "Abdul Alhazred".

> H. P. Lovecraft, "A Confession of Unfaith" (1922)

mythos (*pl.* **mythoi, mythos**), *n.* [< Gr *mŷthos*, story] A myth or system of mythology.

Professor Max Müller, Cox, Gubernatis, and other propounders of the Solar Mythos, have portrayed the primitive myth-maker for us as a sort of German-ised-Hindu metaphysician, projecting his own shadow on a mental mist, and talking ingeniously concerning smoke, or, at least, *cloud;* the sky overhead becoming like the dome of dreamland, scribbled over with the imagery of aboriginal nightmares!

Gerald Massey, "Luniolatry, Ancient and Modern" (1887)

This is a very correct exposition of the lunar-mythos from its astronomical aspect. Selenography, however, is the least esoteric of the divisions of lunar Symbology. To master thoroughly—if one is permitted to coin a new word—*Selenognosis*, one must become proficient in more than its astronomical meaning.

H. P. Blavatsky, *The Secret Doctrine:*
The Synthesis of Science, Religion, and Philosophy (1888)

Hoary "superstitions," such as the fairy-like Atlantis of Plato, the *Garden of Hesperides*, Atlas supporting the world on his shoulders, all of them mythoi connected with the peak of Teneriffe, did not go far with sceptical Science.

H. P. Blavatsky, *The Secret Doctrine:*
The Synthesis of Science, Religion, and Philosophy (1888)

The Greek mythos just alluded to a few pages back, namely the mutilation of *Uranos* by his son *Kronos* in the Greek theogony, is an allusion to this theft by the Son of the Earth and Heavens of the *divine creative fire*.

H. P. Blavatsky, note to *The Secret Doctrine: The Synthesis of Science,*
Religion, and Philosophy (1888)

Did they all symbolise the same experience? Or, were there two experiences, one supernal, and the other, if not infernal, as in Tannhäuser, then at least, dubious, suspect, perilous? All the legends in their essence, no doubt, were pre-Christian: might one take it that those in which the implied experience was held up to reprobation were the stories which had come under the review of the Church; while the Mabinogion mythos (for example) had, for one reason or another, escaped ecclesiastical censure, coming down to us in its original form with its original feeling?

Arthur Machen, *The Green Round* (1932)

With the origin and the occult meaning of the folklore of Poictesme this book at least is in no wise concerned: its unambitious aim has been merely to familiarize English readers with the Jurgen epos for the tale's sake. And this tale of old years is one which, by rare fortune, can be given to English readers almost unabridged, in view of the singular delicacy and pure-mindedness of the Jurgen mythos: in all, not more than a half-dozen deletions have seemed expedient (and have been duly indicated) in order to remove such sparse and unimportant outcroppings of mediæval frankness as might conceivably offend the squeamish.

James Branch Cabell, *Jurgen: A Comedy of Justice* (1919)

Both legends, however (as they have been collated by Professor Afanyakof, of the University of Sorram, in the seven volumes of his somewhat superficial *Smire Mythos*), unite here.

Branch Cabell, *Smire: An Acceptance in the Third Person* (1936)

As to the varying references to the mythos in different tales, I wonder if these weren't designed to suggest the diverse developments and interpretations of old myths and deities that spring up over great periods of time and in variant races and civilizations? I have, intentionally, done something of the sort in my own myth-creation.

Clark Ashton Smith, letter to August Derleth (28 April 1937)

As to the Lovecraft mythos, probably he had no intention or desire of reducing it to a consistent and fully worked out system, but used it according to varying impulse and inspiration. The best way, it seems to me, is to enjoy each tale separately and without trying to link it closely with all the others.

Clark Ashton Smith, letter to August Derleth (13 May 1937)

As for parallelisms between the Cthulhu Mythos and my own cycles, I haven't been able to find that there is really enough for an article, since Laney has now covered my main additions to the Lovecraft Mythology. In common with other weird tales writers, I have the Necronomicon in more than one of my yarns, and have made a few passing references (often under slightly altered names, such as Iog-Sotot for Yog-Sothoth and Kthulhut for Cthulhu) to some of the Lovecraftian deities. My Hyperborean tales, it seems to me, with their primordial, prehuman and sometimes pre-mundane background and figures, are the closest to the Cthulhu Mythos, but most of them are written in a vein of grotesque humor that differentiates them vastly. However, such a tale as "The Coming of the White Worm" might be regarded as a direct contribution to the Mythos. My tales of Averoigne, it seems to me, are all thoroughly medieval in spirit; but two of them, "The Holiness of Azédarac" and "The Beast of Averoigne," contain suggestions drawn from the Lovecraftian cosmos. Offhand, I would say that there is even less correspondence between the Lovecraft Mythos and my main cycle, that of Zothique. But perhaps someone else could trace parallels.

Clark Ashton Smith, letter to August Derleth (26 July 1944)

"But the perils and agonies of withdrawal from the hard drugs have been vastly exaggerated—it's part of the mythos. I learned that when I was a paramedical worker in the great days of the Haight-Ashbury, before I became a nurse, running around and giving Thorazine to hippies who'd O.D.'d or thought they had."

Fritz Leiber, *Our Lady of Darkness* (1977)

The brown face creased into a grimace of laughter. "I'm afraid you're a victim of the same fantasy-projections as poor Blake and your friend Lovecraft. Everyone knows that Nyarlathotep is pure invention—part of the Lovecraft mythos."

> Robert Bloch, "The Shadow from the Steeple" (1950)

As I pressed deeper into the dark mythos which surrounds those terrors from beyond—bloated Cthulhu, indescribable Shub-Niggurath, vast batrachian Dagon—I might have been sucked into the whirlpool of absolute belief, had my engrossment not been interrupted by the librarian, bearing an armful of yellowed volumes.

> Ramsey Campbell, "The Room in the Castle" (1964)

"Oh, yes! I've heard of that pulp-magazine scribbler! Wrote for a penny a word—or less! Lovelock or Lovecrop—or something like that. That whole so-called Mythos is a rambling, rubbish-filled fabrication! Not a word of truth to it!"

> Joseph Payne Brennan, "The Feaster from Afar" (1975)

And this seems as good a place as any to explain precisely what we mean by this term "the Cthulhu Mythos." In the first place, the word *mythos* does not exactly belong to the English language. Neither is it a neologism, a coined word. *Mythos* is Greek and can mean "myth, fable, tale, talk, speech," or so my Webster's Collegiate informs me.

In discussing a certain body of interconnected stories by H. P. Lovecraft and other writers, we use the word in a special sense, which might be defined as: "a corpus of fictitious narratives which share as their common background a system of invented lore."

> Lin Carter, *Lovecraft: A Look Behind the Cthulhu Mythos* (1971)

Eventually, my sense of cult and mythos tells me, Bill [Clinton] himself will surpass mere kings and join the legendary Roman emperors—Caligula, Tiberius, Commdus, et al.—or stand beside the bawdiest tales in the Finn Mac Cool cycle. Hell, give it 3000 years, and with the usual corrosions of time, archeologists will be found in violent dispute over whether certain ithyphallic statues represent Osiris, Priapus, or Our Own Bill; only carbon dating will settle these arguments.

> Robert Anton Wilson, *TSOG: The Thing That Ate the Constitution and
> Other Everyday Monsters* (2002)

N

Naacal, *n.* According to the works of James Churchward, the priestly caste of the lost continent Mu, which sank in the Pacific Ocean some 12,000 years ago. The Naacals colonized Burma, and moved on to India and Tibet, where they left clay tablets, copied from originals in Mu or Burma, which describe the special creation of the human race, in Hindu and Buddhist monasteries, and onward to Egypt, where Moses copied the story. In the Cthulhu Mythos, the language of Mu, in which the Naacal tablets are written; Churchward calls this the Naga-Maya language. [Not in *OED*.]

> The Naacal tablets are written with the Naga symbols and characters—and, legend says, were written in the Motherland and first brought to Burma and then to India. Their extreme age is attested to by the fact that history says the Naacals left Burma more than 15,000 years ago.
>
> James Churchward, *The Lost Continent of Mu* (1931)

> At the commencement of our studies my priestly friend informed me that it would be impossible to decipher ancient tablets and inscriptions without knowledge of what he called the Naga-Maya language; as all of the ancient writing that have to do with Mu are in this language; and as all Naacal writings have an esoteric or hidden meaning, known only to the Naacals and to those whom they taught. To this hidden language he held the key, and, after he had taught me its use, it proved a sesame that unlocked for me many strange doors.
>
> James Churchward, *The Lost Continent of Mu* (1931)

> In two very old Naacal tablets, one of which is in India and the other in Tibet, it is stated that man first appeared on earth in the Land of Mu about 200,000 years ago; and in other Naacal writings it would appear that his religious teaching was not long delayed after his arrival; but, how long was long?
>
> James Churchward, *The Lost Continent of Mu* (1931)

> His career had been a strange and lonely one, and there were those who inferred from his curious novels many episodes more bizarre than any in his recorded history. His association with Harley Warren, the South Carolina mystic whose studies in the primal Naacal language of the Himalayan priests had led to such outrageous conclusions, had been close.
>
> H. P. Lovecraft & E. Hoffmann Price,
> "Through the Gates of the Silver Key" (1932–33)

"No, I have not been able to make anything of the parchment. Mr. Phillips, here, also gives it up. Col. Churchward declares it is not Naacal, and it looks nothing at all like the hieroglyphs on that Easter Island wooden club.

H. P. Lovecraft & E. Hoffmann Price,
"Through the Gates of the Silver Key" (1932–33)

The Naacal tablets and other works that have come down from Mu are the creation of these men, not of the original "gods."

Colin Wilson, "The Return of the Lloigor" (1969)

Naiad (*pl.* **Naiades, Naiads**), **Naïad, Naïd** (*pl.* **Naïds**), **Naïs** (*pl.* **Naïdes**), *n.* & *adj.* In Græco-Roman mythology, the nymphs of rivers, lakes, and springs.

Titles: Thomas Lovell Beddoes, "Song of the Stygian Naiades"

> Then thus the goddess of the skies bespake,
> With sighs and tears, the goddess of the lake,
> King Turnus' sister, once a lovely maid,
> Ere to the lust of lawless Jove betray'd:
> Compress'd by force, but, by the grateful god,
> Now made the Naïs of the neighb'ring flood.
>
> Virgil (trans. John Dryden), *Æneid*

Grimm's Fairy Tales were my delight until at the age of seven I chanced upon Hawthorne's Wonder Book and Tanglewood Tales. Then and there began an undying passion for classical mythology, which was soon increased by Bulfinch's Age of Fable. All the world became ancient Greece to me; I looked for Naiades in the fountain on the lawn, and forebore to break the shrubbery for fear of harming the Dryades.

H. P. Lovecraft, letter to Maurice Moe (1 January 1915)

> What desert naiads, amorous,
> Have drawn me to their sunken strand!
> How many a desert succubus
> Has clasped me on her couch of sand!
> What liches foul, with breast nor face,
> Have seemed to bear thy beauty's grace!
>
> Clark Ashton Smith, "The Outer Land" (1935)

natron, *n.* A crystallized salt of hydrous sodium carbonate, $Na_2CO_3 \cdot 10H_2O$.

Obviously I ought not to walk at random, and perhaps retreat directly from the entrance I sought; so I paused to note the direction of the cold, fœtid, natron-scented air-current which I had never ceased to feel.

H. P. Lovecraft & Harry Houdini, "Under the Pyramids" (1924)

There was, it seemed, no reasonable explanation for the vanishing of the mummies, in whose preservation the powerful spices of the Orient had been employed, together with natron, rendering them virtually incorruptible.

Clark Ashton Smith, "The Weaver in the Vault" (1933)

Lycanthropic sights were revealed as Malcolm hacked away the case-coverings. The stench of natron hung like a miasma above the violated sarcophagi of creatures with human heads and the mummified bodies of apes. There was a hoofed horror with vestigial remnants of a tail, and a Ganesha-like thing with the enormous trunk of an elephant. Some of those we saw were evidently failures: noseless, eyeless, faceless freaks with extra arms; and finally an awful corpse without limbs, whose swollen neck grew into a gaping, headless maw.

Robert Bloch, "The Brood of Bubastis" (1937)

necrophage (*pl.* **necrophagi**), *n.* An eater of the dead. [Not in *OED*.]

> I saw the stretching marshy shore,
> And the foul things those marshes bore:
> Lizards and snakes convuls'd and dying;
> Ravens and vampires putrefying;
> All these, and hov'ring o'er the dead,
> Necrophagi that on them fed.

H. P. Lovecraft, "The Nightmare Lake" (1919)

"It's some sort of necrophage."
"A what?"
"It only eats dead things," Geo explained.

Samuel Delany, *The Jewels of Aptor* (1962)

necrophagous, *adj.* Feeding on corpses or carrion, carrion-eating.

I heard it, and knew no more. Heard it as I sat petrified in that unknown cemetery in the hollow, amidst the crumbling stones and the falling tombs, the rank vegetation and the miasmal vapours. Heard it well up from the innermost depths of that damnable open sepulchre as I watched amorphous, necrophagous shadows dance beneath an accursed waning moon.

H. P. Lovecraft, "The Statement of Randolph Carter" (1919)

I notice that many of the efjeh-weeds on the plain are reaching out necrophagous feelers toward the thing; but I doubt if any are long enough to reach it.

H. P. Lovecraft & Kenneth Sterling, "In the Walls of Eryx" (1936)

necrophile, *n.* One morbidly attracted to corpses; a necrophiliac, a necrophilist.

Art always has a suspicion to fight against; always some poor mad Max Nordau is handy to call everything outside the kitchen the asylum. Here, however, there is a substratum of truth. Consider the intolerable long roll of names, all tainted with glorious madness. Baudelaire the diabolist, debauchee of sadism, whose dreams are nightmares, and whose waking hours delirium; Rollinat the necrophile, the poet of phthisis, the anxiomaniac; Péladan, the high priest—of nonsense; Mendès, frivolous and scoffing sensualist; besides a host of others, most alike in this, that, below the cloak of madness and depravity, the true heart of genius burns. No more terrible period than this is to be found in literature; so many great minds, of which hardly one comes to fruition; such seeds of genius, such a harvest of —whirlwind! Even a barren waste of sea is less saddening than one strewn with wreckage.

> Aleister Crowley, Preface to *White Stains: The Literary Remains of George Archibald Bishop, A Neuropath of the Second Empire* (1898)

necrophilic, *adj.* Of, pertaining to, or characterized by necrophilism or necrophily.

> Thine eyes, Valerian, are full
>   Of sights and sounds of outer space,
> Abomination beautiful,
>   The dark star's necrophilic race.
>
> Donald Wandrei, "Valerian" (1928)

A green sun was crawling over the horizon and bathing him in its necrophilic glare.

> Donald Wandrei, *The Web of Easter Island* (1929–31)

necrophilism, *n.* Necrophilia, the practice of engaging in sexual intercourse with a corpse.

They accorded worship to the Elder One who is known to myth as Nyarlathotep, the "Mighty Messenger." This abominable deity was said to confer wizard's power upon receiving human sacrifices; and while the evil priests reigned supreme they temporarily transformed the religion of Egypt into a bloody shambles. With anthropomancy and necrophilism they sought terrible boons from their demons.

> Robert Bloch, "Fane of the Black Pharaoh" (1937)

necrophilist, *n.* One morbidly attracted to corpses; a necrophiliac, a necrophile.

necrophily, *n.* Necrophilia, the practice of engaging in sexual intercourse with a corpse.

For these quartos dealt with no romantic nonsense such as the phantasms with which novels vitiate the intelligence and the morals of their readers, as Gerald observed with approval. They dealt with really worth-while ethnographic matters like the marriage customs of all lands, and the ways of male and female prostitution among the different races, and with the history, in each country, of pæderasty, and of lesbianism, and of bestiality, and of necrophily, and of incest, and of sodomy, and of onanism, and of all manifestations of the sexual impulse in every era.

> James Branch Cabell, *Something About Eve: A Comedy of Fig-Leaves* (1927)

But I must give over these remarks, for I must take a nap against the afternoon; when (tho' 'tis devilish cold) I am pledg'd to visit my son Eddy in East-Province, and help him with his newest fiction, a pleasing and morbid study in hysterical necrophily, intitul'd *The Lov'd Dead.* . . .

> H. P. Lovecraft, letter to James F. Morton (28 October 1923); ellipsis in original

necropolis (*pl.* **necropoli, necropoles, necropoliseis, necropolises**), **necropole,** *n.* [< Gr *nekrós*, corpse, dead person + *pólis*, city] A cemetery or grave-yard; in particular, one that is large and elaborate.

> Yet, as in some necropolis you find
>> Perchance one mourner to a thousand dead,
> So there: worn faces that look deaf and blind
>> Like tragic masks of stone.
>
> James Thomson, "The City of Dreadful Night" (1870–74)

There is no correct English plural of "necropolis";—the French word *nécropole* is more normal. As the Greek plural could not be used very euphoniously, and as I have tried throughout to render an exact English equivalent for each French word whenever comprehensible, I beg indulgence for the illegitimate plural "necropoli," used to signify more than one necropolis, as an equivalent for the French *nécropoles.*

> Lafcadio Hearn, Addendum to Théophile Gautier,
> "One of Cleopatra's Nights" (1882)

That was to be our climax, and for the present we concentrated on the mediæval Saracenic glories of the Caliphs whose magnificent tomb-mosques form a glittering faery necropolis on the edge of the Arabian Desert.

> H. P. Lovecraft & Harry Houdini, "Under the Pyramids" (1924)

A woman, he wept for the bygone dead in necropoli long-crumbled; an antique wizard, he muttered the rude spells of earlier sorcery; a priest of some pre-human god, he wielded the sacrificial knife in cave-temples of pillared basalt.

> Clark Ashton Smith, "Ubbo-Sathla" (1932)

Gaining the flat expansive ground of the summit, where dwarfish dying yews disputed with leafless briars the intervals of slabs blotched with lichen, he recalled the tale that Famurza had mentioned, anent the lamia who was said to haunt the necropolis. Famurza, he knew well, was no believer in such legendry, and had meant only to mock his funereal mood.

> Clark Ashton Smith, "Morthylla" (1952)

> A waif of day, I wandered beneath stars
> That seemed the unnumbered steely eyes of Death
> Seeking the lost necropoles.
>
> Clark Ashton Smith, "In the Desert"

It might even be that the possessors of these innumerous bones, when the clothing of mortality still enveloped them in far off gulfs of time forgotten, had deliberately entered the subterranean necropolis by way of the four-dimensional seal, not by accident but by compulsion, and their flesh, their intelligence, their life-identity dissolved and transmitted by unknown force to a dimension of time-space-life remote from us, yet possibly quite near at hand under the laws of that hyper-universe, that hyper-space, that hyper-time.

Donald Wandrei, *The Web of Easter Island* (1929–31)

He had not stopped at this corroboration of his visions. Some nights ago he had gone farther. He had entered the necropolis and found the niche in the wall; descended the stairs and come upon—*the rest.*

Robert Bloch, "The Grinning Ghoul" (1936)

necropolitan, *adj.* Of, pertaining to, or resembling a necropolis (q.v.).

That hand! It was hideously cold, and it was crushing me; it was the cold and cramping of the sarcophagus . . . the chill and constriction of unrememberable Egypt. . . . It was nighted, necropolitan Egypt itself . . . that yellow paw . . . and they whisper such things of Khephren. . . .

H. P. Lovecraft & Harry Houdini, "Under the Pyramids"
(1924; ellipses in original)

nefandous, *adj.* [< L *nefandus* < *ne-*, not + *fandus,* gerundive of *fārī,* to speak] Unspeakable, unutterable, infandous.

Also the Dæmon belched forth most horrid and nefandous Blasphemies, exalting himself above the most High.

Increase Mather, *An Essay for the Recording of Illustrious Providences* (1684;
aka *Remarkable Providences*)

Suppose a Man to be suspected for Murder, or for committing a Rape, or the like nefandous Wickedness, if he does freely confess the Accusation, that's ground enough to Condemn him.

Increase Mather, *Cases of Conscience Concerning Evil Spirits Personating Men; Witchcrafts,
Infallible Proofs of Guilt in Such as Are Accused with That Crime: All Considered According
to Scriptures, History, Experience, and the Judgment of Many Learned Men* (1693)

On *Dec.* 17. her Tongue being drawn out of her mouth to an extraordinary Length, a *Dæmon* began manifestly to speak in her; for many Words were distinctly utter'd, wherein are the *Labial Letters,* without any motion of her Lips at all: Words also were utter'd from her Throat sometimes when her mouth was wholly shut; and sometimes Words were utter'd when her mouth was wide open; but no Organs of Speech us'd therein. The chief things that the *Dæmon* spoke, were horrid Railings against the Godly *Minister* of the Town; but sometimes he likewise belch'd out most nefandous Blasphemies against the God of Heaven.

Cotton Mather, *Magnalia Christi Americana; or,
The Ecclesiastical History of New England from Its First Planting* (1701)

Only the bricks of the chimney, the stones of the cellar, some mineral and metallic litter here and there, and the rim of that nefandous well.

> H. P. Lovecraft, "The Colour out of Space" (1927)

It had only horror, because I knew unerringly the monstrous, nefandous analogy that had suggested it.

> H. P. Lovecraft, *At the Mountains of Madness* (1931)

From a legal view-point, this doubly nefandous malefactor was now twice-dead.

> Clark Ashton Smith, "The Testament of Athammaus" (1931)

And Sir Roderick Hagdonne was now deemed a moste infamous warlocke, and hys Ladye Elinore a nefandous witche.

> untitled volume, as quoted in
> Clark Ashton Smith, "The Necromantic Tale" (1930)

> Black Lord of bale and fear, master of all confusion!
> By thee, thy prophet saith,
> New power is given to wizards after death,
> And witches in corruption draw forbidden breath
> And weave such wild enchantment and illusion
> As none but lamiæ may use;
> And through thy grace the charneled corpses lose
> Their horror, and nefandous loves are lighted
> In noisome vaults long nighted;
> And vampires make their sacrifice to thee—
> Disgorging blood as if great urns had poured
> Their bright vermilion hoard
> About the washed and welting sarcophagi.

> "Ludar's Litany to Thasaidon", in
> Clark Ashton Smith, "The Death of Ilalotha" (1937)

Conscience smote him as he did the deed. Black, agonizing waves of guilt washed through his mind, telling him this was a crime beyond forgiveness, a nefandous action from which the universe turned aside in loathing.

> Fritz Leiber, *Gather, Darkness!* (1943)

"Because they were hypocrites," Finkle-McGraw said, after igniting his calabash and shooting a few tremendous fountains of smoke into the air, "the Victorians were despised in the late twentieth century. Many of the persons who held such opinions were, of course, guilty of the most nefandous conduct themselves, and yet saw no paradox in holding such views because they were not hypocrites themselves—they took no moral stancees and lived by none."

> Neal Stephenson, *The Diamond Age* (1995)

Nemesis (*pl.* **Nemeses**), **nemesis**, *pr.n.* & *n.* In Græco-Roman mythology, the goddess of divine justice and retribution; hence, any source of continuing opposition.

Titles: H. P. Lovecraft, "Nemesis" (verse)

> "Tonight I go as a Nemesis bearing just and blazingly cataclysmic vengeance. Watch in the sky close by the *Dæmon-Star*."
>
> > H. P. Lovecraft, "Beyond the Wall of Sleep" (1919)

> Down unlit and illimitable corridors of eldritch phantasy sweeps the black, shapeless Nemesis that drives me to self-annihilation.
>
> > H. P. Lovecraft, "The Hound" (1922)

> His was an Odyssey that took all time and all space for its province, with the stars for witness and the nebulæ as monitors, and Nemesis always at hand in the shape of a wandering comet or a lone asteroid; a labyrinthine plunge through abysms and chasms of night, of stars, of unplumbed wastes and unknown dangers beyond.
>
> > Donald Wandrei, "A Race through Time" (1933)

nepenthe, nepenthes, *n.* [< L *nēpenthes* < Gr *nēpenthés* (*phármakon*), grief-banishing (drug)] In Græco-Roman mythology, a drug that relieves suffering, sorrow, and grief, given to Telemachus by Helen of Troy in Homer's *Odyssey*.

Titles: George Darley, *Nepenthe* (verse); Samuel Loveman, "Nepenthe" (verse)

> Nepenthe is a drinck of souerayne grace,
> > Deuized by the Gods, for to asswage
> > Harts grief, and bitter gall away to chace,
> > Which stirs vp anguish and contentious rage:
> > In stead thereof sweet peace and quiet age
> > It doth establish in the troubled mynd.
> > Few men, but such as sober are and sage,
> > Are by the Gods to drinck thereof assynd;
> But such as drinck, eternall happinesse do fynd.
>
> > Edmund Spenser, *The Faërie Queene* (159-)

> And first behold this cordial Julep here
> That flames, and dances in his crystal bounds
> With spirits of balm, and fragrant Syrops mixt.
> Not that Nepenthes which the wife of Thone,
> In Egypt gave to Jove-born Helena
> Is of such power to stir up joy as this,
> To life so friendly, or so cool to thirst.
>
> > John Milton, *Comus (A Masque Presented at Ludlow Castle, 1634)*

Here was a panacea—a [*pharmakon népenthes*] for all human woes: here was the secret of happiness, about which philosophers had disputed for so many ages, at once discovered: happiness might now be bought for a penny, and carried in the waistcoat pocket: portable ecstasies might be had corked up in a pint bottle: and peace of mind could be sent down in gallons by the mail coach.

> Thomas De Quincey, *Confessions of an English Opium-Eater:*
> *Being an Extract from the Life of a Scholar* (1821)

Then, methought, the air grew denser, perfumed from an unseen censer
Swung by seraphim whose foot-falls tinkled on the tufted floor.
"Wretch," I cried, "thy God hath lent thee—by these angels he hath sent thee
Respite—respite and nepenthe from thy memories of Lenore;
Quaff, oh quaff this kind nepenthe and forget this lost Lenore!"
    Quoth the Raven "Nevermore."

> Edgar Allan Poe, "The Raven" (1844)

But in the cosmos there is balm as well as bitterness, and that balm is nepenthe.

> H. P. Lovecraft, "The Outsider" (1921)

Though we distill
Quintessences of hemlock or nepenthe,
We cannot slay the small, the subtle serpents,
Whose mother is the lamia Melancholy
That feeds upon our breath and sucks our veins,
Stifling us with her velvet volumes.

> Clark Ashton Smith, "Soliloquy in an Ebon Tower" (1951)

nepenthean, *adj.* Of, pertaining to, or resembling nepenthe (q.v.).

Watching the tardy portents of slow change
Prolonged unnotably through changeless days,
I walk in solitude
Where memories return
That die not with a single season's leaves
But still delay the blind nepenthean doom,
And gather stranger hues
Than these that clothe the tree
Or fold the autumnal earth.

> Clark Ashton Smith, "Hesperian Fall" (1951)

nephalotë, *n.* [?< portmanteau of *nephalo-*, cloud + *camalote*] A fantastical flower. [Not in *OED*.]

It was in the pale gardens of Zais,
The mist-shrouded gardens of Zais,

Where blossoms the white nephalotë,
The redolent herald of midnight.

H. P. Lovecraft, "Nathicana"

night-gaunt, nightgaunt, night gaunt, *n.* A fabulous creature inhabiting the Dreamlands of H. P. Lovecraft. [Not in *OED*.]

Titles: H. P. Lovecraft, "Night-Gaunts" in *Fungi from Yuggoth* (verse); Brett Rutherford, *Night Gaunts: An Entertainment Based on the Life and Writings of H. P. Lovecraft* (play)

The captain was not even sure that any person now living had beheld that carven face, for the wrong side of Ngranek is very difficult and barren and sinister, and there are rumours of caves near the peak wherein dwell the night-gaunts. But the captain did not wish to say just what a night-gaunt might be like, since such cattle are known to haunt most persistently the dreams of those who think too often of them.

H. P. Lovecraft, *The Dream-Quest of Unknown Kadath* (1926–27)

Ngranek was a hard mountain with only an accursed valley behind it, and besides, one could never depend on the certainty that night-gaunts are altogether fabulous.

H. P. Lovecraft, *The Dream-Quest of Unknown Kadath* (1927)

No one ever found what the night-gaunts took, though those beasts themselves were so uncertain as to be almost fabulous.

H. P. Lovecraft, *The Dream-Quest of Unknown Kadath* (1927)

In spite of himself his memory began reconstructing the utterly non-human blasphemies that lurked in the obscurer corners, and these lumpish hybrid growths oozed and wriggled toward him as though hunting him down in a circle. Black Tsathoggua moulded itself from a toad-like gargoyle to a long, sinuous line with hundreds of rudimentary feet, and a lean, rubbery night-gaunt spread its wings as if to advance and smother the watcher. Jones braced himself to keep from screaming. He knew he was reverting to the traditional terrors of his childhood, and resolved to use his adult reason to keep the phantoms at bay.

H. P. Lovecraft & Hazel Heald, "The Horror in the Museum" (1932)

I began to have nightmares of the most hideous description, peopled with *things* which I called "night-gaunts"—a compound word of my own coinage. I used to draw them after waking (perhaps the idea of these figures came from an edition de luxe of *Paradise Lost* with illustrations by Doré, which I discovered one day in the east parlour). In dreams they were wont to whirl me through space at a sickening rate of speed, the while fretting & impelling me with their detestable tridents.

H. P. Lovecraft, letter to Reinhardt Kleiner (16 November 1916)

Actual nightmares, though, were another story. We still have one or two per year—though even the worst is pallid beside the real 1896 product. I invented the name of *Night-Gaunts* for the Things I dreamed of in '96 and '97.

H. P. Lovecraft, letter to M. F. Bonner (4 May 1936)

When I was 6 or 7 I used to be tormented constantly with a peculiar type of re-current nightmare in which a monstrous race of entities (called by me "Night-Gaunts"—I don't know where I got hold of the name) used to snatch me up by the stomach (bad digestion?) and carry me off through infinite leagues of black air over the towers of dead and horrible cities. They would finally get me into a grey void where I could see the needlelike pinnacles of enormous mountains miles below. Then they would let drop—and as I gained momentum in my Icarus-like plunge I would start awake in such a panic that I hated to think of sleeping again. The "night-gaunts" were black, lean, rubbery things with bared, barbed tails, batwings, and *no faces at all*. Undoubtedly I derived the image from the jumbled memory of Doré's drawings (largely the illustrations to *Paradise Lost*) which fascinated me in waking hours. They had no voices, and their only form of real torture was their habit of tickling my stomach (digestion again) before snatching me up and swooping away with me. I sometimes had the vague no-tion that they lived in the black burrows honeycombing the pinnacle of some incredibly high mountain somewhere. They seemed to come in flocks of 25 or 50, and would sometimes fling me one to the other.

H. P. Lovecraft, letter to Virgil Finlay (24 October 1936)

As unmoved by this prodigy as by the thunder-stroke, Fafhrd bellowed above the storm toward the doorway, his voice sounding tiny to himself in his thun-der-smitten ears, "Hear me, witch, wizard, nightgaunt, whatever you are!"

Fritz Leiber, "The Circle Curse" (1969)

These were the grisly night-gaunts that he beheld in dreams; these were ghouls.

Robert Bloch, "The Grinning Ghoul" (1936)

And the night-gaunts shall ride, and, crouching at their talons, the great hounds lie a-waiting to leap forth into the world.

Anton Szandor LaVey (Howard Stanton Levey),
"Die elektrischen Vorspiele" in *The Satanic Rituals* (1972)

O dark one, who rideth the winds of the Abyss and cryeth the night gaunts be-tween the living and the dead, send to us the Old One of the World of Horrors, whose word we honor unto the end of the deathless sleep. Hail, Nyarlathotep.

Anton Szandor LaVey (Howard Stanton Levey),
["Ceremony of the Nine Angles" in *The Satanic Rituals* (1972)
[Michael A. Aquino actually wrote the ritual. LaVey altered Aquino's "hounds" (referring to Frank Belknap Long's "The Hounds of Tindalos"; Aquino uses "Ty'h nzal's" as Yuggothic equivalent of "Tindalos") to "night gaunts".]

I nearly reached India, said the Imaginary Mongoose. It was made of olive skin drifting down a windy hall past troglodytes, dwarfs, cavemen, night-gaunts, crabs, giant sunflowers, ticktockticktock trembling.

Robert Anton Wilson, *Masks of the Illuminati* (1981)

"I saw three men on nightgaunts . . . that name sprang into my brain as if placed there."

Gary Gygax, *Artifact of Evil* (1986; ellipsis in original)

Nilotic, *adj.* Of or pertaining to the river Nile in Egypt; Egyptian.

I was stared at, hooted at, grinned at, chattered at by monkeys, by parrakeets, by cockatoos. I ran into pagodas and was fixed for centuries at the summit or in secret rooms; I was the idol; I was the priest; I was worshiped; I was sacrificed. I fled from the wrath of Brahma through all the forests of Asia; Vishnu hated me; Siva laid wait for me. I came suddenly upon Isis and Osiris; I had done a deed, they said, which the ibis and the crocodile trembled at. I was buried, for a thousand years, in stone coffins, with mummies and sphinxes, in narrow chambers at the heart of eternal pyramids. I was kissed, with cancerous kisses, by crocodiles and laid, confounded with all unutterable slimy things, amongst reeds and Nilotic mud.

Thomas De Quincey, *Confessions of an English Opium-Eater:
Being an Extract from the Life of a Scholar* (1821)

I shrieked with terror, and Professor Gregg came running; and as I pointed to Cradock, the boy with one convulsive shudder fell face forward, and lay on the wet earth, his body writhing like a wounded blind worm, and an inconceivable babble of sounds bursting and rattling and hissing from his lips. He seemed to pour forth an infamous jargon, with words, or what seemed words, that might have belonged to a tongue dead since untold ages, and buried deep beneath Nilotic mud, or in the inmost recesses of the Mexican forest.

Arthur Machen, "Novel of the Black Seal" in
The Three Impostors; or, The Transmutations (1895)

> Yet is there more, whereat none guesseth, love!
>   Upon the ending of my deadly night
> (Whereof thou hast not the surmise, and slight
> Is all that any mortal knows thereof),
>   Thou wert to me that earnest of day's light,
> When, like the back of a gold-mailèd saurian
>   Heaving its slow length from Nilotic slime,
> The first long gleaming fissure runs Aurorian
> Athwart the yet dun firmament of prime.

Francis Thompson, *Sister Songs* (1895)

It was then that the smile of the Sphinx vaguely displeased us, and made us wonder about the legends of subterranean passages beneath the monstrous creature, leading down, down, to depths none might dare hint at—depths connected with mysteries older than the dynastic Egypt we excavate, and having a sinister relation to the persistence of abnormal, animal-headed gods in the ancient Nilotic pantheon.

H. P. Lovecraft & Harry Houdini, "Under the Pyramids" (1924)

Nis, *pr.n.* ? [Not in *OED*.]

It is called the valley Nis.
And a Syriac tale there is
Thereabout which Time hath said
Shall not be interpreted.
Something about Satan's dart—
Something about angel wings—
Much about a broken heart—
All about unhappy things:
But "the valley Nis" at best
Means "the valley of unrest."

Edgar Allan Poe, "The Valley Nis" (1831)
[Subsequently re-titled "The Valley of Unrest" and all references to Nis omitted.]

Sometimes, in the throes of a nightmare when unseen powers whirl one over the roofs of strange dead cities toward the grinning chasm of Nis, it is a relief and even a delight to shriek wildly and throw oneself voluntarily along with the hideous vortex of dream-doom into whatever bottomless gulf may yawn.

H. P. Lovecraft, "The Lurking Fear" (1922)

In the valley of Nis the accursed waning moon shines thinly, tearing a path for its light with feeble horns through the lethal foliage of a great upas-tree.

H. P. Lovecraft, "Memory" (1919)

A large body of taste opposes absolutely the use of coined names as applied to strange things & places—thus outlawing my *Yuggoth, Thok, Nithon,* etc., along with Machen's *Voorish domes* & *Aklo letters,* & Poe's *Yaanek, Nis, Auber,* etc.

H. P. Lovecraft, letter to Harold Farnese (22 September 1932)

Here he broke off into a rambling discourse of obscure secret myths, with frequent allusions to such shadows of antique lore as fabled Leng, lightless N'ken, and demon-haunted Nis; spoke too of such blasphemies as the Moon Yiggurath and the secret parable of Byagoona the Faceless One.

Robert Bloch, "The Grinning Ghoul" (1936)

Bloch's failure to develop any of his own invented gods beyond a mere mention or two may, after all, have been deliberate. He had this trick of tossing into his Mythos stories otherwise unexplained and never followed-up-on, fragments of lore. These fascinate a student of the Mythos such as I am—I wish to Karneter I knew what they mean! References to fragments of lore like the Feast of Ulder, the thirteenth covenant, the Moon of Yiggurath, the Soul Chant of Sebek, the Legend of the Elder Saboth, demon-haunted Nis, and the secret parable of Byagoona the Faceless One. I'd love to know what those things were supposed to mean. . . .

> Lin Carter, "Demon-Dreaded Lore: Robert Bloch's Contribution to the Cthulhu My-
> thos", in Robert Bloch, *Mysteries of the Worm* (1981; ellipsis in original)

noctuary, *n.* A record of happenings of the night; a nightly journal, as distinct from a diary.

Titles: Thomas Ligotti, *Noctuary*

"When we had proceeded for a considerable time, (at least so it appeared to me, for minutes are hours in the *noctuary* of terror,—terror has no *diary*), this passage became so narrow and so low, that I could proceed no farther, and wondered how my companion could have advanced beyond me."

> Charles Maturin, *Melmoth the Wanderer: A Tale* (1820)

Nodens, Nodons, Nudens, *pr.n.* [see quotation from Puhvel] In Celtic mythology, a deity pertaining to healing, hunting, and the sea. Roman ruins found in Lydney Park, Gloucestershire, dating from the fourth century CE, include a number of votive tablets bearing well-known inscriptions to this deity. Based on his appearance in H. P. Lovecraft's "The Strange High House in the Mist" and *The Dream-Quest of Unknown Kadath*, August Derleth made Nodens into the head of his pantheon of benignant Elder Gods. [Not in *OED*.]

Titles: J. R. R. Tolkien, "The Name 'Nodens'" in *Report on the Excavation of the Prehistoric, Roman, and Post-Roman Sites in Lydney Park, Gloucestershire* (1932)

Dr. McCaul quotes from a letter from Meyrick to Lysons that "Deus Nodens seems to be Romanised British, which correctly written in the original language would be Deus Noddyns, the 'God of the abyss,' or it may be 'God the preserver,' from the verb *noddi*, to preserve; both words being derived from *nawdd*, which signifies protection." Prof. Jarrett, a profound Celtic scholar, to whom I applied for a translation of "Deus Noddyns" without mentioning Meyrick's explanation, at once rendered it as "God of the deeps," a sense that every circumstance confirms.

> *Roman Antiquities at Lydney Park, Gloucestershire:*
> *Being a Posthumous Work of the Rev. William Hiley Bathurst, M.A.* (1879)

The name of the god, as given in the inscriptions, varies between Nudons and Nodens, the cases actually occurring being the dative Nodonti, Nodenti, and Nudente, and the genitive Nodentis, so I should regard $\bar{o}$ or $\bar{u}$ as optional in the first syllable, and o as preferable, perhaps, to e in the second, for there is no room for reasonably doubting that we have here to do with the same name as Irish *Nuadu*, genitive *Nuadat*, conspicuous in the legendary history of Ireland.

> John Rhŷs, *Celtic Folklore: Welsh and Manx* (1901)

Underlying the stories of Nūadu (genitive Nūadat) and Lug and that of Lludd and Lleuelys we may thus discern a Celtic myth of Lugus bringing relief to Nō-dons; the latter is attested in dedications from Lydney (cf. Lludd!) in Gloucester-shire bordering South Wales (*Deo Nodonti*) and seems to mean 'Fisher' (cf. Gothic *nuta* 'fisherman', from *nudōn[*s*]), the probable ancestor of the Arthurian "Fisher King" of the Grail legend, whose maiming resulted in the Waste Land.

Jaan Puhvel, Comparative Mythology (1987; brackets in original)

After I had seen most of the sculptured stones, the coffins, rings, coins, and frag-ments of tessellated pavement which the place contains, I was shown a small square pillar of white stone, which had been recently discovered in the wood of which I have been speaking, and, as I found on inquiry, in that open space where the Roman road broadens out. On one side of the pillar was an inscription, of which I took a note. Some of the letters have been defaced, but I do not think there can be any doubt as to those which I supply. The inscription is as follows:

devomnodent*i*

fla*v*ivssenilispossv*it*

propternvp*tias*

*qua*sviditsvbvmb*ra*

"To the great god Nodens (the god of the Great Deep or Abyss) Flavius Senilis has erected this pillar on account of the marriage which he saw beneath the shade."

Arthur Machen, "The Great God Pan" (1890)

Down the valley in the distance was Caerleon-on-Usk; over the hill, somewhere in the lower slopes of the forest, Caerwent, also a Roman city, was buried in the earth, and gave up now and again strange relics—fragments of the temple of "Nodens, god of the depths."

Arthur Machen, Far Off Things (1922)

"By Nodens," said Caswallon drily, "your prayer was granted. Tros—"

Talbot Mundy, Tros of Samothrace: Lud of Lunden (1925)

A sea-god of the Britons, later confused with Neptune by the Romans.

Talbot Mundy, note to Tros of Samothrace: Lud of Lunden (1925)

Trident-bearing Neptune was there, and sportive tritons and fantastic nereids, and upon dolphins' backs was balanced a vast crenulate shell wherein rode the grey and awful form of primal Nodens, Lord of the Great Abyss.

H. P. Lovecraft, "The Strange High House in the Mist" (1926)

He spoke, too, of the things he had learnt concerning night-gaunts from the fres-coes in the windowless monastery of the high-priest not to be described; how even the Great Ones fear them, and how their ruler is not the crawling chaos Nyarlathotep at all, but hoary and immemorial Nodens, Lord of the Great Abyss.

H. P. Lovecraft, *The Dream-Quest of Unknown Kadath* (1927)

And with his hideous escort he had half hoped to defy even the Other Gods if need were, knowing as he did that ghouls have no masters, and that night-gaunts own not Nyarlathotep but only archaick Nodens for their lord.

H. P. Lovecraft, *The Dream-Quest of Unknown Kadath* (1927)

> Dear, shall I pray the gulf's great deity,
> Nodens, to bring once more for you and me
> Some love-relinquished hour we could not save
> That westered all too swiftly to the wave,
> Ebbing between the cypress and the grass?

Clark Ashton Smith, "Sea Cycle"

Double doors of green bronze stood open against the wall, and portrayed in high relief the primal allegory of Nodens, the Lord of the Great Abyss: an anthropomorphic god with a beard of tentacles, now hunting winged octopi with a trident, now enthroned in a scallop shell.

Gary Myers & Marc Laidlaw, "The Summons of Nuguth-Yug" (1981)

I come upon a granite pillar. At first I make it for a tombstone, but a tombstone wouldn't be here on the site of an ancient landfill. I flashlight it to read the inscription.

Three parallel inscriptions (shades of Rosetta). Latin, English, and (maybe) Iroquois. English one says:

> I ERECT THIS PILLAR TO THE
> GREAT GOD NODENS
> ON ACCOUNT OF THE MARRIAGE I SEE
> UNDER THE SHADE.

The dog whimpers and backs away. Straight from a B movie. In the shade of the pillar some mushrooms grow. Golden yellow caps, white gills, about seven inches tall. *Pantheria amanita.* Deadly fly agaric. Panthers of the night of the Gods.

Don Webb, "Metamorphosis No. 40" in *Uncle Ovid's Exercise Book* (1988)

The magician commenced to walk around the central hearth, emptying his mind of distracting thoughts and images while reciting an invocation in the secret priestly tongue of the British: *"Coblyanau inniskea baile medb Nodens, Pwyll gwawl connla ballysadare airmid."*

Richard Tierney & Glenn Rahman, *The Gardens of Lucullus* (2001)

noisome, *adj.* Noxious, foul-smelling, stinky, fœtid.

[Tatifart:] A noisome giant, whom Anus, King of Podolia, beat out of his kingdom.

> Robert Anton, note to *Moriomachia* (1613)

> There many a pale and ruthless robber's corse,
>   Noisome and ghast, defiles thy sacred sod;
> O'er mingling man, and horse commix'd with horse,
>   Corruption's heap, the savage spoilers trod.

> George Gordon, Lord Byron, "Elegy on Newstead Abbey" (1807)

It was the most noisome quarter of London, where every thing wore the worst impress of the most deplorable poverty, and of the most desperate crime.

> Edgar Allan Poe, "The Man of the Crowd" (1840)

He peered over the green wall of the fort, and there in the ditch he saw a swarm of noisome children, horrible little stunted creatures with old men's faces, with bloated faces, with little sunken eyes, with leering eyes. It was worse than uncovering a brood of snakes or a nest of worms.

> Arthur Machen, "Out of the Earth" (1915)

For some time I tossed about the bed trying to get the sound of his voice out of my ears, but could not. It filled my head, that muttering sound, like thick oily smoke from a fat-rendering vat or an odor of noisome decay.

> Robert W. Chambers, "The Yellow Sign" (1895)

But they were too late, for in one final spurt of strength which ripped tendon from tendon and sent its noisome bulk floundering to the floor in a state of jellyish dissolution, the staring corpse which had been Robert Suydam achieved its object and its triumph.

> H. P. Lovecraft, "The Horror at Red Hook" (1925)

> Then sank the lake within its bed,
> Suck'd down to caverns of the dead,
> Till from its reeking, new-script earth
> Curl'd fœtid fumes of noisome birth.

> H. P. Lovecraft, "The Nightmare Lake" (1919)

> Let obscene shapes of Darkness ride the earth,
> Let sacrificial smokes blot out the skies,
> Let dying virgins glut the Black Gods' eyes,
> And all the world resound with noisome mirth.

> Robert E. Howard, "Which Will Scarcely Be Understood"

On either side and in front wide fens and mires now lay, stretching away southward and eastward into the dim half-light. Mists curled and smoked from dark and noisome pools. The reek of them hung stifling in the still air.

> J. R. R. Tolkien, *The Two Towers* in *The Lord of the Rings* (1936–49)

All the night-walkers were gone, and the land seemed empty. North amid their noisome pits lay the first of the great heaps and hills of slag and broken rock and blasted earth, the vomit of the maggot-folk of Mordor; but south and now near loomed the great rampart of Cirith Gorgor, and the Black Gate amidmost, and the two Towers of the Teeth tall and dark upon either side.

J. R. R. Tolkien, The Return of the King in The Lord of the Rings (1936–49)

> You sink into the slime, who dare
>   To knock upon their door,
> While down the grinning gargoyles stare
>   And noisome waters pour.

J. R. R. Tolkien, "The Mewlips"

But the tasks Sheelba would set the Mouser at times like these were apt to be peculiarly onerous and even noisome—such as procuring nine white cats with never a black hair among them, or stealing five copies of the same book of magic runes from five widely separated sorcerous libraries or obtaining specimens of the dung of four kings living or dead—so the Mouser had come early, to get the bad news as soon as possible, and he had come alone, for he certainly did not want his comrade Fafhrd to stand snickering by while Sheelba delivered his little wizardly homilies to a dutiful Mouser . . . and perchance thought of extra assignments.

Fritz Leiber, "Bazaar of the Bizarre" (1963; ellipsis in original)

I personally wish to terminate my services as of now in that I cannot continue to sell the raw materials of death. . . . Yours, sir, is a hopeless case and a noisome one. . . .

William S. Burroughs, Naked Lunch (1955–59; ellipses in original)

My old Gothic castle, located high atop the hill of Howth facing Dublin Bay, was not only damp, dank and dark (due to omnipresent clouds) but rapidly becoming decadent, noisome and fœtid.

Robert Anton Wilson, "The Horror on Howth Hill" (1990)

noisomely, *adv.* In a noisome (q.v.) manner.

Of course my resolution to keep my eyes shut had failed. It was foredoomed to failure—for who could crouch blindly while a legion of croaking, baying entities of unknown source flopped noisomely past, scarcely more than a hundred yards away?

H. P. Lovecraft, "The Shadow over Innsmouth" (1931)

noisomeness, *n.* The state or property of being noisome (q.v.).

> Methought the stunted trees with hungry arms
> Grop'd greedily for things I dare not name;
> The while a stifling, wraith-like noisomeness

Fill'd all the dale, and spoke a larger life
Of uncorporeal hideousness awake
In the half-sentient wholeness of the spot.

H. P. Lovecraft, "Aletheia Phrikodes" in
"The Poe-et's Nightmare: A Fable" (1916)

nuclear, *adj.* Of or pertaining to a nucleus or center. (With no reference to nuclear fission prior to WW II.)

I learned whence Cthulhu *first* came, and why half the great temporary stars of history had flared forth. I guessed—from hints which made even my informant pause timidly—the secret behind the Magellanic Clouds and globular nebulæ, and the black truth veiled by the immemorial allegory of Tao. The nature of the Doels was plainly revealed, and I was told the essence (though not the source) of the Hounds of Tindalos. The legend of Yig, Father of Serpents, remained figurative no longer, and I started with loathing when told of the monstrous nuclear chaos beyond angled space which the *Necronomicon* had mercifully cloaked under the name Azathoth.

H. P. Lovecraft, "The Whisperer in Darkness" (1930)

Of all this, only the slightest memory, because of what I saw framed in that opening where I had expected to see but stars, and the charnel, nauseating smell that poured in from *Outside*—not stars, but *suns*, the *suns* seen by Stephen Bates, in his last moments—*great globes of light massing towards the opening, and not alone these, but the breaking apart of the nearest globes, and the protoplasmic flesh that flowed blackly outward to join together and form that eldritch, hideous horror from outer space, that spawn of the blankness of primal time, that tentacled amorphous monster which was the lurker at the threshold, whose mask was as a congeries of iridescent globes, the noxious Yog-Sothoth, who froths as primal slime in nuclear chaos forever beyond the nethermost outposts of space and time!*

August Derleth (as H. P. Lovecraft & August Derleth),
The Lurker at the Threshold (1945)

nugæ, *n.* (*pl.*) [< L] Trifles.

In furnishing my Irish colleague with an account of my vivid and active career I did not think it necessary to mention trifles such as Satanism and neogonophagy—nay, nor my voyage up the Oxus, nor my visit to Samarcand, nor how and why I slew the yellow-veiled priest at Lhasa—that priest whose yellow silken veil stood out too far in front of where his face ought to be, and moved in a manner that I did not like. These nugæ I have pass'd over altogether as unworthy of the career of a man of genius; but I did hint of certain travels through the æther in the dark of the moon, and give broad suggestions regarding certain queerly-dimensioned cities of windowless onyx towers on a planet circling about Antares, which the initiated cannot well read without forming their own conjectures about the first-handedness of my information.

H. P. Lovecraft, letter to Frank Belknap Long (December 1927)

nyctalopic, *adj.* 1. Characterized by night-blindness or the inability to see in the dark; hemeralopic. 2. Characterized by day-blindness or the inability to see in bright light; hemeralopic.

> The wind howled strangely over a midnight tomb. The moon hung like a golden bat over ancient graves, glaring through the wan mist with its baleful, nyctalopic eye.
>
> Robert Bloch, "The Secret in the Tomb" (1934)

nyctalops, *n.* 1. One afflicted with night-blindness. 2. One able to see in the dark.

Titles: Clark Ashton Smith, "Nyctalops" (verse)

> It appears that nearly all of the Maglores had possessed certain physical malformations that had made them conspicuous. Some had been born with veils; others with clubfeet. One or two were dwarfed, and all had at some time or another been accused of possessing the fabled "evil eye." Several of them had been nyctalops—they could see in the dark.
>
> Robert Bloch, "The Mannikin" (1936)

> "Look at the cat—contrary to popular impression a nyctalops."
>
> Robert Bloch, "The Sorcerer's Jewel" (1939)

nyctaloptic, *adj.* Nyctalopic (q.v.). [Not in *OED*.]

> His features were not unusual, from what could be seen of them in the dark, except for his full-lidded and burning eyes, like those of some nyctaloptic animal. But from him there emanated a palpable sense of things that were inconceivably strange and outré and remote—a sense that was more patent, more insistent, than any impression of mere form and odor and sound could have been, and which was well-nigh tactual in its intensity.
>
> Clark Ashton Smith, "The Monster of the Prophecy" (1929)

> He began to resemble his uncle Richard, and his eyes had taken on that lambent cast which hinted of a nyctaloptic power.
>
> Robert Bloch, "The Mannikin" (1936)

O

obscene, *adj.* (1) Ill-omened, inauspicious, impropitious. (2) Offensive and repugnant to the senses, loathsome.

When I had it in my hands it was no common water but a certain kind of oil of
a watery complexion. A viscous, fat, mineral nature it was, bright like pearls and
transparent like crystal. When I had viewed and searched it well, it appeared
somewhat spermatic, and in very truth it was obscene to the sight but much
more to the touch.

Thomas Vaughan, *Lumen de Lumine; or,*
A New Magical Light, Discovered and Communicated to the World (1650)

But at last he found his voice and shrieked at them, and they burst into a yell of
obscene laughter and shrieked back at him, and scattered out of sight.

Arthur Machen, "Out of the Earth" (1915)

Ichthyosauri, plesiosauri, prodigious batrachians, gigantic cuttlefish, sea-spiders
twenty feet high, cobras of the size of the mythical sea-serpent, monsters shaped
almost like some huge bird, yet obviously reptilian in character, ghastly bloodless
creatures like enormously magnified animalculæ—all these and many more
nameless variants defiled before my eyes; and yet no two of the obscene host
were alike, and none seemed perfect; each had some peculiar and awful deform-
ity of its own.

C. W. Leadbeater, "A Test of Courage" (1911)

In that same hour Corund marshalled his folk and assaulted Eshgrar Ogo, placing those of Impland in the van. They prospered not at all. Many a score lay
slain without the walls that night; and the obscene beasts from the desert feasted
on their bodies by the light of the moon.

E. R. Eddison, *The Worm Ouroboros* (1922)

The flag strains furiously to the north. It whips around, with new vigor, eastward, now that the flag and I are visited in our shared isolation by turkey buz-
zards. These circle and slant and glide about us, and they otherwise disport their
obscene bodies with an incredible gracefulness such as would have mightily uplifted the heart of Charles Baudelaire.

Branch Cabell, *These Restless Heads: A Trilogy of Romantics* (1931)

"I can't describe these carvings! No human being could—the human eye cannot
grasp them any more than it can grasp the shapes that haunt the fourth dimen-

sion. Only a subtle sense in the back of the brain sensed them vaguely. They were formless things that gave no conscious image, yet pressed into the mind like small hot seals—ideas of hate—of combats between unthinkable monstrous things—victories in a nebulous hell of steaming, obscene jungles—aspirations and ideals immeasurably loathsome——"

A. Merritt, "The People of the Pit" (1918)

In an alcove near the door reared a squat idol, bulky, taller than a man, half hidden by a heavy lacquer screen, an obscene, brutish travesty of nature, that only a Mongolian brain could conceive.

Robert E. Howard, "Lord of the Dead"

"No words in our language can describe them!" He spoke in a hoarse whisper. "They are symbolized vaguely in the myth of the Fall, and in an obscene form which is occasionally found engraved on ancient tablets. The Greeks had a name for them, which veiled their essential foulness. The tree, the snake, and the apple—these are the vague symbols of a most awful mystery."

Frank Belknap Long, "The Hounds of Tindalos" (1929)

The Hounds of Tindalos, March 1929 . . . No words in our language can describe them . . . symbolized in the myth of the Fall . . . obscene ancient tablets. . . . The Greeks had a name for them to veil their essential foulness. . . . As soon as you name something you reduce its power, of course, the power of a foulness essential to their function. . . . They must be too horrible to name or look at. . . .

William S. Burroughs, *The Place of Dead Roads* (1977–83; ellipses in original)

It was red and dripping; an immensity of pulsing, moving jelly; a scarlet blob with myriad tentacular trunks that waved and waved. There were suckers on the tips of the appendages, and these were opening and closing with ghoulish lust. . . . The thing was bloated and obscene; a headless, faceless, eyeless bulk with the ravenous maw and titanic talons of a starborn monster.

Robert Bloch, "The Shambler from the Stars" (1935; ellipsis in original)

A few hours' work sufficed for the men to uncover the idol. If the crown of its stony head had hinted of horror, the face and body openly proclaimed it. The image was obscene and shockingly malignant.

Robert Bloch, "The Faceless God" (1936)

He would not attempt to describe these creatures save to say that they were very horrible to look upon, in ways peculiarly obscene.

Robert Bloch, "The Grinning Ghoul" (1936)

If tales were true, Nephren-Ka had offered up that final mighty sacrifice upon the obscene laps of these evil idols; offered them up to Nyarlathotep, and buried the dead in the mummy-cases set here in the niches. Then he had gone on to his own sepulcher within.

Robert Bloch, "Fane of the Black Pharaoh" (1937)

Fumbling at the ignition key which I had inserted upside down, I looked back to see an obscene reaching member protruding from the gulf against the fast-misting sky.

Ramsey Campbell, "The Room in the Castle" (1964)

An assortment of plastic surfaces came to light, which were assembled into a distorted semi-solid pentagram; and it was followed by two black candles formed into vaguely obscene shapes, a metal rod carrying an icon, and a skull.

Ramsey Campbell, "The Render of the Veils" (1964)

They whispered, softly and lightly, laughing shrilly, chuckling in obscene ways.

Gardner F. Fox, *Kothar and the Wizard Slayer* (1970)

The wild blackamoor turned then and moved toward the window. Agassiz was astounded to see that the creature's skirt in back was rucked up over enormous fatty buttocks so huge and disproportionate as to render the very term "obscene" an instance of litotes.

Paul Di Filippo, *Hottentots* (1994) in the *Steampunk Trilogy*

obscenely, *adv.* In an obscene (q.v.) manner.

Unseen things not of earth—or at least not of tri-dimensional earth—rushed fœtid and horrible through New England's glens, and brooded obscenely on the mountaintops.

H. P. Lovecraft, "The Dunwich Horror" (1928)

Ocypetean, *adj.* [< *Ocypete,* one of the three harpies of Græco-Roman mythology] Noisome, like the harpy Ocypete. [Not in *OED.*]

The air of the room is saturated with thick, heavy, stifling waves . . . at any moment I expect to feel hot tongues of flame lick eagerly at my useless legs . . . my eyes smart . . . my ears throb . . . I cough and choke to rid my lungs of the Ocypetean fumes . . . smoke such as is associated only with appalling catastrophes . . . acrid, stinking, mephitic smoke permeated with the revolting odor of burning flesh * * *

C. M. Eddy, Jr. & H. P. Lovecraft,
"Deaf, Dumb, and Blind" (1924; ellipses in original)

Odyssey, *n.* [< L *Odyssēa* < Gr *Odýsseia* < *Odysseús,* Ulysses, king of Ithaca, protagonist of the Homeric epic] A long, adventurous journey.

Titles: Stanley Weinbaum, "A Martian Odyssey"; Phillip K. Dick, "A Terran Odyssey"

But the climax of the whole Odyssey was my excursion, by train, to the Endless Caverns in the exquisite Shenandoah Valley. Despite all the fantasy I have written concerning the nether world, I had never beheld a real cave before in all my life—and my sensations upon plunging into one of the finest specimens in the country may be better imagined than described. For over an hour I was led spellbound through illimitable gulfs and chasms of elfin beauty and dæmonic mystery—here and there lighted with wondrous effect by concealed lamps, and in other places displaying awesome grottoes and abysses of unconquered night; black bottomless shafts and galleries where hidden winds and waters course eternally out of this world and all possible worlds of mankind, down, down to the sunless secrets of the gnomes and night-gaunts, and the worlds where web-winged monsters and fabulous gargoyles reign in undisputed horror. . . .

> H. P. Lovecraft, letter to Zealia Brown Reed (Bishop)
> (28 July 1928) (ellipsis in original)

Olieribos, *n.* [?< Gr] Fennel.

The sacrifice must be new bread, pine resin, and the grass Olieribos.

> Abdul Alhazred (trans. "Simon"), *Necronomicon* (1977)

oneirodynia, *n.* [< Gr] An unpleasant or painful dream; a nightmare.

An ordinary man's forehead, under these methods, would register as being hydrocephalic; his eyes might appear as bulging beacons illumined by insane lights. The perspective of nightmare, the nuances of oneirodynia, the hallucinative images of the demented were reproduced by distortion.

> Robert Bloch, "The Sorcerer's Jewel" (1939)

oneiroscopic, *adj.* Of or pertaining to dream-vision. [Not in *OED.*]

When you see my long Randolph Carter novelette you will realise that this fantastic and oneiroscopic mood is a darned hard thing to pry me out of!

> H. P. Lovecraft, letter to Bernard Austin Dwyer (26 March 1927)

[John] Martin's real fame must rest on his febrile & oneiroscopic glimpses of other worlds—or atmospheric emanations of other worlds. In his day he was an idol of the Radcliffe-revering & Lewis-loving herd, but a doubtful question to the sedate & well-bred academicians. Today his favour amongst a microscopic minority of fantaisistes, & his absolute disappearance from the general view, (for he has in truth found what Sadok sought!) constitutes a reversal of the most ironic sort.

> H. P. Lovecraft, letter to Vincent Starrett (10 January 1928)

opalescence, *n.* The state or property of being opalescent (q.v.); a lustrous iridescence like that of an opal.

Upon the brows were caps—and with a fearful certainty I knew that they were *not* caps—long, thick strands of gleaming, yellow, feathered scales thin as sequins! Sharp, curving noses like the beaks of the giant condors; mouths thin, austere; long, powerful, pointed chins; the—*flesh*—of the faces white as whitest marble; and wreathing up to them, covering all their bodies, the shimmering, curdled, misty fires of opalescence!

A. Merritt, *The Moon Pool* (1919)

opalescent, *adj.* Characterized by a milky, lustrous iridescence like that of an opal; opaline, nacreous, pearlescent.

He picked up an Easter lily which Geneviève had brought that morning from Notre Dame and dropped it into the basin. Instantly the liquid lost its crystalline clearness. For a second the lily was enveloped in a milk-white foam, which disappeared, leaving the fluid opalescent. Changing tints of orange and crimson played over the surface, and then what seemed to be a ray of pure sunlight struck through from the bottom where the lily was resting.

Robert W. Chambers, "The Mask" (1895)

On and on it swept toward us—an opalescent mistiness that sped with the suggestion of some winged creature in arrowed flight. Dimly there crept into my mind memory of the Dyak legend of the winged messenger of Buddha—the Akla bird whose feathers are woven of the moon rays, whose heart is a living opal, whose wings in flight echo the crystal clear music of the white stars—but whose beak is of frozen flame and shreds the souls of unbelievers.

A. Merritt, *The Moon Pool* (1919)

The soaring, verdure-clad walls of the cañon had long been steadily marching closer. Between their rims the wide ribbon of sky was like a fantastically shored river, shimmering, dazzling; every cove and headland edged with an opalescent glimmering as of shining pearly beaches. And as though we were sinking in that sky stream's depths its light kept lessening, darkening, imperceptibly with luminous shadows of ghostly beryl, drifting veils of pellucid aquamarine, limpid mists of glaucous chrysolite.

A. Merritt, *The Metal Monster* (1920)

Grayness first, like a pearly, opalescent dawn; then yellowish fingers of sunlight; and finally the hot blaze of a summer afternoon!

Henry Kuttner, "Bells of Horror" (1939)

ophidian, *adj.* [< LL *ophidia*, the suborder of reptiles including snakes or serpents, < Gr *óphis*, a snake or serpent] Of, pertaining to, or resembling a member of the Ophidia, snakes or serpents.

Through years and ages of the ophidian era it returned, and was a thing that crawled in the ooze, that had not yet learned to think and dream and build.

Clark Ashton Smith, "Ubbo-Sathla" (1932)

His limbs, his body, his lineaments were outwardly formed like those of aboriginal man; and one might even have allowed for his utter hairlessness, in which there was a remote and blasphemously caricatural suggestion of the shaven priest; and even the broad, formless mottling of his skin, like that of a huge boa, might somehow have been glossed over as a rather extravagant peculiarity of pigmentation. It was something else, it was the unctuous, verminous ease, the undulant litheness and fluidity of his every movement, seeming to hint at an inner structure and vertebration that were less than human—or, one might almost have said, a sub-ophidian lack of all bony frame-work—which made me view the captive, and also my incumbent task, with an unparallelable distaste.

Clark Ashton Smith, "The Testament of Athammaus" (1931)

opiate, *adj.* & *n.* [< *opium* < Gr *ópion,* dim. of *opós,* vegetable juice] Of, pertaining to, or resembling in effect the drug opium or its derivatives; inducing sleep, sedation, or sopor; acting as an analgesic or anodyne; such a drug.

When her mind was discomposed by the behaviour of Madame La Motte, or by a retrospection of her early misfortunes, a book was the opiate that lulled it to repose.

Ann Radcliffe, *The Romance of the Forest, Interspersed with Some Pieces of Poetry* (1791)

> My heart aches, and a drowsy numbness pains
> My sense, as though of hemlock I had drunk,
> Or emptied some dull opiate to the drains
> One minute past, and Lethe-wards had sunk:
> 'Tis not through envy of thy happiness,—
> That thou, light-winged Dryad of the trees,
> In some melodious plot
> Of beechen green, and shadows numberless,
> Singest of summer in full-throated ease.

John Keats, "Ode to a Nightingale" (1819)

> At midnight, in the month of June,
> I stand beneath the mystic moon.
> An opiate vapour, dewy, dim,
> Exhales from out her golden rim,
> And, softly dripping, drop by drop,
> Upon the quiet mountain top,
> Steals drowsily and musically
> Into the universal valley.

Edgar Allan Poe, "The Sleeper" (1831)

[cf: "There's a drop," said the Peri, "that down from the moon / Falls through the withering airs of June / Upon Egypt's land, of so healing a power, / So balmy a virtue, that e'en in the hour / That drop descends, contagion dies, /

And health reanimates earth and skies!"— Thomas Moore, "Paradise and the Peri" in *Lalla Rookh*.]

> A breath of attar, fallen from the bloom,
>   Made opiate the air,
> Like wafture of an undulant perfume,
>   Flown from enchanted hair.

George Sterling, "The Hidden Pool" (1922)

And they were strange, because they had come as dark furtive folk from opiate southern gardens of orchids, and spoken another tongue before they learnt the tongue of the blue-eyed fishers.

H. P. Lovecraft, "The Festival" (1923)

> There amid the tinted towers,
>   Raptur'd with the opiate spell
> Of the grasses, ferns, and flowers,
>   Poppy, phlox, and pimpernel,
> Long I lay, entranc'd and dreaming,
>   Pleas'd with Nature's bounteous store,
> Till I mark'd the shaded gleaming
>   Of the sky, and yearn'd for more.

H. P. Lovecraft, "Revelation" (1919)

> I look'd upon thee yesternight
> Beneath the drops of yellow light
> That fell from out a poppy moon
> Like notes of some far opiate tune.

H. P. Lovecraft, "To Zara" (1922)

Deeper and deeper I went into the wilderness of colossal architecture, led by that remote, ethereal, opiate music.

Clark Ashton Smith, "The City of the Singing Flame" (1931)

orgiast, *n.* A celebrant of orgies.

A house in the suburbs or an apartment in the city would be assigned him, and he would be initiated into one of the large affection-groups, including many noblewomen of the most extreme and art-enhanced beauty, which in latter-day K'n-yan took the place of family units. Several horned *gyaa-yothn* would be provided for his transportation and errand-running, and ten living slaves of intact body would serve to conduct his establishment and protect him from thieves and sadists and religious orgiasts on the public highways.

H. P. Lovecraft & Zealia Bishop, "The Mound" (1930)

orgiastic, *adj.* Of, pertaining to, or characteristic of an orgy (q.v.).

Animal fury and orgiastic license here whipped themselves to dæmoniac heights by howls and squawking ecstasies that tore and reverberated through those nighted woods like pestilential tempests from the gulfs of hell.

H. P. Lovecraft, "The Call of Cthulhu" (1926)

No one, even those who have the facts concerning the recent horror, can say just what is the matter with Dunwich; though old legends speak of unhallowed rites and conclaves of the Indians, amidst which they called forbidden shapes of shadow out of the great rounded hills, and made wild orgiastic prayers that were answered by loud crackings and rumblings from the ground below.

H. P. Lovecraft, "The Dunwich Horror" (1928)

orgy, orgie, *n.* A religious rite or ceremony, particularly one which involves extravagant feasting, drinking, dancing, singing, or sexual activity.

"The imaginations of the younger members are at once polluted and inflamed, by the idea of the infernal and impure orgies which the demon celebrates in your cell; and of which we know not whether your cries, (which all can hear), announce triumph in, or remorse for."

Charles Maturin, *Melmoth the Wanderer: A Tale* (1820)

"At the end of the table sat an old man, wrapped in a long robe; his head was covered with a black velvet cap, with a broad border of furs, his spectacles were of such size as almost to hide his face, and he turned over some scrolls of parchment with an anxious and trembling hand; then seizing a scull that lay on the table, and grasping it in fingers hardly less bony, and not less yellow, seemed to apostrophize it in the most earnest manner. All my personal fears were lost in the thought of my being the involuntary witness of some infernal orgie."

Charles Maturin, *Melmoth the Wanderer: A Tale* (1820)

A flare of naphtha, burning with a rushing noise, threw a light on one point of the circle, and Lucian watched a lank girl of fifteen as she came round and round to the flash. She was quite drunk, and had kicked her petticoats away, and the crowd howled laughter and applause at her. Her black hair poured down and leapt on her scarlet bodice; she sprang and leapt round the ring, laughing in Bacchic frenzy, and led the orgy to triumph.

Arthur Machen, *The Hill of Dreams* (1897)

But as many years passed without calamity even the priests laughed and cursed and joined in the orgies of the feasters.

H. P. Lovecraft, "The Doom That Came to Sarnath" (1919)

I looked at Zann, and saw that he was past conscious observation. His blue eyes were bulging, glassy, and sightless, and the frantic playing had become a blind, mechanical, unrecognisable orgy that no pen could even suggest.

H. P. Lovecraft, "The Music of Erich Zann" (1921)

Anchester had been the camp of the third Augustan legion, as many remains attest, and it was said that the temple of Cybele was splendid and thronged with worshippers who performed nameless ceremonies at the bidding of a Phrygian priest. Tales added that the fall of the old religion did not end the orgies at the temple, but that the priests lived on in the new faith without real change.

H. P. Lovecraft, "The Rats in the Walls" (1923)

Detectives assigned to follow him reported strange cries and chants and prancing of feet filtering out from these nocturnal rites, and shuddered at their peculiar ecstasy and abandon despite the commonness of weird orgies in that sodden section.

H. P. Lovecraft, "The Horror at Red Hook" (1925)

Then the men, having reached a spot where the trees were thinner, came suddenly in sight of the spectacle itself. Four of them reeled, one fainted, and two were shaken into a frantic cry which the mad cacophony of the orgy fortunately deadened.

H. P. Lovecraft, "The Call of Cthulhu" (1926)

Rumor said that blasphemous rites had flourished during the years of Roman occupation, with orgies to powers and beings greater than mortal, that in other ages Druid rituals had fulfilled the ecstasies and terrors of the forest.

Donald Wandrei, *The Web of Easter Island* (1929–31)

On the *Golconda*'s deck, Stragella was darting erratically among those piles of gleaming bones. But they were bones no longer. They had gathered into shapes, taken on flesh, blood. Before his very eyes they assumed substance, men and beasts alike. And then began an orgy such as Nels Yancy had never before looked upon—an orgy of the undead.

Hugh B. Cave, "Stragella" (1932)

The old days, when Cotton Mather had hunted down the evil cults that worshipped Hecate and the Magna Mater in frightful orgies, had passed; but dark gabled houses still leaned perilously toward each other over narrow cobbled street, and blasphemous secrets and mysteries were said to be hidden in subterranean cellars and caverns.

Henry Kuttner, "The Graveyard Rats" (1936)

"You haven't spent much time with the indole crowd. They're very elitist. They see themselves at the end of a long European dialectic, generations of blighted grain, ergotism, witches on broomsticks, community orgies, cantons lost up there in folds of mountain that haven't known an unhallucinated day in the last 500 years—keepers of a tradition, aristocrats—"

Thomas Pynchon, *Gravity's Rainbow* (1973)

oriel, oriel window, *n.* A bay window projecting out from a wall, supported by a corbel or bracket.

Old Cairo is itself a story-book and a dream—labyrinths of narrow alleys redolent of aromatic secrets; Arabesque balconies and oriels nearly meeting above the cobbled streets; maelstroms of Oriental traffic with strange cries, cracking whips, rattling carts, jingling money, and braying donkeys; kaleidoscopes of polychrome robes, veils, turbans, and tarbushes; water-carriers and dervishes, dogs and cats, soothsayers and barbers; and over all the whining of blind beggars crouched in alcoves, and the sonorous chanting of muezzins from minarets limned delicately against a sky of deep, unchanging blue.

H. P. Lovecraft & Harry Houdini, "Under the Pyramids" (1924)

osseous, *adj.* Of bone.

These were no disarticulated skeletons; these osseous fragments before the sinister altar! These were *fresh* bones!

Robert Bloch, "The Brood of Bubastis" (1937)

ossicle, *n.* A small bone.

White spiders, demon-headed and large as monkeys, had woven their webs in the hollow arches of the bones; and they swarmed out interminably as Nushain approached; and the skeleton seemed to stir and quiver as they seethed over it abnormally and dropped to the ground before the astrologer. Behind them others poured in a countless army, crowding and mantling every ossicle.

Clark Ashton Smith, "The Last Hieroglyph" (1934)

ossuarium, *n.* An ossuary or charnel.

Gnawing curiosity overcame my dread, as I followed him through the ossuarium and into a second chamber.

Robert Bloch, "The Brood of Bubastis" (1937)

ossuary, *n.* A receptacle or repository for the bones of the dead.

ossuary, *adj.* Of or pertaining to the bones of the dead.

He had dwelt alone for two generations in a curious house on the rim of the northern desert of Tasuun: a house whose floor and walls were built from the large bones of dromedaries, and whose roof was a wattling composed of the smaller bones of wild dogs and men and hyenas. These ossuary relics, chosen for their whiteness and symmetry, were bound securely together with well-tanned thongs, and were joined and fitted with marvellous closeness, leaving no space for the blown sand to penetrate.

Clark Ashton Smith, "The Witchcraft of Ulua" (1933)

Henceforward, Nushain followed the mummy without recalcitrance. Returning to the chamber in which stood the immense sarcophagus, he was enjoined by his guide to replace in its socket the black taper he had stolen. Without other light than the phosphorescence of the mummy's cerements, he threaded the foul gloom of those profounder ossuaries which lay beyond.

> Clark Ashton Smith, "The Last Hieroglyph" (1934)

oulothrix, *adj.* [Gr *oulóthrix,* curly-haired] Curly-haired. [Not in *OED.*]

N.B.—K'nath-Hothar was *not* oulothrix—and he had *thin lips,* a *very large* aquiline nose, and a *light* complexion inherited from his *Nordick* stream.

> H. P. Lovecraft, letter to James Ferdinand Morton (30 October 1929)

He turned down The Outpost on the alleged ground of excessive length, but I'm sure the real reason is because he wouldn't believe in the thin-lipp'd non-oulothrixitude of the Great King!

> H. P. Lovecraft, letter to James Ferdinand Morton (6 December 1929)

outré, outré, *adj.* [< Fr < L *ultra,* beyond] Outside of the common and conventional; bizarre and freakish; weird and fantastic.

"You forget you have left Paris," said La Motte to his son, while a faint smile crossed his face, "such a compliment would there be in character with the place—in these solitary woods it is quite *outré.*"

> Ann Radcliffe, *The Romance of the Forest, Interspersed with Some Pieces of Poetry* (1791)

Booths, fantastically hung with lamps, and filled with merchandize of every kind, disposed in the gayest order, were spread out on all sides, and peasants in their holiday cloaths, and parties of masks crowded every avenue. Here was a band of musicians, and there a group of dancers; on one spot the *outré* humour of a zanni provoked the never-failing laugh of an Italian rabble, in another the *improvisatore,* by the pathos of his story, and the persuasive sensibility of his strains, was holding the attention of his auditors, as in the bands of magic.

> Ann Radcliffe, *The Italian; or,*
> *The Confessional of the Black Penitents: A Romance* (1797)

[zanni: a *zany* or clown]

If what I have written appear nonsense to you, or commonplace thoughts in a harlequinade of Outré expressions, suspend your judgment till we see each other.

> S. T. Coleridge, letter to William Godwin (22 September 1800)

The dinner and the ball took place, and what a pity I may not describe that entertainment, the dresses, and the dancers, for they were all exquisite in their way, and *outré* beyond measure. But such details only serve to derange a winter's evening tale such as this.

> James Hogg, "The Mysterious Bride" (1830)

Yet I must believe that my first mental development had in it much of the uncommon—even much of the *outré*.

Edgar Allan Poe, "William Wilson" (1839)

"As I was saying," resumed the visitor—"as I was observing a little while ago, there are some very *outré* notions in that book of yours, Monsieur Bon-Bon. What, for instance, do you mean by all that humbug about the soul?"

Edgar Allan Poe, "Bon-Bon" (1832)

"The 'Gazette,'" he replied, "has not entered, I fear, into the unusual horror of the thing. But dismiss the idle opinions of this print. It appears to me that this mystery is considered insoluble, for the very reason which should cause it to be regarded as easy of solution—I mean for the *outré* character of its features."

Edgar Allan Poe, "The Murders in the Rue Morgue" (1841)

"Here is a woman strangled to death by manual strength, and thrust up a chimney, head downward. Ordinary assassins employ no such modes of murder as this. Least of all, do they thus dispose of the murdered. In the manner of thrusting the corpse up the chimney, you will admit that there was something *excessively outré*—something altogether irreconcilable with our common notions of human action, even when we suppose the actors the most depraved of men."

Edgar Allan Poe, "The Murders in the Rue Morgue" (1841)

"Indeed, I may go further and show you that in all but every instance in which his actions are in themselves *outré*, suspicious, they are rendered, not less *outré*, but less suspicious, by the fact that Lord Pharanx himself knew of them, shared in them."

M. P. Shiel, "The Race of Orven" (1895)

But a rival of Solutré, told the tribe my style was *outré*—
  'Neath a tomahawk, of diorite, he fell.
And I left my views on Art, barbed and tanged, below the heart
  Of a mammothistic etcher at Grenelle.

Rudyard Kipling, "In the Neolithic Age" (1895)

A kind of growing horror, of outré and morbid cast, seemed to possess him.

H. P. Lovecraft, "Cool Air" (1926)

So Gilman climbed upstairs again in a mental turmoil, convinced that he was either still dreaming or that his somnambulism had run to incredible extremes and led him to depredations in unknown places. Where had he got this outré thing?

H. P. Lovecraft, "The Dreams in the Witch House" (1932)

I continued, however, to keep a careful record of the outré dreams which crowded upon me so thickly and vividly.

H. P. Lovecraft, "The Shadow out of Time" (1935)

As an example—a young man I know lately told me that he means to write a story about a scientist who wishes to dominate the earth, and who to accomplish his ends trains and overdevelops germs (à la Anthony Rud's "Ooze"), and leads on armies of them in the manner of the Egyptian plagues. I told him that although this them has promise, it is made utterly commonplace by assigning the scientist a normal motive. There is nothing outré about wanting to conquer the earth; Alexander, Napoleon, and Wilhelm II wanted to do that. Instead, I told my friend, he should conceive a man with a morbid, frantic, shuddering hatred of the life-principle itself, who wishes to extirpate from the planet every trace of biological organism, animal and vegetable alike, including himself. That would be tolerably original.

> H. P. Lovecraft, letter to *Weird Tales* (August 1923)

"I was compelled to make a drawing of it, almost against my will, since anything so *outré* is hardly in my line. In fact, I made two drawings. I'll show them to you, if you like."

> Clark Ashton Smith, "Genius Loci" (1932)

It seemed, however, that he found little to divert or inveigle him in these outré doings and exotic wonders.

> Clark Ashton Smith, "The Flower-Women" (1933)

Smiling impassively at the wild rumors of the court, he continued his search for novel pleasures and violent or rare sensations. In this, however, he met with small success; it seemed that every path, even the most outré and tortuous, led only to the hidden precipice of boredom.

> Clark Ashton Smith, "The Garden of Adompha" (1937)

"My dear girl," said I, "this is a masterpiece of *outré* literature."

> Robert E. Howard, "The Little People" (1928)

Accustomed as I was to the human curiosities, to the often incredible characters and unusual sights to be encountered on the nocturnal walks I took about Providence, the circumstances surrounding the Poesque Mr. Allan and his brothers were so outré that I could not get them out of my mind.

> August Derleth (as H. P. Lovecraft & August Derleth),
> "The Dark Brotherhood" (1966)

"They are not yet matters of record."
"Why not?"
"Because they are too *outré* for belief."

> Alfred Bester, *Golem*[100] (1980)

This was essentially a brainstorming organization, started by an alumnus of the RAND Corporation, which specialized in imagining possible political and military confrontations and their possible outcomes, some of them so *outré* as to require the subcontracting of free-lance science-fiction writers.

James Blish, *Black Easter; or, Faust Aleph-Null* (1968)

Much of what I heard was completely new to me, only recently fathomed or discovered by the Foundation, so that I thrilled to such *outré* names as Sunken Yatta-Uc, a city drowned in the forgotten inner cone of Titicaca's volcano; Doomed Arken Tengri, a derelict aerie of mist-obscured peaks and icy pinnacles in the white wastes of the Kunlun Mountains; and the Jidhauas, savage nomads of Mongolia's Gobi Desert and worshipers of Shudde-M'ell.

Brian Lumley, *The Transition of Titus Crow* (1975)

P

palæogæan, palæogean, paleogean, *adj.* Belonging to a former geologic configuration of the earth, as distinct from its current aspect; ancient, very old.

Usage: Consistency would seem to favor either the form *palæogæan* or *paleogean*.

The Deep Ones could never be destroyed, even though the palæogean magic of the forgotten Old Ones might sometimes check them.

H. P. Lovecraft, "The Shadow over Innsmouth" (1931)

Half way uphill toward our goal we paused for a momentary breathing-spell, and turned to look again at the fantastic palæogean tangle of incredible stone shapes below us—once more outlined mystically against an unknown west.

H. P. Lovecraft, *At the Mountains of Madness* (1931)

Glad you found the *Mts. of Madness* readable. [. . .] There are several inexcusable errors in the text [as printed in *Astounding Stories*]—such as "palæocene" for *palæogean*—but the illustrations are excellent. The artist visualised the archæan entities perfectly from the written description—proving that he really read the text, which is more than most of Satrap Pharnabazus's picture-bunglers do.

H. P. Lovecraft, letter to E. Hoffman Price (12 February 1936)

"It is very old—palæogean, one might say."

Clark Ashton Smith, "Ubbo-Sathla" (1932)

palæography, *n.* The study of ancient writing.

At the library it was easy to find good manuals of palæography, and over these the two men puzzled till the lights of evening shone out from the great chandelier. In the end they found what was needed. The letters were indeed no fantastic invention, but the normal script of a very dark period. They were the pointed Saxon minuscules of the eighth or ninth century A.D., and brought with them memories of an uncouth time when under a fresh Christian veneer ancient faiths and rites stirred stealthily, and the pale moon of Britain looked sometimes on strange deeds in the Roman ruins of Caerleon and Hexham, and by the towers along Hadrian's crumbling wall.

H. P. Lovecraft, *The Case of Charles Dexter Ward* (1927)

palimpsest, *n.* [< L *palimpsēstus* < Gr *palímpsêstos*, scraped again] A manuscript which has been erased and written on a second time; particularly, when the earlier text has been incompletely erased and can be recovered.

Titles: Seabury Quinn, "Satan's Palimpsest"

A palimpsest, then, is a membrane or roll cleansed of its manuscript by reiterated successions.

Thomas De Quincey, *Suspiria de Profundis:*
Being a Sequel to the Confessions of an English Opium-Eater (1821)

As an incident-resemblance, I instance the perception, in both experiences, of the inerasible character of the mind's memorial inscriptions—as De Quincey grandly has it—the Palimpsest characteristic of memory.

Fitz-Hugh Ludlow, *The Hasheesh Eater:*
Being Passages from the Life of a Pythagorean (1857)

Some thirty-odd years ago a young man of twenty-two, the son of a Welsh clergyman, fresh from school and with his head full of a curiously occult mediæval-ism, privately acquired from yellowed palimpsests and dog-eared volumes of black letter, wrote a classic. More, he had it published.

Vincent Starrett, "Arthur Machen: A Novelist of Ecstasy and Sin" (1917) in
Buried Cæsars: Essays in Literary Appreciation (1923)

This new and degenerate work was coarse, bold, and wholly lacking delicacy of detail. It was counter-sunk with exaggerated depth in bands following the same general line as the sparse cartouches of the earlier sections, but the height of the reliefs did not reach the level of the general surface. Danforth had the idea that it was a second carving—a sort of palimpsest formed after the obliteration of a previous design.

H. P. Lovecraft, *At the Mountains of Madness* (1931)

pallid, *adj.* [< L] Pale, wan, ashen.

And the Raven, never flitting, still is sitting, *still* is sitting
On the pallid bust of Pallas just above my chamber door;
And his eyes have all the seeming of a demon's that is dreaming,
And the lamp-light o'er him streaming throws his shadow on the floor;
And my soul from out that shadow that lies floating on the floor
      Shall be lifted—nevermore!

Edgar Allan Poe, "The Raven" (1844)

"Impressive, isn't it?" said my host. "I fancy it is by far the best collection in the entire world of volumes dealing with the macabre and the fantastic. Over there, for instance, under that Grecian marble niche containing a pallid bust of Pallas, is the sort of marvelous accumulation of first editions and manuscripts—along with other, rather more exotic artifacts—of Poe which I had never dared even hope to see, let alone touch, let alone own, back in the days of my obscurity."

Gahan Wilson, "H.P.L." (1990)

pandæmoniac, pandemoniac, *adj.* Of, pertaining to, or resembling Pandæmonium (q.v.).

That Hallowe'en the hill noises sounded louder than ever, and fire burned on Sentinel Hill as usual; but people paid more attention to the rhythmical screaming of vast flocks of unnaturally belated whippoorwills which seemed to be assembled near the unlighted Whateley farmhouse. After midnight their shrill notes burst into a kind of pandæmoniac cachinnation which filled all the countryside, and not until dawn did they finally quiet down.

H. P. Lovecraft, "The Dunwich Horror" (1928)

Then I saw the chasm's edge, leaped frenziedly with every ounce of strength I possessed, and was instantly engulfed in a pandæmoniac vortex of loathsome sound and utter, materially tangible blackness.

H. P. Lovecraft, "The Shadow out of Time" (1935)

> Late in the night it was, when o'er the vale
> The storm-king swept with pandemoniac gale;
> Deep pil'd the cruel snow, yet strange to tell,
> The lightning sputter'd while the white flakes fell;
> A hideous presence seem'd abroad to steal,
> And terror sounded in the thunder's peal.

H. P. Lovecraft, "Psychopompos: A Tale in Rhyme" (1917–18)

Pandæmonian, Pandemonian, pandæmonian, pandemonian, *adj.* Of, pertaining to, or resembling Pandæmonium (q.v.).

But lest they should still shrink back, dazzled by the Pandemonian glare of Illumination which will now burst upon them, he exacts from them, for the first time, a bond of perseverance. But, as Philo says, there is little chance of tergiversation.

John Robison, Proofs of a Conspiracy against All the Religions and Governments of Europe, Carried on in the Secret Meetings of Free Masons, Illuminati, and Reading Societies, Collected from Good Authorities (1798)

Is that a real Elysian brightness, cries many a timid wayfarer, or the reflex of Pandemonian lava? Is it of a truth leading us into beatific Asphodel meadows, or the yellow-burning marl of a Hell-on-Earth?

Thomas Carlyle, Sartor Resartus: The Life and Opinions of Herr Teufelsdröckh (1831)

The remainder of my flight is a blur of pandemonian terror.

Clark Ashton Smith, "The Vaults of Yoh-Vombis" (1931)

> My dreams are turned to some disordered mime:
> A plot that pandemonian shadows feign
> Ravels half told; and dead loves live again
> In settings of distorted place and time:

A broken drama, puerile or sublime,
Whose riddled meaning I must guess in vain;
A masque, whose grey grotesques of mirth and pain
Move randomly through an occulted clime.

Clark Ashton Smith, "The Mime of Sleep" (1941)

Pandæmonium, Pandemonium, pandæmonium, pandemonium, *pr.n.* &
n. [< Gr, "all" + "demon"] An area in a state of extreme and wild uproar and
confused noise. Coined by John Milton, in whose epic *Paradise Lost* it is the
name of the capitol of Hell.

Meanwhile the winged Heralds by command
Of Sovran power, with awful Ceremony
And Trumpets' sound throughout the Host proclaim
A solemn Council forthwith to be held
At *Pandæmonium*, the high Capitol
Of Satan and his Peers: thir summons call'd
From every Band and squared Regiment
By place or choice the worthiest; they anon
With hundreds and with thousands trooping came
Attended: all access was throng'd, the Gates
And Porches wide, but chief the spacious Hall
(Though like a cover'd field, where Champions bold
Wont ride in arm'd, and at the Soldan's chair
Defi'd the best of *Paynim* chivalry
To mortal combat or career with Lance)
Thick swarm'd, both on the ground and in the air,
Brusht with the hiss of rustling wings.

John Milton, Paradise Lost (1667)

"Edward foster passed in," echoed his brother turnkey, who stood at the yard
gate; and the new prisoner, on his appearance among us, was received with a
cheer by the gaping crowd of malefactors, as Lucifer might be by his kith and
kin of fallen angels on his arrival at Pandemonium.

William Godwin the Younger, "The Executioner" (1832)

But I was enchanted by the appearance of the hut; here the snow and rain could
not penetrate; the ground was dry; and it presented to me then as exquisite and
divine a retreat as Pandæmonium appeared to the dæmons of hell after their sufferings in the lake of fire.

Mary Shelley, Frankenstein; or, The Modern Prometheus (1816–17)

Upon the present occasion the debauch had proceeded until the greater part of
the crew were, as usual, displaying inebriation in all its most brutal and disgrace-
ful shapes—swearing empty and unmeaning oaths—venting the most horrid

imprecations in the mere gaiety of their heart—singing songs, the ribaldry of which was only equalled by their profaneness; and, from the middle of this earthly hell, the two captains, together with one or two of their principal adherents, as also the carpenter and boatswain, who always took a lead on such occasions, had drawn together into a pandemonium, or privy council of their own, to consider what was to be done; for, as the boatswain metaphorically observed, they were in a narrow channel, and behoved to keep sounding the tide-way.

Sir Walter Scott, *The Pirate* (1821)

He knew that he deluded himself with imagination, that he had been walking through London suburbs and not through Pandemonium, and that if he could but unlock his bureau all those ugly forms would be resolved into the mist.

Arthur Machen, *The Hill of Dreams* (1897)

"So we spoke together in Pandemonium," said Belial, wistfully, "in the brave days when Pandemonium was newly built and we were all imps together."

James Branch Cabell, *Jurgen: A Comedy of Justice* (1919)

The howl let loose the hounds of Pandemonium. A phantom pack gave tongue in full cry down the valley of hell—pounced on their quarry leagues away—worried it—and vanished into silence.

Talbot Mundy, *Om, the Secret of Ahbor Valley* (1924)

I dream of a day when they may rise above the billows to drag down in their reeking talons the remnants of puny, war-exhausted mankind—of a day when the land shall sink, and the dark ocean floor shall ascend amidst universal pandemonium.

H. P. Lovecraft, "Dagon" (1917)

Then one night as I listened at the door, I heard the shrieking viol swell into a chaotic babel of sound; a pandemonium which would have led me to doubt my own shaking sanity had there not come from behind that barred portal a piteous proof that the horror was real—the awful, inarticulate cry which only a mute can utter, and which rises only in moments of the most terrible fear or anguish.

H. P. Lovecraft, "The Music of Erich Zann" (1921)

His ears were growing sensitive to a preternatural and intolerable degree, and he had long ago stopped the cheap mantel clock whose ticking had come to seem like a thunder of artillery. At night the subtle stirring of the black city outside, the sinister scurrying of rats in the wormy partitions, and the creaking of hidden timbers in the centuried house, were enough to give him a sense of strident pandemonium.

H. P. Lovecraft, "The Dreams in the Witch House" (1932)

Hysteria and pandemonium prevailed in the streets. Pale, panic-stricken faces milled everywhere in an aimless stream. Hurrying torches flared dolorously in the twilight that deepened as if with the shadow of impending wings arisen from Erebus.

Clark Ashton Smith, "The Colossus of Ylourgne" (1932)

I must have gone utterly mad for a while. I remember only a teeming delirium of things too frightful to be endured by a sane mind, that peopled the infinite gulf of hell-born illusion into which I sank with the hopeless precipitancy of the damned. There was a sickness inexpressible, a vertigo of redeemless descent, a pandemonium of ghoulish phantoms that reeled and swayed about the column of malign omnipotent force which presided over all.

Clark Ashton Smith, "The Devotee of Evil" (1930)

A hellish pandemonium of sound burst forth, and the echoes of that hideous yell thundered through the palace and deafened the hearers.

Robert E. Howard, "The Gods of Bal-Sagoth" (1931)

At this point pandemonium broke loose because of something noticed by such of the men as were able to notice anything at all. *The sky had been snuffed out.*

Frank Belknap Long, "The Horror from the Hills" (1930; adapted from a 1927 letter by H. P. Lovecraft)

I stood upon a gentle slope that fell away into the fog-hidden distance, from which came a pandemonium of muffled bellowing and high-pitched, shrill squeakings vaguely akin to obscene laughter.

Henry Kuttner, "The Secret of Kralitz" (1936)

panic, panique, *adj.* & *n.* [< Gr *panikós* < *Pan,* the name of the deity; also *panikón,* panic terror.] Of or pertaining to the god Pan; specifically, in such expressions as panic terror, panic horror, panic fear, etc., of or pertaining to the sudden attack of groundless terror once attributed to the god Pan; the attack of groundless terror itself, or a similar attack of intense terror.

> Ran *Coll* our Dog, and *Talbot* with the Band,
> And *Malkin,* with her Distaff in her Hand:
> Ran Cow and Calf, and Family of Hogs,
> In Panique Horror of pursuing Dogs;
> With many a deadly Grunt and doleful Squeak
> Poor Swine, as if their pretty Hearts would break.

John Dryden, "The Cock and the Fox; or, The Tale of the Nun's Priest"

For death is given in a kiss; the dearest kindnesses are fatal; and into this life, where one thing preys upon another, the child too often makes its entrance from the mother's corpse. It is no wonder, with so traitourous a scheme of things, if the wise people who created for us the idea of Pan thought that of all fears the fear of him was the most terrible, since it embraces all. And still we preserve the phrase: a panic terror. To reckon dangers too curiously, to hearken too intently for the threat that runs through all the winning music of the world, to hold back the hand from the rose because of the thorn, and from life because of death: this it is to be afraid of Pan.

Robert Louis Stevenson, "Pan's Pipes" (1910)

It was something between the pillar and the pyramid in shape, and its grey solemnity amidst the leaves and the grass shone and shone from those early years, always with some hint of wonder. She remembered how, when she was quite a little girl, she had strayed one day, on a hot afternoon, from her nurse's side, and only a little way in the wood the grey stone rose from the grass, and she cried out and ran back in panic terror.

Arthur Machen, "The Ceremony" in Ornaments in Jade (1897)

They were working for panic terror?

Arthur Machen, The Terror (1916)

> So stung by certainty's mistrust,
>   Or tranced in dream of sin,
> Or blinded by some Panic dust,
>   By Dionysian din
> Deafened, arose the laughing lust
>   To fling my body in!

Aleister Crowley, Orpheus: A Lyrical Legend (1905)

Now's the light, the light accurséd: I must get me to the feast,
Stupefy this Panic spirit, throw a posset to the beast.

Aleister Crowley, "The Stone of the Philosophers" in
Konx Om Pax: Essays in Light (1907)

For he wakened in a panic remorse, without at all knowing what he was remorseful about.

Branch Cabell, Smirt: An Urbane Nightmare (1933)

It was merely that these emotions, like tyannizing giants, had dragged him back into panic wakefulness.

Branch Cabell, Smirt: An Urbane Nightmare (1933)

There they stood—that enigmatic row, intent, studying us beneath their god or altar or machine of cones and disks within their cylinder walled with light—and at that moment there crystallized within my consciousness the sublimation of all the strangenesses of all that had gone before, smothering throat and heart; a panic loneliness as though I had wandered into an alien world—a world as unfamiliar to humanity, as unfamiliar with it as our own would seem to a thinking, mobile, crystal adrift among men.

A. Merritt, The Metal Monster (1920)

My muscles tightened for panic flight, held in only by a certain unconscious cau-
tion and half-hypnotic fascination.

> H. P. Lovecraft, "The Shadow over Innsmouth" (1931)

In a moment when no one was looking I reached out and seized the too familiar
sheets, crushing them in my hand without daring to look at their penmanship. I
ought to be sorry now that a kind of panic fear made me burn them that night
with averted eyes.

> H. P. Lovecraft & Adolphe de Castro, "The Electric Executioner" (1929)

Once more the mound was a thing of panic fright, and only the excitement of
the Great War served to restore it to the farther background of Binger folklore.

> H. P. Lovecraft & Zealia Bishop, "The Mound" (1930)

Then I heard a rustle among the food packages brought in yesterday, and that
dæmoniac fly crawled out before my eyes. I grabbed something flat and made
passes at the thing despite my panic fear, but with no more effect than usual.

> H. P. Lovecraft & Hazel Heald, "Winged Death" (1933)

And at that instant the head of Vacharn, in its rolling, bound against Uldulla's
feet; and the head, snarling ferociously, caught the hem of his robe with its teeth
and hung there as he sprang back in panic fright.

> Clark Ashton Smith, "Necromancy in Naat" (1935)

"Quiet!" he commanded, then hurried on: "In the old days when such things
were, my friend, Pan, the god of Nature, was very real to the people. They believed, firmly, that whoso saw Pan after nightfall, that one died instantly. Therefore, when a person is seized with a blind, unreasoning fear, even to this day, we
say he has a panic."

> Seabury Quinn, "The Great God Pan" (1926)

Someday the hill might be bulldozed down, when greed had grown even greater
than it is today and awe of primeval nature even less, but now it could still
awaken panic terror.

> Fritz Leiber, *Our Lady of Darkness* (1977)

I ran from Jason, who clung inexorably to the fabric of my mind, pouring the
black blind panic of his fear into my soul. Such fear as we have no name for today!

It was terror that only primitive peoples know, assailed by the vastness of
the unknown. A fear like an ecstasy that used to fall upon men in the old days
when Pan himself peered out at them, horned and grinning, through the trees.

Panic they called it, because they knew that horned head by name.

> Henry Kuttner, *The Mask of Circe* (1948)

And he told me of Pan, goat-footed, moving through the woodland with laughter running before him and panic behind, the same panic terror which my language and the Shaughnessy's get from his name. *Pânico*, we Brazilians call it.

C. L. Moore, "Dæmon" (1946)

Paniscus (*pl.* **Panisci**), **panis,** *n.* [< L < Gr *paniskos,* little Pan] A little pan; a satyr or faun. [These forms not in *OED*; s.v. panisc, panisk.]

Besides, that they filled almost all places, with spirits called *Dæmons:* the plains, with *Pan,* and *Panises,* or *Satyres;* the Woods, with *Fawnes,* and *Nymphs;* the Sea, with *Tritons,* and other *Nymphs;* every River, and Fountain, with a Ghost of his name, and with *Nymphs;* every house, with its *Lares,* or Familiars; every man, with his *Genius;* Hell, with Ghosts, and spirituall Officers, as *Charon, Cerberus,* and the *Furies;* and in the night time, all places with *Larvæ, Lemures,* Ghosts of men deceased, and a whole kingdome of Fayries, and Bugbears.

Thomas Hobbes, Leviathan; or, The Matter, Forme, and
Power of a Common-Wealth, Ecclesiastical and Civil (1651)

Mount Mænalus is a chosen haunt of dreaded Pan, whose queer companions are many, and simple swains believe that the tree must have some hideous kinship to these weird Panisci; but an old bee-keeper who lives in the neighboring cottage told me a different story.

H. P. Lovecraft, "The Tree" (1920)

paradisal, *adj.* Paradisiacal.

In these views the city and the desert valley were shewn always by moonlight, a golden nimbus hovering over the fallen walls and half revealing the splendid perfection of former times, shewn spectrally and elusively by the artist. The paradisal scenes were almost too extravagant to be believed; portraying a hidden world of eternal day filled with glorious cities and ethereal hills and valleys.

H. P. Lovecraft, "The Nameless City" (1921)

pelf, *n.* Money or riches, particularly when acquired dishonestly; "filthy lucre."

> But all his mind is set on mucky pelfe,
>   To hoord vp heapes of euill gotten masse,
>   For which he others wrongs, and wreckes himself;
>   Yet is he lincked to a louely lasse,
>   Whose beauty doth her bounty far surpasse,
>   The which to him both far vnequall yeares,
>   And also far vnlike conditions has;
>   For she does ioy to play emongst her peares,
> And to be free from hard restraint and gealous feares.

Edmund Spenser, The Faërie Queene (159-)

Immediately upon beholding this amulet we knew that we must possess it; that this treasure alone was our logical pelf from the centuried grave.

H. P. Lovecraft, "The Hound" (1922)

Penanggalan, *n.* [Malay] A vampire.

I return the Ullman-Knopf communication herewith. Knopf should remove the Borzoi from his imprint, and substitute either a Golden Calf or a jackass with brazen posteriors. I wish Herr Hitler had him, along with Gernsback. If I were a practising wizard, like Namirrha or Malygris or Nathaire, I'd devise a behemothian Sending and dispatch it to his office. The Sending would include a brace of penanggalans, and about a dozen rokurokubis with jaws elastic as their necks, and a regiment of poltergeists equipped with sledge-hammers. Callicantzaris and vrykolakes and barguests and Himalayan Snow-Men and Eskimo tupileks and the more unpleasant Aztec gods would form the main body; and a mass formation of shoggoths would bring up the rearguard. After their passing, the Knopf headquarters would be one with the middens of Nineveh.

Clark Ashton Smith, letter to H. P. Lovecraft (mid-October 1933)

pentagram, *n.* [< Gr, consisting of five lines] A five-pointed star. Also known as a pentalpha, pentacle, pentangle, and pentagonon (q.v.).

Three times, and with closed eyes, I invoked Apollonius. When I again looked forth there was a man in front of me, wrapped from head to foot in a species of shroud, which seemed more grey than white. He was lean, melancholy and beardless, and did not altogether correspond to my preconceived notion of Apollonius. I experienced an abnormally cold sensation, and when I endeavoured to question the phantom I could not articulate a syllable. I therefore placed my hand upon the Sign of the Pentagram, and pointed the sword at the figure, commanding it mentally to obey and not alarm me, in virtue of the said sign. The form thereupon became vague, and suddenly disappeared.

Éliphas Lévi (trans. A. E. Waite), *Transcendental Magic: Its Doctrine and Ritual* (1896)

"He closed his eyes, and called three times upon Apollonius. When he opened them, a man stood before him, wholly enveloped in a winding sheet, which seemed more grey than black. His form was lean, melancholy, and beardless. Eliphas felt an intense cold, and when he sought to ask his questions found it impossible to speak. Thereupon, he placed his hand on the Pentagram, and directed the point of his sword toward the figure, adjuring it mentally by that sign not to terrify, but to obey him. The form suddenly grew indistinct and soon it strangely vanished.

W. Somerset Maugham, *The Magician* (1907)

Ward at no time repulsed the doctor, but the latter saw that he could never reach the young man's inner psychology. Frequently he noted peculiar things about; little wax images of grotesque design on the shelves or tables, and the half-erased remnants of circles, triangles, and pentagrams in chalk or charcoal on the cleared central space of the large room.

> H. P. Lovecraft, *The Case of Charles Dexter Ward* (1927)

Dark hangings swathed the walls, their sable folds giving the chamber an elusive quality of spaciousness. Tables, chairs had been pushed back against the walls, and on the bare floor was traced an extraordinary design. Doyle searched his memory; then he recognized it—a pentagram, with its circles and six-pointed star, drawn in some substance that glowed with a faint greenish light.

> Henry Kuttner, "The Hunt" (1939)

Phaleron jug, *n.* A type of small jug so called because a majority of specimens were discovered in the locality of Phaleron. [Not in *OED*.]

(See quotation under **lekythos**.)

phantasm, *n.* An apparition or phantom; a vision, dream, or illusion.

Titles: Clark Ashton Smith, "Thirteen Phantasms" (1929)

It is only in the terrible phantasms of drugs or delirium that any other man can have had such a descent as mine.

> H. P. Lovecraft, "The Nameless City" (1921)

The bent, goatish giant before him seemed like the spawn of another planet or dimension; like something only partly of mankind, and linked to black gulfs of essence and entity that stretch like titan phantasms beyond all spheres of force and matter, space and time.

> H. P. Lovecraft, "The Dunwich Horror" (1928)

phantasma (*pl.* *phantasmata*), **phantasma** (*pl.* **phantasmata**) *n.* A phantasm, apparition, or phantom; a vision, dream, or illusion.

Somnambulism and other nocturnal deceptions frequently lend their aid to the formation of such *phantasmata* as are formed in this middle state, betwixt sleeping and waking.

> Sir Walter Scott, *Letters on Demonology and Witchcraft,*
> *Addressed to J. G. Lockheart, Esq.* (1830)

And the evening closed in upon me thus—and then the darkness came, and tarried, and went—and the day again dawned—and the mists of a second night were now gathering around—and still I sat motionless in that solitary room; and still I sat buried in meditation, and still the *phantasma* of the teeth maintained its terrible ascendancy as, with the most vivid and hideous distinctness, it floated about amid the changing lights and shadows of the chamber.

> Edgar Allan Poe, "Berenice" (1835)

They talk ignorantly of human nature who regard the abolished crime of Witch-craft as having had its origin in the phantasma of the superfluities.

"The Witch" (1827)

In writing, I treated the phantasmata as things seen; but at all other times I brushed them aside like any gossamer illusions of the night.

H. P. Lovecraft, "The Shadow out of Time" (1935)

phantasmagoria, *n.* [< Fr *phantasmagorie*; coined for the exhibition of a device invented by a man named M. Philipstal, and first publicly demonstrated in London in 1802, which created a series of optical illusions using slide projection] An ever-shifting sequence or medley of fantastic and illusive images and pictures, such as that seen in dreams or febrile hallucinations.

Titles: Lewis Carroll, *Phantasmagoria* (verse)

It is an inexplicable Phantasmagoria, capricious, quick-changing; as if our Traveller, instead of limbs and highways, had transported himself by some wishing-carpet, or Fortunatus' Hat.

Thomas Carlyle, *Sartor Resartus: The Life and Opinions of Herr Teufelsdröckh* (1831)

Suddenly at that thought—through this space, in which nothing save one mellow translucent light had been discernible—a swift succession of shadowy landscapes seemed to roll; trees, mountains, cities, seas, glided along, like the changes of a phantasmagoria; and at last, settled and stationary, he saw a cave by the gradual marge of an ocean shore—myrtles and orange-trees clothing the gentle banks.

Sir Edward Bulwer-Lytton, *Zanoni: A Rosicrucian Tale* (1842)

"Are you perfectly sure, Raymond, that your theory is not a phantasmagoria—a splendid vision, certainly, but a mere vision after all?"

Arthur Machen, "The Great God Pan" (1890)

"As men live, I have lived soberly and honestly, in the fear of God, all my days, and all I can do is believe that I suffered from some monstrous delusion, from some phantasmagoria of the bewildered senses."

Arthur Machen, "The Shining Pyramid" (1895)

I was sitting silent in an arm-chair by the fire, wondering over all I had heard, and still vainly speculating as to the secret springs concealed from me under all the phantasmagoria I had witnessed, when I became suddenly aware of a sensation that change of some sort had been at work in the room, and that there was something unfamiliar in its aspect.

Arthur Machen, "Novel of the Black Seal" in *The Three Impostors; or, The Transmutations* (1894)

Lucian tossed and cried out in his sleep that night, and the awakening in the morning was, in a measure, a renewal of the awakening in the fort. But the impression was not so strong, and in a plain room it seemed all delirium, a phantasmagoria.

Arthur Machen, *The Hill of Dreams* (1897)

In great perturbation and confusion of mind, I made my way into the street. Needless to say, no trace of the phantasmagoria that had been displayed before me remained.

Arthur Machen, "N" (1935)

Machen crosses those perilous frontiers. He all but lifts the veil; himself, indeed, passes beyond it. But the curtain drops behind him and we, hesitating to follow, but dimly see the phantasmagoria beyond; the ecstasies of vague shapes with a shining about them, on the one hand; on the other the writhings of animate gargoyles. And we experience, I think, a distinct sense of gratitude toward this terrible guide for that we are permitted no closer view of the mysteries that seem to him so clear.

Vincent Starrett, "Arthur Machen: A Novelist of Ecstasy and Sin" (1917) in
Buried Cæsars: Essays in Literary Appreciation (1923)

It was not noble, not wonderful; but it was better than this nightmare of phantoms, cruel and malignant and hideous, this phantasmagoria of damnation.

Aleister Crowley, *Moonchild* (1917; aka *The Butterfly-Net* or *The Net*)

It was like Night white in death then; and wan as the very realm of death and Hades I have beheld it, most terrifying, that neuter state and limbo of nothingness, when unreal sea and spectral vault, all confines lost, mingled in a void of ghostly phantasmagoria, pale to huelessness, at whose center I, as it were annihilated, seemed to moon aswoon in immensity of space; into which disembodied world would be flirted anon whiffs of that perfume of peach which I knew, and their frequency grew; but onward the *Boreal* moved, traversing, as it were, bottomless Eternity, and I got to latitude 72°, not far now from Northern Europe.

M. P. Shiel, *The Purple Cloud* (1901)

He knew clearly enough that his imagination was growing traitor to him, and yet at times it seemed the ship he sailed in, his fellow-passengers, the sailors, the wide sea, were all part of a filmy phantasmagoria that hung, scarcely veiling it, between him and a horrible real world.

H. G. Wells, "Pollock and the Porroh Man" (1895)

After the body had been taken away, and as I sat waiting for McCann to return, I tried to orient myself to this phantasmagoria through which, it seemed to me, I had been moving for endless time.

A. Merritt, *Burn, Witch, Burn!* (1932)

"There is no Mallare," he whispered. "I am Mallare. I whom you call Julian and who follows you like a shadow, I am all that lives. Everything else in this Kingdom, including you, is a phantasmagoria I tolerate and at which I have smiled too long. It is in my power to blot out this lewd mist. All the horrors and monstrosities at which you are beginning to tremble, I have only to wave my hand and command them and they will crawl back into my mind again, dragging you after them."

Ben Hecht, The Kingdom of Evil: A Continuation of the Journal of
Fantazius Mallare (1924)

Daily life had for him come to be a phantasmagoria of macabre shadow-studies; now glittering and leering with concealed rottenness as in Beardsley's best manner, now hinting terrors behind the commonest shapes and objects as in the subtler and less obvious work of Gustave Doré.

H. P. Lovecraft, "The Horror at Red Hook" (1925)

His sensations were those of a dreamer who is on the verge of waking; and London itself was unreal as the lands that slip from the dreamer's ken, receding in filmy mist and cloudy light. Beyond it all, he felt the looming and crowding of vast imageries, alien but half-familiar. It was as if the phantasmagoria of time and space were dissolving about him, to reveal some veritable reality—or another dream of space and time.

Clark Ashton Smith, "Ubbo-Sathla" (1932)

"I shall never know how we made it. I remember a phantasmagoria of endless pain and agony that racked my body, of thirst and hunger and raving delirium, and the endless ache of muscles that throbbed for rest in our almost incessant flight toward safety."

Donald Wandrei, "The Tree-Men of M'bwa" (1932)

phantasmagoric, *adj.* Of, pertaining to, or resembling a phantasmagoria (q.v.).

While the objects around me—while the carvings of the ceilings, the sombre tapestries of the walls, the ebon blackness of the floors, and the phantasmagoric armorial trophies which rattled as I strode, were but matters to which, or to such as which, I had been accustomed from my infancy—while I hesitated not to acknowledge how familiar was all this—I still wondered to find how unfamiliar were the fancies which ordinary images were stirring up.

Edgar Allan Poe, "The Fall of the House of Usher" (1839)

I can only contemplate such exhibitions of will and spirit and conclude, as I so often conclude, that precisely there resides reality. The spirit only is real. The flesh is phantasmagoric and apparitional.

Jack London, The Star Rover (1915)

Any further impressions belong wholly to the domain of phantasmagoric delirium.

> H. P. Lovecraft, "The Shadow out of Time" (1935)

I simply could not bring myself to mention Chapman's meadow and its baleful influence: the whole thing was too unbelievable, too phantasmagoric, to be offered as an explanation to a modern girl.

> Clark Ashton Smith, "Genius Loci" (1932)

They are figures in dreams. They amuse him. They belong to the opium: they never come if it's anything else. He tries not to smoke the hashish out here, actually, any more than courtesy demands. That chunky, resinous Turkestan phantasmagoric is fine for Russian, Kirghiz, and other barbaric tastes, but give Chu the tears of the poppy any time. The dreams are better, not so geometrical, so apt to turn everything—the air, the sky—to Persian rugs. Chu prefers situations, journeys, comedy.

> Thomas Pynchon, *Gravity's Rainbow* (1973)

phantasmal, *adj.* Of the nature of a phantasm (q.v.) or phantom.

He saw before him a vision of two forms; a faun with tingling and pricking flesh lay expectant in the sunlight, and there was also the likeness of a miserable shamed boy, standing with trembling body and shaking, unsteady hands. It was all confused, a procession of blurred images, now of rapture and ecstasy, and now of terror and shame, floating in a light that was altogether phantasmal and unreal.

> Arthur Machen, *The Hill of Dreams* (1897)

Later I must have dropped asleep again, for it was out of a phantasmal chaos that my mind leaped when the night grew with shrieks beyond anything in my former experience or imagination.

> H. P. Lovecraft, "The Lurking Fear" (1922)

All the dim horror-ridden shadows beyond ancestral fears clawed and whispered at the back of my mind, all the vague phantasmal shapes that lurk in the subconsciousness rose titanic and terrible, all the dim racial memories of grisly prehistoric fears awoke to haunt me. Every reverberation of those lumbering footfalls roused, in the slumbering deeps of my soul, horrific, mist-veiled shapes of near-memory.

> Robert E. Howard, "The Hoofed Thing" (1932)

Submerged in unvarying grayness, distracted and confused by phantasmal intrusions about them, the people of the town felt their world dissolving.

> Thomas Ligotti, "The Mystics of Muelenburg" (1987)

phantasmally, *adv.* In a phantasmal (q.v.) manner.

One could not be sure that the sea and the ground were horizontal, hence the relative position of everything else seemed phantasmally variable.

H. P. Lovecraft, "The Call of Cthulhu" (1926)

Pharos, Pharus, *pr.n.* & *n.* [< L < Gr *Pháros,* an island in the Egyptian Bay of Alexandria which housed a famous lighthouse built under the ruler Ptolemy Philadelphus, one of the Seven Wonders of the World] A lighthouse or tower provided with a beacon to guide passing seaman.

Titles: H. P. Lovecraft, "The Elder Pharos" in *Fungi from Yuggoth*

This is my advice, which if it be well observed, 'tis possible I may communicate more of this nature. I may stand up like a Pharus in a dark night and hold out that lamp which Philalethes hath overcast with that envious phrase of the Rabbins: "Ofttimes the silence of wisdom."

Thomas Vaughan, *Aula Lucis; or, The House of Light: A Discourse Written in the Year 1651*

And Evaine the Fox-Spirit laughed. Such unresponsiveness she declared to be, when manifested by a god, wholly surprising, and comparable to the Seven Wonders of the World, namely: (1) the Pyramids of Egypt; (2) the Hanging Gardens of Babylon; (3) the Tomb of Mausolos; (4) the Temple of Diana at Ephesus; (5) the Colossus of Rhodes; (6) the Statue of Zeus by Phidias; and (7) the Pharos at Alexandria. Yet Evaine continued, she perceived that she might trust him—

James Branch Cabell, *Something About Eve: A Comedy of Fig-Leaves* (1927)

"Will the gull choose, to dash herself against the Pharos light?"

E. R. Eddison, *A Fish Dinner in Memison* (1936–40)

They say (though none has been there) that it comes
Out of a pharos in a tower of stone,
Where the last Elder One lives on alone,
Talking to Chaos with the beat of drums.

H. P. Lovecraft, "The Elder Pharos" in *Fungi from Yuggoth* (1929–30)

He has on rare occasions whispered disjointed and irresponsible things about "the black pit", "the carven rim", "the proto-shoggoths", "the windowless solids with five dimensions", "the nameless cylinder", "the elder pharos", "Yog-Sothoth", "the primal white jelly", "the colour out of space", "the wings", "the eyes in darkness", "the moon-ladder", "the original, the eternal, the undying", "and other bizarre conceptions; but when he is fully himself he repudiates all this and attributes it to his curious and macabre reading of earlier years.

H. P. Lovecraft, *At the Mountains of Madness* (1931)

Star of strange hope,
Pharos beyond our desperate mire,

Lord of unscaleable gulfs,
Lamp of unknowable life.

> Theophilus Alvor, "Ode to Antares" as quoted in
> Clark Ashton Smith, "The Monster of the Prophecy" (1929)

("The carven rim," they are saying now here in my study. "The proto-shoggoths, the diagramed corridor, the elder Pharos, the dreams of Cutlu . . .")

> Fritz Leiber, "The Terror from the Depths" (1975; ellipsis in original)

Phlegethon, Phlegeton, *pr.n.* [< Gr *Phlegéthôn* < *phlegethein,* to blaze.] In Græco-Roman mythology, the river of fire in Hades. Also called **Pyriphlegethon.**

How restless are the ghosts of hellish spirits,
When every charmer with his magic spells
Calls us from nine-fold-trenched Phlegethon,
To scud and over-scour the earth in post
Upon the speedy wings of swiftest winds!

> Robert Greene, *The Honorable History of Friar Bacon and Friar Bungay* (1589)

He was the Sonne of blackest Acheron,
Whear many frozen soules doe chattring lie,
And rul'd the burning waves of Phlegethon,
Whear many more in flaming sulphur frie,
At once compel'd to live and forc't to die,
> Whear nothing can be heard for the loud crie
> Of oh, and ah, and out alas that I
Or once again might live, or once at length might die.

> Giles Fletcher, *Christs Victorie on Earth* (1610)

"And," exclaimed Margrave, no longer with gasp and effort, but with the swell of a voice which drowned all the discords of terror and of agony sent forth from the Phlegethon burning below,—"and this witch, whom I trusted, is a vile slave and impostor, more desiring my death than my life."

> Sir Edward Bulwer-Lytton, *A Strange Story* (1861)

Looking down from this pinnacle upon the howling Phlegethon below, I could not help smiling at the simplicity with which the honest Jonas Ramus records, as a matter difficult of belief, the anecdotes of the whales and the bears; for it appeared to me, in fact, a self-evident thing, that the largest ships of the line in existence, coming within the influence of that deadly attraction, could resist it as little as a feather the hurricane, and must disappear bodily and at once.

> Edgar Allan Poe, "A Descent into the Maelström" (1841)

And now Atal, slipping dizzily up over inconceivable steeps, heard in the dark a loathsome laughing, mixed with such a cry as no man else ever heard save in the

Phlegethon of unrelatable nightmares; a cry wherein reverberated the horror and anguish of a haunted lifetime packed into one atrocious moment [. . .]

H. P. Lovecraft, "The Other Gods" (1921)

Then came the world war. I was one of the first to go across, one of the last to return. Four years of blood-red charnel Hell . . . sickening slime of rain-rotten trenches . . . deafening bursting of hysterical shells . . . monotonous droning of sardonic bullets . . . smoking frenzies of Phlegethon's fountains . . . stifling fumes of murderous gases . . . grotesque remnants of smashed and shredded bodies . . . four years of transcendent satisfaction.

C. M. Eddy, Jr. & H. P. Lovecraft,
"The Loved Dead" (1923; ellipses in original)

An instant more, and he felt that his worst fears had been justified. The wine burned like the liquid flames of Phlegeton in his throat and on his lips; it seemed to fill his veins with a hot, infernal quicksilver.

Clark Ashton Smith, "The Holiness of Azédarac" (1931)

Man had worshipped Iod in older days, under other names. He was one of the oldest gods, and he had come to Earth, the tale went, in pre-human eons when the old gods soared between the stars, and earth was a stopping place for in-credible voyagers. The Greeks knew him as Trophonios; the Etruscans made nameless sacrifices diurnally to Vediovis, the Dweller beyond Phlegethon, the River of Flame.

Henry Kuttner, "The Hunt" (1939)

And then, "Who in Phlegethon are you?"

Gene Wolfe, *The Shadow of the Torturer* (1980)

Phlegethonian, *adj.* Of, pertaining to, or resembling Phlegethon (q.v.). [Not in *OED*.]

To you, my sister in God as well as by consanguinity, I must ease my mind (if this be possible) by writing again of the dread thing that harbors close to Perigon: for this thing has struck once more within the abbey walls, coming in darkness and without sound or other ostent than the Phlegethonian luster that surrounds its body and members.

Clark Ashton Smith, "The Beast of Averoigne" (1932)

Phlegethontic, *adj.* Of or pertaining to Phlegethon (q.v.).

And I remember when good old Mac display'd Hell's Kitchen to Little Belknap and me—a first glimpse for both of us. Morbid nightmare aisles of odorous Abaddon-labyrinths and Phlegethontic shores—accursed hashish-dreams of endless brick walls bulging and bursting with viscous abominations and staring insanely with bleared, geometrical patterns of windows—confused rivers of elemental, simian life with half-Nordic faces twisted and grotesque in the evil flare of bonfires set to signal the nameless gods of dark stars—sinister pigeon-breeders on the flat roofs of unclean teocallis, sending out birds of space with blasphemous messages for the black, elder gods of the cosmic void—death and menace behind furtive doors—frightened policemen in pairs—fumes of hellish brews concocted in obscene crypts—49th St.—11th Ave.—47th St.—10th Ave.—9th Ave. elevated—and through it all the little white-hair'd guide plodding na-ively along with his in a simpler, older, lovelier, and not very possible world . . . . . a sunny, hazy world of Wisconsin farm-days and green shores of romantick boy-adventure and Utopian lands of fixt, un-complex standards and values . . . . . good old Mac!

> H. P. Lovecraft, letter toMaurice W. Moe (18 January 1930) (ellipses as in original)

phobic, *adj.* Of or pertaining to a phobia or fear.

I awoke to red madness and the mockery of diabolism, as farther and farther down inconceivable vistas that phobic and crystalline anguish retreated and re-verberated.

> H. P. Lovecraft, "The Lurking Fear" (1922)

phthisical, *adj.* Afflicted with phthisis, consumption, tuberculosis.

"I am grown phthisical," he began, "from this cursed river air."

> H. P. Lovecraft, *The Case of Charles Dexter Ward* (1927)

plastic, *adj.* Pertaining to molding or shaping; susceptible to being molded or shaped.

In that hall the captive mind of an incredible entity—a half-plastic denizen of the hollow interior of an unknown trans-Plutonian planet eighteen million years in the future—had kept a certain thing which it had modelled from clay.

> H. P. Lovecraft, "The Shadow out of Time" (1935)

plasticity, *n.* The state or property of being plastic (q.v.).

It might be pure energy—a form ethereal and outside the realm of substance—or it might be partly material; some unknown and equivocal mass of plasticity, capable of changing at will to nebulous approximations of the solid, liquid, gaseous, or tenuously unparticled states.

> H. P. Lovecraft, "The Shunned House" (1924)

Plutonian, plutonian, *adj.* [< *Plūto,* the Roman equivalent of Hades, god of the underworld] Of, pertaining to, or resembling the god Pluto or the under-world over which he presides; Plutonic, Acherontic, Hadean, Stygian, Tar-tarean; dark, dismal, gloomy.

> As when the *Tartar* from his *Russian* Foe
> By *Astracan* over the Snowy Plains

Retires, or *Bactrian* Sophi from the horns
Of *Turkish* Crescent, leaves all waste beyond
The Realm of *Aladule*, in his retreat
To *Tauris* or *Casbeen*: So these the late
Heav'n-banisht Host, left desert utmost Hell
Many a dark League, reduc't in careful Watch
Round thir Metropolis, and now expecting
Each hour their great adventurer from the search
Of Foreign Worlds: he through the midst unmark't,
In show Plebeian Angel militant
Of lowest order, pass't; and from the door
Of that *Plutonian* Hall, invisible
Ascended his high Throne, which under state
Of richest texture spread, at th' upper end
Was plac't in regal lustre.

John Milton, Paradise Lost (1667)

Then this ebony bird beguiling my sad fancy into smiling,
By the grave and stern decorum of the countenance it wore,
"Though thy crest be shorn and shaven, thou," I said, "art sure no craven,
Ghastly grim and ancient Raven wandering from the Nightly shore—
Tell me what thy lordly name is on the Night's Plutonian shore!"
    Quoth the Raven "Nevermore."

Edgar Allan Poe, "The Raven" (1844)

Our miner sits in his tent door, meditating on the novel beauty of the scene before, below him. A north breeze has rolled the smoky sea silently away, and left no sign. Beneath the tent outspreads a vast abyss, dark, silent, "the night's Plutonian shore."

Phylos the Thibetan (Frederick S. Oliver),
A Dweller on Two Planets; or, The Dividing of the Way (1886)

Thus horror alone is left as my peculiar kingdom, & in it I must hold my lowly reproduction of a Plutonian court.

H. P. Lovecraft, letter to Elizabeth Toldridge (8 March 1929)

Nay, come! Rise up from grim Plutonian deep,
Ye lesser forms of Evil. Rise and creep
    Before my presence. Say there is a way . . .
Ye will not speak? Ye smirk and mock at me,
And gibbering, titter with disloyal glee?
    Then, go! I'll gain my grave as best I may . . .

Richard F. Searight, "The Wizard's Death" (ellipses in original)

Plutonic, *adj.* [< L *Plūto,* considered the Roman equivalent of Hades, god of the underworld] (1) Of or pertaining to Pluto; Plutonian. (2) In geology, pertaining to the action of great heat at great depths in the formation of igneous rocks in the earth's crust.

I staggered to my feet; looked back. The veils were gone! The precipice walled gateway they had curtained was filled with a Plutonic glare as though it opened into the incandescent heart of a volcano!

A. Merritt, The Metal Monster (1920)

As the cloud of steam from the Plutonic gulf finally concealed the entire surface from my sight, all the firmament shrieked at a sudden agony of mad reverberations which shook the trembling æther.

H. P. Lovecraft & Winifred Virginia Jackson, "The Crawling Chaos" (1920–21)

præternatural, preternatural, *adj.* Beyond the limits of nature; supernatural.

A ghost story, to be a good one, should unite, as much as possible, objects such as they are in life with a preternatural spirit.

Leigh Hunt, "A Tale for a Chimney Corner" (1819)

The fury of the tempest immediately died away, and a dead calm sullenly succeeded. A white flame still enveloped the building like a shroud, and, streaming far away into the quiet atmosphere, shot forth a glare of preternatural light; while a cloud of smoke settled heavily over the battlements in the distinct colossal figure of—*a horse.*

Edgar Allan Poe, "Metzengerstein" (1832)

A great painter of antiquity is said, in a picture of Hades, to have represented the monsters that glide through the ghostly River of the Dead, so artfully, that the eye perceived at once that the river itself was but a spectre, and the bloodless things that tenanted it had no life, their forms blending with the dead waters till, as the eye continued to gaze, it ceased to discern them from the preternatural element they were supposed to inhabit.

Sir Edward Bulwer-Lytton, Zanoni: A Rosicrucian Tale (1842)

On July 22 occurred the first incident which, though lightly dismissed at the time, takes on a preternatural significance in relation to later events.

H. P. Lovecraft, "The Rats in the Walls" (1923)

propylæum (*pl.* **propylæa**), *n.* A vestibule or court leading into a temple or group of buildings.

I saw phantom processions of priests with the heads of bulls, falcons, cats, and ibises; phantom processions marching interminably through subterraneous labyrinths and avenues of titanic propylæa beside which a man is as a fly, and offering unnamable sacrifices to indescribable gods.

H. P. Lovecraft & Harry Houdini, "Under the Pyramids" (1924)

pshent, *n.* [< Gr *pskhént* < Demotic Ancient Egyptian *p-skhent, p-,* the + *skhent* < Hieroglyphic Ancient Egyptian *sekhet*; these three forms are found in the parallel texts on the Rosetta Stone] The double crown of ancient Egypt.

([. . .] On his head is perched an Egyptian pshent. Two quills project over his ears.)

James Joyce, *Ulysses* (1914–21)

And the priests shook their pshent-bearing heads and vowed it would be the death of his soul.

H. P. Lovecraft, *The Dream-Quest of Unknown Kadath* (1926–27)

psychic, *adj.* Of or pertaining to the psyche, the mind or soul; psychical.

That the psychic or intellectual life might be impaired by the slight deterioration of sensitive brain-cells which even a short period of death would be apt to cause, West fully realised.

H. P. Lovecraft, "Herbert West—Reanimator" (1921–22)

psychopomp, psychopompos, *n.* [< Gr *psýkhopompós*] One who leads souls to the afterworld, such as Hermes or Charon.

Titles: H. P. Lovecraft, "Psychopompos: A Tale in Rhyme" (verse); Clark Ashton Smith, "Cattle Salute the Psychopomp" in "Experiments in Haiku: Mortal Essences"

Then too, the natives are mortally afraid of the numerous whippoorwills which grow vocal on warm nights. It is vowed that the birds are psychopomps lying in wait for the souls of the dying, and that they time their eerie cries in unison with the sufferer's struggling breath. If they can catch the fleeing soul when it leaves the body, they instantly flutter away chittering in dæmoniac laughter; but if they fail, they subside gradually into a disappointed silence.

H. P. Lovecraft, "The Dunwich Horror" (1928)

It was not until after the rise of the miasma-distorted moon that an anguished groan came from the dying man, followed by a united rising of affrighted nightjars, from where they perched lengthwise in the trees and watched the house from across the river with glinting eyes. They flew as if escaping from some pursuing horror, which some believe these psychopomps to have attempted to capture.

Ramsey Campbell, "The Horror from the Bridge" (1964)

pthagon, *n.* The inner skin of the Muvian yakith-lizard. [Not in *OED*.]

So T'yog wrote his protective formula on a scroll of *pthagon*-membrane (according to von Junzt, the inner skin of the extinct yakith-lizard) and enclosed it in a carven cylinder of *lagh* metal—the metal brought by the Elder Ones from Yuggoth, and found in no mine of earth.

H. P. Lovecraft & Hazel Heald, "Out of the Æons" (1933)

pulp, *n.* A soft, soggy, and only partially cohering mass of vegetable or animal matter; the substance into which human beings and other creatures are reduced by beating and pounding, and the raw material from which weird fiction and fantasy are made.

> At his feet the old coroner lay dead; Arthwait, his convulsions terminated by exhaustion approximating coma, lay with his head upon the carrion, his tongue, lolling from his mouth, chewed to a bloody pulp.
>
> Aleister Crowley, *Moonchild* (1917; aka *The Butterfly-Net* or *The Net*)

> "The blood seethes and boils in the veins, the brains are boiling in the skull, the heart in the breast glowing and bursting, the bowels a redhot mass of burning pulp, the tender eyes flaming like molten balls."
>
> James Joyce, *A Portrait of the Artist as a Young Man* (1904–14)

> Hail to the carcass, fed, tho' bound in chains;
> Pox on your dreamer's or your poet's pains!
> We drink to flesh in one black Stygian gulp,
> And sink our spirits in a grave of PULP!
>
> H. P. Lovecraft, "Lines upon the Magnates of the Pulp"

> The tremendous mass broke in an entire side of the chapel; and those who had gathered therein were found later, crushed into bloody pulp amid the splinters of their carven Christ.
>
> Clark Ashton Smith, "The Colossus of Ylourgne" (1932)

> Out of the shaft came a slavering mad nightmare which arrows pierced but could not check, which swords carved but could not slay. It fell slobbering upon the warriors, crushing them to crimson pulp, tearing them to bits as an octopus might tear small fishes, sucking their blood from their mangled limbs and devouring them even as they screamed and struggled.
>
> Robert E. Howard, "The Valley of the Worm" (1934)

> Demons, monsters, unnameable things! Nightmare colossi strode bellowing through the murk, and amorphous gray things like giant slugs walked upright on stumpy legs. Creatures of shapeless soft pulp, beings with flame-shot eyes scattered over their misshapen bodies like fabled Argus, writhed and twisted there in the evil glow. Winged things that were not bats swooped and fluttered in the tenebrous air, whispering sibilantly—whispering in *human* voices.
>
> Henry Kuttner, "The Secret of Kralitz" (1936)

> "Truly at this point many a one has failed—Mr Bradly Mr Martin is like pulp beside you—A man walks through dream shirt in another—"
>
> William S. Burroughs, *The Ticket That Exploded* (1957–61)

Glittering eyes peered up and: "Man, like good bye"—Ding dong bell—
Silence—Solitude—Bradly leaning say: "Good bye then in currents waiting for
the carbon dioxide—Truly *adiós*"—Bitter price—Martin is like pulp behind—

> William S. Burroughs, *The Ticket That Exploded* (1957–61)

bitter price—whale stranded—the colors released, Martin is like pulp behind—
Now remove all your gimmicks in setting forth—This dream be your orders—
Your ticket now ended—All Martin's recorded speech fade-out—Mr Bradly
Mr Martin, now show blighted planet the dog tape empty of control—

> William S. Burroughs, *The Ticket That Exploded* (1957–61)

He paced behind the board members like an aroused tom cat. He stopped behind Scamperelli the Pulp King who perfected a process for making pasta from
sawdust. He clamped one hand over Scamperelli's mouth pulled his head back
and applied the hack saw to Scamperelli's throbbing carotid. "Scamperelli do
you like this thing that I have done?"
   "Glub . . glub . . glub . ."
   "I presume that is pulp talk for 'yes.'"

> William S. Burroughs, *The Ticket That Exploded* (1957–61; ellipses as in original)

There was a moist explosion, and the watchers were spattered with a noisome
pulp.

> Ramsey Campbell, "The Horror from the Bridge" (1964)

pulpily, *adv.* In the manner of pulp (q.v.); in a pulpy (q.v.) manner.

Then, rearing the mace like a warrior in battle, he struck down with one crashing
blow the impious thing that wore his own rightful flesh united with the legs and
hooves of a demon courser. And the thing crumpled swiftly down and lay with
the brain spreading pulpily from its shattered skull on the shining jet.

> Clark Ashton Smith, "The Dark Eidolon" (1932)

pulpy, *adj.* Of or resembling pulp (q.v.); consisting of pulp or a pulp-like substance; soft, fleshy, and succulent.

The three friends moved away from the door, and began to walk slowly up and
down what had been a gravel path, but now lay green and pulpy with damp
mosses.

> Arthur Machen, *The Three Impostors; or, The Transmutations* (1894)

The young of the human creature were really too horrible; they defiled the earth,
and made existence unpleasant, as the pulpy growth of a noxious and obscene
fungus spoils an agreeable walk.

> Arthur Machen, *The Hill of Dreams* (1897)

West had greedily seized the lifeless thing which had once been his friend and
fellow-scholar; and I shuddered when he finished severing the head, placed it in

his hellish vat of pulpy reptile-tissue to preserve it for future experiments, and proceeded to treat the decapitated body on the operating table.

H. P. Lovecraft, "Herbert West—Reanimator" (1922)

Amid these hushed throngs I followed my voiceless guides; jostled by elbows that seemed preternaturally soft, and pressed by chests and stomachs that seemed abnormally pulpy; but seeing never a face and hearing never a word.

H. P. Lovecraft, "The Festival" (1923)

If I say that my somewhat extravagant imagination yielded simultaneous pictures of an octopus, a dragon, and a human caricature, I shall not be unfaithful to the spirit of the thing. A pulpy, tentacled head surmounted a grotesque and scaly body with rudimentary wings; but it was the general outline of the whole which made it most shockingly frightful. Behind the figure was a vague suggestion of a Cyclopean architectural background.

H. P. Lovecraft, "The Call of Cthulhu" (1926)

I caught glimpses of glittering eyes, cold and unwinking; pulpy, glowing masses of semi-transparent flesh; monstrous reptilian appendages that swam before my eyes as the things moved loathsomely. I felt contaminated, defiled. I think I shrieked, and my hands flew up to shut out that intolerable vision of lost Abaddon—the dimension of the Invaders.

Henry Kuttner, "The Invaders" (1939)

Even now he did not see them plainly as they sported in the surf, but there were dim suggestions of past horror in their tenebrous outlines. The things were like seals: great, fish-like, bloated monsters with pulpy, shapeless heads.

Robert Bloch & Henry Kuttner, "The Black Kiss" (1937)

And then the hot pulpy lips had pressed against his—the loathsome, slimy lips had kissed him again. Wet, dank, horribly avid kiss!

Robert Bloch & Henry Kuttner, "The Black Kiss" (1937)

"The pulpy, tentacled head," I heard in horror, "*Cthulhu fhtagn*, the *wrong* geometry, the polarizing miasma, the prismatic distortion, *Cthulhu R'lyeh*, the positive blackness, the living nothingness . . ."

Fritz Leiber, "The Terror from the Depths" (1975; ellipsis in original)

purulent, *adj.* [< L *pūs* (root *pūr-*), matter, pus] Infected, generating and discharging pus; suppurating, festering.

How still it was! I dropped a pebble and the little plop as it struck the water echoed cavernously from stone to stone. Envenomed the water was no doubt, that purulent green, filled with slow malevolent thought, memory of tragedy, undercurrent of sighs and terrors and hauntings, triste and inflamed. Here lies buried the wrystone; it is tended her by maidens with hair gray as Spanish moss and breasts moss-green.

Leonard Cline, The Dark Chamber (1927)

And it fluttered not in the wind, but moved with a flowing as of some heavy, thick and purulent liquid; and its color was not blue nor purple nor black, nor any other hue to which man's eyes are habituated, but a hue as of some darker putrescence then that of death; and its form was altogether monstrous, seeming to move as if cast by one that trod erect, but having the squat head and long, undulant body of things that should creep rather than walk.

Clark Ashton Smith, "The Double Shadow" (1932)

The hypochondriac lassoes the passer-by and administers a straitjacket and starts talking about his rotting septum: "An awful purulent discharge is subject to flow out . . . just wait till you see it."

William S. Burroughs, Naked Lunch (1955–59; ellipsis in original)

pustulant, *adj.* Of, pertaining to, or resembling a pustule or pustules.

Gradually the nacreous surface cleared and brightened, so that the crouching creature emerged in bold relief against its background of shadow. The flesh tones became livid blendings of pustulant ochre and myxalike green, and the red eyes flared with renewed intensity. Hitherto-undisclosed details were revealed; the tiny black mites clinging to the furry forearms, the patches of *usnea humana* on the surface of the victim's skull, and the minute gobbets of flesh lodged between the feasting fangs.

Robert Bloch, Strange Eons (1978)

putrefaction, *n.* The process of putrefying (q.v.); the matter resulting from the process of putrefaction.

Most of her visions were simply formless and incoherent horrors. Her foolish thoughts and senseless impulses took shape, usually in some distortion of an animal form, with that power of viscosity which is to vertebrates the most loathsome of all possibilities of life, since it represents the line of development which they have themselves avoided, and is therefore to them excremental in character. But to Iliel's morbidity the fascination of these things was overpowering. She took an unnatural and morose delight in watching the cuttle-fish squeeze itself slowly into a slime as black and oozy as the slug, and that again send trickling feelers as of leaking motor-oil, greasy and repulsive, with a foul scum upon its surface, until the beast looked like some parody of a tarantula; then this again would collapse, as if by mere weariness of struggle against gravitation, and spread itself slowly as a pool of putrefaction, which was yet intensely vital and personal by reason of its power to suck up everything within its sphere of sensation.

Aleister Crowley, Moonchild (1917; aka The Butterfly-Net or The Net)

If men would face the facts of life, including their own constitutions as they are, practically all abuse and perversions would disappear. They are for the most part morbid phantasms of putrefaction, aggravated by the attempt at suppression. The wound of Amfortas will not heal because it has never been properly opened and rendered aseptic.

> Aleister Crowley, *The Confessions of Aleister Crowley: An Autohagiography* (1923)

Drawn by the baleful mesmerism, like a somnambulist led by an unseen demon, I entered the room. I knew with a loathly prescience the sight that awaited me beyond the sill—the *double* heap of human segments, some of them fresh and bloody, and others already blue with beginning putrefaction and marked with earthstains, that were mingled in abhorrent confusion on the rug.

> Clark Ashton Smith, "The Return of the Sorcerer" (1931)

putrefy, *v.intr.* & *v.tr.* To decompose, decay, rot, and become putrid and corrupt.

It is a terrible error to let any natural impulse, physical or mental, stagnate. Crush it out, if you will, and be done with it; or fulfil it, and get it out of the system; but do not allow it to remain there and putrefy. The suppression of the normal sex instinct, for example, is responsible for a thousand ills.

> Aleister Crowley, *Moonchild* (1917; aka *The Butterfly-Net* or *The Net*)

I looked again, as the air putrefied that withered countenance before my eyes.

> Robert Bloch, "The Brood of Bubastis" (1937)

putrescence, *n.* The state or property of being putrescent (q.v.).

Upon the bed, before that whole company, there lay a nearly liquid mass of loathsome—of detestable putrescence.

> Edgar Allan Poe, "The Facts in the Case of M. Valdemar" (1845)
> [Altered to "putridity" in the author's final version.]

No spiritist, once he is wholly enmeshed in sentimentality and Freudian fear-phantasms, is capable of concentrated thought, of persistent will, or of moral character. Devoid of every spark of the divine light which was his birthright, a prey before death to the ghastly tenants of the grave, the wretch, like the mesmerized and living corpse of Poe's Monsieur Valdemar, is a "nearly liquid mass of loathsome, of detestable putrescence."

> Aleister Crowley, *Magick in Theory and Practice*

As my term of servitude draws to a close, I begin to feel the exhilaration of approaching fossildom ... long nights of uninterrupted reading, when I shall slither and wallow in all the diseased and unnatural horrors of nether hells with the putrid and sadistic authors of my choosing—or when, these tame literateurs proving as insipid as a mere Huysmans or Baudelaire, I shall seize a pen made of a condor's wing and dipped in carbonaceous putrescence, and leave on yellow pages a trail of ideographick fœtor which shall be to their superficial dabblings as Poe is to Frances Hodgson Burnett. . . .

H. P. Lovecraft, letter to James Morton (3 May 1923) (ellipses in original)

putrescent, *adj.* Rotting and becoming putrid; putrefying; of or pertaining to the process of putrefaction.

> Now glow'd the ground, and tarn, and cave, and trees,
> And moving forms, and things not spoken of,
> With such a phosphorescence as men glimpse
> In the putrescent thickets of the swamp
> Where logs decaying lie, and rankness reigns.

H. P. Lovecraft, "Aletheia Phrikodes" in
"The Poe-et's Nightmare: A Fable" (1916)

putrid, *adj.* [< L *putridus,* rotten] In a state of loathsome and noxious decomposition, decay, and rottenness that produces an offensively fœtid odor; putrescent.

By the side of three putrid half-corrupted bodies lay the sleeping beauty.

M. G. Lewis, *The Monk: A Romance* (1794)

putridity, *n.* A state of loathsome and noxious decomposition, decay, and rottenness that produces an offensively fœtid odor; loathsomely putrid matter; putrescence.

"For six months he lingered, a hopeless maniac—raving as wildly from the very moment of his discovery as at the moment he died—babbling his visions of the giant horse, the fissured house collapsing into the tarn, the black cat, the pit, the pendulum, the raven on the pallid bust, the beating heart, the pearly teeth, and the nearly liquid mass of loathsome—of detestable putridity from a voice emanated."

Robert Bloch, "The Man Who Collected Poe" (1951)

pylon, *n.* [< Gr] A gateway; in particular, the monumental gateway to an Egyptian temple.

Would it unlock the mystic pylon which his sharp eye had traced amidst the jagged rocks at the back of that inner cave behind the Snake-Den on the hill?

H. P. Lovecraft & E. Hoffmann Price,
"Through the Gates of the Silver Key" (1932–33)

Q

quintessence, *n.* [< Middle English < Middle French < Mediæval Latin, fifth essence] The purest and most highly concentrated essence of a certain thing; the most typical example or instance of a certain thing or quality.

quintessential, *adj.* Of or pertaining to a quintessence (q.v.).

There is a menacing, portentous quality in the tones which they use to describe very ordinary events—a seemingly unjustified tendency to assume a furtive, suggestive, confidential air, and to fall into awesome whispers at certain points—which insidiously disturbs the listener. Old Yankees often talk like that; but in this case the melancholy aspect of the half-mouldering village, and the dismal nature of the story unfolded, give these gloomy, secretive mannerisms an added significance. One feels profoundly the quintessential horror that lurks behind the isolated Puritan and his strange repressions—feels it, and longs to escape precipitately into clearer air.

H. P. Lovecraft & Hazel Heald, "The Horror in the Burying-Ground" (1933–35)

R

rath, rathe, *n.* [< Gaelic] An Irish hill-fort, formerly erroneously attributed to the Danes, and now associated with fairies.

Those with Celtic legendry in their heritage—mainly the Scotch-Irish element of New Hampshire, and their kindred who had settled in Vermont on Governor Wentworth's colonial grants—linked them vaguely with the malign fairies and "little people" of the bogs and raths, and protected themselves with scraps of incantation handed down through many generations.

H. P. Lovecraft, "The Whisperer in Darkness" (1930)

Gabinius had, the rumour ran, come upon a cliffside cavern where strange folk met together and made the Elder Sign in the dark; strange folk whom the Britons knew not save in fear, and who were the last to survive from a great land in the west that had sunk, leaving only the islands with the raths and circles and shrines of which Stonehenge was the greatest.

H. P. Lovecraft, "The Descendant"

This simple peasant sympathy and universal pity stuff will do for adolescents and Slavs—but it simply can't mean a tremendous lot to a Celt or Teuton who has looked into enchanted forests or heard strange music on the raths in the dark of the moon.

H. P. Lovecraft, letter to Frank Belknap Long, 26 October 1926

raven, *v.intr.* & *v.tr.* To consume and devour greedily, voraciously, and ravenously;

And the dragon did not open his ravening mouth, nor rush upon the knight, breathing out fire; for well he knew the fate of those that did these things, but he consented to the terms imposed, and swore to the knight to become his trusty steed.

Lord Dunsany, "The Hoard of the Gibbelins" (1911)

The hatred men feel for every ravening monster that wears fangs and scales, she pointed out, is due to its apparel being not quite the sort of thing to which men are accustomed: whereas people were wholly used to having soldiers and prelates and statesmen ramping about in droves, and so viewed these without any particular wonder or disapproval.

James Branch Cabell, *The High Place: A Comedy of Disenchantment* (1923)

Raw butcher's meat was never fresh enough: it had known the coldness of death and refrigeration, and had lost all vital essence. Long ago there had been other meals, warm, and sauced with still-spurting blood. But now the thin memory merely served to exasperate his ravening.

Clark Ashton Smith, "Monsters in the Night" (1953)

The red men of the isles! By the thousands they had descended on the Isle of the Gods in the night, and whether stealth or treachery let them through the walls, the comrades never knew, but now they ravened through the corpse-strewn streets, glutting their blood-lust in holocaust and massacre wholesale.

Robert E. Howard, "The Gods of Bal-Sagoth" (1931)

Like locusts they came on, from every side, eyes red with blood-lust, teeth bared in hate—beasts of the jungle, ravening for the kill!

P. Schuyler Miller, "Tetrahedra of Space" (1931)

The goblins gathered again in the valley. There a host of Wargs came ravening and with them came the bodyguard of Bolg, goblins of huge size with scimitars of steel. Soon actual darkness was coming into a stormy sky; while still the great bats swirled about the heads and ears of elves and men, or fastened vampire-like on the stricken.

J. R. R. Tolkien, *The Hobbit; or, There and Back Again* (1930–36)

The horror always came next. He would suddenly emerge into a series of dimly lighted chambers, and as he stood undetected in the shadows, he would see *things*. These were the dwellers that laired beneath; the ghastly spawn that ravened on the dead.

Robert Bloch, "The Grinning Ghoul" (1936)

Through the eons this entity has ravened in the abyss beyond our dimension, sending out its call to claim victims where it could.

Henry Kuttner, "Hydra" (1939)

recherché, recherché, *adj.* [< Fr < *chercher*, to seek] Rare, uncommon; of rare quality and choiceness.

>   At Henry's mansion then, in Blank-Blank Square,
>   Was Juan a *recherché*, welcome guest,
>   As many other noble Scions were;
>   And some who had but talent for their crest;
>   Or wealth, which is a passport every where;
>   Or even mere fashion, which indeed's the best
>   Recommendation;—and to be well drest
>   Will very often supersede the rest.

Lord Byron, *Don Juan* (1818–23)

To be less abstract—Let us suppose a game of draughts where the pieces are reduced to four kings, and where, of course, no oversight is to be expected. It is obvious that here the victory can be decided (the players being at all equal) only by some *recherché* movement, the result of some strong exertion of the intellect.

Edgar Allan Poe, "The Murders in the Rue Morgue" (1841)

The duellist accepted my aid with his usual stiff and *ultra recherché* air, and, taking my arm, led me to his apartment.

Edgar Allan Poe, "Mystification" (1837)

During a rainy afternoon, not long ago, being in a mood too listless for continuous study, I sought relief from *ennui* in dipping here and there, at random, among the volumes of my library—no very large one, certainly, but sufficiently miscellaneous; and, I flatter myself, not a little *recherché*.

Edgar Allan Poe, *Marginalia* (1844)

His food was taken to him in the room he had made his habitation, and it was remarked that, though simple before in his gustatory tastes, he now—possibly owing to the sedentary life he led—became fastidious, insisting on *recherché* bits.

M. P. Shiel, "The Race of Orven"

In a fashion almost business-like he laid before me a pile of manuscript which he wanted me to type for him. The familiar click of the keys aided me somewhat in dismissing my apprehensions of vague evil, and I could almost smile at the recherché and terrific information comprised in my employer's notes, which dealt mainly with formulæ for the acquisition of unlawful power.

Clark Ashton Smith, "The Return of the Sorcerer" (1931)

recondite, *adj.* [< L *reconditus*, hidden] Hidden, removed from view; of or pertaining to the erudite obscurity of the scholar, who has plumbed the depths of profound and abstruse matters; profound and abstruse.

Stella took possession of the recondite apartments. Scythrop intended to find her another asylum; but from day to day he postponed his intention, and, by degrees forgot it. The young lady reminded him of it from day to day, till she also forgot it.

Thomas Love Peacock, *Nightmare Abbey* (1817)

For a long time, all my experiments were condemned to failure, because I was groping among mysterious powers and recondite laws whose motive-principle I had not wholly grasped.

Clark Ashton Smith, "Murder in the Fourth Dimension" (1930)

> We have seen fair colors
> That dwell not in the light—
> Intenser gold and iris

Occult and recondite;
We have seen the black suns
Pouring forth the night.

Clark Ashton Smith, "Nyctalops" (1929)

For [Clark Ashton] Smith at his best is a fine creative scholar. I know of no more impressive way to introduce Smith to a stranger than with "The Kingdom of the Worm," which was published in *The Fantasy Fan* many years ago. The episode was perfectly in the style of its ostensible period; it could have been slipped into *The Voyage and Travel of Sir John Mandeville, Knight* without the unwary reader's detecting it in his perusal of that recondite volume; as an entity in itself it helf together beautifully, and preserved throughout that atmosphere of naive wonder mixed with uneasiness which is the literary signature of the great French liar—and a far more difficult thing to achieve than a mere parroting of stylistic tricks.

James Blish, "Eblis in Bakelite" (1943)

Maria knew that Old Kyte had secret & esoteric Knowledge of more than herbal healing; yea, of Arts Arcane and Recondite.

Robert Anton Wilson, *Nature's God* (1991)

redolent, *adj.* Diffusing an odor; suggestive of, reminiscent of, bringing to mind.

Just what it was that I feared or loathed, I could by no means define; but something in the whole atmosphere seemed redolent of unhallowed age, of unpleasant crudeness, and of secrets which should be forgotten.

H. P. Lovecraft, "The Picture in the House" (1920)

Charles, though he was inordinately long in answering the summons and was still redolent of strange and noxious laboratory odours when he did finally make his agitated appearance, proved a far from recalcitrant subject; and admitted freely that his memory and balance had suffered somewhat from close application to abstruse studies.

H. P. Lovecraft, *The Case of Charles Dexter Ward* (1927)

It was whispered about that the Reverend Johannes Vanderhoof had made a compact with the devil, and was preaching his word in the house of God. His sermons had become weird and grotesque—redolent with sinister things which the ignorant people of Daalbergen did not understand. He transported them back over ages of fear and superstition to regions of hideous, unseen spirits, and peopled their fancy with night-haunting ghouls.

Wilfred Blanch Talman & H. P. Lovecraft, "Two Black Bottles" (1926)

A medley of untraceable exotic odors was wafted through the twilight. The perfume was redolent of alien mystery, and it thrilled and troubled the Earthmen, who became silent as they approached the bridge, feeling the oppression of eery strangeness that gathered from all sides in the thickening gloom.

Clark Ashton Smith, "Vulthoom" (1933)

relief, *n.* In the plastic arts, the projection of a design from the plane surface; a work of art characterized by such a relief. A common style of art in fantasy and weird fiction, particularly the low or bas-relief. Cf. **alto-relievo, bas-relief, basso-relievo, high relief, low relief.**

History told of their conquests, triumphs, glories, heroisms, of heart-stirring tragedies and lovely sacrifices. They were all far greater than life-size—like the monarchs and gods in an Assyrian relief—the common people ran about beneath their feet according to the best historical traditions. So it had been.

H. G. Wells, *Star-Begotten: A Biological Fantasia* (1937)

reticulate, reticulated, *adj.* Forming or resembling a network.

Above the waist it was semi-anthropomorphic; though its chest, where the dog's rending paws still rested watchfully, had the leathery, reticulated hide of a crocodile or alligator. The back was piebald with yellow and black, and dimly suggested the squamous covering of certain snakes. Below the waist, though, it was the worst; for here all human resemblance left off and sheer phantasy began.

H. P. Lovecraft, "The Dunwich Horror" (1928)

***revenant,* revenant,** *n.* [< Fr *revenant*, one who returns < *revenir*, to return] One who returns; in particular, one who returns after death; a ghost, specter, or vampire.

Titles: Henry Thomson, "Le Revenant"; Walter de la Mare, "The Revenant" (verse); Clark Ashton Smith, "Revenant" (verse)

"*Sacre—cochon—bleu!*" exclaimed Fatout, giving very deliberate emphasis to every portion of his terrible oath—"I vould not meet de *revenant*, de ghost—*non*—not for all de *bowl-de-punch* in de vorld."

Thomas Love Peacock, *Nightmare Abbey* (1817)

"It was troubled by *revenants*, sir; several were tracked to their graves, there detected by the usual tests, and extinguished in the usual way, by decapitation, by the stake, and by burning; but not until many of the villagers were killed."

J. S. LeFanu, "Carmilla" (1871)

He had at his fingers' ends all the great and little works upon the subject. "Magia Posthuma," "Phlegon de Mirabilibus," "Augustinus de curâ pro Mortuis," "Philosophicæ et Christianæ Cogitationes de Vampiris," by John Christofer Harenberg; and a thousand others, among which I remember only a few of those which he lent to my father. He had a voluminous digest of all the judicial cases, from which he had extracted a system of principles that appear to govern—

some always, and others occasionally only—the condition of the vampire. I may mention, in passing, that the deadly pallor attributed to that sort of *revenants*, is a mere melodramatic fiction. They present, in the grave, and when they show themselves in human society, the appearance of healthy life.

J. S. LeFanu, "Carmilla" (1871)

Did ghosts return or linger from a world that had been buried beneath the waves for unknown ages? Damn it, he had almost felt at times as if he were some sort of revenant himself.

Clark Ashton Smith, "An Offering to the Moon" (1930)

There are things hidden in the great deserts and mountains of the world, and others sunken under the deepest oceans, which never were meant to exist in any sane or ordered universe. Yes, and certain revenants of immemorial horror have even come among men.

Brian Lumley, "The House of the Temple" (1981)

Roodmas, *pr.n.* [< *rood*, cross + *mass*] September 14, (Holy) Rood Day, the Exaltation of the Cross; or May 3, the Invention of the Cross, commemorating the discovery of the Cross (or Rood) by the Emperor Constantine's mother Helena in 326; or, May Eve.

The chief festivals were: in the spring, May Eve (April 30), called Roodmas or Rood Day in Britain and Walpurgis-Nacht in Germany; in the autumn, November Eve (October 31), called in Britain Allhallow Eve. Between these two came: in the winter, Candlemas (February 2); and in the summer, the Gule of August (August 1), called Lammas in Britain. To these were added the festivals of the solstitial invaders, Beltane at midsummer and Yule at midwinter; the movable festival of Easter was also added, but the equinoxes were never observed in Britain. On the advent of Christianity the names of the festivals were changed, and the date of one—Roodmas—was slightly altered so as to fall on May 3; otherwise the dates were observed as before, but with ceremonies of the new religion.

Miss Margaret Murray, *The Witch-Cult in Western Europe* (1921)

Miss Murray mistakenly says (p. 109) that May Eve (30 April) is called Roodmas or Rood Day. Roodmas or Rood Day is 3 May, the Feast of the Invention of Holy Cross. An early English Calendar (702–706) even gives 7 May as Roodmas. The Invention of Holy Cross is found in the Lectionary of Silos and the Bobbio Missal. The date was not slightly altered. The Invention of Holy Cross is among the very early festivals.

Montague Summers, note to *The History of Witchcraft and Demology* (1925)

"Born on Candlemas—nine months after May-Eve of 1912, when the talk about the queer earth noises reached clear to Arkham— What walked on the mountains that May-Night? What Roodmas horror fastened itself on the world in half-human flesh and blood?"

> H. P. Lovecraft, "The Dunwich Horror" (1928)

"But we always managed to get along fine enough till this dirty rat shewed up, even if she did balk at helping me with the Rites on Roodmas and Hallowmass."

> H. P. Lovecraft & Hazel Heald, "The Man of Stone" (1932)

"To summon Yogge-Sothothe from the Outside, be wise to wait upon the Sun in the Fifth House, when Saturn is in trine; draw the pentagram of fire, and speak the Ninth Verse thrice, repeating which each Roodemas and Hallow's Eve causeth the Thing to breed in the Outside Spaces beyond the gate, of which Yogge-Sothothe is the Guardian. The once will not bring Him, but may bring Another Who is likewise desirous of growth, and if He have not the blood of Another, He may seek thine own. Therefore be not unwise in these things."

> August Derleth, "The Whippoorwills in the Hills" (1948) in
> *The Mask of Cthulhu*

All the ancient books agreed that May Eve, or Roodmas, was the prime occasion for such blasphemous doings. And Roodmas was now scarcely a fortnight hence.

> Robert M. Price, "The Round Tower" (1990)

roseal, *adj.* Resembling a rose in color or odor; roseate.

For hours I waited, till the east grew grey and the stars faded, and the grey turned to roseal light edged with gold.

> H. P. Lovecraft, "The Nameless City" (1921)

roseate, *adj.* Resembling a rose in color or odor; roseal.

Just as they galloped up the rising ground to the precipice a golden glare came somewhere out of the east and hid all the landscape in its effulgent draperies. The abyss was now a seething chaos of roseate and cerulean splendour, and invisible voices sang exultantly as the knightly entourage plunged over the edge and floated gracefully down past glittering clouds and silvery coruscations.

> H. P. Lovecraft, "Celephaïs" (1920)

rugose, *adj.* [< L *rūgōsus* < *rūga*, wrinkle] Wrinkled, corrugated, rugate.

The Great Race's members were immense rugose cones ten feet high, and with head and other organs attached to foot-thick, distensible limbs spreading from the apexes.

> H. P. Lovecraft, "The Shadow out of Time" (1934–35)

Retracting this neck and gazing down very sharply, I saw the scaly, rugose, iridescent bulk of a vast cone ten feet tall and ten feet wide at the base.

> H. P. Lovecraft, "The Shadow out of Time" (1934–35)

His descriptions were vague, but startling in what they suggested. None of his beings seemed clearly formed, except for certain rugose cones which might as readily have been vegetable in origin as animal.

> August Derleth (as H. P. Lovecraft & August Derleth),
> "The Shadow out of Space" (1957)

On the rugose upper surface of the thing was a great faceted eye, and below this a puckered orifice that corresponded, perhaps, to a mouth.

> Henry Kuttner, "The Invaders" (1939)

That head was—awful. A slanted, saurian skull, all green and scaly on top; hairless, slimy, slick and nauseous. Great bony ridges socketed the embered eyes, staring from behind a sickening sweep of long, reptilian snout. A rugose muzzle, with great champing jaws half opened to reveal a lolling pinkish tongue and scummy teeth of stiletto-like sharpness.

> Robert Bloch, "The Secret of Sebek" (1937)

rune, *n.* [< Old Norse *rún,* whisper or mystery] Any character of various alphabets used by the ancient Scandinavians, which had a prominent place in their practice of magick; any written character used in the practice of magick; a spell, charm, or incantation.

Titles: M. R. James, "Casting the Runes"

a. General:

"Tell me this thing. What is the rune that is said for the throwing into the sea of the sins of the dead? See here, Maisie Macdonald. There is no money of that man that I would carry a mile with me. Here it is. It is yours, if you will tell me that rune."

> Fiona Macleod (William Sharp), "The Sin-Eater" (1895)

"On your feet before his whip covers your back with the blood runes."

> A. Merritt, *The Ship of Ishtar* (1924)

What he did do was to become an almost fanatical devotee of subterranean magical lore, for which Miskatonic's library was and is famous. Always a dweller on the surface of phantasy and strangeness, he now delved deep into the actual runes and riddles left by a fabulous past for the guidance or puzzlement of posterity. He read things like the frightful Book of Eibon, the Unaussprechlichen Kulten of von Junzt, and the forbidden Necronomicon of the mad Arab Abdul Alhazred, though he did not tell his parents he had seen them.

> H. P. Lovecraft, "The Thing on the Doorstep" (1933)

I felt that those walls and overhanging gables of mildewed brick and fungous plaster and timber—with fishy, eye-like, diamond-paned windows that leered—could hardly desist from advancing and crushing me . . . yet I had read only the least fragment of that blasphemous rune before closing the book and bringing it away.

H. P. Lovecraft, "The Book" (c. 1933; ellipsis in original)

Pondering in vain the significance of the mystery, he seemed to hear in the air about him a sweet and wizard voice. And, speaking in a tongue that he knew not, the voice uttered a rune of slumber. And Evagh could not resist the rune, and upon him fell such numbness of sleep as overcomes the outworn watcher in a place of snow.

Clark Ashton Smith, "The Coming of the White Worm" (1933)

Books were piled everywhere: ancient volumes bound in serpent-skin, with verdigris-eaten clasps, that held the frightful lore of Atlantis, the pentacles that have power upon the demons of the earth and the moon, the spells that transmute or disintegrate the elements; and runes from a lost language of Hyperborea, which, when uttered aloud, were more deadly than poison or more potent than any philter.

Clark Ashton Smith, "The Last Incantation" (1929)

> I met a witch with amber eyes
> Who slowly sang a scarlet rune,
> Shifting to an icy laughter
> Like the laughter of the moon.
>
> Clark Ashton Smith, "The Witch with Eyes of Amber" (1923)

> I will repeat a subtle rune—
>   And thronging suns of Otherwhere
> Shall blaze upon the blinded air,
>   And spectres terrible and fair
> Shall walk the riven world at noon.
>
> Clark Ashton Smith, "Song of the Necromancer" (1937)

> Between the windy, swirling fire
> And all the stillness of the moon,
> Sweet witch, you danced at my desire,
> Turning some weird and lovely rune
> To paces like the swirling fire.
>
> Clark Ashton Smith, "Witch-Dance" (1939)

And then for many a weary moon I labored at the galley's oar
Where men grow maddened by the rune of row-locks clacking every more.

Robert E. Howard, "Thor's Son"

Whenas Aldebaran riseth to the Sixth House, and agreeth in all ways with ye Conjunctions of Phutatorius as shall hereinafter be inscribed, then that is no

Door which openeth on its Rising, but a Gate to ye Outside, through which All may pass but None may return save a Master of ye Runes, or ye Host of Ekron.

Abdul Alhazred (trans. John Dee), Necronomicon,
as quoted in Brian McNaughton, Satan's Mistress (1978)

b. In compounds:

"Did he take her for a witch?" she asked; and "did he want to get her burnt; or perhaps have her tied hand and foot, right thumb to left toe, right toe to left thumb, and thrown into the deep black dub? No, no! No rune-wife was she. The rune-wife that was, she had gone long ago to her own place, and her own master too—anyhow she supposed so—when she herself was young. And her arts and her knowfulness had gone with her."

J. C. Atkinson, The Last of the Giant Killers; or,
The Exploits of Sir Jack of Danby Dale (1891)

[dub: a deep, dark pool in a river]

runic, Runic, *adj.* Of or pertaining to runes (q.v.); of or pertaining to a spell or incantation; of or pertaining to language (esp. verse) of the age that made use of runes, after Olaus Wormius' term Literatura Runica; Scandinavian; also, applied to ancient Scots.

a. General:

> At ev'ry pause, before thy mind possesst,
> Old Runic bards shall seem to rise around,
> With uncouth lyres, in many-coloured vest,
> Their matted hair with boughs fantastic crown'd [. . .]

William Collins, "An Ode on the Popular Superstitions of the
Highlands of Scotland, Considered as the Subject of Poetry" (1749)

Professor Webb had been engaged, forty-eight years before, in a tour of Greenland and Iceland in search of some Runic inscriptions which he failed to unearth; and whilst high up on the West Greenland coast had encountered a singular tribe or cult of degenerate Esquimaux whose religion, a curious form of devil-worship, chilled him with its deliberate bloodthirstiness and repulsiveness. It was a faith of which other Esquimaux knew little, and which they mentioned only with shudders, saying that it had come down from horribly ancient æons before ever the world was made.

H. P. Lovecraft, "The Call of Cthulhu" (1926)

b. In the phrase **runic rhyme, Runic rhyme:**

> Facing to the northern clime,
> Thrice he traced the runic rhyme;
> Thrice pronounced, in accents dread,
> The thrilling verse that wakes the dead;

Till from out the hollow ground
Slowly breathed a sullen sound.

Thomas Gray, "The Descent of Odin: An Ode"

But, on this occasion, it seemed as if her own voice refused all its usual duty, and as if, while she felt herself unable to express the words of the well-known air, it assumed, in her own despite, the deep tones and wild and melancholy notes of Norna of Fitful-head, for the purpose of chanting some wild Runic rhyme, resembling those sung by the heathen priests of old, when the victim (too often human) was bound to the fatal altar of Odin or of Thor.

Sir Walter Scott, The Pirate (1821)

Hear the tolling of the bells—
Iron bells!
What a world of solemn thought their monody compels!
In the silence of the night
How we shiver with affright
At the melancholy meaning of the tone!
For every sound that floats
From the rust within their throats
Is a groan.
And the people—ah, the people
They that dwell up in the steeple
All alone,
And who, tolling, tolling, tolling,
In that muffled monotone,
Feel a glory in so rolling
On the human heart a stone—
They are neither man nor woman—
They are neither brute nor human—
They are Ghouls:—
And their king it is who tolls:—
And he rolls, rolls, rolls, rolls,
A Pæan from the bells!
And his merry bosom swells
With the Pæan of the bells!
And he dances and he yells;
Keeping time, time, time,
In a sort of Runic rhyme,
To the Pæan of the bells—
Of the bells:—
Keeping time, time, time,
In a sort of Runic rhyme,
To the throbbing of the bells—

> Of the bells, bells, bells—
>   To the sobbing of the bells:—
> Keeping time, time, time,
>   As he knells, knells, knells,
> In a happy Runic rhyme,
>   To the rolling of the bells—
> Of the bells, bells, bells:—
>   To the tolling of the bells—
> Of the bells, bells, bells, bells,
>   Bells, bells, bells—
> To the moaning and the groaning of the bells.
>
> Edgar Allan Poe, "The Bells" (1849)

rustication, *n.* A period of residence in the country; particularly, as an act of punishment or banishment.

To hint to unimaginative people of a horror beyond all human conception—a horror of houses and blocks and cities leprous and cancerous with evil dragged from elder worlds—would be merely to invite a padded cell instead of a restful rustication, and Malone was a man of sense despite his mysticism.

H. P. Lovecraft, "The Horror at Red Hook" (1925)

S

Sabaoth, sabaoth, Sabbaoth, *pr.n.* & *n.* [< L < Gr Sabaôth < Hb, TzBAVTh, *pl.* of TzBA, host, army] Hosts, armies, as in the Lord of Sabaoth or Lord Sabaoth, the Lord of Hosts, a Biblical title of God; also, erroneously, in place of Sabbath (q.v.).

a. General:

> "Diabolical contrivance!—Oh, England! beloved country, that gave me birth! nurse of liberty, virtue, and good sense! never shall thy gallant name be deformed with this sabaoth of demons!—"
>
> William Godwin, Fleetwood; or, The New Man of Feeling (1804)

> All's one gift; thou canst grant it moreover, as prompt to my prayer
> As I breathe out this breath, as I open these arms to the air.
> From thy will stream the worlds, life and nature, thy dread Sabaoth;
> I will?—the mere atoms despise me!
>
> Robert Browning, "Saul" (1845/1855)

> For now out of the north came Kjalar, the fair guide of pagan warriors to eternal delights in the Hall of the Chosen; and from the zenith sped, like a shining plummet, Ithuriel to fetch the soul of the brave champion of Christendom to the felicities of the golden city walled about with jasper of the Lord God of Sabaoth.
>
> James Branch Cabell, The Silver Stallion: A Comedy of Redemption (1925)

> The writing was in red, and varied from Arabic to Greek, Roman, and Hebrew letters. Malone could not read much of it, but what he did decipher was portentous and cabbalistic enough. One fequently repeated motto was in a sort of Hebraised Hellenistic Greek, and suggested the most terrible dæmon-evocations of the Alexandrian decadence:

> "HEL * HELOYM * SOTHER * EMMANVEL * SABAOTH * AGLA * TETRAGRAMMATON * AGYROS * OTHEOS * ISCHYROS * ATHANATOS * IEHOVA * VA * ADONAI * SADAY * HOMOVSION * MESSIAS * ESCHEREHEYE."
>
> H. P. Lovecraft, "The Horror at Red Hook" (1925)

Sabaoth is an Hellenised form of the Hebrew Tzebaoth, meaning hosts found in the scriptures in the Lord God of Hosts. It was a favourite word with mediæval occultists and with them probably came to signify hosts or armies of elemental spirits. I have often wondered if this, rather than sabbath (day of rest), is not really the parent-word for the term sabbat (Witches' Sabbath) applied to the hideous secret orgies of the witch-cult followers. Surely a word signifying throngs is much more appropriate for the obscene convocations of May-Eve and Hallowe'en than is a word signifying a weekly rest period.

H. P. Lovecraft, "The Incantation at Red Hook"

They come,
The Sabaoth of retribution, drawn
From all dread spheres that knew my trespassing,
And led by vengeful fiends and dire alastors
That owned my sway aforetime!

Clark Ashton Smith, *The Hashish-Eater; or, The Apocalypse of Evil* (1920)

Sabbat, sabbat, *n.* [< Fr; see under Sabbath for further details.] A Witches' Sabbath. See under Sabbath. Found in compounds such as Black Sabbat, Great Sabbat, Sabbat-chant, Sabbat-night, Sabbat-rite, Sabbat-time, Witches' Sabbath.
Titles: Robert Bloch, "Wine of the Sabbat"; Lin Carter, "The Sabbat" in Dreams from R'lyeh (verse); Richard Tierney, "Sabbat" (verse)

a. Alone:

Lord Bacon suggests that the ointments with which witches anointed themselves might have had the effect of stopping the pores and congesting the brain, and thus impressing the sleep of the unhappy dupes of their own imagination with dreams so vivid that, on waking, they were firmly convinced that they had been borne through the air to the Sabbat.

Sir Edward Bulwer-Lytton, *A Strange Story* (1861)

Though not inclined to be superstitious, nor hitherto believing that man could be brought into bodily communication with demons, I felt the terror and the wild excitement with which, in the Gothic ages, a traveller might have persuaded himself that he witnessed a sabbat of fiends and witches.

Sir Edward Bulwer-Lytton, *The Coming Race* (1871;
aka *Vril: The Power of the Coming Race*)

Like a sound borne in sleep through such dreams as encumber
With haggard emotions the wild wicked slumber
Of some witch when she seeks, through a night-mare, to grab at
The hot hoof of the fiend, on her way to the Sabbat.

Owen Meredith (Robert Bulwer-Lytton), *Lucile* (1860)

"But—to go back a little,—I had thought the Sabbat would be so different! One imagined there would be cauldrons, and hags upon prancing broomsticks, and a black Goat, of course—"

"How much more terrible it is," the girl replied,—"and how beautiful!"

James Branch Cabell, *The Cream of the Jest: A Comedy of Evasion* (1911–15)

"And yes, I have dabbled a bit in forces that aren't as yet thoroughly understood, Mr. Kennaston. I wouldn't go so far as to admit to witchcraft, though. Very certainly I never attended a Sabbat."

I recollect, now, how his face changed. "And what in heaven's name was a Sabbat?" Then he fidgeted, and crossed his legs the other way.

I replied: "Well! it was scarcely Heaven's name that was invoked there, if old tales are to be trusted. Traditionally, the Sabbat was a meeting attended by all witches in satisfactory diabolical standing, lightly attired in smears of various magical ointments; and their vehicle of transportation to these outings was, of course, the traditional broomstick."

James Branch Cabell, *The Cream of the Jest: A Comedy of Evasion* (1911–15)

"That would require a rather lengthy explanation—Why, no," I protested, in answer to his shrug; "the Sabbat is not inexplicable. Hahn-Kraftner's book, or Herbert Perlin's either, will give you a very fair notion of what the Sabbat really was,—something not in the least grotesque, but infinitely more awe-inspiring than is hinted by any traditions in popular use. And Le Bret, whom bookdealers rightly list as 'curious'—"

James Branch Cabell, *The Cream of the Jest: A Comedy of Evasion* (1911–15)

His bearing, which combined abstraction with a touch of boredom, discouraged any advances from phantoms, and made fiends uneasily suspect this little fellow in bottle-green and silver to be one of those terrible magicians who attend sabbats only when they are planning to kidnap with strong conjurations some luckless fiend to slave for them at unconscionable tasks.

James Branch Cabell, *The High Place: A Comedy of Disenchantment* (1923)

Another said: "I study to divine and to make smooth the approach of every evil fortune,—with smoke and arrows and wax, with an egg, with mice, and with the simulacra of dead persons;—but, above all, as you may perceive, I have been most successful with the head of an ass in a brazier of live coals. And my guide is not any bow-legged, swarthy eunuch, but Leonard, the Grand Master of the Sabbat."

James Branch Cabell, *Something About Eve: A Comedy of Fig-Leaves* (1927)

Gerald and Maya did not go out a great deal; but they were on friendly terms with the neighbors; they attended an occasional Sabbat; and they kept in touch generally with the affairs of Turoine.

James Branch Cabell, *Something About Eve: A Comedy of Fig-Leaves* (1927)

And now Dream Maker after Dream Maker followed one another, and dream upon dream unfolded in the web of rays. Some, Graydon watched fascinated, unable to draw his eyes from them, others sent him shuddering into the shelter of the Spider-man's arms, sick of soul. A few were of surpassing beauty, Djinn worlds straight out of the Arabian Nights. There was a world of pure colors, unpeopled, colors that built of themselves gigantic symphonies, vast vistas of harmonies. Such drew little applause from these men and women whose chant was interlude between the dreams. It was carnage and cruelty, diablerie, defiled, monstrous matings, Sabbats; hideous fantasies to which Dante's blackest hell was Paradise itself which stirred them.

A. Merritt, *The Face in the Abyss* (1923)

"I've never seen a place more loaded with traces of magic. I can pick out Mrs. Jennings' very strongly and your own business magic. But after I eliminate them the air is still crowded. You must have had everything but a rain dance and a sabbat going on around you!"

Robert A. Heinlein, "Magic, Inc." (1940)

He spoke of the rites of Osiris, the black worship of Typhon whom the Egyptians also named Set of the Red Hair, the Eleusinian and the Delphic mysteries as though he had witnessed them. Described them in minutest detail—and others more ancient and darker; long buried in age-rotten shrouds of Time. The evil secrets of the Sabbat were open to him, and once he spoke of the worship of Kore, the Daughter, who was known also as Persephone, and in another form as Hecate, and by other names back, back through the endless vistas of the ages— the wife of Hades, the Queen of the Shades, whose daughters were the Furies.

A. Merritt, *Creep, Shadow!* (1934; aka *Creep, Shadow, Creep!*)

Grandfather kept me saying the Dho formula last night, and I think I saw the inner city at the 2 magnetic poles. I shall go to those poles when the earth is cleared off, if I can't break through with the Dho-Hna formula when I commit it. They from the air told me at Sabbat that it will be years before I can clear off the earth, and I guess grandfather will be dead then, so I shall have to learn all the angles of the planes and all the formulas between the Yr and Nhhngr. They from outside will help, but they cannot take body without human blood.

Wilbur Whateley, diary, as quoted in H.P. Lovecraft, "The Dunwich Horror" (1928)

Simaetha would surely seem to be a true heir to the most sorcerous traditions of Hyperborea and Regio Averonum—not unlike those reputedly immortal felines who guarded the shrine of Sadoqua, and whose regular disappearances at New Moon figure so largely in the folklore of mediæval Averoigne. One recalls the disquieting suggestions in Jehan d'Arbois' Roman des Sorciers concerning the huge black cats captured at those very singular Sabbats on the rocky hills behind Vyones—the cats which could not be burned, but which escaped unhurt from the flames, uttering cries which, though not like any known human speech, were

damnably close to the unknown syllables forming part of the Tsath-ritual in the
Livre d'Eibon.

H. P. Lovecraft, letter to Clark Ashton Smith (11 February 1934)

"Here!" Her voice was apocalyptic, a scream on the silence of our sabbat. "Listen, here is another Christmas!"

Leonard Cline, *The Dark Chamber* (1927)

In a pit of granite, in some unhallowed spot, roofed with darkness that was itself swollen with infernal portent, the high chase through the sky came to an end. The Sabbat was gathering before an altar of black marble, lit by double rows of the five-flamed torches with their blue light; and in the blasphemous Holy of Holies on that altar of ill-omen squatted a huge and ugly toad. And ranged in order around this altar were a hundred worshippers, and all of them quite naked now.

Leonard Cline, "The Vampire of Bedlam Hill" (ellipsis in original)

Ere the litter of falling glass had reached the tavern floor, a swart and monstrous form flew into the room, with a beating of heavy vans that caused the tapers to flare troublously, and the shadows to dance like a sabbat of misshapen devils.

Clark Ashton Smith, "The Maker of Gargoyles" (1931)

> Or I, perchance,
> Begot you on some golden succubus
> Amid the madness of the Sabbat's night
> In earlier lives forvowed to Satanry
> And sorcerous dark romance.

Clark Ashton Smith, "Wizard's Love" (1938)

> The owl that whilom
> Hooted his famine to a full-chapped moon,
> Has pounced upon his gopher, or has gone
> To fresher woods behind a farther hill;
> And Hecate has grounded all the witches
> For some glade-hidden Sabbat.

Clark Ashton Smith, "Soliloquy in an Ebon Tower" (1951)

b. In Witches' Sabbat:

To my amazement, I beheld these formal matrons and sober fathers of families forming themselves into a dance, turbulent as a children's ball at Christmas; and when, suddenly desisting from his music, Margrave started up, caught the skeleton hand of lean Miss Brabazon, and whirled her into the centre of the dance, I could have fancied myself at a witch's sabbat.

Sir Edward Bulwer-Lytton, *A Strange Story* (1861)

c. In other compounds:

Former experience had told him that May-Eve—the hideous Sabbat-night of underground European legend—would probably be more fruitful than any other date, and he was not disappointed.

H. P. Lovecraft, "The Whisperer in Darkness" (1930)

And what was that faint suggestion of sound which once in a while seemed to trickle through the maddening confusion of identifiable sounds even in broad daylight and full wakefulness? Its rhythm did not correspond to anything on earth, unless perhaps to the cadence of one or two unmentionable Sabbat-chants, and sometimes he feared it corresponded to certain attributes of the vague shrieking or roaring in those wholly alien abysses of dream.

H. P. Lovecraft, "The Dreams in the Witch House" (1932)

"It must have been one of those things great-grandfather got at the Great Sabbat on Sugar-Loaf in the Catskills."

H. P. Lovecraft & Hazel Heald, "The Man of Stone" (1932)

Sabbath, sabbath, *n.* [< Hb ShBTh, *sabbath* < *shâbath,* to rest; supported by the widespread anti-Semitism of the period in which the word arose, and by the common (and earlier) use of synagogue as a synonym (but cf. "synagogue of Satan" in Rev. II 9). In the case of the witches' sabbath, this derivation has been contested. Other proposed derivations for the latter include: (1) Hb TzBAVTh, Gr sabaôth, hosts; (2) Sabazius (Gr Sabázios), a Phrygian deity identified with Dionysus or Zeus, and worshipped in orgiastic rites; (3) OF s'esbattre, to frolic (cf. esbat); (4) Ar zabbat, the forceful or powerful one.] A midnight meeting of witches, believed to involve worship of the devil, riotous dancing, the exchange of spells, potions, and poisons, and diverse orgies celebrated in conjunction with demons. Often found in compounds such as **Witches' Sabbath, Black Sabbath, Devil's Sabbath. Cf. Esbat, Sabbat, Walpurgis.**

Titles: Donald Wandrei, "Witches' Sabbath" (verse); Black Sabbath, "Black Sabbath" (song) on Black Sabbath (album)

a. General:

however the stories of old Witches, prove beyond contradiction, that all sorts of spirits which assume light aery bodies, or crazed Bodies coacted by forrein spirits, seem to have som pleasure (at least to asswage som pain or Melancholy) by frisking and capering like Satyrs, or whistling and shreecking (like unluckey birds) in their unhallowed Synagogues and Sabbaths: If invited and earnestly required, these companions make them selves known and familiar to men, otherwises, being in a different state and Element, they neither can nor will easily converse with them.

Robert Kirk, Secret Commonwealth; or, A Treatise Displayeing the Chiefe Curiosities
as They Are in Useamong Diverse of the People of Scotland to This Day,
Singularities for the Most Part Peculiar to That Nation (1691)

Italy may be considered as the very focus and parent of superstitious credulity. The materials which Hector had furnished, after all the interrogations of the donzella, were slight compared with the superstructure which was presently erected upon them. My grotto was said to be the appropriated haunt where a thousand devils held their infernal sabbath. The terrified imagination of the rustics, listening with a temper horribly distracted between curiosity and alarm, created to itself fictitious howlings and shrieks, and saw pale and sulphureous flames dancing upon the surface of the stream.

William Godwin, *St. Leon: A Tale of the Sixteenth Century* (1799)

Fenced round with spells, unhurt I venture
   Their sabbath strange where witches keep;
Fearless the sorcerers' circle enter,
   And woundless tread on snakes asleep.

M. G. Lewis, "The Gipsy's Song" in *The Monk: A Romance* (1794)

"I thought of being forced to witness the unnatural revels of a diabolical feast,—of seeing the rotting flesh distributed,—of drinking the dead corrupted blood,—of hearing the anthems of fiends howled in insult, on that awful verge where life and eternity mingle,—of hearing the hallelujahs of the choir, echoed even through the vaults, where demons were yelling the black mass of their infernal Sabbath."

Charles Maturin, *Melmoth the Wanderer: A Tale* (1820)

"As I came through the desert thus it was,
As I came through the desert: Lo you, there,
That hillock burning with a brazen glare;
Those myriad dusky flames with points a-glow
Which writhed and hissed and darted to and fro;
A Sabbath of the Serpents, heaped pell-mell
For Devil's roll-call and the fête of hell."

James Thomson ("B. V."), "The City of Dreadful Night" (1870–74)

Then, again, there were myths darker still; the dread of witch and wizard, the lurid evil of the Sabbath, and the hint of demons who mingled with the daughters of men.

Arthur Machen, "Novel of the Black Seal" in
The Three Impostors; or, The Transmutations (1894)

Ring within ring the awful temple closed around him; unending circles of vast stones, circle within circle, and every circle less throughout all ages. In the centre was the sanctuary of the infernal rite, and he was borne thither as in the eddies of a whirlpool, to consummate his ruin, to celebrate the wedding of the Sabbath.

Arthur Machen, *The Hill of Dreams* (1897)

On every side the wizened witches of religion and morality were shrill in celebration of their obscene sabbath.

Aleister Crowley, *The Confessions of Aleister Crowley: An Autohagiography* (1923)

This was Kora and Persephone, the daughter of Ceres and the Winter Queen:
the child abducted into the underworld of death. Except this child had no supernatural mother to save her, no living mother at all. For the sacrifice I witnessed was an echo of one that had occurred twenty years before, the carnival
feast of the preceding generation—*O carne vale!* Now both mother and daughter
had become victims of this subterranean sabbath.

Thomas Ligotti, "The Last Feast of Harlequin" (1990)

b. In **Witches' Sabbath, Black Sabbath, Devil's Sabbath:**

A number of unfortunate wretches were brought for judgment, fitter, according
to the civilian's opinion, for a course of hellebore, than for the stake. Some were
accused of having dishonoured the crucifix, and denied their salvation; others of
having absconded to keep the Devil's Sabbath, in spite of bolts and bars; others
of having merely joined in the choral dances around the witches' tree of rendezvous.

Sir Walter Scott, *Letters on Demonology and Witchcraft,*
Addressed to J. G. Lockheart, Esq. (1830)

It was the fascination of this process which brought men and women—all sorts
and conditions of both—to the Black Sabbath and the White Sabbath, and
blinded them to the danger of the stake.

A. E. Waite, *The Book of Ceremonial Magic* (1898/1911;
aka *The Book of Black Magic, The Book of Black Magic and of Pacts,*
& *The Book of Black Magic and Ceremonial Magic*)

"Out of the little realities he has so proudly reared, phantoms, ghastly and murderous will launch themselves at him. Everything about him will become laden
with horror. The day and night into which he looks will, like dreadful mirrors,
give him back only the Witches' Sabbath of his mind."

Ben Hecht, *The Kingdom of Evil: A Continuation of the*
Journal of Fantazius Mallare (1924)

Any magazine-cover hack can splash paint around wildly and call it a nightmare
or a Witches' Sabbath or a portrait of the devil, but only a great painter can
make such a thing really scare or ring true. That's because only a real artist
knows the actual anatomy of the terrible or the physiology of fear—the exact
sort of lines and proportions that connect up with latent instincts or hereditary
memories of fright, and the proper colour contrasts and lighting effects to stir
the dormant sense of strangeness.

H. P. Lovecraft, "Pickman's Model" (1926)

A few of the tales were exceedingly picturesque, and made me wish I had learnt more of comparative mythology in my youth. There was, for instance, the belief that a legion of bat-winged devils kept Witches' Sabbath each night at the priory—a legion whose sustenance might explain the disproportionate abundance of coarse vegetables harvested in the vast gardens.

H. P. Lovecraft, "The Rats in the Walls" (1923)

It was as the old man had said—a vaulted, columned hell of mingled Black Masses and Witches' Sabbaths—and what perfect completion could have added to it was beyond my power to guess.

H. P. Lovecraft & Zealia Bishop, "Medusa's Coil" (1930)

The beasts had been holding a devil's sabbath in the forest during the night.

Henry Kuttner, *Valley of the Flame* (1946)

"Did you ever hear of the Goat of Mendes?" continued the voice slowly, he realized, from beyond the door. "Do you know what used to appear at the witches' sabbaths? Do you know about the Land of the Goat in the Pyrenees, or the Great God Pan? What about the Protean God? *And the Black Goat of the Woods with a Thousand Young?*"

Ramsey Campbell, "The Moon-Lens" (1964)

Here are Slothrop and the apprentice witch Geli Tripping, standing up on top of the Brocken, the very plexus of German evil, twenty miles north by northwest of the Mittelwerke, waiting for the sun to rise. Though May Day Eve's come and gone and this frolicking twosome are nearly a month late, relics of the latest Black Sabbath still remain: Kriegsbier empties, lace undergarments, spent rifle cartridges, Swastika-banners of ripped red satin, tattooing-needles and splashes of blue ink— "What the heck was *that* for?" Slothrop wondered.

Thomas Pynchon, *Gravity's Rainbow* (1973)

c. In other compounds or as modifier:

He sought for that magic by which all the glory and glamour of mystic chivalry were made to shine through the burlesque and gross adventures of Don Quixote, by which Hawthorne had lit his infernal Sabbath fires, and fashioned a burning aureole about the village tragedy of the *Scarlet Letter.*

Arthur Machen, *The Hill of Dreams* (1897)

> Come, child of wonder! it is Sabbath Night,
> The speckled twilight and the sombre singing!
> Listen and come: the owl's disastrous flight
> Points out the road! Hail, O propitious sight!
> See! the black gibbet and the murderer swinging!

Aleister Crowley, *The Temple of the Holy Ghost* (1901)

Sabbatial, *adj.* Of or pertaining to a Witches' Sabbat (q.v.). [Not in *OED*.]

There is ample and continuous evidence that children, usually tender babes who were as yet unbaptized, were sacrificed at the Sabbat. These were often the witches' own offspring, and since a witch not unseldom was the midwife or wise-woman of a village she had exceptional opportunities of stifling a child at birth as a non-Sabbatial victim to Satan.

Montague Summers, *The History of Witchcraft and Demology* (1925)

Sabbatic, *adj.* Of or pertaining to a Witches' Sabbat (q.v.). [Not in *OED* in this sense.]

Now as the twilight's doubtful interval
Closes with night's accomplished certainty,
A wizard wind goes crying eerily,
And on the wold misshapen shadows crawl,
Miming the trees, whose voices climb and fall,
Imploring, in Sabbatic ecstacy,
The sky where vapor-mounted phantoms flee
From the scythed moon impendent over all.

Clark Ashton Smith, "The Eldritch Dark" (1912)

Sorceress and sorcerer,
Risen from the sepulcher,
From the deep, unhallowed ground,
We have found and we have bound
Each the other, as before,
With the fatal spells of yore,
With Sabbatic sign, and word
That Thessalian moons have heard.

Clark Ashton Smith, "Resurrection"

sable, *adj.* Black in color; dark, somber, or gloomy. Found in such compounds as: **sable-cinctured, sable-coloured, sable-lettered, sable-suited, sable-plumed, sable-robed, sable-stoled, sable-vested.**

a. Alone:

Was I deceiv'd, or did a sable cloud
Turn forth her silver lining on the night?
I did not err, there does a sable cloud
Turn forth her silver lining on the night,
And casts a gleam over this tufted Grove.

John Milton, *Comus (A Masque Presented at Ludlow Castle, 1634)*

Night, sable goddess! from her ebon throne,
In rayless majesty, now stretches forth

Her leaden sceptre o'er a slumb'ring world:
Silence, how dead! and darkness, how profound!

Edward Young, *The Complaint, and the Consolation; or, Night Thoughts* (1742)

Trembling I write my dream, and recollect
A fearful vision at the midnight hour;
So late, Death o'er me spread his sable wings,
Painted with fancies of malignant power!

Philip Freneau, *The House of Night: A Vision* (1779)

The first thing, that struck Manfred's eyes, was a group of his servants, endeavouring to raise something, that appeared to him a mountain of sable plumes. He gazed, without believing his sight. "What are ye doing?" cried Manfred, wrathfully; "where is my son?" A volley of voices replied, "Oh! my lord! the prince! the prince! the helmet! the helmet!"

Horace Walpole, *The Castle of Otranto: A Gothic Story* (1764)

At length the sated murderers, gorged with prey,
 Retire; the clamour of the fight is o'er:
Silence again resumes her awful sway,
 And sable Horror guards the massy door.

George Gordon, Lord Byron, "Elegy on Newstead Abbey" (1807)

It was a freak of fancy in my friend (for what else shall I call it?) to be enamored of the Night for her own sake; and into this *bizarrerie*, as into all his others, I quietly fell; giving myself up to his wild whims with a perfect *abandon*. The sable divinity would not herself dwell with us always; but we could counterfeit her presence. At the first dawn of the morning we closed all the massy shutters of our old building, lighted a couple of tapers which, strongly perfumed, threw out only the ghastliest and feeblest of rays. By the aid of these we then busied our souls in dreams—reading, writing, or conversing, until warned by the clock of the advent of the true Darkness.

Edgar Allan Poe, "The Murders in the Rue Morgue" (1841)

Now and then, a maid-servant, neatly dressed, and now the shining, sable face of a slave, might be seen bustling across the windows, in the lower part of the house.

Nathaniel Hawthorne, *The House of the Seven Gables* (1850–51)

Now I know the fiendish fable
 That the golden glitter bore;
Now I shun the spangled sable
 That I watch'd and lov'd before;
But the horror, set and stable,
 Haunts my soul for evermore.

H. P. Lovecraft, "Astrophobos" (1917)

All about us I sensed a gloating Presence; a lurking demon who watched our progress with eyes of gleeful mirth, and whose sable soul shook with hell-born laughter as we opened the door of the study and stumbled across that which lay within.

Robert Bloch, "The Mannikin" (1936)

Eliza Ellet considered herself a whole blazing constellation amongst the starry sisterhood and was delighted to tell him of the salon's brilliance, even more delighted to recite little snatches of transcendental verse which she had herself indited "in that hushed hour between midnight and dawn when Morpheus' sable hands touch the rosy finger tips of Aurora and even the fairies are slumbering on their flowery couches," said Mrs. Ellet with a rapt look.

Anya Seton, *Dragonwyck* (1943)

b. In compounds:

> Nor is *Osiris* seen
> In *Memphian* Grove, or Green,
>   Trampling the unshowr'd Grasse with lowings loud:
> Nor can he be at rest
> Within his sacred chest;
>   Naught but profoundest Hell can be his shroud,
> In vain with Timbrel'd Anthems dark
> The sable-stoled Sorcerers bear his worshipt Ark.

John Milton, "On the Morning of Christ's Nativity" (1629)

> My spirit is wrapt in the wind of light;
> It is whirled away on the wings of night,
> Sable-plumed are the wonderful wings,
> But the silver of moonlight subtly springs
> Into the feathers that flash with the pace
> Of our flight to the violate bounds of space.

Aleister Crowley, *The World's Tragedy* (1908)

> Sable-robed, at noon,
> They passed beneath red cherries
> Ripening with June.

Clark Ashton Smith, "Nuns Walking in the Orchard" in
"Experiments in Haiku: Distillations"

salt, salte, *n.* An extremely fine substance contained within the ashes of a burnt plant or animal. Alchemists have professed their ability to extract these salts and perform the process known as palingenesy, which produces from them the plant or animal's latent astral spirit or body, distinct from both the physical body and the soul. (This process seems to have sometimes been mis-understood as re-creating the physical body.) [This sense not in *OED*.]

> This perhaps will seem a Ridiculous story to those, who reade only the Titles of Bookes: but, those that please, may see this Truth confirmed, if they but have recourse to the Workes of *M. du Chesne, S. de la Violette*, one of the best Chymists that our Age hath produced; who affirmes, that himselfe saw an Excellent Pol-ish Physician of *Cracovia*, who kept in Glasses, the Ashes of almost all the Hearbs that are knowne: so that, when any one, out of Curiosity, had a desire to see any of them, as (for example,) a Rose, in one of his Glasses, he tooke That where the Ashes of a Rose were preserved; and holding it over a lighted Candle, so soone as ever it began to feele the Heat, you should presently see the Ashes begin to Move; which afterwards rising up, and dispersing themselves about the Glasse, you should immediately observe a kind of little Dark Cloud; which di-viding it selfe into many parts, it came at length to represent a Rose; but so Faire, so Fresh, and so Perfect a one, that you would have thought it to have been as Substantial, & as Odoriferous a Rose, as any growes on the Rose-tree. This Gentleman sayes, that Himselfe hath often tryed to do the like: but not finding the successe, to answer all the Industry hee could use, Fortune at length gave him a sight of this Prodigy. For, as he was one day practising, with *M. de Luynes*, called otherwise *De Fomentieres*, Counseller to the Parliament, to see the Curiosity of diverse Experiments, having extracted the Salt of certaine Nettles burnt to Ashes, and set the Lye abroad all night in a winter Evening; in the Morning he found it all Frozen; but with this Wonder attending it; that the Net-tles themselves, with their Forme, and Figure, were so Lively and so perfectly represented on the Ice, that the Living Nettles were not more.
>
> James Gaffarel (trans. Edmund Chilmead), *Unheard-of Curiosities:*
> *Concerning the Talismanical Sculpture of the Persians; the Horoscope of the Patriarkes; and the*
> *Reading of the Stars* (1650; original title *Curiositéz inouyes, sur la Sculpture*
> *talismanique des Persans; Horoscope des Patriarches; Et lectures des Estoilles*)

If such a renowned chymist as Quercetanus, with a whole tribe of "labourers in the fire," since that learned man, find it no easie thing to make the common part of mankind believe that they can take a plant in its more vigorous consistence, and after a due *maceration, fermentation* and *separation,* extract the *salt* of that plant, which, as it were, in a *chaos,* invisibly reserves the *form* of the whole, with its vital principle; and, that keeping the *salt* in a *glass* hermetically sealed, they can, by ap-plying a *soft fire* to the glass, make the *vegetable* rise by little and little out of its *ashes,* to surprize the spectators with a notable illustration of that *resurrection,* in the faith whereof the Jews, returning from the graves of their friends, pluck up the *grass* from the earth, using those words of the Scripture thereupon, "Your bones shall flourish like an herb:" 'tis likely, that all the observations of such writers as the incomparable Borellus, will find it hard enough to produce our be-lief that the *essential salts* of *animals* may be so prepared and preserved, that an in-genious man may have the whole *ark* of Noah in his own study, and raise the fine *shape* of an animal out of its ashes at his pleasure: and that, by the like method from the *essential salts of humane dust,* a philosopher may, without any criminal *necromancy,* call up the *shape* of any *dead* ancestor from the dust whereinto his body has been incinerated. The resurrection of the dead will be as just, as great an article of our *creed,* although the *relations* of these learned men should pass for incredible romances: but yet there is an anticipation of that blessed resurrection, carrying in it some resemblance of these curiosities, which is performed, when we do in a *book,* as in a *glass,* reserve the history of our departed friends; and by bringing our *warm affections* unto such an history, we revive, as it were, out of their *ashes,* the true *shape* of those friends, and bring to a fresh view what was memorable and imitable in them.

Cotton Mather, *Magnalia Christi Americana* (1702)

The essential Saltes of Animals may be so prepared and preserved, that an ingenious Man may have the whole Ark of Noah in his own Studie, and raise the fine Shape of an Animal out of its Ashes at his Pleasure; and by the lyke Method from the essential Saltes of humane dust, a Philosopher may, without any criminal Necromancy, call up the Shape of any dead Ancestour from the Dust whereinto his Bodie has been incinerated.

Borellus, as quoted in H. P. Lovecraft, *The Case of Charles Dexter Ward* (1927)

(Those voices *are* continent-wide, of course: "The essential salts, the fane of Dagon, the gray twisted brittle monstrosity, the flute-tormented pandemonium, the coral-encrusted towers of Rulay . . .")

Fritz Leiber, "The Terror from the Depths" (1975; ellipsis in original)

"The dust is gone because I took it and used it—because in the works of wizardry I found the formulæ, the arcana whereby I could raise the flesh, re-create the body from the essential salts of the grave. Poe does not *lie* beneath this house—he *lives!* And the tales are *his posthumous works!*"

Robert Bloch, "The Man Who Collected Poe" (1951)

"He'd purloined the basic notion from a book by none other than good old Cotton Mather—the idea of raising the dead from their 'essential salts'— attributed it to the French scholar Borellus, and used it as th basic modus operandi for his scurvy Frankensteins in *The Case of Charles Dexter Ward.*"

Gahan Wilson, "H.P.L." (1990)

"Dead four hundred years this day, Howard, does your dust lie in ancient ground still? Could some later Curwen not have raised your essential salts?"

Richard A. Lupoff, "Discovery of the Ghooric Zone" (1977)

"He died four hundred years ago today, Howard did. But first he wrote of one Curwen who could restore the dead if only he could obtain their essential salts.

What he called their essential salts." She paused and giggled. "Maybe he had a prevision of cloning!"

Richard A. Lupoff, "Discovery of the Ghooric Zone" (1977)

From a square bottle marked "Essential Salts," Prospero poured a few green crystals into a white ceramic dish; when he had mumbled some words over the bowl, a pink and green cloud began to ascend from the shimmering translucent pebbles. Before long, a definite shape appeared.

"Carnations," said the wizard disgustedly. "Phooey."

John Bellairs, *The Face in the Frost* (1969)

saltant, *adj.* Jumping, leaping.

"Woods and fields are tremulous at twilight with the shimmering of white saltant forms, and immemorial Ocean yields up curious sights beneath thin moons."

H. P. Lovecraft & Anna Helen Crofts, "Poetry and the Gods" (1920)

Flutes shrieked and drums began to beat, and as I watched in awe and terror I thought I saw dark saltant forms silhouetted grotesquely against the vision of marble and effulgence.

H. P. Lovecraft, "The Moon-Bog" (1921)

sanguinary, *adj.* Characterized by slaughter and bloodshed.

Sanguinary baptism becomes some gods. Were the gracious figures of the Grecian pantheon to appear to us with blood upon their garments we should recoil in horror, but we should think the terrible Mithra or the heart-devouring Huitzilopochitli a trifle unconvincing if they came on our dreams untarnished by the ruddy vintage of sacrifice.

Frank Belknap Long, *The Horror from the Hills* (1930)

sanguineous, *adj.* Of or pertaining to bloodshed.

I enjoyed your letter and enclosures very much, and was especially pleased with the glimpse of "Pickman's Model" with its frightful companions at its nefarious feast by the black barn in the accursed wood. I duly note all the details of the terrible scene, including the arachnid horror on the sanguineous stone altar. This thing—which I will duly shield from all the sensitive and impressionable eyes of the household—shall repose broodingly in a wallet of skin taken from a wizard's corpse cut down from the gallows in 1692, in a locked secret cabinet in the vaulted crypt beneath my shunned abode. At Roodmas and All-Hallows' shall I view it, and the Objects squatting on nearby coffins or peering monstrously over my shoulder shall shudder as they gaze upon its forbidden revelations.

H. P. Lovecraft, letter to Bernard Austin Dwyer (3 March 1927)

sanguinolent, *adj.* Of the red color characteristic of blood; blood red.

But in my heart, as in some high-piled press,
Dancing, thou crushest out with thy wan feet

A vintage strong, a wine sanguinolent
That shall restore the summer.

Clark Ashton Smith, "Dancer"

sanies, *n.* A thin, green, fœtid, and serous pus or ichor discharged from suppurating wounds or ulcers.

Vacharn lit the way with a brand of drifwood plucked from the fire. Anon a bloated moon rose red as with sanies-mingled blood, over the wild, racing sea; and before its orb had cleared to a death-like paleness, they emerged from the gorge on stony fell where stood the house of the three necromancers.

Clark Ashton Smith, "Necromancy in Naat" (1935)

The pedestal upon which it squatted was of black onyx: the statute itself, with the exception of the tusks, had apparently been chiseled from a single block of stone, and was so hideously mottled and eroded and discolored that it looked, in spots, as though it had been dipped in sanies.

Frank Belknap Long, *The Horror from the Hills* (1930)

saprophytic, *adj.* Growing and feeding upon dead or decaying organic matter.

And now at last I forget utterly the hall and its emptiness and death; for here life was renewing itself. Not saprophytic, the colorless life that creeps in corpse and rotting trunk, the life that is darkness and death; but life new and fresh and clean, of the sun.

Leonard Cline, *The Dark Chamber* (1927)

The first inkling that I had of the gigantic abomination that was soon to smother the world with its saprophytic obscenity in 192-, was obtained almost by accident.

Bertram Russell, "The Scourge of B'Moth" (1929)

saraband, sarabande, *n.* A slow Spanish dance of Saracenic origin, in triple time; the traditional dance of the Witches' Sabbath.

The dances at the Sabbath were mostly indecent, including the well-known Sarabande, and the women danced in them sometimes in chemise, but much more frequently quite naked.

Thomas Wright, *The Worship of the Generative Powers During the
Middle Ages of Western Europe* (1865)

And when our chaffering all was done,
    All was paid for, sold and done,
We drew a glove on ilka hand,
We sweetly curtsied, each to each,
And deftly danced a saraband.

William Bell Scott, "The Witch's Ballad"

> They took each other by the hand,
> And danced a stately saraband;
> Their laughter echoed thin and shrill.

> Oscar Wilde, "The Harlot's House" (1883)

For the terror had not faded with the silhouette, and in a fearsome instant of deeper darkness the watchers saw wriggling at that treetop height a thousand tiny points of faint and unhallowed radiance, tipping each bough like the fire of St. Elmo or the flames that came down on the apostles' heads at Pentecost. It was a monstrous constellation of unnatural light, like a glutted swarm of corpse-fed fireflies dancing hellish sarabands over an accursed marsh; and its colour was that same nameless intrusion which Ammi had come to recognise and dread.

> H. P. Lovecraft, "The Colour Out of Space" (1927)

And yet I saw them in a limitless stream—flopping, hopping, croaking, bleating—surging inhumanly through the spectral moonlight in a grotesque, malignant saraband of fantastic nightmare.

> H. P. Lovecraft, "The Shadow over Innsmouth" (1931)

Faun and dryad and satyr swung in a mad saraband beyond the shrouding mists.

> Henry Kuttner, "Cursed Be the City" (1939)

For there was no wind, only the cold, soft breeze that billowed ever so gently from the nighted sky above. Only the cold, soft breeze, rustling the curtains and prompting a sarabande of shadows on the wall; shadows that danced in silence over the great bed in the corner.

> Robert Bloch, "The Unspeakable Betrothal" (1949)

Of all the tales collected here, this one ["The Secret in the Tomb"] is the most guilty of the supposed sin of heavily peppering the text with Lovecraftian lingo, a malignant nightmare saraband of eerie adjectives, as it were. Edmund Wilson (in his critical review "Tales of the Marvellous and the Ridiculous") chided Lovecraft's use of such adjectives: "Surely one of the primary rules for writing an effective tale of horror is never to use any of these words." You should not have to tell the reader that what he reads is hideous, loathsome, etc. Let him see it for himself.

A point well taken. But then why do stories like "The Suicide in the Study" work so well anyway? I suspect the use of these words creates a kind of almost hypnotic horror language that functions like a mantra and that, contrary to Wilson, does actually suggest more than it states, in the manner of a word association test. Each use of "hideous" invites you to conjure up your image of the hideous, of the loathsome, etc.

> Robert Price, introduction to "The Secret in the Tomb" (1993), in
> Robert Bloch, *The Mysteries of the Worm*

Saturnalia, saturnalia (*pl., sing.* **Saturnalis,** but *pl.* frequently taken as *sing.,* especially in extended uses), *n.* In the Roman religion, a mid-December harvest festival characterized by riotous and unrestrained merrymaking, drinking, and dancing. By extension, any period or occasion of unrestrained and orgiastic revelry.

The magic bow was drawing forth its last quivering sounds—famous among prodigious musical feats—imitating the precipitate flight of the witches before bright dawn; of the unholy women saturated with the fumes of their nocturnal Saturnalia, when—a strange thing came to pass on the stage.

> H. P. Blavatsky, "The Ensouled Violin" (1880)

Sunset was sombre and splendid; the disc itself was but a vague intensity of angry Indian red. His agony split a murky saffron through the haze; and the edges of the storm-clouds on the horizon, fantastically shapen, cast up a veritable mirage, exaggerated and distorted images of their own scarred crests, that shifted and changed, so that one might have sworn that monsters—dragons, hippogriffs, chimæræ—were moving in the mist, a saturnalia of phantasms.

> Aleister Crowley, *Moonchild* (1917; aka *The Butterfly-Net* or *The Net*)

For the triduum of Saturnalia his goatservant had paraded hiz willingsons in the Forum while the jenny infanted the lass to be greeted raucously (the Yardstated) with houx and epheus and measured with missiles too from a hundred of manhood and a wimmering of weibes.

> James Joyce, *Finnegans Wake* (1922–39)

Then it began—the unnatural scene—the saturnalia of murder.

> Sax Rohmer (Arthur Sarsfield Ward),
> *The Mystery of Dr. Fu-Manchu* (1913; aka *The Insidious Dr. Fu-Manchu*)

The time of the Saturnalia was at hand, that seven-day carousal when master and slave sat equal at table and nothing must be written or said that was not merry.

> Leonard Cline, *The Dark Chamber* (1927)

A short while ago he was Professor Jacobi, a famed and aged man still playing like a fanatic child in his laboratory. He wore a skull cap and occasionally addressed an auditorium filled with dignified and obsequious colleagues. The world paused now and then in its Saturnalia of greed to turn its ears to his voice—a voice that promised calmly and authoritatively that new secrets were being wrested from nature; that science was fashioning new toys out of life.

> Ben Hecht, *The Kingdom of Evil: A Continuation of the
> Journal of Fantazius Mallare* (1924)

I plumbed the blackest pits of hell and came back—laughing. I was one with the rest of those dark warders, and I joined them in the saturnalia of horror until the scarred man spoke to us again.

> Henry Kuttner, "The Secret of Kralitz" (1936)

Thus I passed through streets of saturnalia, my thoughts still wine-wafted and far away.

Robert Bloch, "The Secret of Sebek" (1937)

Ah yes, the first wild Opsday of Ops Week, traditional Opalia (the Women's Movement counter to Saturnalia) dedicated to reckless entertainment . . . as if the Guff needed any additional excuse for madness. Ops, wife of Saturn, Earth Goddess of Plenty (she gave her name to "opulent") in whose honor one touched earth instead of wood for luck, gave earthenware gifts, and fraternized regardless of rank or clout.

Alfred Bester, *Golem*[100] (1980; ellipsis in original)

savant, *n.* [< Fr] An individual of learning or science; a sage or scientist.

Piecing together the tales which Norrys collected for me, and supplementing them with the accounts of several savants who had studied the ruins, I deduced that Exham Priory stood on the site of a prehistoric temple; a Druidical or ante-Druidical thing which must have been contemporary with Stonehenge.

H. P. Lovecraft, "The Rats in the Walls" (1923)

scabrous, *adj.* Rough to the touch, as with raised scales or projections.

I did not faint—though no reader can possibly realise the effort it took to keep me from doing so. I did cry out, but stopped short when I saw the frightened look on the old man's face. As I had expected, the canvas was warped, mouldy, and scabrous from dampness and neglect; but for all that I could trace the monstrous hints of evil cosmic outsideness that lurked all through the nameless scene's morbid content and perverted geometry.

H. P. Lovecraft & Zealia Bishop, "Medusa's Coil" (1930)

What they saw before them was not the living features of a human being, but the shrunken, withered horror of a skull! The flesh had dried and cracked like old leather, revealing patches of scabrous naked bone; the lips were peeled back to bare discolored fangs; the throat was so thin they could actually *see* the bones of the spine.

Robert E. Howard, "Scarlet Tears"

A great grey rat paused and watched him. Its long ragged whiskers twitched, and its scabrous, naked tail was moving slowly from side to side.

Henry Kuttner, "The Graveyard Rats" (1936)

He saw the fish-like scales, the scabrous whiteness of the slimy skin; saw the veined gills.

Robert Bloch & Henry Kuttner, "The Black Kiss" (1937)

Scolopendra, *n.* A fabulous, enormous sea-monster.

Most vgly shapes, and horrible aspects,
    Such as Dame Nature selfe mote feare to see,
Or shame, that euer should so fowle defects
From her most cunning hand escaped bee;
All dreadfull pourtraicts of deformitee:
Spring-headed *Hydraes*, and sea-shouldring Whales,
    Great whirlpools, which all fishes make to flee,
Bright Scolopendraes, arm'd with siluer scales,
Mighty *Monoceros*, with immeasured tayles.

                    Edmund Spenser, *The Faërie Queene* (159-)

[*Monoceros* is usually now amended to *Monoceroses*, despite ruining the scansion.]

Wings

Of white-hot stone along the hissing wind
Bear up the huge and furnace-hearted beasts
Of hells beyond Rutilicus; and things
Whose lightless length would mete the gyre of moons—
Born from the caverns of a dying sun—
Uncoil to the very zenith, half-disclosed
From gulfs below the horizon; octopi
Like blazing moons with countless arms of fire,
Climb from the seas of ever-surging flame
That roll and roar through planets unconsumed,
Beating on coasts of unknown metals; beasts
That range the mighty worlds of Alioth rise,
Afforesting the heavens with multitudinous horns
Amid whose maze the winds are lost; and borne
On cliff-like brows of plunging scolopendras,
The shell-wrought tow'rs of ocean-witches loom,
And griffin-mounted gods, and demons throned
On sable dragons, and the cockodrills
That bear the spleenful pygmies on their backs;
And blue-faced wizards from the worlds of Saiph,
On whom Titanic scorpions fawn; and armies
That move with fronts reverted from the foe,
And strike athwart their shoulders at the shapes
Their shields reflect in crystal; and eidola
Fashioned within unfathomable caves
By hands of eyeless peoples; and the blind
Worm-shapen monsters of a sunless world,
With krakens from the ultimate abyss,
And Demogorgons of the outer dark,
Arising shout with dire multisonous clamors,
And threatening me with dooms ineffable

> In words whereat the heavens leap to flame,
> Advance upon the enchanted palace.

> Clark Ashton Smith, *The Hashish-Eater; or, The Apocalypse of Evil* (1920)

scoriac, *adj.* Of or pertaining to *scoriæ* (*sing. scoria*)—cinder-like, porous fragments of dark lava; scoriaceous. Apparently coined by Edgar Allan Poe.

> He is the apex of the focussed ages,
> The crown of all those labouring powers that warm
> Earth's red hot core, when scoriac sorrow rages.

> Ernest Wheldrake, "Louis Napoleon" as quoted by Algernon Charles Swinburne,
> review of Ernest Wheldrake, *The Monomaniac's Tragedy and Other Poems*

Similar to euphemism and circumlocution is polysyllabicity: besides being clumsy and often imprecise, long Latinate words are very often purged of all color and crispness, and in Alfred Austin's lines on the "umbrageous vicarage." The worst offenders in this area are Edgar Allan Poe and Thomas Holley Chivers, contemporaries who probably borrowed words from one another. Each used exotic diction to convey a sense of the remote, the mystic, and the romantic; Poe's lush style is well known, and probably at its best (or worst) in Ulalume, where such words as "liquescent," "senescent," and "scoriac" are common.

> John Bellairs, "An Anatomy of Abuses: Why Bad Poetry Is Bad"

Carter could see the rifts and ruggedness of that sombre stone, and did not welcome the prospect of climbing it. In places there were solid streams of lava, and scoriac heaps that littered slopes and ledges.

> H. P. Lovecraft, *The Dream-Quest of Unknown Kadath* (1927)

The scoriac peak towered up some 12,700 feet against the eastern sky, like a Japanese print of the sacred Fujiyama; while beyond it rose the white, ghost-like height of Mt. Terror, 10,900 feet in altitude, and now extinct as a volcano. Puffs of smoke from Erebus came intermittently, and one of the graduate assistants—a brilliant young fellow name Danforth—pointed out what looked like lava on the snowy slope; remarking that this mountain, discovered in 1840, had undoubtedly been the source of Poe's image [in "Ulalume"] when he wrote seven years later of

> "—the lavas that restlessly roll
> Their sulphurous currents down Yaanek
> In the ultimate climes of the pole—
> That groan as they roll down Mount Yannek
> In the realms of the boreal pole."

> H. P. Lovecraft, *At the Mountains of Madness* (1931)

sepulcher, sepulchre, *n.* [< OE < OF < L *sepulcrum* or *sepulchrum* < *sepelire*, to bury (the dead)] A vault for the interment of the dead; a grave or tomb.

"The four monks, who had never spoken or lifted up their heads till that moment, now directed their livid eyes at me, and repeated, all together, in a voice that seemed to issue from the bottom of a sepulchre, 'Your crime is—'"

Charles Maturin, *Melmoth the Wanderer: A Tale* (1820)

Musides, weeping, promised him a sepulchre more lovely than the tomb of Mausolus; but Kalos bade him speak no more of marble glories.

H. P. Lovecraft, "The Tree" (1920)

sepulchral, *adj.* Of, pertaining to, or resembling a sepulcher (q.v.); reminiscent of death or the dead; (of a voice or other sound) markedly deep, low, and hollow in tone.

"So saying he hasted away, and Isidora, sinking on a grave for rest, wrapt her veil around her, as if its folds could exclude even thought. In a few moments, gasping for air, she withdrew it; but as her eye encountered only tomb-stones and crosses, and that dark and sepulchral vegetation that loves to shoot its roots, and trail its unlovely verdure amid the joints of grave-stones, she closed it again, and sat shuddering and alone."

Charles Maturin, *Melmoth the Wanderer: A Tale* (1820)

When they had reached the portal, whose deep archway was dimly lighted by a cresset, the stranger paused, and addressed the baron in a hollow tone of voice, which the vaulted roof rendered still more sepulchral.

Washington Irving, "The Specter Bridegroom: A Traveler's Tale" (1820–21)

The eyes, before invisible, now wore an energetic and human expression, while they gleamed with a fiery and unusual red; and the distended lips of the apparently enraged horse left in full view his sepulchral and disgusting teeth.

Edgar Allan Poe, "Metzengerstein" (1832)

There are moments when, even to the sober eye of Reason, the world of our sad Humanity may assume the semblance of a Hell—but the imagination of man is no Carathis, to explore with impunity its every cavern. Alas! the grim legion of sepulchral terrors cannot be regarded as altogether fanciful—but, like the Demons in whose company Afrasiab made his voyage down the Oxus, they must sleep, or they will devour us—they must be suffered to slumber, or we perish.

Edgar Allan Poe, "The Premature Burial" (1844)

"I came to warn thee," answered the sepulchral voice of the Saga.

Sir Edward Bulwer-Lytton, *The Last Days of Pompeii* (1834)

"They have, sir," said David in a sepulchral voice which I hardly recognized.

Robert W. Chambers, "The Maker of Moons" (1896)

Most credibly, she was a wanton who had come out to keep a rendezvous amid the tombs. There were, he knew, certain perverse debauchees who required sepulchral surroundings and furnishings for the titillation of their desires.

Clark Ashton Smith, "Morthylla" (1952)

The incidents of the dream always occurred at nightfall, beneath a waning and sepulchral moon.

Robert Bloch, "The Grinning Ghoul" (1936)

It was my favorite number—the superb and sonorously sepulchral Number One scene from The Swan Lake, by Tchaikowsky. It droned, mocked, shrilled, blared. It whispered, roared, threatened, frightened. It even impressed and quieted the milling geese about me.

Robert Bloch, "The Secret of Sebek" (1937)

"Levi," interrupted the young man in a sepulchral tone. "My name is Eliphas Levi, mage of Sarnath, seer of Unknown Kadath."

Paul Di Filippo, *Hottentots* (1994) in the *Steampunk Trilogy*

sere, *adj.* Dry, withered; (of fabrics) worn, thin.

> And soon I heard a roaring wind:
> It did not come anear;
> But with its sound it shook the sails,
> That were so thin and sere.

S. T. Coleridge, *The Rime of the Ancient Mariner* (1798)

Unhappy is he to whom the memories of childhood bring only fear and sadness. Wretched is he who looks back upon lone hours in vast and dismal chambers with brown hangings and maddening rows of antique books, or upon awed watches in twilight groves of grotesque, gigantic, and vine-encumbered trees that silently wave twisted branches far aloft. Such a lot the gods gave to me—to me, the dazed, the disappointed; the barren, the broken. And yet I am strangely content, and cling desperately to those sere memories, when my mind momentarily threatens to reach beyond to *the other*.

H. P. Lovecraft, "The Outsider" (1921)

shaman, *n.* In "primitive" societies, an individual believed to have access to the spiritual world.

"I know it," Todd answered snappishly. "And the shamans enchanted the bells with their magic. Don't be a fool!"

Henry Kuttner, "Bells of Horror" (1939)

shamanism, *n.* The religion and practice of shamans (q.v.).

Suydam, when questioned, said he thought the ritual was some remnant of Nestorian Christianity tinctured with the Shamanism of Thibet. Most of the people, he conjectured, were of Mongoloid stock, originating somewhere in or near Kurdistan—and Malone could not help recalling that Kurdistan is the land of the Yezidis, last survivors of the Persian devil-worshippers.

H. P. Lovecraft, "The Horror at Red Hook" (1925)

"Mysticism? It is black shamanism, foul as the tundras which bred it."

Robert E. Howard, "The Daughter of Erlik Khan"

shoggoth, *n.* In the Lovecraft Mythos, an artifical lifeform created by the crinoid Elder Things as a race of slaves. Shoggoths are about fifteen feet in diamater when a sphere, and can metamorphose themselves to create sensory organs and limbs of great strength as required. Over time they gained more independent intelligence and became rebellious. [Not in *OED*.]

> Over the jagged peaks of Thok they sweep,
> Heedless of all the cries I try to make,
> And down the nether pits to that foul lake
> Where the puffed shoggoths splash in doleful sleep.

H. P. Lovecraft, "Night-Gaunts" in *Fungi from Yuggoth* (1929–30)

They had done the same on other planets; having manufactured not only necessary foods, but certain multicellular protoplasmic masses capable of moulding their tissues into all sorts of temporary organs under hypnotic influence and thereby forming ideal slaves to perform the heavy work of the community. These viscous masses were without doubt what Abdul Alhazred whispered about as the "shoggoths" in his frightful *Necronomicon*, though even that mad Arab had not hinted that any existed on earth except in the dreams of those who had chewed a certain alkaloidal herb.

H. P. Lovecraft, *At the Mountains of Madness* (1931)

Sculptured images of these shoggoths filled Danforth and me with horror and loathing. They were normally shapeless entities composed of a viscous jelly which looked like an agglutination of bubbles; and each averaged about fifteen feet in diameter when a sphere. They had, however, a constantly shifting shape and volume; throwing out temporary developments or forming apparent organs of sight, hearing, and speech in imitation of their masters, either spontaneously or according to suggestion.

H. P. Lovecraft, *At the Mountains of Madness* (1931)

It's a voice and it's not a voice. That is, it doesn't sound like a voice but more like a buzzing or croaking, deep and droning. But it has to be a voice because it is saying words.

Not words I could understand, but words. Words that made me keep my head down, half afraid I might be seen and half afraid I might see something. I

stayed there sweating and shaking. The smell was making me pretty sick, but that awful, deep droning was worse. Saying over and over something like
"E uh shub nigger ath ngaa ryla neb shoggoth."

Robert Bloch, "Notebook Found in a Deserted House" (1951)

Doris didn't like the *Necronomicon*, although she considered herself an emancipated and free-thinking young woman. There was something sinister, or to be downright honest about it, *perverted* about that book—and not in a nice, exciting way, but in a sick and frightening way. All those strange illustrations, always with five-sided borders just like the Pentagon in Washington, but with those people inside doing all those freaky sex acts with those other creatures who weren't people at all. It was frankly Doris's opinion that old Abdul Alhazred had been smoking some pretty bad grass when he dreamed up those things. Or maybe it was something stronger than grass: she remembered one sentence from the text: "Onlie those who have eaten a certain alkaloid herb, whose name it were wise not to disclose to the unilluminated, maye in the fleshe see a Shoggothe." I wonder what a "Shoggothe" is, Doris thought idly; probably one of those disgusting creatures that the people in the illustrations are doing those horny things with. Yech.

Robert Anton Wilson and Robert Shea,
The Eye in the Pyramid in *The Illuminatus! Trilogy* (1969–71)

The first stained-glass window was worse from inside than outside; he didn't know who Saint Toad was, but if that mosaic with his name on it gave any idea of Saint Toad's appearance and predelictions, then, by God, no self-respecting Christian congregation would ever think of sanctifying him. The next feller, a shoggoth, was even less appetizing; at least they had the common decency not to canonize *him*.

Robert Anton Wilson and Robert Shea,
The Golden Apple in *The Illuminatus! Trilogy* (1969–71)

And by now it wasn't so much like a tunnel or even a chimney but a kind of roller coaster with dips and loops but not the sort you find in a place like Brighton—I think I saw this kind of curve once, on a blackboard, when a class in non-Euclidean geometry had used the room before my own class in Eng Lit Pope to Swinb. and Neo-Raph. Then I passed a shoggoth or it passed me, and let me say that their pictures simply do not do them justice: I am ready to go anywhere and confront any peril on H.M. Service but I pray to the Lord Harry I never have to get that close to one of those chaps again.

Robert Anton Wilson and Robert Shea,
The Golden Apple in *The Illuminatus! Trilogy* (1969–71)

The shoggoth came by again (or was it his twin brother?) and shouted, or I should say, gibbered, "Yog Sothoth Neblod Zin," and I could tell that was something perfectly filthy by the tone of his voice. I mean, after all, I can take a queer proposition without biffing the offender on the nose—one must be cosmopolitan, you know—but I would vastly prefer to have such offers coming out of human mouths, or at the very least out of mouths rather than orifices that shouldn't be talking at all. But you would have to see a shoggoth yourself, God forbid, to appreciate what I mean.

Robert Anton Wilson and Robert Shea,
The Golden Apple in *The Illuminatus! Trilogy* (1969–71)

The little people had had their own experiences with the lloigor, long ago, but all they remembered were confused legends about Orcs (whom Mama Sutra identified with the Tcho-Tchos) and a great hero named Phroto who battled a monster called Zaurn (evidently a shoggoth, Mama Sutra said.)

Robert Anton Wilson and Robert Shea,
The Golden Apple in *The Illuminatus! Trilogy* (1969–71)

It only remains to affirm that *Schrödinger's Cat*, contrary to appearances, is not a mere "routine" or "shaggy shoggoth story."

Robert Anton Wilson, *The Universe Next Door* in the *Schrödinger's Cat Trilogy* (1979)

sificligh, *n.* [< *Sci*ence *Fic*tion *League*] An obnoxious creature native to the planet Venus. [Not in *OED*.]

In the gathering dusk I could see the dim line of the corpse, now the centre of a loathsome cloud of farnoth-flies. Before long, no doubt, the mud-dwelling sificlighs would be oozing in from the plain to complete the ghastly work.

H. P. Lovecraft & Kenneth Sterling, "In the Walls of Eryx" (1936)

sinus, *n.* [< L] A cavity or hole in the earth.

We were on the track ahead as the nightmare plastic column of fœtid black iridescence oozed tightly onward through its fifteen foot sinus; gathering unholy speed and driving before it a spiral, re-thickening cloud of the pallid abyss-vapour. It was a terrible, indescribable thing vaster than any subway train—a shapeless congeries of protoplasmic bubbles, faintly self-luminous, and with myriads of temporary eyes forming and unforming as pustules of greenish light all over the tunnel-filling front that bore down upon us, crushing the frantic penguins and slithering over the glistening floor that it and its kind had swept so evilly free of all litter.

H. P. Lovecraft, *At the Mountains of Madness* (1931)

Siren, Syren, *n.* [< *L Sīrēn (LL Sīrēna) < Gr Seirén*] In Græco-Roman mythology, any of a number (usually three) of sea nymphs who were part bird and part woman, and whose singing was so seductive that it lured sailors to their deaths as they crashed their ships on the rocks in pursuit. In later use, frequently confounded with mermaids.

"The Pestilence doth most risest infect the clearest complection, and the Caterpillar cleaueth vnto the ripest fruite: the most delycate witte is allured with small enticement vnto vice, and most subject to yeeld vnto vanitie. If therefore thou doe but hearken to the *Syrenes* thou wilt be enamoured; if thou haunt their houses and places, thou shalt be enchaunted."

John Lyly, Euphues: The Anatomy of Wit (1578)

What Song the Syrens sang, or what name Achilles assumed when he hid himself among women, though puzling Questions are not beyond all conjecture.

Sir Thomas Browne, Hydriotaphia, Urne-Buriall; or,
A Discourse of the Sepulchrall Urnes Lately Found in Norfolk (1658)

Intoxicated with pleasure, the monk rose from the syren's luxurious couch: he no longer reflected with shame upon his incontinence, or dreaded the vengeance of offended heaven: his only fear was lest death should rob him of enjoyments, for which his long fast had only given a keener edge to his appetite.

M. G. Lewis, The Monk: A Romance (1794)

To consider—as after any such statement seems unavoidable—the possibility that, had Marlowe lived to attain maturity, he might to-day have been as tritely gabbled about as Shakespeare, is rather on a plane with debating "what song the Sirens sang" or the kindred mystery of what becomes of political issues after election.

James Branch Cabell, Beyond Life: Dizain des Démiurges (1919)

The sirens! The story of crafy Ulysses' adventure with those sea women flashed into his memory. How desire had come upon that wanderer to hear the siren song—yet no desire to let it draw him to them. How he had sailed into their domain; had filled his oarsmen's ears with melted wax; had made them bind him to the mast with open ears, and then, cursing, straining at his bonds, mad with desire to leap into their white arms, had heard their enchanted measure—and sailed safe away.

A. Merritt, The Ship of Ishtar (1924)

I tried to keep all my skill and self-possession about me, and stared at the sector of reddish farther sky betwixt the walls of the pass—resolutely refusing to pay attention to the puffs of mountain-top vapour, and wishing that I had wax-stopped ears like Ulysses' men off the Sirens' coast to keep that disturbing wind-piping from my consciousness.

H. P. Lovecraft, At the Mountains of Madness (1931)

But in a moment we understood the source of that music as the same from which had come that weirdly beautiful music we had heard in our dreams in Sandwin House; for the music, on the surface of so beautiful and ethereal, abounded with hellish undertones. It was such as the sirens might have sung to

Ulysses, it was as beautiful as the Venusburg music, but perverted by evil that was horribly manifest.

> August Derleth, "The Sandwin Compact" (1940) in *The Mask of Cthulhu*

In gay Grecian robes the nymphs came, singing the Sirens' Song, the same song that Doctor Browne asserted was not difficult of divination but which, nevertheless, he did not hazard to name, contenting himself merely with the claim he could do so any time he got around to it.

> Charles G. Finney, *The Circus of Dr. Lao* (1934)

Siroc, *n.* [< Fr *siroc, siroch* (now *siroco*) = It *sirocco*] See under **Sirocco**.

> "When the whirlwind's gusts are wheeling,
>   Ours it is the dance to braid;
> Zarah's sands in pillars reeling
>   Join the measure that we tread,
> When the Moon has donned her cloak
>   And the stars are red to see,
> Shrill when pipes the sad Siroc,
>   Music meet for such as we."

> Sir Walter Scott, *The Bridal of Triermain; or, The Vale of Saint John: A Lover's Tale* (1813)

These were wild and miserable thoughts; but I cannot describe to you how the eternal twinkling of the stars weighed upon me, and how I listened to every blast of wind, as if it were a dull ugly siroc on its way to consume me.

> Mary Shelley, *Frankenstein; or, The Modern Prometheus* (1816–17)

> O, human love! thou spirit given,
> On Earth, of all we hope in Heaven!
> Which fall'st into the soul like rain
> Upon the Siroc-wither'd plain,
> And, failing in they power to bless,
> But leav'st the heart a wilderness!

> Edgar Allan Poe, "Tamerlane" (1827)

Sirocco, *n.* [< It *sirocco, scirocco* < Ar *sharq*, east < *sharaqa*, (the sun) rose] A hot, humid wind originating in Libyan deserts, and chiefly experienced in Italy, Sicily, and Malta; any hot wind of cyclonic origin; a windstorm that raises up clouds of sand and dust.

The wind is colder than ever, if such a thing be possible . . . a wind freighted with the stench of dead-alive things * * * O merciful God Who took my sight! * * * a wind so cold it burns where it should freeze . . . it has become a blistering sirocco * * *

> C. M. Eddy, Jr. & H. P. Lovecraft, "Deaf, Dumb, and Blind" (1924;
> ellipses as in original)

"Without you i on pavement—Saw a giant crab snapping—Help me—Sinking ship—You trying Ali God of Street Boys on screen?—So we turn over knife wind voices covered—From the radio interstellar sirocco"—

William S. Burroughs, The Ticket That Exploded (1957–61)

skorah, *n.* [< William F. *Sykora,* science fiction fan & member of the International Scientific Association and the Science Fiction League] An obnoxious creature native to the planet Venus. [Not in *OED*.]

If the things knew this building they would come through it after me, and in this way would form a key to getting out, just as carnivorous skorahs might have done.

H. P. Lovecraft & Kenneth Sterling, "In the Walls of Eryx" (1936)

squamous, *adj.* [< L *squāmōsus* < *squāma,* scale] Covered with scales; scaly.

He was, as many a night before, walking amidst throngs of clawed, snouted beings through the streets of a labyrinth of inexplicably fashioned metal under a blaze of diverse solar colour; and as he looked down he saw that his body was like those of the others—rugose, partly squamous, and curiously articulated in a fashion mainly insect-like yet not without a caricaturish resemblance to the human outline.

H. P. Lovecraft & E. Hoffmann Price,
"Through the Gates of the Silver Key" (1932–33)

Even now I cannot begin to suggest it with any words at my command. I might call it gigantic—tentacled—proboscidian—octopus-eyed—semi-amorphous—plastic—partly squamous and partly rugose—ugh! But nothing I could say could even adumbrate the loathsome, unholy, non-human, extra-galactic horror and hatefulness and unutterable evil of that forbidden spawn of black chaos and illimitable night.

H. P. Lovecraft & Hazel Heald, "Out of the Æons" (1933)

And even Sturgeon's verbal excesses are his own; he does not call upon exotic or obsolete words for their own sakes, or otherwise the multitudinous seas incarnadine; he never says anything is ineffable or unspeakable, the very ideas embodied in those words being foreign to his artistic credo; he does not splash color on with a mop, or use the same colors for everything; and he does not say "partly rugose and partly squamous" when he means "partly rough and partly scaly."

James Blish (as William Atheling, Jr.), More Issues at Hand (1970)

Furthermore, there was out there at the tower a constant flux and flowing; the bat-winged creatures were sometimes to be seen, and sometimes invisible, abruptly vanishing, as if they slipped away into another dimension; the amorphous flute-players on the roof were now great and monstrous, now small and dwarf-like; and the extension in space before my cousin, which I have described as an excrescence, was so hideously in flux that I could not bear to take my eyes from it, convinced as I was that at any moment this illusion and all else would pass, and present once more the calm, moon-lit landscape as I had expected to see it; and by describing it as "in flux" I know that I fall far short of adequately describing what took place before my horrified and incredible eyes, for the *Thing*, which first appeared before me as an angular extension into space, with its focal point before my cousin Ambrose at the tower, became in succession a great amorphous mass of changing flesh, squamous as certain snakes, and putting forth and drawing back constantly and without cessation innumerable tentacular appendages of all lengths and shapes; a horrible, blackly furred thing with great red eyes that opened from all portions of its body; a hellish monstrosity which was octopoid in seeming to have become a small, shrivelled mass of torso with tentacles hundreds of times its size and weight which whipped backward in a fainting motion into space, and the ends of which were literally sloughed or melted away into distance, while the empurpled body opened a great eye to look upon my cousin, and disclosed beneath it a great pit of mouth from which issued a terrible, if muted, screaming, at the sound of which the flute-players on the tower and the piping singers in the marsh increased their wild music in unbearable volume, and my cousin gave voice to terrible, ululant sounds which drifted unmistakably to my ears as a horrible mockery of something less than human, and filled me with such terror and abysmal fright as I have never known before, for among the sounds he made, he uttered one of the dread names which had occurred so often, always fraught with terror unbelievable, in the history of this accursed region—*"N'gai, n'gha'ghaa, y'hah—Yog-Sothoth!"*—all this making such an eldritch and bestial tumult that I thought surely all the world must hear it, and fell away from the window, once again overcome by that terrible malignance, flowing towards me not so much this time from the walls as from that strange window.

August Derleth (as H. P. Lovecraft & August Derleth),
The Lurker at the Threshold (1945)

But now many of the creatures clutched a grisly trophy at their squamous breasts.

Robert Bloch & Henry Kuttner, "The Black Kiss" (1937)

Moving, the squamous horror of the head loomed like a camera close-up.

Robert Bloch, "The Secret of Sebek" (1937)

It rose—huge, black, oozing and bubbling forth from the great volcanic crater where it had watched and waited—its squamous shape silhouetted against the stars as it wriggled up and out, flowing toward her.

Robert Bloch, *Strange Eons* (1978)

Another sailor piped up. "And what about 'squamous'? It got anything to do with Indian squaws?"

> Paul Di Filippo, *Hottentots* (1994) in the *Steampunk Trilogy*

star-jelly, *n.* A slimy mass, believed to have fallen from space; identified by the skeptical as the algæ Nostoc. Also known as pwdre ser, star-fallen, star-shot, star-slime, star-slough, star-slubber, star-slutch, etc.

The cuttings you enclose are of extreme interest—that about the "star jelly" being absorbingly & superlatively so. No idea has ever fascinated me so much as that of the wafting of alien life across space, & I have enjoyed reading about these doubtful phenomena in books like Charles Fort's eccentric *Book of the Damned* & *New Lands*.

> H. P. Lovecraft, letter to Elizabeth Toldridge (1 April 1930)

stay, *v.tr.* To stop, halt, hinder.

I paused for a moment, and then with a rush of fire to my heart I knew that no horror could stay me, but that I must follow my brother and save him, even though all hell rose up against me.

> Arthur Machen, "Adventure of the Missing Brother" in
> *The Three Impostors; or, The Transmutations* (1894)

A wave of nameless fright rolled out to meet him, but he yielded to no whim and deferred to no intuition. There was nothing alive here to harm him, and he would not be stayed in his piercing of the eldritch cloud which engulfed his patient.

> H. P. Lovecraft, *The Case of Charles Dexter Ward* (1927)

> > Who rides a dream, what hand shall stay?
> > What eye shall note or measure mete
> > His passage on a purpose fleet,
> > The thread and weaving of his way!
>
> > Clark Ashton Smith, "The Star-Treader" (1911)

steatopygous, *adj.* [< Gr, *steat-*, fat, tallow + *pygé*, buttocks] Fat-assed; characterized by steatopyga, or an abnormal accumulation of fatty tissue behind the hips and thighs, as characteristic among the Hottentots.

Is this disproportionate, topheavy, steatopygous, or otherwise gibbous and malform'd? Let the Child know and he'll be your debtor æternally.

> H. P. Lovecraft, letter to James F. Morton (22 November 1925)

At the fifteenth floor the lift picked up a foppish steatopygous young man, stylish in well-cut jacket without lapels, tight calf-length trousers, flowery round-necked shirt.

> Anthony Burgess, *The Wanting Seed* (1962)

The guffawing men and tittering women in the audience were particularly struck by her steatopygous traits, those immense gluteal lipoid deposits which Agassiz had noticed in her daughter. This feature was exhibited sans clothing to the audience, who were free to poke and prod it, though, in a gesture of modesty, Saartjie kept her pudendum covered with a loincloth.

> Paul Di Filippo, *Hottentots* (1994) in the *Steampunk Trilogy*

stertor, *n.* A heavy snoring or snoring sound.

stertorous, *adj.* Of, pertaining to, or resembling a stertor (q.v.) or stertors; snoring.

By this time his pulse was imperceptible and his breathing was stertorous, and at intervals of half a minute.

> Edgar Allan Poe, "The Facts in the Case of M. Valdemar" (1845)

He found Old Whateley in a very grave state, with a cardiac action and stertorous breathing that told of an end not far off.

> H. P. Lovecraft, "The Dunwich Horror" (1928)

stertorously, *adv.* In a stertorous (q.v.) manner.

Willet had been breathing stertorously, and opened his eyes slowly when Mr. Ward gave him some brandy fetched from the car. Then he shuddered and screamed, crying out, *"That beard . . . those eyes . . . God, who are you?"* A very strange thing to say to a trim, blue-eyed, clean-shaven gentleman whom he had known from the latter's boyhood.

> H. P. Lovecraft, *The Case of Charles Dexter Ward* (1927; ellipses in original)

stinkard, *n.* A foul-smelling individual.

> 'Sdeath, you abominable Pair of Stinkards,
> Leave off your barking, and grow one again,
> Or, by the light that shines, I'll cut your throats.
>
> Ben Jonson, *The Alchemist: A Comedy* (1610)

Why shouldn't rats eat a de la Poer as a de la Poer eats forbidden things? . . . The war ate my boy, damn them all . . . and the Yanks ate Carfax with flames and burnt Grandsire Delapore and the secret . . . No, no, I tell you, I am *not* that dæmon swineherd in the twilit grotto! It was *not* Edward Norrys' fat face on that flabby, fungous thing! Who says I am a de la Poer? He lived, but my boy died! . . . Shall a Norrys hold the lands of a de la Poer? . . . It's voodoo, I tell you . . . that spotted snake . . . Curse you, Thornton, I'll teach you to faint at what my family do! . . . 'Sblood, thou stinkard, I'll learn ye how to gust . . . wolde ye swynke me thilke wys? . . . *Magna Mater! Magna Mater! . . . Atys . . . Dia ad aghaidh 's ad aodann . . . agus bas dunach ort! Dhonas 's dholas ort, agus leat-sa! . . . Ungl . . . ungl . . . rrlh . . . chchch . . .*

> H. P. Lovecraft, "The Rats in the Walls" (1923; ellipses in original)

Stygian, stygian, *adj.* Of, pertaining to, or resembling the river Styx in Hades; profoundly dark and gloomy; hellish, infernal, Acherontic, Plutonian, Tartarean. **Stygian oath:** an unbreakable oath, as one sworn by the river Styx.

Titles: Thomas Lovell Beddoes, "Song of the Stygian Naiades"

a. General:

> Murder, rape, war, lust, and treachery
> Were with Jove closed in Stygian empery.
>
> Christopher Marlowe, Hero and Leander(1598)

A custome lothsome to the eye, hatefull to the Nose, harmefull to the braine, dangerous to the Lungs, and in the blacke stinking fume thereof, neerest resembling the horrible Stigian smoke of the pit that is bottomlesse.

King James I & VI, "A Counter-Blaste to Tobacco" (1604)

> Hence loathed Melancholy
>   Of *Cerberus*, and blackest midnight born,
> In *Stygian* Cave forlorn
>   'Mongst horrid shapes, and shreiks, and sights unholy,
> Find out some uncouth cell,
>   Where brooding darknes spreads his jealous wings,
> And the night-Raven sings;
>   There under *Ebon* shades, and low-brow'd Rocks,
> As ragged as they Locks,
>   In dark *Cimmerian* desert ever dwell.
>
> John Milton, "L'Allegro" (1631)

> Whose woeful forms yet chill my soul with dread,
> Each wore a vest in Stygian chambers wove,
> Death's kindred all—Death's horses they bestrode,
> And gallop'd fiercely, as the chariot drove.
>
> Philip Freneau, The House of Night: A Vision (1779)

> AH, broken is the golden bowl!
>   The spirit flown forever!
> Let the bell toll!—A saintly soul
>   Glides down the Stygian river!
> And let the burial rite be read—
>   The funeral song be sung—
> A dirge for the most lovely dead
>   That ever died so young!
>
> Edgar Allan Poe, "Lenore" (1843 version)

We were almost over, when, between us and the border of the basin, arose a long neck, on the top of which, like the blossom of some Stygian lily, sat what seemed the head of a corpse, its mouth half open, and full of canine teeth.

George MacDonald, *Lilith: A Romance* (1895)

"'O apostate!' cries the bell-wether, 'O spawn of Beelzebub! excommunicate him with bell, book, and candle. May he be thrust down with Korah, Balaam, and Iscariot, to the most Stygian pot of the sempiternal Tartarus.'"

Charles Kingsley, *Hereward the Wake: "Last of the English"* (1865)

[pot: abyss, pit of hell]
Urged on by an impulse which I cannot definitely analyse, I scrambled with difficulty down the rocks and stood on the gentler slope beneath, gazing into the Stygian deeps where no light had yet penetrated.

H. P. Lovecraft, "Dagon" (1917)

We shall never know what sightless Stygian worlds yawn beyond the little distance we went, for it was decided that such secrets are not good for mankind.

H. P. Lovecraft, "The Rats in the Walls" (1923)

The foul air had now slightly abated, and Willett was able to send a beam of light down the Stygian hole.

H. P. Lovecraft, *The Case of Charles Dexter Ward* (1927)

Many graphic sculptures told of explorations deep underground, and of the final discovery of the Stygian sunless sea that lurked at earth's bowels.

H. P. Lovecraft, *At the Mountains of Madness* (1931)

It was very gradually that I regained my senses after that eldritch flight through Stygian space.

H. P. Lovecraft & Harry Houdini, "Under the Pyramids" (1924)

The inner column grew solid and opaque as ebony; and the face of Averaud, who was standing well within the broad penumbral shadow, became dim as if seen through a film of Stygian water.

Clark Ashton Smith, "The Devotee of Evil" (1930)

Up them he went, stumbling and slipping, and with a deep gasp of relief, came out into the tomb, whose spectral grayness seemed like the blaze of noon in comparison to the stygian depths he had just traversed.

Robert E. Howard, "Worms of the Earth" (1930)

Shadows lurked along the angles darker than the Stygian pits, and the boarded-up door was only a vague splotch in the sheer of the wall.

Robert E. Howard, "Lord of the Dead"

The night was exceptionally dark, and a thin, clammy drizzle had commenced to fall—not a cold rain, but a viscid, penetrating darkness like the breath of some Stygian fury.

> Bertram Russell, "The Scourge of B'Moth" (1929)

It was a mad odyssey through a black hell of shrieking ruin! Flying objects screamed past us, unseen walls and chimneys toppled and smashed nearby. Frightened, hysterical men and women blundered into us in the dark and went shouting away, vainly searching for escape from this stygian death trap.

> Henry Kuttner, "Bells of Horror" (1939)

In the gloom they could not see. The Stygian atmosphere was quite appalling; it was as if they had been born sightless, or there had never been a sun.

> Hannes Bok, "Jewel Quest" (1974)

b. In **Stygian darkness, Stygian blackness, Stygian gloom,** etc.:

Com let us our rights begin,
'Tis onely day-light that makes Sin
Which these dun shades will ne're report.
Hail Goddess of Nocturnal sport
Dark vaild Cotytto, t' whom the secret flame
Of mid-night torches burns; mysterious Dame
That ne're art calld, but when the Dragon woom
Of Stygian darknes spets her thickest gloom,
And makes one blot of all the ayr,
Stay thy cloudy Ebon chair,
Wherein thou rid'st with Hecat', and befriend
Us thy vow'd priests, til utmost end
Of all thy dues be done, and none left out,
Ere the blabbing Eastern scout
The nice Morn on th' Indian steep
From her cabin'd loophole peep,
And to the tel-tale sun discry
Our conceal'd Solemnity.

> John Milton, *Comus (A Masque Presented at Ludlow Castle, 1634)*

While I was still wondering, suddenly, like a great sword of flame, a beam from the setting sun pierced the Stygian gloom, and smote upon the point of rock whereon we lay.

> H. Rider Haggard, *She: A History of Adventure* (1886)

I dreamed that I lay writhing on the floor in agony indescribable. My veins were filled with liquid fire, and but that Stygian darkness was about me, I told myself that I must have seen the smoke arising from my burning body.

> Sax Rohmer (Arthur Sarsfield Ward),
> *The Mystery of Dr. Fu-Manchu* (1913; aka *The Insidious Dr. Fu-Manchu*)

Here and there the brilliant rays penetrated to earth, but for the most part they only served to accentuate the Stygian blackness of the jungle's depths.

> Edgar Rice Burroughs, *Tarzan of the Apes* (1912)

"Come!" Norhala flitted ahead of us, a faintly luminous shape in the now Stygian darkness.

> A. Merritt, *The Metal Monster* (1920)

He discovered a second opening, low, and fanged with broken-off pillar formations, in the opposite wall of the cavern. It was filled with Stygian darkness, and before entering it, he tore a lumpy branch from one of the phosphorescent fungi, to serve him in lieu of other light.

> Clark Ashton Smith, "The Immortals of Mercury" (1932)

Without pausing to retrieve the still burning brand he had left at the entrance, Xeethra plunged incontinently into the dark cave. Through Stygian murk he managed to grope his way upward on the perilous incline.

> Clark Ashton Smith, "Xeethra" (1934)

Then he was gone and a stygian darkness closed about me, buffeting, crushing, squeezing me like toothpaste from a tube out of that . . . that place . . . where I had no right to be.

> Brian Lumley, *The Transition of Titus Crow* (1975; ellipses in original)

How far into that stygian darkness we descended, it was impossible to tell. At times we paused to flash the light from our torches onto the walls, where we discovered that these were engraven with huge reliefs representing creatures which bore no resemblance to anything known to have existed on the Earth.

> John S. Glasby, "The Brooding City"

The detective shined the thin beam of his flashlight into the hole, but Stygian darkness hid the bottom.

> P. H. Cannon, *Pulptime: Being a Singular Adventure of Sherlock Holmes,*
> *H. P. Lovecraft, and the Kalem Club, As if Narrated by Frank Belknap Long, Jr.* (1984)

subterrane, *n.* An underground cave.

Bearing the lit flambeau, he began his investigation. He gave heed to the piled and dusty sarcophagi in the first reaches of the subterrane for, during their past visit, Ilalotha had shown to him a niche at the innermost extreme, where, in due time, she herself would find sepulture among the members of that decaying line.

> Clark Ashton Smith, "The Death of Ilalotha" (1937)

subterraneous, *adj.* Subterranean, subterrene.

An awful silence reigned throughout those subterraneous regions, except, now and then, some blasts of wind that shook the doors she had passed, and which, grating on the rusty hinges, were re-echoed through that long labyrinth of darkness.

          Horace Walpole, *The Castle of Otranto: A Gothic Story* (1764)

Though I could not help conjecturing that a subterraneous cemetery, where the relics of ten centuries reposed, must be a sight too congenial with the morbid temper of my mind, I had no notion of the actual horrors of that mansion for the dead, or in my then distempered state of feeling, I should not have trusted my nerves with the spectacle to be expected.

          Daniel Keyes Sanford, "A Night in the Catacombs" (1818)

The suggestion of dark antiquity, the recurrent hint of unnatural events on Midsummer Night, touched some slumbering instinct in my being, as one senses, rather than hears, the flowing of some dark subterraneous river in the night.

          Robert E. Howard, "The Black Stone" (1931)

What they called themselves, we never knew; for none of our tribe ever learned the accursed hissing sibilances they used as speech; but we called them the Children of the Night. And night-things they were indeed, for they slunk in the depths of the dark forests, and in subterraneous dwellings, venturing forth into the hills only when their conquerors slept.

          Robert E. Howard, "The Children of the Night" (1930)

subterrene, *adj.* Subterraneous, subterranean.

They were twitching morbidly and spasmodically, clawing in convulsive and epileptic madness at the moonlit cloud; scratching impotently in the noxious air as if jerked by some alien and bodiless line of linkage with subterrene horrors writhing and struggling below the black roots.

          H. P. Lovecraft, "The Colour out of Space" (1927)

succubus (*pl.* **succubi**), **succuba** (*pl.* **succubæ**), **succube,** *n.* [< L, one who lies beneath one] A demon or devil that has taken on the form of a human female in order to engage in sexual intercourse with a man.

Usage: The masculine form, *succubus,* is the older form and is preferred by some over the feminine *succuba* because spirits such as demons or devils were not properly believed to have any sex, but could take on either as the need arose.

Titles: Aleister Crowley, "Succubus" (verse); Robert Graves, "The Succubus" (verse)

For they affirme undoubtedlie, that the divell plaieth *Succubus* to the man, and carrieth from him the seed of generation, which he delivereth as *Incubus* to the woman, who manie times that waie is gotten with child; which will verie naturallie (they saie) become a witch, and such a one they affirme *Merline* was.

          Reginald Scot, *The Discoverie of Witchcraft* (1584)

> I will have all my Beds, blown up; not stuft:
> Down is too hard. And then, mine Oval Room
> Fill'd with such Pictures as *Tiberius* took
> From Elephantis, and dull Aretine
> But coldly imitated. Then, my Glasses
> Cut in more subtil Angles, to disperse,
> And multiply the Figures, as I walk
> Naked betweeen my *Succubæ*.
>
> Ben Jonson, *The Alchemist: A Comedy* (1610)

Water-devils are those naiades or water-nymphs which have been heretofore conversant about waters and rivers. The water (as Paracelsus thinks) is their chaos, wherein they live; some call them fairies, and say that Habundia is their queen; these cause inundations, many times shipwrecks, and deceive men divers ways, as succubæ, or otherwise, appearing most part (saith Trithemius) in women's shapes.

> Robert Burton, *The Anatomy of Melancholy: What It Is, With All the Kinds,*
> *Causes, Symptomes, Prognostickes & Severall Cures of It* (1621)

Lucian passed on his way, wondering at the strange contrasts of the Middle Ages. How was it that people who could devise so beautiful a service believed in witchcraft, demoniacal possession and obsession, in the incubus and succubus, and in the Sabbath and in many other horrible absurdities? It seemed astonishing that anybody could even pretend to credit such monstrous tales, but there could be no doubt that the dread of old women who rode broomsticks and liked black cats was once a very genuine terror.

> Arthur Machen, *The Hill of Dreams* (1897)

Companioned by these bitter reflections, I had lost the remainder of the conversation between Nayland Smith and the police officer; now, casting off the succubus memory which threatened to obsess me, I put forth a giant mental effort to purge my mind of this uncleanness, and became again an active participant in the campaign against the master—the director of all things noxious.

> Sax Rohmer (Arthur Sarsfield Ward),
> *The Return of Dr. Fu-Manchu* (1916; aka *The Devil Doctor*)

Poor-spirited, over-easy-going Ninzian sat upon the stone bench, an outcast now in his own garden: and he thought for a while about the pitiless miracles with which this Holmendis had harried the fairies and the elves and the salamanders and the trolls and the calcars and the succubæ and all the other amiable iniquities of Poictesme; and about the Saint's devastating crusades against moral laxity and free-thinking and the curt conclusions which he had made with his ropes and his fires to the existence of mere heresy.

> James Branch Cabell, *The Silver Stallion: A Comedy of Redemption* (1925)

—Wallpurgies! And it's this's your deified city? Norganson? And it's we's to pray for Bigmesser's conversions? Call Kitty the Beads, the Mandame of Tip-knock Castle! Let succuba succumb, the improvable his wealth made possible! He's cookinghagar that rost her prayer to him upon the top of the stairs. She's deep, that one.

> James Joyce, *Finnegans Wake* (1922–39)

"The Hammer Against Witches. The old book of the Inquisition that tells what Succubi and Incubi are, and what they can do, and how to tell witches and what to do against them and all of that. Very interesting. It says that a demon can become a shadow, and becoming one may fasten itself upon a living person and become corporeal—or corporeal enough to beget, as the Bible quaintly puts it. The lady demons are the Succubi."

> A. Merritt, *Creep, Shadow!* (1934; aka *Creep, Shadow, Creep!*)

"I allow her to cover my body with kisses and listen to her laughter. Pollutions result. I am powerless against her lips and terrible fingers. She devours me night after night like a succubus. I lie and masturbate with a phantom."

> Ben Hecht, *Fantazius Mallare: A Mysterious Oath* (1918)

Incubi and succubæ howled praise to Hecate, and headless moon-calves bleated to the Magna Mater.

> H. P. Lovecraft, "The Horror at Red Hook" (1925)

Always he awoke from ill dreams, to find about him the stiffened arms of long-dead succubi, or to feel at his side the amorous trembling of fleshless skeletons. He was choked by the natron and bitumen of mummied breasts; he was crushed by the unremoving weight of gigantic liches; he was kissed nauseously by lips that were oozing tatters of corruption.

> Clark Ashton Smith, "The Witchcraft of Ulua" (1933)

"In the dreams of slumber," mused Valzain, "I have clasped succubi who were more than flesh, have known delights too keen for the waking body to sustain."

> Clark Ashton Smith, "Morthylla" (1952)

> Fair you were as nymph or queen of vision,
> Bosomed like the succubi of dreams. . . .
> All your beauty turns to sad, ironic
> Weariness, and sorrowful derision.

> Clark Ashton Smith, "Satiety" (ellipsis in original)

> We have seen the nightmares
> Winging down the sky,
> Bat-like and silent,
> To where the sleepers lie;

We have seen the bosoms
of the succubi.

Clark Ashton Smith, "Nyctalops" (1929)

The serpent's sting, the smell of goat,
   The blue and scarlet fires,
The succubi who foully gloat
   Upon their lewd desires!

Frank Belknap Long, "An Old Wife Speaketh It"

The books dealt in the fullest detail with such matters as the private life of devils, the secret histories of murderous cults, and—these were illustrated—the
proper dueling techniques to employ against sword-armed demons and the
erotic tricks of lamias, succubi, bacchantes, and hamadryads.

Fritz Leiber, "Bazaar of the Bizarre" (1963)

The crowd began to slip from their robes, to reveal all manner of men and
women, old and young—orange-haired witches of the Cobalt Mountain; forest
sorcerers of Ascolais; white-bearded wizards of the Forlorn Land, with babbling
small succubi.

Jack Vance, "T'sais" in *The Dying Earth* (1950)

Melancthe looked here and there with great interest. Shimrod described two or
three pieces of his paraphernalia, then took her before a tall mirror, which reflected her image in clear detail, and another of Shimrod's misgivings was put to
rest. Had she been a succuba or a harpy, the creature's true image would have
reflected from the mirror.

Jack Vance, *The Green Pearl* (1985)

"I am reminded of a case in fifteenth-century Holland where a young woman
accused an elderly and respectable sorcerer of conjuring up a succubus who then
had uh carnal knowledge of the young person in question with the under the
circumstances regrettable result of pregnancy. So the sorcerer was indicted as an
accomplice and rampant voyeur before during and after the fact. However, gentleman of the jury, we no longer credit such uh legends; and a young woman at-
tributing her uh interesting condition to the attentions of a succubus would be
accounted, in these enlightened days, a romanticist or in plain English a God
damned liar hehe hehe heh. . . ."

William S. Burroughs, *Naked Lunch* (1955–59; ellipsis in original)

He knew that the succubi and incubi of medieval legend were *actual beings* and he
felt sure that these creatures were still in operation. Surveys proved him right.

William S. Burroughs, *The Place of Dead Roads* (1977–83)

Ware ironically called her Gretchen, or Greta, or Rita, and she could be compelled by the word *Cazotte*, but in fact she had no name, nor even any real sex.
She was a demon, alternately playing succubus to Jack and incubus to some
witch on the other side of the world.

James Blish, *The Day after Judgment* (1971) [reference to Jacques Cazotte, author of
Le Diable amoureux (1772; trans. *The Devil in Love*).]

She came to him in the night, long after the moon had gone down and the fireflies had vanished from the fields. He awoke to find her crouching over him like
a succubus, gazing urgently into his face.

T. E. D. Klein, *The Ceremonies* (1984)

Summanus, *pr.n.* [< L *Summānus*] In Roman mythology, god of the night-sky
and thunderstorms. [Not in *OED*.]

> Scorners of the Muse, beware!
> [. . .]
> Gods august you have not known
> Gather to her awful throne,
> Demons that you wot not of
> Serve her with a fearful love;
> Dim Summanus, lord of night,
> Is her moiling minister,
> Demogorgon toils for her
> In the darkling Infinite.

Clark Ashton Smith, "Minatory" (1925)

Research into just such cycles of myth and æon-lost legend, while ostensibly he
had been studying Hittite antiquities in the Middle East and Turkey, had cost
Henley his position as Professor of Archæology and Ethnology at Meldham
University. "Cthulhu, Yibb-Tstll, Yog-Sothoth, Summanus—the Great Old
Ones!" Again an expression of awe flitted across his bespectacled face. To be
confronted with a . . . a *monument* such as this, and in such a place . . .

Brian Lumley, "The Fairground Horror" (1975; ellipses in original)

suppurate, *v.intr.* To generate and discharge pus, as a sore, boil, or abscess.

When vampirism is suspected the thing to do is to go over that person's body
inch by inch with a powerful magnifying glass, and the search will probably be
rewarded by the discovery of numerous minute punctures, so minute that they
are not discovered by an examination with the naked eye unless they reveal
themselves by becoming infected and suppurating, when they are usually mistaken for insect bites. They are bites right enough, but not those of an insect.

Dion Fortune, *Psychic Self-Defence: A Study in Occult Pathology and Criminality* (1930)

He does a strip-tease to operation scars, guiding the reluctant fingers of a victim. "Feel that suppurated swelling in my groin where I got the lymphogranulomas. . . . And now I want you to palpate my internal hæmorrhoids."

William S. Burroughs, *Naked Lunch* (1955–59; ellipsis in original)

He wallows in abominations, unspeakable rites, diseased demon lovers, loathsome secrets imparted in a thick slimy whisper, ancient ruined cities under a purple sky, the smell of unknown excrements, the musky sweet rotten reek of the terrible Red Fever, erogenous sores suppurating in the idiot giggling flesh.

William S. Burroughs, *The Place of Dead Roads* (1977–83)

The ghoul lounged naked on a throne of bones that I recognized from my earlier visit to the underworld, toying shamelessly as might an idiot with his gigantic phallus. To describe this organ, which seemed in a permanent state of inflamed erection, would require a specialist in the maladies said to be inflicted by Filloweela on those who earn her hatred. The pimpled and knobbed and suppurating obscenity served the ghoul as a lord's scepter.

Brian McNaughton, "The Tale of the Zaxoin Siblings" (1997)

In 1933, some thirty-five years later, Howard Lovecraft, in a letter to his friend James Morton, claims light-heartedly to be descended from his Elder deities: from Azathoth, Cthulhu and Yog Sothoth. There, four years before his end, he almost managed to decrypt the bas-reliefs raised in the R'lyeh of his sunken mind; almost exposed the Lurker at the Threshold as a travelling salesman, nothing more. Would he have screamed his father's name, like Wilbur Whately's brother, from a hilltop: College Hill, or Sentinel? Would he have recognized himself, his nature and his mannerisms captured in the frail, fore-doomed procession of his fictive victims; his narrators, driven mad or torn apart by Old Ones, things that suppurate and bellow in the sloughs of night?

Alan Moore, "Recognition" (1995)

surcease, *n.* Cessation, suspension, relief.

> Eagerly I wished the morrow;—vainly I had sought to borrow
> From my books surcease of sorrow—sorrow for the lost Lenore—
> For the rare and radiant maiden whom the angels name Lenore—
>   Nameless *here* for evermore.

Edgar Allan Poe, "The Raven" (1844)

O the terror of sleep and of me who am blotted, erased and spun
Into things that are vile and gross.
And the long death of me that drank of this hemlock of earth that brings not the
    death that is surcease—
Only a death of vile dreaming, a lapsing without a forgetting:
O my Soul, my Soul, awake thou!

Benjamin De Casseres, "The Sleeper" in *The Shadow-Eater* (1916)

One night, reading over what is perhaps the most sensational of my books—
"The Poppies and Primulas of Southern Tibet," the result of my travels of
1910–1911, I determined to return to that quiet, once-forbidden land. There, if
anywhere, might I find surcease of sorrow.

> A. Merritt, *The Metal Monster* (1920)

I tried morphine; but the drug has given only transient surcease, and has drawn
me into its clutches as a hopeless slave.

> H. P. Lovecraft, "Dagon" (1917)

> Not while the woods are redolent with spring,
> Or scentless immortelles of autumn blow,
> Shall I evade your loveliness, or know
> Surcease of love and love's remembering.
>
> > Clark Ashton Smith, "The Last Oblivion" (1924)

> I turn away from diamonds, rubies, emeralds, pearls,
> I find no surcease in the unrelieving wine;
> I clap, and at the sign
> Come forth my slaves and eunuchs and the dancing girls;
> I hear the music's plaintive sob, watch spins and whirls,
> But ennui still is mine.
>
> > Donald Wandrei, "Somewhere Past Ispahan"

He was motionless, not sobbing, but hopelessly weeping and weeping, without
sign of surcease.

> Fred Chappell, *Dagon* (1968)

T

tarn, *n.* A mountain or highland lake or pool; in particular, one which has no major outlet and is therefore stagnant. A frequent feature of Gothic landscape.

Titles: Clark Ashton Smith, "The Nightmare Tarn" (verse)

> It was possible, I reflected, that a mere different arrangement of the particulars of the scene, of the details of the picture, would be sufficient to modify, or perhaps to annihilate its capacity for sorrowful impression; and, acting upon this idea, I reined my horse to the precipitous brink of a black and lurid tarn that lay in unruffled lustre by the dwelling, and gazed down—but with a shudder even more thrilling than before—upon the remodelled and inverted images of the gray sedge, and the ghastly tree-stems, and the vacant and eye-like windows.
>
> Edgar Allan Poe, "The Fall of the House of Usher" (1839)

> Our talk had been serious and sober,
>   But our thoughts they were palsied and sere—
>   Our memories were treacherous and sere;
> For we knew not the month was October,
>   And we marked not the night of the year—
>   (Ah, night of all nights in the year!)
> We noted not the dim lake of Auber,
>   (Though once we had journeyed down here)
> We remembered not the dank tarn of Auber,
>   Nor the ghoul-haunted woodland of Weir.
>
> Edgar Allan Poe, "Ulalume—A Ballad" (1847)

> So pin'd Lucullus with his lofty woe,
> Till one drear day he bought a set of Poe:
> Charm'd with the cheerful horrors there display'd,
> He vow'd with gloom to woo the Heav'nly Maid.
> Of Auber's tarn and Yaanek's slope he dreams,
> And weaves an hundred Ravens in his schemes.
>
> H. P. Lovecraft, "The Poe-et's Nightmare: A Fable" (1916)

Apropos of your unholy feast by the tarn of black blood—I am reminded of what Baudelaire once asked an aspiring decadent poet who copied—and even exceeded his colourful Satanism without reflecting to any dangerous extent his genius. A trifle exasperated by the ostentatious "shockingness" of the young man, Baudelaire "went him one better" by asking very gravely—"Have you ever tasted young children's brains? They're quite delightful, and taste exactly like walnuts!"

H. P. Lovecraft, letter to Bernard Austin Dwyer (3 March 1927)

In lieu of the purling brook there lay before him a tarn of waters that were dark and dull as clotting blood, and which gave back no reflection of the brown autumnal sedges that trailed therein like the hair of suicides, and the skeletons of rotting osiers that writhed above them.

Clark Ashton Smith, "A Rendezvous in Averoigne" (1930)

The Conrad affair is no longer simply a missing persons case; it is a crime whose hideous memory still lurks in the mirror of the tarn that separates the Castle from the deserted village of Zengerstein.

C. Hall Thompson, "The Pale Criminal" (1947)

Tartarean, Tartarian, *adj.* Of, pertaining to, or resembling Tartarus (q.v.); hellish, infernal; profoundly dark; Stygian, Plutonian.

> And o'er his head flew jealousies and cares,
> Ghosts, imps, and half the black Tartarian crew,
> Arch-angels damn'd, nor was their Prince remote,
> Borne on the vaporous wings of Stygian dew.

Philip Freneau, *The House of Night: A Vision* (1779)

"Drink wine with me, and be less Tartarean."

M. P. Shiel, "Xélucha" (1896)

Out of the unimaginable blackness beyond the gangrenous glare of that cold flame, out of the Tartarean leagues through which that oily river rolled uncannily, unheard, and unsuspected, there flopped rhythmically a horde of tame, trained, hybrid winged things that no sound eye could ever wholly grasp, or sound brain ever wholly remember.

H. P. Lovecraft, "The Festival" (1923)

He screamed and screamed and screamed in a voice whose falsetto panic no acquaintance of his would ever have recognised; and though he could not rise to his feet he crawled and rolled desperately away over the damp pavement where dozens of Tartarean wells poured forth their exhausted whining and yelping to answer his own insane cries.

H. P. Lovecraft, *The Case of Charles Dexter Ward* (1927)

And at the bottom of all—far, far down—still trickles the waters that carved the whole chain of gulfs out of the primal soluble limestone. Whence it comes and whither it trickles—to what awesome deeps of Tartarean nighted horror it bears the doom-fraught messages of the hoary hills—no being of human mould can say. Only They which gibber down There can answer.

H. P. Lovecraft, "A Descent to Avernus" (1929)

The moon's bloodying horn was dragged down by sable boughs, and the dig-
gings became an unfathomable gulf of Tartarean blackness.

Clark Ashton Smith, "The Ice-Demon" (1932)

The hollow eye sockets, deep as Tartarean wells, appeared to seethe with myriad, mocking lights, like the eyes of elementals swimming upward in obscene
shadow.

Clark Ashton Smith, "The Colossus of Ylourgne" (1932)

Only the most redoubtable of men or demons could have made away with
Dwerulas, who was said to have lived through a whole millennium, never sleeping for one night, and crowding all his hours with iniquities and sorceries of a
sub-tartarean blackness.

Clark Ashton Smith, "The Garden of Adompha" (1937)

Tartarus, *pr.n.* [< L < Gr *Tártaros*] In Greek and Roman mythology, the lowest
and worst of the hells, held to be as far below Hades as Hades is below the
world of the living, and three times as dark as the darkest night.

Titles: Herman Melville, "The Paradise of Bachelors and the Tartarus of
Maids"; Clark Ashton Smith, "The Titans in Tartarus" (verse)

No sooner did Mr. ―― make his appearance, than she went below stairs,
brushed his shoes, coat, &c.; and, except when she was summoned to run an er-
rand, she never emerged from the dismal Tartarus of the kitchens, to the upper
air, until my welcome knock at night called up her little trembling footsteps to
the front door.

Thomas De Quincey, Confessions of an English Opium-Eater:
Being an Extract from the Life of a Scholar (1821)

"Filth, unhand me," said Spitfire, "else shall I presently thrust thee through
with my sword, and send thee to the Tartarus of hell, where I doubt not the
devils there too long await thee."

E. R. Eddison, The Worm Ouroboros (1922)

"In Tartarus the Titans writhe, and beneath the fiery Ætna groan the children of
Uranus and Gæa."

H. P. Lovecraft & Anna Helen Crofts, "Poetry and the Gods" (1920)

And then had come the scourge, grinning and lethal, from the nightmare caverns of Tartarus.

H. P. Lovecraft, "Herbert West—Reanimator" (1921–22)

The push had been tremendous, but the force had held out; and as the pusher
collapsed to a muddy blotch of corruption the pedestal he had pushed tottered,
tipped, and finally careened from its onyx base into the thick waters below,

sending up a parting gleam of carven gold as it sank heavily to undreamable
gulfs of lower Tartarus.

> H. P. Lovecraft, "The Horror at Red Hook" (1925)

What, I thought, of the hapless rats that stumbled into such traps amidst the
blackness of their quests in this grisly Tartarus?

> H. P. Lovecraft, "The Rats in the Walls" (1923)

But Ezra Weeden, who watched him closely, sneered cynically at all this outward
activity; and freely swore it was no more than a mask for some nameless traffick
with the blackest gulfs of Tartarus.

> H. P. Lovecraft, *The Case of Charles Dexter Ward* (1927)

There is a sense of spectral whirling through liquid gulfs of infinity, of dizzying
rides through reeling universes on a comet's tail, and of hysterical plunges from
the pit to the moon and from the moon back again to the pit, all livened by a
cachinnating chorus of the distorted, hilarious elder gods and the green, bat-
winged mocking imps of Tartarus.

> H. P. Lovecraft, "The Call of Cthulhu" (1926)

> Ebbing, the battle left those elder gods
> Thrown back on iron shores of their despair,
> A darker and a vaster Tartarus.

> Clark Ashton Smith, "Saturn" (1912)

Each face was alike in its blood-red, sensual lips and its expression of gnawing
agony, and burning black eyes like the abysmal pits of Tartarus stared at me until
I felt the short hairs stir on my neck.

> Henry Kuttner, "The Secret of Kralitz" (1936)

tattoo, *n.* A repetitive beating sound, as of drumming or a finger tapping.
Sometimes given as the (or a) **devil's tattoo**.

a. General:

Meantime the hellish tattoo of the heart increased. It grew quicker and quicker,
and louder and louder every instant. The old man's terror *must* have been extreme! It grew louder, I say louder every moment!—do you mark me well?

> Edgar Allan Poe, "The Tell-Tale Heart" (1843)

The downpour was increasing, and beating now a regular tattoo upon the gutter-
way.

> Sax Rohmer (Arthur Sarsfield Ward),
> *The Return of Dr. Fu-Manchu* (1916; aka *The Devil Doctor*)

The baying of the dogs was close, and with it a tattoo of hoofs, the drumming
of a strong horse, galloping.

> A. Merritt, *Creep, Shadow!* (1934; aka *Creep, Shadow, Creep!*)

Satan—or maybe his lieutenant Momus, fiend of mockery—peered from the solitary unregenerate eye of the wizened stall keeper; gnarled fingers beat a whimsical tattoo on either side of the bright gaud, and a wisp of beard wagged knowingly toward the girl's ear.

Leslie Barringer, *Joris of the Rock* (1928)

"'I am the victim of an overwhelming desire to masturbate,' I said to her, 'since I find it difficult to resist you. But if I yield to the mysterious reality you have assumed I will become too grotesque for my vanity to tolerate. I will remain aware while possessng you that my penis is beating a ludicrous tattoo on a sofa cushion. I choose rather to emulate the pride of St. Anthony, who shrewdly refused to play the whoremonger with shadows.'"

Ben Hecht, *Fantazius Mallare: A Mysterious Oath* (1918)

As though his words had been a cue the sounds again burst forth—no longer muffled nor faint. They roared; they seemed to pelt through air and down upon us; they beat about our ears with thunderous tattoo like covered caverns drummed upon by Titans with trunks of great trees.

A. Merritt, *The Metal Monster* (1920)

As usual, no use. It merely flew across the room to a lamp and began beating the same tattoo on the stiff cardboard shade.

H. P. Lovecraft & Hazel Heald, "Winged Death" (1933)

If that creature attempts another tattoo, it will be its last!

H. P. Lovecraft & Hazel Heald, "Winged Death" (1933)

Nightsticks beat a lusty tattoo upon the door.

C. M. Eddy, Jr. & H. P. Lovecraft, "The Loved Dead" (1923)

As I anticipated, the tattoo upon my ears has ceased and a low whisper has caught my attention . . . the overwhelming significance of the thing has just registered itself upon my bewildered brain . . . *I can hear!*

C. M. Eddy, Jr. & H. P. Lovecraft,
"Deaf, Dumb, and Blind" (1924; ellipses in original)

Meanwhile the wind howled and roared and rain battered in a steady hard tattoo on the turf roof.

Jack Vance, *The Green Pearl* (1985)

Along the narrow, dusty little roads of Nirvalla the iron hooves of the great warhorse carried thunder in a rolling tattoo as its long strides ate up ground.

Gardner F. Fox, "The Helix from Beyond" in *Kothar of the Magic Sword* (1969)

The earth was blasted from the spot as thunder boomed and lightning beat a frenzied tattoo roundabout, while tornadic winds howled and roared so that no vegetation within a mile stood whole and green when their work was finished.

Gary Gygax, *Artifact of Evil* (1986)

Morrigan's breath came hard and trembly. Her pulse rate elevated, drumming a tattoo of lust in her ears, her temples, and her sleek throat.

t. Winter-Damon, "City in the Torrid Waste"

b. In the phrase the/a **devil's tattoo:**

The young knight beat the devil's tattoo upon the open casement.

Alfred Crowquill, "Crochet" (1848)

For a moment I heard nothing; the hail was playing the devil's tattoo on the corrugated zinc of the roof.

H. G. Wells, "The Story of Davidson's Eyes" (1895)

I hurled myself out of the hotel, my pulse pounding a devil's tattoo.

Robert E. Howard, "The Little People" (1928)

There commenced a rattle of windows like the devil's own tattoo.

Robert Sheckley, "The New Horla" (2000)

Tekeli-li, ?. [< Theodore Hook, *Tekeli; or, The Siege of Montgatz,* a play in which Edgar Allan Poe's mother performed. *Tekeli* seems to be a common Turkish name.] See quotations. [Not in *OED*.]

Titles: Tekeli-li! (periodical); J. Guy & D. Peters, "Tekelili hyperalbum gen. et sp. nov., an interesting new bird from the Antarctic Tsalal Formation" in the *New England Journal of Science* (hoax)

From absolute stupor they appeared to be, all at once, aroused to the highest pitch of excitement, and rushed wildly about, going to and from a certain point on the beach, with the strangest expressions of mingled horror, rage, and intense curiosity depicted on their countenances, and shouting, at the top of their voices, *Tekeli-li! Tekeli-li!*

Edgar Allan Poe, *The Narrative of Arthur Gordon Pym of Nantucket* (1838)

By-and-by the men with the stakes drove them in a circle around it, and, no sooner was this arrangement completed, than the whole of the vast assembly rushed into the interior of the island, with loud screams of *Tekeli-li! Tekeli-li!*

Edgar Allan Poe, *The Narrative of Arthur Gordon Pym of Nantucket* (1838)

The sight of the linen seemed to affect him in a very singular manner. He could not be prevailed upon to touch it or go near it, shuddering when we attempted to force him, and shrieking out *Tekeli-li!*

Edgar Allan Poe, *The Narrative of Arthur Gordon Pym of Nantucket* (1838)

Many gigantic and pallidly white birds flew continuously now from beyond the veil, and their scream was the eternal *Tekeli-li!* as they retreated from our vision.

Edgar Allan Poe, *The Narrative of Arthur Gordon Pym of Nantucket* (1838)

They could see big turtles crawling on the beach, but how could they venture to go thither, with hundreds of natives coming and going about their several occupations, with their constant cry of tekeli-li?

Jules Verne (trans. Harold Beaver), *The Sphinx of the Ice Fields*
(orig. *Le Sphinx des glaces*).
[In *The Antarktos Cycle* (ed. Robert M. Price), garbled into "t$\geq$ k$\geq$ li-li".]

At the risk of seeming puerile I will add another thing, too; if only because of the surprising way Danforth's impression chimed with mine. Of course common reading is what prepared us both to make the interpretation, though Danforth has hinted at queer notions about unsuspected and forbidden sources to which Poe may have had access when writing his Arthur Gordon Pym a century ago. It will be remembered that in that fantastic tale there is a word of unknown but terrible and prodigious significance connected with the antarctic and screamed eternally by the gigantic, spectrally snowy birds of that malign region's core. "*Tekeli-li! Tekeli-li!*" That, I may admit, is exactly what we thought we heard conveyed by that sudden sound behind the advancing white mist—that insidious musical piping over a singularly wide range.

H. P. Lovecraft, *At the Mountains of Madness* (1931)

Again came that insidious musical piping—"*Tekeli-li! Tekeli-li!*"

H. P. Lovecraft, *At the Mountains of Madness* (1931)

Once more came that sinister, wide-ranged piping—"*Tekeli-li! Tekeli-li!*"

H. P. Lovecraft, *At the Mountains of Madness* (1931)

Unhappy act! Not Orpheus himself, or Lot's wife, paid much more dearly for a backward glance. And again came that shocking, wide-ranged piping—"*Tekeli-li! Tekeli-li!*"

H. P. Lovecraft, *At the Mountains of Madness* (1931)

Still came that eldritch, mocking cry—"*Tekeli-li! Tekeli-li!*" And at last we remembered that the dæmoniac shoggoths—given life, thought, and plastic organ patterns solely by the Old Ones, and having no language save that which the dot-groups expressed—*had likewise no voice save the imitated accents of their bygone masters.*

H. P. Lovecraft, *At the Mountains of Madness* (1931)

At the time his shrieks were confined to the repetition of a single mad word of all too obvious source:
"Tekeli-li! Tekeli-li!"

H. P. Lovecraft, *At the Mountains of Madness* (1931)

They may have heard, as I did, that thin, far whistling sound, that maddening ululation from the deep, immeasurable gulf of cosmic space, the wailing that fell back along the wind, and the syllables that floated down the slopes of air: *Tekeli-li, tekeli-li, tekeli-li* . . . And certainly they say the thing that came crying out at us from the sinking ruins behind, the distorted caricature of a human being, with its eyes sunk to invisibility in thick masses of scaly flesh, the thing that flailed its arms bonelessly at us like the appendages of an octopus, *the thing that shrieked and gibbered in Paul Tuttle's voice!*

> August Derleth, "The Return of Hastur" (1929)
> in *The Mask of Cthulhu* (ellipsis in original)

"I can hear it! The very sound recorded by Poe and Lovecraft: Tekeli-li, tekeli-li! It must be close."

> Robert Anton Wilson & Robert Shea,
> *The Golden Apple* in *The Illuminatus! Trilogy* (1969–71)

All the while, there was this bleating or squealing that seemed to say "Tekeli-li! Tekeli-li!"

> Robert Anton Wilson & Robert Shea,
> *The Golden Apple* in *The Illuminatus! Trilogy* (1969–71)

The next stop was quite a refrigerator, miles and miles of it, and that's where the creature who kept up that howling of "Tekeli-li! Tekeli-li!" hung his hat. Or its hat. I shan't attempt to do him, or it, justice. That *Necronomicon* said about Yog Sothoth that "Kadath in the cold waste hath known him," and now I realized that "known" was used there in the Biblical sense.

> Robert Anton Wilson & Robert Shea,
> *The Golden Apple* in *The Illuminatus! Trilogy* (1969–71)

In the Antarctic a great land-reclamation project had been undertaken. Geothermal power was used to melt the ice in a circle centered on the south pole. The cleared area measured 1.5 million square kilometers. The soil ws found to be incredibly rich in minerals. It was hugely fertile. The scenic beauty of the region was incomparable. There were mountains, lakes, glaciers, to shame those of New Zealand or Switzerland or Tibet. Forests were planted and grew rapidly and luxuriantly. Imported wildlife throve. The few native species—penguins, amphibian mammals, a strange variety of bird newly discovered and named the tekeli-li—*were protected.*

> Richard A. Lupoff, "Discovery of the Ghooric Zone" (1977)

To be fair, Randolph's lyrics get better when she gives up English completely halfway through the third verse: "Crash bridgelict eyeolins, crobble yog sothoth ngh'haa ygnaiith fhtagn in cractory whine-yards / beloke sleepled R'lyeh nga'haa tekeli-li."

> Alan Moore, "The Courtyard" (1994)

N'gaii fhtagn e'hucunechh R'lyeh. Iä, G'harne ep ygg Rhan Teggoth n'thyleii yr gnh'gua? Shagghai, humuk Dho-Hna, g'yll-gnaii ygg yr nhhngr shoggoth, hrr yll'ngngr Nyarlathotep. Gh'll mhhg-gthaa tekeli-li Y'golonac rrthnaa.

H'rrnai Cthulhu. H'rrnai Cthulhu nnh'gtep . . .

Alan Moore, "The Courtyard" (1994; ellipsis in original)

Then, from somewhere deep in the woods, came a faint, whistling cry, not unlike a whipporwill: "Tekeliiii-liiiii . . . Tekeliii-liiiiii."

Stephen M. Rainey, "The Pit of the Shoggoths" (ellipsis in original)

The shrill, keening cry he'd heard this morning from the forest:
Tekelliiii-lleeeee . . . Tekelliiii-lleeeee . . .

Stephen M. Rainey, "The Pit of the Shoggoths" (ellipses in original)

Just then, the two odd men dematerialized and reappeared standing over Glory. Howard was hardly halfway there.

"*Tekeli-li!*" said the larger shadow.

A puzzled expression crossed Howard's face. He hesitated momentarily.

"*Tekeli-li!*" said the other shadow.

"Oh, my God!" cried Lovecraft. "It's true! It's true!"

"*Tekeli-li!*" the odd men said in unison, and they leaped forward.

David Barbour & Richard Raleigh, Shadows Bend:
A Novel of the Fantastic and Unspeakable (2000)

tenebrific, *adj.* Rendering dark and gloomy; dark and gloomy; tenebrous.

Level with the light, their tenebrific brows preserve a pride as of Titan kings.

Clark Ashton Smith, "The Memnons of the Night" (1915)

At the question, a veil seemed to fall between us, impalpable but tenebrific. He shook his head morosely and made no reply.

Clark Ashton Smith, "Genius Loci" (1932)

tenebrous, *adj.* Dark and gloomy.

> Over their heads the towering and tenebrous boughs of the cypress
> Met in a dusky arch, and trailing mosses in mid-air
> Waved like banners that hang on the walls of ancient cathedrals.

Henry Wadsworth Longfellow, Evangeline (1847)

A few days later he saw at his club a gentleman of his acquaintance, named Austin, who was famous for his intimate knowledge of London life, both in its tenebrous and luminous phases.

Arthur Machen, "The Great God Pan" (1890)

"She was savage and superb, wild-eyed and magnificent; there was something ominous and stately in her deliberate progress. And in the hush that had fallen suddenly upon the whole sorrowful land, the immense wilderness, the colossal body of the fecund and mysterious life seemed to look at her, pensive, as though it had been looking at the image of its own tenebrous and passionate soul."

Joseph Conrad, *Heart of Darkness* (1902)

"The pilgrims looked upon me with disfavor. I was, so to speak, numbered with the dead. It is strange how I accepted this unforeseen partnership, this choice of nightmares forced upon me in the tenebrous land invaded by these mean and greedy phantoms."

Joseph Conrad, *Heart of Darkness* (1902)

> Woe is me! the brow of a brazen morning
> Breaks in blood on water athirst of Hebrus.
> Sanguine horror starts on her hills tenebrous:
> Hell hath not heard her!

Aleister Crowley, *Orpheus: A Lyrical Legend* (1905)

And through this revolving graveyard of the universe the muffled, maddening beating of drums, and thin, monotonous whine of blasphemous flutes from inconceivable, unlighted chambers beyond Time; the detestable pounding and piping whereunto dance slowly, awkwardly, and absurdly the gigantic, tenebrous ultimate gods—the blind, voiceless, mindless gargoyles whose soul is Nyarlathotep.

H. P. Lovecraft, "Nyarlathotep" (1920)

And before the day was done Carter saw that the steersman could have no other goal than the Basalt Pillars of the West, beyond which simple folk say splendid Cathuria lies, but which wise dreamers well know are the gates of a monstrous cataract wherein the oceans of earth's dreamland drop wholly to abysmal nothingness and shoot through the empty spaces toward other worlds and other stars and the awful voids outside the ordered universe where the dæmon-sultan Azathoth gnaws hungrily in chaos amid pounding and piping and the hellish dancing of the Other Gods, blind, voiceless, tenebrous, and mindless, with their soul and messenger Nyarlathotep.

H. P. Lovecraft, *The Dream-Quest of Unknown Kadath* (1927)

Long, long we shouted and sang and caroused there in the great cavern, and after a time we arose together and trooped to where a narrow, high-arched bridge spanned the tenebrous waters of the lake. But I may not speak of what was at the other end of the bridge, nor of the unnameable things I saw—and did!

Henry Kuttner, "The Secret of Kralitz" (1936)

teratological, *adj.* Of or pertaining to teratology (q.v.).

And then he began to see Uncle Pietro much thinner and much taller, so that he looked like Don Quixote in the illustrations, and then Sancho Panza came in, but he didn't look like the illustrations at all, in fact there was something dark and teratological about him, and then Sigismundo realized it was not Sancho Panza at all but the violet-eyed assassin in the church.

Robert Anton Wilson, *The Earth Will Shake* (1982)

teratologically, *adv.* In a teratological (q.v.) manner. [Not in *OED*.]

It was partly human, beyond a doubt, with very man-like hands and head, and the goatish, chinless face had the stamp of the Whateleys upon it. But the torso and lower parts of the body were teratologically fabulous, so that only generous clothing could ever have enabled it to walk on earth unchallenged or uneradicated.

H. P. Lovecraft, "The Dunwich Horror" (1928)

Why not write a tale about some extraplanetary being who has undergone (either at the hands of his own kind, or of some human plastic surgeon) a facial transformation which enables him to pass as a human. His body, of course, would be "teratologically fabulous" beneath his clothing; and there would be all sorts of disquieting suggestions about his personality.

Clark Ashton Smith, letter to H. P. Lovecraft (c. 24 October, 1930)

I must have new subject matter, truly unusual plot material. If only I could conceive of something that was teratologically incredible!

Robert Bloch, "The Shambler from the Stars" (1935)

Here were the misshapen skulls of an ancient order of sub-man, and the teratologically fabulous remains of things which had never been men; bottles of multi-hued liquids, some bubbling and others quiescent; flutes made of the hollow bones of *pteranodon primus*, capable of notes which would transmute silver into gold and vice-versa; shelf upon shelf of books in black leather and umber skins, at least one of which was tattooed!

Brian Lumley, *Elysia: The Coming of Cthulhu* (1989)

Wilbur's spectacular ending parallels Helen's just as strikingly as does his beginning. Both are observed in terrible death throes in which their physiognomies and anatomies are revealed as "teratologically fabulous" (to use Lovecraft's adjectivally fabulous expression), manifesting the anatomy of various evolutionary stages, Helen's in turn, Wilbur's simultaneously, and finally resolving themselves into disintegrating ooze.

Robert M. Price, introduction to Arthur Machen, "The Great God Pan" in
Robert M. Price, ed., *The Dunwich Cycle: Where the Old Gods Wait* (1995)

teratology, *n.* That branch of science which takes the study of monsters and abnormalities as its purview.

There were aspersions on his sanity and tales of his crazy forms of secret worship—though latterly his success with his own basement museum had dulled the edge of some criticisms while sharpening the insidious point of others. Teratology and the iconography of nightmare were his hobbies, and even he had had the prudence to screen off some of his worst effigies in a special alcove for adults only.

H. P. Lovecraft & Hazel Heald, "The Horror in the Museum" (1932)

Terminus, terminus, *pr.n.* & *n.* In Roman mythology, the god who presides over boundaries and landmarks; a statue or bust of the god Terminus used as a boundary post; hence, a border, boundary, or endpoint marker; the border, boundary, or endpoint itself.

The seven arched gates of that garden, each having over it a carven face like those on the city's gates, are always open; and the people roam reverently at will down the tiled paths and through the little lanes lined with grotesque termini and the shrines of modest gods.

H. P. Lovecraft, *The Dream-Quest of Unknown Kadath* (1926–27)

Then, in a flaring as of infernal levin, he remembered all, and knew the grim shadow that towered above him like a Terminus reared in hell.

Clark Ashton Smith, "Xeethra" (1934)

Said Smygo, the iconoclast of Zothique: "Bear a hammer with thee always, and break down any terminus on which it is written: 'So far shalt thou pass but no farther go.'"

Clark Ashton Smith, "Epigrams and Apothegms"

terraqueous, *adj.* Consisting of land and water.

> A part how small of the terraqueous globe
> Is tenanted by man! the rest a waste:
> Rocks, deserts, frozen seas, and burning sands—
> Wild haunts of monsters, poisons, stings, and death:
> Such is earth's melancholy map! but, far
> More sad, this earth is a true map of man:
> So bounded are its haughty lord's delights
> To woe's wide empire; where deep troubles toss,
> Loud sorrows howl, envenom'd passions bite,
> Ravenous calamities our vitals seize,
> And threatening fate wide opens to devour.

Edward Young, *The Complaint, and the Consolation; or, Night Thoughts* (1742)

Sometimes I believe that this less material life is our truer life, and that our vain presence on the terraqueous globe is itself the secondary or merely virtual phenomenon.

H. P. Lovecraft, "Beyond the Wall of Sleep" (1919)

"Too hardily, O filth of mankind, thou hast intruded on the peace of Ornava, isle that is sacred to the birds, and wantonly thou hast slain one of my subjects. For know that I am the monarch of all birds that fly, walk, wade or swim on this terraqueous globe of Earth; and in Ornava is my seat and my capital. Verily, justice shall be done upon thee for thy crime."

Clark Ashton Smith, "The Voyage of King Euvoran" (1933)

terrible, *adj.* Inspiring terror, terrifying.

Whatever is fitted in any sort to excite the ideas of pain, and danger, that is to say, whatever is in any sort terrible, or is conversant about terrible objects, or operates in a manner analogous to terror, is a source of the *sublime*; that is, it is productive of the strongest emotion which the mind is capable of feeling.

Edmund Burke, *A Philosophical Enquiry into the Origin of Our Ideas of the Sublime and Beautiful* (1757)

One of his most remarkable stories—certainly, I think, his most terrible story— is "The Great God Pan," at first published separately with "The Inmost Light;" now included in "The House of Souls."

Vincent Starrett, "Arthur Machen: A Novelist of Ecstasy and Sin" (1917) in *Buried Cæsars: Essays in Literary Appreciation* (1923)

I shuddered oddly in some of the far corners; for certain altars and stones suggested forgotten rites of terrible, revolting, and inexplicable nature, and made me wonder what manner of men could have made and frequented such a temple.

H. P. Lovecraft, "The Nameless City" (1921)

The story is overwritten, over-dramatic, and the mood of mounting horror is applied in a very artificial manner. Rather than creating in the reader a mood of terror, Lovecraft *describes* a mood of terror: the emotion is applied in the adjectives—the valley in which the city lies is "terrible"; the ruins themselves are of an "unwholesome" antiquity; certain of the altars and stones "suggested forbidden rites of terrible, revolting, and inexplicable nature." Of course, if you stop to think about it, such terms are meaningless. A stone is a stone, a valley is a valley, and ruins are merely ruins. Decking them out with a variety of shuddersome adjectives does not make them intrinsically shuddersome.

Lin Carter, *Lovecraft: A Look Behind the Cthulhu Mythos* (1971)

"When their city was completed, they slew all the black slaves. And their magicians made a terrible magic to guard the city; for by their necromantic arts they re-created the dragons which had once dwelt in this lost land, and whose monstrous bones they found in the forest."

Robert E. Howard, "Red Nails" (1935)

"And you have a voice in the government, and enough people voting the same way you vote could change the face of the world. There is something terrible in that thought."

Charles G. Finney, *The Circus of Dr. Lao* (1934)

terrific, *adj.* Inspiring terror, terrifying.

What she had read of the MS. awakened a dreadful interest in the fate of the writer, and called up terrific images to her mind. "In these apartments!"—said she, and she closed her eyes. At length, she heard Madame La Motte enter her chamber, and the phantoms of fear beginning to dissipate, left her to repose.

Ann Radcliffe, *The Romance of the Forest, Interspersed with Some Pieces of Poetry* (1791)

The road, therefore, was carried high among the cliffs, that impended over the river, and seemed as if suspended in air; while the gloom and vastness of the precipices, which towered above and sunk below it, together with the amazing force and uproar of the falling waters, combined to render the pass more terrific than the pencil could describe, or language can express. Ellena ascended it, not with indifference but with calmness; she experienced somewhat of a dreadful pleasure in looking down upon the irresistible flood; but this emotion was heightened into awe, when she perceived that the road led to a slight bridge, which, thrown across the chasm at an immense height, united two opposite cliffs, between which the whole cataract of the river descended.

Ann Radcliffe, *The Italian; or,*
The Confessional of the Black Penitents: A Romance (1797)

At length a third horror, more horrible than the rest, presented itself to the af- frighted eyes of Edwin. He saw a figure, larger than the human, that walked among the clouds, and piloted the storm. Its appearance was dreadful, and its shape, loose and undistinguishable, seemed to be blended with the encircling darkness. From its countenance gleamed a barbarous smile, ten times more ter- rific than the frown of any other being. Triumph, inhuman triumph, glistened in its eye, and, with relentless delight, it brewed the tempest, and hurled the de- structive lightning. Edwin gazed upon this astonishing apparition, and knew it for a goblin of darkness.

William Godwin, *Imogen: A Pastoral Romance from the Ancient British* (1784)

"Think of wandering amid sepulchral ruins, of stumbling over the bones of the dead, of encountering what I cannot describe,—the horror of being among those who are neither the living or the dead;—those dark and shadowless things that sport themselves with the reliques of the dead, and feast and love amid cor- ruption,—ghastly, mocking, and terrific. *Must* we pass near the vaults?"

Charles Maturin, *Melmoth the Wanderer: A Tale* (1820)

"When a north-wester, as it is termed, visited the island, with all its terrific ac- companiments of midnight darkness, clouds of suffocating dust, and thunders like the trumpet of doom, she stood amid the leafy colonnades of the banyan-tree, ignorant of her danger, watching the cowering wings and dropping heads of the birds, and the ludicrous terror of the monkeys, as they skipt from branch to branch with their young."

Charles Maturin, *Melmoth the Wanderer: A Tale* (1820)

To be buried while alive is, beyond question, the most terrific of these extremes which has ever fallen to the lot of mere mortality.

Edgar Allan Poe, "The Premature Burial" (1844)

"Oh, my God! when the justice of Heaven permits the Evil one to carry out a scheme of vengeance—when its execution is committed to the lost and terrible victim of sin, who owes his own ruin to the man, the very man, whom he is commissioned to pursue—then, indeed, the torments and terrors of hell are anticipated on earth. But heaven has dealt mercifully with me—hope has opened to me at last; and if death could come without the dreadful sight I am doomed to see, I would gladly close my eyes this moment upon the world. But though death is welcome, I shrink with an agony you cannot understand—an actual frenzy of terror—from the last encounter with that—that DEMON, who has drawn me thus to the verge of the chasm, and who is himself to plunge me down. I am to see him again—once more—but under circumstances unutterably more terrific than ever."

J. S. LeFanu, "The Familiar" (1847)

"But the Americans had their own saints," Zeus reminded him. "I very well recollect how quite recently the Pilgrim Fathers—Englishmen—took to the rising nation a most melancholy and terrific variant of Jaweh worship and ruled their generation with rods of terror. It oppressed me at the time."

Eden Phillpotts, *The Miniature* (1927)

And while there are those who have dared to seek glimpses beyond the Veil, and to accept HIM as a Guide, they would have been more prudent had they avoided commerce with HIM; for it is written in the Book of Thoth how terrific is the price of a single glimpse. Nor may those who pass ever return, for in the Vastnesses transcending our world are Shapes of darkness that seize and bind. The Affair that shambleth about in the night, the Evil that defieth the Elder Sign, the Herd that stand watch at the secret portal each tomb is known to have, and that thrive on that which groweth out of the tenants within—all these Blacknesses are lesser than HE Who guardeth the Gateway; HE Who will guide the rash one beyond all the worlds into the Abyss of unnamable Devourers. For HE is 'UMR-AT-TAWIL, the Most Ancient One, which the scribe rendereth as THE PROLONGED OF LIFE.

Abdul Alhazred, *Necronomicon*, as quoted in H. P. Lovecraft & E. Hoffmann Price, "Through the Gates of the Silver Key" (1932–33)

tessellated, tesselated, *adj.* Decorated with a mosaic or checkerboard pattern of small squares of stone or glass fitted together. The quintessential style of flooring in fantasy and weird fiction.

After I had seen most of the sculptured stones, the coffins, rings, coins, and fragments of tessellated pavement which the place contains, I was shown a small square pillar of white stone, which had been recently discovered in the wood of which I have been speaking, and, as I found on inquiry, in that open space where the Roman road broadens out.

Arthur Machen, "The Great God Pan" (1890)

He loved his garden and the view of the tessellated city from the vineyard on the hill, the strange clamour of the tavern, and white Fotis appearing on the torch-lit stage.

Arthur Machen, *The Hill of Dreams* (1897)

The room was built of rose-colored marble excepting the floor which was tesselated in rose and gray.

Robert W. Chambers, "The Mask" (1895)

The floor of the chamber was tessellated of marble and green tourmaline, and on every square of tourmaline was carven the image of a fish: as the dolphin, the conger, the cat-fish, the salmon, the tunny, the squid, and other wonders of the deep.

E. R. Eddison, *The Worm Ouroboros* (1922)

He piously crossed himself, and went into the hut. Inside, the walls were adorned with very old-looking frescoes that were equally innocent of perspective and reticence: the floor was of tessellated bronze.

James Branch Cabell, *Figures of Earth: A Comedy of Appearances* (1920)

Norrys now took a lantern close to the altar and examined the place where Nigger-Man was pawing; silently kneeling and scraping away the lichens of centuries which joined the massive pre-Roman block to the tessellated floor.

H. P. Lovecraft, "The Rats in the Walls" (1923)

With the night came song, and Carter nodded as the lutanists praised ancient days from beyond the filigreed balconies and tessellated courts of simple Ulthar.

H. P. Lovecraft, *The Dream-Quest of Unknown Kadath* (1927)

I saw tremendous tessellated pools, and rooms of curious and inexplicable utensils of myriad sorts.

H. P. Lovecraft, "The Shadow out of Time" (1935)

In my chess sessions with Gaston I saw the board as a square pool of limpid water with rare shells and stratagems rosily visible upon the smooth tessellated bottom, which to my confused adversary was all ooze and squid-cloud.

Vladimir Nabokov, *Lolita* (1954)

testudineous, testudinous, *adj.* Of, pertaining to, or resembling the shell of a tortoise.

But Clarendon did not reply. He only smiled, while his singular clinic-man Surama indulged in many a deep, testudinous chuckle.

H. P. Lovecraft & Adolphe de Castro, "The Last Test" (1927)

thagweed, *n.* A smokable narcotic herb native to H. P. Lovecraft's Dreamlands. [Not in *OED*.]

And the odours from those galleys which the south wind blew in from the wharves are not to be described. Only by constantly smoking strong thagweed could even the hardiest denizens of the old sea-taverns bear them.

H. P. Lovecraft, *The Dream-Quest of Unknown Kadath* (1927)

". . . Dylath-Leen," she mused, "where the wide-mouthed traders with the strange turbans come for their slaves and gold, anchoring black galleys whose stench only the smoking of thagweed can kill, paying with rubies, departing with the powerful oar strokes of invisible rowers. Southwest then to Thran of the sloping alabaster walls, unjoined, and its cloud-catching towers all white and gold, there by the River Shai, wharves all of marble. . ."

Roger Zelazny, *A Night in the Lonesome October* (1993; ellipses in original)

thaumatropically, *adv.* In the manner of a thaumatrope, a scientific toy that presents a primitive form of animation. [Not in *OED*.]

I wondered whether I should ever reach the world again, and at times would furtively open my eyes to see if I could discern any feature of the place other than the wind of spiced putrefaction, the topless columns, and the thaumatropically grotesque shadows of abnormal horror.

H. P. Lovecraft & Harry Houdini, "Under the Pyramids" (1924)

thaumaturge, *n.* [< Gr *thaumatourgós* < *thauma* (root *thaumat-*), wonder + *ergon*, work] A wonder- or miracle-worker; a practitioner of thaumaturgy or the art magical, a mage, wizard, sorcerer, necromancer, enchanter, thaumaturgist.

> Astarte, known nigh threescore years,
>   Me to no speechless rapture urges;
> Them in Elysium she enspheres,
>   Queen, from of old, of thaumaturges.

James Russell Lowell, "Arcadia Rediviva"

From nameless valleys far below,
And hills and plains no man may know,
The mystic swells and sullen surges
Hint like accursed thaumaturges
A thousand horrors, big with awe,
That long-forgotten ages saw.

H. P. Lovecraft, "Oceanus" in "A Cycle of Verse" (1918)

thaumaturgic, *adj.* Of or pertaining to thaumaturgy (q.v.).

"It appears that, now I am a saint, I enjoy, by approved precedents, all thaumaturgic powers, with especial proficiency in blasting, cursing and smiting my opponents with terrible afflictions; and have moreover the gift of tongues, of vision and of prophecy, and the power of expelling demons, of healing the sick, and of raising the dead. The situation is extraordinary, and I know not what to do with so many talents."

James Branch Cabell, The High Place: A Comedy of Disenchantment (1923)

"The release of the soul," Julian smiles at me, "is a diversion pleasing to crystal gazers and drug addicts. But you, Mallare, how can you play with such childish and thaumaturgic fancies? . ."

Ben Hecht, The Kingdom of Evil: A Continuation of the Journal
of Fantazius Mallare (1924; ellipsis in original)

thaumaturgical, *adj.* Thaumaturgic (q.v.). (H. P. Lovecraft's fragment "Of Evill Sorceries done in New-England of Dæmons in no Humane Shape" purports to come from *THAUMATURGICALL PRODIGIES in the New-English Canaan* by the Rev. Ward Phillips, Pastor of the Second Church in Arkham, in the Maſsachusetts-Bay—Boston, 1697.)

Mr. Merritt always confessed to seeing nothing really horrible at the farmhouse, but maintained that the titles of the books in the special library of thaumaturgical, alchemical, and theological subjects which Curwen kept in a front room were alone sufficient to inspire him with a lasting loathing. Perhaps, however, the facial expression of the owner in exhibiting them contributed much of the prejudice. This bizarre collection, besides a host of standard works which Mr. Merritt was not too alarmed to envy, embraced nearly all the cabbalists, dæmonologists, and magicians known to man; and was a treasure-house of lore in the doubtful realms of alchemy and astrology.

H. P. Lovecraft, The Case of Charles Dexter Ward (1927)

Appended to this curious document was a note, evidently hastily scrawled: "See the Rev. Ward Phillips, *Thau. Prod.*"

August Derleth (as H. P. Lovecraft & August Derleth),
The Lurker at the Threshold (1945)

It was entitled Thaumaturgical Prodigies in the New-English Canaan, by the
Rev. Ward Phillips, described on the title-page as "Pastor of the Second Church
in Arkham in the Massachusetts-Bay." The volume was clearly a reprint of an
earlier book, for its date was Boston, 1801.

> August Derleth (as H. P. Lovecraft & August Derleth),
> *The Lurker at the Threshold* (1945)

Only a wizard would possess those moldering, maggoty volumes of monstrous
and fantastic lore; only a thaumaturgical adept would dare the darker mysteries
of the *Necronomicon*, Ludvig Prinn's *Mysteries of the Worm*, the *Black Rites* of mad
Luveh-Keraph, priest of Bast, or Comte d'Erlette's ghastly *Cultes des Goules*.

> Robert Bloch, "The Suicide in the Study" (1935)

Ningauble stood to Fafhrd very much as Sheelba stood to the Mouser except
that the Seven-Eyed One was a somewhat more pretentious archimage, whose
taste in the thaumaturgical tasks he set Fafhrd ran in larger directions, such as
the slaying of dragons, the sinking of four-masted magic ships, and the kidnap-
ping of ogre-gaurded enchanted queens.

> Fritz Leiber, "Bazaar of the Bizarre" (1963)

Hektor snorted. "No fancy thaumaturgical titles?"

> John Jakes, "Ghoul's Garden" (1973)

thaumaturgist, *n.* A wonder- or miracle-worker; a practitioner of thaumaturgy
or the art magical, a mage, wizard, sorcerer, necromancer, enchanter, thaumaturge.

"Equally," Gonfal continued, "where now is your Thorston or your Merlin? All
which to-day remains of any one of these thaumaturgists may well, at this very
instant, be passing us as dust in that bland and persistent wind which now
courses over Inis Dahut: but the mage goes undiscerned, unhonored, impotent,
and goes as the wind wills, not as he elects. Ah, no, madame!"

> James Branch Cabell, *The Silver Stallion: A Comedy of Redemption* (1925)

thaumaturgy, *n.* The art or act of performing wonders, miracles, or feats of
magick; the art magical.

Such were the achievements of rude monastic chemistry. But the more elaborate
chemistry of our own days has reversed all these motions of our simple ancestors, with results in every stage that to *them* would have realized the most fantastic among the promises of thaumaturgy.

> Thomas De Quincey, *Suspiria de Profundis: Being a Sequel to the*
> *Confessions of an English Opium-Eater* (1845)

So extreme was his humility, that he would not claim to have been consciously
united to the Divinity more than four times in his life; without condemning
magic and thaumaturgy, he left their practice to more adventurous spirits, and

contented himself with the occasional visits of a familiar demon in the shape of a serpent.

Richard Garnett, "The City of the Philosophers" (1888)

"In the art of magic, which I chose to be my art, I have performed no earth-shaking wonders, yet in small thaumaturgies I have had some hand."

James Branch Cabell, *Something About Eve: A Comedy of Fig-Leaves* (1927)

He had regarded them with a curious and morbid esthetic pleasure, had found in them the infallible attraction of things enormous and hypernatural. Now, for the first time, he passed among them with a languid interest. He began to apprehend that fatal hour when the garden, with its novel thaumaturgies, would offer no longer a refuge from his inexorable ennui.

Clark Ashton Smith, "The Garden of Adompha" (1937)

theosophist, *n.* An adherent of theosophy (q.v.).

Theosophists have guessed at the awesome grandeur of the cosmic cycle wherein our world and human race form transient incidents. They have hinted at strange survivals in terms which would freeze the blood if not masked by a bland optimism. But it is not from them that there came the single glimpse of forbidden æons which chills me when I think of it and maddens me when I dream of it.

H. P. Lovecraft, "The Call of Cthulhu" (1926)

theosophy, *n.* [< Gr *theós,* god + *sophia,* wisdom, "divine wisdom"] Any of various systems of mysticism claiming a profounder source of knowledge than empirical science, such as Neo-Platonism, Qabalah, or that of the Christian mystic Jacob Böhme (1575–1624) , known as the "Teutonic Theosopher." In particular, that associated with the Theosophical Society, founded 1875 by H. P. Blavatsky, Colonel Henry S. Olcott, and W. Q. Judge. While disdaining dogma and requiring no particular beliefs of its members, the society's esoteric teachings include revelations transmitted by trans-Himalayan Mahatmas, the astral plane, various psychical phenomena, and an anti-Darwinian theory of evolution involving vast cosmic cycles and lost continents.

I am impelled to remark at this point that what goes under the name of "theosophy" in the world to-day is an article so far removed from the genuine that the name has even thus early been laid aside by the silent nature student, who, now as ever, is a Son of the Solitude.

Phylos the Thibetan (Frederick S. Oliver),
A Dweller on Two Planets; or, The Dividing of the Way (1886)

Here Lila found herself pausing, puzzling, then peering in perplexity at the incongruous contents of Norman Bates's library. *A New Model of the Universe, The Extension of Consciousness. The Witch-Cult in Western Europe, Dimension and Being.*

These were not the books of a small boy, and they were equally out of place in the home of a rural motel proprietor. She scanned the shelves rapidly. Abnormal psychology, occultism, theosophy. Translations of *Là Bas, Justine.* And here, on the bottom shelf, a nondescript assortment of untitled volumes, poorly bound. Lila pulled one out at random and opened it. The illustration that leaped out at her was almost pathologically pornographic.

Robert Bloch, Psycho (1959)

Subucule, the most devout of the pilgrims, stated his credo in detail. Essentially he professed the orthodox Gilfigite theosophy, in which Zo Zam, the eight-headed deity, after creating cosmos, struck off his toe, which then became Gilfig, while the drops of blood dispersed to form the eight races of mankind.

Jack Vance, The Eyes of the Overworld (1966)

Thule, *pr.n.* [< L *Thūlē* < Gr *Thoúlē*] In Greek and Roman mythology, an island six days' sail north of Britain, variously identified as Iceland, Greenland, or the Shetland Islands. Occasionally adopted in fantasy literature as the name for a lost continent and prehistorical civilization. Figuratively, an extreme limit of travel or attainment; a zenith or nadir. Frequently in the phrase **Ultima Thule,** farthest Thule.

Titles: Walter de la Mare, "Thule" (verse); George Sterling, "Ultima Thule" (verse); Manly Wade Wellman, "Sorcery from Thule"; Eric Frank Russell, "Ultima Thule"; Avram Davidson, *Ursus of Ultima Thule,* "Arnten of Ultima Thule"

> In Artick Climes, an Isle that *Thule* hight
> Famous for snowy monts, whose hoary head's
> Sure signe of cold, yet from their fiery feet
> They strike out burning stones with thunders dread,
> And all the Land with smoak, and ashes spread:
> Here wandring Ghosts themselves have often shown,
> As if it were the region of the dead.
> And men departed met with whom they've known,
> In seemly sort shake hands, and ancient friendship own.

Henry More, The Præexistency of the Soul (1647)

My cognizance of the pit had become known to the inquisitorial agents—*the pit* whose horrors had been destined for so bold a recusant as myself—*the pit,* typical of hell, and regarded by rumor as the Ultima Thule of all their punishments.

Edgar Allan Poe, "The Pit and the Pendulum" (1842)

There is a provocative imaginative fascination about *Ultima Thule* which has affected me profoundly since childhood.

H. P. Lovecraft, letter to Elizabeth Toldridge (10 March 1930)

And through Zothique and primal Thule wandering,
A pilgrim to the shrines where elder Shadows dwell,
Perhaps I shall behold such lusters visible
As turn to ash the living opal of thy wing.

Clark Ashton Smith, "Farewell to Eros" (1937)

Thulean, *adj.* Of or pertaining to (Ultima) Thule (q.v.). [Not in *OED*.]

I have but known
The silence of Thulean lands extreme—
A silence all-attending and supreme
As is the sea's enormous monotone.

Clark Ashton Smith, "Desolation" (1916)

Tikkun, Tikkoun, *n.* [< Hb] See quotations.

The "Heavenly man," who is the Protogonos, Tikkun, the first-born of God, or the universal Form and Idea, engenders Adam. Hence the latter is god-born in humanity, and endowed with the attributes of all the ten Sephiroth.

H. P. Blavatsky, *Isis Unveiled: A Master-Key to the Mysteries of
Ancient and Modern Science and Theology* (1877)

The "Heavenly Man" (Tetragrammaton) who is the Protogonos, Tikkoun, the firstborn from the passive deity and the first manifestation of that deity's shadow, is the universal form and idea, which engenders the manifested Logos, Adam Kadmon, or the four-lettered symbol, in the Kabala, of the *Universe itself,* also called the *second Logos.*

H. P. Blavatsky, *The Secret Doctrine:
The Synthesis of Science, Religion, and Philosophy* (1888)

The *form* of *Tikkun* or the *Protogonos*, the "first-born," i.e., the universal form and idea, had not yet been mirrored in *Chaos.*

H. P. Blavatsky, note to *The Secret Doctrine:
The Synthesis of Science, Religion, and Philosophy* (1888)

Men know him as the Dweller in Darkness, that brother of the Old Ones called Nyogtha, the Thing that should not be. He can be called to Earth's surface through certain secret caverns and fissures, and sorcerers have seen him in Syria and below the black tower of Leng; from the Thang Grotto of Tartary he has come ravening to bring terror and destruction among the pavilions of the great Khan. Only by the looped cross, by the Vach-Viraj incantation and by the Tikkoun elixir may he be driven back to the nighted caverns of hidden foulness where he dwelleth.

Abdul Alhazred, *Necronomicon*, as quoted in
Henry Kuttner, "The Salem Horror" (1937)

Eventually Crow and I had been able to add to the list of such defenses many weird and wonderful devices. Among them was the Tikkoun Elixir, which was nothing less than water blessed in a holy font; the *Vach Viraj* Incantation, a chant of particular power against Nyogtha, one of the more ethereal, but nonetheless deadly, Cthonians, and to a lesser extent against others of the burrowers beneath; the previously mentioned five-pointed star-stones of ancient Mnar, which were not only powerful protective devices in their own right but often formed the actual "bars" of Cthonian prisons; the Crux Ansata or Tau Cross, being of course the Ankh of olden Khem, a great protection of life and soul against all evils, which, incidentally, if its loop is broken, gives a figure of five extremities, a five-pointed "star" in effect; the *Shad'asahn* Liturgy of the Namoha nomads, potent against thirst and the heat of the sun, and of course against fire elementals in general, and so on.

Brian Lumley, *The Transition of Titus Crow* (1975)

tlath, *n.* A type of tree native to the lost continent of Mu. [Not in *OED.*]

It was dawn on the Day of the Sky-Flames (nomenclature undefined by von Junzt) that T'yog, amidst the prayers and chanting of the people and with King Thabon's blessing on his head, started up the dreaded mountain with a staff of tlath-wood in his right hand.

H. P. Lovecraft & Hazel Heald, "Out of the Æons" (1933)

trans-dimensional, *adj.* Of or pertaining to dimensions beyond the usual. [Not in *OED.*]

The Fear, Loathing & Paranoia juice can be alchemically transformed into psychoactive compounds (adrenochrome, related to mescaline) for intense dream (nightmare) work. The important and significant aspect of this glory in the horrific, scary, & alien nature of extra-terrestrial/trans-dimensional contact/communion symbiosis-&-metamorphosis is that this is the outward, common interpretation which, with its repulsive/forbidding mask, keeps the merely curious and dabblers outside the Lion-Serpent Gate of the Abyss and this fear of Initiation acts as an insurmountable barrier to those unprepared and unwilling to transcend the "ugliness" of the necessary transformation to be undergone.

Soror Azenath, XXIII*, *The Esoteric Order of Dagon: An Introduction* (1987)

trapezohedron (*pl.* **trapezohedra, trapezohedrons**), *n.* A solid geometrical figure whose faces are trapezoids or trapeziums, such as the 24-faced icositetrahedron.

"Fr. O'Malley tells of devil-worship with box found in great Egyptian ruins—says they call up something that can't exist in light. Then has to be summoned again. Probably got this from deathbed confession of Francis X. Feeney, who had joined Starry Wisdom in '49. These people say the Shining Trapazohedron shews them heaven & other worlds, & that the Haunter of the Dark tells them secrets in some way."

H.P. Lovecraft, "The Haunter of the Dark" (1935)

It was then, in the gathering twilight, that he thought he saw a faint trace of luminosity in the crazily angled stone. He had tried to look away from it, but some obscure compulsion drew his eyes back. Was there a subtle phosphorescence of radio-activity about the thing? What was it that the dead man's notes had said concerning a *Shining Trapazohedron?* What, anyway, was this abandoned lair of cosmic evil?

H.P. Lovecraft, "The Haunter of the Dark" (1935)

Of the Shining Trapazohedron he speaks often, calling it a window on all time and space, and tracing its history from the days it was fashioned on dark Yuggoth, before ever the Old Ones brought it to earth. It was treasured and placed in its curious box by the crinoid things of Antarctica, salvaged from their ruins by the serpent-men of Valusia, and peered at æons later in Lemuria by the first human beings. It crossed strange lands and stranger seas, and sank with Atlantis before a Minoan fisher meshed it in his net and sold it to swarthy merchants from nighted Khem. The Pharaoh Nephren-Ka built around it a temple with a windowless crypt, and did that which caused his name to be stricken from all monuments and records. Then it slept in the ruins of that evil fane which the priests an the new Pharaoh destroyed, till the delver's spade once more brought it forth to curse mankind.

H.P. Lovecraft, "The Haunter of the Dark" (1935)

The fire of Hell doth provide and the thoughts from within doth prevail. Open the portals of darkness, O Great Opener of the Way. Come forth into this cycle. Blast ye forth through the gates of the shining Trapezohedron, for the blood hath been offered!

Anton Szandor LaVey (Howard Stanton Levey),
"Die elektrischen Vorspiele" in *The Satanic Rituals* (1972)

tumulus (*pl.* **tumuli**), *n.* An artificial hillock, especially a grave mound or barrow.

Here, far above the waters, are solemn, mighty walls, turf-grown; circumvallations rounded and smooth with the passing of many thousand years. At one end of this most ancient place there is a tumulus, a tower of observation, perhaps, and underneath it slinks the green, deceiving ditch that seems to wind into the heart of the camp, but in reality rushes down to sheer rock and a precipice over the waters.

Arthur Machen, "Out of the Earth" (1915)

There were buildings and other architectural remains—in one terrified glance I saw a weird pattern of tumuli, a savage circle of monoliths, a low-domed Roman ruin, a sprawling Saxon pile, and an early English edifice of wood—but all these were dwarfed by the ghoulish spectacle presented by the general surface of the ground.

H. P. Lovecraft, "The Rats in the Walls" (1923)

Instantly, as once before, my visions faded, and I saw again only the evil moonlight, the brooding desert, and the spreading tumulus of palæogean masonry.

H. P. Lovecraft, "The Shadow out of Time" (1935)

tukah, *n.* [< Wilson "Bob" *Tucker,* science fiction fan & writer from whose practice of incorporating the names of fellow fans sprang the term *tuckerization*] An obnoxious flying creature native to the planet Venus. [Not in *OED.*]

(See quotation under **akman.**)

Turanian, *adj.* & *n.* [< Persian *Turân,* name used by Firdausi in *The Shah Namah* for a realm beyond the Oxus, as opposed to Irân (Persia) < *Tur,* in Iranian mythology one of the three mythical brothers from which mankind is supposedly descended.] Of or pertaining to the (mostly Asian) languages of the Ural-Altaic family, as opposed to those of the Indo-European ("Aryan") and Semitic families; of or pertaining to the speakers of these Ural-Altaic languages, particularly when considered as a race. Formerly also used in an extended sense that included various non-Indo-European-speaking (or otherwise suspect) peoples such as the Lapps, Finns, Basques, Picts, Berbers, Dravidians, Gypsies, etc. According to the so-called "pygmy" theory, folk memories of Turanian peoples account for the European folklore concerning fairies, elves, dwarfs, etc. By some post-Blavatsky Theosophists, the name was given to the fourth Sub-race of the fourth Root Race.

Titles: Arthur Machen, "The Turanians" in *Ornaments of Jade* (1897)

The very title of Tur, which they give to their supreme magistrate, indicates theft from a tongue akin to the Turanian.

Sir Edward Bulwer-Lytton, *The Coming Race* (1871; aka *Vril: The Power of the Coming Race*)

The appropriate definition of the name "Turanian" is: any family that ethnologists know nothing about.

H. P. Blavatsky, note to *Isis Unveiled: A Master-Key to the Mysteries of Ancient and Modern Science and Theology* (1877)

The occult doctrine admits of no such divisions as the Aryan and the Semite, accepting even the Turanian with ample reservations.

H. P. Blavatsky, *The Secret Doctrine: The Synthesis of Science, Religion, and Philosophy* (1888)

Granting that the Turanian races were typified by the dwarfs (Dwergar), and that a dark, round-headed, and dwarfish race was driven northward by the fair-faced Scandinavians, or Æsir, the gods being like unto men, there still exists neither in history nor any other scientific work any anthropological proof whatever of the existence in time or space of a race of giants.

> H. P. Blavatsky, *The Secret Doctrine: The Synthesis of Science,*
> *Religion, and Philosophy* (1888)

This was the Shaman. He seems to have had a Tartar-Mongol-mongrel-Turanian origin, somewhere in Central Asia, and to have spread with his magic drum, and songs, and stinking smoke, exorcising his fiends all over the face of the earth.

> Charles Godfrey Leland, *Gypsy Sorcery and Fortune Telling* (1891)

A further and rather terrible development of the Turanian times must still be referred to. With the practice of sorcery many of the inhabitants had, of course, become aware of the existence of powerful elementals—creatures who had been called into being, or at least animated by their own powerful wills, which being directed towards maleficent ends, naturally produced elementals of power and malignity. So degraded had then become man's feelings of reverence and worship, that they actually began to adore these semi-conscious creations of their own malignant thought. The ritual with which these beings were worshipped was bloodstained from the very start, and of course every sacrifice offered at their shrines gave vitality and persistence to these vampire-like creations—so much so, that even to the present day in various parts of the world, the elementals formed by the powerful will of these old Atlantean sorcerers still continue to exact their tribute from unoffending village communities.

> W. Scott-Elliot, *Legends of Atlantis and the Lost Lemuria* (1896/1904)

"And the hint came of the old name of fairies, 'the little people,' and the very probable belief that they represent a tradition of the prehistoric Turanian inhabitants of the country, who were cave dwellers: and then I realized with a shock that I was looking for a being under four feet in height, accustomed to live in darkness, possessing stone instruments, and familiar with the Mongolian cast of features!"

> Arthur Machen, "The Shining Pyramid" (1895)

But as I idly scanned the paragraph, a flash of thought passed through me with the violence of an electric shock: what if the obscure and horrible race of the hills still survived, still remained haunting the wild places and barren hills, and now and then repeating the evil of Gothic legend, unchanged and unchangeable as the Turanian Shelta, or the Basques of Spain?

> Arthur Machen, "Novel of the Black Seal" in
> *The Three Impostors; or, The Transmutations* (1894)

Though everybody called them gipsies, they were in reality Turanian metal-workers, degenerated into wandering tinkers; their ancestors had fashioned the bronze battle-axes, and they mended pots and kettles.

Arthur Machen, "The Turanians" in *Ornaments in Jade* (1897)

M. Pineau, very properly, interprets these dwarfs to mean the aboriginal Turanian race which inhabited Europe before the coming of the Aryans, and passes on, without dwelling on the subject.

Arthur Machen, "Folklore and Legends of the North" (1898)

That these hellish vestiges of old Turanian-Asiatic magic and fertility-cults were even now wholly dead he could not for a moment suppose, and he frequently wondered how much older and how much blacker than the very worst of the muttered tales some of them might really be.

H. P. Lovecraft, "The Horror at Red Hook" (1925)

"They are known variously as Turanians, Picts, Mediterraneans, and Garlic Eaters. A race of small dark people, traces of their type may be found in primitive sections of Europe and Asia today, among the Basques of Spain, the Scotch of Galloway, and the Lapps."

Robert E. Howard, "The Little People" (1928)

U

ugrat, *n.* [< *"Hugo* the *Rat,"* nickname for Hugo Gernsback due to his failure to pay writers.] An obnoxious creature native to the planet Venus. [Not in *OED.*]

(See quotation under **daroh**.)

ululant, *adj.* Ululating.

> The deep chuckle ceased, and in its place came a frantic, ululant yelp as of a thousand ghouls and werewolves in torment. It died away with long, reverberant echoes, and slowly the flames resumed their normal shape.
>
> H. P. Lovecraft & Adolphe de Castro, "The Last Test" (1927)

ululantly, *adv.* Ululatingly.

> A wailing distinctly different from the scream now burst out, and was protracted ululantly in rising and falling paroxysms.
>
> H. P. Lovecraft, *The Case of Charles Dexter Ward* (1927)

ululate, *v.intr.* [< L *ululāre,* cf. *ulula,* screech-owl] To howl or wail in a prolonged and emphatic manner.

> We fled, I say, so shaken that it was only by a supreme effort of will that we were able to take flight in the right direction. And behind us the voice rose, the blasphemous voice of Nyarlathotep, the Blind, Faceless One, the Mighty Messenger, even while there rang in the channels of memory the frightened words of the half-breed, Old Peter—*It was a Thing—didn't have no face, hollered there till I thought my eardrums 'd bust, and them things that was with it—Gawd!*—echoed there while the voice of that Being from outermost space shrieked and gibbered to the hellish music of the hideous attending flute-players, rising to ululate through the forest and leave its mark forever in memory!
> *Ygnaiih! Ygnaiih! EEE-yayayayayaaa-haaahaaahaaahaaa-ngh'aaa-ngh'aaa-ya-ya-yaaa!*
> Then all was still.
>
> August Derleth, "The Dweller in Darkness" (1944)

> At a bookstore he chose volumes they would both devour: Muir, Renault, Steinbeck, Sturgeon. The Lovecraft, he thought with a lewd grin, was for nights when the wind ululated in the eaves of the cabin, when she would nestle against him for more than physical warmth.
>
> Dean Ing, *Soft Targets* (1979)

ululation, *n.* A prolonged and emphatic howling or wailing.

Sobs they sighdid at Fillagain's chrissormiss wake, all the hoolivans of the nation, prostrated in their consternation and their duodisimally profusive plethora
of ululation. There was plumbs and grumes and cheriffs and citherers and raid-
ers and cinemen too. And the all gianed in with the shoutmost shoviality. Agog
and magog and the round of them agrog.

James Joyce, Finnegans Wake (1922–39)

All in the fort could hear it now—a vast ululation of mad exultation and blood-
lust, from the depths of the dark forest.

Robert E. Howard, "The Black Stranger" (c. 1934;
aka "The Treasure of Tranicos")

*For, where but a moment before there had been nothing, there was now a gigantic protoplasmic
mass, a colossal being who towered upward toward the stars, and whose actual physical being
was in constant flux; and flanking it on either side were two lesser beings, equally amorphous,
holding pipes or flutes in appendages and making that demoniac music which echoed and reech-
oed in the enclosing forest. But the thing on the slab, the Dweller in Darkness, was the ultimate in horror; for from its mass of amorphous flesh there grew at will before our eyes tentacles,
claws, hands, and withdrew again; the mass itself diminished and swelled effortlessly, and
where its head was and its features should have been there was only a blank facelessness all the
more horrible because even as we looked there rose from its blind mass a low ululation in that
half-bestial, half-human voice so familiar to us from the record made in the night!*

August Derleth, "The Dweller in Darkness" (1944)

Words—or perhaps I had better write sounds, bestial sounds—rose from be-
low, a kind of awe-inspiring ululation:
   *"Iä! Iä! Ithaqua! Ithaqua cf'ayak vulgtmm. Iä! Uhg! Cthulhu fhtagn! Shub-Niggurath!
Ithaqua naflfhtagn!"*

August Derleth, "Beyond the Threshold" (1941)

Even as I remembered, everything was driven from my mind by a frightful cho-
rus of ululation, the triumphant chanting as of a thousand bestial mouths—
   *"Iä! Iä! Ithaqua, Ithaqua! Ai! Ai! Ai! Ithaqua cf'ayak 'vulgtmm, vugtlagln vulgtmm.
Ithaqua fhtagn! Ugh! Iä! Iä! Ai! Ai! Ai!"*

August Derleth, "Beyond the Threshold" (1941)

On the roof, as it were one on each side of him, were two toad-like creatures which
seemed constantly to be changing shape and appearance, and from whom emanated, by some means I could not distinguish, a ghastly ululation, a piping which was
matched only by the shrill choir of the frogs, now risen to a truly cacophonous
height. And in the air about him were great viperine creatures, which had curiously
distorted heads, and grotesquely great clawed appendages, supporting themselves
with ease by the aid of black rubbery wings of singularly monstrous dimensions.

August Derleth (as H. P. Lovecraft & August Derleth),
The Lurker at the Threshold (1945)

uncial, *n.* & *adj.* A letter in a style of writing in use primarily from the fourth through the eighth century, characterized by rounded capital letters and up-strokes and downstrokes slightly inclining.

> This, also written in black letter, we found inscribed on a second parchment that was in the coffer, apparently somewhat older in date than that on which was written the mediæval Latin translation of the uncial Greek of which I shall speak presently.
>
> H. Rider Haggard, *She: A History of Adventure* (1886)

> Further on was a complete set of pictures from a Psalter of English execution, of the very finest kind that the thirteenth century could produce; and perhaps best of all, there were twenty leaves of uncial writing in Latin, which, as a few words seen here and there told him at once, must belong to some very early patristic treatise. Could it possibly be a fragment of the copy of Papias *On the Words of Our Lord* which was known to have existed as late as the twelfth century at Nîmes?
>
> M. R. James, "Canon Alberic's Scrap-book" (c. 1893)

> No printing-press, but the hand of some half-crazed monk, had traced these ominous Latin phrases in uncials of awesome antiquity.
>
> H. P. Lovecraft, "The Book" (c. 1933)

> When he came back he was holding a bundle of rain-spotted foolscap sheets that were covered on both sides with his neat uncial script.
>
> John Bellairs, *The Face in the Frost* (1969)

unheimlich, *adj.* [< German] Uncanny, weird, eerie, eldritch.

> UNHEIMLICH. Urvater whose art's uneven, horrid be thine aim. Harpoons in him, corpus whalem: take ye and hate.
>
> Robert Anton Wilson & Robert Shea,
> *The Eye in the Pyramid* in *The Illuminatus! Trilogy* (1969–71)

> Ingolstadt always reminds me of the set of a bleeding Frankenstein movie, and, after Saint Toad and that shoggoth chap and the old Lama with his wog metaphysics, it was no help at all to have an invisible voice ask me to join him in a bawdy card game. I've faced some weird scenes in H. M. Service but this Fernando Poo caper was turning out to be outright unwholesome, in fact *unheimlich* as these krauts would say.
>
> Robert Anton Wilson & Robert Shea,
> *The Golden Apple* in *The Illuminatus! Trilogy* (1969–71)

unreverberate, *adj.* That does not reverberate; giving back no echo or reflection. [Not in *OED*.]

And Sippy very unwisely attempted flight, and Slorg even as unwisely tried to hide; but Slith, knowing well why that light was lit in that secret upper chamber and *who* it was that lit it, leaped over the edge of the World and is falling from us still through the unreverberate blackness of the abyss.

> Lord Dunsany, "Probable Adventure of the Three Literary Men" (1912)

In the darkness there flashed before my mind fragments of my cherished treasury of dæmoniac lore; sentences from Alhazred the mad Arab, paragraphs from the apocryphal nightmares of Damascius, and infamous lines from the delirious *Image du Monde* of Gauthier de Metz. I repeated queer extracts, and muttered of Afrasiab and the dæmons that floated with him down the Oxus; later chanting over and over again a phrase from one of Lord Dunsany's tales—"the unreverberate blackness of the abyss".

> H. P. Lovecraft, "The Nameless City" (1921)

And he would mew an invitation for me to follow him through the archway— beyond which lay (as saith Dunsany) "the unreverberate darkness of the abyss."

> H. P. Lovecraft, letter to Duane W. Rimel (22 December 1934)

Hope I succeeded in saving you and Herr Ludwig on that cliff—it would be a pity for two such promising celebrities to be lost in "the unreverberate blackness of the abyss"!

> H. P. Lovecraft, letter to Willis Conover (10 January 1937)

For many people, perhaps most people, there is a deep, ineradicable desire not to cease to exist. Perhaps this desire, this fear of falling into what Lord Dunsany once called the "unreverberate blackness of the abyss," is no more than an expression of genetic mechanisms for avoiding death.

> Martin Gardner, *The Whys of a Philosophical Scrivener* (1983)

upas-tree, upas, *n.* [< Malay, *pôhun úpas,* poison-tree] A deciduous tree, *Antiaris toxicaria,* native to Southeast Asia, which exudes a venomous sap whose toxicity has occasionally been slightly exaggerated.

Usage: Proper usage requires the form **upas-tree** except in those cases where the term refers to the tree's poison rather than to the tree itself.

> Our life is a false nature—'tis not in
> The harmony of things,—this hard decree,
> This uneradicable taint of sin,
> This boundless upas, this all-blasting tree,
> Whose root is earth, whose leaves and branches be
> The skies which rain their plagues on men like dew—
> Disease, death, bondage—all the woes we see—
> And worse, the woes we see not—which throb through
> The immedicable soil, with heart-aches ever new.
>
> Lord Byron, *Childe Harold's Pilgrimage: A Romaunt* (1809–18)

"I have no hope for myself or for others. Our life is a false nature; it is not in the harmony of things; it is an all-blasting upas, whose root is earth, and whose leaves are the skies which rain their poison-dews upon mankind. We wither from our youth; we gasp with unslaked thirst for unattainable good; lured from the first to the last by phantoms—love, fame, ambition, avarice—all idle, and all ill—one meteor of many names, that vanishes in the smoke of death."

Thomas Love Peacock, *Nightmare Abbey* (1817)

"You are a thousand times more culpable than I am, guilty as you think me. I stand a blasted tree,—I am struck to the heart, to the root,—I wither alone,—but you are the Upas, under whose poisonous droppings all things living have perished,—father—mother—brother, and last yourself;—the erosions of the poison, having nothing left to consume, strike inward, and prey on your own heart."

Charles Maturin, *Melmoth the Wanderer: A Tale* (1820)

> At last a father! In Mathilde's womb
> The poison quickens, and the tare-seeds shoot;
> On my old upas-tree a bastard fruit
> Is grafted. One more generation's doom
> Fixes its fangs. Crime's flame, disease's gloom,
> Are thy birth-dower. Another prostitute
> Predestined, born man, damned to grow a brute!
> Another travels tainted to the tomb!

Aleister Crowley, "To My First-Born" in *White Stains: The Literary Remains of George Archibald Bishop, a Neuropath of the Second Empire* (1898)

> Yea, o thou terrible magician,
> I see the black wings of suspicion
> Fanning each bud with tales of spite,
> Blasting each bud with bitter blight.
> I see the poisonous upas-tree,
> Its shade the ghastly trinity
> —Religion, law, morality—
> Sicken with its stifling breath
> Human loveliness to death.

Aleister Crowley, *The World's Tragedy* (1908)

Frantic efforts to stay the progress of the plant were made by armies with bombs and cannon, with lethal sprays and gasses; but all in vain. Everywhere humanity was smothered beneath the vast leaves, like those of some omnipresent upas, which emitted a stupefying and narcotic odor that conferred upon all who inhaled it a swift euthanasia.

Clark Ashton Smith, "Seedling of Mars" (1931)

One said: "I have seen, from cliffs of doom,
The seven hells flame up in flower
Like a million upas trees that tower,
Massing their realms of poisonous bloom."

Clark Ashton Smith, "Dialogue" (1941)

Thus
We triumph; thus the laurel overtops
The upas and the yew; and we decline
No toil, no dolor of our votive doom.

Clark Ashton Smith, "Soliloquy in an Ebon Tower" (1951)

When the world was young and mean were weak, and the fiends
of the night walked free,
I strove with Set by fire and steel and the juice of the upas-tree;
Now that I sleep in the mount's black heart, and the ages take
their toll,
Forget ye him who fought with the Snake to save the human
soul?

Robert E. Howard, "The Road of Kings"

Rarer even than this was the stark white upas that soared in the center of the sorcerer's garden; Pteron had enclosed it under an unbroken dome of transparent crystal, for so deadly is the wood of the Upas if left bare to the ambient vapors of the atmosphere that no human dare come within twelve miles of it on peril of his life.

Lin Carter, *Kesrick* (1982)

urhag, *n.* A fabulous creature that inhabits the Dreamlands of H. P. Lovecraft. [Not in *OED*.]

High over its jagged rim huge ravens flapped and croaked, and vague whirrings in the unseen depths told of bats or urhags or less mentionable presences haunting the endless blackness.

H. P. Lovecraft, *The Dream-Quest of Unknown Kadath* (1926–27)

V

Vâch, Vach, *n.* [< Skr, voice, speech, word] In Theosophy, the female principle of speech that corresponds to the male principle Virâj. See under **Vâch-Virâj.** [Not in *OED*.]

Vâch-Virâj, Vach-Viraj, *n.* [< Skr, "voice resplendent," the name of a "serpent queen" mentioned in the *Rig Veda* (10.189) perhaps to be identified with the Kundalini.] In Theosophy, the feminine aspect of the god Brahma, when considered as the Second Logos emanating Virâj, the Third Logos. [Not in *OED*.] (See quotations under **kadishtu** and **Tikkun.**)

vacuum (*pl.* **vacua, vacuums**), *n.* [< L] A void and empty space.

> There was a night when winds from unknown spaces whirled us irresistably into limitless vacua beyond all thought and sanity.
>
> > H. P. Lovecraft, "Hypnos" (1922)

> Only the steady low fall of his steps broke the appalling silence; all things that lay on every side as far as he could see conspired to give him a sense of minuteness in an infinitude that extended, ceaseless, upward and outward through the vacua overhead.
>
> > Donald Wandrei, "A Fragment of a Dream" (1926)

vasty, *adj.* Vast, immense.

> GLENDOWER: I can call Spirits from the vastie Deepe.
> HOTSPUR: Why so can I, or so can any man:
> But will they come, when you doe call for them?
>
> > William Shakespeare, *Henry IV, Part I* (1598)

> "Down, down, Dagon! Chthulu commands it! Back to your vasty deeps! Sleep for eons yet to come!"
>
> > Paul Di Filippo, *Hottentots* (1994) in the *Steampunk Trilogy*

Venerian, *adj.* & *n.* [< L *Venus* (root: *Vener-*)] Of or pertaining to the planet Venus; originating from the planet Venus; a native or inhabitant of the planet Venus; the language spoken by Venerians; Venusian. [Not in *OED*.]

> Evidently there must be intelligent life somewhere in the ocean of Venus. Evidently the marine Venerians resented the steady depletion of their aqueous world, and were determined to stop it.
>
> > Olaf Stapledon, *Last and First Men* (1930)

545

They want their conventional best-seller values and motives kept paramount throughout the abysses of apocalyptic vision and extra-Einsteinian chaos, and would not deem an "interplanetary" tale in the least interesting if it did not have its Martian (or Jovian or Venerian or Saturnian) heroine fall in love with the young voyager from Earth, and thereby incur the jealousy of the inevitable Prince Kongros (or Zeelar or Hoshgosh or Norkog) who at once proceeds to usurp the throne etc.; or if it did not have its Martian (or etc.) nomenclature follow a closely terrestrial pattern, with an indo-Germanic '-*a*' name for the Princess, and something disagreeable and Semitic for the villain.

> H. P. Lovecraft, letter to Farnsworth Wright (5 July 1927)

"Some of the extraplanetary drugs haven't been so beneficial to mankind, have they?" queried Balcoth. "I seem to have heard of a Martian poison that has greatly facilitated the gentle art of murder. And I am told that *mnophka*, the Venerian narcotic, is far worse, in its effects on the human system, than is any terrestrial alkaloid."

> Clark Ashton Smith, "The Plutonian Drug" (1932)

"Venerian" is the right adjective derived from "Venus," whose Latin genitive is *Veneris*. The term "Venusian," often heard, properly refers to an inhabitant of the ancient Italian city of Venusia.

> L. Sprague de Camp & Catherine Crook de Camp, *Science Fiction Handbook, Revised: A Guide to Writing Imaginative Literature* (1953/1975)

veridical, *adj.* Truthful, corresponding to the truth, veracious.

Those statues were too life-like, too veridical in all their features, in their poses that preserved a lethal fear, their faces marked with a deadly but undying torment. No human sculptor could have wrought them, could have reproduced the physiognomies and the costumes with a fidelity so consummate and so atrocious.

> Clark Ashton Smith, "The Gorgon" (1930)

Add to this the seemingly impossible and incredible nature of the whole tale, and my hesitancy in accepting it as veridical will easily be understood.

> Clark Ashton Smith, "Beyond the Singing Flame" (1931)

"Tetrahedra of Space," incidentally, contains another common characteristic of early magazine science fiction: elephantiasis of the adjectives. Especially in the first portion of the story, every sentence carries a load of them that breaks it in two. Combine that with inverted word order and unnecessary italics, and you find yourself breathing heavily and losing track of the sense.

To me in my younger days, and to others in theirs, and to some, I fear, in all their days, this thick layer of fatty adjectival froth seems to be a mark of good writing. And, indeed, in such admired writers as A. Merritt, H. P. Lovecraft, and

Clark Ashton Smith (whom, however, I am afraid I never admired, even when I was young and might have been excused the error).

Clark Ashton Smith, in particular, had a second interesting literary aberration. He used long and unfamiliar words as another way of impressing the naïve with the quality of his writing. In the same issue with "Tetrahedra of Space," for instance, there is Smith's "Beyond the Singing Flame," and since Sam Moskowitz had sent me the complete issue in this particular case, I looked at the Smith story for old times' sake.

In the very second paragraph, I found him using "veridical" when he meant "true," and I read no further. Yes, "veridical" does mean "true," but I cannot imagine any occasion (outside a certain specialized use among psychologists) when "true" is not very greatly to be preferred.

Isaac Asimov, *Before the Golden Age:*
A Science Fiction Anthology of the 1930s (1974)

veriest, *adj.* Truest, merest.

The fireside tales were of the most grisly description, all the ghastlier because of their frightened reticence and cloudy evasiveness. They represented my ancestors as a race of hereditary dæmons beside whom Gilles de Retz and the Marquis de Sade would seem the veriest tyros, and hinted whisperingly at their responsibility for the occasional disappearances of villagers through several generations.

H. P. Lovecraft, "The Rats in the Walls" (1923)

vertiginous, *adj.* Causing a sensation of dizziness or vertigo, as by rapidly revolving, whirling, or spinning; afflicted with dizziness or vertigo.

Copernicus, Atlas his successor, is of opinion the earth is a planet, moves and shines to others, as the moon doth to us. Digges, Gilbert, Keplerus, Origanus, and others, defend this hypothesis of his in sober sadness, and that the moon is inhabited: if it be so that the earth is a moon, then are we also giddy, vertiginous and lunatic within this sublunary maze.

Robert Burton, *The Anatomy of Melancholy: What It Is, With All the Kinds,*
Causes, Symptomes, Prognostickes & Severall Cures of It (1621)

We were rapidly approaching; now upon the platform; my bearers were striding closely along the side; I leaned far out—a giddiness seized me! I gazed down into depth upon vertiginous depth; an abyss indeed—an abyss dropping to world's base like that in which the Babylonians believed writhed Talaat, the serpent mother of Chaos; a pit that struck down into earth's heart itself.

A. Merritt, *The Moon Pool* (1919)

The condition and scattering of the blocks told mutely of vertiginous cycles and geologic upheavals of cosmic savagery.

H. P. Lovecraft, "The Shadow out of Time" (1935)

viewless, *adj.* Invisible; unseen; not perceptible to the eye.

> Fear spoke from the age-worn stones of this hoary survivor of the deluge, this great-grandmother of the eldest pyramid; and a viewless aura repelled me and bade me retreat from antique and sinister secrets that no man should see, and no man else had ever dared to see.
>
> H. P. Lovecraft, "The Nameless City" (1921)

> A single lightning-bolt shot from the purple zenith to the altar-stone, and a great tidal wave of viewless force and indescribable stench swept down from the hill to all the countryside. Trees, grass, and underbrush were whipped into a fury; and the frightened crowd at the mountain's base, weakened by the lethal fœtor that seemed about to asphyxiate them, were almost hurled off their feet.
>
> H. P. Lovecraft, "The Dunwich Horror" (1928)

vigintillion, *n.* The cardinal number equal to 10^{63}; or, the cardinal number equal to 10^{120}.

> After vigintillions of years great Cthulhu was loose again, and ravening for delight.
>
> H. P. Lovecraft, "The Call of Cthulhu" (1926)

> He would shout that the world was in danger, since the Elder Things wished to strip it and drag it away from the solar system and cosmos of matter into some other plane or phase of entity from which it had once fallen, vigintillions of æons ago. At other times he would call for the dreaded *Necronomicon* and the *Dæmonolatreia* of Remigius, in which he seemed hopeful of finding some formula to check the peril he conjured up.
>
> H. P. Lovecraft, "The Dunwich Horror" (1928)

viol, *n.* An archaic cello-like instrument held between the legs. A fairly common musical instrument in fantasy and weird fiction.

> No rays from the holy heaven come down
> On the long night-time of that town;
> But light from out the lurid sea
> Streams up the turrets silently—
> Gleams up the pinnacles far and free
> Up domes—up spires—up kingly halls—
> Up fanes—up Babylon-like walls—
> Up shadowy long-forgotten bowers
> Of sculptured ivy and stone flowers—
> Up many and many a marvellous shrine
> Whose wreathèd friezes intertwine
> The viol, the violet, and the vine.
>
> Edgar Allan Poe, "The City in the Sea" (1831)

The town seemed very attractive in the afternoon sunlight as we swept up an incline and turned to the right into the main street. It drowsed like the older New England cities which one remembers from boyhood, and something in the collocation of roofs and steeples and chimneys and brick walls formed contours touching deep viol-strings of ancestral emotion.

> H. P. Lovecraft, "The Whisperer in Darkness" (1930)

Roofs and steeples and chimneys, prosaic enough in the telling, here cluster together on the green river-bluff in some magical collocation that stirs dim memories. Something in the contours, something in the setting, has power to touch deep viol-strings of feeling which are ancestral if one be young and personal if one be old.

> H. P. Lovecraft, "Vermont—A First Impression" (1927)

Upon Zann the effect was terrible, for, dropping his pencil, suddenly he rose, seized his viol, and commenced to rend the night with the wildest playing I had ever heard from his bow save when listening at the barred door.

> H. P. Lovecraft, "The Music of Erich Zann" (1921)

Yet when I looked from that highest of all gable windows, looked while the candles sputtered and the insane viol howled with the night-wind, I saw no city spread below, and no friendly lights gleamed from remembered streets, but only the blackness of space illimitable; unimagined space alive with motion and music, and having no semblance of anything on earth. And as I stood there looking in terror, the wind blew out both the candles in that ancient peaked garret, leaving me in savage and impenetrable darkness with chaos and pandemonium before me, and the dæmon madness of that night-baying viol behind me.

> H. P. Lovecraft, "The Music of Erich Zann" (1921)

The very name of Erich Zann broke us up. Then again, Zann, the crazy old musician, played a viol. Come on, guys, viola is serious. Violin is serious. *Viol* is FUNNY! Sounds like VILE, right?

> Brian Aldiss, "The Adjectives of Erich Zann: A Tale of Horror"

Kili and Fili rushed for their bags and brought back little fiddles; Dori, Nori, and Ori brought out flutes from somewhere inside their coats; Bombur produced a drum from the hall; Bifur and Bofur went out too, and came back with clarinets that they had left among the walking-sticks. Dwalin and Balin said: "Excuse me, I left mine in the porch!" "Just bring mine in with you!" said Thorin. They came back with viols as big as themselves, and with Thorin's harp wrapped in a green cloth.

> J. R. R. Tolkien, The Hobbit; or, There and Back Again (1930–36)

voonith, *n.* An amphibious creature that inhabits the Dreamlands of H. P. Lovecraft. [Not in *OED*.]

At evening Carter reached the farthermost pile of embers and camped for the night, tethering his zebra to a sapling and wrapping himself well in his blanket before going to sleep. And all through the night a voonith howled distantly from the shore of some hidden pool, but Carter felt no fear of that amphibious terror, since he had been told with certainty that not one of them dares even approach the slopes of Ngranek.

H. P. Lovecraft, *The Dream-Quest of Unknown Kadath* (1926–27)

W

Walpurga, Walburga, *pr.n.* An eighth-century English saint and missionary to Heidenheim, Germany, whose feast day falls on 30 April, May Day Eve, on which witches reputedly celebrate their Sabbath.

"Good Friday night," I continued, seeing they all seemed willing enough to listen, "was the favorite time for such gatherings, which were likewise held after dusk on St. John's Eve, on Walburga's Eve, and on Hallowe'en Night. The diversions were numerous: there was feasting, with somewhat unusual fare, and music, and dancing, with the Devil performing obbligatos on the pipes or a cittern, and not infrequently preaching a burlesque sermon. He usually attended in the form of a monstrous goat; and—when not amorously inclined,—often thrashed the witches with their own broomsticks. The more practical pursuits of the evening included the opening of graves, to despoil dead bodies of finger- and toe-joints, and portions of the winding-sheet, with which to prepare a powder that had strange uses . . . But the less said of that, the better."

James Branch Cabell, *The Cream of the Jest:*
A Comedy of Evasion (1911–15; ellipsis in original)

The Witches' Sabbat, my friend Richard Harrowby informs me, was "traditionally a meeting attended by all witches in satisfactory diabolical standing, lightly attired in smears of various magical ointments: and their vehicle of transportation to these outings was of course the traditional broomstick. Good Friday night was the favorite time for such gatherings, which were likewise held after dark on St. John's Eve, on Walburga's Eve, and on Hallowe'en Night."

James Branch Cabell, *Beyond Life: Dizain des Démiurges* (1919)

For the hound squatted upon his haunches, and seemed to grin at Jurgen; and there were other creatures abroad, that flew low in the twilight, keeping close to the ground, like owls; but they were larger than owls and were more discomforting. And, moreover, all this was just after sunset upon Walburga's Eve, when almost anything is rather more than likely to happen.

James Branch Cabell, *Jurgen: A Comedy of Justice* (1919)

What he did there so often was not known but the seasons came and went and the winter merged into spring and in time it was Walburga's Eve. That night the town gates were tightly closed and bolted and all cowered behind locked doors. Strange shapes flew screeching through the air and sniffed most horribly at the doorsteps.

R. H. Barlow, "The Black Tower" (1933)
in "Annals of the Jinns"

Walpurgis, Walburgis, *pr.n.* [< St. *Walpurga* or *Walburga,* whose feast day falls on 30 April, when almost anything is rather more than likely to happen.] St. Walpurga (q.v.); the orgiastic Witches' Sabbath held on May Day Eve, known as **Walpurgis-night** or (after the German) **Walpurgisnacht.** The most famous Walpurgis-night revels take place at the Brocken (or Blocksberg) in the Harz (or Hartz) Mountains; other renowned locations include Iceland's Hecla, Sweden's Blåkulla, and Norway's Blaakolle or Troms. Also found in other compounds, such as **Walpurgis-dance, Walpurgis Eve, Walpurgis-revel, Walpurgis-rhythm, Walpurgis-riot, Walpurgis Sabbat, Walpurgis Time**.

Titles: Johann Wolfgang von Gœthe, "Walpurgis-Night" ("*Walpurgisnacht*") & "Walpurgis-Night's Dream; or, Oberon's and Titania's Golden Wedding" ("*Walpurgisnachtstraum; oder, Oberons und Titanias Goldne Hochzeit*") in *Faust;* Paul Verlaine, "*Nuit de Walpurgis classique*" (verse); Gustav Meyrink, *Walpurgisnacht;* Dorothy Quick, "Walpurgis Night" (verse); Lin Carter, "Walpurgisnacht" (verse)

a. Alone:

> Golnitz further tells us that a figure of Priapus was placed over the entrance gate to the enclosure of the temple of St. Walburgis at Antwerp, which some antiquaries imagined to have been built on the site of a temple dedicated to that deity.
>
> Thomas Wright, *The Worship of the Generative Powers During the Middle Ages of Western Europe* (1786)

> Over the stepping-stones, pulling up her dress, she skipped with her long, lank legs, like a witch joining a Walpurgis.
>
> J. S. LeFanu, *Uncle Silas: A Tale of Bartram-Haugh* (1864)

> This the lamp ancestral hands have lit
> Deep in the doorless crypts of blood and bone. . . .
> For you and me, it is a witch-fire blown
> Where secret airs and obscure pinions flit,
> That has outburned Walpurgis and the moon
> And lifts in quenchless rose to a cloudy noon.
>
> Clark Ashton Smith, "Amor" (1943; ellipsis in original)

> The men of Ulthar and Nir and Hatheg would have been content to leave such unpleasant neighbors alone in their high valley were it not for the disappearance of several of their young maidens each Walpurgis and Yule and of plump specimens of both sexes at odd times throughout the year.
>
> Walter C. DeBill, Jr., "In 'Ygiroth" (1975)

b. In **Walpurgis-night** or **Walpurgisnacht:**

> The poppy visions of Cathay,
>   The heavy beer-trance of the Suabian;

The wizard lights and demon play
    Of nights Walpurgis and Arabian!
                John Greenleaf Whittier, "The Haschish" (c. 1853)

Ukalepe. Loathers' leave. Had Days. Nemo in Patria. The Luncher Out. Skilly
and Carubdish. A Wondering Wreck. From the Mermaids' Tavern. Bullyfamous.
Naughtsycalves. Mother of Misery. Walpurgas Nackt.
                James Joyce, *Finnegans Wake* (1922–39)

Little by little the Old Lady beguiled Iliel, and one day, while they were setting a
trap to catch a viper, and a vineyard, and a violin with their unicorn, and their
umbrella, and their ukulele, she suddenly stopped short, and asked Iliel point-
blank if she would like to attend the Sabbath on Walpurgis-night—the eve of
May-day—for "there's a short cut to it, my dear, from this country."
                Aleister Crowley, *Moonchild* (1917; aka *The Butterfly-Net* or *The Net*)

Now he was praying because the Witches' Sabbath was drawing near. May-Eve
was Walpurgis-Night, when hell's blackest evil roamed the earth and all the
slaves of Satan gathered for nameless rites and deeds.
                H. P. Lovecraft, "The Dreams in the Witch House" (1932)

In popular folklore Walpurgis Night—the night of April 30–May1—is regarded as
a time of spectral manifestations much as its autumnal counterpart Hallowe'en is
. . . . But why, you will ask, were April 30 & Oct. 31 the chosen times for the
witch-cult's nocturnal celebrations? The answer is that these dates have been connected with rites & ceremonies of some sort since the very dawn of the human
race. It is well known that all new cults & religions seize on old festival-dates to
celebrate—translating the observances into the terms of the new faith. Thus the
primitive winter festival of late December, which celebrates the northward turning
of the sun & the prophecy of spring contained in that event, has been adopted
successively by the Roman & Christian religions, appearing respectively under the
names of "Saturnalia" & "Christmas". Well—in prehistoric & pre-agricultural
times there is ever reason to believe that April 30 & Oct. 31 were celebrated as
marking the two annual breeding seasons of the flocks & herds. Since these flocks
& herds were all-important to a wandering race who depended wholly on them
for food, it is natural that these dates should seem very significant. They must
have been marked by vivid & perhaps repulsive fertility-rites, & it is known that
they continued to be observed among the peasantry long after the dawn of agri-
culture had made them obsolete in the race's main religions.
                H. P. Lovecraft, letter to Margaret Sylvester,
                (13 January 1934) (ellipses as in original)

And now for the *name* "Walpurgis Night". Famous as this is, . . it is really a mere
matter of *accidental coincidence* due to the falling of a certain saint's day on the date
of the horrible spring "Sabbat" of the witch-cult. May 1st is the day sacred to St.

Walburga or Walpurgis, an English nun of the 8th century who helped to introduce Christianity into Germany. Among the Germans the old weird memories
& still-surviving Sabbat-rites of May-Eve became very easily fused with the worship of the saint—especially since certain miracles were associated with her . . .
or rather, with her tomb. Hence—with typical cosmic irony—one of the two
most anti-Christian festivals in Europe became known by the name of a Christian saint! The Germans always regarded "Walpurgis-Nacht" with fear, & associated its reputed phenomena with the well-known mountain (highest in the
Harz range) called the Brocken—whose circling cloud of mist causes visitors to
behold their magnified shadows at the summit under rather spectral circumstances. It is possible that actual Sabbats of the witch-cult were held on the
Brocken. The reason why this essentially German term, "Walpurgis Night", has
been transferred to modern English folklore is that much of our weird-library
tradition stems from German ballads & romances of the 18th & early 19th centuries. One does not meet the term in our older literature—but by 1820 or 1830 it
seems to be firmly fixed among us.

H. P. Lovecraft, letter to Margaret Sylvester,
(13 January 1934) (ellipses as in original)

"*Exactement.* Tomorrow is May Eve, Witch-Night—Walpurgis-Nacht. Of all the
nights which go to make the year, they are most likely to try their deviltry then."

Seabury Quinn, "The Hand of Glory" (1933)

"Have you been up to the Brocken yet?"
    "Just hit town, actually."
"I've been up there every Walpurgisnacht since I had my first period."

Thomas Pynchon, *Gravity's Rainbow* (1973)

It was April 30, Walpurgisnacht (pause for thunder on the soundtrack), and I was
rapping with some of the crowd at the Friendly Stranger. H. P. Lovecraft (the rock
group, not the writer) was conducting services in the back room, pounding away at
the door to Acid Land in the gallant effort, new and striking that year, to break in
on waves of sound without any chemical skeleton key at all and I am in no position
to evaluate their success objectively since I was, as is often the case with me, 99 and
44/100ths percent stoned out of my gourd before they began operations.

Robert Shea & Robert Anton Wilson,
The Eye in the Pyramid in *The Illuminatus! Trilogy* (1969–71)

c. In other compounds or as modifier:

She could not tell how I might take it; but she quickly rallied, burst into a loud
screeching laugh, and, with her old Walpurgis gaiety, danced some fantastic
steps in her bare wet feet, tracking the floor with water, and holding out with
finger and thumb, in dainty caricature, her slammakin old skirt, while she sang
some of her nasal patois with an abominable hilarity and emphasis.

J. S. LeFanu, *Uncle Silas: A Tale of Bartram-Haugh* (1864)

I had no reply but shrieks of laughter, and one of those Walpurgis dances in which she excelled.

J. S. LeFanu, *Uncle Silas: A Tale of Bartram-Haugh* (1864)

Moloch and Ashtaroth were not absent; for in this quintessence of all damnation the bounds of consciousness were let down, and man's fancy lay open to vistas of every realm of horror and every forbidden dimension that evil had power to mould. The world and Nature were helpless against such assaults from unsealed wells of night, nor could any sign or prayer check the Walpurgis-riot of horror which had come when a sage with the hateful key had stumbled on a horde with the locked and brimming coffer of transmitted dæmon-lore.

H. P. Lovecraft, "The Horror at Red Hook" (1925)

He seemed to know what was coming—the hideous burst of Walpurgis-rhythm in whose cosmic timbre would be concentrated all the primal, ultimate space-time seethings which lie behind the massed spheres of matter and sometimes break forth in measured reverberations that penetrate faintly to every layer of entity and give hideous significance throughout the worlds to certain dreaded periods.

H. P. Lovecraft, "The Dreams in the Witch House" (1932)

The passage through the vague abysses would be frightful, for the Walpurgis-rhythm would be vibrating, and at last he would have to hear that hitherto veiled cosmic pulsing which he so mortally dreaded. Even now he could detect a low, monstrous shaking whose tempo he suspected all too well. At Sabbat-time it always mounted and reached through the worlds to summon the initiate to nameless rites. Half the chants of the Sabbat were patterned on this faintly overheard pulsing which no earthly ear could endure in its unveiled spatial fulness.

H. P. Lovecraft, "The Dreams in the Witch House" (1932)

This was April 30th, and with the dusk would come the hellish Sabbat-time which all the foreigners and the superstitious old folk feared. Mazurewicz came home at six o'clock and said people at the mill were whispering that the Walpurgis-revels would be held in the dark ravine beyond Meadow Hill where the old white stone stands in a place queerly void of all plant-life.

H. P. Lovecraft, "The Dreams in the Witch House" (1932)

Late in April, just before the æon-shadowed Walpurgis time, Blake made his first trip into the unknown.

H. P. Lovecraft, "The Haunter of the Dark" (1935)

> There are whispers from groves auroral
> To blood half-afraid to hear,
> While the evening star's faint choral
> Is an ecstasy touch'd with fear.

> And at night where the hill-wraiths rally
>> Glows the far Walpurgis flame,
> Which the lonely swain in the valley
>> Beholds, tho' he dare not name.
>
> H. P. Lovecraft, "Primavera" (1925)

> Phantasmal fire burns the band of sorcery,
>> The bat-things weave,
> And taloned shapes of evil stalk, for one night free,
>> Walpurgis Eve.
>
> Donald Wandrei, "Witches' Sabbath"

"Morgan writes that the effects are quite rapid," he said. "First drowsiness, then sleep, and then hopefully dreams. He's tried it twice himself with Rice and doughty old Armitage, who laid the Dunwich Horror with him. The first time they visited in dream Gilman's Walpurgis hyperspace; the second, the inner city at the two magnetic poles—an area topologically unique."

Fritz Leiber, "The Terror from the Depths" (1975)

> Where gnarled gnomes and where haggard hags convene
> In some huge sepulchre deep in the earth;
> There, were the lovely lamia reigns as queen
> Amid Walpurgis revelry and mirth;
> There, where the basilisk gives loathsome birth
> To monstrous brood; there, there I met my love,
> That Atlantean solace for all dearth,
> That primal goddess from domains above,—
> Fair Lilith,—she wherein unite the serpent and the dove: [. . .]
>
> Donald Sidney-Fryer, "Connaissance Fatale"

He well knew from his activity in the witch-cult that at the time of the monstrous Sabbat-rites held at Walpurgis Time and Hallowmass, curious numbers of unfamiliar guests turned up at the old inn; he well understood that these were in reality departed shades seeking entrance to the nether world, and he knew also that the monstrous being under the pool, especially vigilant on these occasions to prevent unwarranted passages into the underworld, was itself frustrated in not being able to attend the hellish rites so dear to it.

Donald R. Burleson, "The Pool" (1987)

wamp, *n.* A fantastic creature that inhabits the Dreamlands of H. P. Lovecraft. [Not in *OED*.]

When it learned that Carter wished to get to the enchanted wood and from there to the city Celephaïs in Ooth-Nargai beyond the Tanarian Hills, it seemed rather doubtful; for these ghouls of the waking world do no business in the graveyards of upper dreamland (leaving that to the web-footed wamps that are spawned in dead cities), and many things intervene betwixt their gulf and the enchanted wood, including the terrible kingdom of the gugs.

H. P. Lovecraft, *The Dream-Quest of Unknown Kadath* (1926–27)

weird, (wyrd, weïrd, wëird, weyard, weyward, wayward), *n. & adj.* [< OE *Wyrd*, goddess of fate; cognate of Old Norse *Urð*, one of the three Norns] Fate, fortune, destiny; particularly, when personified as a goddess or a Norn (q.v.); an evil fate inflicted upon one through magic, particularly in retribution for some offense; a spell or enchantment. As an adjective, deriving from the foregoing, and specifically from the Weird Sisters in William Shakespeare's *Tragedie of Macbeth*: eerie, eldritch, strange, uncanny, unearthly, *Unheimlich*. Shakespeare's spellings "weyard" and "weyward" led to confusion with the word "wayward"; Lewis Theobald, in his edition of Shakespeare's works, amended the spelling to weïrd, adding the diæresis in order to indicate the bisyllabic pronunciation required by the prosody. **weird-man, weird-woman:** A fortuneteller, soothsayer; a witch, wizard. See also under **dree.**

Titles: Mrs. J. H. Riddell, *Weird Stories* (aka *Weird Tales*); M. E. Bradden, *Wyllard's Weird;* Clark Ashton Smith, "The Weird of Avoosl Wuthoqquan"; Donald A. Wollheim, "Miss McWhortle's Weird"; Michael Moorcock, *The Weird of the White Wolf;* D. F. Lewis, "The Weirdmonger"; Terry Pratchett, *The Wyrd Sisters*

a. General:

> *Mista* black, terrific maid,
> Sangrida and Hilda see,
> Join the wayward work to aid:
> 'Tis the woof of victory.
>
> Thomas Gray, "The Fatal Sisters: An Ode" (1761)

> "She who sits by haunted well,
> Is subject to the Nixie's spell.
> She who walks on lonely beach
> To the Mermaid's charmed speech;
> She walks round ring of green,
> Offends the peevish Fairy Queen;
> And she who takes rest in the Dwarfie's cave,
> A weary weird of woe shall have."
>
> Sir Walter Scott, *The Pirate* (1821)

> Ane nychte he darnit in Maisry's cot;
>   The fearless haggs came in;
> And he heard the word of awsome weird,
>   And he saw their deedis of synn.
>
> James Hogg, "The Witch of Fife" in *The Queen's Wake: A Legendary Poem* (1813)

Pale grew her immortality, for woe
Of all these lovers, and she grieved so
I took compassion on her, bade her steep
Her hair in weïrd syrops, that would keep
Her loveliness invisible, yet free
To wander as she loves, in liberty.

John Keats, *Lamia* (1819)

"I wot not, beloved," said he; "must we not go and dwell where deeds shall lead us? and the hand of Weird is mighty."

William Morris, *The Well at the World's End* (1893)

"But we lived on in hope, and trusted to what weird had wrought for us."

William Morris, *The Sundering Flood* (1896)

There were, indeed, a good many cronies already about the house, full of the mood of funerals—the last will of the grandfather Macdougal consisting mainly of instructions as to his burial, he never dreaming that it was his weird never to be buried at all!

M. P. Shiel, "The Globe of Gold-Fish"

Till later Lammas is led in by baith our washwives, a weird of wonder tenebrous as that evil thorn~garth, a field of faery blithe as this flowing wind.

James Joyce, *Finnegans Wake* (1922–39)

"Harken to your weird: the godless and exceeding love which you bear to all material things, and your lust therefor, shall lead you on a strange quest and bring you to a doom whereof the stars and the sun will alike be ignorant. The hidden opulence of earth shall allure you and ensnare you; and earth itself shall devour you at the last."

"The weird is more than a trifle cryptic in its earlier clauses; and the final clause is somewhat platitudinous."

Clark Ashton Smith, "The Weird of Avoosl Wuthoqquan" (1931)

So these young men, led by one Bragi, my brother-in-arms, took their girls and venturing to the southwest, took up their abode in the Valley of Broken Stones. The Picts expostulated, hinting vaguely of a monstrous doom that haunted the vale, but the Æsir laughed. We had left our own demons and weirds in the icy wastes of the far blue north, and the devils of other races did not much impress us.

Robert E. Howard, "The Valley of the Worm" (1934)

"I come here," the Weirdmonger roared, "to sell Weirds, and Weirds are merely Words that materialize into all sorts of true existence the moment I release them from between my lips. . . ."

D. F. Lewis, "The Weirdmonger" (ellipsis in original)

b. In compounds or as modifier, as **Weird Sisters,** etc.:

> The weyward Sisters, hand in hand,
> Posters of the Sea and Land,
> Thus doe goe, about, about,
> Thrice to thine, and thrice to mine,
> And thrice againe, to make vp nine.

> William Shakespeare, *The Tragedie of Macbeth* (1606)

> Thou hast it now, King, Cawdor, Glamis, all,
> As the weyard Women promis'd, and I feare
> Thou playd'st most fowly for't: yet it was saide
> It should not stand in thy Posterity,
> But that my selfe should be the Roote, and Father
> Of many Kings.

> William Shakespeare, *The Tragedie of Macbeth* (1606)

> I will to morrow
> (And betimes I will) to the weyard Sisters.

> William Shakespeare, *The Tragedie of Macbeth* (1606)

"The warlock men and the weird wemyng,

> And the fays of the wood and the steep,
> And the phantom hunteris all war there,
> And the mermaidis of the deep."

James Hogg, "The Witch of Fife" in *The Queen's Wake: A Legendary Poem* (1813)

> The mysterious Sisters then severally requested what he sought to know. "Ask!"—
> "Require!"—"Demand!"—exclaimed the Weird Beings.

> Francis Lathom, "The Water Spectre" (1809)

—That's folk, he said very earnestly, for your book, Haines. Five lines of text and ten pages of notes about the folk and the fishgods of Dundrum. Printed by the weird sisters in the year of the big wind.

> James Joyce, *Ulysses* (1914–21)

One stormy afternoon, as the nobles of Caduz sat in conclave, a weird-woman dressed in white entered the chamber holding high a glass vessel which exuded a flux of colors swirling behind her like smoke. As if in a trance she picked up the crown, set it on the head of Duke Thirlach, husband to Etaine, younger sister to Casmir. The woman in white departed the chamber and was seen no more. After some contention, the omen was accepted at face value and Thirlach was enthroned as the new king.

> Jack Vance, *Lyonesse: Suldrun's Garden* (1983)

It seemed to be fact, however, that he had booked the Weird Sisters. Exactly who or what the Weird Sisters were Harry didn't know, never having had access to a wizard's wireless, but he deduced from the wild excitement of those who had grown up listening to the WWN (Wizarding Wireless Network) that they were a very famous musical group.

> J. K. Rowling, *Harry Potter and the Goblet of Fire* (2000)

Wendigo, Windigo, witiko, Wiindigo, Witiko, *n.* [< Ojibway *wintiko*, Cree *wihtikow*] In Algonquian mythology, a man-eating giant.

Titles: William Henry Drummond, "The Windigo" (verse); Mary Hartwell Catherwood, "The Windigo"; Algernon Blackwood, "The Wendigo"; Ogden Nash, "The Wendigo" (verse); Richard Tierney, "The Wendigo" (verse)

> "Go back to your home and people,
> Live among them, toil among them,
> Cleanse the earth from all that harms it,
> Clear the fishing-grounds and rivers,
> Slay all monsters and magicians,
> All the Wendigoes, the giants,
> All the serpents, the Kenabeeks,
> As I slew the Mishe-Mokwa,
> Slew the Great Bear of the mountains."
>
> Henry Wadsworth Longfellow, *The Song of Hiawatha* (1855)

That grene ray of earong it waves us to yonder as the red, blue and yellow flogs time on the domisole, with a blewy blow and a windigo.

> James Joyce, *Finnegans Wake* (1922–39)

> The Wendigo, the Wendigo!
> Its eyes are ice and indigo!
> Its blood is rank and yellowish!
> Its voice is hoarse and bellowish!
>
> Ogden Nash, "The Wendigo" (1936)

witch-fire, witchfire, *n.* A corposant, St. Elmo's fire; a will-o'-the-wisp, *ignis fatuus.*

Titles: George Sterling, "Witch-Fire" (verse)

Witch-fires [*Des feux follets*] ever and anon flitted across the road before us; and the night-birds shrieked fearsomely in the depth of the woods beyond, where we beheld at intervals glow the phosphorescent eyes of wild cats.

> Théophile Gautier (trans. Lafcadio Hearn), "Clarimonde" (1882;
> orig. "*La Morte amoureuse*")

> "As a breath on glass,—
>   As witch-fires that burn,

    The gods and monsters pass,
        Are dust, and return."

George Sterling, "The Face of the Skies" (1919)

Here we shall find none or little of the sentimental fat with which so much of our literature is larded. Rather shall one in Imagination's "mystic mid-region," see elfin rubies burn at his feet, witch-fires glow in the nearer cypresses, and feel upon his brow a wind from the unknown.

George Sterling, Preface to Clark Ashton Smith, Ebony and Crystal (1922)

A wave of pity swept through him, quenching the witch-fires in his blood.

A. Merritt, The Face in the Abyss (1923)

"*La strega!*" he muttered. "The Witch! The Witch-fire!"

A. Merritt, Burn, Witch, Burn! (1932)

Those fungi, grotesquely like the vegetation in the yard outside, were truly horrible in their outlines; detestable parodies of toadstools and Indian pipes, whose like we had never seen in any other situation. They rotted quickly, and at one stage became slightly phosphorescent; so that nocturnal passers-by sometimes spoke of witch-fires glowing behind the broken panes of the fœtor-spreading windows.

H. P. Lovecraft, "The Shunned House" (1924)

At noon we would be in Pompelo, & at night we would go into the horrible hills where witch-fires flamed & drums & howling echoed.

H. P. Lovecraft, letter to Bernard Austin Dwyer (4 November 1927)

He came to eerie pools, alight with coiling and wreathing witch-fires, in dim arboreal grottoes.

Clark Ashton Smith, "The Maze of Maal Dweb" (1932)

"But what thing is it that can cry like a woman and laugh like a devil, and shines like witch-fire as it glides through the trees?" gasped Balthus, mopping the sweat from his pale face.

Robert E. Howard, "Beyond the Black River" (1935)

A weird glow burned through the trees. It moved toward him, shimmering weirdly—a green witch-fire that moved with purpose and intent.

Robert E. Howard, "Beyond the Black River" (1935)

As he approached the ring, he saw an eerie glow within, so that the gaunt stone stood etched like the ribs of a skeleton in which the witch-fire burns.

Robert E. Howard, "Worms of the Earth" (1930)

    In a marsh that even the water-snakes spurn,
    Mandrakes writhe and witch-fires burn,

> Swart talons toward the ruby turn,
>> In Marmora.

Donald Wandrei, "Marmora" (1930)

The luminous energy bathing the corridor with elfin witchfire in the color that had no name became the play of unimaginable powers surging into tortured vision.

Donald Wandrei, The Web of Easter Island (1929–31)

Wizard's Bane pulsed with a corposant of blue witch-fire. Shadows stark and unreal cringed away from the lambent blade.

Karl Edward Wagner, "Undertow"

witch-light, witchlight, witch light, *n.* A will-o'-the-wisp, *ignis fatuus*; the aurora borealis (Northern Lights); St. Elmo's fire; etc.. [Not in *OED*.]

"We are saved, Gudruda, and thus far indeed thou wast fey. Now rise, ere thy limbs stiffen, and I will set thee on the horse, if he still can run, and lead thee down to Middalhof before the witchlights fail us."

H. Rider Haggard, Eric Brighteyes (1889)

"I thought certainly thou wast perishing with Gudruda in the snow, and now men go to seek thee while the witchlights burn."

H. Rider Haggard, Eric Brighteyes (1889)

A minute later the steamer was a dark mass to the nor'-west, with a sheet of white writhing after her, and a swirl of flaming cinders from her funnel riding down the night like a shoal of witch-lights.

Fiona Macleod (William Sharp), Pharais: The Mountain Lovers (1909)

"That extraordinary American with his tales of witch-lights and haunted abbeys has been playing the devil with our nerves."

Sax Rohmer (Arthur Sarsfield Ward),
The Return of Dr. Fu-Manchu (1916; aka The Devil Doctor)

A light was dancing out upon the moor, a witch-light that came and went unaccountably, up and down, in and out, now clearly visible, now masked in the darkness!

Sax Rohmer (Arthur Sarsfield Ward),
The Return of Dr. Fu-Manchu (1916; aka The Devil Doctor)

"There's something about them like St. Elmo's fire, witch lights—condensation of atmospheric electricity."

A. Merritt, The Metal Monster (1920)

But I, having determinedly dismissed the idea, was more interested in the fantastic lights that flooded this columned hall with their buttercup radiance. Still they were, and unwinking; not disks, I could see now, but globes. Great and small they floated motionless, their rays extending rigidly and as still as the orbs that shed them. Yet rigid as they were there was nothing about either rays or orbs that suggested either hardness or the metallic. They were vaporous, soft as the St. Elmo's fire, the witch lights that cling at times to the spars of ships, weird gleaming visitors from the invisible ocean of atmospheric electricity.

A. Merrit, *The Metal Monster* (1920)

The color of its water was pale emerald, and like an emerald it gleamed, placid, untroubled. But beneath that untroubled surface there was movement—luminous circles of silvery green that spread swiftly and vanished, rays that laced and interlaced in fantastic yet ordered, geometric forms; luminous spirallings, none of which ever came quite to the surface to disturb its serenity. And here and there were clusters of soft lights, like vaporous rubies, misted sapphires and opals and glimmering pearls—witch-lights. The luminous lilies of the Lake of the Ghosts.

A. Merritt, *Dwellers in the Mirage* (1932)

The witch-lights flickered in her eyes; a flash of green shone through them.

A. Merritt, *Dwellers in the Mirage* (1932)

The servants had quenched their torches, for now the corposants had begun to glimmer over the standing stones. The witch lights. The lamps of the dead. Faintly at first, but growing ever stronger. Glimmering, shifting orbs of gray but phosphorescence of the grayness of the dead. Decaying lights, and putrescent.

A. Merritt, *Creep, Shadow!* (1934; aka *Creep, Shadow, Creep!*)

Mazurewicz was waiting for him at the door, and seemed both anxious and reluctant to whisper some fresh bit of superstition. It was about the witch light. Joe had been out celebrating the night before—it was Patriots' Day in Massachusetts—and had come home after midnight. Looking up at the house from outside, he had thought at first that Gilman's window was dark; but then he had seen the faint violet glow within. He wanted to warn the gentleman about that glow, for everybody in Arkham knew it was Keziah's witch light which played near Brown Jenkin and the ghost of the old crone herself.

H. P. Lovecraft, "The Dreams in the Witch House" (1932)

A ghostly trumpet echoes from a barren mountain head;
Through the fen the wandering witch-lights gleam like phantom arrows sped;
There is silence in the valleys and the moon is rising red.

Robert E. Howard, "The Ghost Kings"

While creatures cower in their burrows, silent all,
    Strange witch-lights flare,
Demonic revel holds dark, writhing forms in thrall,
    Their wild eyes glare.

Donald Wandrei, "Witches' Sabbath"

Elfa smiled and the witch-lights danced in her blue eyes.

Gardner F. Fox, *Kothar: Barbarian Swordsman* (1969)

Wormian, *adj.* [< L *(ossa) Wormiana* < Olaus *Wormius,* Latinized form of Ole *Wurm,* Danish physician (1588–1664)] Of or pertaining to the small, irregularly shaped bones found in the skull's sutures.

"Look, this might seem a bit queer, but I'm looking for something on worm worship."

The other frowned. "Worm worship? Man or beast?"

"I'm sorry?" Crow looked puzzled.

"Worship of the annelid—family, *Lumbricidæ*—or of the man, Worm.?"

"The man-worm?"

"Worm with a capital 'W'," Sedgewick grinned. "He was a Danish physician, an anatomist. Olaus Worm. Around the turn of the 16th Century, I believe. Had a number of followers. Hence the word 'Wormian', relating to his discoveries."

"You get more like a dictionary every day!" Crow jokingly complained. But his smile quickly turned to a frown. "Olaus Worm, eh? Could a Latinized version of that be Olaus Wormius, I wonder?"

"What, old Wormius who translated the Greek *Necronomicon*? No, not possible, for he was 13th Century."

Brian Lumley, *Lord of the Worms* (1987)

X

xanthic, *adj.* [< Gr xanthós, yellow] Yellow in color.

Never yet has man profaned it, never printed Xanthic sands whereover duskier flames the blue For tall marble cliffs whereon the hippogriffin Rears his head and gazes seaward, unalarmed, and all replete with grainy grasses.

Clark Ashton Smith, "The Isle of Saturn"

Y

Yahoo, yahoo, *n.* In the language of the Houyhnhnns, a human being. Reported in Jonathan Swift, *Travels into Several Remote Nations of the World, in Four Parts* (aka *Gulliver's Travels*).

> YAHOOS.—See Swift's Voyage to Laputa. It is to be feared that the mad Dean intended to satirize mankind, the race for which the Lord of Glory died!
>
> Rev. C. Verey (Aleister Crowley), note to *Clouds Without Water* (1909)

> So he lay well back in the shade of the hedge, and thought whether some sort of an article could not be made by vindicating the terrible Yahoos; one might point out that they were in many respects a simple and unsophisticated race, whose faults were the result of their enslaved position, while such virtues as they had were all their own.
>
> Arthur Machen, *The Hill of Dreams* (1897)

> Swift surely had a sound basis for his account of the Yahoos—which indeed I found fascinating from childhood onward.
>
> H. P. Lovecraft, letter to William Lumley (21 December 1931)

yakith-lizard, *n.* A type of lizard native to the lost continent of Mu. [Not in *OED.*]

(See quotation under *pthagon.*)

y'm-bhi, *n.* [Cf. *zombi, jumbee* < Kongo *zumbi,* fetish, or *nzambi,* god] In the society of the Mound-dwellers, a zombi-like animated corpse serving as a slave. [Not in *OED.*]

> He likewise observed the more manlike shapes that toiled along the furrows, and felt a curious fright and disgust toward certain of them whose motions were more mechanical than those of the rest. These, Gll'-Hthaa-Ynn explained, were what men called the *y'm-bhi*—organisms which had died, but which had been mechanically reanimated for industrial purposes by means of atomic energy and thought-power. The slave-class did not share the immortality of the freemen of Tsath, so that with time the number of *y'm-bhi* had become very large.
>
> H. P. Lovecraft & Zealia Bishop, "The Mound" (1930)

Z

Zimimar, Zymymar, Ziminar, Ziminiar, Zimimay, *n.* [?] According to such demonologists as John Wierus, the demon monarch assigned to the north. (Supposedly referred to in these lines from William Shakespeare, *Henry VI, Part I*: "Now helpe ye charming Spelles and Periapts, / And ye choise spirits that admonish me, / And giue me signes of future accidents. / You speedy helpers, that are substitutes / Vnder the Lordly Monarch of the North, / Appeare, and ayde me in this enterprize." Other candidates for the demon monarch of the north given by various demonologists include Eltzen, Cham, Amaymon, Egin, and Mahazuel.) [Not in *OED*.]

> *Amaymon* king of the east, *Gorson* king of the south, *Zimimar* king of the north, *Goap* king and prince of the west, may be bound from the third houre, till noone, and from the ninth houre till evening.
>
> Reginald Scot, The Discoverie of Witchcraft (1584)

> Bowing reversely, Gorson, Goap, Zimimar and Amaimon, lords of the four quarters, went out one after one, leaving their prince alone.
>
> Clark Ashton Smith, "Schizoid Creator" (1952)

> Within your arms I will forget
> The horror that Zimimar brings
> Between his vast and vampire wings
> From out his frozen oubliette.
>
> Clark Ashton Smith, "The Sorcerer to His Love" (1941)

Zmargad, Zemargad, *n.* [< Hb ZMRGD; Graves & Patai suggest a connection with Gr *smáragdos*, emerald, aquamarine, and suggest on this basis that it is a submarine kingdom.] A fabulous land ruled by Lilith. [Not in *OED*.]

> Help! Don't shoot! I surrender! *Zemargad* is in neither the *Necronomicon* nor in von Junzt's *Unaussprechlichen Kulten*, unless perchance it be in that passage (*Nec.* xii, 58—p. 984) in Naacal hieroglyphics, whose fullest purport I was never able to unravel. The Yashish passage in von Junzt (footnote, p. 751, ed. 1839)—
>
> ◁ ∪ ⸓∶ Υ ? ◿ ⸰ ⸗ ∵ △ ◊ ⸒∶ Υ ◻ ⸕ ∵⸑ ⸙ ∪ ∶?
>
> etc.—hints at a vague, ultra-dimensional realm of nameless horror best transliterated as *H'mar*; but the resemblance of this word to *Zemargad* is too strained to be other than fortuitous. Nor is the doubtful allusion to *Khad* in the *Book of Eibon* any real clue. The *Pnakotic Manuscripts* mention the subterrene gulf of *Zim*, but all scholars from de Galimatias and Zu Dumkopf onward have agreed that

this is really a reference to the Vaults of *Zin*, so well known to all students of Alhazred and von Junzt. No—there's no use in concealing plain ignorance; and I must flatly admit that I never heard the name *Zemargad* before, and that the volumes in my library are unanimous in failing to solve the mystery.

H. P. Lovecraft, letter to E. Hoffmann Price (20 December 1932)

Incidentally—Klarkash-Ton tells me that his Semitic oracle de Casseres never heard of *Zemargad*. Tough luck! But the hint so strongly appeals to High-Priest Klarkash that he is going to use the name *Zemargad*—in conjunction with more synthetic nomenclature—in his new and hellish conception, *The Infernal Star*.

H. P. Lovecraft, letter to E. Hoffman Price (15 February 1933)

Zemargad—never did figure THAT one out.

E. Hoffman Price, letter to Steve Behrends (17 July 1984)

The erudition of the unknown writer was remarkable even if misguided: as he turned the leaves impatiently, the attention of Woadley was caught by unheard-of names and terms wholly obscure to him. He frowned over casual mention-ings of Lomar, Eibon, Zemargad, the Ghooric Zone, Zothique, the Table of Mordiggian, Thilil, Psollantha, Vermazbor, and the Black Flame of Yuzh.

Clark Ashton Smith, *The Infernal Star* (1933)

DAN CLORE is a free-lance writer and scholar. He has had articles published in *Lovecraft Studies, Studies in Weird Fiction, Necrofile: The Review of Horror Fiction, Weird Times*, and the anthologies *A Century Less a Dream: Selected Criticism on H.P. Lovecraft, The Freedom of Fantastic Things: Selected Criticism on Clark Ashton Smith*, and *Supernatural Literature of the World: An Encyclopedia*. His fiction has appeared in *The Urbanite, Deathrealm, Terminal Fright, Lore, Epitaph, Black October Magazine, Cosmic Visions, Cthulhu Sex, Creatio ex Nihilo, The NetherReal*, and the anthologies *The Last Continent: New Tales of Zothique* and *Eldritch Horrors: Dark Tales*. It was collected in *The Unspeakable and Others*, first published in the fall of 2001, undoubtedly the most terrifying incident to occur in the period. A revised and expanded edition will appear in 2009.